D1552260

INTRODUCTION to
COMMUNICATION STUDIES

Translating Scholarship into Meaningful Practice

Alan K. Goodboy
Kara Shultz

Kendall Hunt
publishing company

Cover image © Shutterstock, Inc.

Kendall Hunt
publishing company

www.kendallhunt.com
Send all inquiries to:
4050 Westmark Drive
Dubuque, IA 52004-1840

Printed in the United States of America
10 9 8 7 6 5 4 3 2

CONTENTS

INTRODUCTION

EDITED BY ALAN K. GOODBOY & KARA SHULTZ

OUR VISION

The field of communication studies is arguably one of the most exciting disciplines to study. Many students agree with this assertion as communication is one of the 10 most popular majors in college (Kramer, 2010). And many employers agree that this major equips students with a variety of competencies that are valued in the workplace including interpersonal skills, organizational skills, presentational skills, leadership, teamwork, critical thinking, reasoning, and cultural awareness (Bertelsen & Goodboy, 2009). With research topics ranging from understanding relational maintenance and dating, to learning about nonverbal deception and lying, to persuading healthcare consumers to live better lives, communication research has produced findings that may profoundly enhance our daily lives if we understand them. This textbook is designed to help you as a student, understand some important communication research findings published in our peer-reviewed journals. As Kramer (2010) noted, "unless we believe that students do not learn anything from our classes, then our research makes a difference in their personal and professional lives" (p. 435). We want to make a difference in your life with information you are likely to care about, because we, like many other scholars, believe communication scholarship does make a difference in helping people become more effective communicators (Hummert, 2009).

This edited volume is unique because no other introductory book has attempted to translate entire research programs of complicated findings into simple real life practices across the major communication contexts. Most introductory texts are written for the "basic course", which typically focuses on public speaking, group communication, and interpersonal communication. However, as the editors of this volume, it is our contention that the field has so much more to offer students beyond the basic course. We want to offer students "translational research" findings. As Frey (2009) noted, "because of its perceived lack of relevance and accessibility, to make a difference, scholarship typically has to be *translated* for use by other audiences" (p. 267). Petronio (1999) explained that "translating means that we take the knowledge discovered through research or theory and interpret it for everyday use. Translators develop pathways for converting research knowledge into practice" (p. 88). This book does precisely that; it translates some of the best research findings into practice so you can be an effective communicator in a variety of real life situations and contexts.

We believe that students who are introduced to our field for the first time should leave their introductory course with practical knowledge they can actually use in their daily lives. This perspective is rooted in the tradition of applied communication research. According to Wood (2000), applied communication scholarship adopts a particularly pragmatic focus by insisting on "putting theory and research into the service of practice and, equally, of studying practices to refine theory in order to gain new understandings of how communication functions and how it might function differently, or better" (p. 189). Therefore, this book provides real research findings from published studies that have practical implications, if not direct advice on how to communicate more appropriately and effectively. We do not believe that an introduction to our field should expose students to the hybrid/basic course (although we believe that public speaking, small group communication, and interpersonal communication are still important courses that should be taught separately). Since we know how fun and exciting the field is, we believe that students should be exposed to actual research findings that are directly relevant to them.

We are very fortunate to publish 44 brief mini-chapters that highlight major programs of communication research. And we are even more fortunate to feature chapters from the most published and prolific communication researchers in the field. Literally, every chapter in this book is written by the most *famous* experts who are noteworthy scholars with impressive research agendas. We are proud to say that we have the "all-star team" of communication researchers writing and translating in this book. These scholars have the biggest names in our field and it is an honor to feature their work in one edited volume. No other textbook has such impressive scholars and applied findings for an introductory course. It is our hope, that more universities will adopt our approach of exposing undergraduate students to translational research in the introductory course to orient them with the field, instead of relying on the basic course. Such an approach will leave students with better "take-aways" from an introductory course, show students a good cross-section of the state of the art research that is being conducted, allow students to recognize major programs of research and the prolific scholars who do this research, and ultimately give students practical real life advice grounded in scholarship. For additional information about these ideas, we asked Dr. Sandra Petronio, who was cited earlier in this introduction, to offer a brief history of translational research in the field for those of you who are interested in the origins of the translational movement. This brief history is offered next.

We know that translational communication scholarship can make a difference in your lives if you apply the principles and findings featured in this book. It is also our hope that you enjoy what you learn from this book and find this translational research to be helpful advice that can aid you in the meaningful practice of communication in life.

Cheers!

Alan K. Goodboy
West Virginia University

Kara Shultz
Bloomsburg University

REFERENCES

Bertelsen, D., A., & Goodboy, A. K. (2009). Curriculum planning: Trends in communication studies, workplace competencies, and current programs at four-year colleges and universities. *Communication Education, 58*, 262–275.

Frey, L. R. (2009). What a difference more difference-making communication scholarship might make: Making a difference from and through communication research. *Journal of Applied Communication Research, 37*, 205–214.

Hummert, M. L. (2009). Not just preaching to the choir: Communication scholarship does make a difference. *Journal of Applied Communication Research, 37*, 215–224.

Kramer, M. W. (2010). It depends on your criteria. *Communication Monographs, 77*, 435–437.

Petronio, S. (1999). "Translating scholarship into practice": An alternative metaphor. *Journal of Applied Communication Research, 27*, 87–91.

Wood, J.T. (2000). Applied communication research: Unbounded and for good reason. *Journal of Applied Communication Research, 28*, 188–191.

TRANSLATING COMMUNICATION SCHOLARSHIP INTO MEANINGFUL PRACTICES: HISTORICAL OVERVIEW IN THE DISCIPLINE OF COMMUNICATION

SANDRA PETRONIO, IUPUI

The editors of this volume, Alan Goodboy and Kara Shultz asked me to write about the historical place of translational scholarship in the discipline of communication. In 1996, as the Chair of the Interpersonal and Small Group Division of the Speech Communication Association (SCA now NCA) held in San Diego, CA, along with colleagues, I organized a pre-conference focusing on "Translating Scholarship into Practice." Though the concept is now a trend, it was a new way of thinking about scholarship at that time. Over 60 professors and students discussed the meaning of translating scholarship with an emphasis on seeking a new framework for the research enterprise that promised to emphasize purposeful research to improve lives. Because it was clear that "evidence" was essential to translation, as the then current Editor of the *Western Journal of Communication,* a call was issued for articles discussing the meaning of evidence in translational scholarship. Many excellent examples were published early in our exploration of translational research within the discipline of communication. Subsequently, several other special issues featuring translational research were published (see, Petronio, 1999, 2002, 2007a, 2007b for additional information). In particular, *Journal of Applied Communication Research volume 35, issue 3,* 2007, presents examples of translational scholarship in the discipline of communication. Continuing to advocate for translating research into practice, as the Founding Director of the IUPUI Chancellor's campus-wide Initiative on Translating Research into Practice, the aim is to celebrate and generate translational research conducted by Indiana University-Purdue University, Indianapolis faculty across all Schools on the campus.

The concept of research translation gained prominence as the National Institute of Research, a US government institution under the Director Elias Zerhouni, in 2004, established the NIH Roadmap for Medical Research calling for scientific discoveries to be translated into practical applications using the phrase, "from bench to bedside" meaning from the lab to treating the patient.

In a very simple way, the notion of translating research into practice focuses on conducting investigations of real life problems that can potentially change lives and make a meaningful difference to people. As needs for better ways to meet the demands of our world have grown over the last several decades, it has become clear that much of the research enterprise has focused on only half of the issue—knowledge generation. While it is obviously important to generate new ideas, in many cases, it may not be enough. We also need applications, systems, new approaches, and methods capable of converting knowledge from research findings into productive opportunities to help people cope with cancer, improve communication skills, give parents better guidance about educating their children, and other important challenges facing people in their lives. We need to know how to take the "evidence" of research findings and turn them into useable information to help people in the everyday world (Petronio, 1999). Knowledge generation is most productive when it is aimed at the outcome of knowledge utilization. As you can see, translating research into practice necessitates taking research findings and turning them into intervention, new practices, and using the findings as potential change agents that can transform how people live in productive ways. Knowing that people do not talk about engaging in safer sex practices is useful information. But, so what? These findings are only half of the puzzle. The next question asks: How can we help people change their communication interaction patterns? When these two issues are combined, we see that research findings provide insights (evidence) into patterns that help direct productive changes. These changes lead to implementing new ways to facilitate engaging in more effective safe sex behavior, the end goal of translational scholarship. Making lives better.

This book illustrates numerous examples of translating scholarship into practice. The move to a translational approach for research investigations continues and extends a rich history in the discipline of communication that is; our discipline actively conducts practical research and teaches important skills to people. From training public speakers to developing persuasive arguments, to improving interpersonal communication, to giving organizations ways to accomplish conflict mediation, and beyond, our discipline has been at the forefront of keeping the mission of practical needs, based on evidence, as a mainstay throughout its over 100 year history.

REFERENCES

Petronio, S. (1999). "Translating scholarship into practice": An alternative metaphor. *Journal of Applied Communication Research, 27*, 87–91.

Petronio, S. (2002). The new world and scholarship translation practices: Necessary changes in defining evidence. *Western Journal of Communication, 66*, 507–512.

Petronio, S. (2007a). JACR commentaries on translating research into practice: Introduction. *Journal of Applied Communication Research, 35*, 215–217.

Petronio, S. (2007b). Translational research endeavors and practices of communication privacy management. *Journal of Applied Communication Research, 35*, 218–222.

AUTHOR BIOGRAPHIES

Tamara Afifi is a Professor in the Department of Communication at the University of California, Santa Barbara. Most of her research focuses on how family members cope communicatively with various challenges they face. When examining her research program, two primary themes emerge: (1) information regulation (privacy, secrets, disclosure, avoidance) in parent-child and dating relationships, and (2) communication processes related to uncertainty, loss, stress and coping in families, with particular emphasis on post-divorce families. Professor Afifi was the recipient of the Young Scholar Award from the International Communication Association in 2006 and the Brommel Award from the National Communication Association (NCA) for a distinguished career of research in family communication in 2011. She has also won several other research awards, including the Franklin Knower Article Award in 2004 from the Interpersonal Communication Division of NCA and the Distinguished Article Award from the Family Communication Division of NCA in 2008.

Mark Andrejevic is an ARC Research Fellow at the Centre for Critical and Cultural Studies at The University of Queensland, Brisbane, Australia. As a media scholar, he writes about surveillance, new media, and popular culture with an interest in the ways in which forms of surveillance and monitoring enabled by the development of new media technologies impact the realms of economics, politics, and culture. His first book, *Reality TV: The Work of Being Watched* (2003), explores the way in which this popular programming genre equates participation with willing submission to comprehensive monitoring. His second book, *iSpy: Surveillance and Power in the Interactive Era* (2007), considers the role of surveillance in the era of networked digital technology and explores the consequences for politics, policing, popular culture, and commerce. He is also the author of numerous book chapters and journal articles on surveillance and media. He is currently working on a five-year, ARC funded project that looks at public attitudes towards measures to regulate the collection and use of personal information online and over mobile networks.

Leslie A. Baxter has been a Professor of Communication Studies at the University of Iowa for 17 years; and before that, she had appointments at the University of California-Davis, Lewis & Clark College, and the University of Montana. She has published 150 articles, chapters in edited books, and books on a range of topics in interpersonal and family communication. She is particularly interested in the contradictory discourses that animate relating. She is honored to be the recipient of many awards, including the NCA Carroll Arnold Distinguished Lecturer Award, the NCA

Distinguished Scholar Award, The Bernard Brommel Award for family communication research, the Gerald Miller Book Award for interpersonal communication, the Franklin Knower Article Award for interpersonal communication, the inaugural WSCA Distinguished Scholar Award, and the F. Wendell Miller Distinguished Professorship from the University of Iowa.

Carole Blair is Professor of Communication Studies and Fellow of the Institute for the Arts and Humanities at the University of North Carolina at Chapel Hill. She is also affiliated with the American Studies Department and the Curriculum in Global Studies. She teaches courses in rhetorical theory and criticism, public memory, and the rhetorics of public places. Her research focuses upon U.S. public commemorative places and artworks and their endorsements of particular versions of nationalism and citizenship. She is a Distinguished Scholar of the National Communication Association.

Patrice M. Buzzanell (Ph.D., Purdue University) is Professor in the Brian Lamb School of Communication at Purdue University and an International Communication Association Fellow. Dr. Buzzanell has served as President of the International Communication Association, the Council of Communication Associations, and the Organization for the Study of Communication, Language and Gender. Her primary area is organizational communication with specific interests in career, leadership, and work-life processes. Dr. Buzzanell has edited three books, *Management Communication Quarterly,* and special issues; she has published over 100 articles and chapters in top communication and interdisciplinary journals and handbooks. Recent research and teaching delve into communicative constructions of resilience, work-personal life sustainability, and gendered career processes for children, as well as men and women in STEM (science, technology, engineering, and math). She has taught workshops and seminars in Europe, Asia, and the U.S. at different institutions and organizations. She has taught in the Engineering Projects for Community Service (EPICS) for over a decade and in the Purdue (NSF) ADVANCE initiative to educate the majority about diversity and inclusion to create institutional transformation.

Carma Bylund, Ph.D., is Associate Attending Behavioral Scientist in the Department of Psychiatry and Behavioral Sciences at Memorial Sloan-Kettering Cancer Center. Dr. Bylund directs the Communication Skills Training and Research Laboratory, and her work focuses on improving healthcare communication.

Donal Carbaugh is Professor of Communication, Samuel F. Conti Faculty Research Fellow, past Chair of the International Studies Council (2004–2010), and past Co-Chair of the Five College Committee on Native American Indian Studies (2003–2004). His recent book, *Cultures in Conversation,* was awarded the Outstanding Book of the Year by the International and Intercultural Division of the National Communication Association. During 2007 to 2008, he was Distinguished Fulbright Professor and Bicentennial Chair of American Studies at the University of Helsinki, Finland. He has been Chair of both the International Communication Association's Language and Social Interaction Division, and the National Communication Association's International and Intercultural Communication Division. In 1992, he was elected Visiting Senior Member at Linacre College, Oxford University, England, which is a lifetime appointment. He has held academic appointments at the University of Pittsburgh, the University of Helsinki, the Turku School of Economics in Finland, and at other universities in the United States, Europe, and Asia.

His general interests focus upon cultural philosophies of communication and, more specifically, the ways culturally distinctive practices get woven into international and intercultural interactions. His studies focus upon Native American, popular American, Russian, and Finnish communication practices, with special attention to the relationship between language use, culture, spirit, and nature.

John P. Caughlin (Ph.D., University of Texas at Austin, 1997) is Conrad Professorial Scholar, Associate Professor, and Associate Head of Communication at the University of Illinois at Urbana-Champaign. His research focuses on the avoidance of communication in various contexts, such as when relational partners or families deal with health challenges. He has published recently in journals such as *Communication Monographs, Health Communication, Human Communication Research,* and *Journal of Social and Personal Relationships.* His awards include the Brommel Award from the National Communication Association for contributions to family communication, the Garrison Award for the Analysis of Interpersonal Communication in Applied Settings, the Miller Early Career Achievement Award from the International Association for Relationship Research, the Arnold O. Beckman Research Award from the University of Illinois Research Board, and the Franklin H. Knower Article Award from the Interpersonal Communication Division of the National Communication Association.

Guo-Ming Chen is Professor of Communication Studies at the University of Rhode Island. He was the recipient of the 1987 outstanding dissertation award and the founding president of the Association for Chinese Communication Studies. He served as Chair of the ECA Intercultural Communication Interest Group and the co-editor of the *International and Intercultural Communication Annual.* In addition to serving as an editorial board member of several professional journals, presently Chen is the Executive Director of the International Association for Intercultural Communication Studies and the co-editor of *China Media Research.* His primary research interests are in intercultural/organizational/global communication. Chen has published numerous articles, books, book chapters, and essays. Those books include *Foundations of Intercultural Communication, Introduction to Human Communication, Communication and Global Society, A Study of Intercultural Communication Competence, Chinese Conflict Management and Resolution,* and *Theories and Principles of Chinese Communication.*

George Cheney (Ph.D., Purdue University, 1985) is Professor of Communication Studies incoming Coordinator of Doctoral Education and Research for the College of Communication and Information, both at Kent State University. Previously, he held faculty positions at the universities of Illinois at Urbana-Champaign, Colorado-Boulder, Montana-Missoula, Utah, and Texas-Austin. George has held administrative positions in communication departments, a campus quality-of-worklife program, an interdisciplinary peace and conflict studies program, a human rights center, and a service-learning institute. George has had opportunities to teach, lecture, conduct research, or consult in Denmark, Spain, the Netherlands, Mexico, and Colombia, in addition to holding a position as adjunct professor at the University of Waikato in Hamilton, New Zealand since 1998. George has authored or co-authored eight books and nearly 100 articles, chapters, and reviews. His most recent book is the *Handbook of Communication Ethics* (Cheney, May & Munshi, 2011) commissioned by the International Communication Association and published by Routledge. Together with three colleagues in Europe, he is editing the Routledge *Companion* *to Alternative Organization* (for 2013). George is the recipient of numerous professional awards, regularly contributes to public discourse through speeches and op-eds, and is a strong proponent of service learning.

Celeste Condit is a professor at the University of Georgia in the department of Communication Studies, where she teaches courses in rhetoric. For the past decade and a half she has studied communication about genetics; the National Institutes of Health and the Centers for Disease Control have funded much of this research. She has published several books and dozens of academic articles. She is currently focusing her attention on ways to expand our pro-social emotions through public address. She gets great joy from getting outside on her mountain bike with her spouse, and she expands her imagination by reading science fiction.

Renee L. Cowan is an Assistant Professor in the Department of Communication at the University of Texas at San Antonio. Her primary research interests lie in investigating contemporary organizational issues, such as workplace bullying, work/life issues, and communication technology use in organizations (electronic mail and weblogs). Dr. Cowan's recent research focuses on workplace bullying and the human resource professional and work/life issues of blue-collar employees. Her research appears in such peer-reviewed journals as the *Journal of Computer-Mediated Communication, Communication Education, Communication Studies, Women & Language, Communication Quarterly, Qualitative Research Reports in Communication, Communication Research Reports,* and *Human Communication.*

Marianne Dainton (Ph.D., The Ohio State University) is a Professor of Communication at La Salle University in Philadelphia. She teaches interpersonal communication, group communication, and communication theory. Marianne's research focuses on relationship maintenance. She is the author of two books, with one more on the way: *Maintaining Relationships through Communication* (co-edited with Dan Canary, published by LEA) and *Applying Communication Theory for Professional Life* (co-authored with Elaine Zelley, published by Sage); and she has another book in press, *Conducting Research for Problem-Solving: A Professional Communication Perspective* (co-authored with Lynne Texter, published by Sage). Her personal life is spent exploring the city of Philadelphia, hanging at the Jersey Shore (but she refuses to fist pump), and trying to pass as a local while visiting foreign countries.

Amber N. Finn (Ph.D., University of North Texas, 2007) is an assistant professor in the Department of Communication Studies at Texas Christian University. She serves as the director of the basic course and facilitates instructional communication training for new graduate teaching assistants. In addition, she teaches undergraduate courses in training and development and graduate seminars in instructional communication. Her research focuses on communication apprehension and communication in the instructional process. Her research has appeared in *Communication Education, Communication Quarterly, Southern Communication Journal,* and other communication journals. Dr. Finn can be reached at a.n.finn@tcu.edu.

Jennifer Gibbs (Ph.D., University of Southern California) is an Associate Professor of Communication at Rutgers University's School of Communication and Information. Her research interests include the use of the Internet and social media for online self-presentation and relationship formation as well as collaboration and knowledge sharing in virtual, multicultural work contexts. She has studied such contexts as online dating, online communities, and globally distributed teams and organizations. Her work has been published in such leading journals as *Administrative Science Quarterly, Communication Research, Communication Yearbook, Human Relations, Journal of Computer-Mediated Communication, Journal of Social and Personal Relationships,* and *Organization Science,* among others.

Cindy L. Griffin is a professor in the department of Communication Studies and a member of the Women's Studies affiliate faculty at Colorado State University. Throughout her academic career, she has focused on questions of who can or is speaking, why those individuals can and do speak, whose voices and ideas have been ignored or neglected, and why those voices and ideas are ignored or silenced. Her communication scholarship is centered in feminist theories and practices, a commitment to invitational rhetoric and civility, and a desire for collaboration and respectful exchanges. She and her husband recently established the GriffinHarte Foundation, a nonprofit organization designed to provide support and resources for people interested in similar questions, research projects, and teaching efforts.

Alan K. Goodboy (Ph.D., West Virginia University, 2007) is an Associate Professor at West Virginia University. His research interests focus on instructional communication (e.g., instructional dissent) and interpersonal communication (e.g., relational maintenance). His research appears in such journals as *Communication Education, Communication Quarterly, Journal of Applied Communication, Communication Research Reports,* and *Communication Reports,* and in several other journals.

Dennis S. Gouran (Ph.D., University of Iowa, 1968) is Professor of Communication Arts and Sciences and Labor Studies and Employment Relations at The Pennsylvania State University. Professor Gouran has been President of both the Central States Communication Association and the National Communication Association. Additionally, he has served as Editor of Communication Studies and Communication Monographs. A specialist in the area of communication in decision-making and problem-solving groups, Professor Gouran has published in excess of 180 books, chapters, refereed articles, and reviews dealing with these and related subjects. He has directed to completion nearly 90 Ph.D., M.A., and Honors theses while serving as chair or member of numerous university, college, departmental, and professional association committees, as well as being a member of three to eleven editorial boards concurrently for every year from 1970 to the present.

Laura K. Guerrero (Ph.D., University of Arizona) is a professor in the Hugh Downs School of Human Communication at Arizona State University where she teaches courses in relational communication, nonverbal communication, and research methods. Her research focuses on both the "dark" and the "bright" sides of communication in relationships, including such topics as jealousy, hurtful events, conflict, nonverbal intimacy, relational maintenance, forgiveness, and attachment. Her book credits include *Close Encounters: Communication in Relationships* (coauthored with P. Andersen & W. Afifi), *Nonverbal Communication in Close Relationships* (coauthored with K. Floyd), *Nonverbal Communication* (coauthored with J. Burgoon & K. Floyd), *The Handbook of Communication and Emotion* (co-edited with P. Andersen), and *The Nonverbal Communication Reader* (co-edited with M. Hecht). She has received several research awards, including the Early Career Achievement Award from the International Association for Relationship Research and the Western States Communication Association's Dickens Award for outstanding research.

Ashley A. Hanna is a doctoral student in the Department of Communication at Michigan State University. Her research interests focus on interpersonal relationships, especially relating to disclosure behaviors and computer-mediated communication.

Michael Hecht is Distinguished Professor of Communication Arts and Sciences, and Crime, Law, and Justice at the Pennsylvania State University. A researcher in health and intercultural communication, he has been involved in many community-based research programs and collaborations, conducting research for federally funded drug abuse and treatment programs, crime prevention organizations, and mental health agencies. His current focus is co-directing the Drug Resistance Strategies Project, which studies how and why adolescents use drugs. The project is engaged in three major collaborative effort, including the first rural substance abuse prevention curriculum for rural middle schools. Second, the project is partnering with D.A.R.E. America to distribute rural, suburban, and urban versions of its effective multicultural middle school drug resistance curriculum, titled *keepin' it REAL.* Finally, the same curriculum is being nationally distributed through the Web-based Discovery Health, Penn State, and ETR Publishers to reach more schools and communities. The Drug Resistances Strategies Project is a model for the integration of teaching, research, and outreach at the university and for engaged scholarship by conducting research in collaboration with various communities to effect important social problems.

Lawrence A. Hosman is a Professor of Communication Studies at the University of Southern Mississippi. He received his Ph.D. from the University of Iowa. His areas of research interest are language, persuasion, and interpersonal communication, with a particular interest in powerful and powerless language.

Marian L. Houser is an Associate Professor in the Communication Studies Department at Texas State University–San Marcos. Her primary research interest is in the area of communication in relationships with a focus on teacher-student relationships (traditional versus nontraditional students and face-to-face versus electronic) and student learning indicators, as well as interpersonal communication with a focus on dating initiation and relational conflict. In addition to receiving numerous departmental teaching awards, Dr. Houser was the recent recipient of the President's Award for Scholarly and Creative Activities. In 2010, she received the Eastern Communication Association's Past-President's Award for her contributions to research and teaching. Dr. Houser has published and/or presented over 60 research studies and takes great pride in the 20-plus manuscripts she has published and/or presented with her students.

Robert L. Ivie is Professor of American Studies & Communication and Culture at Indiana University, Bloomington, USA, and Honorary Professor of Rhetoric at the University of Copenhagen in Denmark. He teaches courses on political communication, democratic dissent, war propaganda, and peace-building communication, as well as graduate seminars on rhetorical criticism, rhetorical theory, war rhetoric, and discourses of democracy. He has served as the editor of *Communication and Critical/Cultural Studies,* the *Quarterly Journal of Speech,* and the *Western Journal of Communication.* His research focuses on the rhetorical critique of U.S. political culture with particular emphasis on democracy and its relationship to the problem of war. His current research project is a study of political myth, which examines the cultural origins of the post-9/11 rhetoric of evil. It constructs a genealogy of the American image of the devil embedded in ritual wars of redemption and explores democracy's untapped potential for resisting the projection of evil. Ivie's 90 articles, chapters, and reviews are published in a wide range of national and international journals and books of communication, historical, political, and cultural scholarship. He is the author or coauthor of four books, including most recently *Dissent from War* (2007) and Democracy and *America's War on Terror* (2005).

Ronald L. Jackson II is Dean of the McMicken College of Arts and Sciences at the University of Cincinnati. Dr. Ronald L. Jackson II is one of the leading communication and identity scholars in the nation. He is Past President of the Eastern Communication Association and currently co-editor (with Kent Ono) of the widely cited journal *Critical Studies in Media Communication.* His research examines how theories of identity relate to intercultural and gender communication. In his teaching and research, he explores how and why people negotiate and define themselves as they do. Additionally, Professor Jackson's research includes empirical, conceptual, and critical approaches to the study of masculinity, identity negotiation, Whiteness, and Afrocentricity. He is author or editor of twelve books including the recently released *Global Masculinities and Manhood* (with Murali Balaji, University of Illinois Press). He is already working on his next book (with Jamel Bell) titled *The Tyler Perry Reader.*

Jeffrey W. Kassing is Professor of Communication Studies at Arizona State University where he teaches graduate and undergraduate courses in organizational, applied, and environmental communication, as well as research methods. He earned his Ph.D. from Kent State University in 1997 with an emphasis in organizational communication. Dr. Kassing's primary line of research concerns how employees express dissent about organizational policies and practices. This work, which began with his dissertation and the development of the Organizational Dissent Scale, now spans over a decade and appears in numerous scholarly outlets. He is the author of *Dissent in Organizations* (2011) and coauthor with Vincent Waldron of *Managing Risk in Communication Encounters: Strategies for the Workplace.*

Lisa Keränen (Ph.D., University of Pittsburgh, 2003) is Associate Professor and Director of Graduate Studies in the Department of Communication and Associate of the Program for Arts & Humanities in Health Care at the University of Colorado Denver. Her research and teaching principally concern the rhetorics of medicine, health, and bioethics. In addition to her book, *Scientific Characters: Rhetoric, Politics, and Trust in Breast Cancer Research* (2010, University of Alabama Press), her publications appear in *Academic Medicine, Argumentation & Advocacy, Quarterly Journal of Speech, Rhetoric & Public Affairs,* and *Journal of Medical Humanities,* among other venues. Keränen received the 2010 Karl R. Wallace Memorial Research Award from the National Communication Association (NCA) and currently serves as Second Vice-President of the Association for the Rhetoric of Science & Technology (ARST).

Gary L. Kreps (Ph.D., University of Southern California, 1979) is a University Distinguished Professor and Chair of the Department of Communication at George Mason University in Fairfax, Virginia, where he directs the Center for Health and Risk Communication. His research examines the role of communication in providing high quality care, promoting public health, reducing health disparities, and informing effective health decision-making related to such health issues as cancer, HIV/AIDS, and chronic disease. He is an active scholar, who has published more than 300 books, articles, and chapters concerning the applications of communication knowledge in society. A number of federal and international government agencies, foundations, and corporations have funded his research, and he has received many awards for his scholarship.

Kenneth A. Lachlan (Ph.D., Michigan State University) is Associate Professor and Chair of the Communication Department at the University of Massachusetts Boston. His research focuses on psychological responses to mediated information, with a particular emphasis on crisis and risk communication campaigns, and on new media technologies. His research on video games has included studies examining the uses and gratifications associated with console gaming, the role of user attributes in the production of interactive content, the impact of violent games on aggressive cognition and mood states, and video game content characteristics that lend themselves well to behavioral modeling. He teaches a broad range of courses on media psychology and media effects in both macro and micro level processes.

Betty H. La France Ph.D. (Michigan State University) is a communication scientist whose expertise is in social influence. Her specific interest area is the expression of intimacy and sexual communication in interpersonal relationships. She is a quantitative methodologist who focuses on measurement, modeling, and meta-analysis. Her publications have appeared in such academic journals as *Communication Monographs, Communication Quarterly, Southern Communication Journal, Communication Reports,* and *Communication Studies.* She is currently a faculty member in the Department of Communication at Northern Illinois University.

Timothy R. Levine is a professor in the Department of Communication at Michigan State University where he received his Ph.D. in 1992. Besides deception, his teaching and research interests include interpersonal communication, persuasion, cross-cultural communication, and quantitative (especially experimental) research methods. Levine has authored more than 100 journal articles. In 2011, he received MSU's Distinguished Faculty Award.

Sean Luechtefeld is a doctoral student in the Department of Communication at the University of Maryland, College Park. His research explores rhetoric and political culture, particularly as it relates to presidential rhetoric during times of economic downturn.

Jennifer A. Malkowski (M.A., San Diego State University, 2008) is a doctoral student in the Department of Communication Studies at the University of Colorado Boulder. Her research pays particular attention to how identity, gender, and inequality influence healthcare decision-making processes. Most broadly, she examines stages of disease messaging that contribute to public understandings of autonomy, risk, and responsibility. More specifically, her work examines the tension between a physician's obligation to safeguard public health and the rights of individuals to make decisions concerning vaccination. She currently serves as a Communication Coach with the Foundations of Doctoring Program at the University of Colorado Denver's School of Medicine and as an Assistant Coordinator with Community Health, a division of the Wardenberg Health Center at the University of Colorado at Boulder.

Matthew M. Martin (Ph.D., Kent State University, 1992) is a Professor and Chair in the Department of Communication Studies at West Virginia University. His teaching and research focus on instructional and interpersonal communication. He is the coauthor or author of over 100 scholarly articles and book chapters.

Raymie E. McKerrow is the Charles E. Zumkehr Professor of Communication, School of Communication Studies, Ohio University, Athens, OH 45701. A past president of the Eastern Communication Association and the National Communication Association, he is the current editor of the *Quarterly Journal of Speech*. His research has focused on the intersection of postmodernism, rhetoric, and culture. He teaches graduate seminars in feminist rhetoric, rhetoric and culture, and Foucault and social change.

Mitchell S. McKinney is the co-author/editor of five books, including *Communication in the 2008 U.S. Election: Digital Natives Elect a President* (with Mary C. Banwart), *The 1992 Presidential Debates in Focus* (with Diana B. Carlin), *Civic Dialogue in the 1996 Presidential Campaign* (with Lynda Lee Kaid & John C. Tedesco), and two edited volumes of political communication studies, including *The Millennium Election: Communication in the 2000 Campaign,* and *Communicating Politics: Engaging the Public in Democratic Life.* His research appears in major communication, journalism, and political science journals, including the *Journal of Communication, Communication Monographs, Communication Studies, Journalism Studies,* and *American Behavioral Scientist.* McKinney has combined practical political experience with his training as a political communication scholar, having served as a staff member in the U.S. Senate and at the White House. He has served as a consultant to C-SPAN and also the U.S. Commission on Presidential Debates, advising the Commission on how debates might be structured in order to better educate voters. Dr. McKinney has provided expert political commentary for such national media as the *New York Times, USA Today, CNN* and *NPR.*

Ashley Middleton is a doctoral student at the University of Illinois, Urbana-Champaign. She received her M.A. from the University of Texas at Austin in 2008. She is interested in family communication and alcohol/drug problems. Her work has been published in *Communication Monographs, Health Communication,* and the *Journal of Social and Personal Relationships.*

Michelle Miller-Day is Michelle Miller-Day is Professor of Communication Studies at Chapman University. Her research addresses human communication and health, including such areas as substance use prevention, suicide, and issues related to families and mental health. Her community-embedded research has involved numerous creative projects to translate research findings into social change. For the past 20 years she has served as the principal qualitative methodologist for a National Institute on Drug Abuse line of research. This work has developed one of the most successful evidence-based substance use prevention programs in the United States and reaches youth in 43 countries worldwide.

Paul Mongeau (Ph.D., Michigan State University) is a Professor in the Hugh Downs School of Human Communication at Arizona State University in Tempe. His primary research interests are in interpersonal communication (e.g., dating, romantic relationship initiation; and friends with benefits) and social influence (e.g., message processing and emotional appeals). He previously taught at Miami University (Oxford, Ohio) and is the former editor of the *Journal of Social and Personal Relationships* and *Communication Studies.*

Scott A. Myers (Ph.D., Kent State University, 1995) is a Professor in the Department of Communication Studies at West Virginia University. He teaches courses in instructional communication, small group communication, and interpersonal communication. His research interests center primarily on the student-instructor relationship in the college classroom and the adult sibling relationship. His research appears in such journals as *Communication Education, Journal of Family Communication, Communication Research Reports,* and *Communication Quarterly,* among others. He is a former editor of *Communication Teacher* and a former Executive Director of the Central States Communication Association (CSCA), where he currently serves as the President.

Robin L. Nabi (Ph.D., Annenberg School for Communication, University of Pennsylvania, 1998) is a professor of communication at the University of California, Santa Barbara. Her research interests focus on the influence of discrete emotions on message processing and decision making in response to media messages that concern health or social issues. She has published over 50 articles and book chapters and co-edited the *SAGE Handbook of Media Processes and Effects.* She has served on several editorial boards, as the chair of the Mass Communication Division of the International Communication Association, and as a co-editor of *Media Psychology.*

Thomas K. Nakayama (Ph.D., University of Iowa) is professor of Communication Studies at Northeastern University. He is a fellow of the International Association of Intercultural Research, a former Libra Professor at the University of Maine, and a former Fulbrighter at the Université de Mons in Belgium. His research interests lie at the intersection of rhetoric, intercultural communication, and critical theory. His work addresses how racial difference functions rhetorically in society, as well as how larger economic, political, cultural, and social contexts function to structure intercultural communication and interaction in particular ways. He is the co-author of *Intercultural Communication in Contexts, Experiencing Intercultural Communication, Human Communication in Society,* and *Communication in Society.* He is the co-editor of *Whiteness: The Communication of Social Identity* and *The Handbook of Critical Intercultural Communication.* He is the founding editor of the *Journal of International and Intercultural Communication.*

Daniel J. O'Keefe is the Owen L. Coon Professor in the Department of Communication Studies at Northwestern University. He received his Ph.D. from the University of Illinois at Urbana-Champaign, and has been a faculty member at the University of Michigan, Pennsylvania State University, and the University of Illinois at Urbana-Champaign. His research focuses on persuasion and argumentation. He has received the National Communication Association's Charles Woolbert Research Award, its Golden Anniversary Monograph Award, its Rhetorical and Communication Theory Division Distinguished Scholar Award, and its Health Communication Division Article of the Year Award; the International Communication Association's Best Article Award and its Division 1 John E. Hunter Meta-Analysis Award; the American Forensic Association's Daniel Rohrer Memorial Research Award, the International Society for the Study of Argumentation's Distinguished Research Award, and teaching awards from Northwestern University, the University of Illinois, and the Central States Communication Association. He is the author of *Persuasion: Theory and Research* (Sage Publications).

Kent Ono is the Chairperson of the Department of Communication at the University of Utah. He studies rhetoric and discourse, media and film, and race, ethnic, and cultural studies. He authored *Contemporary MediaCulture and the Remnants of a Colonial Past* (Peter Lang, 2009); co-authored *Asian Americans and the Media* with Vincent Pham (Polity, 2009); and *Shifting*

Borders: Rhetoric, Immigration, and California's Proposition 187 with John Sloop (Temple University Press, 2002). He edited *Asian American Studies after Critical Mass* (Blackwell, 2005) and *A Companion to Asian American Studies* (Blackwell, 2005) and co-edited *Critical Rhetorics of Race* with Michael Lacy (New York University Press, 2011) and *Enterprise Zones: Critical Positions on Star Trek* with Taylor Harrison, Sarah Projansky, and Elyce Helford (Westview Press, 1996). He co-edits the book series "Critical Cultural Communication" with Sarah Banet-Weiser at New York University Press and also co-edits the *Critical Studies in Media Communication* journal with Ronald L. Jackson II.

Trevor Parry-Giles is an Associate Director for Academic & Professional Affairs at the National Communication Association. Prior to working at the NCA, he was a professor in the Department of Communication at the University of Maryland. He is the co-author *The Prime-Time Presidency: The West Wing and U.S. Nationalism* (University of Illinois Press) and *Constructing Clinton: Hyperreality and Presidential Image-Making in Postmodern Politics* (Peter Lang). Dr. Parry-Giles is also the author of *The Character of Justice: Rhetoric, Law, and Politics in the Supreme Court Confirmation Process* (Michigan State University Press). His research has appeared in the *Quarterly Journal of Speech, Rhetoric & Public Affairs, Critical Studies in Mass Communication,* and elsewhere.

Sandra Petronio, Ph.D., is a Professor in the Department of Communication Studies at IUPUI and in the IU School of Medicine, a senior affiliate faculty in the Charles Warren Fairbanks Center for Medical Ethics, IU Health, an adjunct faculty in the IU Schools of Nursing and Informatics. She has a B.A. in interdisciplinary social science from State University of New York at Stony Brook, as well as an M.A. in social psychology and a Ph.D. in communication studies, both from The University of Michigan. Dr. Petronio has held faculty positions at the University of Minnesota, Arizona State University, and Wayne State University, Detroit. Her areas of expertise are in health and family communication. She has published five books and numerous research articles. She studies privacy, disclosure, and confidentiality within family, health, and interpersonal contexts. Over the last 32 years she has developed, applied, and tested the evidenced-based theory of "*Communication Privacy Management*"; in 2002, she published, "Boundaries of Privacy: Dialectics of Disclosure" on this theory. This book won several national and international awards. Petronio continues to serve as the Director of the IUPUI *Translation into Practice* campus-wide initiative, which was launched six years ago.

Linda L. Putnam is a Professor in the Department of Communication at the University of California, Santa Barbara. Her current research interests include organizational conflict, discourse analysis in organizations, and gender and organizational communication. She is the co-editor of eight books and over 150 articles and book chapters. She is a Distinguished Scholar of the National Communication Association, a Fellow of the International Communication Association, and the recipient of a Lifetime Achievement Award from the International Association for Conflict Management and a Distinguished Service Award from the Academy of Management.

Michael E. Roloff (Ph.D., Michigan State University) is professor of Communication Studies. His research and teaching interests are in the general area of interpersonal influence. He has published articles and offers courses focused on persuasion, interpersonal compliance gaining, conflict management, organizational change and bargaining and negotiation. His current research is focused on conflict avoidance and serial arguing in intimate relationships, the interpretation and construction of persuasive messages, and the effects of planning and alternatives on negotiation processes. He has co-edited five research volumes: (1) *Persuasion: New Directions in Theory and Research,* (2) *Social Cognition and Communication,* (3) *Interpersonal Processes,* (4) *Communication and Negotiation,* and (5) *The Handbook of Communication Science.* He wrote *Interpersonal Communication: The Social Exchange Approach.* He completed a term as the editor of *Communication Yearbook* and is currently the co-editor of *Communication Research.* He is a Fellow of the International Communication Association and was selected to be a Distinguished Scholar of the National Communication Association. He was co-recipient of the Woolbert Award for Outstanding Contribution to Communication Research from the Speech Communication Association and of a publication award from the Social Cognition and Communication Division of the National Communication Association. In 2011, he received from the National Communication Association the Donald H. Ecroyd Award for Outstanding Teaching in Higher Education and the Mark L. Knapp Award for his contribution to research in Interpersonal Communication. He has been the Chair of the Interpersonal Communication Division of the National Communication Association. He served as the Director of the National Communication Association Publications Board and as a member of the Executive Committee of NCA. Professor Roloff has received several teaching awards from groups at Northwestern, including the Associated Student Government, the Mortar Board, and the Alumni Association. He is a member of the American Psychological Association, the American Sociological Association, the International Association for Relationship Research, the International Communication Association, the National Communication Association, and the Society for Personality and Social Psychology.

Chris Sawyer is currently ranked among the top 100 most published scholars in the field of Communication Studies and maintains an active research program into the causes, symptoms, and treatments of speech anxiety. A former Chair of NCA's Communication Apprehension and Avoidance Commission, Dr. Sawyer has received recognition as a teacher-scholar, including a nomination for the prestigious Minnie Stephens Piper Foundation Award for college teaching excellence; and he was a recent recipient is a past recipient of the College of Communication Distinguished Research and Creative Activity Award. In 1983, Dr. Sawyer began his college teaching career as an instructor at Tarrant County Junior College, Northwest Campus in Fort Worth, TX. In 1999, he joined the Communication Studies Department at Texas Christian University. He served as director of the Basic Speech Communication course from his appointment until 2005. A former department Chair, Dr. Sawyer currently holds the rank of Professor at TCU. He resides in Fort Worth with his wife, daughter, and two grandchildren.

Scott M. Schönfeldt-Aultman (Ph.D., Cultural Studies, University of California Davis; M.A., Speech and Communication Studies, San Francisco State University) is Associate Professor in the Communication Department at Saint Mary's College of California. His research, while broadly concerned with culture and communication, focuses on whiteness and rhetoric. He has published in *African Identities,* the *Journal of African Cultural Studies,* and *Applied Semiotics/Sémiotique Appliquée.* He is the co-author, with Gust A. Yep, of a chapter on South Africa's Heritage Day in *National Days/National Ways: Historical, Political, and Religious Celebrations around the World* (2004). He is the co-author of *Communication & Social Understanding* (2009) with M. K. Dick, E. M. Rigsby, & E. E. Tywoniak.

Ashleigh K. Shelton (M.A., University of Minnesota), a Ph.D. student at the University of Minnesota's School of Journalism and Mass Communication, joined the UMass Boston faculty as a lecturer in the spring of 2011. Her research focuses on the social and psychological dimensions of digital media technologies and, in particular, the entertainment value and effects of video games. Recent projects have included book chapters and articles examining the impact of naturally mapped controllers on presence; the linkage points between advergames, tourism and major mass communication theories; the relationship between virtual identities, virtual consumption and real world consumption; and the potential for presence to positively and negatively affect outcomes of media exposure. She also teaches courses on popular culture, media effects, and visual communication at both UMass Boston and the University of Minnesota.

Natasha Shrikant completed her masters in Communication at the University of Illinois at Urbana-Champaign and is currently a doctoral student at the University of Massachusetts at Amherst. In her research, Natasha examines the expression of ethnic and cultural identity in everyday interaction. Additionally, Natasha's research explores how the media portrays minority groups and how minority groups use different forms of media (i.e., social media) to constitute aspects of their own identities.

Kara Shultz is a Professor and Chairperson of the Department of Communication Studies at Bloomsburg University of Pennsylvania. She teaches a variety of courses in rhetoric and public advocacy and intercultural communication. Her research explores the use of rhetoric in constructing and contesting identity for marginalized cultural communities. Her essay "Every Child a Star" (And Some Other Failures): Rhetorical Trajectories of Guilt and Shame in the Cochlear Implant Debates" appeared in the August 2000 *Quarterly Journal of Speech.* In addition, she has a co-authored article that appeared in *The Howard Journal of Communication* (1998, July-September); two book chapters in the edited volumes *Conflict and Diversity* and *Handbook of Communication and People with Disabilities;* and an article "On Establishing a More Authentic Relationship with Food: From Heidegger to Oprah on Slowing Down Fast Food" in the forthcoming book on *The Rhetoric of Food.*

Brian Spitzberg received his B.A. at the University of Texas at Arlington (1978), and his M.A. (1980) and Ph.D. (1981) in Communication Arts and Sciences at the University of Southern California. He has taught at San Diego State since 1989, where he was promoted to Full Professor in 1995, and honored with the title Senate Distinguished Professor in 2009. His areas of research include communication assessment, interpersonal communication skills, conflict, jealousy, infidelity, intimate violence, sexual coercion, and stalking. He is the author or co-author of three scholarly books, the co-editor of three scholarly books, and the author or coauthor of over 100 scholarly articles and chapters. His coauthored 2004 book, *The Dark Side of Relationship Pursuit: From Attraction to Obsession and Stalking,* won the 2006 International Association for Relationship Research Book Award. He is currently working on a multidisciplinary National Science Foundation grant project on mapping the diffusion of ideas on the Internet. He is also an active member of the Association for Threat Assessment Professionals.

Keri K. Stephens is an Assistant Professor of Communication Studies at the University of Texas at Austin. Her research examines how people use information and communication technologies (ICTs) in organizations and how that affects overload and emergency/crisis communication. Her published work appears in places like *Communication Theory, Management Communication Quarterly,* the *Journal of Computer-Mediated Communication, Communication Education,* the *Journal* of *Health Communication, Communication Research,* the *Journal of Public Relations Research,* and *The Handbook of Crisis Communication.* She is a co-author of the book, *Information and Communication Technology in Action: Linking Theory and Narratives of Practice.* She has won several teaching awards, taught research methods courses in Norway, and currently teaches organizational communication, sales communication, and workplace technology use. She has also advised four undergraduate research teams that have studied topics like using mobile devices in meetings, college student ICT use, and crisis communication uses of Twitter.

Paul D. Turman (Ph.D. University of Nebraska-Lincoln, 2000) is the Associate Vice President for Academic Affairs with the South Dakota Board of Regents. In his position, Dr. Turman performs a range of assessment, institutional research, and program management responsibilities. Before joining the South Dakota Board of Regents staff, Dr. Turman taught as an assistant professor at the University of Northern Iowa (UNI), having received promotion and tenure at the associate level before assuming his current position in 2006. Prior to his work at UNI, he taught at the collegiate level for six years in various capacities as instructor and graduate teaching assistant at South Dakota State University and the University of Nebraska-Lincoln and was recognized for outstanding teaching. Throughout his academic career Dr. Turman has maintained an active research agenda in the areas of instructional and group communication, focusing his research efforts on communication variables that impact student classroom outcomes. He has published 34 peer reviewed research articles, as well as three co-authored books published by Sage. In his current role, Dr. Turman continues to find a number of avenues for advancing his research interests working with colleagues on the intersections between communication and sport.

Joseph B. Walther is a professor in the Department of Communication and the Department of Telecommunication, Information Studies & Media at Michigan State University. His research and teaching focus on interpersonal and group relations via computer-mediated communication, in personal, organizational, and educational settings.

Myra Washington is an assistant professor. Myra Washington is an assistant professor in the Communication and Journalism department at the University of New Mexico. She writes about race and mixed-race in popular culture, and focuses specifically on mixed-race Blasians (Black & Asians).

Benjamin Wiedmaier (M.A., San Diego State University) is a doctoral student in the Hugh Downs School of Human Communication at Arizona State University. His research interests focus primarily on initial stages of romantic relationships and their formation, as well as translational work aimed at bringing the wealth of knowledge housed within the academy to the public.

SunWolf (M.A., Ph.D., J.D.) is a former trial attorney and performing storyteller. Now Professor at Santa Clara University, she teaches persuasion, groups, friendships & romances, multicultural folktales, interpersonal communication, and the science of happiness. She is also Visiting Professor at her university's law school. Her scholarship focuses on communication in groups, storytelling, persuasion, and the neuroscience of social behaviors. She has served on the editorial boards of *Communication Monographs, Small Group Research,* the *Journal of Applied Communication Research,* and *Communication Studies.* She is the originator of Decisional Regret Theory, and her scholarship about juries and childhood peer groups has won numerous national awards. Her book, *Practical Jury Dynamics2: From One Juror's Trial Perceptions to the Group's Decision-Making Processes,* won NCA's Ernest Bormann Book Award. In 2008, she received her university's Achievement in Scholarship Award for scholarly work over the previous five years that represents a major contribution to a field of knowledge. The book now in her typewriter is *Naming,* describing the complex social rules and consequences of what we call ourselves and others. In the remaining cracks of her life, she's a collector of antique typewriters, multicultural ghost tales, and a poet. She's on Twitter as @TheSocialBrain with a web site that invites new thinking in diverse fields: ProfessorSunWolf.com

Gust A. Yep (Ph.D. University of Southern California) is Professor of Communication Studies, Core Graduate Faculty of Sexuality Studies, and Faculty of the Ed. D. Program in Educational Leadership at San Francisco State University. He has three ongoing research programs: (1) Communication at the intersection of race, class, gender, sexuality, ability, and nation with a focus on queer theory and quare studies; (2) communication and HIV/AIDS education and prevention with a focus on communities of color and gender and sexual minorities; and, (3) critical intercultural communication with a focus on whiteness, culture, and pedagogy. He has authored over 60 articles in interdisciplinary journals and anthologies. He has co-authored and/or co-edited three books, including *Queer Theory and Communication: From Disciplining Queers to Queering the Discipline(s).* He served as the editor of the National Communication Association Non-serial Publications Program (Book Series) during 2006 to 2008. Finally, he has received a number of teaching, mentoring, community service, and research awards, including the National Communication Association Randy Majors Memorial Award for "outstanding scholarship in lesbian, gay, bisexual, and transgender studies in communication" in 2006 and the San Francisco State University Distinguished Faculty Award for Professional Achievement in Research in 2011.

Priscilla Young is adjunct faculty in the Department of Communication Studies at the University of Rhode Island and in the Department of English at Johnson and Wales University. A graduate of the University of Rhode Island's master's program in Communication Studies, she received the department's Graduate Excellence Award and also its Community Scholar Award, the only student in her class to receive two awards. Young is secretary/treasurer of the International Association for Intercultural Communication Studies and is the organization's newsletter editor and designer. Her previous careers include executive management, public relations, fund development, and radio broadcasting. Young has freelanced as a news feature writer over three decades and continues to do so currently.

Ted Zorn is Pro Vice-Chancellor of the College of Business at Massey University, New Zealand. His teaching and research interests are organizational change processes, such as information technology implementation, change-related communication, and enhancing workplace well being. Ted has received more than $3M in research grant funding, and has been appointed chair of the Business & Economics panel for the 2012 New Zealand national Performance Based Research Assessment exercise. He is the incoming chair of the Organizational Communication Division of the International Communication Association (ICA), past editor of *Management Communication Quarterly,* past chair of the Organizational Communication Division of the National Communication Association (NCA), and the 2006 recipient of ICA's Frederic Jablin Award for Outstanding Contribution to Organizational Communication. He has published more than 80 books, articles, and chapters, including recent articles in *Human Communication Research, Public Understanding of Science,* the *Journal of Applied Communication Research, Management Communication Quarterly, New Media & Society,* and *Information, Communication & Society.* He is also the co-author of the textbook *Organizational Communication in an Age of Globalization,* now in its second edition.

SECTION 1

COMPUTER-MEDIATED COMMUNICATION

The computer-mediated communication (CMC) context focuses on communication that occurs using computer technologies as the medium to convey messages. Accordingly, CMC scholars examine mediated communication across personal computers, Internet technologies, video/audio recordings, mobile devices, and wireless technologies. Some major areas of research in CMC include cyberbullying, chat rooms, texting, online support groups, blogging, email, social networking sites, and podcasting. This chapter focuses on three important areas of CMC research: (1) online dating, (2) Facebook, and (3) Internet privacy. First, Jennifer Gibbs (Rutgers University) examines the dating scene in online personals to answer the question: How can online daters be more successful in meeting a potential romantic partner? Second, Ashley Hanna and Joseph Walther (Michigan State University) examine how Facebook communicates to receivers by answering the question: What perceptions do people form after viewing Facebook profiles? Third, Sandra Petronio (IUPUI) reviews communication privacy management research to answer the question: What are we giving up and what are we risking when we disclose our private information online? With CMC and online communication increasing exponentially through mediums such as Facebook, Google +, Skype, Twitter, Youtube, iPAD/Droid apps, and even plain "old" email, it is ever important to understand the messages we send through computers. These research programs will help you navigate your Facebook profile choices, online disclosures, and online dating profiles. Only time will tell how computer mediated technologies will continue to change after the publication of this chapter!

HOW TO BE SUCCESSFUL IN ONLINE DATING

JENNIFER L. GIBBS, RUTGERS UNIVERSITY

When I began studying online dating in 2003, I had no idea it would turn into an ongoing research program with such importance for the field of communication. It all started when two of my friends and fellow graduate students at USC, Nicole Ellison and Rebecca Heino, invited me to collaborate with them on a project on online dating. It made sense as we all had interests in new technologies and how they were changing the way we communicate. At the time, the World Wide Web was relatively new and there was little scholarship on online communication, and even less published research on Internet dating. I also had a personal interest in this topic, as I had met my husband on Match.com back in 1998, when very few people had ever tried online matchmaking. I've heard it said (and I fully agree) that research is "me-search," and the best research topics tend to be ones that are rooted in your own personal experience and passions. This is so because studying something about which you have particular knowledge and insight generally leads to more informed research, and choosing a topic that excites you provides motivation to drive and sustain your interest in the research.

Although you—as a college student who probably has many opportunities to meet people in your peer group—might not understand the appeal of going online and paying a web site in order to find a date, online dating has become a popular dating option for several reasons. First, young people are waiting until they get older to settle down and get married, and once one is out of school and in the workplace it becomes increasingly difficult to meet potential romantic partners. Second, many people are busy and spend much of their day in front of the computer, and the ease of browsing through profiles and corresponding with prospective mates at their convenience is appealing. Finally, the Internet has become a very social tool that plays a significant role in our lives—as evidenced by the rise of social media such as Facebook and Twitter—and thus using it for dating purposes is becoming seen as natural as well. Online dating is particularly attractive for groups such as gays, lesbians, and middle-aged heterosexuals (including those who are divorced or widowed) who may find it more difficult to meet people offline. But it has gone from a once stigmatized to a mainstream practice within the population more broadly. And it does seem to work: A survey commissioned by Match.

com found that one in every five relationships now begins online (Chadwick Martin Bailey, 2010), and a survey commissioned by eHarmony even found that 5% of all marriages in the U.S. today are the result of an eHarmony connection (Harris Interactive, 2009). Online daters' goals range from simply wanting to meet new people to wanting to get married, although it is fair to say that most are looking for some kind of romantic or sexual relationship.

More than just a fad or a popular trend, online dating is an interesting topic for communication scholars to study, since it requires individuals to form relationships with virtual strangers in a mediated environment in which they have less visual and contextual information and fewer social cues about one another. A number of communication scholars (including myself and my colleagues) have studied questions related to how online daters present themselves, form impressions of others, and establish relationships with potential partners. This chapter reviews our knowledge on this topic, focusing on the following question: How can online daters be more successful in meeting a potential romantic partner?

PRESENTING ONESELF ONLINE

Presenting oneself and assessing others in online dating can be challenging. When you meet someone face-to-face, you have many visual and social cues to provide clues about the person and their relationship to you. The way they are dressed, physical objects they are carrying (such as a book), and the physical location in which you meet may tell you about their background and interests.

You can read their body language and facial expressions to gauge their mood and how they feel about you. The other person can also use these cues to learn about you. But what about when you are just looking at a profile online? How should you present yourself in a way that is accurate yet garners attention? How do you know if someone is lying about their age, appearance, or marital status?

My colleagues and I have addressed such questions in our research. We have found that online daters navigate a tension between presenting an ideal self and an actual self (Ellison, Heino, & Gibbs, 2006). On one hand, they face pressure to portray themselves in the most positive, attractive light possible in their profile, in order to stand out and be noticed amidst hundreds of other profiles. On the other hand, there are competing pressures to create honest and accurate self-portrayals if one desires a romantic relationship, since the truth will eventually come out on an in-person date. The desire to view oneself as honest may also limit the amount of deception that takes place (Mazar & Ariely, 2006). In research with a national sample of Match.com users, we found that a full 94% of our respondents strongly disagreed they had intentionally misrepresented themselves in their profile or online communication, and 87% felt such misrepresentation was unacceptable. Despite these strong claims of their own honesty, they felt that other online daters routinely misrepresented aspects such as their physical appearance, relationship goals, age, income, and marital status (Gibbs, Ellison, & Heino, 2006).

Since people are unlikely to admit to something as socially undesirable as lying in an interview or even in an anonymous survey, several of my colleagues decided to measure how much online daters lie in their profiles in a more objective way, by bringing them into a lab and comparing their actual age, height, and weight with what they had claimed in their profiles. They found that a majority had indeed misrepresented one or more of these features, but that most lies were minor—such as shaving off five pounds or adding an inch to their height (Toma, Hancock, & Ellison, 2008). Although blatant deception is rare, online daters do tend to exaggerate and embellish the truth (Whitty, 2008). While this certainly happens offline as well, the online dating context offers certain features that allow for increased exaggeration and embellishment. First, users are anonymous and the information they have about one another is initially limited to the profile. Without a shared social network (in the form of shared friends and acquaintances) to temper misinformation, online daters are free to exaggerate their virtues in order to maximize their attractiveness (Fiore & Donath, 2004). They are also communicating asynchronously (at least initially), which allows them to engage in 'selective self-presentation' (Walther & Burgoon, 1992) by consciously controlling and editing their profiles to emphasize the positive and mask their negative attributes. This is not unique to online dating; we do this in other contexts, such as job interviews and writing a resume. Research has found that an online dating profile is similar to a 'resume' in which one tries to sell oneself to potential romantic partners rather than to employers (Heino, Ellison, & Gibbs, 2010).

Through qualitative interviews with online dating participants, we were able to explore this issue in more depth. We found that honesty online is complicated and that misrepresentation occurs in both intentional and unintentional ways (Ellison et al., 2006). First, online daters often portray an idealized or potential future version of the self, through strategies such as identifying themselves as active in a laundry list of activities (such as hiking, surfing, rollerblading) in which they rarely participate but which are in line with how they would like to see themselves. They may also describe themselves in euphemistic terms such as "curvy" or "average" rather than admitting they are overweight. Ellison and her colleagues conceive of the profile as a "promise made to an imagined audience that future face-to-face interaction will take place with someone who does not differ fundamentally from the person represented by the profile" (Ellison, Hancock, & Toma, 2012, p. 56). In this sense, the profile is like a 'psychological contract' that the online dater could be held to by potential future dates, and it is not considered deceptive as long as it *could* be true in the future.

Misrepresentation also occurs as an attempt to circumvent technological constraints of the site. For example, online daters often "fudge" demographic information such as their age by subtracting a few years in order to avoid being "filtered out" of searches. Many online dating sites allow users to perform searches on basic demographic criteria, such as age, height, weight, and geographic location. Since many users tend to perform searches using natural breakpoints (e.g., 35), it is common practice for those a few years older (36, 37, or 38) to list their age as 35 on their profile in order to appeal to a wider audience. They justify this by saying they tend to look younger or date younger people, and they often regard this as socially acceptable as long as they disclose their real age early on in their correspondence (Ellison et al., 2006). This is confirmed by an analysis of Match.com profiles, which found that spikes occurred at certain (more desirable) age points that were much higher than would be expected by chance. For example, there were a disproportionate number of 29-year-old female users, eight times higher than the number of females aged 30 to 34 (Epstein, 2007).

Finally, online daters may unintentionally misrepresent themselves due to the limits of their own self-knowledge. We call this the "foggy mirror" effect, in which individuals represent themselves on the basis of an inaccurate self-concept that may not correspond with how others see them (Ellison et al., 2006). That is, they may not be able to accurately describe themselves because there are blind spots in their self-concept, or things about themselves that they don't know. As one of our interviewees put it, "sometimes you will see a person who weighs 900 pounds and—this is just an exaggeration—and they will have on spandex, you'll think, 'God, I wish I had their mirror, because obviously their mirror tells them they look great.' It's the same thing with online" (Ellison et al., 2006, p. 13). Thus, users often unintentionally misrepresent themselves out of lack of awareness of themselves and how others may perceive them.

ASSESSING OTHERS AND FORMING RELATIONSHIPS ONLINE

Meeting people through online dating is fraught with uncertainty. There is usually no shared social network, and rather than meeting through a friend or an acquaintance, users are interacting with virtual strangers. They thus face privacy risks in disclosing intimate information. Given the relative anonymity and ease of deception online, it is important for online daters to assess and vet the credibility of potential partners in order to verify their identity claims. This is more difficult since there are fewer traditional identity cues and less immediate feedback (Gibbs, Ellison, & Lai, 2011), but online environments do allow for a variety of information seeking strategies, which refer to ways in which we seek information about others (Ramirez, Walther, Burgoon, & Sunnafrank, 2002).

Although less information is available from nonverbal and social context cues, online dating participants do scrutinize the cues that are present and use them to form impressions of others. As a result, small cues may become exaggerated or take on greater importance. For example, a profile with a typo or a misspelling may be rejected based on the assumption that the profile creator is lazy or uneducated (Ellison et al., 2006). As Walther's (1996) hyperpersonal effect predicts, online daters have the tendency to idealize potential partners on the basis of limited cues, and they fill in the gaps by building up a fantasy persona that may be inaccurate and unrealistic. This may explain why the longer communicators wait to meet in person, the more likely their first meeting is to end up in rejection (Ramirez & Zhang, 2007).

The process of verifying identity claims online is known as "warranting" (Walther & Parks, 2002). Warranting involves establishing a reliable link between an online persona and a "corporeally-anchored person in the physical world" (Walther, Van Der Heide, Hamel, & Shulman, 2009, p. 232). Generally, messages generated by others carry more weight than information we report about ourselves (which is easier to manipulate). Support for the warranting principle has been found in several experiments that found other-generated claims about qualities such as one's attractiveness and extraversion are more compelling than self-generated claims in social network sites (Walther et al., 2008; 2009; Utz, 2010).

A few sites exist, such as truedater.com, where online daters can write reviews of their online dates and caution others against fake profiles or users to be avoided for other reasons. But, for the most part, online dating participants cannot rely on other-generated accounts to warrant their identity claims. They can, however, engage in tactics such as "showing" rather than "telling" (Ellison et al., 2006); for example, it is more credible to demonstrate one's sense of humor by writing a clever, witty profile than by simply stating "I am hilarious" in an otherwise dull profile (Gibbs et al., 2011). Our research found evidence that online dating participants used a variety of tactics to reduce uncertainty and verify the credibility of potential partners, by gathering information from both online and offline sources.

These tactics—classified as passive, active, interactive, and extractive (Ramirez et al., 2002)—include comparing profiles on multiple web sites or saving emails to check for consistency, checking public records such as white pages, and "Googling" people to warrant their online claims. Some of our participants even went as far as to perform home property value searches, drawing on the rich stores of personal information accessible online. The most common strategies, however, were interactive and involved asking direct questions of the other person. Those who used more strategies to reduce uncertainty about others tended to disclose more personal information about themselves, perhaps because such "detective work" reduced their privacy concerns and made them more comfortable revealing intimate information to strangers they met online (Gibbs et al., 2011). Such individuals were also likely to have a higher sense of self-efficacy (or confidence in their own abilities) and more Internet experience.

Assessing others online is also complicated by the level of choice available, or what is known as the "paradox of choice." Having access to a large pool of eligible dating partners is convenient and affords users a great deal of choice, but this choice can also be paralyzing and lead to poor decisions. Online dating models vary from sites like Match.com that allow users to browse through all user profiles and choose whom to contact to sites like eHarmony, in which users go through extensive personality tests and are then matched up with others according to scientific algorithms that assess their compatibility. Both models provide a great deal more choice of potential dating partners than most individuals encounter in their offline lives. Related to the notion of expanded choice, my colleagues and I (Heino et al., 2010) observed a prevalent "market" metaphor in how online dating participants talked about their experiences. Our interviewees talked about online dating as "people shopping" and used terms like "sales pipeline," "catalog," and "supermarket" to describe the process. They described viewing profiles as resumes and mentally accounting for embellishments of others, as well as trying to sell themselves. Our interviews revealed that the market metaphor encouraged a mentality in which people became more picky and rejected profiles on the basis of trivial criteria, such as privileged demographic fields (age, height, weight), rather than getting a holistic sense of the person; and that they regarded others as well as themselves as commodities or products to buy and sell, with an emphasis on "relationshopping" (shopping for a mate) rather than "relationshipping" (getting to know someone and developing a relationship). As one male put it, "the downside of it is, I think, that the expectations are very much of a consumer—that sort of instant karma expectation, expecting a connection with less effort" (Heino et al., 2010, p. 440).

ADVICE FOR ONLINE DATERS

Based on what we know about online dating, how can online daters be more successful? The research on misrepresentation in online dating suggests that in order to be successful, online daters should strive to present themselves in a positive and attractive yet still honest and accurate light. As in offline situations, such as job interviews and first dates, it is helpful to think carefully about how you present yourself in your profile; first impressions count for a lot and are hard to change. Since many people are not always aware of how others perceive them, a good strategy is to ask a friend or a family member to read over one's profile and give input. Many online dating sites provide tips, and we found that online daters often engage in their own recursive process of assessing others and then applying the rules to their own self-presentation (Ellison et al., 2006). For example, one may become disillusioned with profiles that only include one or two (unrealistic) photos, and then make an effort to post multiple photos of oneself in a variety of situations to portray oneself more accurately. Despite the prevalence of at least minor misrepresentation (e.g., fudging one's age or accentuating one's appearance) in online dating, honesty is still the best policy. Gibbs et al. (2006) found that online daters who were more honest and disclosed more personal feelings and information were more likely to consider themselves successful in achieving their goals; and Baker (2005) also found that being open and honest in one's self-disclosures was one of the factors in developing successful long-term relationships. Given that others are often not completely honest in their profiles, however, it is important to find ways to "warrant" others' identity claims by looking for multiple photos, asking questions and checking for consistency, or Googling them. Don't wait too long to meet in person, since it is easy to build up a fantasy persona based on limited cues that may not be completely accurate. Finally, emphasizing "relationshopping" may provide more choice and convenience in selecting potential partners, but online daters should not neglect the "relationshipping" aspect and expect to have an instant connection with little effort. Online dating has real advantages in providing a portal or an initial introduction to individuals who may never meet otherwise, but it is just the first step. Finding the right person requires making good choices (and being able to identify which criteria will make one a good partner) initially, but the bulk of relationship development occurs offline, beyond the online dating site itself.

REFERENCES

Baker, A. J. (2005). *Double click: Romance and commitment among online couples.* Cresskill, NJ: Hampton Press.

Chadwick, Martin Bailey. (2010). *Recent trends: Online dating.* Available at http://blog.match.com/2010/05/17/stay-up-to-date-introducing-the-official-match-com-blog/

Ellison, N. B., Heino, R. D., & Gibbs, J. L. (2006). Managing impressions online: Self-presentation processes in the online dating environment. *Journal of Computer-Mediated Communication 11*(2), article 2. Available at http://jcmc.indiana.edu/vol11/issue2/ellison.html.

Ellison, N. B., Hancock, J. T., & Toma, C. L. (2012). Profile as promise: A framework for conceptualizing veracity in online dating self- presentations. *New Media & Society 14,* 45–62.

Epstein, R. (2007). The truth about online dating. *Scientific American Mind, 18,* 1, 8–35.

Fiore, A. T., & Donath, J. S. (2004). Online personals: An overview. In *Proceedings of the Conference on Human Factors in Computing Systems*. New York: ACM, 1395–1398.

Gibbs, J. L., Ellison, N. B., & Heino, R. D. (2006). Self-presentation in online personals: The role of anticipated future interaction, self-disclosure, and perceived success in Internet dating. *Communication Research, 33,* 152–177.

Gibbs, J. L., Ellison, N. B., & Lai, C. H. (2011). First comes love, then comes Google: An investigation of uncertainty reduction strategies and self-disclosure in online dating. *Communication Research, 38,* 70–100.

Harris Interactive. (2009). *eHarmony Marriage Metrics Study.* Available at http://download.eharmony.com/pdf/Harris-09-Executive-Summary.pdf.

Heino, R. D., Ellison, N. B., & Gibbs, J. L. (2010). Relationshopping: Investigating the market metaphor in online dating. *Journal of Social and Personal Relationships, 27,* 427–447.

Mazar, N., & Ariely, D. (2006). Dishonesty in everyday life and its policy implications. *Journal of Public Policy & Marketing, 25,* 1–21.

Ramirez, A., Walther, J. B., Burgoon, J. K., & Sunnafrank, M. (2002). Information-seeking strategies, uncertainty, and computer-mediated communication: Toward a conceptual model. *Human Communication Research, 28,* 213–228.

Ramirez, A., & Zhang, S. (2007). When online meets offline: The effect of modality switching on relational communication. *Communication Monographs, 74,* 287–310.

Toma C. L., Hancock, J. T., & Ellison, N. B. (2008). Separating fact from fiction: An examination of deceptive self-presentation in online dating profiles. *Personality and Social Psychology Bulletin, 34,* 1023–1036.

Utz, S. (2010). Show me your friends and I will tell you what type of person you are: How one's profile, number of friends, and type of friends influence impression formation on social network sites. *Journal of Computer-Mediated Communication, 15,* 314–335.

Walther, J. B. (1996). Computer-mediated communication: Impersonal, interpersonal, and hyperpersonal interaction. *Communication Research, 23,* 3–43.

Walther, J. B., & Burgoon, J. K. (1992). Relational communication in computer-mediated interaction. *Human Communication Research, 19,* 50–88.

Walther, J. B., & Parks, M. R. (2002). Cues filtered out, cues filtered in: Computer-mediated communication and relationships. In M. L. Knapp & J. A. Daly (Eds.), *Handbook of interpersonal communication* (3rd ed., pp. 529–563). Thousand Oaks, CA: Sage.

Walther, J. B., Van Der Heide, B., Hamel, L. & Shulman, H. (2009). Self-generated versus other-generated statements and impressions in computer-mediated communication: A test of warranting theory using Facebook. *Communication Research, 36,* 229–253.

Walther, J. B., Van Der Heide, B., Kim, S., Westerman, D., & Tong, S. T. (2008). The role of friends' behavior on evaluations of individuals' Facebook profiles: Are we known by the company we keep? *Human Communication Research, 34,* 28–49.

Whitty, M. (2008). Revealing the 'Real' me, searching for the 'Actual' you: Presentations of self on an Internet dating site. *Computers in Human Behavior, 24,* 1707–1723.

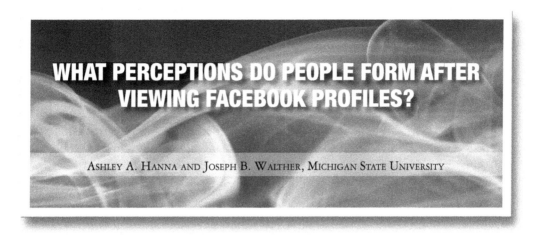

WHAT PERCEPTIONS DO PEOPLE FORM AFTER VIEWING FACEBOOK PROFILES?

ASHLEY A. HANNA AND JOSEPH B. WALTHER, MICHIGAN STATE UNIVERSITY

For many college students, it seems that the World Wide Web has always existed (Beloit Mindset list, 2011). You probably use the Web to shop and study, and to entertain and inform yourselves. You may also use *social network sites* on the Web as an important communication tool with which to manage your social relationships. Joinson (2008) defined social network sites (SNS) as web sites that "provide users with a profile space, facilities for uploading content (e.g., photos, music), messaging in various forms, and the ability to make connections with other people" (p. 1027). The most popular SNS is Facebook.com (Alexa.com, 2011), with over 750 million active users worldwide (Facebook.com, August 26, 2011). While Facebook helps people make and sustain these connections, the structure and content of the messages people post on Facebook also shape people's perceptions of us in subtle and interesting ways. Some of these influences on perceptions come from the messages that profile owners deliberately place on their profiles. Other influences come from Facebook's underlying computations about users' activities. Yet other influences come from what one's Facebook friends do, say, or picture. This chapter reviews what recent research has found with respect to *what perceptions people form after viewing Facebook profiles.*

Individuals use Facebook for a variety of purposes, from viewing photos of friends and family members, to sharing awareness about and coordinating upcoming social events, to checking the relationship status of a new acquaintance. Research has identified seven key purposes of Facebook use (Joinson, 2008). First, users employ Facebook for *social connection,* that is, to maintain existing relationships. You may use Facebook to communicate with a friend who is studying abroad or to reconnect with a friend from elementary school. Second, users *share identities* on Facebook by connecting with others who hold similar interests and beliefs. When fans of a sports team "like" a team's profile page online, they signal something about themselves and their similarity to other like-minded people. Third, Facebook serves a *photograph* function when users upload and view each other's pictures. Previous generations have little photographic traces of their college days (since dad owned and used the old camera), but digital cameras and Facebook have made college life an ongoing photo-documentary (Mendelsohn & Papacharissi, 2011). Fourth, people utilize Facebook for *content gratifications* that involve applications such as games and quizzes. These applications provide an opportunity for users to interact with each other and to develop shared interests. Fifth, Facebook serves a *social investigation* function, such that users gather information about people they have gotten to know offline, or do not know well offline. Someone might look up the profile of the attractive student who sits next to him in class, for instance. Sixth, users go *social network surfing* by following the connections or links (i.e., Facebook friends) between their own friends and their friends' friends. Seventh, Facebook serves the function of *status updates* through which users disclose information to their friends or gather information from their friends about their friends. One may use Facebook to announce that she has a new job, or to discover that a friend has recently become engaged, did great on a test, or broke up a relationship.

But how does using Facebook affect the perceptions we maintain about the people whose profiles we see? A growing amount of research studies have found that forming impressions about other people by looking at various aspects of their Facebook profiles leads to certain kinds of information processing patterns and judgments that are somewhat unlike impression formation patterns elsewhere.

In some ways, Facebook resembles other venues where we control what we say about ourselves. People who see what we put online, and only what we say about ourselves, seem to get a pretty accurate view of who we are (Back et al., 2010; Gosling, Gaddis, & Vazire, 2007). The things that Facebook users deliberately say about themselves and how they arrange their profiles (when they indicate their music, book, TV, and movie preferences, fan groups, and other voluntary disclosures) reveal not only the things they like, but glimpses into their own personalities as well. Profile owners who alphabetize their interests may reveal their preference for organization, while users who do not share a phone number or address seem to signal a preference for privacy. Gosling and colleagues refer to the clues about one's personality that come from the way people go about arranging their possessions—in this case, their virtual possessions, or profile space—as *behavioral residue.* That is, the ways that people went about doing things leaves clues about the ways they think and feel. In Gosling et al.'s studies, independent observers (i.e., strangers) rated Facebook users' personalities. Those ratings were compared to personality ratings that the profile owners completed about themselves, and, additionally, to ratings of the profile owners that were provided from the profile owners' offline friends. The independent observers looked at Facebook profiles that reflected both the owners' intentional statements as well as their "behavioral residue"; observers also looked at a random sample of the profile owners' photographs. They then rated the profile owners on each of the Big Five personality traits: extraversion, agreeableness, conscientiousness, emotional stability, and openness to experience. The researchers found that the group of observers rated profile owners pretty consistently among themselves. Moreover, the observers' personality assessments of the profile owners were accurate, in that they matched with the assessments by the profile owners and their friends on each of the profile owner's personality dimensions, except for the personality dimension of emotional stability.

In addition to what Facebook users indicate about themselves, purposefully or less intentionally, there are other sources of information that affect observers' impressions of Facebook users. Some of these information sources are automatically generated by Facebook's underlying computation system. One of these clues is the automatic display Facebook provides indicating how many Facebook friends an individual has. In traditional, offline relating, people tend to maintain some kind of relationship with about 150 people, while the number of Facebook friends one has may be considerably greater (see for review Tong, Van Der Heide, Langwell, & Walther, 2008).

In a recent study, researchers sought to determine if a person can appear to have too many friends, that is, whether others doubt the authenticity of a person with too great a number of people linked as a Facebook friend (Tong et al., 2008). If an individual appears to waste time and gratuitously "friend" other people, observers may actually think less of someone apparently exhibiting such superficial behavior than they do of more moderate levels of friending. The study involved an experiment that showed one of several different versions of Facebook profile mock-ups to a number of different college students. The only difference between these versions of the profiles was the number of friends that the Facebook system seemed to say that the profile owner possessed: about a hundred, three hundred, five hundred, seven hundred, or nine hundred. As the number of friends increased, there was a general trend in perceptions of the profile owner's level of extraversion, although this increase leveled off after 500 friends. The most stark finding was on the subjects' judgments of the profile owner's "social attractiveness," a measure assessing how much a subject can imagine being friends with someone, having a social conversation with someone, or seeing that person in a subject's social circle. Social attractiveness was greatest when a profile owner appeared to have about 500 friends. Profile owners with less than 500 friends were less socially attractive. Likewise, profile owners with more than 500 friends also were seen as less socially attractive than the 500-friend apex.

In addition to what one indicates about his or herself on Facebook, and what the system reveals about one's network, the characteristics and messaging actions of one's network also affect how others perceive Facebook users. Additional research has examined how the comments and appearances of one's friends affect how one is evaluated by observers.

One's Facebook friends contribute to individuals' Facebook wall, and append comments to users' status updates. A research study asked, "are we known by the company we keep?" and it explored how one's friends' comments on one's Facebook wall affect perceptions of the profile owner's social attractiveness (Walther, Van Der Heide, Kim, Westerman, & Tong, 2008). Because a friend's comment on one's wall is displayed alongside that friend's photograph, the same study looked at how good looking or bad looking one's friends are affects observers' perceptions of how physically attractive the profile owner is. This experiment also involved Facebook profile mock-ups, which showed subjects one of several different sets of wall posting statements ostensibly contributed by two of the profile owner's friends. One set of statements stressed the profile owner's positive social behavior, for example, "I just gotta say you rock!!! u were the life of the party last night. all my friends from home thought you were great!" The other set of statements reflected negative social behavior, such as, "WOW were you ever trashed last night! Im not sure Taylor was that impressed." The comments had a significant effect on viewers' evaluations of the profile owner. When positive messages appeared, observers rated the profile owner as more credible and more socially attractive than when the negative comments were displayed.

The effects of one's friends' physical attractiveness, as shown in the pictures that accompanied wall postings, had a significant effect on the profile owners' attractiveness. Although some previous research predicts a contrast effect—one looks better by contrast when one's picture is displayed next to people who are worse-looking—the opposite effect pertains to one's Facebook friends: The better looking one's friends are, the better looking a profile owner appears to be, too.

Yet a third experiment sought to find out which has a more potent effect on observers' perceptions of Facebook profile owners—the information that the profile owners indicate about themselves, or the statements that their friends post about them. This research drew on a relatively new theory of computer-mediated communication known as warranting theory (Walther & Parks, 2002). Warranting theory addresses concerns that people have about the authenticity of what people say about themselves online, a concern that has troubled chat room users, online dating site subscribers, and others on the Internet who need to establish whether what people say about themselves online is actually true or not. The term *warranting* refers to a connection. In this case, it is the connection between how people present themselves online and what they are really like offline. Because people often suspect that others distort their self-descriptions and tend to self-aggrandize, it may be hard to figure out how real people's self-descriptions might really be. The basic premise of warranting theory is that people put more faith in information about a person when it seems that the person it is about could not have manipulated it him- or herself. That is, the more immune information is from tampering by the person it refers to, the more true people perceive it to be.

One application of warranting theory suggests that people are less likely to trust information that individuals provide about themselves and more likely to trust information provided by third party sources. This is consistent with warranting theory because what others say about an individual is relatively less open to that individual's manipulations. These principles apply to Facebook because, as we discussed above, Facebook pages feature information that individuals provide about themselves (having less warranting value) as well as information generated by third parties or Facebook friends (having greater warranting value as far as other observers may be concerned).

An experiment tested which had more influence on observers' impressions: the information that Facebook profile owners said themselves, or what their Facebook friends said about them (Walther, Van Der Heide, Hamel, & Shulman, 2009). In one version of the experiment, a Facebook page was made up so that the profile owner provided indications that his favorite activities were socializing and going out with friends. Yet his Facebook friends' wall comments asked why he hadn't come out the last few weekends, and if he was still locked away studying. In another case, a Facebook owner's self-statements suggested she was not very attractive. She claimed she was trying to lose weight, and her favorite quotation was "Judge not a book by its cover," but her friends' wall comments indicated that they thought she was hot. One friend said that the profile owner's pictures made it clear that she was the better looking of the two of them. When observers viewed these and other test stimuli, more often than not the friends' comments were more influential in affecting observers' perceptions than what the profile owner had suggested about his or her own characteristics. Warranting theory appears to offer a useful perspective on how people weigh conflicting information about Facebook users, when information from the users or from their friends doesn't agree.

The findings presented in the preceding discussion may pertain most strongly to situations in which observers have little other information about the profile owners on which to base their perceptions. After all, these experiments featured unfamiliar observers looking at and rating the profiles of people who they did not know. While it is the case that some social browsing on Facebook involves looking at the profiles of people we do not personally know, or know well, it is also the case that most of the people one demarcates as a Facebook "friend" are people already known, to some extent, offline (Ellison, Steinfeld, & Lampe, 2007; Joinson, 2008). The strength of these relationships varies. Long before Facebook, sociologist Mark Granovetter (1973) conceptualized our associations with other people as comprising strong ties or weak ties. Strong ties are connections people have to others with whom they a have close relationship; individuals who they spend time with, confide in, have an emotional bond with, and provide favors for. Being Facebook friends with your best friend is an example of a strong tie. Weak ties originally referred to people who one does not know directly, such as a friend of a friend. The Internet has "disintermediated" indirect ties—we can easily communicate directly with people we don't personally know—so now the term weak ties is used to refer to people in one's social network who are less familiar or intimate at the present time. Weak ties therefore include people one has not yet gotten to know too well (such as new acquaintances), or people with whom one is less close than formerly (such as friends who were close at some time in the past).

According to Ellison et al. (2007), weak ties allow a Facebook user to maintain a larger set of potential resources from whom to ask for information or other forms of help. Facebook may be especially conducive to weak tie relationships due to the relatively small effort required to maintain these connections online, compared to maintaining connections via traditional communication or one-to-one messaging systems. For example, the time and energy associated with congratulating a distant relative on a job promotion is greatly reduced on Facebook (e.g., posting a quick message on a Facebook wall or "liking" a job promotion status update) compared to offline (e.g., calling the individual or sending a card).

Whether an individual Facebook friend is a strong tie or a weak tie—well-known or barely-known to an observer—should have some impact on how much the material on the person's Facebook sites affect an observer's perceptions of that person. Yet even among people who know each other well, research has shown that information people present on Facebook can trigger perceptions of insincerity and hypocrisy under some circumstances. DeAndrea and Walther (2011) asked college students to identify one of their Facebook friends with whom they were relatively less familiar, who the students knew had some inconsistency on his profile between the way he presented himself on Facebook and the way he was to people who knew him offline. In addition, the researchers asked students to identify close friends who also had discrepancies between their Facebook profiles and their actual natures.

Students had no trouble finding examples for the researchers; it appears that everyone knows people whose Facebook personae and their offline personae do not quite match. Examples of these discrepancies included individuals whose profile pictures suggested they liked to party or who posed in sexually suggestive manners, whose real friends knew them not to drink or to be sexually active. The researchers also surveyed the students' perceptions about these friends with distorted self-presentations. When the person was less well acquainted with the student, the student rated the friend as more hypocritical and less trustworthy than when rating a close friend who had been equally as deceptive. It seems that we are more forgiving of our close friends for minor distortions in their online self-presentations, but when a friend is not a close friend, watch out for significantly more negative perceptions. This is especially important news since many people assume that Facebook friends already know each other offline, and because of that it may not matter what a person says online; they already know better because of their offline acquaintance. Not so; even when people know one another, their perceptions can be changed when they see each other presenting themselves in ways that deviate precisely from what they know of each other outside of Facebook.

The lessons and recommendations someone could draw from this research are in some ways easy to discern and in other ways more difficult to apply. One lesson seems clear: Individuals' efforts to convey who they are and what they are like via Facebook are not entirely up to them. People can be careful about what they say, and try to make as positive or desirable, or as personable an impression as they wish, but their efforts can only go so far. The residue of their online and offline behaviors, such as how they arrange their profile and how many friends they attempt to have, also affect what people think of them. Moreover, trying to enhance one's image in a less than truthful way can backfire; your friends know it when you're faking, and if your friends aren't close friends, you lose standing in their estimation when there is a gap between the Facebook you and the real you.

We would never suggest that someone should pick friends on the basis of how good-looking they are, even though the attractiveness of people's Facebook friends, as reflected on others' profiles or walls, affects others' perceptions of people's attractiveness. More reasonable advice might be not to "friend" other people indiscriminately. It seems reasonable to recommend grooming one's networks on occasion, combing out partners who have shown themselves to be sources of embarrassment, who like to tease or to give you a hard time about yourself even if it is all in fun, since others who see your profile might not understand the context or irony of their comments. People might ask certain friends not to be critical or negative in their wall postings or public comments. That's what private messaging is for.

REFERENCES

Back, M. D., Stopfer, J. M., Vazire, S., Gaddis, S., Schmukle, S. C., Egloff, B., & Gosling, S. D. (2010). Facebook profiles reflect actual personality, not self-idealization. *Psychological Science, 21,* 372–374.

"Beloit College 2015 Mindset List" (2011). Retrieved from http://www.beloit.edu/mindset/2015/

DeAndrea, D. C., & Walther, J. B. (2011). Attributions for inconsistencies between online and offline self-presentations. *Communication Research, 38,* 805–825.

Ellison, N. B., Steinfeld, C., & Lampe, C. (2007). The benefits of Facebook "friends": Social capital and college students' use of online social network sites. *Journal of Computer-Mediated Communication, 12,* 1143–1168.

"Facebook.com Site Info" (2011). Retrieved from http://www.alexa.com/siteinfo/facebook.com

Gosling, S. D., Gaddis, S., & Vazire, S. (2007, March). *Personality impressions on Facebook profiles.* Paper presented at the International Conference on Weblogs and Social Media, Boulder, CO. Retrieved August 2, 2011 from http://www.icwsm.org/papers/paper30.html

Granovetter, M. S. (1973). The strength of weak ties. *American Journal of Sociology, 78,* 1360–1380.

Joinson, A. N. (2008). 'Looking at', 'looking up' or 'keeping up with' people? Motives and uses of Facebook. *CHI '08: Proceedings of the twenty-fifth annual SIGCHI conference on human factors in computing systems* (pp. 1027–1036). New York: ACM.

Mendelsohn, A. L., & Papacharissi, Z. (2011). Look at us: Collective narcissism in college student Facebook photo galleries. In Z. Papacharissi (Ed.), *A networked self* (pp. 251–273). New York: Routledge.

"Statistics" (2011). Retrieved from http://www.facebook.com/press/info.php?statistics

Tong, S. T., Van Der Heide, B., Langwell, L., & Walther, J. B. (2008). Too much of a good thing? The relationship between number of friends and interpersonal impressions on Facebook. *Journal of Computer-Mediated Communication, 13,* 531–549.

Walther, J. B., & Parks, M. R. (2002). Cues filtered out, cues filtered in: Computer-mediated communication and relationships. In M. L. Knapp & J. A. Daly (Eds.), *Handbook of interpersonal communication* (3rd ed., pp. 529–563). Thousand Oaks, CA: Sage.

Walther, J. B., Van Der Heide, B., Hamel, L., & Shulman, H. (2009). Self-generated versus other-generated statements and impressions in computer-mediated communication: A test of warranting theory using Facebook. *Communication Research, 36,* 229–253.

Walther, J. B., Van Der Heide, B., Kim, S.-Y., Westerman, D., & Tong, S. T. (2008). The role of friends' appearance and behavior on evaluations of individuals on Facebook: Are we known by the company we keep? *Human Communication Research, 34,* 28–49.

COMMUNICATION PRIVACY MANAGEMENT THEORY AND KNOWING HOW PEOPLE REGULATE TELLING AND NOT TELLING THEIR PRIVATE INFORMATION

SANDRA PETRONIO, IUPUI

For the last 32 years, I have been working on the development, testing, expansion, and refinement of an evidenced-based theoretical perspective called *Communication Privacy Management* (CPM). Many colleagues have joined me in contributing to the empirical testing and application of CPM. At this point, we know a great deal about how people make decisions to control and manage their private information. In developing CPM, I intentionally created the theory to be translational in nature.

By translational I mean that the CPM theoretical perspective had to accomplish more than crafting a way to understand how people manage private information. There are several criteria necessary to meet the parameters of translating scholarship into practice. First, CPM theory had to be grounded in research. For every finding supporting the principles of this theory, there were contradictions to those principles. Those contradictions were important because they helped pave the way to new discoveries about what people were doing with their private information. Much research has been conducted over the years leading to a predictive set of axioms that give us confidence the theory tells us how people act and react to regulating private information (e.g., Petronio, 2010a). Second, CPM had to be interdisciplinary in scope. In other words, to be translational, this theory had to be relevant not only to the communication discipline, but also relevant to many other disciplines. In other words, CPM theory had to be developed so that people could use the principles in all the contexts in which people manage private information to better understand the patterns of choice. CPM has been successfully applied to many areas of relationships and family life (e.g., Afifi, 2003; Hawk, Keijsers, Hale, & Meeus, 2009; Matsunaga, 2009; Petronio, 2010b; Petronio & Jones, 2006; Petronio, Jones, & Morr, 2003; Serewicz & Canary, 2008). Many people have applied CPM to health communication issues (e.g., Bevan & Pecchioni, 2008; Helft & Petronio, 2007; Petronio & Gaff, 2010; Petronio & Lewis, 2010; Petronio & Sargent, 2011; Wittenberg-Lyles, Goldsmith, Ragan, & Sanchez-Reilly, 2010). More recently, the CPM perspective has been applied to understand online privacy issues, including cross-cultural comparisons (e.g., Azza Abdel-Azim Mohamed, 2010; Child & Petronio, 2011).

Third, CPM theory had to succeed in applications that: (1) change dysfunctional practices (e.g., Petronio, Reeder, Hecht, Ros-Mont Mendoza, 1996—program for child sexual abuse), (2) determine interventions so that behaviors can be modified in productive ways (Helft & Petronio, 2007, training medical residents), and/or (3) identify successful practices to use as models (Child, Petronio, Agyeman-Budu, & Westermann, 2011, identifying blog-scrubbing patterns). Currently, CPM has met the expectations of a translational perspective and continues to grow.

While there are many different areas in which to explore the CPM perspective, this chapter gives an overview of how we can better understand communication privacy management in online environments guided by the following question posed by the editors: *"What are we giving up and what are we risking when we disclose our private information online?"* The answers to this question are situated within active attempts at managing private information. Clearly, there are circumstances where unauthorized people, businesses, or some entity intentionally violates our privacy and security. Individuals may not be able to always control those situations; they may only attempt to repair their privacy boundaries to once again regain jurisdiction of their information. But, in the scheme of privacy issues, these extraordinary circumstances happen less frequently than you might think. They are sensationalized to make you feel you are always at risk. To some extent you are, but you have more control than you might think. How you manage your information is therefore more critical to understand to preempt unwanted privacy breakdowns.

ANSWERING THE QUESTION BY UNDERSTANDING THE NATURE OF COMMUNICATION PRIVACY MANAGEMENT

The Communication Privacy Management perspective gives several tools to understand privacy management problems and regulation processes in any context, not just online. All the tools discussed below have evolved from research and subsequent adjustments to the theory. We can trust that these steps reflect what happens with privacy management. Our mission in this chapter is to think about applications to online environments. The first step is to examine the way privacy management works from a CPM perspective. The second step is to delve more deeply into how the CPM perspective answers the questions about online privacy management behavior.

Consider this situation:

> The other day, John wrote a blog to a friend. His family is having a hard time financially and he was telling his friend, Rachel, that his father might lose his job. John worried that he would have to drop out of school. He told Rachel that he thought maybe it was as much his Dad's fault as it was the economy that he might be laid off. He felt angry and confused about his feelings toward his Dad, he disclosed to Rachel. But, he told Rachel that since this was so personal he did not want other people to know about what he told her. He also told her that in his family, things like financial issues were taboo and no one was supposed to talk about them outside the family. After he finished writing his blog and sent it he recalled that his Dad had recently mentioned he started to look at his son's blog. He wasn't sure what to do.

Let's understand the axioms and principles of CPM predicting privacy management behaviors to diagnosis John's experience and privacy dilemma.

CPM Framework. There are two components that help build scaffolding for the CPM perspective. *First,* to make it easier to envision how the privacy management system functions, CPM uses a privacy boundary metaphor to mark the borders around the private information. Before John shared the information with Rachel on his blog, he was keeping these thoughts private and secure within his own personal privacy boundary. Everyone has these boundaries around information that could potentially make them feel vulnerable. *Second,* it is important to recognize that like most people, John had a need to share his feeling; consequently he revealed it to Rachel. Giving access to this personal information that is considered private allows us to see some of the complications people face with managing private information. Thinking about this behavior and the potential ramifications illustrates that privacy management is complicated by the fact that people need to be autonomous and separate from others. At the same time, they need to be social and connected to others typically through sharing private information. The CPM perspective, through the use of a privacy management system, is constructed to help us see how people navigate having both autonomy and relationships with other people regarding revealing and concealing private information.

CPM Management System. There are six axioms or predictions for how the privacy management system works according to CPM (Petronio, 2002, 2010a). *Axiom #1* states that people believe they own their private information and it belongs to them individually. Individuals believe they are the original and rightful owners of the information. In other words, people are the "original owners" of their information. This axiom tells us that ownership of information defines what is private and is presumed by people in the way that John presumed he had the right to decide in whom to confide. The condition of ownership impacts the second axiom.

Axiom #2 states that when people make a decision to grant access to others (disclose or give permission for others to see private information), they define those privileged to know as "authorized co-owners" of their information. When access is granted, the privacy boundary around that information metaphorically changes. Since the information has been shared the personal privacy boundary transforms into a dyadic privacy boundary signifying a co-owner has been made privy to the information. Co-owners given information by original owners are seen as authorized because the original owner selects and permits them to know the owner's private information. They did not overhear the information by accident, they did not pry into someone's business, nor did they steal the information. Instead, they were chosen by the original owner.

However, becoming an "authorized co-owner" carries some weight of responsibility. The original owner expects the co-owner to take care of his or her private information restricting access to anyone the owner thinks might make him or her vulnerable. In CPM terms, this is called the principle of "fiduciary responsibilities." In other words, knowing someone's private information makes you responsible for that information and what happens to it after you know. Although not everyone who is told private information understands this assumption about responsibility, the fact is, everyone disclosing believes that "authorized co-owners" should get that point. For our example, this assumption means that John likely believes that Rachel will not disclose John's feelings he discussed on his blog concerning his family's financial troubles and his concerns about his Dad.

Axiom #3 states that because people believe they own their private information, they justifiably feel that they have the right to maintain *control* over their private information. This is true even after people give others access to their information. The big question is how do individuals accomplish that control? The next axiom gives us direction.

Axiom #4 states that the way people exercise control over their private information is through the use of privacy rules. In the example above, John stated a privacy rule. He told Rachel not to talk to anyone about the revelations he made in his blog. People develop privacy rules in a number of ways. They can learn privacy rules from their families since families have "privacy orientations" (Petronio, 2002; Serewicz & Canary, 2008). For example, some families are more open about private matters than others. In John's family, they clearly use rules that restrict the disclosure of private information about family issues, particularly finances. The development and implementation of privacy rules can be triggered by situations or motivations that call for new rules or adjustments to existing rules. As you see with John in this example. His need to talk about his feelings triggered a set of new privacy rules about family issues that were different than what he had learned in his family.

Axiom #5 states that successful and continued control post-access is accomplished through coordinating and negotiating privacy rules with authorized co-owners regarding third-party access. These negotiations revolve around decisions about who else may be privy to the information, how much others outside the shared privacy boundary know the information, and the extent to which co-owners have independent rights to make judgments about who else can know the information. In other words, the decisions include who knows, how much they know, if they know, and whether it is ok for someone else to tell them. In our story, John clearly stated his privacy rule for Rachel telling her not to tell anyone. He presumes she would follow that rule. However since his negotiation was conducted on-line, it may not have been clear that Rachel agreed to the conditions. John, likely assumed she did.

Axiom #6 states that while people believe that they have the right to control the management of their private information, privacy regulation can be unpredictable. Therefore, there is a likelihood that privacy turbulence will erupt that can ultimately lead to privacy breakdowns. Not all states of turbulence end in a complete privacy breakdown. Sometimes a turbulent state helps people realize that their privacy management rules are not working the way they want and they take action to change their expectations altering their rules. At other times, people may not pay attention or realize that there are signs of turbulence and the result is a complete privacy management failure or breakdown. In our story about John, there are several places where privacy turbulence could result in a problem. Can you determine where problems might erupt and how they might lead to privacy turbulence? Here are some clues: (1) family privacy rules; (2) John's privacy rules; (3) Rachel's judgments; (4) publicness of the blog; (5) access John's father has to the blog; (6) John's expectations about how others treat his private information.

PRIVACY TURBULENCE

In diagnosing the potential for privacy turbulence in John's case, one of the issues that potentially makes John's blog a problem is that he revealed negative feelings about his Dad and his father has access to his blog. Often people can preempt problems with co-ownership if they coordinate privacy rules with people authorized to know the information. "For most users, the creation of a blog establishes an online privileged community where granting access to the blog functions as an authorization to contribute thought, feeling, and evaluations with the online community" (Child, Petronio, Agyeman-Budu, & Westermann, 2011, p. 2019). In John's case, while he gave his father access, he likely did not think about that when he was venting his feelings. *This is one of the risks that has less to do with privacy settings and more to do with how we use the technology.* Blogs, in particular, often function as online diaries where we "talk through" our feelings. Disclosure research says that revealing can be helpful to us (Pennebaker, 1990). We need to talk some things out. Many times people face situations where they feel if they do not talk they might explode. Stiles (1987) tells us that conditions like this reflect the "Fever Model" of disclosure; we boil over if we cannot talk.

Nevertheless, the risks of disclosing are personal, involve a loved one, and compromise privacy for John in ways that are not easy to overcome. Making the situation more difficult is the fact that John blogged about a forbidden topic of family finances to someone outside the family. By doing so, he violated his parents' family privacy rules that collectively members are expected to follow (Petronio, 2010).

John was mindful of the family restrictions and told Rachel about these rules. People do try to negotiate privacy rules either before or after they disclosure or give access to private information with authorized co-owners (Petronio, 2002). This same behavior occurs in online communities (Child & Petronio, 2011). John not only stipulated his family privacy rules, he also articulated his own privacy rules in his blog to Rachel. He told her two things. First, he qualified the nature of the private information he disclosed telling her it was highly personal. Second, he told her how she was to regulate it as a co-owner of the information. However, we do not know anything further about the level of coordination between Rachel and John regarding his information. Although John made his rules clear, Rachel may not fully understand whether certain mutual friends could know what John told her. Sometimes people take many things for granted. If they feel comfortable having their friends know something they likely share the information with someone else. They might not worry about telling a mutual friend, as Rachel might with John's information. It is in these cases that privacy is often violated, and even though Rachel may be forgiven by John, John still has to live with the fall-out of the violation.

Interestingly, John's blog behavior also violated his own privacy. He used the assumption that he was talking to Rachel within a protected blog privacy boundary forgetting about the potential for his father and others to see these revelations he made. Research shows that people often make this kind of mistake treating public domain space as private (Child & Agyeman-Budu, 2010; Child & Petronio, 2011; Child, Pearson, Petronio, 2009; Petronio, 2002). John used criteria to select Rachel likely based on trusting her and was highly motivated to talk given his unhappiness about the situation. Nevertheless, since we see at the end of the story John has a realization that his father might see his blog message triggering feelings of anger and hurt, John is likely to attempt rectifying the situation.

In recent research, a study using the CPM perspective found that while there appears to be a wide variety of how people decide to disclose and manage their privacy on blogs, including whether they leave them permanently visible or retrieve them, there are certain patterns (Child, Petronio,

Agyeman-Budu, & Westermann, 2011). There are certain conditions that are more likely to lead to "blog scrubbing," that is, times when people remove the messages from their blogs, as John in our story might consider (Child et al., 2011). Blog scrubbing represents times when people recalibrate the risk-benefit ratio of leaving the written message on the blog versus removing it and changing their privacy rules to accommodate the risk-benefit assessment. In John's case, it is likely he sees the risk too high to leave the message up because his father could see the message on his blog. It is possible that he will scrub the blog message. For example, one respondent stated that:

My friend was talking about illegal substances and I just became friends on my blog with little cousins. I wanted to be a good example to them, so I deleted it hoping they didn't see it before hand (Child et al., 2011, p. 2022).

We know from this research there are triggers that change the typical privacy rules people use to reveal or conceal on blogs (Child et al., 2011). They include impression management triggers, such as the above example shows. There are also identity safety triggers when bloggers are worried about others knowing too much about their everyday lives and feel unsafe, relational triggers, and fear of legal or disciplinary actions. This study also showed that there are three types of privacy management bloggers: *Cautious bloggers* who pre-empt scrubbing problems by carefully selecting privacy management practices. When they post their blogs, they never worry about the ramifications because they have already addressed the inevitabilities. *High risk-taking bloggers* also do not scrub their blogs because they are not worried by potential consequences. It is possible that this category of people do not have high privacy needs in general. *Normative bloggers* are more receptive to the triggers than either cautious or high risk-taking bloggers and adjust their privacy practices to accommodate the needs of the situations as they arise.

This overview of CPM and particularly the discussion of online blogging help illustrate two issues that address this earlier question: "*What are we giving up and what are we risking when we disclose our private information online?* First, many of our privacy concerns may be addressed by better understanding the way we think about privacy management and control over information that we define as belonging to us. We calculate the risk against the benefits either proactively so that we protect ourselves by anticipating what might happen. Or, we might also realize the risks after we have posted a message or disclosed, then we likely try to repair the potential or actual damage to ourselves or others. Second, while we calculate risks versus benefits, it is important to realize that as social animals, we have two competing needs. We both need connections with others and the ability to maintain our autonomy apart from others. These competing needs, at times, complicate the calculus we use to decide whether to post a blog or put a message on our Facebook. Our difficulties tend to arise when we wish to engage others in our lives and one of the ways we do that is to reveal private matters, feelings, emotions, and situations. If we did not want relationships with other people, we would never have any problems with privacy. However, think how lonely it would be if we did not have relationships with partners, friends, family, the local bank where we keep our money, the hairdresser, our teachers, physicians, and so on. While we need others, it is the balance of also needing to be our own person. As part of that tension, we regulate how much of ourselves we give over to someone for those relationships to work. People are certainly different in how much they are willing to tell or conceal. Nevertheless, we all regulate our public and private selves in ways that make us feel like we have some control over what people know. As this chapter has shows, we do so with a set of rules and a privacy management system that guides us in the best way we know how to have both connections with people and a sense of autonomy. When one need grows too big, our self-regulating communication privacy management system adjusts to accommodate the other need. Hopefully, this chapter gives you some issues about privacy management to think about the next time you go on Facebook or blog someone revealing or concealing private information.

REFERENCES

Afifi, T. D. (2003). "Feeling caught" in stepfamilies: Managing boundary turbulence through appropriate communication privacy rules. *Journal of Social and Personal Relationships, 20,* 729–755.

Azza Abdel-Azim Mohamed (2010). Online privacy concerns among social networks' users. *Cross-Cultural Communication, 6,* 74–89.

Bevan, J. L., & Pecchioni, L. L. (2008). Understanding the impact of family caregiver cancer literacy on patient health outcomes. *Patient Education and Counseling, 71,* 356–364.

Child, J., & Petronio, S. (2011). Unpacking the paradoxes of privacy in CMC relationships: The challenges of blogging and relational communication on the Internet. In K. Wright & L. Webb (Eds.). *Computer Mediated Communication in Personal Relationships,* (pp. 21–40). New York, NY: Peter Lang Publishing, Inc.

Child, J., Petronio, S., Agyeman-Budu, E., & Westermann, D. (2011). Blog scrubbing: Exploring triggers that change privacy rules. *Computers in Human Behavior, 27,* 2017–2027.

Hawk, S. T., Keijsers, L., Hale, W. W. & Meeus, W. (2009). Mind your own business! Longitudinal relations between perceived privacy invasion and adolescent-parent conflict. *Journal of Family Psychology, 23,* 511–520.

Helft, P., & Petronio, S. (2007). Communication pitfalls with cancer patients: Hit and run delivery of bad news. *Journal of American College of Surgeons, 205,* 6, 807–811.

Matsunaga, M. (2009). Parents don't (always) know their children have been bullied: Child-parent discrepancy on bullying and family-level profile of communication standards. *Human Communication Research, 35,* 221–247.

Pennebaker, J. (1990). *Opening up: The healing power of confiding in others.* New York: Avon.

Petronio, S. (2010a). Embarrassment of disclosing private information in public: Newly married couples. In D. Braithwaite & J. Wood (Eds.). *Casing Interpersonal Communication: Case Studies in Personal and Social Relationships,* (pp. 95–102). Dubuque, IA: Kendall Hunt Publishing.

Petronio, S. (2010b). Communication privacy management theory: What do we know about family privacy regulation? *Journal of Family Theory and Review, 2,* 175–196.

Petronio, S. (2002). *Boundaries of privacy: Dialectics of disclosure.* New York: SUNY Press.

Petronio, S., & Sargent, J. (2011). Disclosure predicaments arising during the course of patient care: Nurses privacy management. *Health Communication, 26,* 255–266.

Petronio, S., & Gaff, C. (2010). Managing privacy ownership and disclosure. In C. Gaff & C. Bylund (Eds.). *Family Communication About Genetics: Theory and Practice,* (pp. 120–135). London, England: Oxford Press.

Petronio, S., & Lewis, S. S. (2010). Medical disclosure in oncology: Families, patients, and providers. In M. Miller-Day (Ed.), Family Communication and Health Transitions. New York: Peter Lang Publishing, Inc.

Petronio, S., & Jones, S. M. (2006). When "friendly advice" becomes a privacy dilemma for pregnant couples: Applying CPM theory. In R. West &, L. Turner (Eds.), *Family Communication: Sourcebook,* (pp. 201–218). Thousand Oaks, CA: Sage Publications.

Petronio, S., Jones, S. M., & Morr, M. C. (2003). Family privacy dilemmas: Managing communication boundaries within family groups. In L. Frey (Ed.), *Group Communication in Context: Studies of Bona Fide Groups* (pp. 23–56). Mahwah, NJ: LEA Publishers.

Petronio, S., Reeder, H. M., Hecht, M., & Mon't Ros-Mendoza, T. (1996). Disclosure of sexual abuse by children and adolescents. *Journal of Applied Communication Research, 24,* 181–199.

Serewicz, M.C.M., & Canary, D.J. (2008). Assessments of disclosure from the in-laws: Links among disclosure topics, family privacy orientations, and relational quality. *Journal of Social and Personal Relationships, 25,* 333–357.

Stiles, W.B. (1987). "I have to talk to somebody": A fever model of disclosure. In V. J. Derlega & J. H. Berg (Eds.). *Self-disclosure: Theory research and therapy* (pp. 2–7). New York: Plenum Press.

Wittenberg-Lyles, E., Goldsmith, J., Ragan, S., & Sanchez-Reilly, S. (2010). *Dying with comfort.* Cresskill, NJ: Hampton Press.

SECTION 2
CONFLICT COMMUNICATION

The conflict communication context focuses on how we manage and resolve conflict effectively. All of us end up in arguments, fights, disputes, tiffs, or whatever label you'd like to use, and research on conflict communication helps us understand how these conflict episodes unfold and how to communicate effectively to achieve resolution. Generally speaking, many conflict scholars examine the causes of conflict in different relationships (e.g., romantic, family, roommate, etc.), the functional and dysfunctional conflict tactics, strategies, or styles that are used, and the short and long term consequences of conflict patterns. Some major areas of research in conflict communication include serial arguing, conflict avoidance, conflict mediation, physiological outcomes of conflict, and emotional responses to conflict. This chapter focuses on three important areas of conflict communication research: (1) conflict management, (2) demand/withdraw patterns, and (3) workplace conflict. First, Michael Roloff (Northwestern University) reviews how people can make better conflict decisions by answering the question: *What are the most effective ways for individuals to manage their interpersonal conflicts?* Second, John Caughlin and Ashley Middleton (University of Illinois, Urbana-Champaign) review a common conflict pattern communicated in families by answering the question: *How do demand/withdraw patterns affect family members?* Third, Linda Putnam (University of California, Santa Barbara) examines conflict unfolding at work by answering: *What are major conflict issues in the workplace and how can workplace conflict be managed more effectively?* Everyone gets into arguments. Sometimes, we fight over major issues that need resolving and sometimes our fights are pointless and useless. But, rest assured, you will need to manage conflict effectively throughout your lifetime, you will encounter demand/withdraw patterns from your romantic partner and your children, and you will have some nasty conflict episodes at work. The research reviewed in this chapter will help you handle these common conflict situations, because the difference between functional and dysfunctional fighting is dependent upon one thing: communication.

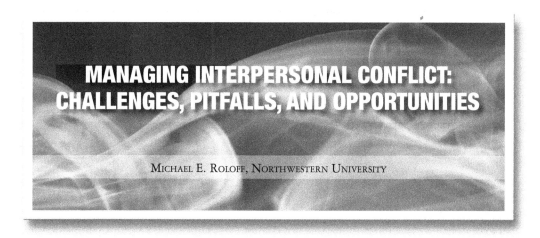

MANAGING INTERPERSONAL CONFLICT: CHALLENGES, PITFALLS, AND OPPORTUNITIES

Michael E. Roloff, Northwestern University

It is obvious that people need one another. Individuals have insufficient resources, time, and energy to go it alone. Consequently, we form relationships that help us achieve our needs. However, as our relationships develop, we find that our partners not only facilitate achieving our goals but that they also can interfere (Solomon & Theiss, 2008). Indeed, researchers have long noted that even in the happiest of relationships, individuals report that their partners engage in unpleasant activities on a daily basis (Birchler, Weiss, & Vincent, 1975). In a sense, this reflects an interdependency paradox. As relational partners grow closer, their outcomes become more interrelated, which can sometimes be enjoyable (e.g., doing things together is more enjoyable than doing them alone), but at other times extremely irritating (e.g., partners don't enjoy doing the same things). Because an individual's negative actions seem to have a much larger impact on his or her partner's feelings about a relationship than does the partner's positive behaviors, individuals must find ways to deal with negativity (Seidman, 2011). To help individuals with this task, a great of research has focused on conflict management, which is the area in which I research. My research addresses the following question: What are the most effective ways for individuals to manage their interpersonal conflicts? This question is quite broad. There are many ways that individuals might manage their disagreements. My research has focused on three ways in which individuals try to manage conflict. In the remaining portion of this paper, I will describe each one.

CONFLICT AVOIDANCE

Conflict arises from an individual's perception that another had engaged in a provocative action (e.g., Vuchinich, 1987). A provocative action is one that is incompatible with or that interferes with one's own behavior or standards for evaluating behavior (e.g., Deutsch, 1973). Given that provocations are by their nature negative, one might expect that individuals often confront them with the aim of stopping them and perhaps gaining restitution. However, not all individuals are confrontational and some actually have an avoidant conflict style (e.g., Rahim, 1997). These individuals seem to let provocations pass without comment. I have been interested in what motivates avoidance and whether can it be an effective way of managing conflict.

In our research, we ask individuals who are in a relationship to make a list of their partners' annoying or irritating behaviors (e.g., Roloff & Solomon, 2002). We then ask them to identify which ones that they have told the partner about and, if they have not complained, why they have not. We find that most individuals have unexpressed complaints and their reasons for withholding them vary (see Roloff & Wright, 2009). Some reasons reflect powerlessness. For example, some individuals withhold complaints because they fear that the partners will respond in a physically or verbally aggressive response (Cloven & Roloff, 1993). Others remain silent because they believe that their partners might react to the complaint by terminating the relationships and, as a result, they would be left alone (Roloff & Solomon, 1990). Still others avoid expressing their displeasure because they feel that they lack the communication skills to complain to the partner (Makoul & Roloff, 1998). Certainly, all of these reasons imply that avoidance results from an unpleasant set of circumstances that force individuals to withhold their concerns.

However, not all reasons imply relational or personal powerlessness. For example, some reasons indicate that individuals intend to complain to their partners but not until the time is right (Wright & Roloff, 2009). Hence, withholding is merely temporary. For example, as relationships become more intimate, it becomes more appropriate to disclose feelings, including negative ones (e.g., Altman & Taylor, 1973). Indeed, a person who complains about a partner's behavior early in a relationship may be viewed as overstepping bounds. Hence, we find that some individuals withhold complaints because the relationships are not sufficiently developed and that when the relationships are better established, they will confront the partners (Cloven & Roloff, 1994). Still others withhold because they feel that the opportunity for discussing the issue has not yet occurred and they are waiting for an appropriate time (Roloff & Wright, 2009). This may occur because the partner is currently under stress and complaining would simply add to that stress. Individuals feel it is better to wait for things to settle before they discuss their concerns.

Other reasons imply that the decision to withhold complaints is a pragmatic one. Some individuals feel that withholding may be a more appropriate way of managing the dispute than confronting the partner.   A confrontation can have negative consequences. Indeed, an intense argument can lead to violent escalation (see Roloff 1996). Hence, when deciding whether to confront the partner, individuals may consider whether it is worth it. We have found that individuals who are strongly committed to the continuation of their relationships are willing to confront their partners about their provocative behavior but withhold complaints when they believe the provocations are minor and when they believe their partners won't change (Roloff & Solomon, 2002). In a sense, these individuals may have learned to "pick their battles." Only complain when a problematic behavior is serious and there is a chance that partner will change. Otherwise, find a way to cope with the irritation.

There are several ways that may help individuals live with minor, irresolvable problems. First, accentuate the positive. For example, Gottman (1994) argues that married couples that are satisfied with their relationships are able to maintain a ratio of five positive behaviors for every negative one. This implies that to keep a relationship healthy, one must overwhelm negative actions with positive ones. That could mean individuals need to routinely enact positive behaviors so as to overcome negative ones that their partners are withholding and that partners should remain mindful of the good things that their partners do for them. Second, be forgiving. There is a growing literature on forgiveness that indicates that responding to a partner's transgressions in a forgiving manner can enhance an individual's well being as well as the relationship (McCullough, Pargament, & Thoresen, 2000; Waldron & Kelley, 2008). Of course, one must be mindful that frequent and unconditional forgiveness can lead to exploitation (McNulty, 2008). Finally, avoid mulling about the behavior. Let it go. Continued rumination about the event can make it seem more serious than it was and prompt individuals to blame their partners (Cloven & Roloff, 1991).

Certainly, avoidance is not a cure-all for conflict. It leaves an issue unaddressed and there is the possibility that it may grow. It also could reflect a sense of powerlessness. However, it may also reflect a temporary state of affairs or a pragmatic decision that the benefits of withholding outweigh the risks. In such cases, it might be used effectively to manage conflicts.

NEGOTIATING AGREEMENTS

In some cases, provocations are sufficiently bothersome that individuals choose to confront their partners. If a problem has been building, individuals may confront their partner in an assertive or even an aggressive way. Partners do not always respond positively to such influence attempts and may enact strategies to avoid being influenced (Belk & Snell, 1988). In part, this resistance could result from the partner's perception that his or her freedoms are being unfairly restricted, which can prompt immediate reactance (Chartrand, Dalton, & Fitzsimons, 2006). Negotiation may provide a better means to deal with negativity.

Negotiation is a process by which two or more parties interact with the goal of creating an agreement that will guide and regulate their future interaction (Sawyer & Guetzkow, 1965). When negotiating, individuals make offers which, if approved, become informal agreements or even formal contacts. They often will make arguments for why their partners should accept their proposals.

Traditionally, negotiation strategies are divided into two broad categories. One type is distributive. These strategies are focused on how to best divide resources. One distributive approach is to argue that one deserves the largest portion of the resources and apply pressure on others to give up their shares. This tough approach can result in deadlocks and bad feelings (Fisher & Ury, 1991). Another distributive approach is to try to be friendly, understanding, and undemanding with the hope that the other partner will reciprocate or at least an agreement will be reached. Unfortunately, this softer approach can result in exploitation (Fisher & Ury, 1991).

Because of the disadvantages of tough and soft approaches, scholars have proposed a second set of negotiation strategies that are integrative. Integrative strategies are focused on developing agreements that integrate the needs of two parties. They produce what are thought to be "win-win" agreements. Dean Pruitt (1981) developed one of the most useful integrative approaches.

Pruitt argues that integrative agreements are most likely to occur when both parties are committed to achieving reasonably high goals while being flexible as to the best way to achieve them. High goals are difficult to achieve and individuals must exert considerable energy constructing agreements that will meet them. If they are able to do so, they avoid the trap of reaching a "split the difference" agreement or a compromise that may result in a quick agreement but one in which each side has to sacrifice something of value. A truly integrative agreement is not a compromise.

Logrolling is an effective strategy for finding integrative agreements. In order to logroll, individuals should negotiate several issues at the same time. When proposing a package of issues, negotiators can prioritize their relative importance and propose tradeoffs by which they receive what they want on high priority issues in exchange for concessions on issues that are of low priority to them but are high priority to their partners. When only considering a single issue, the best negotiators can do is to compromise and often fall into a pattern in which they attack one another. In addition, Pruitt argues that integrative agreements are most likely to be achieved when negotiators exchange information about their priorities while avoiding pressuring each other to accept their individual proposals.

I conducted research with several colleagues that tested some of Pruitt's notions, and although not all were confirmed, aspects of his framework appear valid and provide useful insights into how to negotiate integrative agreements. First, negotiators who are skillful planners are more likely to reach integrative agreements than are those who lack planning skills (Jordan & Roloff, 1997). Second, setting high goals increases the likelihood that negotiators will plan to logroll prior to a negotiation. Although not anticipated by Pruitt, negotiators who have a great deal of experience negotiating in a given context are more likely to discover the logrolling potential in a given situation and plan to take advantage of it (Roloff & Jordan, 1991). Third, negotiators who have high goals are more likely to logroll and thereby achieve integrative agreements than are those who have low goals (Tutzauer & Roloff, 1988). Fourth, regardless of their goals, negotiators who gain insight into how each other prioritizes the importance of issues are more likely to reach integrative agreements than are those who do not (Tuzauer & Roloff, 1988). Finally, using pressure tactics such as coercion or arguing reduces the likelihood of reaching integrative agreements (Tutzauer & Roloff, 1988). Negotiators seem to know this and plan to be coercive only if their other strategies fail (Roloff & Jordan, 1991)

So, assuming that you wish to confront your partner, what should you do to maximize the chance of a win-win outcome? First, plan what you intend to do during the negotiation. This means you should set relatively high goals and be committed to achieving them; identify issues that are important to you and your partner and package them so you can logroll. So, if you want to go out with your partner this weekend, identify the various things you could do together and which one you might most enjoy. Second, when negotiation begins, present the issues that you wish to discuss, including how you prioritize them, and ask how your partner prioritizes them. Indicate that you want to do something together but that you are flexible as to what that might be. You can suggest alternatives, but allow the partner to suggest some as well. That leaves open the possibility that you can find something both of you enjoy doing. Third, once you gain insights into your partner's priorities, offer tradeoffs so that both of you gain something.

Perhaps you can arrange to do what your partner wants this weekend but do what you want the following one. In that manner, you both walk away with something of value. Finally, avoid being coercive or argumentative.

SERIAL ARGUING

Although negotiating integrative agreements is an effective way of managing conflicts, they do not always work. Even if one tries to be a problem solver, the partner may refuse to be influenced and the confrontation ends with no resolution. Indeed, research on conflict management indicates that a surprisingly large number of arguments end with no resolution (e.g., Benoit & Benoit, 1987; Vuchinich, 1987). Because the issue remains unresolved, arguments may occur again and individuals may enter into what is known as serial arguing (Trapp & Hoff, 1985). Serial arguing constitutes repeated disagreements about the same issue. In some cases, serial arguments may become intractable and become part of the ongoing tapestry of the relationship (see Miller, Roloff, & Malis, 2007). Indeed, individuals typically can report at least one serial argument in their relationships and some note that it has been going on for a lengthy period of time (e.g., Johnson & Roloff, 1998).

Because serial arguments are repetitive, they have certain features. First, individuals report that they can often tell when an argumentative episode may occur (Johnson & Roloff, 1998, 2000a). The partner may be acting out of sorts. An event related to the argument is about to occur (e.g., if a married couple regularly argues about their in-laws, an upcoming visit by the in-laws may stimulate an argument). Second, individuals often adopt regular roles within a serial argument. One partner typically initiates an argumentative episode hoping that the other will change (Johnson & Roloff, 2000b). Third, the communication enacted during an argument sometimes becomes scripted (Johnson & Roloff, 2000b). Individuals believe that they can predict what each will say during an argumentative episode and some communication patterns become repeated across the history of arguing. Finally, if not managed effectively, serial arguing can threaten both relational and personal well-being (Johnson & Roloff, 2000b; Malis & Roloff, 2006a, 2006b).

Because serial arguing is common and could be harmful, individuals must effectively manage it. This can be done in several ways. First, prevent an argument from becoming serial. In effect, "nip it in the bud." Arguments become serial partly because they were not handled well in the first episode (Reznick & Roloff, 2011). Enacting dysfunctional communication patterns in the initial argumentative episodes leads to future episodes. One of the most damaging is demand-withdraw (see Eldridge & Christensen, 2002). This pattern involves one partner demanding that the other change and the other responds by withdrawing. Often demand-withdraw result from one partner delaying a confrontation until he or she believes that the problem has become serious (Malis & Roloff, 2006a). Another destructive pattern that leads to serial arguing is mutual hostility during which two individuals verbally attack one another (Reznik & Roloff, 2011). Hence, try to avoid getting off to a bad start.

Second, try to remain positive. Individuals who believe they are making progress toward resolving the argument seem to avoid the relational problems associated with serial arguing (Johnson &

Roloff, 2000a). Individuals who believe they are making progress toward resolving the serial argument engage in constructive communication during argumentative episodes while avoiding demand-withdraw sequences, counter-complaining, and scripted statements (Johnson & Roloff, 2000a). After an episode has ended, they avoid mulling about what happened and they focus on how their relationship is better than most others (Johnson & Roloff. 2000a).

Third, recognize that your partner may not see the argument like you do. Individuals who typically adopt the initiator role in a serial argument tend to be more optimistic about resolvability than are those who resist being influenced (Johnson & Roloff, 2000b). Resistors tend to see frequent serial arguing as irresolvable and harmful to the relationship.

Fourth, make sure that serial arguing does not stress you out. Serial arguing may result in residual stress after an argumentative episode ends and this stress could create health issues, albeit minor ones (Malis & Roloff, 2006a). Arguing can be arousing and some individuals leave episodes in a hyper-aroused state. This extreme arousal can lead to ongoing intrusive thoughts about the episode as well as active attempts to stop thinking about it. Moreover, post-episodic arousal is positively related to stress-related health problems (Malis & Roloff, 2006a). Interestingly, hyper-arousal seems to result from active engagement in an argument rather than from any particular conflict management technique. Individuals who report that they tried to avoid disagreeing during an argument, demanded that their partner change, or tried to develop solutions for the problem all reported greater stress after the episode than did those who were less engaged (Reznick, Roloff, & Miller, 2010). The finding related to problem solving is troubling. Being constructive or integrative is an effective way to solve problems and to protect a relationship (Johnson & Roloff, 2000a). However, because of the cognitive effort expended when problem solving, it is possible that trying to develop solutions creates stress. One way to offset stress is to engage in a coping strategy (Malis & Roloff, 2006b). Although making optimistic comparisons after an argument may help reduce the impact of serial arguing on relational quality (Johnson & Roloff, 2000a), it does not seen to reduce stress; and adopting a resigned stance (i.e., the conflict cannot be prevented) seems to enhance stress (Malis & Roloff, 2006b). The most effective way to cope with residual stress after a conflict seems to be ignoring it (e.g., convincing oneself that the argument is not important).

Finally, one possible way to end a serial argument is to declare it taboo. Sometimes relational partners agree to never talk about something again (Baxter & Wilmot, 1985). When a conflict has been ongoing and shows no signs of being resolved, relational partners may reach the conclusion that they should simply stop discussing it (Roloff & Ifert, 1998). In effect, keep the topic off of the table. Some individuals effectively remove topics from discussion; and, in some cases, topics can be returned to the table if the situation requires (Roloff & Ifert, 2001). However, to be effective, individuals cannot formally declare that a topic can never be discussed. In such cases, such a declaration could appear to be a power move and such contracts might make it difficult ever to return to the topic even if the situation requires it. Such agreements must be done implicitly whereby each partner understands that the topic should be avoided without having to say so.

SUMMARY

In some ways, conflict is a dark topic. Indeed, when asked to describe their everyday disagreements, individuals often use metaphors such as war and natural disasters (McCorkle & Mills, 1992). Certainly, some individuals characterize their arguments as play, but very few do that. In many cases, conflicts are serious business.

Consequently, individuals must make good decisions about whether to address them. Avoiding conflict because of a sense of powerlessness may avoid the negative consequences of an argument but suggests helplessness to stop a problem. That could indicate that one is trapped in a bad relationship. On the other hand, temporarily avoiding conflict or doing so because the problem isn't important or is likely to be unsuccessful may be good reasons to withhold complaints.

When the situation requires a confrontation, it is best to approach it integratively. Do not focus just on one's own needs but consider how the situation might be resolved to the satisfaction of both. That could entail expanding the issues to include some that are important to one's partner and offering to trade. This process can be enhanced if both partners are willing to disclose what issues are most important to them and if they avoid being coercive.

Unfortunately, even integrative bargaining can fail. In such cases, a conflict may repeat and partners become involved in serial arguing. One of the best ways to avoid serial arguing is to avoid negative communication in the first episode. The first episode of an argument seems to set the tone for the future. When serial arguing begins, one must avoid letting the communication become scripted and especially avoid repeating dysfunctional communication patterns. If we can remain optimistic that progress is being made toward resolution, then negative consequences to the relationship may be lessened. However, depending on whether you are someone who typically initiates an argument or someone who resists, you may not be especially optimistic. To remain optimistic, it helps to engage in constructive communication and cope with the argument by making optimistic comparisons. Unfortunately, being integrative may be stressful and optimistic comparisons do not seem to reduce stress. Instead, it might be more effective for relational partners to informally agree to quit talking about the issue and for both to focus on the positive aspects of their relationship while noting how unimportant the problem is in the grand scheme of things. However, if the problem is serious, the best solution might be to end the relationship.

REFERENCES

Altman, I. & Taylor, D. (1973). *Social penetration: The development of interpersonal relationships*. New York: Holt.

Baxter, L. A., & Wilmot, W. W. (1985). Taboo topics in close relationships. *Journal of Social and Personal Relationships, 2*, 253–269.

Belk, S. S., & Snell, W. E., Jr. (1988). Avoidance of strategy use in intimate relationships. *Journal of Social and Clinical Psychology, 7*, 80–96.

Benoit, W. L., & Benoit, P. J. (1987). Everyday argument practices of native social actors. In J. W. Wenzel (Ed.), *Argument and critical practices: Proceedings of the Fifth SCA/AFA Conference on Argumentation* (pp. 465–473). Annandale, VA: Speech Communication Association.

Birchler, G. R., Weiss, R. L., & Vincent, J. P. (1975). A multimethod analysis of social reinforcement exchange between martially distressed and nondistressed spouse and stranger dyads. *Journal of Personality and Social Psychology, 31,* 349–360.

Chartrand, T. L., Dalton, A. N., & Fitzsimons, G. J. (2006). Nonconscious relationship reactance: When significant others prime opposing goals. *Journal of Experimental Social Psychology, 43,* 719–726.

Cloven, D. H., & Roloff, M. E. (1991). Sense-making activities and interpersonal conflict: Communicative cures for the mulling blues. *Western Journal of Speech Communication, 55,* 134–158.

Cloven, D. H., & Roloff, M. E. (1993). The chilling effect of aggressive potential on theexpression of complaints in intimate relationships. *Communication Monographs, 60,* 199–219.

Cloven, D. H., & Roloff, M. E. (1994). A developmental model of decisions to withhold relational irritations in romantic relationships. *Personal Relationships, 1,* 143–164.

Deutsch, M. (1973). *The resolution of conflict: Constructive and destructive processes.* New Haven, CT: Yale University Press.

Eldridge, K. A., & Christensen, A. (2002). Demand-withdraw communication during couple conflict: A review and analysis. In P. Noller, & J. A. Feeney (Eds.), *Understanding marriage: Developments in the study of couple interaction* (pp. 289–322). Cambridge, UK: Cambridge University Press.

Fisher, R., & Ury, W. (1991). *Getting to yes: Negotiating agreement without giving in* (2nd ed.). New York: Penguin Books

Gottman, J. M. (1994). *What predicts divorce? The relationship between marital processes and marital outcomes.* Hillsdale, NJ: Lawrence Erlbaum.

Hample, D. Han, B., & Payne, D. (2010). The aggressiveness of playful arguments. *Argumentation, 24,* 405–421.

Johnson, K. L., & Roloff, M. E. (1998). Serial arguing and relational quality: Determinants and consequences of perceived resolvability. *Communication Research, 25,* 327–343.

Johnson, K. L., & Roloff, M. E. (2000a). Correlates of the perceived resolvability and relational consequences of serial arguing in dating relationships: Argumentative features and the use of coping strategies. *Journal of Social and Personal Relationships, 17,* 676–686.

Johnson, K. L., & Roloff, M. E. (2000b). The influence of argumentative role (initiator vs resistor) on perceptions of serial argument resolvability and relational harm. *Argumentation, 14,* 1–15.

Jordan, J. M., & Roloff, M. E. (1997). Planning skills and negotiator goal accomplishment: the relationship between self-monitoring and plan generation, plan enactment, and plan consequences. *Communication Research, 24,* 31–64.

Makoul, G., & Roloff, M. E. (1998). The role of efficacy and outcome expectations in the decision to withhold relational complaints. *Communication Research, 25,* 5–29.

Malis, R. S., & Roloff, M. E. (2006a). Demand/withdraw patterns in serial arguing: Implications for well-being. *Human Communication Research, 32,* 198–216.

Malis, R. S., & Roloff, M. E. (2006b). Features of serial arguing and coping strategies: Links with stress and well-being. In R.M. Dailey, & B.A. Le Poire (Eds.) *Applied interpersonal communication matters: Family, health, and community relations* (pp. 39–65). New York: Peter Lang.

McCorkle, S., & Mills, J. L. (1992). Rowboat in a hurricane: Metaphors of interpersonal conflict management. *Communication Reports, 5,* 57–66.

McCullough, M. E., Pargament, K. I., & Thoresen, C. E. (Eds.) (2000). *Forgiveness: Theory, research, and practice.* New York: Guilford.

McNulty, J. (2008). Forgiveness increases the likelihood of subsequent partner transgressions in marriage. *Journal of Family Psychology, 22,* 171–175.

Miller, C. W., Roloff, M. E., & Malis, R. S. (2007). Understanding interpersonal conflicts that are difficult to resolve: A review of literature and presentation of an integrated model. In C. S. Beck (Ed.), *Communication Yearbook 31* (pp. 118–173). New York: Erlbaum.

Pruitt, D. G. (1981). *Negotiation behavior.* New York: Academic Press.

Rahim, M. A. (1997). Styles of managing organizational conflict: A critical review and synthesis of theory and research. In M. A. Rahim, R. T. Golembiewski, & L E. Pate (Eds.), *Current topics in management* (pp. 61–77). Greenwich, CT: JAI Press.

Reznick, R. M., Roloff, M. E., & Miller, C. W. (2010). Communication during interpersonal arguing: Implications for stress symptoms. *Argumentation and Advocacy, 46,* 193–213.

Reznick, R. M., & Roloff, M. E. (2011). Getting off to a bad start: The relationship between communication during an initial episode of a serial argument and argument frequency. *Communication Studies, 62,* 291–306.

Roloff, M. (1996). The catalyst hypothesis: Conditions under which coercive communication leads to physical aggression." In D. Cahn & S. Floyd (Ed.), *Family violence from a communication perspective* (pp. 20–36). Thousand Oaks, CA: Sage Publications.

Roloff, M. E., & Cloven, D. H. (1990). The chilling effect in interpersonal relationships: The reluctance to speak one's mind. In D. D. Cahn (Ed.), *Intimates in conflict: A communication perspective* (pp. 49–76). Hillsdale, NJ: Lawrence Erlbaum.

Roloff, M. E., & Ifert, D. E. (1998). Antecedents and consequences of explicit agreements to declare a topic taboo in dating relationships. *Personal Relationships, 5,* 191–206.

Roloff, M. E., & Ifert, D. E. (2001). Reintroducing taboo topics: Antecedents and consquences of putting topics back on the table. *Communication Studies, 52,* 37–50.

Roloff, M. E., & Jordan, J. M. (1991). The influence of effort, experience and persistence on the elements of bargaining plans. *Communication Research, 18,* 306–332.

Roloff, M. E., & Reznik, R. M. (2008). Communication during serial arguments: Connections with individuals' mental and physical well-being. In M. Motley (Ed.). *Studies in applied interpersonal communication* (pp. 97–120). Sage.

Roloff, M. E., & Solomon, D. H. (2002). Conditions under which relational commitment leads to expressing relational complaints. *International Journal for Conflict Management, 13,* 276–391.

Roloff, M. E., Tutzauer, F., & Dailey, W. O. (1989). The role of argumentation in distributive and integrative bargaining contexts: Seeking relative advantage but at what cost? In M.A. Rahim (Ed.), *Managing conflict: An interdisciplinary approach* (pp. 109–120). New York: Praeger.

Roloff, M. E., & Wright C. N. (2009). Conflict avoidance: A functional analysis. In T. T. Afifi, & W. Afifi (Eds.), *Uncertainty and information regulation in interpersonal contexts: Theories and applications.* (pp. 320–340). New York: Routledge.

Sawyer, J., & Guetzkow, H. (1965). Bargaining and negotiation in international relations. In HC Kelman (Ed.), *International behavior: A social-psychological analysis* (pp. 466–520). New York: Holt, Rinehart and Winston.

Seidman. G. (2011). Positive and negative: Partner derogation and enhancement differentially related to relationship satisfaction. *Personal Relationships.* Advance online publication. DOI: 10.1111/j.1475-6811.2010.01337.

Solomon, D. H., & Theiss, J. A. (2008). A longitudinal test of the relational turbulence model of romantic relationship development. *Personal Relationships, 15,* 339–357.

Trapp, R., & Hoff, N. (1985). A model of serial argument in interpersonal relationships. *Argumentation and Advocacy, 22,* 1–11.

Tutzauer, F., & Roloff, M. E. (1988). Communication processes leading to integrative agreements: Three paths to joint benefits. *Communication Research, 15,* 360–380.

Vuchinich, S. (1987). Starting and stopping spontaneous family conflicts. *Journal of Marriage and Family, 49,* 591–601.

Waldron, V. R., & Kelley, D. L. (2008). *Communicating forgiveness.* Thousand Oaks: SAGE.

DEMAND/WITHDRAW IN FAMILY RELATIONSHIPS: UNDERSTANDING A CONFLICT PATTERN THAT IS OFTEN (BUT NOT ALWAYS) PROBLEMATIC

JOHN P. CAUGHLIN & ASHLEY V. MIDDLETON, UNIVERSITY OF ILLINOIS, URBANA-CHAMPAIGN

If you are closely connected with somebody else, chances are you will eventually have some conflicts with that person (e.g., Canary, 2003; Deutsch, 1973). Maybe you do not have conflicts often, but most people experience conflicts at least some of the time in their close relationships, including those with parents, romantic partners, siblings, or friends. Because some conflict is nearly inevitable, many researchers have studied the effects of conflict on people and on their relationships.

Conflict is usually unpleasant, so we often think of it in negative terms. Yet, the impact of conflict depends on a number of factors. Generally speaking, people who have lots of intense conflict tend to be unhappy with their relationships; for example, the more conflicts married people have, the less happy they tend to be with their marriage (Caughlin, Vangelisti, & Mikucki-Enyart, in press). Although it is usually unpleasant, sometimes conflict can be useful, such as when it helps people learn about issues they need to resolve (Canary, 2003) or when it helps adolescents learn to be more independent from their parents (Smetana, 1989). Because conflict is common but has varying effects, it is very important to understand how to minimize the negative impact of conflicts while fostering the benefits.

This chapter addresses one aspect of conflict by focusing on a particular pattern of conflict in families, the demand/withdraw pattern. First, we describe demand/withdraw and provide examples to demonstrate how this pattern manifests in interactions between family members. Next, we briefly review some of the outcomes of demand/withdraw in family relationships, including negative consequences for the emotional and physiological health of individuals who engage in this behavior. Then, we highlight the importance of understanding demand/withdraw, particularly as it relates to understanding family interaction. We suggest that there are a number of factors that determine the extent to which demand/withdraw is problematic in family relationships. We close the chapter with some comments about both the demand/withdraw pattern specifically and conflict in family relationships generally.

DEFINITION AND EXAMPLES OF DEMAND/WITHDRAW

To begin, let's define and describe demand/withdraw. Demand/withdraw is a pattern of communication that involves two individuals' behaviors. Specifically, demand/withdraw occurs when one person in a relationship demands or "nags" while the other person avoids or withdraws (Christensen & Heavey, 1993). When we say one person avoids while the other demands, we are emphasizing that these behaviors happen at roughly the same time, but this does not mean that the demanding and withdrawing are happening at exactly the same time. In fact, what often happens is one person's demands lead to the other person avoiding and then that person's avoidance leads to more demands (e.g., Klinetob & Smith, 1996).

This situation in which both the demander and the withdrawer influence each other is one of the reasons why demand/withdraw is thought of as a dyadic pattern that two people do together, rather than simply a description of the sum of two people's behaviors. Scholars who have studied marriage noticed this pattern in some couples many years ago (e.g., Watzlawick, Beavin, & Jackson, 1967), and they have also noted that the back and forth between demander and withdrawer can happen so many times that nobody can really tell which person started the pattern. One partner might say, "I only started nagging because she was avoiding me," but the avoider would say, "I only need to avoid because he nags me." In such circumstances, who started it is not only impossible to determine but also not very important because, regardless of who first started it, it has become a pattern that both individuals enact together. Once such a pattern becomes routine in a relationship, it is difficult to stop because each person's behavior tends to reinforce the other person's (Christensen & Heavey, 1993).

Demand/withdraw can be a feature of one conversation, or it can happen across many episodes. Many relationships have occasional conflicts that fall into a pattern where one person raises complaints while the other person avoids talking about them. However, demand/withdraw can also become a common way that two relational partners deal with conflict in general, with the pattern occurring over repeated conversations or conflict episodes (Christensen & Heavey, 1993). Demand/withdraw patterns also can occur over many days. For example, imagine a spouse who stays at work later than expected and returns home to a partner who complains about the late arrival. In some cases, the negative feelings elicited from those complaints could make the person reluctant to return home the next day, and another delayed arrival may elicit even more intense complaining. Eventually, this could lead to a pattern in which the one spouse frequently nags about this issue while the other spouse tries to avoid home as much as possible.

Although early scholarship sometimes assumed that that "nagging" was something wives do and withdrawing is something husbands do, people in different family roles can do both demanding and withdrawing. In marriages, both husband and wives can demand or withdraw (Eldridge & Christensen, 2002; Heavey, Layne, & Christensen, 1993; Papp, Kouros, & Cummings, 2009). Depending on the issue at hand, spouses may trade who demands depending on the issue (Caughlin & Malis, 2004a; Heavey et al., 1993). Also, demand/withdraw happens in other family relationships besides marital ones; for example, demand/withdraw can happen between parents and adolescents (Caughlin & Malis, 2004a, 2004b; Caughlin & Ramey, 2005).

Although we have offered a basic definition and description, let's take an example to illustrate one form that demand/withdraw can take in interaction. We will use an example from an actual conversation between relational partners (Caughlin & Scott, 2010). This is an excerpt from a conversation in which a husband and wife were told to talk about their relationship, and the husband was indicating that he wished they had more affectionate communication:

1   **H:**   It's just nice to have a little conversation about issues like—

2   **W:**   Yeah, but you get so wrapped up and take it all so personally.

3   **H:**   Where are you going?

4   **W:**   I'm shutting this window.

5   [Pause]

6   **W:**   I understand what you are saying, but I really don't see how that has anything to do with this question.

7   **H:**   I do, 'cause it's kind of like talking is a way of showing affection and a lot of times we just don't just sit down and talk about stuff that much.

In this example, we see the husband attempt to begin a conversation about issues in his relationship with his wife. Applying the demand/withdraw perspective, the husband's utterance at Turn 1 constitutes the "demand" portion of the pattern because in this case he is trying to raise a complaint. At first the wife explains why she does not want to have such conversations, then, at Turn 4, we see the wife's attempt to avoid discussion by physically moving away from her husband and toward the window. Although she initially acknowledges her husband's desire to talk about their relationship at Turn 2, her move to close the window represents withdrawal from the conversation and a failure to truly acknowledge her husband's concerns.

After the pause at Turn 5, the wife makes a more overt attempt to avoid discussion of their relationship by denying the legitimacy of her husband's demand and arguing for its irrelevance to the topic that they were told to discuss. Finally, the husband presses for discussion of the issue by insisting on their relevance to the topic. Although this is but one example of demand/withdraw, it demonstrates one way that it can manifest in a conversation.

Demand/withdraw is interesting to recognize in its own right, but it is particularly important because of its impact on conflict dynamics and relationships. In the next section, we turn our attention to describing the consequences of demand/withdraw.

OUTCOMES AND CORRELATES OF DEMAND/WITHDRAW

Overall, demand/withdraw tends to have negative effects on both individuals and relationship quality. Although we will argue below that it is important to consider a number of factors to understand the impact of demand/withdraw, the pattern often has detrimental effects on individuals and family relationships.

As you might suspect, demand/withdraw exacts stress on individuals (Malis & Roloff, 2006). In married couples that engage in demand/withdraw, cortisol, which is a hormonal indicator of physiological stress, tends to be elevated (Heffner et al., 2006). That is, partners who engage in this behavior tend to show physical symptoms of stress. Further, depressed romantic partners are more likely to engage in demand/withdraw than non-depressed partners (Byrne, Carr, & Clark, 2004; Papp et al., 2009). Although most of the research on demand/withdraw has looked at it in marriage, when demand/withdraw happens in other family relationships, it is related to negative outcomes. For example, frequent use of demand/withdraw by parents and their adolescent children is associated with both their diminished self-esteem and increased use of drugs and alcohol (Caughlin & Malis, 2004b).

Unfortunately, this relatively bleak picture also holds for the connection between demand/withdraw and relationship quality. Demand/withdraw is correlated with concurrent dissatisfaction and relationship instability (Gottman & Levenson, 2000; Heavey et al., 1993). Demand/withdraw is associated with relationship dissatisfaction in both romantic and parent-child dyads (Caughlin & Malis, 2004b). However, as we will discuss below, under certain circumstances, demand/withdraw has also been shown to predict increases in satisfaction over time (Caughlin, 2002).

Whereas the focus of our chapter is on demand/withdraw, it is also worth noting that this pattern is related to other negative conflict behaviors and patterns. For example, couples that engage in demand/withdraw are also prone to serial arguing, or the tendency to have repeated conflicts over the same issue (Roloff & Johnson, 2002). Serial arguing can be problematic because people can get the sense that they can never resolve their problems, leading to dissatisfaction or frustration (Roloff & Johnson, 2002). Additionally, in romantic relationships, male demand/partner withdraw is associated with male domestic violence (Feldman & Ridley, 2000). If we consider that, in some relationships, the demand/withdraw pattern may be indicative of a profound lack of communication and problem-solving skills (Noller, Feeney, Sheehan, & Peterson, 2000), it is perhaps not surprising that male partners who frequently demand while their partner withdraws would also be prone to resort to physical violence.

FACTORS THAT MITIGATE NEGATIVE EFFECTS OF DEMAND/WITHDRAW

Although our argument thus far may make it seem that the effects of demand/withdraw are consistently negative, it is important to consider several issues. First, despite the persuasiveness of the findings we have presented thus far, no communication pattern has a clear and simple meaning. Most communication behaviors and patterns do not have an inherent meaning or outcome; thus, what may be a poor strategy in general might be the best thing to do in a particular circumstance. For example, it may generally be a poor idea for family members to criticize each other frequently, but the right criticism given at the right moment with the right tone might be just what a family member needs in a particular conflict. In other words, communication and conflict are much too complex to be understood in terms of patterns that are inherently constructive and destructive: There are multiple factors that can affect the outcomes of conflict behaviors. To illustrate this broader point, we review several contextual and relational features that can affect the meaning and outcomes of demand/withdraw.

One important factor to consider is the overall emotional climate of family relationships. Demand/withdraw is one behavioral pattern, but it is situated within the larger context of a given relationship (Caughlin & Huston, 2002, 2006). The overall nature of the relationship can influence whether demand/withdraw is problematic. For example, let us contrast two married couples, both of whom regularly enact demand/withdraw during conflicts over how much time they should spend as a couple versus apart. In the first couple, demand/withdraw is commonplace and they are rarely affectionate with each other before, during, or after conflicts. The second couple also frequently engages in demand/withdraw over the same issue, but happens to be highly affectionate with each other in their relationship generally. Demand/withdraw seems to have less of a negative impact on couples who also are highly affectionate with each other by complimenting each other, doing nice things for each other, expressing their love, and so forth (Caughlin & Huston, 2002). This is not to suggest that demand/withdraw has no negative effects when coupled with affection, but it does demonstrate the importance of considering other potentially positive behaviors as they may influence relational partners' interpretations and perceptions of demand/withdraw. It is possible, for example, that even though demand/withdraw tends to be unpleasant, it does not seem so bad or serious if it happens in an otherwise positive relationship.

Another factor to consider is that there are many ways to "demand" and many ways to "withdraw" (Caughlin, 2002). We offered one illustration of demand/withdraw above, but you may be able to think of many other ways that demand/withdraw could occur in a given interaction. Indeed, this variation is even reflected in the practice of researching demand/withdraw. One important distinction to consider is the way in which the "withdrawer" withdraws, or how conflict is avoided (Caughlin, Hardesty, & Middleton, 2012; Roloff & Ifert, 2000). As we have previously noted, withdrawing can include conversational moves that attempt to minimize or change the topic of discussion as well as physically leaving the room or the scene of an interaction to stop the conversation. For example, a relational partner might explicitly avoid conversation by saying, "I don't want to talk about that" or implicitly avoid it by remaining silent in the face of a demand. When people avoid in really obvious ways, it appears to be more problematic than when they avoid in more implicit ways (Caughlin & Scott, 2010).

Avoidance behaviors can also be differentiated by their emotional tone. For example, Roberts (2000) found that marital partners who tended to withdraw from conflicts in anger were less happy that those where partners avoided conflicts without expressing anger. The affective tone of demanding may also influence the impact of demand/withdraw. For example, Gottman and Krokoff (1989) differentiated happy and unhappy couples on the basis of the emotions that accompanied wives' engaging or demanding behaviors. Unhappy couples were characterized by wives who expressed fear or sadness when initiating a topic for discussion. Thus, there are many ways to engage in or avoid conflicts, and overlooking these differences may lead to erroneous conclusions about the impact of demand/withdraw on family relationships.

Consistent with, and related to, the view that there are multiple ways to enact demand/withdraw, we might also consider the reasons why partners demand or withdraw. Relational partners' goals for a given interaction, and their perceptions of their partners' goals probably shape the impact of demand/withdraw (Caughlin, 2010; Caughlin & Scott, 2010; Caughlin, Vangelisti, & Mikucki-Enyart, in press). For example, individuals who are trying to avoid a partner's demands to make healthier lifestyle choices may be only slightly annoyed (or even somewhat appreciative) if they think the demands are motivated by a genuine desire to be helpful, but the exact same demands could be viewed in much worse terms if the assumed motivation involves trying to be controlling or dominant.

Finally, it also may be valuable to situate demand/withdraw within the relationship over time. For example, we might consider that demand/withdraw can be indicative of the ability of relational partners to address and work through problems. That is, like other communication processes, demand/withdraw can be a pathway to bring about change in a relationship. If this is the case, then, over time, some individuals should be fairly successful at accommodating to their relational partners' requests for change (Caughlin, 2002). For instance, a father may consistently initiate discussions with his daughter about cleaning her room, an act that may initially produce withdrawal and resistance by his daughter, thereby leading to the demand/withdraw pattern. But over time, the father's demand may resonate with his daughter and, despite her attempts to withdraw, she may indeed keep her room clean. In these instances, demand/withdraw may be frustrating in the short term, but it probably would not diminish satisfaction over time (and may even predict increases in satisfaction over time) because the conflict episode would presage more mutually satisfactory behaviors (Caughlin, 2002). Thus, a willingness to confront and work through issues may be indicative of relationship functioning (Gottman & Krokoff, 1989), particularly if it eventually elicits welcome changes within the relationship.

In sum, we suggest that in order to understand the impact of demand/withdraw on family relationships, it is essential to consider what it means to family members who engage in this behavior. To provide context and thus highlight the multiple potential meanings of demand/withdraw, we should take into account the emotional climate and relationship processes surrounding demand/withdraw. Further, it is important to consider the various ways of enacting as well as the potential, multiple reasons underlying demand/withdraw.

CONCLUSION

This chapter has focused on the demand/withdraw pattern because it is a particularly important pattern of conflict. Generally, it is associated with negative outcomes, such as dissatisfying relationships and adverse effects on individuals. Yet, we also argue that knowing the overall or average effects does not really provide an adequate understanding of demand/withdraw or its impact on relationships. There are times and conditions when it can be functional. Demand/withdraw is not just a pattern of behavior—it is also a communicative phenomenon, and the meanings that people ascribe to the pattern are important. Thus, factors such as the particular way the pattern is enacted, the larger relational context, and the perceived goals ascribed to each person matter.

Even though our focus has been on demand/withdraw, similar points can be made about conflict behaviors in general. Conflict is a common part of relating, and it is therefore important to understand how to manage it well. Yet, this is not a simple task. There are certain types of behaviors that are often functional in conflict and certain behaviors and patterns (like demand/withdraw) that often make conflict unproductive. However, knowing which behaviors are usually constructive or destructive provides only a limited understanding of what makes conflict management successful because even behaviors that are often constructive will not be in every situation, and even behaviors that are often destructive will not be in every situation. As individuals interested in the ways in which communication creates and sustains close relationships, we should consider an array of features and factors associated with conflict generally, and demand/withdraw specifically, before drawing any firm conclusions about possible effects of conflict behaviors and patterns. We hope that this chapter will motivate you to consider such factors in understanding conflict on both a scholarly and a personal level.

REFERENCES

Byrne, M., Carr, A., & Clark, M. (2004). Power in relationships of women with depression. *Journal of Family Therapy, 26,* 407–429.

Canary, D. J. (2003). Managing interpersonal conflict: A model of events related to strategic choices. In J. O. Greene & B. R. Burleson (Eds.), *Handbook of communication and social interaction skills* (pp. 515–549). Mahwah, NJ: Erlbaum.

Caughlin, J. P. (2002). The demand/withdraw pattern of communication as a predictor of marital satisfaction over time: Unresolved issues and future directions. *Human Communication Research, 28,* 49–85.

Caughlin, J. P. (2010). A multiple goals theory of personal relationships: Conceptual integration and program overview. *Journal of Social and Personal Relationships, 27,* 824–848.

Caughlin, J. P., Hardesty, J. L., & Middleton, A. V. (2012). Conflict avoidance in families: Functions, outcomes, and applied implications. In P. Noller & G. Karantzas (Eds.), *Wiley-Blackwell handbook of couples and family relationships* (pp. 115–128). New York: Wiley-Blackwell.

Caughlin, J. P., & Huston, T. L. (2002). A contextual analysis of the association between demand/withdraw and marital satisfaction. *Personal Relationships, 9,* 95–119.

Caughlin, J. P., & Huston, T. L. (2006). The affective structure of marriage. In A. L. Vangelisti & D. Perlman (Eds.), The Cambridge handbook of personal relationships (pp. 131–155). New York: Cambridge University Press.

Caughlin, J. P., & Malis, R. S. (2004a). Demand/withdraw between parents and adolescents as a correlate of relational satisfaction. *Communication Reports, 17,* 59–71.

Caughlin, J. P., & Malis, R. S. (2004b). Demand/withdraw communication between parents and adolescents: Connections with self-esteem and substance use. *Journal of Social and Personal Relationships, 21,* 125–148.

Caughlin, J. P., & Ramey, M. E. (2005). The demand/withdraw pattern of communication in parent-adolescent dyads. *Personal Relationships, 12,* 337–356.

Caughlin, J. P., & Scott, A. M. (2010). Toward a communication theory of the demand/withdraw pattern of interaction in interpersonal relationships. In S. W. Smith & S. R. Wilson (Eds.), *New directions in interpersonal communication research* (pp. 180–200). Thousand Oaks, CA: Sage.

Caughlin, J. P., & Vangelisti, A. L. (1999). Desire for change in one's partner as a predictor of the demand/withdraw pattern of marital communication. *Communication Monographs, 66,* 66–89.

Caughlin, J. P., Vangelisti, A. L., & Mikucki-Enyart, S. (in press). Conflict in dating and marital relationships. In J. G. Oetzel & S. Ting-Toomey (Eds.), *Sage handbook of conflict communication: Integrating theory, research, and practice* (2nd ed.). Thousand Oaks, CA: Sage.

Christensen, A., & Heavey, C. L. (1993). Gender differences in marital conflict: The demand/withdraw interaction pattern. In S. Oskamp & M. Costanzo (Eds.), *Gender issues in contemporary society* (pp. 113–141). Newbury Park, CA: Sage.

Deutsch, M. (1973). *The resolution of conflict.* New Haven, CT: Yale University Press.

Eldridge, K. A., & Christensen, A. (2002). Demand-withdraw communication during couple conflict: A review and analysis. In P. Noller & J. A. Feeney (Eds.), *Understanding marriage: Developments in the study of couple interaction* (pp. 289–322). New York: Cambridge University Press.

Feldman, C. M., & Ridley, C. A. (2000). The role of conflict-based communication responses and outcomes in male domestic violence toward female partners. *Journal of Social and Personal Relationships, 17,* 552–573.

Gottman, J. M., & Krokoff, L. J. (1989). Marital interaction and satisfaction: A longitudinal view. *Journal of Consulting and Clinical Psychology, 57,* 47–52.

Gottman, J. M., & Levenson, R. W. (2000). The timing of divorce: Predicting when a couple will divorce over a 14-year period. *Journal of Marriage and the Family, 62,* 737–745.

Heavey, C. L., Layne, C., & Christensen, A. (1993). Gender and conflict structure in marital interaction: A replication and extension. *Journal of Consulting and Clinical Psychology, 61,* 16–27.

Heffner, K. L., Loving, T. J., Kiecolt-Glaser, J. K., Himawan, L. K., Glaser, R., & Malarkey, W. B. (2006). Older spouses' cortisol responses to marital conflict: Associations with demand/withdraw communication patterns. *Journal of Behavioral Medicine, 29,* 317–325.

Klinetob, N. A., & Smith, D. A. (1996). Demand-withdraw communication in marital interaction: Tests of interspousal contingency and gender role hypotheses. *Journal of Marriage and the Family, 58,* 945–958.

Malis, R. S., & Roloff, M. E. (2006). Features of serial arguing and coping strategies: Links with stress and well-being. In R. M. Dailey & B. A. Le Poire (Eds.), *Applied interpersonal communication matters: Family, health, and community relations* (pp. 39–65). New York: Lang.

Noller, P., Feeney, J. A., Sheehan, G., & Peterson, C. (2000). Marital conflict patterns: Links with family conflict and family members' perceptions of one another. *Personal Relationships, 7,* 79–94.

Papp, L. M., Kouros, C. D., & Cummings, E. M. (2009). Demand-withdraw patterns in marital conflict in the home. *Personal Relationships, 16,* 285–300.

Roberts, L. J. (2000). Fire and ice in marital communication: Hostile and distancing behaviors as predictors of marital distress. *Journal of Marriage and the Family, 62,* 693–707.

Roloff, M. E., & Ifert, D. E. (2000). Conflict management through avoidance: Withholding complaints, suppressing arguments, and declaring topics taboo. In S. Petronio (Ed.), *Balancing the secrets of private disclosures* (pp. 151–163). Mahwah, NJ: Erlbaum.

Roloff, M. E., & Johnson, K. L. (2002). Serial arguing over the relational life course: Antecedents and consequences. In A. L. Vangelisti, H. T. Reis, & M. A. Fitzpatrick (Eds.), *Stability and change in relationships* (pp. 107–128). New York: Cambridge University Press.

Smetana, J. G. (1989). Adolescents' and parents' reasoning about actual family conflict. *Child Development, 60,* 1052–1067.

Watzlawick, P., Beavin, J. H., & Jackson, D. D. (1967). *Pragmatics of human communication: A study of interactional patterns, pathologies and paradoxes.* New York: Norton.

MANAGING CONFLICT AT WORK

LINDA L. PUTNAM, UNIVERSITY OF CALIFORNIA-SANTA BARBARA

One of the major challenges in any work setting is managing conflict with supervisors, employees, and other work units. Managers spend more than half of their time on conflicts related to personnel issues, requests for resources, and responses to decisions (Kolb & Putnam, 1992). Moreover, chief executives, attorneys, and consultants have become increasingly interested in improving the management of organizational conflicts. At one time, organizations were reactive and waited for an organizational conflict to become a problem, but the growing costs of litigation have led companies to respond differently. In an effort to be proactive, many corporations have adopted formal dispute systems to address conflicts (Lipsky & Seeber, 2006). Concerns for fairness and voice in managing grievances have also led to new policies regarding conflict management. Communication is clearly central to these changes, particularly in shaping how a conflict develops over time as well as enacting approaches to dispute management.

This chapter examines two problematic types of workplace conflicts—the management of differences and work-life conflict. It begins by defining conflict, identifying its characteristics, examining two central types of workplace conflict, and exploring how to manage them effectively. In this chapter, communication is the driving force of conflict regardless of the issues, arenas, and approaches for managing it. In effect, conflict is constituted by and enacted through communication.

DEFINITION AND KEY CHARACTERISTICS OF CONFLICT

Conflict is a particular type of social interaction—one characterized by perceptions of incompatible positions or goals. Incompatibility means that one or both parties see their positions as diametrically opposed or as oppositional in goals, values, or beliefs. The parties engaged in the conflict, however, are interdependent and need each other to achieve their goals; thus, they enter into the situation with a mixture of competition and cooperation. They compete for what seems to be opposite positions; yet they cooperate to accomplish their tasks together. For example, if a company appoints a committee of software engineers to make a recommendation on a new email system, the parties are interdependent with each other in deciding which system to purchase. If one unit wants a system to satisfy its own departmental needs and another group needs an entirely different package, the conflict seeds are planted regarding making a choice as to which system to select. The need to work cooperatively to recommend an organization-wide system and the competition between units regarding the type of system to choose become the source of conflict for the participants.

Moreover, in conflict situations, participants often walk a tightrope between escalating a conflict and being exploited by the other unit. Escalation refers to having the conflict become increasingly intense and highly competitive while exploitation means that one or both parties feels defeated, as if their needs have not been met. Thus, the evolving conflict process is like a balancing act. Similar to walking a tightrope, the parties do not want to swing too far to the competitive side and escalate the conflict or too far to the cooperative side and become exploited (Putnam, 2009). The way that communication enacts the conflict shapes this pattern of push-pull between competition and cooperation.

Furthermore, a highly escalated conflict can evolve into a destructive spiral when recurring patterns of communication gain momentum on their own. This spiral is like a vicious cycle in which parties become rigid in working with each other and fight to defeat the other participants. Disputants who respond to each other with continued attacks on each other's behaviors or with the use of threats and counter threats are more likely to produce a conflict spiral (Putnam, 2001). Parties can recognize the potential development of a spiral through noticing that a conflict begins to include more issues, more participants, or greater costs that participants are willing to bare (Deutsch, 1973). Hence, parties need to observe the communication process and recognize how social interaction constructs the conflict. They need to take steps to break up patterns of messages that start to spiral before they gain a momentum of their own and become destructive and hard to manage.

The workplace is a particularly problematic area for conflicts because ways of managing them can become part of workplace culture that get transmitted to new employees. New employees may enter a work environment in which a group has a history of escalating its conflicts with another department. These patterns become repetitive and influence future interactions between the two units. In this instance, the parties need to alter the conflict spirals that are historically and contextually defined and to develop new patterns of interacting with each other.

CONTEMPORARY ISSUES IN WORKPLACE CONFLICTS

Historically, the research on organizational conflict has focused on three major areas: 1) interpersonal conflicts at work, 2) the distribution of scarce resources between units, and 3) grievances between labor and management (De Dreu & Gelfand, 2008). These topics have often aligned with different approaches to conflict management. Interpersonal approaches center on conflict styles and strategies, specifically the ways that organizational roles and relationships contribute to preferences for using particular strategies or modes of conflict management (Nicotera & Dorsey, 2006). Negotiation scholars, in contrast, examine disputes over scarce resources, also known as conflicts of interest (Olekalns, Putnam, Weingart, & Metcalf, 2008). This body of work centers on exchanging offers and counteroffers and the role of interaction patterns and sequences in reaching mutual agreements. Finally, at the organization level, scholars focus on collective bargaining in labor-management disputes and on the design and use of organizational dispute systems (Lipsky & Seeber, 2006; Putnam, 1994). These approaches treat the origins of workplace conflicts as emanating from different organizational levels.

Rather than adopting an approach based on organizational levels, this chapter focuses on two topics or central problems at work, ones that raise new challenges in addressing workplace conflicts. The two problems, managing differences at work and work-life conflicts, are critical because of major changes in the nature of the workplace. Moreover, they often evolve into hidden conflicts that call for creative approaches to manage them. Each of these central issues will be examined through defining the workplace problem, discussing the unique challenges it poses, and exploring alternatives for addressing these conflicts.

The Management of Differences at Work

As the workplace has become increasingly multicultural and multifaceted, the management of differences in organizations has become a particularly prevalent concern. Difference not only refers to diversity in demographics, such as gender, race, age, and ethnicity, but also to variation in occupations, specialties, and values (Gelfand & Brett, 2004). In an age of new technologies, organizational teams are often comprised of employees from around the globe who work in different time zones and with different cultural traditions. These teams are highly diverse in occupational specialties as well as in gender and ethnicity. Companies often engage in multicultural contractual negotiations and this pattern of globalization has forced organizations to adopt collaborative strategies for managing disputes (Lipsky & Seeber, 2006). In this workplace complexity, conflict has become the state of being challenged by human differences (Littlejohn & Domenici, 2007).

Conflicts rooted in differences are linked to social identity categories, that is, to social categories defined by identity features, for example, race, gender, or profession. The key issue in organizations is whether members see their differences as salient, problematic, or natural. When members view difference as the source of conflicts, they are more likely to locate organizational problems in social opposition, blame the other person or group, and intensify the dispute (Poole & Garner, 2006). Conflicts are managed more effectively when employees respond to each other as individuals rather than as members of social categories.

The use of interdisciplinary teams comprised of different specialties or occupational categories serves as an example of conflicts based on differences. For example, health care teams are often comprised of employees with different occupational training and status, such as doctors, technicians, social workers, and nurses. Members of these teams are often hesitant to confront a professional outside of their own discipline; hence, avoidance and suppression are typical responses to these types of conflicts. In this case, the interdisciplinary team needs to develop a norm of direct confrontation, one that overrides the status hierarchies linked to professional identities. Engaging in these confrontations as task and information problems allows members to view diversity conflicts as enhancing team performance.

Managing diversity conflicts in an organization can be particularly problematic when they become embedded in daily routines. In addition to impacting performance, diversity disputes often increase stress, emotional anxiety, and dissatisfaction at work (Pelled, 1996). While some research suggests that talking through differences can help manage diversity disputes (Ayoko, Hartel, & Callan, 2002), other studies report that direct communication is not particularly effective, especially in multicultural contexts (Von Glinow, Shapiro, & Brett, 2004). Cultural variation, racial, and gender sensitivities, and deep-seated value differences, call for creative ways to approach diversity conflicts. Managing conflict through sharing activities or using pictures and images that substitute for talk are effective ways to address multicultural conflicts. In highly volatile racial or gender conflicts, getting the parties to construct alternative narratives or to envision a different kind of workplace also helps them work through conflicts. Disputants can also reorient to difference through giving people voice in the process and agreeing to develop new practices that embrace rather than contest differences. In effect, diversity conflicts in the workplace are not easy to resolve. Managing them effectively focuses on options aimed at enhancing dignity, finding ways to value differences, and recognizing diversity as a vital resource for enriching organizational life (Littlejohn & Domenici, 2007).

The Negotiation of Work-Life Conflict

Work-life conflict is an issue that is equally as sensitive in organizational life as the management of differences (Kirby, Wieland, & McBride, 2006). Work-life conflict refers to the stress that employees feel in trying to manage work, family, elder care, and life activities. The issue has become prominent through the rise of dual career employment, life complexities, and workaholic routines linked to physical and emotional ill health. To address this type of conflict, organizations have introduced optional work arrangements, including flexible time schedules, telecommuting, job rotation, part-time work, and personal leaves (Myers, Galliard, & Putnam, 2012). However, employees are often reluctant to use these arrangements because of pressures to excel in their jobs, fear of supervisor or co-worker disapproval, or the desire to be viewed as an ideal worker. Employees who take advantage of flexible work arrangements are often seen as less committed to the organization than are those who never use them. Thus, even though the policies for flexible work exist, employees may not use them for fear that they will affect their performance evaluations, opportunities for promotion, and relationships with colleagues and supervisors (Kirby & Krone, 2002).

The challenge in managing work-life conflict stems from the dilemma of "damned if you do and damned if you don't"; that is, if employees fail to use the benefits, they often encounter higher levels of stress through increased work-life conflict, but if they use them, they may feel marginalized and devalued for taking time away from work. In a similar way, employees who engage in telecommuting often feel that they must work longer and harder than they do when they are in the office; hence their work-life conflict increases through additional multitasking between work and family (Hylmo, 2004). Supervisors may also feel trapped in administering these policies. For example, the desire to "always be fair" and to offer flexibility to all employees (e.g., single, married, parents) can result in discrimination because some employees may not need these optional work arrangements. In contrast, when supervisors make decisions on a case by case basis, they often deny requests that do not seem like "good reasons" and thus convey the mixed message of encouraging yet discouraging the use of these policies.

Communication becomes a critical factor in addressing work-life conflicts. Organizations often expect employees to make requests for special arrangements; thus, individuals must raise these issues and actively negotiate for workplace flexibility. These negotiations are most effective when employees adopt a win-win strategy and emphasize shared values that help both the organization and the individual. In addition, these give and take negotiations work best when supervisors are supportive and employees feel that they are valuable contributors who cannot easily be replaced (Buzzanell & Liu, 2007). Of importance, this approach places the onus of resolving work-life conflict on the individual rather than on the organization.

An alternative to relying on the employee to initiate negotiations is to reframe work-life conflict. Communicative reframing refers to redefining the problem, labeling it differently, and, in this case, developing a common approach to balancing work and life concerns. Reframing alters the ways that parties conceptualize a problem through renaming it and/or locating it at different organizational levels (Putnam, 2010). One way to reframe work-life conflict is to shift to a discourse of adaptability. Adaptability customizes workplace arrangements to employees' needs at different stages in their careers (Myers et al., 2012). It involves getting workers into regular communication to set expectations, develop arrangements, and evaluate performances. Flexibility in schedules, location, and work arrangements becomes an entitlement or right of employment rather than an optional benefit that employees have to negotiate. Through new communicative practices, adaptability has the potential to transform workers' needs and organizational objectives into shared goals that meet both work and life commitments. Although not a panacea for resolving work-life conflict, the discourse of adaptability transcends the contradictions embedded in current policies and recasts work and life as compatible rather than in conflict.

Unveiling Hidden Conflicts

The management of workplace differences and the negotiation of work-life conflicts are two issues that challenge traditional approaches to conflict management. They differ from conflicts about resource allocations, grievances, or task coordination because they exist on the fringe of routine work practices and often become suppressed or hidden conflicts (Kolb & Putnam, 1992). Hidden conflicts reside in the crevices of organizations as covert or unofficial interactions governed by situational norms rather than by formal policies. Unlike traditional conflicts, they are emotionally charged and can surface spontaneously rather than through planned and strategic interactions open to public deliberations.

Hidden conflicts tend to be managed through covert communication practices, such as gossip, venting, or avoidance. For instance, in diversity conflicts, employees might complain to other colleagues about how they are being treated or they might gossip about being marginalized and devalued, but when interacting with supervisors or work group members, they avoid or suppress the conflict. Similarly, in work-life conflicts, employees often conceal their reasons for needing flexible work arrangements. Specifically, in a study of women corporate leaders, 91% believed that flexible work arrangements were available to them, but only 24% felt that they could invoke family as a reason for using them (Moe & Shandy, 2010). Suppressed conflicts are particularly problematic because they can be ignored; that is, supervisors and work group members can ignore them or embed them in hidden agendas. For example, workgroups often manage difference conflicts through privilege for one faction over another in decision making as opposed to addressing the underlying diversity concerns. Diversity conflicts are also open to coalition building when the majority factions unite to counter initiatives from minority members.

Hidden conflicts also escalate when they grow in issues and costs that participants are willing to accept. In conflicts over difference, employees are willing to quit their jobs in lieu of openly confronting colleagues about suppressed issues. Hidden conflicts then may become protracted and uncontrolled through continual avoidance that leads to blurred and distorted issues, decreased communication, and misperceptions. For example, in work-life conflicts, issues regarding maternity leaves can become blurred and distorted when they are managed through the use of avoidance and misperception (Buzzanell & Liu, 2007). Specifically, Jana, a sales representative in a broadcast organization, accepted her supervisor's proposal that she work from home during her pregnancy leave. But while on leave away from work, Jana received telephone calls from her boss and coworkers at least three times a day. She answered numerous emails and went into the office for various meetings. Incompatibilities in the "meaning" of maternity leave continued to build until she quit her job. Rather than confront her supervisor, hidden conflict escalated to a point where she was willing to leave.

A key to addressing diversity and work-life conflicts is to bring them out of the organizational crevices, to confront them, and to use alternative modes of communication to manage them. Suppression and avoidance reinforce existing power relationships and replicate routine ways of doing business. If the issue is important and likely to resurface, it is best to approach the other party and discuss it. The earlier a conflict is addressed, the easier it is to prevent a pattern of spiraling through either escalation or avoidance. In conflicts about differences, it is best to state your concerns with the use of "I" messages. Making a statement, such as, "I feel as if I am not getting the same challenging work assignments as some of my co-workers," allows an employee to get the issue on the table without accusing the other party. "You" messages such as, "You have not given me the best work assignments," puts the other party on the defensive and lays the foundation for potentially escalating the conflict.

An optional way to approach diversity and work-life conflicts is to ask open-ended questions about the larger context that may have created the situation. For example, an employee might say, "I've been uncomfortable with my work assignments. Could you tell me more about how work assignments are handled in the unit and what challenges you face in making them?" Talking about the larger context that frames the situation gets both parties in a position to share narratives from different points of view. After these different stories are shared, the parties can look for gaps in the narratives and try to build a story together that would meet both their respective needs.

Another alternative is to reframe the conflict based on information about the source of it. For example, once an employee learns how work gets assigned, she could reframe the conflict as a scheduling problem, not one of discrimination in job assignment. Then both parties can shift their conversation to a new topic that might be less contentious than realigning work assignments. Another option is to shift the conversation from the unit to the organizational level. For example, employees from two different departments might see their conflict as a budget dispute. However, after exploring the larger context of the dispute, they might be able to reframe their conflict as one of priorities in funding at the organizational level. Reframing the conflict at the organizational level allows the parties to work collectively to change the system rather than struggling against each other.

This chapter presents some options for addressing diversity conflicts and work-life dilemmas. Specifically, employees can envision a new type of workplace through constructing new narratives; they can alter conflict framing, and they can situate conflicts at different organizational levels. Managing conflicts creatively involves learning from other disputants, embracing differences rather than resolving them, and bringing hidden conflicts out of the organizational crevices. Change can only occur through challenging the organizational structures and cultures that foster these conflicts (Bartunek, Kolb, & Lewicki, 1992). Communication holds the key to managing differences effectively and to redefining issues as common ground rather than as perceived incompatibilities.

REFERENCES

Ayoko, O. B., Hartel, C. E. J., & Callan, V. J. (2002). Resolving the puzzle of productive and destructive conflict in culturally heterogeneous workgroups: A communication accommodation theory approach. *International Journal of Conflict Management, 13,* 165–195.

Bartunek, J. M., Kolb, D. M., & Lewicki, R. J. (1992). Bringing conflict out from behind the scenes: Private, informal, and nonrational dimensions of conflict in organizations. In D. M. Kolb & J. M. Bartunek (Eds.), *Hidden conflict in organizations: Uncovering behind-the-scenes disputes* (pp. 209–228). Newbury Park, CA: Sage.

Buzzanell, P. M., & Liu, M. (2007). It's "give and take": Maternity leave as a conflict management process. *Human Relations, 60,* 453–495.

Deutsch, M. (1973). *The resolution of conflict.* New Haven, CT: Yale University Press.

De Dreu, C. K. W., & Gelfand, M. J. (2008). Conflict in the workplace: Sources, functions, and dynamics across multiple levels of analysis. In C. K. W. De Dreu & M. G. Gelfand (Eds.), *The psychology of conflict and conflict management in organizations* (pp. 3–54). New York: Lawrence Erlbaum.

Gelfand, M. J., & Brett, J. (Eds.). (2004). *The handbook of negotiation and culture.* Stanford, CA: Stanford University Press.

Hylmo, A. (2004). Women, men, and changing organizations: An organizational culture examination of gendered experiences of telecommuting. In P. M. Buzzanell, H. Sterk, & L. Turner (Eds.), *Gender in applied communication contexts* (pp. 47–68). Thousand Oaks, CA: Sage.

Kirby, E. L. & Krone, K. (2002). "The policy exists but you can't really use it": Communication and the structuration of work-family policies. *Journal of Applied Communication Research, 30,* 50–77.

Kirby, E. L., Wieland, S. M., & McBride, M. C. (2006). Work/life conflict. In J. G. Oetzel & S. Ting-Toomey (Eds.), *The Sage handbook of conflict and communication* (pp. 327–357). Thousand Oaks, CA: Sage.

Kolb, D. M. & Putnam, L. L. (1992). Introduction: The dialectics of disputing. In D. M. Kolb & J. M. Bartunek (Eds.), *Hidden conflict in organizations: Uncovering behind-the-scenes disputes* (pp. 1–31). Newbury Park, CA: Sage.

Lipsky, D. B. & Seeber, R. L. (2006). Managing organizational conflicts. In J. G. Oetzel & S. Ting-Toomey (Eds.), *The Sage handbook of conflict and communication* (pp. 359–390). Thousand Oaks, CA: Sage.

Littlejohn, S. W. & Domenici, K. (2007). *Communication, conflict and the management of difference.* Long Grove, IL: Waveland Press.

Moe, K. & Shandy, D. (2010). *Glass ceilings & 100-hour couples: What the opt-out phenomenon can teach us about work and family.* Athens, GA: University of Georgia Press.

Myers, K. K., Gailliard, B. M., & Putnam, L. L. (2012). Reconsidering the concept of workplace flexibility: Is adaptability a better solution? In C. T. Salmon (Ed.), *Communication Yearbook 36* (pp. 195–230). New York: Routledge/Taylor Frances.

Nicotera, A. M., & Dorsey, L. K. (2006). Individual and interactive processes in organizational conflict. In J. G. Oetzel & S. Ting-Toomey (Eds.), *The Sage handbook of conflict and communication* (pp. 293–325). Thousand Oaks, CA: Sage.

Olekalns, M., Putnam, L. L., Weingart, L. R., & Metcalf, L. (2008). Conflict management and communication processes. In C. K. W. De Dreu and M. J. Gelfand (Eds.), *The psychology of conflict and conflict management in organizations* (pp. 81–114). New York: Lawrence Erlbaum/Taylor & Francis.

Pelled, L. H. (1996). Demographic diversity, conflict, and work group outcomes. An intervening process theory. *Organization Science, 7,* 615–631.

Poole, M.S., & Garner, J. T. (2006). Perspectives on workgroup conflict and communication. In J. G. Oetzel & S. Ting-Toomey (Eds.), *The Sage handbook of conflict and communication* (pp. 267–292). Thousand Oaks, CA: Sage.

Putnam, L. L. (1994). Productive conflict: Negotiation as implicit coordination. *The International Journal of Conflict Management, 5,* 284–298.

Putnam, L. L. (2001). The language of opposition: Challenges in organizational dispute resolution. In W. Eadie & P. Nelson (Eds.), *The language of conflict and resolution* (pp. 10–20). Newbury Park, CA: Sage.

Putnam, L. L. (2009). Exploring the role of communication in transforming conflict situations: A social construction approach. In G. J. Galanes & W. Leeds-Hurwitz (Eds.), *Socially constructing communication* (pp. 189–209). Cresskill, NJ: Hampton Press.

Putnam, L. L. (2010). In point of practice: Communication as changing the negotiation game. *Journal of Applied Communication Research, 38* (4), 325–335.

Von Glinow, M.A., Shapiro, D. L., & Brett, J. M. (2004). Can we talk, and should we? Managing emotional conflict in multicultural teams. *Academy of Management Review, 29,* 578–592.

SECTION 3
FAMILY COMMUNICATION

The family communication context focuses on how family members (husband/wives, children, siblings, parents, etc.) communicate with one another. Family communication scholars often examine how family members' communication maintains these familial bonds, helps with socializing each other, or disrupts family functioning. Some major areas of research in family communication include communication in stepfamilies, parenting communication, divorced families/single parent families, childhood socialization, family rituals, and marriage. This chapter focuses on three important areas of family communication research: (1) risky behaviors of kids, (2) sibling communication and closeness, and (3) information regulation between parents and kids. First, Leslie Baxter (University of Iowa) and Carma Bylund (Memorial Sloan Kettering Cancer Center) review how parents can make a difference with their children in lifestyle choices by answering the question: *How do we talk to children about healthy lifestyle choices?* Second, Scott Myers (West Virginia University) reviews sibling communication research to answer the question: *How do siblings communicate to remain close throughout the lifespan?* Third, Tamara Afifi (University of California, Santa Barbara) reviews family information regulation research to answer the question: *What roles and what impact do topic avoidance and secrets play in family relationships?* Most of you are stuck with your family members for the rest of your lives because these are not typically relationships of choice. You don't get to choose your parents or your siblings, and you won't get to disown your kids when they act up. These family relationships can be some of the longest lasting and most important relationships in your life. It is important to consider how we can have better familial relationships and this research can help you navigate kids' bad behavior, understand secrets in the family, and maintain closeness with a brother or sister even after many years.

PARENT-ADOLESCENT COMMUNICATION AND HEALTHY LIFESTYLE CHOICES

LESLIE A. BAXTER, UNIVERSITY OF IOWA AND
CARMA BYLUND, MEMORIAL SLOAN KETTERING CANCER CENTER

What is a "healthy lifestyle choice" and what does research in parent-adolescent communication tell us about how parents can influence their adolescents to make these healthy choices? We use the phrase "healthy lifestyle choice" to refer to two broad categories of behaviors about which adolescents make healthy or unhealthy decisions: (1) risky health behaviors of alcohol and other illicit drug use, tobacco use, and unsafe sex; and (2) preventive health behaviors related to nutrition, exercise, and sun protection. Too often, adolescents make decisions that compromise their physical health. According to the 2009 Youth Risk Behavior Survey (YRBS; Centers for Disease Control and Prevention, 2010), many high school-aged adolescents are engaged in behaviors that increase their likelihood for the leading causes of death among the 10–24 age group: Within the 30 day period prior to completing the survey, 28.3% rode in a car in which the driver had been drinking alcohol, 41.8% had consumed alcohol, and 20.8% had used marijuana. Overall, 34.2% of high school adolescents reported in the survey that they were sexually active, and 39.8% of these had not used a condom during their most recent sexual intercourse. Many adolescents also engage in behaviors associated with the leading causes of death for persons 25 years or older: According to the YRBS, 19.5% had smoked cigarettes within the prior 30-day period and 9.3% failed to use sunscreen; 77.7% had not eaten the recommended servings of fruits and vegetables in the prior 7-day period, and 81.6% were not physically active for at least 60 minutes per day during this same time period. Public health media campaigns that address parents, such as the Partnership for a Drug-Free America, often oversimplify matters, urging parents to talk more to their teens about the health risks associated with their lifestyle choices (Stephenson, 2002). Research suggests that parent-adolescent communication is more complicated than merely talking more. Our purpose is to understand some of those complications related to parent-adolescent communication.

Parent-child communication can be understood along two underlying dimensions: a supportiveness/warmth/openness dimension and a regulation/control dimension (Maccoby, 1992; Steinberg, 2001). The labels for these two dimensions vary from scholar to scholar but the same general features are being referred to. Parental communication along the first dimension can be described along a continuum anchored by expressive, open, caring, supportive, friendly, and supportive behaviors, on the one hand, or non-expressive, cold, and critical behaviors, on the other hand. Parental communication along the second dimension also refers to a continuum of behaviors anchored at one end by behavior that seeks to regulate and control a child's behavior as opposed to the other endpoint in which a child experiences autonomy free of parental constraints. These two dimensions, when combined, can be visualized as the X- and Y-axes in a graph that has four quadrants; thus, parental communication can be located on this graph simultaneously on both dimensions. Both dimensions hold relevance for promoting healthy lifestyle choices in adolescents. Our own research has emphasized the second dimension, but we will also review research on the first dimension.

Research suggests that adolescents are well served when the general parent-child communication climate is characterized by warmth and openness. Such a climate appears to have spillover effects in every facet of a child's socialization, including a child's healthy lifestyle decision-making, and it probably reflects a general parent-child relationship that is positive, honest, and trusting. When this type of climate is missing, it could affect adolescents' decision making. For instance, one study showed that everyday conflict in families is associated with adolescents' use of alcohol and drugs (Caughlin & Malis, 2004). Interestingly, in this study, the content of the conflict wasn't important— the arguments could be about cleaning one's room, about allowance, or about alcohol and drugs—but the association with alcohol and drug use was still present.

However, parents shouldn't put all their eggs in the single basket of creating a general climate of warmth and openness in the family. Research tells us that parents should additionally engage in specific, targeted communication exchanges with their adolescents on topics of healthy lifestyle choices. Researchers have particularly focused on how parents' targeted communication about alcohol is associated with beliefs and decisions about alcohol use (Turrisi, Mastroleo, Mallett, Larimer, & Kilmer, 2007; Turrisi, Wiersma, & Hughes, 2000). One study found that when parents frequently have targeted communication with their adolescents about alcohol, adolescents are less likely to use alcohol (Miller-Day & Kam, 2010). One research group recruited and trained parents to talk to their teens about alcohol use before the teens went to college. The students whose parents used the training materials to talk to their teens drank less and were less likely to get drunk (Turrisi, Jaccard, Taki, Dunnam, & Grimes, 2001).

Too often, parents avoid communicating in specific, targeted ways about healthy lifestyle choices. For example, in one study, parent-child dyads demonstrated limited openness toward discussions about sexual issues and less than ideal openness about other risky behaviors, such as alcohol, drug, and tobacco use (Baxter & Akkoor, 2011). In part, this topic avoidance could reflect a motivational problem in which parents underestimate the poor decisions made by their adolescents when it comes to risky health or preventive health behaviors. In a study of parent-child dyads, we asked 164 dyads of parents and their college-aged children about the child's current health behaviors (Bylund, Imes & Baxter, 2005). When we compared parents and their children, we found that parents significantly underestimated the extent to which their young adult child participated in risky behaviors, such as smoking, marijuana use, and unprotected sex.

To this point, we have been addressing the first underlying dimension of parent-child communication—the warmth/openness dimension. Let's now turn to the other dimension of parental regulation/control. We are especially interested in what has been termed "behavioral control," that is, the "rules, regulations, and restrictions that parents have for their children" (Smetana & Daddis, 2002, p. 563). Behavioral control involves four elements: (1) clarity about rules and expectations for adolescent behavior; (2) reasons and justifications for the rules and expectations; (3) monitoring or surveillance in order to gain knowledge of the adolescent's compliance with the rules/expectations; and (4) parental discipline, or the use of positive and negative reinforcements when expectations are met or violated (Peterson & Hann, 1999).

In general terms, parental communication that displays so-called "firm control" increases the likelihood of a variety of positive social outcomes for adolescents (Peterson & Hann, 1999). More specifically, firm control has been associated with delayed initiation of sexual activity (e.g., Jacobson & Crockett, 2000; Rose, Koo, Bhaskar, Anderson, White, & Jenkins, 2005), safer sex practices (e.g., Miller, Forehand, & Kotchick, 1999; Rodgers, 1999), reduced likelihood of substance abuse (e.g., Li, Stanton, & Feigelman, 2000; Stephenson, Quick, Atkinson, & Tschida, 2005), and reduced use of tobacco smoking (e.g., Dick, Viken, Purcell, Kaprio, Pulkkinen, & Rose, 2007; Forrester, Biglan, Severson, & Smoklowski, 2007). "Firm control" is centered in a warm, open communication climate in which the parent is seen as supportive and caring. It involves communication from parents that creates reasonable expectations and limit setting. Parents monitor and restrict adolescent behavior in a firm way but not in an overly demanding or punitive way. Firm control is motivated by parental desire to have adolescents internalize standards and expectations so that they eventually can monitor their own behavior and self-discipline themselves. In order to internalize parental standards, adolescents need to experience parental communication that explains why the expectations or rules are necessary, how their behavior affects others, and how they can make amends for any harm they have done (Peterson & Hann, p. 334).

In two studies, we have sought to refine our understanding of "firm control" by studying the content of rules and expectations related to healthy lifestyle choices. We noticed that existing research tended to study parental expectations and rules in a general way, usually by simply asking adolescents how frequently their parents communicated rules for health-related behaviors (e.g., Stephenson et al., 2005, van der Vorst et al., 2005). In fact, this inattention to the details of communication is a general pattern in the research related to adolescent healthy lifestyle choices (Miller-Day, 2008).

For the risky behaviors of alcohol use, tobacco use, and unsafe sex (Baxter, Bylund, Imes, & Routsong, 2009), we asked parents and their college-aged children to report all of the health-related rules parents had for the children's adolescent years, in addition to soliciting numerical reports of the extent to which other elements of firm control were present for each reported rule. We found two basic types of rules by which parents communicated their expectations—abstinence and contingency—and additionally found that the type of rule communicated by parents varied by the particular risky health behavior. Abstinence rules and expectations refer to absolute rules designed to prevent the risky behavior; they are similar to what Miller-Day (2008) identified as "no tolerance" messages from parents. By contrast, contingency rules allowed the behavior but only under a set of specific circumstances. For example, an abstinence rule for alcohol use might be "No alcohol, period." A contingency rule for alcohol use might be "You can have one beer but only if there are adults present."

Our results suggested that parents articulate both kinds of rules, but variations exist by risky health behavior. Alcohol use was dominated by four rules, two contingency and two abstinence. The two dominant contingency rules were the prohibition of drinking when driving or riding as a passenger when the driver had been drinking, and the use of alcohol if the adolescent showed good judgment by only consuming a moderate amount. The two abstinence rules were the prohibition of alcohol under any circumstances until the adolescent was of age, or the simple prohibition of alcohol, period. The sexual activity domain also was dominated by two contingency rules and two abstinence rules. The contingency rules were allowing sexual activity if protection was used, and allowing sexual activity if the relationship with the partner was sufficiently close. The two abstinence rules were the prohibition of sex until after marriage and the prohibition of sex until the adolescent was older. By contrast, tobacco use was dominated by a single abstinence rule prohibiting the use of tobacco in any form and under all circumstances.

For the preventive health domains of nutrition, exercise, and sun protection, we similarly asked a sample of adolescents and their parents to report all of the rules and expectations present in the family during the child's adolescence (Bylund, Baxter, Imes, & Wolf, 2010). For these domains, rules varied not so much by their abstinence-contingency nature as by their generality-specificity. General rules expressed the overall value of a healthy practice, for example, "Eat healthy." By contrast, specific rules offered detailed guidelines that addressed how that healthy practice should be accomplished, for example, "Eat four servings of fruits and vegetables every day." We think that general preventive rules function to promote the adolescent's internalization of health-promoting values, whereas specific rules might function in a more narrowly focused way to regulate specific behavioral practices.

Parental rules articulated both general and specific rules across nutrition, exercise, and sun protection domains. Reported nutrition rules were both general and specific in our sample, dominated by an expectation that imposed a limit on the amount of unhealthy food that could be consumed, an expectation about fruit and vegetable consumption, an expectation for a well-balanced diet, and an expectation that imposed a temporal constraint on when unhealthy foods could or could not be consumed (e.g., "No sweets before dinner"). The exercise domain was dominated by a general rule that encouraged physical activity of some kind and a more specific rule that encouraged involvement in some organized physical activity, such as team sports. The sun protection domain was dominated by a single general expectation—the use of sunblock and sunscreen, period. Secondarily, parents and adolescents identified a more specific variation of this rule in which time of use (e.g., between 10 a.m. and 4 p.m.), location of use (e.g., when you go swimming), and amount or type of product to use (e.g., the SPF value).

In addition to examining the content of rules and expectations related to several health lifestyle choices, we have examined how parents communicate their rules or expectations (Baxter et al., 2009; Bylund et al., 2010). In general, across the health domains, parents perceive themselves to communicate more directly and with greater justification than their adolescents perceive is the case. This suggests to us that parents should increase their communicative efforts even more to ensure that their expectations are conveyed with clarity and with justification. In addition, for many health domains, parents perceived themselves to enforce their rules more so than adolescents perceived to be the case. Parents should work harder to maintain consistency in their disciplining of adolescents when rules and expectations are violated. As we mentioned earlier, parents may be overestimating the extent to which their adolescents comply with their expectations, and adolescents might experience this as a lack of consistency in enforcement of rules. Thus, parents need to do a better job of monitoring their adolescent's behaviors, not just monitoring the consistency of their own disciplinary practices; monitoring and discipline are interrelated.

An additional kind of consistency appears to be important, as well: the extent to which parents themselves model healthy lifestyles. Bylund et al. (2010) found that this was an important factor in adolescent compliance with nutrition and sun protection rules and expectations. Other researchers have identified the importance of parental modeling for alcohol, tobacco, and other drug use (e.g., Ennett, Bauman, Foshee, Pemberton, & Hicks, 2001; Kilpatrick et al., 2000). Parental modeling can work in two ways. First, modeling can exert influence but in a subtle manner by allowing the adolescent to observe the consequence of others' actions through social learning (Bandura, 1977). Second, and more relevant to a communication perspective, modeling addresses parental credibility—a clear antidote to the suspect "do as I say, not what I do" double standard of rules that apply only to adolescents but not to parents.

Overall, our findings (Baxter et al., 2009; Bylund et al., 2010) suggest that compliance with rules and expectations during adolescence is greater when parents express rules and expectations clearly and directly, with justification, with consistency in the application of sanctions, and by selectively modeling the desired lifestyle choices. This general pattern is one supported in the research of other scholars, as well (e.g., Miller-Day, 2008). But what, specifically, can parents do to achieve these abstract qualities of clarity, reason giving, discipline, and modeling?

When it comes to discussing healthy and risky behaviors, sometimes it can feel difficult to start a discussion. One approach that is in line with developing a supportive/warm/open environment is to understand the child's perspective before discussing rules, reasons, and sanctions. Parents might choose to start with a simple open request, e.g., "Tell me about what you know about sexually transmitted diseases," or "Why do you think it might be important to wear sunscreen when you go to the pool this summer?" or "Do a lot of your classmates smoke? What do you think about smoking?" Restating in one's own words what parents understood the child to say can also be helpful, e.g., "So it sounds like you're saying that you think some kids smoke, but not any of those that do are your friends?"

A parent might also choose to use an empathic approach in discussions with adolescents about healthy lifestyle choices, acknowledging that sometimes it's difficult to make the healthy choice and praising their efforts, e.g., "I know it can be hard to be at a party when someone offers you a beer" or "I'm really impressed with the nutritious food choices you make."

When explaining rules, the reasons behind the rules, and the sanctions if the rules are broken, it is helpful to involve the adolescent in the decision making process. "Nicholas, your dad and I feel that it's very important that you not smoke cigarettes. We have seen how harmful smoking can be with Uncle Mark. What do you think should happen if you started smoking?"

A final and important step is to check the adolescents' understanding of rules surrounding healthy and risky behavior, e.g., "Anna, I know that sometimes you feel like I haven't explained things to you very well. I just want to check in with you about some things. What do you understand to be our family's rules about drinking?" Again, as the research shows, these conversations are not just one-time conversations but they should happen multiple times.

Parents likely vary in their ability to implement any suggestions for communication behaviors. We, and others, have found that parents have habituated ways of communicating with their adolescents on the topic of healthy lifestyle choices (Baxter, Bylund, Imes, & Scheive, 2005; Booth-Butterfield & Sidelinger, 1998; Koesten & Anderson, 2004; Miller-Day, 2008; Miller-Day & Kam, 2010). Family communication environments vary in underlying parent-child norms of conversation orientation (how open and expressive family members are encouraged to be), similar to the supportiveness/warmth/openness dimension discussed earlier, and conformity-orientation (the extent to which family members feel required to conform to the same opinion, usually that of the parents) (Koerner & Fitzpatrick, 2002). Suggestions for parental openness are easier to accomplish in families with a high conversation orientation, and mandated rules play a more salient role in families high in conformity orientation.

An important caveat is that benefits of effective communication practices might be short-lived. Bylund et al. (2010) found that parent-adolescent communication during the child's adolescence failed to predict health practices related to nutrition, exercise, and sun protection when those adolescents went off to college. Arnett (2004) has observed that emerging adulthood is a developmental period from 18 to 25 years in which the adolescent transitions to adulthood. It is a potential "age of susceptibility" (Miller-Day, 2008, p. 2) for unhealthy lifestyle choices related to both risky health behaviors and preventive lifestyle choices. Communication practices that successfully gain rule compliance during adolescence might not continue into young adulthood. Some parents might be satisfied with a goal of delaying the onset of some risky health-related behaviors, for example sexual activity. However, other health-related behaviors establish habits of living that can affect the adolescents throughout their lives, for example, healthy eating and exercise. The key element at play in this discrepancy between short-term rule compliance and long-term compliance is probably the extent to which the adolescent has internalized the values and justifications that underlie adolescent healthy lifestyle rules. More research is needed in which the focus is how parents can influence the lifelong healthy lifestyle choices of their adolescents.

REFERENCES

Arnett, J. J. (2004). *Emerging adulthood: The winding road from the late teens through the twenties.* New York: Oxford University Press.

Bandura, A. (1977). *Social learning theory.* Upper Saddle River, NJ: Prentice Hall.

Baxter, L. A., Bylund, C. L., Imes, R., & Routsong, T. (2009). Parent-child perceptions of parental behavioral control through rule-setting for risky health choices during adolescence. *Journal of Family Communication, 9,* 251–271.

Baxter, L. A., Bylund, C. L., Imes, R. S., & Scheive, D. M. (2005). Family communication environments and rule-based social control of adolescents' healthy lifestyle choices. *Journal of Family Communication, 5,* 209–227.

Baxter, L. A., & Akkoor, C. A. (2011). Topic expansiveness and family communication patterns. *Journal of Family Communication, 11,* 1–20.

Booth-Butterfield, M., & Sidelinger, R. (1998). The influence of family communication on the college-aged child. *Communication Quarterly, 46,* 295–312.

Bylund, C. L., Baxter, L. A., Imes, R. S., & Wolf, B. (2010). Parental rule socialization for preventive health and adolescent rule compliance. *Family Relations, 59,* 1–13.

Bylund, C. L., Imes, R. S., & Baxter, L. A. (2005). Accuracy of parents' perceptions of their college student children's health and health risk behaviors. *Journal of American College Health, 54,* 31–37.

Caughlin, J. P., & Malis, R. S. (2004). Demand/withdraw communication between parents and adolescents: Connections with self-esteem and substance abuse. *Journal of Social and Personal Relationships, 17,* 523–551.

Centers for Disease Control and Prevention (2010). Youth risk behavior surveillance—United States, 2009. Surveillance Summaries, June 4, 2010. *Morbidity and Mortality Weekly Report, 59* (SS-5), pp. 1–148.

Dick, D. M., Viken, R., Purcell, S., Kaprio, J., Pulkkinen, L., & Rose, R. J. (2007). Parental monitoring moderates the importance of genetic and environmental influences on adolescent smoking. *Journal of Abnormal Psychology, 116,* 213–218.

Ennett, S. T., Bauman, K. E., Foshee, V. A., Pemberton, M., & Hicks, K. A. (2001). Parent-child communication about adolescent tobacco and alcohol use: What do parents say and does it affect youth behavior? *Journal of Marriage and the Family, 63,* 48–62.

Forester, K., Biglan, A., Severson, J. J., & Smolkowski, K. (2007). Predictors of smoking onset over two years. *Nicotine & Tobacco Research, 9,* 1259–1267.

Jacobson, K. C., & Crockett, L. J. (2000). Parental monitoring and adolescent adjustment: An ecological perspective. *Journal of Research on Adolescence, 10,* 65–97.

Kilpatrick, D. G., Acierno, R., Saunders, B., Resnick, H. S., Best, C. L., & Schnurr, P. P. (2000). Risk factors for adolescent substance abuse and dependence: Data from a national sample. *Journal of Consulting and Clinical Psychology, 68,* 19–30.

Koerner, A. F., & Fitzpatrick, M.A. (2002). Understanding family communication patterns and family functioning: The roles of conversation orientation and conformity orientation. *Communication Yearbook, 26,* 37–68.

Koesten, J., & Anderson, K. (2004). Exploring the influence of family communication patterns, cognitive complexity, and interpersonal competence on adolescent risk behaviors. *Journal of Family Communication, 4,* 99–121.

Li, X., Stanton, B., & Feigelman, S. (2000). Impact of perceived parental monitoring on adolescent risk behavior over 4 years. *Journal of Adolescent Health, 27,* 49–56.

Maccoby, E. E. (1992). The role of parents in the socialization of children: An historical overview. *Developmental Psychology, 28,* 1006–1017.

Miller, K. S., Forehand, R., & Kotchick, B. A. (1999). Adolescent sexual behavior in two ethnic minority samples: The role of family variables. *Journal of Marriage and the Family, 61,* 85–98.

Miller-Day, M. (2008). Talking to youth about drugs: What do late adolescents say about parental strategies? *Family Relations, 57,* 1–12.

Miller-Day, M., & Kam, J. A. (2010). More than just openness: Developing and validating a measure of targeted parent-child communication about alcohol. *Health Communication, 25,* 293–302.

Peterson, G. W., & Hann, D. (1999). Socializing children and parents in families. In M. B. Sussman, S. K. Steinmetz, & G. W. Peterson (Eds.), *Handbook of marriage and the family* (2nd ed., pp. 327–370). New York: Plenum Press.

Rodgers, K. B. (1999). Parenting processes related to sexual risk-taking behaviors of adolescent males and females. *Journal of Marriage and the Family, 61,* 99–109.

Rose, A., Koo, H. P., Bhaskar, B., Anderson, K., White, G., & Jenkins, R. R. (2005). The influence of primary caregivers on the sexual behavior of early adolescents. *Journal of Adolescent Health, 37,* 135–144.

Smetana, J. G., & Daddis, C. (2002). Domain-specific antecedents of parental psychological control and monitoring: The role of parenting beliefs and practices. *Child Development, 73,* 563–580.

Steinberg, L. (2001). We know some things: Parent-adolescent relationships in retrospect and prospect. *Journal of Research on Adolescence, 11,* 1–19.

Stephenson, M. T. (2002). Anti-drug public service announcements targeting parents: An analysis and evaluation. *Southern Communication Journal, 67,* 335–350.

Stephenson, M. T., Quick, B. L., Atkinson, J., & Tschida, D. (2005). Authoritative parenting and drug-prevention practices: Implications for antidrug ads for parents. *Health Communication, 17,* 301–321.

Turrisi, R., Jaccard, J. Taki, R., Dunnam, H., & Grimes, J. (2001). Examination of the short-term efficacy of a parent intervention to reduce college student drinking tendencies. *Psychology of Addictive Behaviors, 15,* 366–372.

Turrisi, R., Mastroleo, N. R., Mallet, K. A., Larimer, M. E., & Kilmer, J. R. (2007). Examination of the meditational influences of peer norms, environmental influences, and parent communications on heavy drinking in athletes and nonathletes. *Psychology of Addictive Behavior, 21,* 453–461.

Turrisi, R., Wiersma, K. A., Hughes, K. K. (2000). Binge-drinking-related consequences in college students: Role of drinking beliefs and mother-teen communication. *Psychology of Addictive Behaviors, 14,* 342–355.

van der Vorst, K., Engels, R., Meeus, W., Dekovic, M., & Van Leeuwe, J. (2005). The role of alcohol-specific socialization in adolescents' drinking behavior. *Addiction, 100,* 1464–1476.

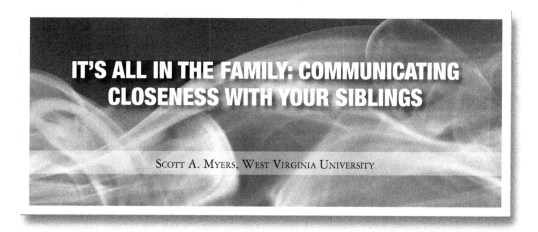

IT'S ALL IN THE FAMILY: COMMUNICATING CLOSENESS WITH YOUR SIBLINGS

SCOTT A. MYERS, WEST VIRGINIA UNIVERSITY

If you are like most people, you have at least one sibling. I happen to have three siblings, all of whom are younger than me. My sister Michelle, who is three years younger, works at State Farm Insurance headquarters where she is a member of upper management. Twice divorced, she is a wonderful mother to a 10-year-old daughter and an 18-year-old daughter. My sister Susan, who is five years younger, is a social worker for the Illinois Department of Children and Family Services. Single, Susan has two dogs, Bella and Sage, who are quite demanding (her third and oldest dog, Pepsi, recently passed away from congestive heart failure), and she is the primary caregiver for our ill mother. My brother Mark, who is seven years younger, passed away in 1998. At the time of his passing, he was a sous chef at a fine dining establishment and was attending college part-time.

As children and adolescents, the four of us spent a lot of time together. Being raised several miles outside a tiny Midwestern, Illinois town with a population of 1,500 residents at a time when cable television was not yet available, when Atari was a crude predecessor of Xbox, and when both cell phones and the Internet had yet to be invented, we relied on each other to fulfill our needs for affection, companionship, and entertainment. Living in the country meant that we had a slew of animals that required daily care, acres of pasture that had to be maintained, and crops that had to be cultivated in the summer, not to mention that almost all of our friends lived in town and largely were inaccessible to us on a daily basis. These conditions meant that we also relied on each other for both instrumental and social support. During this time, our relationships were important and the four of us—despite the occasional fighting, bickering, or even hitting, slapping, or scratching—formed a tight and cohesive bond.

As we moved into emerging adulthood, however, our relationships began to change. Emerging adulthood, which begins when a person reaches the age of 18 and ends when a person turns 25, is a time period when individuals begin to decrease their physical and emotional involvement in their siblings' lives (Scharf, Shulman, & Avigad-Spitz, 2005). While our bond was not necessarily broken, it also was not as tight or cohesive as it was during childhood and adolescence. Consistent with the research findings conducted on emerging adult siblings (Arnett, 2001; Pulakos, 1989), our priorities shifted and we became more focused on our romantic partners, our friends, our part-time jobs, and our education. At the same time, we began to gain a deeper understanding of the importance of our sibling bond, which, too, is consistent with the research literature (Scharf et al., 2005) and we were forced to discover new ways in which we could communicate closeness to each other. This research question—"How do adult siblings communicate closeness with each other across the lifespan?" —is the focus of this chapter. To answer this question, I will examine three communicative behaviors that are particularly salient to how adult siblings communicate closeness to each other. These behaviors are relational maintenance behaviors, behavioral expressions of commitment, and verbal aggressiveness.

SIBLING RELATIONAL MAINTENANCE BEHAVIORS

One way in which siblings communicate closeness across the lifespan is through their use of relational maintenance behaviors. Relational maintenance behaviors are the actions and activities in which individuals engage to sustain desired relational definitions (Canary & Stafford, 1994). In other words, relational maintenance behaviors are the things that people do and say in order to keep their relationships moving forward or to prevent their relationships from becoming stagnant.

Before examining the specific behaviors adult siblings use to maintain their relationships, it is important to identify why adults siblings are motivated to maintain their relationships in the first place. Not surprisingly, adult siblings are motivated to maintain their relationships for one of two reasons: circumstance or choice (Myers, 2011). *Circumstance* refers to the sense of obligation that pervades many sibling relationships. Because the sibling relationship is considered to be involuntary, obligatory, and enduring (Mikkelson, 2006) —as evidenced by the genetic, legal, or cultural bonds that link siblings to each other—some siblings believe it is their duty to both themselves and their immediate families (namely, their parents) to maintain their relationships. In some cases, parents purposely remind their children that they need to maintain a presence in each other's lives (Medved, Brogan, McClanahan, Morris, & Shepherd, 2006). For instance, whenever I visit my siblings (usually twice a year because I do not live in the same state as my sisters and mother), my mother always makes it a point to remind me to keep in contact with Michelle and Susan because, as she likes to say, "they're all you've got." Usually, she says this when we are having a family dinner and the three of us respond by either rolling our eyes or playfully informing her that once she is dead, the three of us will never talk to each other again. (We're a bit verbally aggressive as a unit, which will be discussed in greater detail later in this chapter.)

Conversely, some adult siblings are motivated to maintain their relationships due to choice, which refers to the conscious decision made by siblings to remain involved in each other's lives. Siblings who voluntarily choose to maintain their relationships typically report that their relationships with each other are enjoyable and that their relationships resemble a friendship. I'm always amazed at how much time my sisters spend together and the number of activities they share. For example, before Michelle had her first child, the two of them would travel extensively together. Whether it was driving to Chicago to go shopping or taking a vacation to London and Paris, they did so together willingly. Every several years, the three of us, along with my nieces and mother, go to Walt Disney World. While this is not a place that I want to go, I do so because I want to be able to spend time with my sisters, even if we end up disagreeing about where to eat, arguing about the sleeping arrangements, or fighting over the temperature of the air conditioner in the hotel room (I'm always hot, they're always cold)—which, by the way, we always do.

Regardless of why adult siblings maintain their relationships, researchers have found that adult siblings typically use five behaviors to maintain their relationships. These five behaviors are positivity, assurances, openness, networks, and tasks. (It should be noted that these same five behaviors are used by marital partners, romantic partners, and friends to maintain their relationships.) *Positivity* refers to communicating with a relational partner in a cheerful and optimistic manner, *assurances* refers to expressing a desire to remain involved in the relationship, *openness* refers to directly discussing the nature of the relationship, *networks* refers to sharing common affiliations and memberships, and *tasks* refers to sharing and completing activities unique to the relationship (Canary & Stafford, 1992; Stafford & Canary, 1991). Across the lifespan, adult siblings report using the tasks relational maintenance behavior the most frequently, followed (in descending order) by their use of the positivity, assurances, networks, and openness relational maintenance behaviors (Myers & Members of COM 200, 2001).

Within each stage of the sibling lifespan, similar results have been obtained. Not only do siblings report using all five relational maintenance behaviors, but siblings in both the emerging adulthood lifespan stage (recall that this is ages 18 to 25 years) and the early and middle adulthood lifespan stage (i.e., siblings who are between the ages of 26 and 54 years) report using the tasks relational maintenance behavior the most frequently and the openness relational maintenance behavior the least frequently (Eidsness & Myers, 2008; Myers, Brann, & Rittenour, 2008), whereas siblings in the late adulthood stage (i.e., siblings who are ages 55 years and older) report using the positivity relational maintenance behavior the most frequently and the openness relational maintenance behavior the least frequently (Goodboy, Myers, & Patterson, 2009). At the same time—both across the sibling lifespan and within each of the three stages of the sibling lifespan—when adult siblings trust and like each other, experience relational closeness, are committed to each other, and are satisfied with their relationships, they use these relational maintenance behaviors in their relationships (Myers & Members of COM 200, 2001; Myers & Rittenour, 2012; Myers & Weber, 2004). With my sisters, I rely heavily on the tasks and positivity relational maintenance behaviors because (a) I want to assist my sisters in any way I can, particularly when I visit, with helping take care of my mother or helping them with chores that need to be completed around their homes, and (b) I want to ensure that we have cheerful face-to-face, telephone, or e-mail conversations so that we are motivated to continue communicating with each other. At the same time, I rarely use openness or assurances because I do not feel a strong need to express either my emotions or how I feel about our relationship with them.

Whether siblings choose to use these relational maintenance behaviors, however, may be dependent on the perceived quality of the relationship or the genetic bond that governs most sibling relationships. According to researcher Deborah Gold (1989), sibling relationships can be classified into one of five types: *intimate* (i.e., siblings are considered to be best friends based on mutual feelings of emotional interdependence and psychological closeness); *congenial* (i.e., siblings are considered to be good friends, but their positive feelings are less intense than intimate sibling relationships); *loyal* (i.e., siblings are governed by feelings of familial obligation); *apathetic* (i.e., siblings are indifferent toward each other); and *hostile* (i.e., siblings resent and dislike each other). Myers and Goodboy (2010) found that adult siblings who consider their relationships to be intimate not only use relational maintenance behaviors at a higher rate than adult siblings who consider their relationships to be congenial, loyal, apathetic, or hostile, but they also more frequently use a greater variety of communication channels (e.g., e-mail, telephone, and face-to-face) to maintain their relationships. Mikkelson, Myers, and Hannawa (2011) found that adults use the positivity, openness, and assurances relational maintenance behaviors more frequently with more genetically related (i.e., twins, full sibling, or half sibling) siblings than with less genetically related (i.e., stepsibling, adopted sibling) siblings. They also discovered that individuals use the positivity, openness, assurances, networks, and tasks relational maintenance behaviors at a higher rate with full siblings than with stepsiblings.

BEHAVIORAL EXPRESSIONS OF COMMITMENT

A second way in which adult siblings communicate closeness across the lifespan is through their expressions of commitment. Commitment is considered to be a psychological attachment through which individuals indicate their desire to continue in a relationship indefinitely (Rusbult, 1980), which is marked by their investment of time, effort, and resources in the relationship (Lund, 1985). In an investigation of whether sibling commitment remains stable or fluctuates across the lifespan, Rittenour, Myers, and Brann (2007) found that commitment remained stable across the emerging adult lifespan stage, the early and middle adulthood lifespan stage, and the late adulthood lifespan stage. That is, regardless of the stage of the adult sibling lifespan, siblings report that they are committed to their relationships. They also found that across the three stages of the lifespan, siblings who provided each other with communication-based emotional support and used social support behaviors (i.e., a dimension of affectionate communication) were more highly committed to the sibling relationship. In a related vein, Myers, Byrnes, Frisby, and Mansson (2011) most recently discovered that across the lifespan, adult siblings strategically use three dimensions of affectionate communication—verbal statements, nonverbal gestures, and social support behaviors—as additional ways to maintain and remain committed to their relationships.

With Rittenour et al. findings in mind, Myers and Bryant (2008b) were interested in identifying the ways that emerging adult siblings express their commitment behaviorally to each other, recalling that it is during this stage when familial obligations begin to decline and relationships with romantic partners and friends take precedence over relationships with siblings. Generally, they found that not only do emerging adult siblings report using 11 categories of behaviors to express their commitment to each other, but also that they use these behaviors regularly and that their use of these behaviors is tied positively to the communication and relational satisfaction they associate with their sibling relationships. The first five categories centered on the provision of some form of social support. *Tangible support* occurred when siblings provided each other with needed goods or services. Some of these goods or services included preparing or purchasing meals, providing transportation, loaning money, or purchasing gifts. *Emotional support* consisted of expressions of caring and concern directed toward each other (e.g., "I offer him support and positivity" and "He has not always made the right decisions, but I always support him. He is emotionally there for me, therefore I will be there for him").

Informational support occurred when siblings needed advice, guidance, or feedback about the events occurring in their lives (e.g., their school work, their jobs, and their relationships). *Esteem support* arose when siblings wanted to demonstrate their positive affect for each other. Several participants noted that this included attending activities at which their siblings were participating (e.g., sporting events, band concerts, and school functions) or providing an ego boost that they believed their sibling desperately needed (e.g., "To show my commitment, I often compliment him and give him confidence"). *Network support* emerged when siblings included each other in their activities and same groups of friends. Interestingly, Mikkelson, Floyd, and Pauley (2011) found that emerging adults provide greater amounts of tangible, emotional, informational, and network support to their more genetically related siblings than to their less genetically related siblings.

The sixth and seventh categories centered on how siblings expressed intimacy with each other through their daily routines. *Everyday talk* referenced the communication that occurred between siblings on a regular basis (whether it was face-to-face, cell phone, e-mail, or text messaging) about their daily mundane activities (e.g., jobs, school, chores, and errands). *Shared activities* centered on activities in which siblings participated together on a regular basis that are just as mundane, such as playing video games, watching television, or having the same interests (e.g., "We both like the same music so I am constantly introducing her to new bands that I think she might like"). While both of these categories involved routine behaviors through which commitment was conveyed indirectly, the eighth and ninth categories involved the communication of messages that strategically and specifically expressed commitment toward a sibling. *Verbal expressions* consisted of direct verbal statements (e.g., "I tell my brother I love him every time I see him") whereas *nonverbal expressions* consisted of direct nonverbal behaviors (e.g., "Every time I see my sister, as a sign of greeting we give a kiss on the cheek to each other and a hug").

The tenth category is *protection,* which involves the purposeful efforts made to shield siblings from negative or hurtful people, situations, or influences. Protection was used generally (e.g., "I will always have his back, whether he is right or wrong. Blood is thicker than water, and I will defend him in any situation") or would arise when the sibling was in a potentially troublesome or bothersome situation (e.g., "Being the only girl, and the youngest, he is very protective of me and keeps a close eye on me, particularly with males or potential boyfriends"). The eleventh category is *intimate play,* which involves the physical (and sometimes antisocial) behaviors siblings used with each other. Two examples are "we usually pretend like we're fighting and we'll chase each other around the house and laugh" and "it's just playful fighting between brothers. A punch to say hello and a punch to say goodbye. Most often I get put in a headlock just walking by."

One thing to consider is that Myers' and Bryant's (2008b) research focused solely on one stage of the adult sibling lifespan—emerging adulthood—and researchers have yet to explore how siblings in either the early and middle adulthood stage or the late adulthood stage behaviorally express their commitment to each other. For instance, as my sisters and I now reside in the early and middle adulthood stage, how we express our commitment to each other is reflective of our life circumstances in that, typically during this stage, individuals focus on their marital relationships, their children, and their careers (Connidis, 1992). Because our focus on each other is not as sharp as it once was, we do not have the opportunity to always provide each other with various forms of social support or to engage in the similar amount of everyday contact and shared activities as we once did. Yet, because I am committed to my relationships with my siblings, we do spend a lot of time together when I go to visit them and we do remain in contact with each other, although it can be sporadic and it is usually through e-mail, text messaging, and the occasional gift or card sent through the mail.

VERBAL AGGRESSIVENESS

A third way in which adult siblings communicate closeness across the lifespan—albeit a lack of closeness—is through their use of verbal aggressiveness. Considered to be a destructive communication trait, verbal aggressiveness is a message behavior that attacks an individual's self-concept in order to deliver psychological pain (Infante & Wigley, 1986). Generally, when siblings are perceived to behave in a verbally aggressive manner, their relationships are considered to be less satisfying and less trusting (Martin, Anderson, Burant, & Weber, 1997; Martin, Anderson, & Rocca, 2005; Teven, Martin, & Neupauer, 1998). Across the three stages of the adult sibling lifespan, when adults use verbally aggressive messages with their siblings, they like and trust their siblings less and are less committed to their sibling relationships (Myers & Goodboy, 2006).

In a study that probed the frequency with which adults use verbally aggressive messages with their siblings across the three stages of the adult sibling lifespan, Myers and Goodboy (2006) found that siblings in the emerging adulthood stage reported using verbally aggressive messages at a higher rate than siblings in both the early and middle adulthood stage and in the late adulthood stage. That is, emerging adult siblings stated that they are more likely to utilize verbally aggressive messages that attack their siblings' intelligence, tease their siblings about their relationships with others, call their siblings uncomplimentary nicknames, make fun of their siblings' physical appearance, threaten to get their siblings in trouble, point out their siblings' faults, and tell their siblings that they lack common sense. Furthermore, they found that emerging adult siblings are more likely to make fun of the ways that their siblings talk as well as to embarrass their siblings in front of others than early and middle adulthood siblings. Reflecting on my own sibling relationships, I can attest that my siblings and I used many of these messages, with regularity, during emerging adulthood. For instance, Susan, Mark, and I used to enjoy teasing Michelle about her boyfriend Nello (yes, that was his name) and the way he dressed (he wore sleeveless t-shirts and parachute pants; keep in mind this was during the 1980s), the way he spoke (he was quite soft-spoken and we had to keep asking Michelle "what did he say?"), and the way he acted (he had a lot of facial tics; it would be years later before we all—including Nello—found out that he had Tourette's Syndrome). All four of us would taunt each other about our own intellectual abilities and argue over who was the smartest. To this day, Susan is incredulous that Michelle and I were surprised that she earned a Master's of Social Work degree, given that we apparently would remind her that she was the least intelligent of the four of us. The fact that she hated college and refused to attend the first day of any class because "all professors do is go over the syllabus" certainly did not help her case, particularly because we both loved college and always went to class! And like most siblings, we had no problem critiquing each other's choice of clothing, hairstyles, or hair color.

To explore whether adult siblings consider verbally aggressive messages to be hurtful, Myers and Bryant (2008a) asked a sample of emerging adult siblings to provide one example of a verbally aggressive message directed toward them by one of their siblings and to indicate the extent to which they considered the message to be hurtful, intense, and intentional. While they found that siblings use seven categories of verbally aggressive messages, they also found that no significant differences in perceived hurtfulness, intensity, or intent existed among any of the seven categories of messages. That is, no one type of message was considered more hurtful, intense, or intentional than any other type of message.

The first category is *name calling,* which involved the use of a derogatory, disparaging, or malevolent term directed toward a sibling. These terms could be general (e.g., "My sister called me an idiot") or based on a behavior the sibling did not like or appreciate (e.g., "He called me 'gay' because I wouldn't go get his phone charger"). The second category is *insults,* which identified siblings' ineptitude in some aspect of their lives and often centered on attacking their abilities, intelligence, or appearance. For example, one participant noted her brother's attack on her physical appearance: "My older brother told me that I needed to lose weight and I asked him 'why?' and he said that '[your] ass [is] bigger than J-Lo's and not in a good way!'" The third category is *withdrawal,* which occurred when siblings wanted to make it clear that they did not want to be in the presence of one another. These messages were conveyed verbally (e.g., "Why don't you just stay at school because no one wants you here") and nonverbally (e.g., "My sister will go weeks without speaking to me if she is upset").

The fourth category is *physical acts or threats (real or implied),* which involved the threat of engaging in a violent or aggressive act with a sibling. While most threats were physical (e.g., "Roger told me he would 'punch me in the face' if I interfered with his relationship again"), other threats resembled intimidation or blackmail (e.g., "One time, my brother threatened me, and told me that if I didn't drive him to his friend's house he would tell our mom something that I had done in the past that he knows that she wouldn't approve"). The fifth category is *repudiating the relationship,* which siblings used as a way to either deny or reject the sibling relationship (e.g., "Your opinion doesn't count since you don't live here anymore") or as a way to question the sibling's place in the family (e.g., "She told me . . . that she wished she could have a different sister, because if I was a real sister I wouldn't have treated her the way that I did").

The sixth category is *unfair comparison,* which unjustly compared one sibling's situation to another sibling's situation. These comparisons often revolved around siblings' education and academic prowess: "While I was telling my sister about a hard test that I had just taken, she rolled her eyes and sighed repeatedly. Then she proceeded to tell me how much harder her classes were then [sic] mine and said that I have nothing to complain about." The seventh category is *negative affect,* which conveyed a dislike, hatred, or general disdain toward the sibling, such as "I hate you, I can't wait until you go back to school" and "Within the last month, my little sister told me she hated me. Truthfully, this is no surprise."

Similar to the research conducted on adult sibling commitment, researchers have yet to examine the types of verbally aggressive messages used specifically by siblings in either the early and middle adulthood lifespan stage or the late adulthood lifespan stage. Given the categories uncovered by Myers and Bryant (2008a), it is likely that adult siblings across the lifespan use the same, or similar, types of verbally aggressive messages because the sibling relationship is one of the few relationships in which participants can engage in antisocial relational behaviors without fear of the relationship ending. My siblings and I continue to make fun of each other's physical appearance, point out each other's faults, and call each other uncomplimentary nicknames. For instance, Susan and I know when Michelle either does not like something we have done or disagrees with something we have said, she refers to the two of us as "you people"; when Susan tells us she is bloated, we tell her she is fat; and both sisters still laugh over a perm I got several years ago and do not hesitate to describe to me repeatedly (i.e., each time I visit) how awful, apparently, it looked.

CONCLUSION

The research findings are clear: When adult siblings use relational maintenance behaviors with each other, behaviorally express their commitment to each other, and refrain from using verbally aggressive messages with each other, their relationships are more satisfying and ultimately reflect a higher level of relational closeness. To sustain your current level of closeness—or perhaps to increase your feelings of closeness—take a moment and consider the behaviors you currently use to communicate closeness with your siblings. Based on what you have read in this chapter, answer these questions:

- Which relational maintenance behaviors do you use to maintain your relationships? Why?

- How does this use of relational maintenance behaviors accurately portray the type of relationship you have?

- What types of behaviors do you use to express commitment?

- How do these behaviors mirror how satisfied you are with your relationship?

- How often do you use verbally aggressive messages?

- What is the content of these messages?

- Are these messages intended to be hurtful, intense, or intentional?

More importantly, you need to consider how these three behaviors can be used to communicate closeness as you and your siblings grow older and move through the three stages of the adult sibling lifespan. As sibling researcher Lynn White (2001) noted, adult siblings are considered to be "permanent but flexible members of [their] social networks, whose roles . . . are renegotiated in light of changing circumstances and competing obligations" (p. 557). To successfully renegotiate your role in your sibling relationships as you move across the three stages of the adult sibling lifespan, consider using relational maintenance behaviors and behavioral expressions of commitment, but not verbally aggressive messages, strategically as a way to remain involved in each other's lives. Doing so may not only reaffirm the level of importance that these relationships play in your life, but also may prevent you and your siblings from viewing your relationships as a low priority.

REFERENCES

Arnett, J. J. (2001). Conceptions of the transition to adulthood: Perspectives from adolescence through midlife. *Journal of Adult Development, 8,* 133–143.

Canary, D. J., & Stafford, L. (1992). Relational maintenance strategies and equity in marriage. *Communication Monographs, 59,* 244–267.

Canary, D. J., & Stafford, L. (1994). Maintaining relationships through strategic and routine interactions. In D. J. Canary & L. Stafford (Eds.), *Communication and relational maintenance* (pp. 1–22). New York: Academic Press.

Connidis, I. A. (1992). Life transitions and the adult sibling tie: A qualitative study. *Journal of Marriage and the Family, 54,* 972–982.

Eidsness, M. A., & Myers, S. A. (2008). The use of sibling relational maintenance behaviors among emerging adults. *Journal of the Speech and Theatre Association of Missouri, 38,* 1–14.

Gold, D. T. (1989). Sibling relationships in old age: A typology. *International Journal of Aging and Human Development, 28,* 37–51.

Goodboy, A. K., Myers, S. A., & Patterson, B. P. (2009). Investigating elderly sibling types, relational maintenance, and lifespan affect, cognition, and behavior. *Atlantic Journal of Communication, 17,* 1–9.

Infante, D. A., & Wigley, C. J., III. (1986). Verbal aggressiveness: An interpersonal model and measure. *Communication Monographs, 53,* 61–69.

Lund, M. (1985). The development of investment and commitment scales for predicting continuity of personal relationships. *Journal of Social and Personal Relationships, 2,* 3–23.

Martin, M. M., Anderson, C. M., Burant, P. A., & Weber, K. (1997). Verbal aggression in sibling relationships. *Communication Quarterly, 45,* 304–317.

Martin, M. M., Anderson, C. M., & Rocca, K. A. (2005). Perceptions of the adult sibling relationship. *North American Journal of Psychology, 7,* 107–116.

Medved, C. E., Brogan, S. M., McClanahan, A. M., Morris, J. F., & Shepherd, G. J. (2006). Family and work socializing communication: Messages, gender, and ideological implications. *Journal of Family Communication, 6,* 161–180.

Mikkelson, A. C. (2006). Communication among peers: Adult sibling relationships. In K. Floyd & M. T. Morman (Eds.), *Widening the family circle: New research on family communication* (pp. 21–35). Thousand Oaks, CA: Sage.

Mikkelson, A. C., Floyd, K., & Pauley, P. M. (2011). Differential solicitude of social support in different types of adult sibling relationships. *Journal of Family Communication, 11,* 220–236.

Mikkelson, A. C., Myers, S. A., & Hannawa, A. F. (2011). The differential use of relational maintenance behaviors in adult sibling relationships. *Communication Studies, 62,* 258–271.

Myers, S. A. (2011). "I have to love her, even if sometimes I may not like her": The reasons why adults maintain their sibling relationships. *North American Journal of Psychology, 13,* 51–62.

Myers, S. A., Brann, M., & Rittenour, C. E. (2008). Interpersonal communication motives as a predictor of early and middle adulthood siblings' use of relational maintenance behaviors. *Communication Research Reports, 25,* 155–167.

Myers, S. A., & Bryant, L. E. (2008a). Emerging adult siblings' use of verbally aggressive messages as hurtful messages. *Communication Quarterly, 56,* 268–283.

Myers, S. A., & Bryant, L. E. (2008b). The use of behavioral indicators of sibling commitment among emerging adults. *Journal of Family Communication, 8,* 101–125.

Myers, S. A., Byrnes, K. A., Frisby, B. N., & Mansson, D. H. (2011). Adult siblings' use of affectionate communication as a strategic and routine relational maintenance behavior. *Communication Research Reports, 28,* 151–158.

Myers, S. A., & Goodboy, A. K. (2006). Perceived sibling use of verbally aggressive messages across the lifespan. *Communication Research Reports, 23,* 1–11.

Myers, S. A., & Goodboy, A. K. (2010). Relational maintenance behaviors and communication channel use among adult siblings. *North American Journal of Psychology, 12,* 103–116.

Myers, S. A., & Members of COM 200. (2001). Relational maintenance behaviors in the sibling relationship. *Communication Quarterly, 49,* 19–34.

Myers, S. A., & Rittenour, C. E. (2012). Demographic and relational predictors of adult siblings' use of relational maintenance behaviors. *Journal of the Communication, Speech & Theatre Association of North Dakota, 24,* 1–17.

Myers, S. A., & Weber, K. D. (2004). Preliminary development of a measure of sibling relational maintenance behaviors: Scale development and initial findings. *Communication Quarterly, 52,* 334–346.

Pulakos, J. (1989). Young adult sibling relationships: Siblings and friends. *Journal of Psychology, 123,* 237–244.

Rittenour, C. E., Myers, S. A., & Brann, M. (2007). Commitment and emotional closeness in the sibling relationship. *Southern Communication Journal, 72,* 169–183.

Rusbult, C. E. (1980). Commitment and satisfaction in romantic associations: A test of the investment model. *Journal of Experimental Social Psychology, 16,* 172–186.

Scharf, M., Shulman, S., & Avigad-Spitz, L. (2005). Sibling relationships in emerging adulthood and in adolescence. *Journal of Adolescent Research, 20,* 64–90.

Stafford, L., & Canary, D. J. (1991). Maintenance strategies and romantic relationship type, gender and relational characteristics. *Journal of Social and Personal Relationships, 8,* 217–242.

Teven, J. J., Martin, M. M., & Neupauer, N. C. (1998). Sibling relationships: Verbally aggressive messages and their effect on relational satisfaction. *Communication Reports, 11,* 179–186.

White, L. (2001). Sibling relationships over the life course: A panel analysis. *Journal of Marriage and Family, 63,* 555–568.

WHY CAN'T I JUST OPEN UP TO YOU? IMPLICATIONS FOR TOPIC AVOIDANCE AND SECRETS IN PARENT-ADOLESCENT RELATIONSHIPS

Tamara D. Afifi, University of California, Santa Barbara

Do you tell your parents everything about what you do with your friends? How openly do you talk to your parents about your sexual attitudes and behaviors? Would you tell your parent about a bad grade you received? What makes some adolescents and young adults more likely than others to talk to their parents about important issues? There are likely good reasons why adolescents and young adults do not tell their parents everything. Many parents may actually prefer that their children not tell them everything! There may also be circumstances where children want to tell their parents something and know that they should talk to them about it, but still choose to avoid it or keep it secret.

This chapter highlights some of the recent research in the field of communication on topic avoidance and secrets. In particular, this chapter will illustrate the socially meaningful nature of this work in families, and in parent-adolescent relationships, specifically. The goal if this chapter is to answer the questions: "What role do topic avoidance and secrets play in parent-adolescent/young adult relationships? What impact do topic avoidance and secrecy have on family relationships? In order to answer these questions, differences among related concepts will briefly be addressed, followed by a discussion of topics that are commonly avoided and kept secret in families, the reasons why they are avoided or kept secret, and examples of the application of these concepts within parent-adolescent relationships.

TOPICS THAT ARE COMMONLY AVOIDED OR KEPT SECRET AND THE IMPORTANCE OF CONTEXT

Before diving into the research in this area, it is important to distinguish among a few concepts. One of the primary distinctions that needs to be made is between topic avoidance and secrets. Topic avoidance refers to a topic that people purposefully refrain from discussing with someone, but that the other person typically knows exists (Afifi, Caughlin, & Afifi, 2007). Secrets, on the other hand, involve information that is purposefully withheld or concealed from another. For example, if Maggie's parents know she is dating Dan, but she does not bring up the topic of Dan very much because her parents do not like him, this would be topic avoidance. On the other hand, if Maggie is cohabitating or living with Dan and her parents do not know it, this would be a secret. Because secret keeping requires that information be hidden from others, secrets tend to be more negative than topics that are avoided and often have more negative consequences if they are revealed. Keeping a secret also requires a lot more mental energy than choosing not to talk about something (Bok, 1983). Nevertheless, not all secrets are deceptive. Secrets are deceptive if the person who is keeping the secret is creating a false impression. Sometimes, however, people are keeping secrets simply because they are not close enough to someone to share the information or they do not believe it is any of the other person's business (privacy concerns). It is also important to remember that not all secrets are negative and that secrets and topic avoidance are very common. In fact, approximately 95% of people have a secret of some sort (Afifi et al., 2007; Afifi, Olson, & Armstrong, 2007; Vangelisti, 1994).

Topic avoidance and secrets are also ways people keep information private. Privacy is often a larger umbrella term that encompasses topic avoidance and secrets and involves information that people think they "own" (Petronio, 2002). For example, people often think they own the information they put on their Facebook page. They can partially control the information they share with others by enabling or denying certain people access to the information (i.e., through privacy control settings). However, in the end, Facebook personnel and other people (e.g., the police) can still access, and consequently "co-own," information people put on their Facebook pages. The only real way to protect their private information from being shared is to avoid sharing it. Avoidance, secrecy, and disclosure become ways in which people regulate their private information.

Much of the research on topic avoidance in the field of communication studies has examined it in the context of families, especially within the parent-child relationship. There are many topics adolescents avoid talking about with their parents. Earlier work by Guerrero and Afifi (1995) found that adolescents commonly avoid the topics of sex, friendships, and activities they engage in with their friends, dating relationships, negative things that have happened or failure events, and the state of their relationships, with their parents. Parents also refrain from talking about certain topics with their children. In particular, they often withhold information about their health, finances, and conflict with their spouses from their children (Afifi et al., 2005). Some topics become "off limits" or taboo because they might cause conflict or hurt feelings or they are identity threatening. For example, some families do not talk about politics or religion if family members disagree about them because it is easier to maintain good relationships if these topics are not discussed.

Just as there are different topics that are avoided, there are different types of secrets. Vangelisti (1994) notes in her research on family secrets that there are intra-family secrets or secrets that certain family members keep from other family members, and whole family secrets or secrets that the entire family keeps from "outsiders" or from people outside the family. For example, if someone within the family has an addiction, the family might try to protect that person's identity or the identity of the family by keeping it a secret within the family (whole family secret). Or, within the family, siblings may keep a secret from their parents that one of them broke their mother's favorite lamp while their parents were away on a trip (intra family secret). There are also different types of topics that are kept secret. Vanglisti (1994) identified three types of secrets: (1) taboo topics, (2) rule violations, and (3) conventional secrets. Taboo secrets are potentially the most hurtful in families because they tend to be stigmatizing or condemned by society. Examples of taboo secrets include addictions, violence, and adultery. Rule violations involve breaking family rules, such as if you were cohabitating against your parents' wishes or were partying when you were living with your parents and you were not supposed to be partying. Conventional secrets are topics, such as getting bad grades or health problems, which some people might consider inappropriate to bring up for conversation.

Not surprisingly, sex tends to be the topic that adolescents avoid most with their parents (e.g., Guerrero & Afifi, 1995). Research also shows that parents think talking about sex with their children is important, but they don't know how to talk with them about it. Parents typically lack communication efficacy when it comes to sex or the ability to talk about sex with their children. Parents often feel as if their children will reject them if they bring up the topic of sex. They also fear that they lack the knowledge to talk about it and do not know how to talk about it in the "right" way. Parents often think that if they talk about sex or other risky behaviors like drugs with their children that their children will want to engage in them. To the contrary, most research shows just the opposite—that the more parents talk with their children about risky behaviors like sex, drugs, and alcohol use, the less likely they are to engage in them (e.g., Regnerus, 2005). Nevertheless, some research has found that the more that parents talk about sex, the more likely their children are to engage in risky sexual behaviors. However, one has to be careful when examining this research because it is not the quantity of talk that is important as much as the quality of the talk (see Miller-Day, 2008). If parents themselves are promiscuous and talk about this with their children, their children may be likely to model this behavior. In general, however, talking about sex and other risky behaviors tends to help children.

Additional research is required that can better delineate what parents and children actually talk about regarding risky behaviors, what communication patterns facilitate these kinds of discussions, and how this dialogue transpires over the course of their relationship. Because of their sensitive nature, it is difficult to actually observe parents and children talking with each other about risky behaviors. Afifi, Joseph, and Aldeis (2008) conducted one of the few observational studies of sex discussions among parents and adolescents. They had 118 parents and adolescent/young adult pairs (ages 14–21) come into the laboratory. They asked them to choose three out of four commonly avoided topics to talk about with each other: (1) the child's sexual attitudes and behaviors, (2) negative things the child has done, (3) the parents' relationship, and (4) marriage and divorce in general. To make the parents and children more comfortable (and for ethical reasons), they were allowed to omit one of the topics. Of the four topics, 60% of the sample chose not to talk about the topic of sex, which is a fairly good indication itself of how much this topic is avoided in parent-child relationships! However, the authors took the remaining dyads and analyzed their communication patterns when talking about the child's sexual attitudes and behaviors. The quantitative portion of the study revealed that when parents were receptive, informal, and composed during the conversation, their adolescents were less anxious and, in turn, were less avoidant. When the child also perceived that the parent was a competent communicator, the child was less anxious and less avoidant during the conversation. The quality of the relationship between the parent and the child also influenced how anxious and avoidant the child was during the discussion. The closer the parent-child relationship, the less anxious and avoidant the child felt during the talk. Qualitative findings also revealed that religiosity, the gender of the child, humor, peer groups, the parent's use of fear appeals, and whether the parent and child had an enmeshed relationship affected the nature of the conversations. In particular, male children tended to use more sarcasm when talking with the parent, perhaps as a way to avoid talking about the topic or to make the topic less serious. When the families were highly religious, the conversations also tended to be much shorter because the perception was that there was "nothing to talk about."

While sex tends to be the most commonly avoided topic with parents, risky behaviors in general tend to be highly avoided. As suggested above, researchers need more information on how parents and their children talk about risky behaviors with each other and the types of parental responses that help children disclose them (see Miller, 2001; Miller-Day 2002; Miller-Day, 2008). Aldeis and Afifi (2011) examined how college students' perceptions of confirming, disconfirming, and challenging messages from parents, siblings, and peers shaped their decisions to reveal or conceal their risky behaviors. Five hundred college students reported on a risky behavior they were keeping from a parent, sibling, or friend and were asked two months later whether they revealed it. Participants were more *willing* to reveal their risky behaviors to peers and siblings than to parents and were more likely to *actually* reveal their risky behavior to peers than to parents. They were also more likely to reveal to peers who were more confirming and challenging, compared to parents and siblings with similar responses. Finally, the college students were less likely to reveal their risky behavior to their siblings when they were disconfirming compared to peers when they were disconfirming.

The type of topic avoided or kept secret, however, largely depends upon the context of the avoidance and secrecy. Even though Guerrero and Afifi (1995) found that sex was the most commonly avoided topic by adolescents with parents, it may depend upon the type of family they are in and the method of data collection. For example, Golish and Caughlin (2002) found that when adolescents and young adults from divorced families were asked with Afifi and Guerrero's Likert-type scale how often they avoid certain topics with their parents, sex was the most commonly avoided topic. When asked to write down (in an open-ended fashion) topics they avoid the most with their parents, the adolescents and young adults from divorced families said they avoided talking about their parents' relationship the most, followed by money, and then deep conversations with their stepparent. Topics like these might not have surfaced in Afifi and Guerrero's findings because they were not a part of their scale. It could also be that the topics that are commonly avoided depend upon the type of family. Children from divorced families and stepfamilies are more likely to avoid talking about their parents' relationship compared to children whose parents are still married because it can be conflict-inducing (Afifi & Schrodt, 2003a). They avoid talking about their parents' relationship to preserve their relationships with their parents (Afifi & Schrodt, 2003b), to minimize their feelings of being caught between their parents (Afifi, 2003; Amato & Afifi, 2006;

Buchanan, Maccoby & Dornbusch, 1991), and to prevent conflict between their parents from escalating (Afifi, Afifi, Morse, & Hamrick, 2008).

REASONS FOR AVOIDANCE AND SECRETS

A primary question to consider is why adolescents and young adults avoid or keep certain topics secret from their parents. People avoid or keep secrets for many reasons, which can serve both positive and negative functions. Individuals often withhold information because they are not close to someone, are afraid of getting hurt or being judged (self protection), are afraid of hurting the relationship (relationship protection), want to protect another person from being hurt (other protection), or simply want to maintain their privacy (Afifi & Olson, 2005; Afifi et al., 2005; Afifi et al., 2007; Golish & Caughlin, 2002). For example, adolescents and young adults might be afraid to tell their parents that they received a bad grade on an exam for fear of being judged or looked down upon by their parents (self-protection). Or, if a child is a staunch Democrat and the parent is a staunch Republican, neither one of them might talk about politics to preserve their relationship (relationship protection).

When people are deciding whether to disclose something, they weigh the risk involved with disclosing it. According to communication privacy management (CPM) theory (Petronio, 1991, 2000, 2002), revealing private information is risky and people create metaphorical boundaries around themselves that ebb and flow with the degree of risk involved with a disclosure. The less that people trust others, the more rigid their privacy boundaries become and the less likely they are to disclose private information to them. When the information being withheld is negative or potential harmful, people often engage in avoidance or secrecy for protection reasons: protection of the self, their relationship, and/or other people (Afifi et al., 2005).

Avoidance and secrets, however, can also serve important and positive functions. According to relational dialectics theory (Baxter, 2010; Baxter & Montgomery, 1996) and CPM theory (Petronio, 2002), people need a balance of openness and closedness to maintain healthy relationships. Within romantic relationships, partners need to disclose information to learn more about their partner and to grow closer. However, they also need to keep some information to themselves to maintain a sense of privacy. Research on long-term marriages also shows that people in long-term, happy marriages learn not to tell their partner about every criticism they have—but learn how to choose their "battles" wisely and not "sweat the small stuff" (Pearson, 1992; see also Roloff & Ifert, 2000). There are many instances where a secret is neutral or positive (e.g., a surprise birthday party) and there is very little risk involved with revealing it. When people are privy to a secret, it can also create a cohesive bond between the people who are keeping the secret (Vangelisti & Caughlin, 1997). Secrecy in adolescence can sometimes help maintain boundaries and close connections (Finkenauer, Frijns, Engels, & Kerkhof, 2005; Finkenauer & Hazam, 2000). For example, adolescents often have secrets that they keep from their parents. Sometimes these secrets can give adolescents a feeling of autonomy from their parents (Finkenauer, Kubacka, Engels, & Kerkhof, 2009). Secrets that are shared among adolescents can also create feelings of closeness among them (Finkenauer et al.). However, when secrets are kept from others, it can also create feelings of exclusion and prohibit adolescents from forming close relationships with those from whom the secrets are being kept (Finkenauer et al.). Consequently, while adolescents may become closer to each other if they are keeping secrets from other adolescents and their parents, it could create an emotional wedge between the parents and adolescents (Finkenauer et al.).

CONSEQUENCES FOR PERSONAL AND RELATIONAL HEALTH

Even though avoidance and secrets do serve positive functions, they can have negative health and relational consequences. Topic avoidance and secrets are often associated with dissatisfaction in families and romantic relationships. For instance, when people think their family has more secrets than other families, they tend to be more dissatisfied with their family (Caughlin et al., 2000; Vangelisti & Caughlin, 1997). When a newlywed thinks that the partner is keeping a secret, it often makes the person feel rejected and excluded (Finkenauer, Kerkhof, Righetti, & Branje, 2009). Even though secrets are natural and expected in adolescence, they can create a sense of distance between parents and adolescents (Finkenauer et al.). Topic avoidance has also been found to be dissatisfying in a variety of relationships, including dating relationships and parent-child relationships (Afifi, Joseph, & Aldeis, in press; Afifi, McManus, Steuber, & Coho, 2009; Caughlin & Golish, 2002). People are bothered by their own avoidance, but they tend to be especially bothered if they believe others are avoiding with them (Caughlin & Afifi, 2004). If someone thinks another person is avoiding or keeping something secret, he or she may wonder what it means about their relationship, given that healthy relationships in the United States are often equated with openness (Afifi et al., in press).

A significant amount of research has also shown that the disclosure of secrets, particularly secrets that are traumatic, tends to be health promoting (e.g., Gortner, Rude, & Pennebaker, 2006; Pennebaker & Beall, 1986; Petrie, Booth, & Pennebaker, 1998). The act of sharing a secret, whether it is done verbally or through writing, is beneficial to one's health . For example, Pennebaker et al. (1986) assigned fifty healthy undergraduates to either write about a painful traumatic experience or a superficial topic for four consecutive days. Writing about traumatic experiences was associated with improved immune system functioning in the weeks that followed. Whether the disclosure is beneficial, however, also depends upon the purpose of the disclosure. Catharsis alone may not be that beneficial, but if the catharsis is meaningful and helps a person provide a sense of closure or make sense of something, then it may be beneficial (Kelly & Macready, 2009).

Nevertheless, disclosures can also be harmful to one's health. For example, research has shown that parents' inappropriate disclosures about one another can be associated with more negative mental health symptoms in adolescents (Afifi, McManus, Hutchinson, & Baker, 2007). In addition, when parents talk badly about each other, it can negatively impact their adolescents' and young adults' physiological stress responses (Afifi, Granger, Denes, Joseph, & Aldeis, in press). Research shows that when people disclose too much negative information to each other, it can result in stress contagion effects where one person's stress spills over onto another (Rose, Carson, & Waller, 2007). In short, topic avoidance, secrets, and disclosures can have positive or negative effects on relationships. It is how they are used, and their functions, that are important.

REFERENCES

Afifi, T. D. (2003). "Feeling caught" in stepfamilies: Managing boundary turbulence through appropriate privacy coordination rules. *Journal of Social and Personal Relationships, 20,* 729–756.

Afifi, T. D., Afifi, W. A., Morse, C., & Hamrick, K. (2008). Adolescents' avoidance tendencies and physiological reactions to discussions about their parents' relationship: Implications for post-divorce and non-divorced families. *Communication Monographs, 75,* 290–317.

Afifi, T. D., Caughlin, J., & Afifi, W. A. (2007). Exploring the dark side (and light side) of avoidance and secrets. In B. Spitzberg and B. Cupach (Eds.), *The dark side of interpersonal relationships* (2nd ed., pp. 61–92). Mahwah, NJ: Erlbaum.

Afifi, T. D., Granger, D., Denes, A., Joseph, A., & Aldeis, D. (in press). Parents' communication skills and adolescents' salivary -amylase and cortisol response patterns. *Communication Monographs.*

Afifi, T. D., Joseph, A., & Aldeis, D. (2008). Why Can't We Just Talk about It?: An Observational Study of Parents' and Adolescents' Conversations about Sex. *Journal of Adolescent Research, 23,* 689–721.

Afifi, T. D., Joseph, A., & Aldeis, D. (in press). Why can't you open up to me? The associations among conflict avoidance, rumination, and relationship satisfaction. *Journal of Social and Personal Relationships.*

Afifi, T. D., McManus, T., Hutchinson, S., & Baker, B. (2007). Parental divorce disclosures, the factors that prompt them, and their impact on parents' and adolescents' well-being. *Communication Monographs, 74,* 78–103.

Afifi, T. D., McManus, T., Steuber, K., & Coho, A. (2009). Verbal avoidance and dissatisfaction in intimate conflict situations. *Human Communication Research, 35,* 357–383.

Afifi, T. D., & Olson, L. N. (2005). The chilling effect in families and the pressure to conceal secrets. *Communication Monographs, 72,* 192–216.

Afifi, T. D., Olson, L., & Armstrong, C. (2005). The chilling effect and family secrets: Examining the role of self protection, other protection, and communication efficacy. *Human Communication Research, 31,* 564–598.

Afifi, T. D., & Schrodt, P. (2003). Uncertainty and the avoidance of the state of one's family/relationships in stepfamilies, post-divorce single parent families, and first marriage families. *Human Communication Research, 29,* 516–533.

Afifi, T. D., & Schrodt, P. (2003). "Feeling caught" as a mediator of adolescents' and young adults' avoidance and satisfaction with their parents in divorced and non-divorced households. *Communication Monographs, 70,* 142–173.

Aldeis, D., & Afifi, T. D. (in press). College students' willingness to reveal their risky behaviors: The influence of relationship and message type. *Journal of Family Communication.*

Amato, P. & Afifi, T. D. (2006). Feeling caught between parents: Adult children's relations with parents and subjective well-being. *Journal of Marriage and Family, 68,* 222–236.

Baxter, L. (2010). *Voicing relationships: A dialogic perspective.* Thousand Oaks, CA: Sage.

Baxter, L. A., & Montgomery, B. M. (1996). *Relating: Dialogues and dialectics.* New York: The Guilford Press.Bok, S. (1983). *Secrets: On the ethics of concealment and revelation.* New York: Vintage Books.

Buchanan, C. M., Maccoby, E. E., & Dornbusch, S. M. (1991). Caught between parents: Adolescents' experience in divorced homes. *Child Development, 62,* 1008–1029.

Caughlin, J. & Golish, T. (2002). An analysis of the association between topic avoidance and dissatisfaction: Comparing perceptual and interpersonal explanations. *Communication Monographs, 69,* 275–296.

Caughlin, J., & Afifi, T. D. (2004). When is topic avoidance unsatisfying?: A more complete investigating into the underlying links between avoidance and dissatisfaction in parent-child and dating relationships. *Human Communication Research, 30,* 479-514.

Finkenauer, C., Frijns, T., Engels, R. C. M. E., & Kerkhof, P. (2005). Perceiving concealment in relationships between parents and adolescents: links with parental behavior. *Personal Relationships, 12,* 387–406.

Finkenauer, C., & Hazam, H. (2000). Disclosure and secrecy in marriage: Do both contribute to marital satisfaction? *Journal of Social and Personal Relationships, 17,* 245–263.

Finkenauer, C., Kerkhof, P., Righetti, F., & Branje, S. (2009). Living together apart: Perceived concealment as a signal of exclusion in marital relationships. *Personality and Social Psychology Bulletin, 35,* 1410-1422.

Finkenauer, C., Kubacka, K. E., Engels, R., & Kerkhof, P. (2009). Secrecy in close relationships: Investigating its intrapersonal and interpersonal effects. In T. Afifi and W. Afifi (Eds.), *Uncertainty, information management, and disclosure decisions* (pp. 300–320). New York: Routledge.

Golish, T. D., & Caughlin, J. (2002). "I'd rather not talk about it": Adolescents' and young adults' use of topic avoidance in stepfamilies. *Journal of Applied Communication Research, 30,* 78–106.

Gortner, E. M., Rude, S. S., & Pennebaker, J. W. (2006). Benefits of expressive writing in lowering rumination and depressive symptoms. *Behavior Therapy, 37,* 292–303.

Guerrero, L. K., & Afifi, W. A. (1995). Some things are better left unsaid: Topic avoidance in family relationships. *Communication Quarterly, 43,* 276–296.

Kelly, A., & Macready, D. (2009). Why disclosing to a confidant can be so good (or bad) for us. In T. Afifi and W. Afifi (Eds.), *Uncertainty, information management, and disclosure decisions* (pp. 384–403). New York: Routledge.

Miller, M. (2001). Parent-adolescent communication about alcohol, tobacco, and other drug use. *Journal of Adolescent Research, 17,* 355–374.

Miller-Day, M. (2002). Parent-adolescent communication about alcohol, tobacco, and other drug use. *Journal of Adolescent Research, 17,* 604–616.

Miller-Day, M. (2008). Talking to youth about drugs: What do late adolescents say about parental strategies? *Family Relations, 57,* 1–12.

Pearson, J. C. (1992). *Lasting love: What keeps couples together.* Dubuque, IA: William C. Brown.

Pennebaker, J. W., & Beall, S. K. (1986). Confronting a traumatic event: Toward an understanding of inhibition and disease. *Journal of Abnormal Psychology, 95,* 274–281.

Petrie, K. J., Booth, R. J., & Pennebaker, J. W. (1998). The immunological effects of thought suppression. *Journal of Personality and Social Psychology, 75,* 1264–1272.

Petronio, S. (1991). Communication boundary management: A theoretical model of managing disclosure of private information between marital couples. *Communication Theory, 1,* 311–335.

Petronio, S. (2000). The boundaries of privacy: Praxis of everyday life. In S. Petronio (Ed.), *Balancing the secrets of private disclosures* (pp. 37–49). Mahwah, NJ: Lawrence Erlbaum Associates, Inc.

Petronio, S. (2002). *Boundaries of privacy: Dialectics of disclosure.* Albany, NY: SUNY Press.

Regnerus, M. D. (2005). Talking about sex: Religion and patterns of parent-child communication about sex and contraception. *The Sociological Quarterly, 46,* 79–105.

Roloff, M. E., & Ifert, D. E. (2000). Conflict management through avoidance: Withholding complaints, suppressing arguments and declaring topics taboo. In S. Petronio (Ed.), *Balancing the secrets of private disclosures* (pp. 151–164). Mahwah, NJ: Erlbaum.

Rose, A. J., Carlson, W., & Waller, E. M. (2007). Prospective associations of co-rumination with friendship and emotional adjustment: Considering the socioemotional trade-offs of co-rumination. *Developmental Psychology, 43,* 1019–1031.

Vangelisti, A. L. (1994). Family secrets: Forms, functions and correlates. *Journal of Social and Personal Relationships, 11,* 113–135.

Vangelisti, A. L. & Caughlin, J. P. (1997). Revealing family secrets: The influence of topic, function, and relationship. *Journal of Social and Personal Relationships, 14,* 679–705.

SECTION 4
GENDER COMMUNICATION

The gender communication context offers us a unique opportunity to investigate one of the most fundamental parts of ourselves—our gender identities. The study of gender and communication allows us to learn about how these gender identities influence our personal and public communication with others. Gender communication researchers explore the constructed nature of gender roles as situated within a particular culture. Although our understandings of the ideas "masculine" and "feminine" have come to seem natural and unchanging, these concepts may alternatively be understood as flexible and as created through communicative practices. In the following readings you will be asked to explore how our own communicative practices can condone, contribute to, or resist the cultural construction of gender stereotypes. This chapter focuses on three topics representative of gender communication research: (1) feminist contributions to public discourse theory, (2) critical perspectives on the ways in which popular media script our gender, and (3) queer communication theory and research. First, Cindy Griffin (Colorado State University) responds to the question: *How might feminist ideals help us to shape a more civil public discourse?* by examining the ways in which damaging stereotypes of feminism have silenced alternative contributions and how her research led her to work with others in the construction of "invitational rhetorical" theory. Second, Ronald Jackson III (University of Cincinnati) and Natasha Shrikant (University of Massachusetts, Amherst) show how negative portrayals of Black men in the media can affect individual stereotypes and everyday interracial interactions among the public in answering the question: *How do the popular media script our bodies, our race, and our gender?* Third, Gust Yep (San Francisco State University) and Scott Schönfeldt-Aultman (Saint Mary's College of California) respond to the question: *What is queer theory and how can understanding it help us to better understand our own sexual identity and the ways in which our prejudices influence our interactions with others?* In their dialogue they explore and highlight the efforts of queer theory to analyze power, gender, and sexuality and their shaping of social relations/hierarchies and normalization so that we might learn how our own assumptions and practices reinforce or disrupt heteronormativity and heteropatriarchy. Throughout these three essays you are challenged to become a more critical receiver of communicative messages of all sorts and to use your critical insights to examine your own communication habits.

HOW MIGHT FEMINIST IDEALS HELP US TO SHAPE MORE CIVIL PUBLIC DISCOURSE?

CINDY L. GRIFFIN, COLORADO STATE UNIVERSITY

For many people, the word "feminist" brings to mind images of angry and ugly women who shout slogans and slander men for being "sexist," who demand rights and privileges at the expense of others, have no sense of humor, and even refuse to let anyone show the small kindness of opening a door for them. These unpleasant images are fueled by many things, among them our media, popular comedians, YouTube videos, and news outlets. In fact, these images are so powerful that most people have trouble even imagining that feminism and feminists might have positive and productive ideas to add to any conversation, social or political issue, or relationship. And, the idea of linking feminism and feminists to civility and civil public discourse seems preposterous. Feminists often are viewed as the most uncivil of people, and the image of angry and humorless feminists makes the connection between them and productive public conversation, discussion, and discourse feel highly unlikely.

For most of my life, however, I've had a very different view of, and experience with, feminism and feminists. As I watched the world around me and participated in the things most of us participate in (family, school, sports, religion, entertainment and recreation, for example), I came to understand that, although we often say that we all are "created equal," or even "the same," these familiar and important phrases did not ring true in far too many situations. I experienced and observed many unequal moments, and saw that those inequities were neither logical or natural, nor necessary or productive (Chávez & Griffin, 2009). I also observed that they were often based on stereotypical assumptions about sex and gender, and even race, sexuality, and physical ability. Of course, there are angry and rude people in the world, women and men alike, but my early experiences and ongoing research have helped me to understand that, contrary to what many people have been told, at its very heart feminism is about civility and civil public discourse. Most of our feminist work, ideas, and theories are grounded in these concepts. And many of the day-to-day examples of feminism (the real "doing" of feminism) actually serve as models for civil public discourse. So, a question that I'll explore here is "how might feminist ideals help us to shape more civil public discourse?" I believe they can and do, and I'll map out the ways my own research has attempted to illustrate this.

FEMINISM AND FEMINISTS

In my research, I began my exploration of feminism and feminists with a guiding question: "How can something so important and appealing to both women and men be as awful as some of the critics suggest?" Feminist ideas have been around, literally, for thousands of years (Sappho is the first known feminist, and the fragments we have of her work are over 2,000 years old). And, although their ideas have too often been ignored, for centuries and in very civil ways, women have been advocating for the right to receive a quality education, own property, keep their children after a marriage ends, vote in elections and hold public offices, work at jobs in all the fields men can and get paid equally, serve in the military and as religious officials, walk safely in their towns and cities, and even love openly who they want to love. But I wondered, as Dale Spender (1982) has asked: Why didn't I know about these women and their ideas? Why are their ideas criticized so harshly? And, I asked myself, what might this tell us about communication?

To try to answer these questions, I wrote two essays about Mary Wollstonecraft, a British feminist writing in the late 1700s; an essay about the ideas of a very radical contemporary feminist, Mary Daly (Griffin, 1996, 1994, 1993; Foss, Foss and Griffin, 1999); and a chapter on Angela Davis, who wrote about the oppression of African American women (Griffin, 1996/2005). Working with two other feminist scholars, I also co-wrote two books that showcased the ideas of nine contemporary feminists (Foss, Foss & Griffin, 2004, 1999). These projects helped me articulate some very interesting things about feminism and begin to understand the nature of civil communication. Writing two hundred years apart, Mary Wollstonecraft and Angela Davis both argued that women's subordinate status was and is actually based on a lack of education rather than on anything inherent in their biology, as was the common assumption of their repspective times. Provide women with a decent education, Wollstonecraft argued, and they would be better citizens, wives, and mothers. Both Davis and Wollstonecraft saw that women were not "naturally" inferior or less intelligent than men, but social expectations, norms, and codes had made them so (Griffin, 1994, 2005).

As I read Wollstonecraft's work and explored her ideas further, I saw that she also helped us understand that women's identities as subordinate to men actually were alienating (Griffin, 1996). By "alienating," Wollstonecraft meant that society had constructed this inferior identity for women; it was not one that most women would have constructed for themselves, nor was it one women easily identified with (it's difficult to see oneself as "naturally" inferior to others, she argued). What she argued was that our *communication about* women constructed this "false" or "alienating" inferior identity, and that language and social norms defined women's place, rather than biology. So, Wollstonecraft's and Davis' ideas helped me understand how inaccurate communication about someone or a group of people can create a very definite or binding identity for that person or group, and then how that identity is very hard to alter.

My essay on Mary Daly, a radical feminist philosopher and theologian, helped me understand the harsh resistance to feminist ideas and the ways we can silence those ideas (Griffin, 1993). Daly was fascinated with the ways we talked about women and men, the ways our talk constructed certain ways of viewing the world, and the ways we silence views we don't want to hear. Because she was so radical for her time, she was harshly criticized throughout her career. She was the first woman to be hired in the theology department at Boston University and, when women were finally admitted to BU, she insisted on teaching sex-segregated classes. Daly's work and experiences helped me write about the ways society criticizes women when they disagree with patriarchal ideals, and the ways women's voices and ideas, when they speak out against oppressions, are labeled very negatively. Her work helped me think about how we silence other people and the communication strategies we use to do so.

One of the most common silencing strategies is to call women and feminists "man haters" whenever we raise questions about inequality, discrimination, and sexism. This label (which is usually untrue, very few women really do "hate men") works to flip the argument so that instead of talking about the real life discrimination of women and how we might prevent it, we talk about whether the person or group naming the discrimination "hates men." So, when we say "women still get paid less for the same work men do" and get the response, "you must be one of those angry women who hate men," we are prevented from looking at salary inequities and the reasons for them. We end up locked in a conversation about anger, whether real or not (in all honesty, most people would be a bit upset at getting paid less for the same work). This prevents us from having an open discussion about the fact that there still are pay inequities. Not only does this strategy silence individuals who raise the issue, it also often stops people from even risking speaking up at all.

Another very popular silencing strategy Daly identifies is to say, "well, yes, I see that women are oppressed, but isn't the problem really a *human* problem—shouldn't we be freeing all people?" Daly suggests that while many other people are oppressed, this strategy takes the focus away from the real harms done to women (assault, physical violence, sexual harassment, and fewer opportunities in professions like politics and the military, among others) and prevents us from identifying specific strategies we might use to eliminate the inequities leveled at women. My work on Daly helped me identify strategies like these, and to see that communication is a powerful tool that can derail conversations and even cause people to be afraid of speaking out and naming the harms that are being done to them. When I put Daly, Davis, and Wollstonecraft together, I discovered powerful insights about language and communication, the ways they shape our abilities to speak out, and construct particular identities for us.

With Sonja Foss and Karen Foss, two other communication scholars, I then worked on an anthology of nine different feminists and an edited collection of their readings (Foss, Foss and Griffin, 2004, 1999). In these two books, we wanted to introduce our field to feminist communication theories, to illustrate the diversity of feminism and feminist theories, and to explore the different insights feminist communication theories can bring to communication. The theorists we wrote about came from very different backgrounds and academic fields—and they were racially diverse as well as lesbian and heterosexual. We wrote about the cultural critic, bell hooks; the writer and poet, Gloria Anzaldua; an environmental activist and Wiccan, Starhawk; the filmmaker, Trinh T.

Minha; Native American studies scholar and writer, Paula Gunn Allen; activist and writer, Sonia Johnson; theologian and philosopher, Mary Daly; and two scholars from the communication field, Cheris Kramarae and Sally Miller Gearhart.

In these books, we showcased the diversity of feminist perspectives, the ways those perspectives shed new light on familiar communication concepts like language, metaphors, myth and ritual, resistance, conflict, dialogue, relationships, activism, change, and media. Although all of the scholars we included were identified as feminists, they all had different definitions of feminism, different views of how the world works, how it could work, and how feminists could work to change the inequalities they experienced. Considered together, or individually, they helped us suggest that feminism is a very complex philosophy and approach to the world. At its heart, feminism is focused on actively seeking to find ways to eliminate the discrimination of women that occurs in all walks of life—personal, educational, professional, social, political, and cultural—and to not oppress others while doing so. We were also able to illustrate that much has been left out of our understanding of communication, and that it is to our benefit as a field to consider the ideas of those we have learned to silence.

The insights I gained from these feminist theorists helped me think about how change works and the role of communication in creating change. I began to ask: "What can feminist theories tell us about communication theory and the way we conceptualize change?" This question led me to consider carefully the relationship between feminism and civility and about civil discourse in the public realm.

INVITING CIVIL PUBLIC DISCOURSE

One of the central questions that communication scholars ask is "how do we use our communication to change others?" That question, which causes us to focus on persuasion and persuading others, has intrigued me for some time. Working with Sonja Foss (Foss & Griffin, 1995), as well as Jennifer Bone and Linda Scholz (2008), and also on my own (Griffin, 2005/2010), I explored an idea offered by Sally Miller Gearhart (1979), one of the theorists we included in our books: "What does it mean to change others and when do I have the right to do so?" Gearhart said that to try to persuade another person, to actively try to change someone else, was actually the same thing as violence. Gearhart suggested that "any act of persuasion is an act of violence," and to attempt to change another person is a violation of that person. Rather than scorn or mock her idea, as others had, we listened to her idea and explored its potential for communication research. Gearhart linked the need to change others to patriarchy, a very hierarchical and competitive system in which "conquest" and dominating others are seen as inevitable and natural. She suggested that we had not yet begun to think carefully about the implications of this top-down, individualistic, and rather invasive view of communication, or what it might mean for our relationships to others and to ourselves.

We wondered if Gearhart was actually onto something quite feminist, and whether or not her ideas challenged one of the foundations of our field: that persuading others of the rightness of your ideas is always a noble and desirable goal (Foss & Griffin, 1995). We began to explore the idea of change, when we actually successfully changed other people, and what it felt like to have someone try to persuade us that they were right and we were wrong. Through our conversations and writing together, we began to believe that true change—change that does not come through coercion, force, or manipulation—actually was quite rare and that when people actively sought to change others, those they sought to change often did feel violated. When we imagined (and remembered) parents trying to persuade children to do (or not do) something, politicians trying to persuade us that their ideas were better than those of the other candidates, or even debates over complex issues like poverty, gun control, or abortion, we knew that people often felt violated. Even more, they often felt misunderstood, and that opportunities for understanding and respectful exchanges were rare. We mapped out several foundational principles that we saw as inherent to feminism, such as collaboration and working with others, the importance of process over product (sometimes described as the means are the ends), the importance of collective thinking when issues are complex, and respecting others to make decisions that work for them (even though they might not be the choice we would have made) (Benhabib, 1992; Foss & Griffin, 1992; Rakow, 1992; Harding, 1991; Hill Collins, 1991; Hooks, 1991; Belenky, Clinchy, Goldberger, & Tarule, 1986; Noddings, 1984; Gilligan, 1982; Moraga & Anzaldua, 1981).

We then developed a theory of "invitational rhetoric," or communication, based on these feminist principles, in which the goal was not to try to change the other person, but instead to use communication to create an environment in which mutual understanding could occur (Foss & Griffin, 1995). That environment required that the people involved in the communication respect one another, see each other as equals, and value the other person's ability to choose what is right. We did not suggest that people had to agree, nor did they have to take on the other person's views to engage invitationally. In fact, we suggested that when people are the most different, but still need to interact, live, and work together, invitational rhetoric might be a very effective form of communication. We did not suggest that people should always use invitational communication, but we did suggest that there are many times in our lives when we won't change someone's mind, yet we still have to associate with them. We suggested that invitational rhetoric was an approach to communication in which people 1) offer perspectives honestly and without the goal of persuading another, 2) exchange ideas and reasons with respect and openness, and 3) explore the other person's position and views in order to understand the person (rather than change him or her). Invitational communication might just enable us to live and work together civilly across our differences.

I then began to articulate the link I saw between invitational rhetoric and civil discourse (Bone, Griffin, & Scholz, 2008; Griffin, 2010). As I explored the literature on civility and civil dialogue, I found several ideas about these concepts that clarified this connection for me. Yale Law Professor Stephen Carter (1998) suggests that although civility often gets attacked and discredited (much like feminism), it actually is more than "good manners"; civility is a code of conduct for living in a world where differences and disagreements proliferate. Civility comes from the words "civilized" and "civilization" and is essential to democracy. This is because, as Carter states, when we are civil, we recognize that as members of a society, we are, in fact, "members of a household" (p. 15). When we are civil, we aren't pretending to like someone we despise or to agree with a view when we don't. Instead, we are acknowledging that we are on a "common journey," and that because we are sharing this ride, we are willing to acknowledge that "for the sake of our common journey with others, and out of love and respect for the very idea there are others" (p. 35), we will listen to them and try to understand them.

As Kathleen Ryan and Elizabeth Natalle (2001) explain, "when we are civil, we attempt to understand profound differences that divide us and to 'transcend difference in deep and humane ways'" (p. 83). And, as Harold Barrett (1991) states, when we are civil, we give the world a chance to explain itself (p. 147). When we are civil, we "do not allow others to carry on with their own self-interested and hurtful actions"; in fact, we do try to prevent them from hurting others or themselves. But "we cannot pretend we journey alone, that others are unworthy or without voice, or that our view is the only 'right' view." Invitational rhetoric helps us recognize that, although we disagree, a "profound understanding of the reasons other people believe and behave in the ways they do is a most productive endeavor and that a profound understanding of other people might inform our own choices in important ways" (Bone et al., 2008, p. 457).

CONCLUSION: FEMINISM AND CIVILITY

Feminist ideas have a long history and, contrary to what many people think, that history models civil public discourse for us. Feminists have had to sort through inaccurate labels and damaging messages and to find ways to respond to injustices and inequities, and they have provided students of communication with strategies for speaking civilly to others. Feminism helps us understand the ways identities are constructed and negotiated through communication. It helps us recognize the ways we silence others when we think we might be uncomfortable with their message. And, it helps us think about ways we might communicate invitationally and civilly and across vast differences, always keeping in mind the ways our words and views might affect others negatively or positively.

When we use feminist ideas to explore the ways we might communicate invitationally, we see that when we communicate with others we can 1) identify and understand our own views and reasons for them before we enter the communication exchange, 2) agree to listen fully, with respect, and without interruption, 3) agree to ask for clarification, when needed, and display a willingness to understand views vastly different from our own, 4) agree to share our perspectives openly and honestly, without trying to convince the other person of "rightness" for anyone beyond our own self, and 5) to continually ask ourselves two questions: "At what point do I know what is best for another person?" and, "as a member of a household (society), how do my views affect others?"

REFERENCES

Barrett, H. (1991). *Rhetoric and civility: Human development, narcissism, and the good audience.* New York: State University of New York Press.

Belenky, M. F., Clinchy, B. M., Goldberger, N. R., & Tarule, J. M. (1986). *Women's ways of knowing: The development of self, voice, and mind.* New York: Basic.

Benhabib, S. (1992). *Situating the self: Gender, community and postmodernism in contemporary ethics.* New York: Routledge.

Bone, J. E., Griffin, C. L., & Scholz, T. M. L. (2008). Beyond traditional conceptualizations of rhetoric: Invitational rhetoric and a move towards civility. *Western Journal of Communication, 72,* 434–462.

Carter, S. L. (1998). *Civility: Manners, morals, and the etiquette of democracy.* New York: Basic.

Chávez, K. R., & Griffin, C. L. (2009). Power, feminisms, and coalitional agency: Inviting and enacting difficult dialogues. *Women's Studies in Communication, 32,* 1–11.

Foss, K. A., Foss, S. K., & Griffin, C. L. (2004). *Readings in feminist rhetorical theory.* Thousand Oaks, CA: Sage.

Foss, S. K., Foss, K. A., & Griffin, C. L. (1999). *Feminist rhetorical theories.* Thousand Oaks, CA: Sage.

Foss, S.K., & Griffin, C. L. (1992). A feminist perspective on rhetorical theory: Toward a clarification of boundaries. *Western Journal of Communication, 56,* 330–349.

Foss, S. K., & Griffin, C. L. (1995). Beyond persuasion: A proposal for an invitational rhetoric. *Communication Monographs, 62,* 2–18.

Gearhart, S. M. (1979). The womanization of rhetoric. *Women's Studies International Quarterly, 2,* 195–201.

Gilligan, C. (1982). *In a different voice: Psychological theory and women's development.* Cambridge, MA: Harvard University Press.

Griffin, C. L. (1993). Women as communicators: Mary Daly's hagography as mistake. *Communication Monographs, 60,* 158–177.

Griffin, C. L. (1994). Rhetoricizing alienation: Mary Wollstonecraft and the rhetorical construction of women's oppression. *Quarterly Journal of Speech, 80,* 293–312.

Griffin, C. L. (1996/2005). Angela Y. Davis. In R. W. Leeman (Ed.), *African-American Orators: A bio-critical sourcebook* (pp. 60–70). Westport, CT: Greenwood Press.

Griffin, C. L. (1996). A web of reasons: Mary Wollstonecraft's *A Vindication of the Right of Woman* and the re-weaving of form. *Communication Studies, 47,* 272–288.

Griffin, C. L. (2005/2010). *Invitation to public speaking* (4th ed.). Boston: Wadsworth/Cengage.

Harding, S. (1991). *Whose science? Whose knowledge? Thinking from women's lives.* Ithaca, New York: Cornell University Press.

Hill Collins, P. (1991). *Black feminist thought: Knowledge, consciousness, and the politics of empowerment.* New York: Routledge.

Hooks, B. (1984). *Feminist theory: From margin to center.* Boston: South End.

Moraga, C., & Anzaldua, G. (1981). *This bridge called my back: Radical writings by women of color.* New York: Kitchen Table.

Noddings, N. (1984). *Caring: A feminine approach to ethics and moral education.* Berkeley: University of California Press.

Rakow, L. F. Ed. (1992). *Women making meaning: New feminist directions in communication.* New York: Routledge.

Ryan, K. J., & Natalle, E. J. (2001). Fusing horizons: Standpoint hermeneutics and invitational rhetoric. *Rhetoric Society Quarterly, 31,* 69–90.

Spender, D. (1982). *Women of ideas and what men have done to them.* London: Pandora Press.

SCRIPTING THE BLACK MASCULINE BODY

RONALD JACKSON II, UNIVERSITY OF CINCINNATI AND
NATASHA SHRIKANT, UNIVERSITY OF MASSACHUSETTS, AMHERST

At the moment a child is plopped down in front of the television while mommy and daddy go off and do things around the house, that child begins to learn things not previously introduced by the family. Of course there are messages that are consistent with what he or she has already learned at home, but there are new messages as well. According to TV-Free America, a Washington, DC based think tank and advocacy organization, kids will have watched nearly 15,000 hours of television by the age of 10. They further explain that by the age of 65 the average American has watched a sum total of 9 years worth of television. That's 4,733,538.90 minutes of TV! That's a lot of consumption by anyone's standards; however, this chapter is not so much interested in proving how many hours one watches TV or even whether one is actually ever exposed to media. It's clear already that we are major consumers of all media, not the least of which is television. Instead, this chapter is about what messages, narratives, and stereotypes individuals are taught by the media and how these messages shape social perceptions of cultural others. Quite simply put, there are three overarching points you must remember from this chapter:

- All media teach messages—some good and some bad.

- Every prominent message is like a script that you are expected to play out.

- If you are oblivious to what you're being taught, you will subconsciously consume messages that ultimately affect your behavior and perceptions toward others.

In order to address these themes we have selected to discuss the scripting theory or paradigm. Although this concept has been discussed by many scholars, most notably Duke University professor Robyn Wiegman in her book *American Anatomies,* Ronald Jackson's work has applied the idea of scripting to communication studies.

As with any theatrical script, the script is the text, and the act of scripting is the writing of the text. Therefore, to script someone else's body is to actively inscribe or figuratively place oneself, one's worldview or perceptions onto someone else. To put it another way, the concept of scripting is whole lot like what happens with graffiti or even film production. The graffiti artist finds a canvas or a wall and begins to mark all over it with creative inscriptions. Oftentimes the end product is a sign or a symbol that reflects something about who the artist is or who the artist is representing. Likewise when a film producer develops a movie that is stereotypical, he or she is scripting the lives of each character. In the act of writing the script the producer is also imposing his or her own presumptions, perhaps through research, about how people might act who look like that character. This may eerily resemble real life, and oftentimes that is the intention. Even in a fictive story there has to be some recognizable real life elements with which audiences can resonate. So, with the theory of scripting, the body is theorized as a canvas, which is figuratively written upon by another. The term "scripting" is used to signify that human beings, through all kinds of discourse including media, assign meaning to their perceptions of others in an effort to structure their observations and reflections concerning difference. This is really fascinating when applied to race and culture and it happens every single day!

Imagine for a moment you are watching television and a commercial comes on. Keep in mind you are not in "critical" or "intellectual" mode. You are really relaxing when you are suddenly startled by what you see on television. In this commercial, a white hand reaches down to pick up a toothbrush; the other hand is used to glide on the toothpaste in a swirl-like fashion. As the toothbrush with the white swirl toothpaste is lifted to the teeth, the camera gets a tight, close-up shot of a black outlined medium-sized, bodiless, transparent figure dancing all over the teeth. The white toothpaste is applied to the agitated teeth, and as the black outlined figure is being dissolved, the voiceover script reads, in a most frantic tone, "Oh no, we have to get rid of the evil plaque man." The commercial closes. No face is ever shown. This commercial may seem rather innocent on the surface, but if you are attuned to hearing commercials and other media that disparage minority groups it is actually quite disappointing. The advertisement has several implications. First, from a critical perspective, after the voiceover was heard it became clear that this figure, which appeared to be without body or gender, was actually a man. And, no matter how much the viewer wanted to believe that the black outline meant nothing, the commercial implicitly suggested via both the symbolic black outline and the voiceover that the figure is Black. If you say the concluding line enough times, you'll notice how your tongue is inclined to replace "plaque" with "Black." Some may dismiss this interpretation as mere paranoia, but we contend it is beyond coincidence that the other mechanics of the commercial work hand in hand with what is depicted in the commercial. This is one example of how scripting works.

There are many ways in which racial scripts emerge in the media. One only needs to think about feel-good movies like *The Blind Side* and *Our Family Wedding* or more serious dramas like *Precious* to see how racialized bodies are often treated and understood. To put it bluntly, the notions of race and racial scripting are about bodies that have been assigned social meanings. As a result, we as media consumers unknowingly or subconsciously set up social cognitions about race that conform to mass mediated stereotypes. Through this process of social conformity and media reinforcement, we gradually come to know dialectically what it means to be Black by negating what it means to be quintessentially White; and similarly we also come to know what it means to be female in relation to what it dialectically means to be male. The media rarely offers a complete composite of blackness or femaleness. Consequently, this act of negation is the linchpin of soured interracial and cross-gendered relations in the United States. In our research we study how Black bodies have become surfaces of racial representation.

Unfortunately, much of the mass media represents African Americans as out of control, undereducated, poor, violent, angry, incapacitated, and criminal. There are a few ways that these stereotypes are countered and replaced in the media with more positive stereotypes like the talented and athletic Black person. Seldom do we see successful, positive, healthy, educated, normal Black citizens in the media. If it is true that media teach audiences via messages and that communication scholars George Gerbner and Larry Gross were correct when they indicated that there is a direct relationship between television viewing and cultivated effects in viewers' attitudes and behaviors, then it is no wonder that racism, sexism, and all forms of social exclusion persist in American society. As a consequence of the previously mentioned racial representations of Blacks in media, in real life, non-Black people are extremely knowledgeable about negative African American stereotypes, while many other possible characterizations of African Americans are swept under the rug. Presently, the mass media are currently the primary channels through which race is socially constructed by society.

Once the scripting of different races or racialized bodies begins, it is like a machine that is difficult to turn off. People's minds automatically or subconsciously activate the stereotypes they have learned in the media. They may not even know they are acting on those stereotypes. For example, have you ever gone to a store or a mall in a predominantly Black or Hispanic poor neighborhood and found yourself suddenly afraid to leave your door unlocked or your electronics exposed on the front seat? Now take a moment to recall whether you do the same thing at a store or mall in what appears to be a predominantly White, middle to upper middle class neighborhood. Your reaction in each scenario is a subconscious (and maybe even a conscious) reflex that instinctively combines your personal background with what you think you know about the people who live in that vicinity. If you have not grown up around Blacks or Latinos, but you do recall hearing plenty of crime news stories about these groups, or you recall images from movies or other media that reinforce negative stereotypes about these groups as being violent, then naturally you will be scared.

Interestingly, the way humans perceive the differences between racial bodies is by observing bodies' corporeal zones, or parts of the body that mark it as being of a particular type. This is what we call preverbal communication. For Black bodies, these corporeal zones sometimes include nappy hair, thick lips, and darker-than-white skin complexion. Although perceptions of these visual individual differences may not always have negative consequences, people cannot ignore corporeal zones. They perceive them and from them script the body with particular ideologies. One very ordinary set of scripts in our society is that of blackness and whiteness, which are often presented racially as though they are the complete opposite of one another. Of course the colors themselves in a crayon box do seem quite opposite, but you must admit this is an odd way to think of human beings, particularly of entire cultures.

Yet, the Black-White dichotomy continues to live, even in what some have called our "postracial society." You should know there is no such thing. Here are a couple of illustrations of this Black-White dialectic at work. As mentioned earlier, Black bodies have been characterized as violent; by contrast White bodies have been socially constituted as non-violent, normal, kind, mild-mannered, humane, educated, and often middle class or affluent. The news perpetuates these characterizations, chastising Black bodies for violent behavior, and glossing over White bodies' acts of violence. A primary example of this is in the coverage of the Columbine school shootings. On Tuesday, April 20, 1999, "two young men" entered Columbine High School in Littleton, Colorado (a suburb of Denver) wearing black trench coats, armed with sawed-off shotguns, a semiautomatic rifle, a pistol, and 32 homemade bombs stuffed with nails and shotgun shells. One of these bombs was a 20-pound propane tank with nails and BBs taped to it so that when it exploded, it would send projectiles flying into the air. The two shooters that entered Columbine were reported as "two young men" and "gentlemen" in the majority of news reports. When this daylong tragedy came to an end, the two "gentlemen" had killed 12 students, one teacher, and themselves. The public discourse about this tragedy was very intriguing. As critical observers of the media, we have noticed that when the media reports crimes perpetrated by Black males, negative projections are revealed in the language of the report. Terms like "juvenile" and "delinquent" are common referents to young Black male assailants. In addition, the race of the criminal is always clarified at the beginning of the broadcast. In reports of White criminals, race is not mentioned, and neutral-to-positive language is used. Furthermore, in this particular case, different news broadcasts kept emphasizing how this type of incident does not occur in the suburbs. However, after the Columbine shooting, twelve other shootings occurred, all in the suburbs. All of these shootings were initiated by White males that were a part of a high school group that called themselves the "trench coat mafia." The news initially failed to report the connections among these shootings and the fact that the "trench coat mafia" was an organized gang of which all the shooters, including the Columbine shooters, were a part. To add insult to injury, President Clinton donated money to the families of the murdered students, communicating that some lives, the lives of White people who live in the suburbs, are valued over others, the lives of Black people who live in the inner city. This is noted only because there were concurrent shootings where non-White kids were shot in schools in lower-income communities. Clinton never offered money to the families of victims of those other heinous inner city crimes.

Interestingly, other studies have examined how Blacks, Whites, and Latinos are portrayed in the news. In 2000, Travis Dixon and Dan Linz analyzed how Blacks, Latinos, and Whites are portrayed as lawbreakers. In Los Angeles news stations, Blacks were found to be almost two and a half times more likely to be portrayed as lawbreakers than Whites. However, in reality, Blacks were arrested less frequently than Whites and Latinos. Dixon and Linz argue that these news representations serve to further ingrain the stereotype of the Black male as a violent criminal. In 2004, another study by Mary Beth Oliver and associates examined people's perception of the "typical criminal." Participants had to read a mix of positive and negative news stories about different cultural groups, and then afterward try to recall the pictures of the people associated with each story as a memory test. Participants misidentified Blacks with "Afrocentric" features (i.e., darker skin, thick lips, and/or wide noses) as being associated with more violent crimes. Thus, news reports play a large role in scripting the Black male body as violent and criminal. This inscription has large implications for the African American community because it encourages racial profiling and police brutality towards African American males.

Racial profiling is a very pervasive part of society. Although racial profiling is only acknowledged after a heinous occurrence of police brutality, it actually exists in many different contexts, such as shopping, banking, housing, and academics (Davis, 2001; Kincheloe, Steinberg, & Gresson, 1997; MacDonald, 2003; Meeks, 2000). Davis (2001) provides numerous statistics about the occurrence of racial profiling that occurs with Black drivers, and Meeks (2000) presents narratives and testimony about Black male experience with racial profiling, thus validating that racial profiling is indeed extremely prevalent. Police brutality towards Black male youth is also a widespread phenomenon. In 2003, a young Black male, Nathaniel Jones, was killed by the police because he resisted arrest (Norman, 2003). Nathaniel was the eighteenth Black male to die during a routine police stop since 1995. In 2003, there were 16 cases pending in Cincinnati, 14 for racial profiling, and 2 for wrongful death (Jackson, 2006). A more recent example of racial profiling occurred in 2009 when Harvard professor Henry Louis Gates, Jr. was arrested at his own home for breaking and entering. Gates was reported to be already in his home when the police arrived, and even though he showed the police his driver's license and Harvard identification card, he was still handcuffed and taken to jail (Jan, 2009). Gates accused the police of racial profiling.

The importance of news stories like these is that "these cases are not about police making arrests; they are about people's humanity being seized" (Jackson, 2006, p. 65). Racial profiling is a new form of lynching, or, as Jackson terms it, symbolic lynching. Racial profiling, and the mass media's contribution to it, in essence, characterizes Black male bodies in a particular way, just as slaves were characterized as violent bucks, and then imposes penalties on this particular, marginalized group. After all, after Black bodies have been established as generally violent, who will question the disproportionate amount of Black arrests made in the U.S.? Or the representation of criminals as being primarily Black on the news? The anxiety created by the media has led to a reciprocal relationship between the media and community relations. One feeds off the other and, in the end, the inscription of the violent Black brute becomes more and more difficult to resist. The other stereotypes work in the same way. Think about a euphemism like "urban," which signifies lower income, inner city communities where minorities live. Now, consider the recent release of the board game called Ghettopoloy, in which players build crack houses and projects on their stolen properties. Wealth consists of a ghetto stash and hustler cards. Examples of characters include a Pimp and a Hoe. This board game capitalizes on what outsiders see as the "ghetto experience." Video games such as *Grand Theft Auto* perform the same function, using a "virtual ghettocentric imagination," (p. 250) to allow players to control and exploit their own voyeurism via virtual gangstas. If one becomes proficient at the game, there are levels where racial epithets are quite common. Here, the scripts about minorities are devastating, and laced within an entertainment device where it can appeal to the subconscious mind.

SUMMARY

Scripting is a complicated process that occurs over time. Although scripts can be challenged, changed, and re-constructed, they often still hold remnants of older scripts. The complete process of scripting bodies is referred to as body politics. In body politics, there is a scripter (i.e., the mass media, or someone who holds authority), the scripted (e.g., the Black male body), and the inscription (i.e., violent, incapacitated, exotic, etc.). All of these aspects come together to characterize a body in a particular way. Furthermore, scripting is a historical process. One needs to examine both the history of inscriptions and the current consequences of those inscriptions in order to properly explore Black male corporeal politics.

There are several stereotypical scripts that currently characterize black males: exotic and strange, violent, incompetent and uneducated, sexual, exploitable, and innately incapacitated. These scripts are a combination of racial scripts, characterizing black male bodies as foreign, and gender scripts, attributing a particular type of masculinity to the Black male body. As a result of these inscriptions, some people have xenophobic attitudes towards Black males. These attitudes, however, are not a recent invention that can be accredited solely to mass media representations. The survival of these attitudes and stereotypes is also dependent on people preserving them over time through messages presented to children at the earliest ages all the way through adulthood.

The purpose of this chapter was to explore the process of scripting and the inscription of meanings onto Black male bodies; however, you can substitute any marginalized group and find similar results. We can imagine scripting studies that analyze scripts about gay people, women, or any cultural group. Scripting, or how people characterize and make sense of the Other, is a historical process that can be rewritten over time. In this chapter, we have seen examples of how the process of inscription occurs. Most importantly, we have explained how mass media portrayals of marginalized groups link to everyday race relations in the U.S. We've shown that negative portrayals of Black men in the media can affect individual stereotypes and everyday interracial interactions among the public. Furthermore, on a larger scale, these negative representations are connected to disproportionate mistreatment of marginalized groups as evidenced by mediated racial (mis)representations, crime news reports, racial profiling, and police brutality. As communication scholars, it is important to note the impact that communicative media can have on society, and to be critical of the information presented to us, and not to allow scripts to control how we treat others, but instead to always treat our fellow citizens humanely and with dignity and respect.

REFERENCES

Davis, K. R. (2001). *Driving while black: Cover up.* Cincinnati, OH: Interstate International Publishing of Cincinnati.

Jackson, R. L. (2006). *Scripting the black masculine body: Identity, discourse, and racial politics in popular media.* Albany, NY: State University of New York Press.

Jan, T. (2009, July 20). Harvard professor Gates arrested at Cambridge home. *MetroDesk.* Retrieved from http://www.boston.com/news/local/breaking_news/2009/07/harvard.html

Kincheloe, J. L., Steinberg, S. R., & Gresson, A. D. (1997). *Measured lies: The bell curve examined.* New York: St. Martin's Press.

MacDonald, H. (2003). *Are cops racist?: How the war against the police harms black Americans.* New York: Ivan R. Dee Publisher.

Meeks, K. (2000). *Driving while black: What to do if you are a victim of racial profiling.* New York: Broadway Press.

Norman, T. (2003, December 5). Accomplices to a killing by Cincinnati police. *Pittsburgh Post Gazette.* (http://old.post-gazette.com/columnists/20031205tony107col2p2.asp).

Wiegman, R. (1995). *American anatomies: Theorizing race and gender.* Durham, NC: Duke University Press.

COMMUNICATION, POWER, AND POLITICS: QUEER THEORY AND THE ANALYSIS OF NORMALIZATION

GUST A. YEP, SAN FRANCISCO STATE UNIVERSITY AND
SCOTT M. SCHÖNFELDT-AULTMAN, SAINT MARY'S COLLEGE OF CALIFORNIA

Since its emergence more than two decades ago, queer theory has become an important theoretical tradition in the humanities and social sciences. Although its influence has been noted in communication since the nineties, the first comprehensive collection of research using queer theory (Yep, Lovaas, & Elia, 2003a) was not published in the discipline until the twenty-first century. Since then, a number of studies has appeared in communication journals and edited volumes. This chapter focuses on one of Gust's research programs—his work on queer theory in the field of communication (Elia, Lovaas, & Yep, 2003; Elia & Yep, in press; Slagle & Yep, 2007; Yep, 2002a, 2003, 2005, 2007, 2009a, b, 2010a; Yep & Conkle, 2013; Yep & Elia, 2007; Yep & Elia, in press; Yep, Lovaas, & Elia, 2003a, b, c; Yep & Ochoa Camacho, 2004; Yep, Olzman, & Conkle, in press; Yep & Shimanoff, in press). A lot of the research in queer theory, however, has been characterized, in Gamson's words, as "speaking some kind of high-falutin' pig Latin" (Gamson, 2003, p. 385). To provide a friendly introduction to queer theory in communication, we decided to "queer" this chapter. To do so, we are presenting the ideas in the form of a dialogue between two colleagues rather than using the format of a more traditional expository essay. Our conversation was broadly guided by the question "How might queer theory tell us more about communication at the intersections of gender and sexuality along with race, class, and nation?"

LOCATING OURSELVES IN THE DIALOGUE

We have always found it important to situate our selves and to be self-reflexive in the work and writing that we do. Gust grew up in three cultures—Chinese, Peruvian, and U.S. American—and identifies as "Asianlatinoamerican" (Yep, 2002b, p. 60). He lives in the San Francisco Bay Area with Yogi, his affectionate and inquisitive Pomeranian he adopted from a local dog rescue organization. He is a Professor of Communication Studies, Core Graduate Faculty of Sexuality Studies, and Faculty in the doctoral program in Educational Leadership at San Francisco State University. Scott grew up in the southern United States most of his life, and has lived in the San Francisco Bay Area for the past sixteen years. He is an Associate Professor of Communication at

Saint Mary's College of California. He identifies as a white, middle-upper class, heterosexual, able-bodied male. Scott and Gust met when Scott was a student of Gust's in a masters program in communication in the late nineties. Since then, we have been co-authors and co-presenters on conference panels and have had many conversations together. We share similarities in our approaches to teaching (employing critical pedagogy) and in politics, as well as a love of good food and tea. The dialogue is a distillation of the conversations we have had over the years regarding matters such as gender, sexuality, race, and identity.

A DIALOGUE ABOUT QUEER THEORY IN COMMUNICATION

SCOTT: Most of us have heard the term "queer" before, perhaps most commonly in a derogatory sense. But "queer theory" is less about being negative and more imbued with a political sense. As an area of academic study, queer theory emerged in the early 1990s in the academy, distinct from Gay & Lesbian Studies, and some cite Judith Butler, Eve Kosofsky Sedgwick, and Teresa de Lauretis as originators of the field. I wonder if you can say more about what queer theory is and does, and if you can also say something about how queer theory gets employed by you and others in the field of communication.

GUST: The first thing I want to say is that queer theory is not a traditional theory per se; most people think of a theory as a kind of contained system and logic of description and explanation of a specific kind of phenomenon. Queer theory is not that exactly. Queer theory is more of an interdisciplinary, intellectual movement influenced by critical theory, cultural studies, feminism, postmodernism and poststructuralism. It offers us specific ways of looking, understanding, and explaining power relations in society, so, in that sense, it is theory. Queer theory has affected the way we think about identity, social relationships, social structures, cultural institutions, and power relations in society.

SCOTT: What do you mean when you say that queer theory has something to do with power relations in society?

GUST: First, I want to clarify that I'm using power in a Foucauldian sense—power as relational, ubiquitous, and productive and not simply repressive (Foucault, 1990). So, based on this notion of power, we can see that power is always already embedded in all of our relationships, such as interpersonal relations (e.g., relationship with our boss), social relations (e.g., the ways we group and categorize people), social institutions (e.g., family), or cultural ideologies (e.g., heteropatriarchy). The way that we employ power is not always visible, so in that sense we are not always aware of it. As Foucault (1990) suggests, the power of power is to maintain its invisibility. We are always affected by power. The project of queer theory is to use specific tools for us to become more conscious of how power is operating in our social relationships, with particular attention to how gender and sexuality structure social life.

Queer theorists recognize and acknowledge the history of the term "queer" that is deployed to degrade, to dehumanize, and to pathologize sexual minority subjects. But they are reclaiming the term to resignify it and to give it new meaning and to gesture toward a political project of social justice. The term "queer" can be used as a noun and as a verb. Most people think of "queer" as a noun—as someone who is odd (strangeness) or someone who is lesbian or gay (identity). As a verb, queer theory uses the term to describe a process of making something familiar and taken for granted into something unfamiliar and strange so that it can be analyzed and examined.

SCOTT: Analyzed and examined for what?

GUST: In terms of how power might be operating in a text, in a social relation, in a specific situation. For instance, most people think about marriage as something naturally occurring when two individuals are in love which each other and want to build a life together. Marriage, for these people, is simply a natural part of the life cycle. Most people probably don't think about marriage as something to be analyzed. What queer theory does is look at marriage and its power relations. It would look at the history of marriage, pointing out that marriage was really not so much about love, but about property ownership and the maintenance of wealth, and that it wasn't until the early twentieth century that marriage was seen as the culmination and expression of love between two individuals. This whole notion of marrying for love is a relatively new concept that permeates the way that we think about dating and romantic relationships (Yep, in press).

Traditionally, marriage has been conceived of as between a man and a woman. The process of "queering" marriage is to make it unfamiliar so that we can analyze it to understand its history, evolving meanings, and its relationship to gender and heterosexuality. In addition, through the process of marriage, we set up all kinds of social hierarchies. For example, people that are married may be set up as having more social status than those who are not married. Those that cohabitate have lower social status than married people. In the process, women in love with women and men in love with men cannot get married because of federal law. Same-sex couples are second-class citizens in the United States. Basically, what I'm saying is that the taken-for-granted institution of marriage has all kinds of power relationships that have both symbolic and material consequences for everyone in society.

SCOTT: So many people don't think about all of these consequences because they feel they are not—or don't think they are—affected by them.

GUST: But everyone is affected, but in different ways.

Let me finish this thought about queer theory. It was originally credited to Teresa de Lauretis in the early nineties. But actually Gloria Anzaldúa used the term before that.

SCOTT: Really, I didn't know. Why don't we hear about that?

GUST: I suspect it was because Anzaldúa was seen as a woman of color writing about issues of race, and not about sexuality. In fact, her contribution has been about the lived experiences of people living at the intersections of race, class, gender, sexuality, ability, and nation.

SCOTT: You've just mentioned intersectionality of different identities. I sometimes like to think in metaphors, so what metaphor would you use to describe intersectionality?

GUST: Intersectionality is like a cake. It is made out of a lot of different ingredients, like flour, sugar, eggs, perhaps chocolate chips. None of those are in themselves the cake. The egg is not the cake, the sugar is not the cake. The cake is more than each of the individual ingredients. So, when we talk about race, class, gender, sexuality, ability, and nation, a person is not just his or her race, because s/he also has gender, sexuality, and so on. We can't just say this person is a woman without also looking at the other elements that make her a whole person.

In mainstream U.S. culture, we tend to think of identity in additive ways. So, for example, we might ask a lesbian of color if her race is more important than her gender or sexuality. In the process, we are asking her to fragment herself into parts and to determine what aspects of her identity are more important, when, in fact, she is a whole person, which means that all of these factors are operating simultaneously in any given social situation. In this sense, intersectional identities are multiplicative rather than additive (Yep, 2002b).

SCOTT: I've also heard you talk about "thick intersectionalities," about biographies and lived experiences. I wonder if you can talk about how thick intersectionalities differ from the intersections we were just talking about.

GUST: Well, there are different ways of doing intersectionalities and of doing race, class, gender, sexuality, ability, and nation. One way is the "roster-like" approach to intersectionality when one simply lists the various different identities of a person, which is, in my view, simplistic and superficial (Yep, 2010b).

SCOTT: Why simplistic and superficial? And what makes the kind of intersectionality you're advocating "thick"?

GUST: Because it is a process of listing several identity markers without paying attention to how a person lives and how the person's history and biography affect their communication and relationships. So, for instance, we might have someone whose identities might be labeled as white, middle-class, male, straight, able-bodied, and U.S. American.

SCOTT: You mean, like me.

GUST: Yes. On the surface, one can make a number of assumptions about your life, privileges, and politics—if we simply stayed with those superficial markers. But as we have gotten to know each other, we have learned about each other's biographies, histories, and personal and social struggles, and in that process, I could say that we have a lot of similarities, even though on the surface we appear very different. Thick intersectionalities pay attention to the particularities of our lives and our life journeys and how they are affected by the intersections of race, class, gender, sexuality, ability, and nation (Yep, 2010b).

SCOTT: In other words, thick intersectionalities avoid essentializing, while also recognizing the reality of differences as lived by people.

GUST: We get to know people as unique individuals rather than as a simple combination of social categories. That's not to suggest that race, class, gender, sexuality, ability, and nation don't matter but that we need to attend to the ways that they are embodied and lived in the world.

SCOTT: It seems to me that making assumptions about people based on an additive approach or from a simplistic intersectional perspective is pretty commonplace. There doesn't appear to me to be lots of interrogation of discourses of race, class, gender, sexuality, ability, and nation in mainstream U.S. media or in many everyday relationships and conversations. If we think specifically about discourses of sexuality and normalization, this brings us to the notions of heteronormativity and heteropatriarchy. I know you've thought, spoken, and written a lot about these. Can you talk more about them?

GUST: One of the aims of queer theory is to examine the process of normalization, that is, the process by which we make certain practices unquestionable and taken-for-granted in a culture. Earlier I mentioned that marriage is normalized and so is heterosexuality. Queer theory examines them so that they can be understood in terms of power relations in society. One of the primary concerns of what I have called elsewhere "first-generation" queer theory (Yep, 2009b, p. 820) is to uncover the processes of normalization in general, and normalization in relationship to gender and sexuality in particular. But normalization isn't just a queer theory project; it's an aim of critical theory. So one way to think about it is that queer theory is using the normalization of gender and sexuality as a starting point for the analysis of social relations. Thus, one of the concerns of first-generation queer theory has been about the notion of heteronormativity, which is the normalization of heterosexuality (Yep, 2002a, 2003, 2005, 2009b). When I say normalization of heterosexuality, I mean the seemingly natural, given, assumed, unquestionable status given to heterosexuality in social relations (Yep, 2002a, 2003). For example, a person might assume that his little niece is going to grow up, get married to a man, and have that man's children. Implicit in this set of assumptions is that the normal and natural way to be in the world is to be heterosexual. Such assumptions imply that heterosexuality is unquestionable and inevitable and can be used to call his niece's identity into question when she deviates from it (e.g., she does not want to get married, she does not want to have children, she is not attracted to men). So, I'm posing this question: What happens to this young woman, the niece, when she finds that she is discovering her sexuality, her wishes, and her aspirations as a person? Some would suggest that she may see heterosexuality as the only "right" option. This is what we might term "compulsory heterosexuality." In this sense, the normalization of heterosexuality, or heteronormativity, becomes a site of violence (Yep, 2002a, 2003).

SCOTT: A site of violence? You mean that violence might be inflicted upon her? By her uncle? By society? By family?

GUST: Well, I want to use the notion of violence more broadly. Violence is, in my view, the process of harming someone—it could be symbolic, physical, or both (Yep, 2003). For example, if her uncle calls her a "fucking dyke" to discipline her for not being a "proper young woman," he is inflicting injury on her personhood.

SCOTT: Yes, but the uncle wasn't the originator of the name "fucking dyke"—or the source of the implications and meanings of that name. All of that came from society and the discourses circulating within it. Those discourses, and the social structures from which they emerge and within which they circulate contribute to the valuation of what is appropriate personal and social activity. You're suggesting that the uncle's comments and the social structure work to impose upon people, not just upon the niece, but upon the uncle, too, a sense of what is proper, appropriate, and normative, and that these are a violent enforcement of heteronormativity, not in the least because of the emotional and psychological experience and repercussions of such enforcement upon both the niece and uncle. One might also suggest that patriarchy allows more space for the uncle to make such comments without obvious consequences, and that he might even benefit by making such comments in that it reaffirms his own heterosexuality and status as a man.

GUST: Absolutely! The uncle is operating not just within the structures of heteronormativity, but also within the structures of heteropatriarchy. By heteropatriarchy, I mean a systemic social arrangement that upholds the dominance of men over women through the institution of heterosexuality (Yep, 2003).

SCOTT: So the social structures of heteronormativity and heteropatriarchy we are talking about are the traditional family (e.g., breadwinning husband and housewife, husband as head of household); the church (e.g., predominantly male-led, literal interpretations of scripture regarding gender, sexual, and marital relations); the legal system (e.g., inheritance benefits for married couples, definition of rape); the educational system (e.g., selective study of male-dominant and heterosexual histories, the predominance of male heroes and straight characters in children's books); the mass media (e.g., the focus on male sports, the news coverage of Hillary Rodham Clinton and Sarah Palin), and the like.

GUST: Yes. Here we see how gender and sexuality might work to mutually reinforce each other to create and maintain normativity. As I mentioned earlier, work in queer theory can be characterized by generations (Yep, 2009b). A primary concern of first-generation queer theory, as I indicated, is the violence of heteronormativity in its various forms. Second-generation queer theory has been concerned with the whiteness of much of the first-generation work and the U.S.-centrism of this research. Second-generation work has attempted to look at the process of normalization more broadly ranging from local (e.g., Fisher, 2003) to transnational and global (e.g., Lee, 2003) levels. Another concern of second-generation work is on other forms of normativity. An example of that is the emergence of the notion of homonormativity, which is the normalization of gay and lesbian lives based on a depoliticized, privatized, and consumerist orientation (Yep & Conkle, 2013). So what we end up with is a gay and lesbian consumer in the global marketplace. It's the production of a visible gay and lesbian consumer identity (e.g., gay markets) that gets mistaken as a sign of liberation. We have to recognize that increased LGBT visibility is not synonymous with true gay and lesbian acceptance and liberation. Look at the incidences of hate crimes and homophobic bullying against LGBT people. If we have true acceptance and liberation, these numbers would disappear, but they certainly have not.

Let me also say at this point that, aside from homonormativity, some of the current second-generation queer theory work is focusing on other forms of normativity, such as urban normativity, body normativity, and certain forms of sexual normativity.

SCOTT: There seems to be a real uphill battle for folks not wanting to buy into all these forms of normativity and for folks wanting to transgress. Any suggestions or thoughts about this struggle?

GUST: I want to make a distinction between transgression and intervention. Trangression is the process through which individuals either consciously or less consciously break away from or do not conform to normativities. One example would be dressing differently, such as going to class to teach in shorts and a T-shirt when you normally wear more formal attire, to call attention to the performativity of the various dimensions of identity (of a professor, in this case). A transgression is essentially an act (or acts) that fails to conform to normativities. Intervention, on the other hand, is a deliberate act (or series of acts) that calls our attention to the underlying power dynamics that govern specific forms of normativity (Yep, 2008).

SCOTT: So interventions are intentional efforts to disrupt normativity . . .

GUST: . . . and to call attention to its underlying aims and purposes.

SCOTT: I wonder if such calling attention requires specific mention of what one is challenging. For instance, I wear lots of pink and coordinate my clothing, earring, and hair tie, with intent to have students question normative practices of gender and sexuality broadly. I don't always tell them why I'm dressing as such. I also employ the term "partner" when referring to the woman I married and with whom I have children in order to have students, and others, think about marriage politically and ideologically and to call attention to heterosexual privilege. I wonder if these two examples are interventions or transgressions? I'm asking because it seems to me that interventions, and the two instances I mention here, are marked by political intention and motivation for progressive change. Perhaps my constant dressing differently with political intent and motivation for progressive change is more transgression than intervention, though when I specifically comment on why I dress the way I do, it moves into intervention because I am deliberating attempting to undermine my own privileges and power that I receive as a white, heterosexual male. My use of "partner" is a clearer example of intervention I believe, particularly when students inquire about why I use "partner" instead of "wife," and I then expand on the underlying power dynamics that govern heteronormative marriage. I suppose I am suggesting that acts marked by political intention and motive for progressive change are not in themselves interventions unless they actually serve to call attention (be it through specific mention or not) to the underlying power dynamics that govern specific forms of normativity.

GUST: Yes, interventions are deliberate acts to produce progressive social change. These changes can be small or large. They can also occur at the individual level—like some of your heterosexual students starting to think about their heterosexual privilege—and at the systemic level—like some of your students, regardless of gender or sexual orientation, getting together to organize to promote and support marriage rights for lesbians and gays in their state.

CONCLUSION

In this dialogue we discussed the origins of queer theory and its interdisciplinary nature. We highlighted its efforts to analyze power, gender, and sexuality and their shaping of social relations/ hierarchies and normalization. We also explored the concepts of intersectionality and thick intersectionalities, which pay attention to histories and biographies and to the particularities of race, class, gender, sexuality, ability, and nation. In our discussion we noted queer theory's examination of heteronormativity and the violence inherent in it. We mentioned the concerns of first and second-generation queer theory and the latter's treatment of homonormativity. We concluded with an explanation of transgressions and interventions.

There are several direct communicative implications of our dialogue. These consist of (1) becoming more conscious of the significance of power in everyday interactions and in social structures and institutions; (2) striving to be more aware of one's own and each person's particular social realities that shape their lived experiences; (3) recognizing that intersections of identity complicate our understanding of people and of everyday communicative encounters; (4) becoming more aware of how gender and sexuality are normalized; (5) not assuming that gender and sexuality are clear categories and not making simplistic assumptions about them; (6) observing how we reinforce normalization for ourselves and others via personal, cultural, and social practices; and (7) seeking to practice transgressions and interventions, and to acknowledge them, in efforts to disrupt normativity, even when one is benefitting or receiving privilege from heteronormativity and heteropatriarchy.

REFERENCES

Elia, J. P., Lovaas, K. E., & Yep, G. A. (2003). Reflections on queer theory: Disparate points of view. In G. A. Yep, K. E. Lovaas, & J. P. Elia (Eds.), *Queer theory and communication: From disciplining queers to queering the discipline(s)* (pp. 335–337). Binghamton, NY: Harrington Park Press.

Elia, J. P., & Yep, G. A. (in press). Sexualities and genders in an age of neoterrorism. *Journal of Homosexuality, 59*(7).

Fisher, D. (2003). Immigrant closets: Tactical-micro-practices-in-the-hyphen. In G. A. Yep, K. E. Lovaas, & J. P. Elia (Eds.), *Queer theory and communication: From disciplining queers to queering the discipline(s)* (pp. 171–192). Binghamton, NY: Harrington Park Press.

Foucault, M. (1990). *The history of sexuality: Vol. 1. An introduction.* New York: Vintage. (Original work published 1978.)

Gamson, J. (2003). Reflections on queer theory and communication. In G. A. Yep, K. E. Lovaas, & J. P. Elia (Eds.), *Queer theory and communication: From disciplining queers to queering the discipline(s)* (pp. 385–389). Binghamton, NY: Harrington Park Press.

Lee, W. (2003). Kauering queer theory: My autocritography and a race-conscious, womanist, transnational turn. In G. A. Yep, K. E. Lovaas, & J. P. Elia (Eds.), *Queer theory and communication: From disciplining queers to queering the discipline(s)* (pp. 147–170). Binghamton, NY: Harrington Park Press.

Slagle, R. A., & Yep, G. A. (2007). Taming Brian: Sex, love, and romance in *Queer as Folk.* In M. L. Galician, & D. Merskin (Eds.), *Critical thinking about sex, love, and romance in the mass media: Media literacy applications* (pp. 189–202). Mahwah, NJ: Lawrence Erlbaum.

Yep, G. A. (2002a). From homophobia and heterosexism to heteronormativity: Toward the development of a model of queer interventions in the university classroom. *Journal of Lesbian Studies, 6*(3/4), 163–176.

Yep, G. A. (2002b). My three cultures: Navigating the multicultural identity landscape. In J. N. Martin, T. K. Nakayama, & L. A. Flores (Eds.), *Readings in intercultural communication: Experiences and contexts* (2nd ed., pp. 60–66). Boston, MA: McGraw-Hill.

Yep, G. A. (2003). The violence of heteronormativity in communication studies: Notes on violence, healing, and queer-world making. In G. A. Yep, K. E. Lovaas, & J. P. Elia (Eds.), *Queer theory and communication: From disciplining queers to queering the discipline(s)* (pp. 11–59). Binghamton, NY: Harrington Park Press.

Yep, G. A. (2005). Heteronormativity. In J. T. Sears (Ed.), *Youth, education, and sexualities: An international encyclopedia* (pp. 395–398). Westport, CT: Greenwood.

Yep, G. A. (2007). The politics of loss and its remains in *Common Threads: Stories from the Quilt. Rhetoric & Public Affairs, 10*(4), 681–700.

Yep, G. A. (2008). The dialectics of intervention: Toward a reconceptualization of the theory/activism divide in communication scholarship and beyond. In O. Swartz (Ed.), *Transformative communication studies: Culture, hierarchy and the human condition* (pp. 191–207). Leicester, UK: Troubador.

Yep, G. A. (2009a). Gay, lesbian, bisexual, and transgender theories. In S. W. Littlejohn & K. A. Foss (Eds.), *Encyclopedia of communication theory* (Vol. 1, pp. 421–426). Thousand Oaks, CA: Sage.

Yep, G. A. (2009b). Queer theory. In S. W. Littlejohn & K. A. Foss (Eds.), *Encyclopedia of communication theory* (Vol. 2, pp. 817–821). Thousand Oaks, CA: Sage.

Yep, G. A. (2010a). Rolando and Tatiana: Living at the intersections of race, class, gender, sexuality, and nation. In C. M. Noland, J. Manning, & J. MacLennan (Eds.), *Case studies of communication about sex* (pp. 46–54). Newcastle, UK: Cambridge.

Yep, G. A. (2010b). Toward the de-subjugation of racially marked knowledges in communication. *Southern Communication Journal, 75*(2), 171–175.

Yep, G. A. (in press). Privilege and culture. In A. Kurylo (Ed.), *Inter/Cultural Communication: Representation and construction of culture in everyday interaction.* Thousand Oaks, CA: Sage.

Yep, G. A., & Conkle, A. (2013). The new gay domesticity: Homonormativity in ABC's *Brothers and Sisters.* In R. A. Lind (Ed.), *Race/Gender/Media 3.0: Considering diversity across audiences, content, and producers* (3rd ed.) (pp. 218–224). Boston, MA: Pearson.

Yep, G. A., & Elia, J. P. (2007). Queering/quaring blackness in *Noah's Arc.* In T. Peele (Ed.), *Queer popular culture: Literature, media, film, and television* (pp. 27–40). New York: Palgrave-Macmillan.

Yep, G. A., & Elia, J. P. (in press). Racialized masculinities and the new homonormativity in LOGO's Noah's Arc. *Journal of Homosexuality, 59*(7).

Yep, G. A., Lovaas, K. E., & Elia, J. P. (Eds.). (2003a). *Queer theory and communication: From disciplining queers to queering the discipline(s)* (pp. 11–59). Binghamton, NY: Harrington Park Press.

Yep, G. A., Lovaas, K. E., & Elia, J. P. (2003b). Queering Communication: Starting the Conversation. In G. A. Yep, K. E. Lovaas, & J. P. Elia (Eds.), *Queer theory and communication: From disciplining queers to queering the discipline(s)* (pp. 1–10). Binghamton, NY: Harrington Park Press.

Yep, G. A., Lovaas, K. E., & Elia, J. P. (2003c). A critical reappraisal of assimilationist and radical ideologies underlying same-sex marriage in LGBT communities in the United States. *Journal of Homosexuality, 45*(1), 45–64.

Yep, G. A., Ochoa Camacho, A. (2004). The normalization of heterogendered relations in The Bachelor. *Feminist Media Studies, 4*(3), 338–341.

Yep, G. A., Olzman, M., & Conkle, A. (in press). Seven stories from the "It Gets Better" Project: Progress narratives, politics of affect, and the question of queer world-making. In R. A. Lind (Ed.), *Producing Theory: The Intersection of audiences and production in a digital world.* New York: Peter Lang.

Yep, G. A., & Shimanoff, S. B. (in press). The U.S. Day of Silence: Sexualities, silences and the will to unsay in the age of empire. In S. Malhotra & A. Carrillo-Rowe (Eds.), *Silence and power: Feminist reflections at the edges of sound.* New York: Palgrave Macmillan.

SECTION 5
GROUP COMMUNICATION

The group communication context (often referred to as small group communication) focuses on how we communicate in a group setting. These groups of three people or more (such as work groups, social groups, support groups) function differently than dyads (two people). Therefore, group communication scholars examine how group decisions are made, how groups accomplish a task, the roles that each group member plays, and group outcomes, such as group consensus or groupthink. Some major areas of research in group communication include group norms, group socialization, group climate, group leadership, and group development. This chapter focuses on three important areas of group communication research: (1) peer groups, (2) group/team play in athletics, and (3) group decision-making. First, SunWolf (Santa Clara University) reviews peer group research to answer: *What theories and concepts explain the communication and behaviors of peer groups, where members consider one another to be equals in some relevant way?* Second, Paul Turman (South Dakota Board of Regents) examines coaching athletic teams as a group to answer: *What effects do coaches' communicative messages have on their athletes/team?* Third, Dennis Gouran (The Pennsylvania State University) reviews research on group decision-making by answering: *How can we have better decision-making in small groups?* Throughout your life, you will be required to work in groups, whether it be for school work, for a career, or for a social event. Many of you will need to make effective group decisions to succeed in life. Some of you are already athletes, or are currently members of a peer group. It is important to consider how group research can help us have better group member interactions in these common group gatherings.

PEER GROUPS

SUNWOLF, SANTA CLARA UNIVERSITY

peer *n.* 1. a person who is the equal of another in abilities, qualifications, responsibilities, or social status, 2. a person of the same legal status, privilege, or rights as another.

You are a member of at least one and probably several peer groups: clans, cliques, clubs, or choirs; teams, travelers, taskers, or tribes. An aerospace executive described the euphoric culture of his group:

> We even walked differently than anybody else. We felt we were way out there, ahead of the whole world (Lipman-Blumen & Leavitt, 1999, p. 9).

At the same time, a 79-year old juror in the 2005 Michael Jackson trial described the jury deliberations as toxic:

> The air reeked of hatred and people were angry and I had never been in an atmosphere like that before (SunWolf, 2008, p. 132).

Peer groups have goals that are social, task, or both. Membership can be short term ("We've got to find a way out!") or long term ("Semper Fidelis," Marines). However, the glue-like premise of a peer group is *member sameness*—sameness in some way that is important to that group. Peer groups affect us even when we are *not* members—as a 14-year-old African American teen poignantly pointed out (SunWolf & Leets, 2003, p. 355):

> I think that they excluded me because they just judge people by the outside, but those people are wrong. You should get to know people more.

Peer groups construct boundaries, create identity, engage in tasks, resolve conflict, enact rituals, and exclude outsiders through *communication.* What theories and concepts, then, explain the communication and behaviors of peer groups, where members consider one another to be equals in some relevant way?

OUR LIVES ARE EMBEDDED IN PEER GROUPS

Peer groups are worth our attention because we will belong to them across our lifespan. Peer groups consider members to be equals, even though *not all members agree about the equality of all other members at all times.* When some members have more power, privilege, or status, they are not peers. Consider a coach and team, a commander and soldiers, or parents and children. Subtract the members who have extraordinary power, however, then the remaining members might be peers.

Theoretical Lights That Explain Peer Group Processes

We are all theorists. This includes you. Our ideas about why things happen or what causes people to behave in certain ways are parts of our everyday thinking. Our personal theories might be wrong, but they make other people seem (a little) more predictable.

Scholars who study groups from the *symbolic-interpretive perspective* (Frey & SunWolf, 2004, 2005) are concerned with how group members use symbols (language, stories, rituals, dress, objects, music, humor, and practices) to create and sustain group identity. Peer groups both produce *and are products of* the group's symbolic communication practices. Formal theories attempt to describe, explain, or predict behaviors. *Social comparison theory* (Festinger, 1957) assumes that people wonder how they are doing, so they compare themselves to others. Applied to peer groups, social comparison theory suggests that group members ask each other: Was my behavior or my effort better or worse than my peers? Am I similar or different? *Structuration theory* (Poole, Seibold, & McPhee, 1996) assumes that groups are created by rules and structures. It examines the resources each member brings, looks at rules that are created, and casts light on practices that a group produces and reproduces. *Decisional regret theory* (SunWolf, 2006) assumes that decision-making produces anxiety. Members of a decision-making group will attempt to reduce their decisional anxiety by imagining stories about *what might happen* with each possible choice, searching for a decision that has an imagined *positive* outcome, while rejecting choices that have imagined *negative* outcomes. These theories invite us to take a closer look at the practices, rules, rituals, and outcomes of the communication that occurs in real world peer groups.

Peer Groups in Childhood and Adolescence: Freaks, Geeks, Jocks, and Stars

Ever been picked last? If your family moved a lot, if your face sprouted freckles or scars, if you were clumsy, spoke with an accent, or dressed differently, you probably have been picked last by your peers. Your height, weight, or skin color may have been a convenient target for exclusion by other children.

Continued peer exclusion triggers poor school performance, delinquent behavior, depression, physical illness, and impaired adult relationships (Buhs & Ladd, 2001). Peer-rejected children become more aggressive or more socially withdrawn and lonely (Wood, Cowan, & Baker, 2002). Researchers use brain imaging (fMRI) to see what happens in our brains when we experience social rejection, finding that the same area of our brain that lights up when we experience *physical pain* lights up when we experience *social rejection* (Eisenberger, Lieberman, & Williams, 2003). Peer group rejection hurts.

Remember high school? You knew immediately how you fit into the social hierarchy. Visit any school bus stop, playground, or cafeteria. Sounds of exclusion, sneers, and cutting remarks announce peer group boundaries that cannot be penetrated. In one study, 682 adolescents shared accounts of being excluded (SunWolf & Leets, 2004). Peer groups used five primary *communication tactics for refusing group entry to an outsider,* as shown in Table 1:

Did gender or ethnicity affect group rejection? Both White and non-White teens reported being told they were not wanted because of their race or skin color; both males and females were ridiculed or told they were not good enough to join; and all reported incidents of being silently ignored when they tried to gain entry to a group of their peers.

Leets and SunWolf (2005) also found that teens had rules for when it would be morally right to reject an outsider: if the person was unattractive, unqualified, or dangerous; as punishment (paybacks); or as benevolent protection (the person might get hurt in the activity). A group's decision to reject doesn't always reflect what each member thinks is fair, though. When teens were asked to think about a time their group rejected someone, but they didn't agree (yet kept silent), heartfelt *regrets* were described (SunWolf & Leets, 2003, p. 16), such as:

- I wish I made my group think different about her, not because of the way she dressed.
- I wish I had said, "No, it's alright, you can stay, you are my friend."
- I wish I had told the group to be quiet and include the person.
- I wish I would have been the bigger man and worked with the person excluded.
- I wish I would have left the group and made my own, in which everyone was welcome.

Why don't we speak up when we disagree with our peers? *Rejection contagion* is the perception that an outsider's negative social stigma is capable of being transferred to us. *Inclusion fragility* is the perception that our own group inclusion is so fragile that if we disagree, we might also be rejected (SunWolf & Leets, 2003).

Peer Groups in Neighborhoods: Hoodies and Homies

> Kings is not only like a gang, it's a family. Everybody cares about one another. Everywhere we go we watch each other's back. We never leave nobody running behind. 'Cause, see, the same way we watch their back, they're watching our back.
>
> —Latino Boy, talking to a professor on a Chicago rooftop

Street gangs struggle for survival in the city by creating an intricate culture of communication practices that sustain identity and protect geographic boundaries (Conquergood, 1994; SunWolf, 2008). A gang of girls might be autonomous, allied with a male gang, or part of a gender-integrated gang (Miller, 2000), although female gangs often hold more firmly to an egalitarian norm (Quicker, 1983).

Table 1. Adolescents' Stories of Communication Tactics Peer Groups Used to Reject Them

Peer Rejection Tactics ↓	Responses: What did someone in that group say or do that let you know you would not be included?			
	Males		Females	
	White	NonWhite	White	NonWhite
Ignoring	• They pretty much ignored my presence.	• Walked away. • I was talking and they would make a comment like, "is that the wind?"	• The group wouldn't look at me, they seemed to be avoiding looking at my face and they turned their backs.	• They all gave me an awkward look and continued to talk among themselves. • They pretended I wasn't there.
Disqualifying	• They needed an extra person, so I offered. The person making the team said I was not good enough, even though we played on the same school football team.	• Because of some difficulty I have with my heart, they mocked me and made fun of my situation telling me that I'll die or have a heart attack.	• They said I couldn't play cuz I wasn't good enough of a player. They were mean.	• Basically, that I wouldn't understand what they were talking about because I was scholastically far behind them.
Insulting	• Get out of here, stupid, you're gay. • They said I was fat and stupid, so they didn't want to include me in anything. I walked away crying.	• Someone was making fun of my head's shape. They were making fun of me by saying "E.T., phone home."	• The boys said I couldn't play with them because I was a girl and I had cooties.	• Other kids did not want to play with me because I had a mole. They'd call me mole face. • They said, hey, look at the ugly girl how she dresses.
Blaming	• They said we have even teams and that I could not play very well. Because no one knew me and because of all my freckles.	• They said that I sucked at baseball. • Because I don't look good enough. I'm not a good dresser kind of person.	• Back in grade school I was really large (fat) and people would exclude me all the time. It hurt me a lot.	• I wasn't a fun or smart person to be with. • A group of girls didn't want me to hang around with them because I wasn't a girly girl.
Creating New Rules	• They said I didn't get there in time and they already started. I would have to get another person in order to play. • They ignored me and left me for last pick. Then they told me I couldn't play because it was uneven.	• One time I ask to play football with some people and they said that I was too late, we have too many people, then you're too small. Next time I got there early and asked if I could play and they act like they did not hear me.	• They said "Sorry no more room," but I knew that there was 5 spaces left. I saw someone else ask if they could play and they let that person in. • They said that they had to go home, they were leaving. I thought it was 'cause they didn't like us.	• One time we were getting into groups of 4 people. I went over to this one group to ask them if I could be in their group because they only had 3. When I asked them, they were like, "No, because Amanda was going to be in our group."

Adapted with permission of Sage Publications, from *Peer Groups: Expanding our Study of Small Group Communication.* Copyright © 2008. Permission conveyed through Copyright Clearance Center, Inc.

Members of street gangs develop unique communication practices. Scholars have studied group rituals, graffiti, dress, and the physical performances of walking and throwing signals.

"Playing the dozens" is an oral tradition performed on urban streets, in which two people go head-to-head, taking turns insulting one another (SunWolf, 2008). The goal is to verbally abuse an opponent until the opponent loses control, becomes angry, gets rattled, or gets physical. This proves one player is weak—defeat is humiliating. The Dozens is nonviolent; it resolves social conflict by structuring communicative self-control. While demonized as vandalism, graffiti is *visual peer talk* performed by a *designated artist*. Graffiti performs symbolic functions for the group: designating safe areas, putting down enemies, honoring deceased members, and celebrating triumphs. *Reppin'* refers to communication in which members perform their group's identity by the wearing of colors, throwing up hand signs, and calling out code words. Stylized rites of handshaking enact peer bonding. "Shaking the crown," for example (Conquergood, 1994), is a graceful series of co-performed hand gestures representing the Latin King's crown, in which both partners throw their right fist on their heart, kiss their fingertips, then tap their heart with tips of fingers now extended in the shape of a crown. Hand gestures reestablish affiliation, restore respect, repair loss of face, and redress daily humiliations of poverty and prejudice (SunWolf, 2008).

Peer Groups that Super-Task: Hot Groups

You may have been part of a *hot group*. Maybe you called yourselves a team, a task force, a band, a study group, occupiers, or protestors, or maybe your group never had a specific name. Members of hot groups are overachievers: fast, focused, flaming. Hot groups are tightly-knit peer groups, task-obsessed, full of passion, with a self-sacrificing dedication to doing something together that each member believes is important (Lipman, Blumen, & Leavitt, 1999; SunWolf, 2008). Examples are in the media everyday: elite military teams rescue troops behind enemy lines, rescue teams pull victims from avalanches, law enforcement squads rescue hostages. In hot groups, the work of one is considered to be the work of all.

Imagine a movie opening with a scene showing black cowboys hard at work at a cattle ranch, on the western plains. You've never seen that film—yet thousands of black, Native American, and Hispanic cowboys helped shape the West before and after the Civil War (Durham & Jones, 1965; Katz, 1986; SunWolf, 2008). Interviews with these cowboys reveal the power of a hot group of peers (University of Texas Institute of Texan Cultures, 1995). They worked "from can't to can't," which meant their days started from before the sun was up and ended long after sunset—a work ethic typical of a hot group. One cowboy described loyalty to the group: "It was, just, 'I gotta nickel, you gotta nickel.'" This *collectivistic culture* of property and resources continued into task roles. One cowboy described an owner out looking for another hand named Bill; this cowboy told him, "You lookin' for Bill, you found him." Both the owner and the cowboy knew he was saying, "Whatever work Bill was supposed to do for you, I'm now Bill, I'll do it." Cowboys are an example of super-task peer groups that are both task and social, because they live together (such as Navy SEALS, astronauts, soldiers, firefighters).

What happens when the flame that fires a hot group fizzles? That extraordinary level of effort cannot be maintained. Hot groups wilt in cultures that require permanence.

Peer Groups as Decision Makers: Juries

Sooner or later, chances are that you will be asked to serve on a jury or someone you know will request a jury trial. Juries are a modern tradition; defendants were once subjected to trials by ordeal, dunkings, or fire. Jury experiences can be infuriating, however, as illustrated by this juror's description of the fifth day of deliberations:

> I screamed that I couldn't believe this was happening, that we were possibly going to be a hung jury when in my mind the case was so obvious. Everything was there, DNA evidence, witness testimony. There was no room for interpretation. I was angry. There were words of profanity that came out of my mouth (SunWolf, 2008, p. xi).

Uniquely, peers in juries do not select one another as members; they come involuntarily and are strangers to one another. These groups do their task in secret, behind closed doors. Juries have consulted a Ouija board to ask the victim who the murderer was, flipped a coin to decide between murder and manslaughter, complained of threats from one another, and tried to get some of their members removed by the judge (SunWolf, 2008).

If you end up being on a jury, how do you think the group should pick its leader? This question was asked of citizens called to jury duty at a local courthouse (SunWolf & Seibold, 1998). Almost half suggested selecting a foreperson on a voluntary or random basis—ignoring traits, skills, or experience. *Once selected, does the foreperson differ from his or her peers during deliberations?* While jurors are told that the foreperson just signs the verdict form and "presides" over deliberations, studies find the leader may get communication privileges in the discussion (such as one-fourth of the turns in 12-person juries, more than their fair share) (SunWolf, 2008).

The challenge of any jury is to successfully communicate with one another, yet jurors are given no instructions about how to do this. How should they start? How do you get a speaking turn? Jurors try taking straw votes, going in a circle, or opening discussions as a free-for-all, where people struggle to speak at the same time or are ignored (SunWolf, 2007). The structuring of who talks and for how long, when voting occurs, and how to resolve conflict must be resolved by the group. Some jurors become peers in name only (*nominal* peers), as dominant personalities seize more turns. A jury may have to cope with *task loafers, silent members,* or *slackers,* along with *turn-hoggers.* (If you've been assigned to do a group class project, you know what this can be like.)

It turns out that jurors become storytellers during deliberation. When the court in Arizona allowed the filming of four jury trials, a study of their deliberations revealed that jurors created stories to help them talk about the evidence. Figure 1 shows the seven story types that showed up.

Jurors engaged in what is known as *counterfactual thinking,* in an attempt to resolve their anticipated anxiety about the right verdict (SunWolf, 2006, 2010a, 2010b). Counterfactual thinking occurs when we imagine how a past event could have been different (if-only) or how a future event might turn out (what-if). You've done this thinking throughout your life: What if your grandparents had

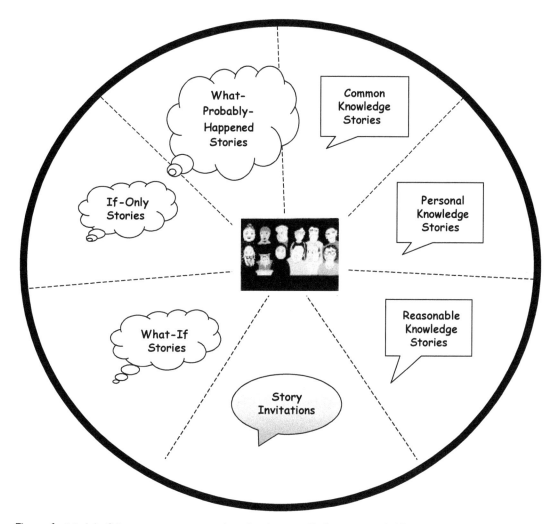

Figure 1. Model of the seven story types shared as jurors talk during jury deliberations. Cloud-shaped cut-outs represent imagined storytelling, box-shaped cut-outs represent *really-happened* storytelling. Reprinted from *Practical Jury Dynamics 2* with permission. Copyright 2007 Matthew Bender & Company, Inc. a part of LexisNexis. All rights reserved.

never met? What if you won a million dollars? What if you had spoken up? What if you chose a different college?

The most important decision any group of peers has to make might be when citizens are asked to serve as jurors on a death penalty trial. A study examining the way jurors talked in deciding between a life sentence and death in an Ohio trial showed how jurors engaging in storytelling (SunWolf, 2010b), for example:

- Now this is what I'm thinking. He always had something planned.

- Somebody who's been in prison for 25 years doesn't, cause my brother-in-law was in prison for 4 years.

- If I'm accused of killing somebody and I didn't feel in my heart I killed them, why would I apologize?

- If not for drugs, he might have made a better choice.

- Now why wasn't that damn door locked. And why didn't he get up and walk Mr. Watson to the door and lock him out?

Each citizen comes to jury duty with a decision-making style. You already have one. The group's challenge is to see how diverse decision-making styles come together. *What happens if the peers in a jury cannot agree on a verdict?* In criminal trials, a unanimous verdict is required, but the law anticipates that some trials will not produce jury agreement. Some jurors suffer from "deadlock phobia," becoming anxious when their peers do not agree. This can result in coercion within the group, as those in the majority pressure the others to change their votes. If you serve on a jury that cannot reach an agreed verdict, you can send a note to the judge asking for guidance.

After announcing a verdict, members of the jury sometimes experience *verdict regret.* A group verdict is more likely to be regretted by a juror when the consequences were public, the trial was lengthy, or when there was coercion and lack of respect for divergent opinions in deliberations. In the Michael Jackson trial (five months of testimony, seven days of deliberation, and a not guilty verdict), two jurors claimed that they regretted their verdicts (SunWolf, 2008), as one blamed threats from the foreperson:

> He said if I could not change my mind or go with the group that he would have to notify the bailiff, the bailiff would notify the judge, and the judge would have me removed (p. 133).

Peer pressure emerges in every group of peers. No one can entirely escape its power.

EPILOGUE: SURVIVING AND THRIVING IN A FOREST OF PEER GROUPS

Members of peer groups consider one another to be equals, without hierarchy or privilege. Theoretical lenses help us understand peer groups (the symbolic-interpretive perspective, social comparison theory, structuration theory, and decisional regret theory). Peer groups communicate their boundaries to outsiders and establish rules for inclusion. Some create rituals to establish identity, claim territory, eulogize members, and put down enemies. Members of hot groups give up individual goals for a fast-paced sustained commitment to task (that eventually fizzles). Juries are temporary decision-making groups of peers who begin as strangers—who tell stories, experience verdict regret, or reach deadlock.

Unless you are now (or have plans to be) a hermit or a lone dweller-on-mountaintops, peer groups will be a part of your life. We do not study peer groups because other people need to know about them.

The core, heart, sticky-gooey center of peer group research involves us. We need to understand the dynamics of these groups because we will be embedded in them for the rest of our lives. Peer groups watch our backs, lift our task burdens, applaud our successes, and commiserate with our losses. They help us practice how to be together.

If you want to go quickly, go alone.

If you want to go far, go with others.

—*African proverb*

REFERENCES

Buhs, E., & Ladd, G. W. (2001). Peer rejection as an antecedent of young children's school adjustment: An examination of mediating processes. *Developmental Psychology, 37,* 550–560.

Conquergood, D. (1994). Homeboys and hoods: Gangs and cultural space. In L. R. Frey (Ed.), *Group communication in context: Studies of natural groups* (pp. 23–52). Hillsdale, NJ: Lawrence Erlbaum.

Durham, P., & Jones, E. L. (1965). *The Negro cowboys.* Lincoln, NE: University of Nebraska Press.

Eisenberger, N. I., Lieberman, M. D., & Williams, K. D. (2003). Does rejection hurt? An fMRI study of social exclusion. *Science, 302,* 290–292.

Festinger, L. (1957). *A theory of cognitive dissonance.* Stanford, CA: Stanford University Press.

Frey, L. R., & SunWolf (2004). A symbolic-interpretive perspective on group dynamics. *Small Group Research, 35*(3), 277–306.

Frey, L. R., & SunWolf (2005). The symbolic-interpretive perspective on group life. In M. S. Poole & A. Hollingshead (Eds.), *Theories of small groups: Interdisciplinary perspectives* (pp. 185–239). Thousand Oaks, CA: Sage.

Katz, W. L. (1986). *Black Indians: A hidden heritage.* New York: Simon Pulse.

Leets, L., & SunWolf. (2005). Adolescent rules for social exclusion: When is it fair to exclude someone else? *Journal of Moral Education, 34*(3), 343–362.

Lipman-Blumen, J., & Leavitt, H. J. (1999). *Hot groups: Seeding them, feeding them, and using them to ignite your organization.* New York: Oxford University Press.

Miller, J. (2000). Gender dynamics in youth gangs: A comparison of males' and females' accounts. *Justice Quarterly, 17,* 419–448.

Padilla, F. (1992). *The gang as an American enterprise.* New Brunswick, NJ: Rutgers University Press.

Poole, M. S., Seibold, D. R., & McPhee, R. D. (1996). The structuration of group decisions. In R. Y. Hirokawa & M. S. Poole (Eds.), *Communication and group decision making* (2nd ed., pp. 114–146). Thousand Oaks, CA: Sage.

Quicker, J. (1983). *Homegirls: Characterizing Chicana gangs.* San Pedro, CA: International Universities Press.

SunWolf. (2006). Decisional regret theory: Reducing the anxiety about uncertain outcomes during group decision making through shared counterfactual storytelling. *Communication Studies, 57*(2), 1–29.

SunWolf (2007). *Practical Jury Dynamics2: From one juror's trial perceptions to the group's decision making processes.* Charlottesville, VA: LexisNexis Publishing.

SunWolf (2008). *Peer groups: Expanding or study of small group communication.* Thousand Oaks, CA: Sage.

SunWolf (2010a). Investigating jury deliberation in a capital murder case. *Small Group Research, 41*(4), 380–385.

SunWolf. (2010b). Counterfactual thinking in the jury room. *Small Group Research, 41*(4), 474–494.

SunWolf (2012). Understanding group dynamics using narrative methods. In A. B. Hollingshead, & M. S. Poole (Eds.), *Research methods for studying groups and teams: A guide to approaches, tools, and technologies* (pp. 235–259). New York: Routledge.

SunWolf, & Leets, L. (2003). Communication paralysis during peer group exclusion: Social dynamics that prevent children and adolescents from expressing disagreement. *Journal of Language and Social Psychology, 22,* 355–384.

SunWolf, & Leets, L. (2004). Being left out: Rejecting outsiders and communicating group boundaries in childhood and adolescent peer groups. *Journal of Applied Communication Research, 32*(3), 195–223.

SunWolf, & Seibold, D. R. (1998). Jurors' intuitive rules for deliberation: A structurational approach to the study of communication in jury decision making. *Communication Monographs, 65,* 282–307.

University of Texas Institute of Texan Cultures at San Antonio (Video Producers). (1995). *Workin' from can't to can't: African-American cowboys in Texas.* San Antonio, TX: The Institute of Texan Cultures.

Wood, J. J., Cowan, P. A., & Baker, B. L. (2002). Behavior problems and peer rejection in preschool boys and girls. *Journal of Genetic Psychology, 163,* 72–89.

WHAT EFFECTS DO COACHES' COMMUNICATIVE MESSAGES HAVE ON THEIR ATHLETES/TEAM?

PAUL D. TURMAN, SOUTH DAKOTA BOARD OF REGENTS

It is not uncommon for people to assume that being a talented athlete will translate easily to being a successful coach. If you know how to play, you should be able to teach the game, right? Unfortunately, history has shown that being a "Hall of Fame" caliber player does not always correlate with the ability to coach. Focus your attention for a minute on just the National Basketball Association (NBA). For every Larry Bird (who coached the Indiana Pacers to the NBA finals), there are numerous star players who have struggled to achieve NBA coaching success. Can you recall the coaching feats of Isaiah Thomas, Irving Johnson, or even Michael Jordan? While their exploits as players may be widely known, their experience as coaches was short-lived. The inverse can also be true. Can you highlight the playing careers of great coaches like Phil Jackson, Red Auerbach, or Larry Brown? While there are a number of talented players who have made the transition into coaching, sometimes the most prominent coaching figures are those individuals who embrace a stronger understanding of what it takes to work with and connect with athletes. Just as effective teaching has more to do with only showing students what to do, coaching requires a set of soft-skills with a much stronger emphasis on communication than one would think. The capacities to shape team goals, enhance athletic skill, and relate to players are essential attributes that can escape even the most talented athletes who seek to transition into the instructional side of sports after their playing days are over.

It is important to note early in this chapter that the coach–athlete relationship is often challenged by the fact that winning is an important outcome in sports. For example, Vince Lombardi is often criticized for suggesting that "Winning isn't everything, it's the only thing." While many coaches might be unwilling to acknowledge the fact publicly, the outcome for every contest does matter. Scoreboards, "most valuable player" titles, and team/player rankings were created for this purpose, as we are predisposed to consider our achievements in relation to those around us. Ask high school coaches if winning matters when they arrive home after a loss to a collection of "For Sale" signs in their lawn. Pressure to achieve from supporters and boosters is higher than ever. So much so that Mondays during the NFL season have often been referred to as "Black Monday" because so many firings occur after losses on Sunday. In spite of his statement about winning early in his career, Lombardi was later quoted as saying, "I wish to hell I'd never said that damned thing (that winning is everything). What really counts is the effort (having a goal). That sure as hell doesn't mean for people to crush human values and morality" (Masin, 2007, p. 5). As coaches work to determine the best communicative approach for interacting with athletes, they face a number of choices in selecting the appropriate style or orientation to best lead their teams across a variety of contexts. This chapter seeks to provide you with an introductory look at what some of the research says about the impact coaches' communicative messages can have on their teams.

COACH COMMUNICATION STYLES

For those not familiar with the sport of wrestling, there is no coach more revered than Dan Gable. An undefeated high school wrestler, Gable went on to win three national NCAA championships (losing only one match his entire collegiate career in the finals as a senior), and then walked through the world competition without giving up a point to win the Olympic gold medal during the 1972 Munich games. With his wrestling career behind him, Gable began coaching the Hawkeye wrestling program at the University of Iowa, going on to develop one of the most accomplished sports dynasties in the history of collegiate sports. His teams won 21 consecutive Big 10 team titles and 15 NCAA championship titles (winning 9 consecutives team titles from 1978–86). During dual competition, his teams went 98–1 at home, and 29 of his wrestlers won individual titles (many of the multiple times), claiming 152 All-American trophies. Many of his athletes have gone on to fill the coaching ranks of current NCAA wrestling programs at institutions like Minnesota, Ohio State, Illinois, Indiana, and Wisconsin, as well as the current Iowa program. Gable coached the current Hawkeye team coach (Tom Brands) to three individual NCAA titles, as well as an Olympic gold medal. As the head coach at Iowa, Brands now has two NCAA titles under his belt, and when he talks about his experience with Gable, he emphasizes the authoritarian styles that Gable often employed. Brands recently noted "(Gable) ran some guys out of town. He was a hard guy to wrestle for. You had to be tough to wrestle for him" (Hamilton, 2011, p. 7).

The above narrative about Gable is used as a lead into our discussion about coach communication styles, because it emphasizes the impact that a coach with the right style can have on his or her athletes. The Multidimensional Leadership Theory (MLT) proposed by Chelladurai and Saleh (1978) operationalizes effective sport leadership by examining the way coaches understand member characteristics (e.g., the athlete's need for achievement or affiliation in the sport), situational characteristics (e.g., the size of the team and the amount of formal structure involved in the sport, task), and the required leader behavior. To examine how coaches utilized these three variables in determining appropriate coaching behaviors, five sets of coaching styles have been proposed. These styles include (a) *autocratic behaviors,* or the extent to which coaches create a separation among athletes by establishing their position and authority over the team; (b) *democratic behaviors* utilized by coaches to foster participation by the athletes when making decisions related to the sport; (c) *social support* to satisfy interpersonal needs of the athletes; (d) displays of *positive feedback* to motivate athletes and demonstrate appreciation; and (e) *training and instruction* to foster the development of athletes' skill and knowledge aimed at improving performance in the sport.

MLT is premised on an assumption that a coach must be cognizant of the leadership preferences of his or her athletes, as well as understanding their maturity level, in order to adjust the leadership style that is most appropriate for the time. Overall, a number of team and athlete characteristics have been found to influence preferences for coaching styles, with collegiate and professional athletes preferring more autocratic behaviors, youth and high school athletes preferring training and instruction, and athletes with limited performance expectations having a stronger preference for positive feedback. Others have concluded that teams with high cohesion were likely to perceive their coaches as using relatively elevated levels of training and instruction.

Studies have found that, when collapsing four of the five styles (democratic, training and instruction, social support, and positive feedback) into one general pro-social style, this type of behavior is positively associated with athletes' ability to positively acquire sport knowledge (Turman & Schrodt, 2004). Contrary to pro-social behaviors enacted by coaches, an autocratic leadership style (e.g., antisocial or custodial behaviors enacted by coaches) is inversely correlated with athletes' affective learning, suggesting that coaches who rely solely on autocratic leadership behaviors may find their athletes demonstrating less appreciation for the sport, their teammates, and, most importantly, their coach. Even when accounting for success, it has been found that autocratic leadership in the presence of moderate to high levels of positive feedback may actually increase an athletes' developmental learning, whereas the sole use of autocratic leadership behaviors may lead to a decline. This tends to support "traditional," anecdotal notions that effective coaching is inherently a form of "tough love." In other words, coaches can enact autocratic leadership as long as athletes know that their coaches have their best interests in mind and can occasionally communicate some form of positive feedback. At the very least, coaches who rely solely on the use of autocratic leadership may find that the deleterious effects of such behavior greatly outweigh athletes' need for positive feedback.

This brings us back to the example about Dan Gable that was used at the beginning of this section. The above quote given by Tom Brands (about his former coach) reinforced the authoritative style that Gable used with his wrestlers. Yet, consistent with the research on coach communication styles, Gable tended to embody an uncanny ability to use varying styles depending on which approach he felt would work best with his wrestlers. After a series of in-depth interviews with three of Gable's most prolific wrestlers, Hamilton (2011) noted that:

> There are dozens of other stories, but the one these three tell describe Gable as a man who was overtly demanding yet compassionate, a coach who had the elasticity to serve the individual needs of his roster without sacrificing the standards of the team, a leader who could see the brightest characteristics in his athletes during the darkest times. Gable's best trait may have been his uncanny ability to push the right motivational button. He knew who needed a pat on the back and who could handle a kick in the pants. (pp. 7—8).

Although it is difficult to attribute the overall success of the teams Gable produced solely on his coaching style, the heightened need for positive feedback at the right time from coaches is one of the central premises set forth by those involved in a new approach to coaching referred to as the positive coaching movement.

CONSTRUCTIVE COACH COMMUNICATION

In the opening section of this chapter, we discussed the constant tension that coaches face because of the importance our society places on winning. Recognizing this tension, a group of coaches from varying sports throughout the United States have joined together to form the *Positive Coaching Alliance.* The mission of this organization is to engage coaches to encourage athletes to enjoy sports as a positive character-building experience. This movement has been geared toward youth sport organizations, but the efforts of this organization carry over into both the collegiate and professional levels. Phil Jackson, head coach of the Los Angeles Lakers and coach of 10 NBA championship teams, has been an avid supporter of the program since its inception in 1998. He affirms that his coaching philosophy centers around the ability to use positive feedback with his players by ensuring that approximately 75% of his comments to players focus on positive rather than negative statements and messages.

When coaches draw upon punitive actions to influence their athletes, they invite stress; yet positive feedback and reinforcement strategies have been found to have a greater impact on athletes' optimal performance, satisfaction levels, enjoyment, and self-esteem. Coaches' positive orientation toward players also has an impact on the self-fulfilling prophecies for their players. A self-fulfilling prophecy occurs in sports when coaches view athletes differently (based on gender, ability, level of enthusiasm) and provide differential treatment. Soloman, DiMarco, Ohlson, and Reece (1998) state, "When coaches' perceptions of an athlete are consistently communicated and understood by the athlete they can impact the athlete's future performance and psychological growth in a positive or negative manner" (p. 445). Coaches have an uncanny ability to use the way they communicate with athletes to help establish winning as a self-fulfilling prophecy. To emphasize this point, another story about Dan Gable is warranted. Although Gable produced numerous three and four time individual NCAA national champions, one individual champion stands out as a testament to his skill as a coach. In 1997, Gable made a bold prediction that Jesse Whitmer was destined to become Iowa's next NCAA champion, a statement that he reiterated at every possible opportunity throughout the season. With the success that Gable had produced up to this time, it might not seem bold that he would accurately predict that one of his wrestlers would go on to win a national title. However, Whitmer was a fifth-year senior who had failed to ever crack the varsity lineup in Iowa, and was not ranked among the top 10 wrestlers at his weight in the country. After losing 18–7 to the topped ranked wrestler early in the season, Whitmer noted that "Instead of pointing out all the things I did wrong in the match, he pointed out everything I did right and what we learned from the match in a positive light. . . By the time he got done talking, you would've thought I won" (Hamilton, 2011, p. 9). Whitmer went on to win the national championship that year, easily defeating the topped ranked contender during his quarterfinals match.

CONTEXT AND COACHING MESSAGES

As noted from the example above, coach-athlete interaction can occur in a variety of contexts (i.e., informal coaching sessions, during practice, halftime, etc.), giving coaches a range of options for communicating with athletes. The type of performance feedback offered by Gable to Whitmer served as an important feature of any instructional process whereby coaches are afforded the opportunity to provide an assessment of athletes' overall performance in a way that best suits their goals. As the positive coaching movement might attest, the messages coaches select to frame their feedback can directly influence the attributions athletes make about their athletic experience. For example, a coach's decision to place the blame on the team's star athlete after a loss is quite different from one who might choose to encourage the player who missed the final shot that marked the end of the season. The coach may also place the blame on him- or herself or even make a point to build up players who have been struggling by using the pregame speech to challenge them to perform beyond their means. Gallmeier (1987) followed a professional hockey team throughout the season and noted that the coach relied upon the pregame speech to "psych up" players, especially in situations where the coach didn't have access to the players throughout the day. Players exposed to these speeches were found to have higher levels of self-efficacy and larger margins of victory. Not only are athlete outcomes influenced, they self-report that the pregame speech is an important function that the coach fulfills for the team, with most athletes noting a strong desire for an emotional response from their coach.

The messages coaches select can be powerful predictors for how athletes view their athletic experiences, and most individuals are predisposed to interpret behaviors, actions, and events that occur around them in connection with their causes. People have an innate need to find an explanation for "why" an event occurred, which allows us to better control our surroundings, and when one is unable to understand the reason why, the world is rendered unpredictable. The messages that coaches employ during these competitive situations have also been found to produce feelings of regret as athletes are challenged to reflect upon what could have or should have happened. *Regret* is defined as a complex emotion causing individuals to make judgments about events they take part in, and they have the ability to feel regretful not only about their participation in past experiences but also about how decisions concerning future events are made.

The need to use messages that connect antecedents and outcomes is likely to increase as individuals or groups are faced with winning and losing situations. For instance, Turman (2005, 2007) identified six types of regret messages used by coaches during their pregame, halftime, and postgame speeches. The most predominant was *accountability regret,* which represented coaches' need to assign blame or praise following their team's first-half performance. By focusing their players' attention on factors that reduced the team's ability to win, coaches were able to implicitly demonstrate that if these antecedents were addressed by the team, a more positive outcome would result at the end of the contest ("If we just would have gone for it on fourth down, we could have won the game"). *Individual performance regret* messages were used to help magnify the potential self-regret felt by athletes after a poor performance/outcome. A majority of these messages occurred during the coaches' pregame comments to the team and included a combination of counterfactual antecedents (e.g., "If you play hard") and upward counterfactual outcomes (e.g.,

"You will feel satisfied"). Thirdly, *collective failure regret* signified messages that demonstrated how athlete performance was potentially linked to the disappointment of their teammates or coach ("If you don't give 100% on every play, you will be letting this team down"). *Social significance regret* was derived from the coaches' efforts to construct the game as socially significant for their players. For instance, as the season drew to a close, a number of coaches began to call attention to the fact that athletes in their senior year were drawing closer to their final game or to direct their athletes' attention toward the significance of the upcoming event for both the team and their school ("Letting them come in here and push you around isn't something our fans will accept"). Fifth, coaches relied on *regret reduction* primarily during the postgame interaction; it characterized coaches' attempts to reduce the potential regret felt by athletes after a loss ("If we hadn't tried for that long pass, we still would have lost the game"). Finally, as the season drew to a close, a number of coaches relied on regret messages that described the *future regret* players would experience as a result of a team loss. It appeared that coaches used this foreshadowing of events and the potential emotional response athletes would feel afterward to identify antecedents that athletes could employ to control their future outcome ("Lose this game and you'll take it to the grave").

CONCLUSION

This chapter has attempted to explore how coaches' communicative messages affect their athletes and teams. The rhetorical and communicative resources that a coach draws upon determine not only a team's success but also how athletes view and interpret their sport experience. Having a coach who emphasizes a positive orientation toward coaching could be important for young athletes who are seeking an enjoyable experience from their sport participation. On the other hand, collegiate or professional athletes are more inclined to have coaches who draw upon the authority of their position to ensure the highest levels of success. This does not mean that coaches have to take a punitive approach to obtain the desired response from their athletes, as even professional coaches must understand the emotional turmoil that athletes can experience in the "just business" model for professional and collegiate athletics. Although he is often vilified by the media for his antics during games and his harsh treatment of players, Bob Knight (former NCAA basketball coach who currently holds the all-time record for most career wins in NCAA men's basketball) is often described by his former players in affectionate terms. His autocratic behavior was a function of the competitive nature of NCAA basketball, but he also possessed skills for teaching the fundamentals of the sport while producing some of the highest player graduation rates in the nation. Developing a suitable balance in one's communication style is what marks the difference between coaches who effectively foster positive relationships with their athletes and those who don't.

REFERENCES

Chelladurai, P., & Saleh, S. D. (1978). Preferred leadership in sports. *Canadian Journal of Applied Sport Science, 3,* 85–92.

Gallmeier, C. P. (1987). Putting on the game face: The staging of emotions in professional hockey. *Sociology of Sport Journal, 4,* 347–362.

Hamilton, A. (2011, August). Dan Gable: Hall of famer is retired now, but he's left a lasting legacy as one of the best wrestlers and coaches in history. *USA Wrestling, 39*(5), 6–9.

Masin, H. L. (2007, September) Remember the "only thing"? *Coach & Athletic Director,* p. 5.

Soloman, G. B., DiMarco, A. M., Ohlson, C. J., & Reece, S. D. (1998). Expectations and coaching experience: Is more better? *Journal of Sport Behavior, 21,* 444–455.

Turman, P. D. (2005). Coaches' use of anticipatory and counterfactual regret messages during competition. *Journal of Applied Communication Research, 33,* 116–138.

Turman, P. (2007). Coach regret messages: The influence of athlete sex, context, and performance on high school basketball coaches' use of regret messages during competition. *Communication Education, 56,* 333–353.

Turman, P., & Schrodt, P. (2004). Coaching as an instructional communication context: Relationships among coaches' leadership behaviors and athletes' affective learning. *Communication Research Reports, 21,* 130–143.

MAKING BETTER DECISIONS IN SMALL GROUPS

DENNIS S. GOURAN, THE PENNSYLVANIA STATE UNIVERSITY

If you were to ask an acquaintance, "When is the last time you were part of a group that set out to make a bad decision?" my guess is that, after displaying a perplexed look, the person would say something like, "Why, never, of course. What group would?" On the other hand, if the question had been, "When is the last time you were in a group that made a bad decision?" I would not be surprised to hear you report a response along the lines of, "Last week, as a matter of fact." This duality raises an interesting anomaly concerning human behavior in groups. Although we want to make good decisions, we often do not. Why? Clearly, having the right motivation, while important, is not enough to achieve the desired outcome.

For most of my career, I have been pursuing an interest in how communication contributes to the performance of decision-making and problem-solving groups. As has been the case with many others who write about these processes, much of my attention has been drawn to determining why such groups frequently have so much difficulty in arriving at appropriate choices despite the desire their members have to do so (see Bazerman & Moore, 2009, for an interesting discussion of the frequent disconnect between our intentions and choice-making practices).

Much of what I have published relates to a perspective on communication in groups that my frequent co-author, Randy Hirokawa, and I have been developing since the early 1980s and that we call "The Functional Theory of Communication in Decision-Making and Problem-Solving Groups" (see Gouran & Hirokawa, 1996, 2003). It is not my intention in this document, however, to attempt a reconstruction of the theory or to provide a comprehensive overview of all of the work that has gone into the origination, evolution, and products of the theory. That would be far beyond the scope of this volume, not to mention the specific charge the editors gave to all of the contributors. Rather, my focus in this fairly abbreviated discussion is on what is the basis of groups' frequent difficulties in achieving decisional outcomes that are commensurate with their members' aspirations, as well as how some of the insights to which work relating to it and in allied areas of study (see Gouran, 2012) can contribute to better performance. Specifically, I address the following question: How can we improve decision making and problem solving in groups? (Note that I refer throughout to both decision making and problem solving in groups. Although there are conceptual differences in the two, for the most part, what applies to one also applies to the other.) To appreciate the answer to the question I have posed, however, it is helpful if one first has a grasp of some of the principal reasons for the often demonstrated lack of success in group decision-making and problem-solving activity. In this overview, I consider the misunderstanding of task requirements, restricted awareness of the influence of cognitive and social constraints on choice, and deficiencies in leadership. Following that, I introduce and discuss several measures for producing better outcomes, including: (1) developing an understanding of task requirements and the functions of communication in fulfilling them; (2) identifying objectives, necessary resources, and procedures at the outset; (3) recognizing and appreciating the importance of the role of reminders; and (4) cultivating respect for procedural champions.

REASONS FOR LACK OF SUCCESS IN GROUP DECISION-MAKING

Misunderstanding of Task Requirements

In his book, *Crucial Decisions: Leadership in Policymaking and Crisis Management,* Irving Janis (1989) observes that decision makers frequently arrive at choices of questionable merit as a result of relative inattention to the issue(s) they need to resolve to make genuinely informed choices (see also, Hirokawa & Rost, 1992). I often am witness to this phenomenon in an introductory performance-based course involving group decision making and problem solving that I regularly teach. For instance, it is not uncommon in a group discussing a question such as, "How can we best address the problem of climate change?" for some member to begin almost immediately talking about solutions with virtually no attention to what precisely the problem is. To attempt to solve a problem before one has clearly established what it is makes little sense on logical grounds, of course, but this is precisely how the members of many groups initiate the discussion of a decision-making or problem-solving task.

It should be obvious, one would think, that if the members of a group do not understand the requirements of the task they are attempting to perform, the chances of their making a sound decision are not very promising. The tendency that I have just noted is the product of what increasing numbers of those interested in human judgment refer to as "System I Thinking" (see, for instance, Bazerman & Moore, 2009, p. 3; Kahneman, 2011, p. 13). According to Bazerman and Moore (2009), this type of thinking refers to "our intuitive system, which is typically fast, automatic, effortless, implicit, and emotional" (p. 3). Such thinking is also characteristic of extroverts, who interestingly often find themselves in positions of leadership because others take their outspokenness as signs of their knowing what to do and as being more effective in directing the actions of a group than their more introverted counterparts (Cain, 2012). Personality differences and the question of whether or not extroverts are more given than introverts to "System

I Thinking" aside, the fact is that far too many members of groups neglect to determine that they have a correct understanding of what it is they are supposed to be accomplishing, with the unfortunate consequence of wasting time or making decisions and generating solutions to problems that are either unwarranted or that go well beyond what they are responsible for doing.

Restricted Awareness of Cognitive and Social Constraints on Choice

In addition to the impact that deficient understandings of task requirements can have on choice making among the members of groups, there are influences stemming from the cognitive and social constraints to which all are susceptible in some degree (see Bazerman & Moore, 2009). Irving Janis (1989) assigned the labels of "cognitive," "affiliative," and "egocentric" to the three with which I deal here, and which Professor Hirokawa and I examine in much greater detail in publications relating specifically to our theory (see Gouran & Hirokawa, 1996, 2003, 2005). Cognitive constraints arise when the members of groups feel pressured to produce but when they also see themselves limited by a lack of time, knowledge, or other pertinent resources. Affiliative constraints may be operative when the members of groups find themselves being more concerned about maintaining a positive climate than making the best decisions. Egocentric constraints have to do with the needs for control that can drive the interaction in a decision-making or problem-solving group.

The presence of any of the three categories of constraints can increase the likelihood of the members of a group taking mental shortcuts known as "heuristics" that may contribute to less than sound judgments. For example, a group that feels it has little time to act might overreact and seize on the first decision option that is intuitively appealing and that appears on its face to be a good solution to a problem rather than exert effort to examine its merits carefully. Group endorsement is all that is necessary for choice. Susan Cain (2012) refers to this as the "New Groupthink" (p. 71). As another illustration, a group member concerned about poor relations could acquiesce in a decision that is ill-advised on the grounds that decisions reached in harmony are probably better than ones that have elicited disagreement. Finally, a group member with high needs for control could easily overestimate the value of the choice option he or she favors and conclude that it is sound because no one has challenged it even though, if the truth be known, the reason is that no one has had the nerve to do so.

A reliance on heuristics does not always lead to poor outcomes (Kahneman, 2011). It is the exclusive reliance on them about which decision makers need to be worried because they so frequently function at levels beneath normal thresholds of critical thinking. For instance, a person might lean in the direction of endorsing a particular decision option without appreciating the extent to which he or she is doing that largely because a strong proponent seems to be so obviously convinced. "After all," the person says to him or herself, "Could anyone be that strongly committed if there were not some merit to the stance she [he] is taking?" Such surmises, when unaccompanied by other data and careful analysis, do not augur well for the prospects of a group's making even a defensible choice, let alone the best possible one.

Deficiencies in Leadership

The third and final in my list of reasons why decision-making groups and problem-solving groups perform at suboptimal levels, or perhaps not even that well in many instances, is that they suffer from a variety of deficiencies in leadership. Mind you, leadership is possibly the most written about subject in the social sciences (see Bass, 2008 if you doubt the veracity of this claim). Consequently, what I am able to say about the subject constitutes even less than the proverbial "scratching of the surface" of the enormous literature relating to the subject that exists. Nevertheless, I hope that what little I am able to address will help you to understand why I have identified deficiencies in leadership as one of the "principal reasons" for why the members of decision-making and problem-solving groups so easily can fall short of what they presumably are capable of achieving more frequently than they or we would hope. I say "we" because the choices decision-making and problem-solving groups make typically affect the well-being of more people than simply their members, and we "others" should be concerned about that.

We tend to equate leadership with the individual who has been designated to serve as the leader of a decision-making or a problem-solving group. However, there is nothing in the mere act of designation that provides assurance that the designate will function in ways that enhance the prospects for choice making of high quality. There is a substantial body of work suggesting either directly or indirectly that such a likelihood is often the result of the presence of one or more members who have qualities that enable them to make clear to the other members what the requirements of their task entail, along with keeping them actively engaged in satisfying those requirements and doing whatever is necessary to develop the sort of climate that promotes strong commitments to make choices that have desired consequences (see Bass, 2008).

Peter Northouse (2013) defines leadership as "a process whereby an individual influences a group of individuals to achieve a common goal" (p. 5). Warren Bennis (2007) adds, "[L]eadership exists only with the consensus of followers" (p. 3). Some individuals seem to be more adept in achieving such consensus than others. However, many of those who find themselves in positions of leadership do not appear to be aware of the importance of such consensus and instead attempt to impose their views, if not their will, on others. Under these conditions, if there is no one equipped to counteract this type of unhealthy influence, or who is willing to step forward in an attempt to do so, poor rather than good choices are the probable outcome (see Gouran, 2003b). In my experience, it is more often the case that the problem resides in the reluctance of other members to take the risk of offending the designated leader than in their lack of capability to do what is necessary to move the group in the right directions. This can be very unfortunate for all concerned.

Effective leaders of decision-making and problem-solving groups seem to be more successful in keeping the members focused on the fulfillment of their fundamental task requirements when they possess personal qualities of the types that Steven Zaccaro (2007) has catalogued. These include, among other attributes, "cognitive complexity, cognitive flexibility, metacognitive skills, social intelligence, emotional intelligence, adaptability, openness, and tolerance for ambiguity" (p. 10). They also appear to have considerable interpersonal adeptness, or what Robert Katz (1955) calls "Human Skills" and Michael Mumford, Stephen Zaccaro, Francis Harding, Owen Jacobs, and Edwin Fleishman (2000) refer to as "Social Judgment Skills," when it comes to stressing the importance of staying on task without being offensive. Robert House (1996) sees the ability to read levels of motivation, as well as what may be limiting it, and skill in adjusting one's style accordingly, as the key to maximizing successful performance. Those lacking such qualities have considerably greater difficulty striking a responsive chord among the members of decision-making and problem-solving groups

MEASURES FOR PRODUCING BETTER OUTCOMES

Developing an Understanding of Task Requirements and the Functions of Communication in Fulfilling Them

A source of inspiration for the development of The Functional Theory of Communication in Decision-Making and Problem-Solving Groups was the eminent American philosopher John Dewey (1910) and his identification of what came to be known as the "Method of Reflective Thinking." Dewey was interested in what habits of mind distinguish those who succeed in solving complex problems from those who do not, or who experience great difficulty in the process. His inquiries led to the formation of a model that portrays a rational systematic sequence of activity that has spawned versions that one can find in various forms in economics, management, psychology, and communication (see, for example, Bazerman & Moore, 2009, pp. 2–3; Gouran, 2012; Janis & Mann, 1977, p. 11). In the most current version of Functional Theory, one finds a Dewey-based representation of the requirements that a decision-making or problem-solving group, when dealing with a complex issue, needs to satisfy if it is to have much chance of making the most appropriate choices. The formulation is as follows. Effective group decision making and problem solving are more likely when participants:

> (a) show a correct understanding of the issues to be resolved, (b) determine the minimal characteristics any acceptable alternative must possess, (c) identify a relevant and realistic set of alternatives, (d) examine carefully the alternatives in relationship to each previously agreed-upon characteristic of an acceptable choice, and (e) select the alternative that analysis reveals to be most like to have the desired characteristics. (Gouran & Hirokawa, 2003, p. 29)

This formulation resonates with what Bazerman and Moore (2009), among others refer to as "System II Thinking," which, in comparison to "System I Thinking," is "slower, conscious, effortful, explicit, and logical" (Kahneman, 2003, p. 3). It is also applicable to any of the four types of questions (Gouran & Hirokawa, 2003) the members of a decision-making or problem-solving group may find themselves addressing, namely questions of fact (which concern the determination of what is true), conjecture (or what is probable), value (what is acceptable or defensible—usually in a moral sense), and policy (what actions should be taken).

Given this general set of requirements and the types of questions to which it applies, it is fairly easy to see that the functions of communication in decision-making and problem-solving groups are to ensure that the members adequately fulfill the requirements, regardless of the matter under consideration. Those having this understanding are at an advantage relative to those who do not seem to know what is necessary for achieving success in group decision-making and problem-solving activity or who are prone to approach their tasks in an intuitive or possibly haphazard manner.

Identifying Objectives, Necessary Resources, and Procedures at the Outset

In addition to developing the sort of understanding the preceding section emphasizes, the members of decision-making and problem-solving groups can do a better job of choosing appropriately with a little forethought concerning what precisely they seek to achieve, what it will take in the way of resources to succeed, and how they are best advised to go about their task. One cannot simply assume that those comprising a group, merely by virtue of membership, somehow have a firm grasp on their responsibilities and how they should behave. Rather than operate from such an assumption, even in groups having a history of collaboration, it is probably wise to confirm that everyone taking part understands what it is the group is to accomplish, what the task requires of the members, and how they should go about performing it. There is a moderate correlation between the quality of procedures a decision-making group employs and the outcomes it achieves (Gouran & Hirokawa, 2005; Herek, Janis, & Huth, 1987). Paying attention in advance to such matters, as Seibold and Krikorian (1997) have observed, can have positive payoffs, if not necessarily in respect to the quality of choices, at least in respect to efficiency in respect to arriving at them. There is evidence from different venues suggesting that taking care to impose structure in advance of the actual undertaking of a task can be especially useful when a group has not achieved a very high level of maturity or development (see Hersey & Blanchard, 1993).

Recognizing and Appreciating the Importance of the Role of Reminders

Despite the value of understanding requirements and advanced planning measures, one cannot rely exclusively on them for keeping a group on track. This recognition led me some years ago to begin viewing leadership in decision-making and problem-solving groups as a form of corrective action that I began referring to as "counteractive influence" (see Gouran, 1982, 2003b). This form of influence consists of communicative acts that serve to restore movement to a group's goal path under conditions in which members are straying from it. Such interventions can become necessary in substantive, relational, and procedural spheres. However, it is the procedural domain that digressions from the goal path are often most apparent, but ironically resistant to restoration.

Regardless of the type of digression from the goal path, one form of counteractive influence that seems to be useful is reminding group members of their roles and responsibilities when they are behaving in ways that are not in line with expectations and prior understandings. This "procedural enactment" (see Gouran, 2003a) that reminding represents is a corrective for which there is some impressive research evidence in a study of decision-making groups including members trained to engage in such behavior. When they had such members, digressive tendencies were much less pronounced (Schultz, Ketrow, & Urban, 1995). In comparison to groups lacking such individuals, the groups with those enacting the role of reminders also functioned more effectively—in fact, at a qualitatively superior level.

I have observed similar outcomes in decision-making and problem-solving groups in which particular individuals having no designated responsibility simply took it upon themselves to function as reminders. Sometimes, they did this diplomatically (e.g., "I think that we may be a little off point here"). On other occasions, they were blunt (e.g., "We are supposed to be assessing probable impact of the decision option, not our personal likes and dislikes"). I find it interesting that both types of behavior, that is, indirect or oblique and direct, can have the same consequence—getting members to return to doing what they are supposed to be doing.

Cultivating Respect for Procedural Champions

Marshall Scott Poole (1991) has observed that we are frequently averse to following procedures for a variety of reasons, but primarily because we consider them sources of interference or hindrances to the performance of tasks. In my membership as a Faculty Senator in the institution where I reside, I have heard such disparaging remarks concerning procedures as, "I have no patience with those who are caught up in 'parliamentary niceties,'" and, "We're letting procedures keep us from doing what we know is right." The fact is, however, that following sound procedures increases rather than diminishes the likelihood of group members' exercising good judgment and making sound choices. Overcoming the negative perceptions and inappropriate attendant behavior, in Poole's view, requires the presence of "procedural champions," that is, participants who commit themselves to systematic ways of examining issues and who are willing to insist on conformity in decision-making and problem-solving groups to agreed-upon approaches to the performance of their tasks. I agree with Professor Poole. Rather than being critical of and irritated by these sorts of group members, we should applaud their willingness to enact the roles and keep the rest of us from making serious errors in judgment and potentially costly choices.

CONCLUSION

In this brief overview relating to the study of decision making and problem solving in groups in which I have been engaged throughout my professional career, I have attempted to isolate three reasons why such groups often fail to perform well. Specifically, (1) members are not fully cognizant of the requirements of their tasks, (2) they are also often unaware of the impact the various forms of cognitive and social constraints are exerting on their judgment and their actions, and (3) they suffer from deficiencies in leadership. I have also identified measures that can help members of decision-making and problem-solving groups improve their performance. These include (1) developing an understanding of task requirements and the functions communication serves in their fulfillment, (2) identifying objectives, necessary resources, procedures to be followed in the performance of a decision-making or problem-solving task at the outset, (3) recognizing and appreciating the importance of the role of reminders, and (4) cultivating respect for procedural champions. Such measures will not guarantee success, but I hope that I have made clear why and how they can be of help.

REFERENCES

Bass, B. M. (2008). *The Bass handbook of leadership: Theory, research, and managerial applications* (4th ed.). New York: Free Press.

Bazerman, M. H., & Moore, D. A. (2009). *Judgment in managerial decision making* (7th ed.). Hoboken, NJ: John Wiley & Sons.

Bennis, W. (2007). The challenges of leadership in the modern world. *American Psychologist, 62,* 2–5.

Cain, S. (2012). *Quiet: The power of introverts in a world that can't stop talking.* New York: Crown.

Dewey, J. (1910). *How we think.* Boston: Heath.

Gouran, D. S. (1982). *Making decisions in groups: Choices and consequences.* Glenview, IL: Scott, Foresman.

Gouran, D. S. (2003a). Communication skills for group decision making. In J. O. Greene, & B. R. Burleson (Eds.), *Handbook of communication and social interaction skills* (pp. 835–870). Mahwah, NJ: Lawrence Erlbaum.

Gouran, D. S. (2003b). Leadership as the art of counteractive influence in decision-making and problem-solving groups. In R. Y. Hirokawa, R. S. Cathcart, L. A. Samovar, & L. D. Henman (Eds.), *Small group communication theory and practice: An anthology* (8th ed., pp. 172–183). New York: Oxford University Press.

Gouran, D. S. (2010). Overcoming sources of irrationality that complicate working in decision-making groups. In S. Schuman (Ed.), *The handbook of working with difficult groups: How they are difficult, why they are difficult, and what you can do about it* (pp. 137–152, 379–381). San Francisco: Jossey-Bass.

Gouran, D. S. (2012). The heuristic value of work by significant figures in other disciplines relating to the role of communication in decision-making and problem-solving groups. *Review of Communication, 12,* 86–100.

Gouran, D. S., & Hirokawa, R. Y. (1996). Functional theory and communication in decision-making and problem-solving groups. In R. Y. Hirokawa, & M. S. Poole (Eds.), *Communication and group decision making* (2nd ed., pp. 55–80). Thousand Oaks, CA: Sage.

Gouran, D. S., & Hirokawa, R. Y (2003). Effective decision making and problem solving in groups. In R. Y. Hirokawa, R. S. Cathcart, L. A. Samovar, & L. D. Henman (Eds.), *Small group communication theory and practice: An anthology* (8th ed., pp. 27–38). New York: Oxford University Press.

Gouran, D. S., & Hirokawa, R. Y. (2005). Facilitating communication in group decision-making discussions. In S. Schuman (Ed.), *The IAF handbook of group facilitation* (pp. 351–360). San Francisco: Jossey-Bass.

Herek, G., Janis, I. L., & Huth, P. (1987). Decision making during international crises: Is quality of process related to outcome? *Journal of Conflict Resolution, 31,* 203–226.

Hersey, P., & Blanchard, K. H. (1993). *Management of organizational behavior: Using human resources* (6th ed.). Englewood Cliffs, NJ: Prentice Hall.

Hirokawa, R. Y., & Rost, K. M. (1992). Effective group decision making in organizations: Field test of the vigilant interaction theory. *Management Communication Quarterly, 5,* 267–288.

House, R. J. (1996). Path-goal theory of leadership: Lessons, legacy, and a reformulated theory. *Leadership Quarterly, 7,* 323–352.

Janis, I. L. (1989). *Crucial decisions: Leadership in policymaking and crisis management.* New York: Free Press.

Janis, I. L., & Mann, L. (1977). *Decision making: A psychological analysis of conflict, choice, & commitment.* New York: Free Press.

Kahneman, D. (1973). A perspective on judgment and choice: Mapping bounded rationality. *American Psychologist, 58,* 697–720.

Kahneman, D. (2011). *Thinking fast and slow.* New York: Farrar, Straus and Giroux.

Katz, R. L. (1955). Skills of an effective administrator. *Harvard Business Review, 33*(1), 33–42.

Mumford, M. D., Zaccaro, S. J., Harding, F. D., Jacobs, T. O., & Fleishman, E. A. (2000). Leadership skills for a changing world: Solving complex social problems. *Leadership Quarterly, 11,* 11–35.

Northouse, P. G. (2013). Introduction. In P. G. Northouse (Ed.), *Leadership: Theory and practice* (6th ed., pp. 1–17). Thousand Oaks, CA: Sage.

Poole, M. S. (1991). Procedures for managing meetings: Social and technological innovations. In R. A. Swenson, & B. O. Knapp (Eds.), *Innovative meeting management.* Austin, TX: 3M Meeting Management Institute.

Schultz, B., Ketrow, S. M., & Urban, D. M. (1995). Improving decision quality in the small group: The role of the reminder. *Small Group Research, 26,* 521–541.

Seibold, D. R., & Krikorian, D. H. (1997). Planning and facilitating group meetings. In L. R. Frey, & J. K. Barge (Eds.), *Managing group life: Communicating in decision-making groups* (pp. 270–305). Boston: Houghton Mifflin.

Zaccaro, S. J. (2007). Trait-based perspectives of leadership. *American Psychologist, 62,* 7–16.

SECTION 6
HEALTH COMMUNICATION

The health communication context focuses on how we interpret and talk about health-related information. As active consumers of healthcare, we decide on how we process health messages directed toward us and how we respond. Health communication scholars study communication that occurs in the healthcare context by examining such major areas of research as patient-caregiver communication, ethical considerations of healthcare delivery, patient compliance and satisfaction, illness identity, and health promotion campaigns. This chapter focuses on three important areas of health communication research: (1) strategic health communication, (2) drug use prevention, and (3) illness and patient role construction. First, Gary Kreps (George Mason University) discusses how health outcomes can be influenced by answering the question: *How can we use health communication inquiry to enhance health outcomes?* Second, Michelle Miller-Day (Chapman University) and Michael Hecht (Penn State University) explore their major drug prevention project and curriculum entitled Keepin' it REAL to answer: *How can we keep kids off drugs using communication?* Third, Lisa Keränen (University of Colorado Denver) and Jennifer Malkowski (University of Colorado Boulder) explore the rhetoric of health to answer: *What roles do science and medicine play in constructing our views on illness and our role as patients?* Our health is one of the most important things to cherish in our lives. Fortunately, healthy decisions and outcomes can be enhanced when the right communication frames people's decision-making. Health communication research provides us with many answers that can literally save thousands of lives (if people listen). We hope you consider the role that communication plays in your health or the health of your loved ones after reading these chapters.

STRATEGIC HEALTH COMMUNICATION AND HEALTH OUTCOMES

GARY L. KREPS, GEORGE MASON UNIVERSITY

This chapter examines the applications of the study of health communication to enhance the delivery of care and the promotion of health. There are many complex health promotion efforts that might benefit from better understanding and strategic use of health communication. However, good intentions, precedent, and expedience guide health care and health promotion efforts more often than strategic health communication knowledge. The complexity of achieving health goals, such as informing health behaviors and health-related decision making, demands strategic guidance from relevant health communication research and theory.

Health communication has developed as a rapidly growing and exciting applied area of inquiry that examines the powerful influences of human and mediated communication on health care and health promotion (Kreps & Bonaguro, 2009). Health communication inquiry is typically problem-based, focused on explicating, examining, and addressing important and troubling health care and health promotion issues. These issues often include difficulties in the following: promoting active coordination and collaboration in the delivery of health care, challenges to promoting adoption of recommended health behaviors, demands to reduce and ultimately eliminate inadvertent errors that jeopardize the quality of health care, attempts to meet unmet health information needs for supporting informed health decision making, and the quest to overcome serious inequities in care that lead to health disparities and poor health outcomes (Kreps, 2011a; Neuhauser & Kreps, 2010). These are serious issues that demand attention from health communication scholars to help refine health promotion activities and improve health outcomes! How can we use health communication inquiry to enhance health outcomes?

COMMUNICATION AND HEALTH OUTCOMES

The applied nature of health communication inquiry is firmly grounded in the implicitly accepted goal that by facilitating improvements in the delivery of care and the promotion of health, health communication scholars can ultimately help enhance health outcomes (Kreps & Maibach, 2008;

Parrott, 2008). Unfortunately, it appears that health care and health promotion practitioners have often been slow to recognize and adopt health communication knowledge to help them accomplish their complex health promotion goals. How often is health communication research used to guide the development, implementation, and evaluation of public health education and promotion programs? How often does health communication research guide health care delivery strategies for eliciting full diagnostic information, accomplishing informed consent, or promoting adherence with health care recommendations? Too often, the answer to these questions is that these programs and practices are not guided at all by health communication research. The complexity of achieving desired health communication goals, such as influencing entrenched health behaviors (e.g., smoking, nutrition, exercise, and safer sexual practices) and promoting informed health-related decision making, demands strategic guidance from relevant and rigorous research and theory.

A large and developing body of health communication research has already begun to powerfully illustrate the centrality of communication processes in achieving important health-care and health-promotion goals (Kreps, 2011a; Kreps & Bonaguro, 2009). Kreps and O'Hair (1995), for example, report a series of seminal studies illustrating the powerful influences of communication strategies and programs on health knowledge, behaviors, and outcomes. Research by Greenfield, Kaplan, and Ware (1985) clearly demonstrates the positive influences of increased patient/provider participation in directing health care treatment on achieving desired health outcomes. Kreps and Chapelsky Massimilla (2002) also report a number of studies that illustrate the positive effects of communication interventions on cancer-related health outcomes.

Communication research increasingly informs the development of public health policies and legislation, including policies to prevent and respond to serious health risks, to promote equity in health care, and to improve media coverage of important health issues (Atkin & Smith, 2010; Guttman, 2010; Kunkel, 2010; National Cancer Institute, 2008; Noar, Palmgreen, Chabot, Dobransky, & Zimmerman, 2009; Siu, 2010). Yet, there is so much more that can be done by health communication scholars to improve public health and wellness. While health communication scholarship has already made important contributions to improving health promotion, health communication inquiry has the potential to make even more important and wide-ranging contributions to improving public health.

ADDRESSING IMPORTANT HEALTH COMMUNICATION ISSUES

To really make a positive difference in health outcomes, health communication scholars must carefully identify and examine the critical issues confronting at-risk populations, health care providers, family caregivers, and others participating in the modern health care system and then design studies to address these important health problems. We need studies that will examine the key communication factors that influence these critical health issues. Major health issues in modern society are covered regularly by the popular media (radio, television, magazines, and newspapers), reported by independent agencies in major reports and news conferences (such as reports prepared by the Institute of Medicine), and studied by important federal health agencies like the National Institutes of Health and the Centers for Disease Control and Prevention. A sampling of these serious problems includes poor access to care, low quality of health care services provided for many consumers, medical errors in the delivery of care, inequities in health outcomes between privileged and less privileged populations, limited availability and access to relevant health information, lack of sensitivity in the delivery of care, ineffective health education and health promotion programs, poor consumer adherence with health recommendations, and failure to engage in recommended behaviors to help detect and avoid health risks. Health communication scholars should design studies to examine the communication factors that are related to these important public health issues.

Current evidence suggests that most, if not all, of these important health issues are directly related to the effectiveness of health communication. For example, some of the serious issues that threaten the delivery of high quality care have all been linked to the effectiveness of health communication. This includes the insidious recurrence of medical errors, the lack of consumer adherence with treatment recommendations, and poor levels of active consumer participation in health care decision-making (Greenfield, Kaplan, & Ware, 1985; Kreps & Bonaguro, 2009). Evidence suggests that these health care delivery issues are closely related to miscommunication and misinformation, lack of provider-consumer cooperation, and poor health information sharing (DiMatteo & Lepper, 1998; Kreps, Villagran, Zhao, McHorney, Ledford, Weathers, & Keefe, 2011). Similarly, serious disparities in health outcomes for poor, at-risk, vulnerable, and minority populations have also been related to the effectiveness of health communication. Evidence suggests that disparities in health outcomes are closely related to poor consumer access to relevant health information, lack of consumer understanding about prevention and treatment opportunities, and ineffective communication relationships between health care providers and consumers, as well as to mistrust and intercultural communication barriers within the modern health care system (Eysenbach & Kohnler, 2002; Kreps, 2006). Challenges with achieving health promotion goals have also been connected to the effectiveness of public health communication education, campaign, and intervention programs designed to influence health behaviors (Dutta-Bergman, 2005; Hornik, 2002; Kreps, 2011a, 2007). These are all critical communication issues that deserve close attention by health communication researchers. Ambitious health communication studies need to be designed to directly address the serious communication problems that limit the effectiveness of health care and health promotion. Such studies should focus on examining the critical communication processes at play in the delivery of care and promotion of health, while also examining the larger societal, institutional, and cultural communication influences on health and health care.

THE NEED TO CAREFULLY STUDY HEALTH COMMUNICATION ISSUES

To improve health care and health promotion, health communication scholars must take their work seriously and go the extra mile to translate health communication research into practice (Kreps, Viswanath, & Harris, 2002). Taking health communication scholarship seriously means not only asking important health communication research questions, but also conducting rigorous and far-reaching studies that generate valid, reliable, and generalizable data that can effectively inform health care and health promotion practices (Kreps, 2001; Kreps, 2011b). Serious health communication researchers take great care to meticulously design studies to accurately measure key health communication concepts, processes, and outcomes with both precision and depth. Serious health communication scholars work to actively translate and transform raw health communication research findings into practical and usable health care/promotion programs and policies. They carefully test the efficacy of interventions by monitoring the outcomes (both positive and negative outcomes) of implemented health communication programs within representative health care systems with at-risk populations.

To really make a difference, health communication scholars must provide important insights into the best practices for delivering health care and promoting health. Research must chronicle what works well and what is causing problems in the delivery of care and the promotion of health. The quality of research that health communication scholars conduct is directly related to the potential for this research to inform health policies and practices. Care must be taken to rigorously design and conduct health communication studies to generate the most accurate, valid, and revealing data to demystify the many complexities of health care and health promotion. New models and theories should be developed, tested, and refined to help describe and predict the intricate influences of communication within health systems. Innovative methods should be employed to study the complex communication processes that enable the effective delivery of care and the promotion of health.

ESTABLISHING RELEVANT PARTNERSHIPS

A major strategy for translating health communication inquiry into practice depends on developing meaningful interdisciplinary, inter-professional, and community-based partnerships with scholars, health care providers, consumers, administrators, government agency representatives, support organization members, and public policymakers. These collaborative partnerships are instrumental in helping health communication scholars effectively design, implement, and institutionalize the best evidence-based health communication strategies and interventions within society. It is clear that although health communication scholars have important expertise concerning the process of communication, they certainly do not have many of the answers needed about how health care systems work, how consumers behave, and how to influence institutional and public health policies. Establishing collaborations with key health care system partners can help provide the needed expertise and answers for addressing these important application issues effectively.

A good first step for developing meaningful health communication research partnerships is to establish research collaborations with scholars from other related disciplines, such as public health, health education, epidemiology, the social sciences, and health professional fields. For example, Kreps and Maibach (2008) make a strong case for the synergistic opportunities that can derive from collaborations between health communication and public health scholars, citing complementary, yet distinct, areas of expertise, theoretical grounding, methodological orientation, and intervention strategies. Major federal funding agencies have begun requesting grant applications from researchers that represent different, yet complementary, disciplines and research areas (Kreps, 2012). These funding agencies recognize the unique contributions, benefits, and insights that multidisciplinary research cooperation can provide.

Community-based collaborations are also critically important for supporting the applications of health communication research into practice. Good partners for increasing the applications of health communication knowledge include representatives from government agencies, health care delivery systems, non-profit associations, social service agencies, advocacy organizations, consumer groups, at-risk populations, and even corporations. It is only through these community-based collaborations that we can effectively translate compelling research findings into products, programs, policies, and practices that will be adopted within the modern health care system. Community partners have the embedded health system expertise that communication scholars desperately need to collaboratively introduce new health communication programs into health systems and help to refine these programs so they will work effectively over time.

Community participative research and intervention programs have shown great potential to facilitate applications of research results into health care practices (Minkler, 2000; Minkler & Wallerstein, 2002). Community partners can help health communication scholars learn the best inside strategies for gathering meaningful data from respondents, for interpreting research results within the framework of cultural contexts, for designing usable and effective communication interventions, for testing these interventions in action within real health settings, and for implementing and sustaining these interventions within social systems (Neuhauser, 2001; Neuhauser & Kreps, 2011). Actively engaging community partners in the applied research process can impart a strong sense of ownership in the research and intervention processes among these community partners, which can have major influences on minimizing potential community resistance to accepting the interventions and encouraging cooperation in the implementation and institutionalization of health communication programs, tools, and policies (Kreps, 2007).

DEVELOPING, SUSTAINING, AND DISSEMINATING EFFECTIVE HEALTH COMMUNICATION PROGRAMS

It is imperative that health communication scholars not only conduct relevant health communication research, but also take concerted efforts to use their research findings to guide the development of evidence-based health communication programs to enhance the delivery of care and promotion of health. Exemplary health communication programs can include evidence based policies and practices for the delivery of care (such as protocols for conducting patient interviews, guidelines for making decisions about triaging patients for treatment priority in emergency rooms, and forms for guiding and recording informed consent for treatment); health education tools and media (such as interactive tailored web sites for helping smokers learn about strategies for smoking cessation, video games for sensitizing adolescents about the importance of good nutrition, and online training programs for helping health care providers develop skills for communicating with patients from diverse backgrounds); and strategic health communication campaigns (such as media campaigns that encourage parents to get their children vaccinated, school-based programs to educate children about the dangers of drug abuse, and comprehensive multimedia education programs to help new parents care for their children). Not only can health communication scholars provide relevant data for guiding the development of these health care and health promotion programs, they can also gather formative evaluation data for refining these programs and summative evaluation data for assessing program impact and value (Abbatangelo-Gray, Kennedy, Cole, Baur, Bernhardt, Cho, et al., 2007; Kreps, 2002; Maibach, et al., 1993).

It is also important to develop new and effective strategies for disseminating relevant health communication knowledge to health care system participants who can use this information for accessing needed care, guiding health-related decision making, and promoting health and well being. A first step for the broad dissemination of health communication research findings is to expand the publication and presentation of health communication research in scholarly outlets outside of the communication discipline. This includes at relevant conferences and in important journals from related disciplines (such as public health, health education, health psychology, health sociology, medicine, nursing, and other health professional fields), as well as at interdisciplinary conferences and in health journals. These presentations and publications can help spur interdisciplinary collaborations, and many of these scholarly outlets have greater exposure to the popular media and health professionals than most communication conferences and journals. However, scholarly conferences and journals may be unfamiliar venues for those without advanced scientific training, and they are not likely to reach many health care consumers, caregivers, health care administrators, public health officials, or policymakers.

Efforts need to be taken to identify appropriate communication channels for easily reaching and influencing broader audiences of consumers, caregivers, administrators, government officials, and other policymakers. For example, popular magazines, web sites, blogs, radio and television programs, newspapers, and special audience presentations can have greater public reach than typical scholarly outlets. Moreover, health communication research must be translated out of academic jargon and into language and images that are familiar and meaningful to targeted audiences (see, for example, Kreps & Goldin, 2009). Health communication scholars must learn how to become public scholars and develop needed communication skills to reach and influence diverse audiences, including communicating effectively with vulnerable and at-risk populations. Participation in health fairs, media interviews, briefings for administrators and government representatives, as well as public presentations, public forums, training programs for health care providers and consumers, and the publication of popular articles in different online and print outlets can go a long way in broadening the dissemination of health communication knowledge. Interactive dissemination programs can encourage the exchange of questions and answers about health communication issues that can clarify the meanings and implications of health communication research. Some fruitful interactive channels for health communication dissemination include participation in support groups (both online and in-person groups), training programs, and web sites that allow information exchange.

CONCLUSION

By conducting relevant research and disseminating this work widely, health communication scholars can develop, implement, and sustain important health communication programs, tools, policies, practices, and interventions to enhance health outcomes. As a student of health communication, you can learn how to access relevant information to promote your own health, to navigate the health care system, and to serve as an effective advocate for your friends and family who may be confronting health issues. Health communication inquiry is a most relevant and exciting area of study that has direct implications for improving health outcomes!

REFERENCES

Abbatangelo-Gray, J., Kennedy, M. G., Cole, G. E., Baur, C., Bernhardt, J., Cho, H., Denniston, R., Farrelly, M., Figueroa, M. E., Hornik, R., Kreps, G. L., Middlestadt, S., Parrott, R., Slater, M., Snyder, L., & Storey, D. (2007). Guidance for evaluating mass communication health initiatives: Summary of an expert panel discussion sponsored by the Centers for Disease Control and Prevention. *Evaluation and the Health Professions, 30,* 229–253.

Atkin, C. K., & Smith, S. W. (2010). Improving communication practices to reduce breast cancer environmental risks. *Health Communication, 25,* 587–588.

DiMatteo, M. R., & Lepper, H. S. (1998). Promoting adherence to courses of treatment: Mutual collaboration in the physician-patient relationship. In L. D. Jackson, & B. K. Duffy (Eds.). *Health communication research: A guide to developments and directions.* (pp. 75–86). Westport, CT: Greenwood Press.

Dutta-Bergman, M. J. (2005). Theory and practice in health communication campaigns: A critical interrogation. *Health Communication, 18,* 103–122.

Eysenbach, G., & Kohnler, C. (2002). How do consumers search for and appraise health information on the world wide web? Qualitative study using focus groups, usability tests, and in-depth interviews. *British Medical Journal, 324m,* 573–577.

Frey, L. R., Botan, C. H., & Kreps, G. L. (2000). *Investigating communication: An introduction to research methods* (2nd ed.). Boston: Allyn & Bacon.

Guttman, N. (2010). Using communication research to advance the goals of the National Health Insurance law in Israel. *Health Communication. 5,* 613–614.

Greenfield, S., Kaplan, S., & Ware, J. Jr. (1985). Expanding patient involvement in care: Effects on patient outcomes. *Annals of Internal Medicine, 102,* 520–528.

Hornik, R. C. (2002). *Public health communication: Evidence for behavior change.* Mahwah, NJ: Lawrence Erlbaum.

Kreps, G. L. (2001). Consumer/provider communication research: A personal plea to address issues of ecological validity, relational development, message diversity, and situational constraints. *Journal of Health Psychology, 6,* 597–601.

Kreps, G. L. (2003). Opportunities for health communication scholarship to shape public health policy and practice: Examples from the National Cancer Institute. In T. Thompson, R. Parrott, K. Miller, and A. Dorsey, (Eds.), *The handbook of health communication* (pp. 609–624), Hillsdale, NJ: Lawrence Erlbaum.

Kreps, G. L. (2006). Communication and racial inequities in health care. *American Behavioral Scientist, 49,* 760–774.

Kreps, G. L. (2007). Health communication at the population level—Principles, methods and results. In L. Epstein (Ed.), *Culturally appropriate health care by culturally competent health professionals: International workshop report.* Caesarea, Israel: The Israel National Institute for Health Policy and Health Services Research, pp. 112–120.

Kreps, G. L. (2008). Qualitative inquiry and the future of health communication research. *Qualitative Research Reports in Communication, 9,* 2–12.

Kreps, G. L. (2011a). Translating health communication research into practice: The influence of health communication scholarship on health policy, practice, and outcomes. In T. Thompson, R. Parrott, and J. Nussbaum, (Eds.), *The handbook of health communication,* 2nd Ed. (pp. 595–608). New York: Routledge.

Kreps, G. L. (2011b). Methodological diversity and integration in health communication inquiry. *Patient Education and Counseling, 82,* 285–291.

Kreps, G. L. (2012). Translating health communication research into practice: The importance of implementing and sustaining evidence-based health communication interventions. *Atlantic Communication Journal 20,* 5–15.

Kreps, G. L., & Bonaguro, E. (2009). Health communication as applied communication inquiry. In L. Frey, & K. Cissna (Eds.), *The handbook of applied communication research* (pp. 970–993). Hillsdale, NJ: Lawrence Erlbaum Associates.

Kreps, G. L., & Chapelsky Massimilla, D. (2002). Cancer communications research and health outcomes: Review and challenge. *Communication Studies, 53*(4), 318–336.

Kreps, G. L., & Goldin, R. (2009). Why you should vaccinate your child against H1N1. STATS. http://stats.org/stories/2009/vaccinate_child_h1n1_nov17_09.html (accessed 1/10/2011).

Kreps, G. L., Gustafson, D., Salovey, P., Perocchia, R. S., Wilbright, W., Bright, M. A., & Muha, C. (2007). The NCI Digital Divide Pilot Projects: Implications for cancer education. *Journal of Cancer Education, 22* (Supplement 1), S56–S60.

Kreps, G. L., & Maibach, E. W. (2008). Transdisciplinary science: The nexus between communication and public health. *Journal of Communication, 58*(4), 732–748.

Kreps, G. L., & O'Hair, D. (Eds.). (1995). *Communication and health outcomes.* Cresskill, NJ: Hampton Press.

Kreps, G. L., Villagran, M. M., Zhao, X., McHorney, C., Ledford, C., Weathers, M., & Keefe, B. P. (2011). Development and validation of motivational messages to improve prescription medication adherence for patients with chronic health problems. *Patient Education and Counseling, 83,* 365–371.

Kreps, G. L., Viswanath, K., & Harris, L. M. (2002). Advancing communication as a science: Opportunities from the federal sector. *Journal of Applied Communication Research, 30,* 369–381.

Kunkel, D. (2010). Media research contributes to the battle against childhood obesity. *Health Communication, 25,* 595–596.

Minkler, M. (2000). Using participatory action research to build healthy communities. *Public Health Reports, 115,* 191–197.

Minkler, M., & Wallerstein, N. (2002). *Community based participatory research for health.* Indianapolis: Jossey-Bass.

National Cancer Institute. (2008). *The Role of the Media in Promoting and Reducing Tobacco Use.* Tobacco Control Monograph No. 19. Bethesda, MD: U.S. Department of Health and Human Services, National Institutes of Health, National Cancer Institute. NIH Pub. No. 07-6242.

Neuhauser, L. (2001). Participatory design for better interactive health communication: A statewide model in the USA. *The Electronic Journal of Communication, 11* (3 & 4).

Neuhauser, L., & Kreps, G. L. (2010). Ehealth communication and behavior change: Promise and performance. *Social Semiotics, 20*(1), 7–24.

Neuhauser, L., & Kreps, G. L. (2011). Participatory design and artificial intelligence: Strategies to improve health communication for diverse audiences. In N. Green, S. Rubinelli, & D. Scott. (Eds.), *Artificial intelligence and health communication* (pp. 49–52). Cambridge, MA: American Association of Artificial Intelligence Press.

Noar, S. M., Palmgreen, P., Chabot, M., Dobransky, N., & Zimmerman, R. S. (2009). A 10-year systematic review of HIV/AIDS mass communication campaigns: Have we made progress? *Journal of Health Communication, 14,* 15–42.

Parrott, R. (2008). A multiple discourse approach to health communication: Translational research and ethical practice. *Journal of Applied Communication Research, 36,* 1–7.

Siu, W. (2010). Fear appeals and public service advertising: Applications to influenza in Hong Kong. *Health Communication, 25,* 580.

KEEPIN' IT REAL WHEN DEVELOPING NARRATIVE HEALTH MESSAGES

Michelle A. Miller-Day, Chapman University and Michael L. Hecht, Penn State University

INTRODUCTION

The Drug Resistance Strategies Project (DRS) is a line of research at the intersection of interpersonal, intercultural, and health communication. This drug prevention research grew out of one of the author's (Michelle) work on personal narratives and health. She was part of a group interested in seeing if people's stories could be shaped into health promotion performances—and preliminary evidence focusing on topics like stepfamilies (Miller-Rassulo & Hecht, 1988), date rape (Mann, Hecht, & Valentine, 1988), and reading (Valentine & Valentine, 1983) showed that this approach worked well. Even as a student, she wanted to develop her own brand of narrative theory and help people lead healthier and happier lives. She joined forces with the other author (Michael) to develop DRS as a way of helping adolescents lead healthier and happy lives through enhancing their communication and other life skills.

As we've written elsewhere (Hecht & Miller-Day, 2010), this line of research has evolved into a new approach to research and practice. Actually, it involved breaking down distinctions between research and practice, along with the separation of teaching and research to develop a new, engaged way of working and thinking. This new approach is built around community-based participatory research that seeks to actively involve community members, organizational representatives, and researchers in all aspects of the research process (Israel, Schultz, Parker, & Becker, 1998). Our basic assumption is that community-based work requires collaboration between and among the key stakeholders. In our initial work, this meant working with middle and high school principals, teachers, and students, as well as an interdisciplinary group of university faculty, graduate students, and undergraduate students. Our current work involves an even broader range of constituencies and crosses traditional lines within communication—involving theory, research, and practice.

The translational process we employ starts with a focus on the personal stories (narratives) of youth regarding their experiences with substances. We then identify common narratives across the youth and "center" these experiences within individual lessons of a substance abuse prevention curriculum. Our prevention curriculum, *keepin' it REAL (kiR)*, is now believed to be the most widely used curriculum of its kind. However, we are jumping ahead—we start our DRS story at the beginning with kids, their stories, and their lives. From there we will take you into a collaborative, community-based process of developing health messages, and then, finally, how these messages are reaching over 1.75 million youth per year in the U.S., as well as hundreds of thousands around the world. But, the kids…

NARRATIVES ABOUT DRUGS—HOW WE LEARNED TO KEEP IT REAL

We say that our DRS and *kiR* curricula are "kid-centric." This means they are built around kids and their stories. To make this happen, of course as academics we read about research on kids and their lives (see for example, Johnston, O'Malley, Bachman, & Schulenberg, 2009). But, most importantly, we talked to hundreds and hundreds of kids from all around the U.S. We asked them to tell us stories about their experiences in risky situations, particularly when they were offered drugs. These stories told us a lot about what happens when drugs are offered, how the kids see drugs, and what we can do to prevent drug use.

Narratives are powerful tools because they are both a way of thinking as well as a style of communicating (Hecht & Miller-Day, 2007). What do we mean by this? People are inherently storytellers. Think of the cave pictures and the stories they tell about hunts and other events. Think about how we learn about our families and the world—through the stories family members tell us about our ancestors and about their lives, through stories they read to us that teach us about values and beliefs, and through the stories we see in the media. In fact, we remember things in story form. Try remembering a historical fact—it will often be in the context of a story about an event and people. And, while not everyone is a storyteller, most of us talk in story form at least some of the time. Think about the last time you met someone—did you try to understand each other's story (i.e., where they are from, what is their major, what's a nice man/women like them doing in a place like that). So, understanding the stories kids tell us about drugs is likely to reveal how they see drugs and drug use and the choices they make, as well as what can be done to influence them to make healthy choices.

Drug Narratives

While youth are a diverse group, our research all across the U.S. has shown us that there are some patterns to what happens when adolescents are offered drugs. Over the years we conducted interviews with youth in Arizona, Tennessee, Ohio, Pennsylvania, Alaska, North Carolina, and Louisiana, as well as many of the other states in the U.S. Our analyses of these stories tells us about the "who, what, where, and how" of drug offers.[1]

---

[1]See Alberts, Miller-Rassulo, & Hecht (1991) and Pettigrew, Miller-Day, Hecht, & Krieger (2011) for examples of more detailed information on these analyses.

Who Offers. Contrary to the stereotype, most drug offers come from friends and family rather than strangers. While acquaintances and strangers are responsible for a certain portion of the offers, a large majority comes from those who are close to the kids with whom we talked. As a result of offers occurring in the context of personal relationships, there can be a lot of implicit pressure to accept these offers.

What Gets Offered. Again, in contrast to public images of a meth or prescription drug epidemic, alcohol and tobacco (both smoked and chewed) are far and away the most frequently offered substances for most groups of youth under the age of 18. For example, in a recent rural study, over 70% of the offers involved these substances (Pettigrew, Miller-Day, Hecht, & Krieger, 2011). One exception is our work among Mexican American youth, where marijuana is offered with relatively higher frequency than tobacco (but not alcohol).

How Offered. Our research suggests that while a variety of strategies are used to offer substances, the most frequent style is what we call a simple offer or mere availability. In both, the substance is made available without pressure or influence. For example, a simple offer might be, "You want a dip?" or "Do you want a beer?"

When influence is used, the offerer will try to minimize risks, to appeal to group norms or to talk about benefits, or some combination strategy (e.g., to minimize risks and to show benefits). For example, someone might minimize risks by saying, "Just do it, just do it, you won't get caught if you're with me" or "Aw, come on. It's just, it's harmless."

Others might appeal to group norms, utilizing a bandwagon strategy of "everyone's doing it." For example, someone might say, "Come on, we're all smoking" or "Awww, you're such a wuss." Sometimes, the normative pressure is internal, that is, coming from personal pressure. Kids pressure themselves to act a certain way so they will fit in or be liked. In this situation, offerers don't put pressure on the kids to use (although that pressure can be implicit), but rather, the kids brings it on themselves. For example, one kid told us:

> Like, the first thing that goes through your mind is that if you don't do it, will your friends still like you? And then, you have that second thought, like, "Well, maybe it's not that bad." But then, like, it's, like, your body's telling you, "No, don't do it because it'll hurt you." Like, "Don't do it, 'cause you'll hurt me." But then your mind's telling you, "Well, maybe your friends won't like you if you don't do it." So it's like a mind-over-matter type thing.

Others talk about benefits of use. For example, one kid reported being told, "Oh, did you guys try this? It's so awesome, like, it's good, it tastes like fruit and stuff." Another was offered pot and told, "It feels good to be like that."

How Substances are Resisted or Refused. Drug resistance or refusal strategies have been at the heart of adolescent substance use prevention since the 1980s when Nancy Reagan coined the "Just Say No" campaign strategy. Our research suggests that there are four ways of refusing drug offers. These became known as "real," an acronym for remembering Refuse (simple no), Explain (no with an explanation), Avoid (avoid the situation or the offer), and Leave (leave the situation) (Alberts, Miller-Rassulo, & Hecht, 1991; Pettigrew et al., 2011). We have found these strategies used by people from kindergarten through college and recently found they also were used to resist sexual pressure. But we were not the only ones to find these strategies—Harrington (1995) and others confirmed their existence.

Refuse. Refuse is the simplest strategy—at least, the least complex one. All it requires is saying "no" or shaking one's head "no." However, one's style of communication is particularly important. To be effective, this must be done with confidence, assertiveness, or even with an element of aggression.

Explain. Explain is a little more complex communication strategy because it requires us to justify our reasoning. An example might be, "No thanks, I have to pick my parents up at the airport and cannot be high when I see them." However, as Langer (1989) has shown, even a "nonreason" reason can work. A simple example would be saying, when asking for a pencil, "Can I have a pencil? I need one." Not really an explanation but in explanation form (I want "x" because "y"). So, some kids say, "No, I don't want a beer because I don't drink."

Avoid. Avoid is the most complex strategy. We know that means it should come last, but RELA does not make for a good acronym. In any case, there are both proactive and reactive avoidance strategies. Proactive strategies prepare for or anticipate drug offers. One proactive way to avoid is by not putting yourself in a situation where an offer will be made. Think about a typical Friday night—do you know what party is likely to have lots of alcohol? Other substances? Avoiding would mean not going to the party. Perhaps a bit risky and more complicated are reactive strategies such as avoiding the rooms at the party where beer is served or consumed. Even more complicated is a verbal avoid. For example, when offered a beer at a party, one young woman said she wanted to dance instead. Others accept the offered beer, but don't drink it. Still others carry a beer (or apple juice that looks like beer) around a party so they won't be asked again.

Leave. The final strategy, leave, involves removing yourself from a situation in which drugs are offered. While sometimes this is paired with an explanation of why you are leaving, it is largely about the action of going. Some kids employ elaborate leave strategies. At a younger age, they may arrange for their parents to be the reason they have to leave. Some even think of a texting code so their friends can help them get out of the situation (e.g., inviting them to another party; making it so their ride is going).

All of these strategies can be relatively straightforward. Our research suggests that leave is used most frequently by older adolescents and young adults who have the means to leave by themselves or by more sophisticated younger communicators who can figure out how to get out of the situation.

Relationships. Regardless of the strategy, one of the key challenges for all age groups is how to refuse without insulting others or losing friends. Sometimes the issue is all in our head—it's an internal or personal pressure because we think people won't like us unless we fit in. Other times, however, it is real. Kids really do say to each other, you can't hang out with us unless you drink or smoke. Then people may have to choose between being part of a certain group and doing what they think is best. Tough choices, but nobody said being healthy was easy.

TRANSLATING NARRATIVES INTO DRUG PREVENTION MESSAGES

As we said from the start, we were interested not only in describing the social process of drug offers as academic research but also how to translate that knowledge into health promotion. Fortunately, there were some theories to guide us and we were developing others to perfect this approach, such as communication competence theory (Spitzberg & Cupach, 1984) and narrative engagement (Polkinghorne, 1988).

Our goal, then, is to teach knowledge, motivation, and skills (communication competence theory) through engaging, narrative role models. We do this by using indigenous narratives to construct lessons. In other words, the information and skills we want to convey, and the motivation we want to provide, is to depict stories told by other youth—kids telling about real events that occurred to real kids. We describe this kid-centric approach as "from kids through kids to kids." These stories create narrative engagement (i.e., they create interest, realism, and identification) because the youth recognize themselves and their peers in the stories and find them appealing. The narratives also provide role models (using social cognitive theory)[2] that teach youth how to resist drug offers (knowledge), enhance the perceived need to resist through social norms (motivation), and the strategies for accomplishing this (skills of competent communication). Since the narratives come from other kids, they are not "preachy," and we avoid using fear appeals because research shows they are less effective for this age group (Hastings, Stead, & Webb, 2004). The narratives ground the curriculum in a kids-eye view of the world, making them kid-centric while reflecting ethnic, gender, regional and other identities (cultural grounding) (see Hecht & Krieger, 2006).

You are probably thinking, this is all well in theory, but how can you do all these things at once? It all starts with the effective presentation of stories. If the narrative research is done well, we will have identified prototypical narratives reflecting cultural styles of thought and conversation that can be used to develop classroom materials. Elsewhere, the overall curriculum development has been described (Gosin, Marsiglia, & Hecht, 2003). But, here we focus on effectively translating the adolescents' narratives into videos illustrating and teaching resistance skills.

REAL Videos

The goal of the videos in the *keepin' it REAL* curriculum is to teach communication and life skills while communicating an anti-drug norm. While the videos focus on the four refusal skills (REAL), they also teach decision-making and risk assessment. At the same time, by showing youth refusing offers, they convey the impression that "cool" kids are not doing drugs and it is OK to be drug free. Finally, we hope that after they practice these skills, they will feel like they can resist and resist effectively. This is called "efficacy." All this is accomplished by creating realistic and interesting models for the four resistance skills with which youth can identify.

---

[2]For more about the use of role models and Social Cognitive Theory, see Bandura (1986, 1989).

To achieve this, we recruited students and faculty from high schools in the local communities. We conducted training sessions with the video production teams in which we overviewed the narrative philosophy of kiR and then presented the four refusal strategies conceptually and provided exemplar narratives elicited in interviews with students from the community. The teams then created dramatic recreations of the strategies through an iterative process. Students drafted script concepts and received feedback from the project team. Then they drafted scripts and again received feedback. We finalized scripts and the videos were shot. A "rough cut" or draft video was reviewed before the final edit.

Finally, we produced a "making of the videos" that introduced the high school students who created the videos and talked about their reasons for being involved with the production. This video was used to start the curriculum and not only introduce the concepts but also to increase identification. We chose high school students as the source of the message because they are "near peers" —slightly older members of their own community and age cohort. We are proud to report that some of the students who produced the videos won regional Emmy awards for their work. At the same time, not only did the overall 10 lessons reduce alcohol, tobacco, and marijuana use (Hecht, Graham, & Elek, 2006), but our analyses indicates that if students watched at least four videos with no other content, the curriculum had a similar effect (Warren, Hecht, Wagstaff, Elek, Ndiaye, Dustman, & Marsiglia, 2006). As a result, the curriculum was selected for the National Registry of Evidence-based Programs and Practices. It was initially distributed nationally by Discovery Health and ETR Publishing and then was adopted for national and international distribution by D.A.R.E. America.

keepin' it D.A.R.E.

D.A.R.E. America has a long history in school-based drug prevention. Started in 1983 in Los Angeles, California, D.A.R.E. has grown into what is believed to be the largest school-based drug prevention program in the world. While they have had great success disseminating their programs and their D.A.R.E. officers have proven to be highly effective prevention teachers (Hammond, Sloboda, Tonkin, Stephens, Teasdale, Grey, & Williams, 2008), the outcomes from their programs have been less than desirable. As a result, D.A.R.E. decided to adopt an existing evidence-based prevention program rather than create a new program of their own. We felt honored with the selected kiR. However, we did not realize what this meant for the further translation of the curriculum.

All school-based curricula involve three constituencies—the kids, the schools, and the prevention scientists. We had a long history of working with these in our community-based research practices. We view these constituencies as collaborators rather than as clients or merely as our target audience. As prevention scientists, we are committed to a curriculum that works for the kids that the teachers can teach. D.A.R.E., however, brings in other communities.

The first of these is D.A.R.E. America, itself a private, nonprofit organization led by former law enforcement officials. D.A.R.E. also consists of educators, mostly former and current teachers, as well as active law enforcement officers around the country. In existence as an organization for almost 30 years at the time we write, D.A.R.E. has developed its own culture, which reflects, in part, the law enforcement community. While they see themselves as involved in what is known as "community-based policing," they are still cops residing within a cop culture. As result, the organization does not change rapidly. In addition, it has lived with constant criticism from the press and the scientific community due to unfavorable research results in the past. As you can imagine, a trusting partnership was slow to build.

In addition to D.A.R.E. itself, the program utilizes officers to deliver the curriculum in schools, and they constitute a separate constituency. These officers work for local police forces that provide this service to the schools. This is sometimes part of their larger role as school resource officers. Within their own police organizations, they are sometimes derisively referred to a "kiddy cops," making their jobs a bit harder. As preventionists, they face the unique challenge of coming into someone else's classroom for a limited time, usually for a 10-week period. Thus they are typically "outsiders" who represent authority and are unfamiliar with the students when the lessons start. They are still quintessential cops, yet at the same time, they have extensive training in public presentations, drug prevention, and classroom facilitation, making them more open to prevention science than many of their contemporaries. However, they are not teachers, and thus the curriculum itself—the written and visual resources that make up the lessons—needs to reflect the officers' needs as implementers;—a process we came to call "DARE-ification" or "DARIFYING" the lessons.

In DARIFYing our research-based curriculum, we fortunately had Margaret (Magi) Colby[3] to facilitate this translation. Working primarily with one of the D.A.R.E. educators, Anita Bryan, and one of the officers, Bobby Robinson, the team interviewed officers, educators, and other stakeholders. We produced new videos that represented the national scope of the program, including rural, suburban, and urban versions. We drafted, revised, pilot tested, redrafted, revised, and kept going until everyone was satisfied. Ultimately, the curriculum was implemented by D.A.R.E. in 2009 to very positive feedback within the organization and schools.

While we do not know yet if this collaboration has improved D.A.R.E.'s outcomes, we do know that there has been a 25% increase in participation by middle school students since adopting *kiR*. We also know that the partnership has expanded to a new elementary curriculum that goes into the field starting January 2012. This means that in the U.S., alone, over 1.75 million youth will be enrolled in kiR. This is in addition to youth in 45 countries around the world. This is an incredible opportunity to really see communication theory in practice; to teach about safe and responsible choices; and to improve self-control, planning, communication, and relationship skills. It also can help them understand risks and consequences, as well as the perspective of others, and learn to get and give help. Of course, in the end, we hope that students who receive the curriculum will lead healthier and safer drug free lives. We are not naïve enough to think the kiR is the be all and end all in prevention or that we can save the world. But if we can "move the curve" on their skills and decrease unhealthy behaviors, it will all be worth it.

---

[3]Ms. Colby was an integral member of our research team until her untimely death in 2010.

REFERENCES

Alberts, J. K., Miller-Rassulo, M., & Hecht, M. L. (1991). A typology of drug resistance strategies. *Journal of Applied Communication Research, 19,* 129–151.

Bandura, A. (1986). *Social foundations of thought and action: A social cognitive theory.* Englewood Cliffs, NJ: Prentice Hall.

Bandura, A. (1989). Human agency in social cognitive theory. *American Psychologist, 44,* 1175–1184.

Gosin, M., Marsiglia, F. F., & Hecht, M. L. (2003). keepin' it REAL: A drug resistance curriculum tailored to the strengths and needs of pre-adolescents of the Southwest. The Journal of Drug Education, 33, 119–142.

Hammond, A., Sloboda, Z., Tonkin, P., Stephens, R., Teasdale, B., Grey, S. F., & Williams, J. (2008). Do adolescents perceive police officers as credible instructors of substance abuse prevention programs? *Health Education Research, 23,* 682–696.

Harrington. N. G. (1995). The effects of college students' alcohol resistance strategies. *Health Communication, 7,* 371–391.

Hastings, G., Stead, M., & Webb, J. (2004) Fear appeals in social marketing: Strategic and ethical reasons for concern. *Psychology and Marketing, 21,* 961–86.

Hecht, M. L., Graham, J. W., & Elek, E. (2006). The drug resistance strategies intervention: Program effects on substance abuse. *Health Communication, 20,* 267-276.

Hecht, M. L., & Krieger, J. K. (2006). The principle of cultural grounding in school based substance use prevention: The Drug Resistance Strategies Project. *Journal of Language and Social Psychology, 25,* 301–319.

Hecht, M. L. & Miller-Day, M. (2007). The Drug Resistance Strategies Project as translational research. *Journal of Applied Communication Research, 35,* 343-349.

Hecht, M. L., & Miller-Day, M. (2010). "Applied" aspects of the Drug Resistance Strategies Project, Special Issue of the *Journal of Applied Communication Research, 38,* 215–229.

Israel, B. A., Schultz, A. J., Parker, E. A., & Becker, A. B. (1998). Review of community-based research: Assessing partnership approaches to improve public health. *Annual Review of Public Health, 19,* 173–202.

Johnston, L. D., O'Malley, P. M., Bachman, J. G., & Schulenberg, J. E. (2009). *Monitoring the Future national results on adolescent drug use: Overview of key findings, 2008.* (NIH Publication Number 09-7401). Bethesda, MD: National Institute on Drug Abuse.

Langer, Ellen J. (1989). *Mindfulness.* Reading, MA: Addison Wesley.

Mann, C., Hecht, M. L., & Valentine, K.B. (1988). Performance in a social context: Date rape versus date right. *Central States Speech Journal, 39,* 269–280.

Michaels, S. (2006). Narrative presentations: An oral preparation for literacy with first graders. In J. Cook-Gumperz (Ed.), *The social construction of literacy* (pp. 110–137). Cambridge, Maryland: Cambridge University Press.

Miller-Rassulo, M. & Hecht, M.L. (1988). Performance as persuasion: Trigger scripting as a tool for education and persuasion. *Literature in Performance, 8,* 40–55.

Pettigrew, J., Miller-Day, M., Hecht, M.L., & Krieger, J. (2011). Alcohol and other drug resistance strategies employed by rural adolescents. *Journal of Applied Communication Research, 39,* 103–122.

Polkinghorne, D. 1988. *Narrative knowing and the human sciences.* Albany: State University of New York Press.

Spitzberg, B. H., & Cupach, W. R. (1984). *Interpersonal communication competence.* Beverly Hills, CA: Sage.

Valentine, K. B., & Valentine, D. E. (1983). Facilitation of intercultural communication through performed literature. *Communication Education, 32,* 303–307.

Warren, J. R., Hecht, M. L., Wagstaff, D. A., Elek, E., Ndiaye, K., Dustman, P., & Marsiglia, F. F. (2006). Communication prevention: The effects of keepin' it REAL classroom videotapes and televised PSAs on middle-school students' substance abuse. *Journal of Applied Communication Research, 34,* 209-227.

WHAT DOES A RHETORICAL PERSPECTIVE OFFER OUR UNDERSTANDING OF HEALTH AND MEDICINE?

LISA KERÄNEN, UNIVERSITY OF COLORADO DENVER AND
JENNIFER MALKOWSKI, UNIVERSITY OF COLORADO BOULDER

Our lives are steeped in health and medical concerns even from before we are born to the moment we die. On any given day, the average American is surrounded by health messages. You might flip through a magazine advertisement for an antidepressant or a heart pill, catch a television show about plastic surgery, listen to a radio spot advertising Lasik surgery or weight loss remedies, chat with a friend on a social networking site about a medical condition, or surf the web for health information. You are not alone. According to the Pew Internet and American Life Project (2011), 80% of adult U.S. Internet users search the Internet for health information each day, while 34% have read about another's health condition online. In addition to the growing scope of medical authority over everyday life, health care constitutes a booming business: The U.S. government spends more than 15% of its gross domestic product on health care, representing the largest expenditure on health care of any nation and one of the highest per capita expenditures in the world (WHO, 2009). These developments mean that our communication about health and medical concerns comprises a significant part of public and private, corporate and nonprofit, and national and global affairs.

Unlike health communication researchers who apply social science methods to understand and improve health messages (see, for example, the other chapters in this section), researchers in a growing area known as the rhetoric of medicine study health and medical discourses and practices using the lens of persuasion and the tools of humanistic rhetorical analysis. This chapter explains how a rhetorical perspective can help us understand the roles of science and medicine in shaping our views of illness and our roles as patients. To do so, it begins by reviewing major research themes in the rhetoric of medicine and closes with an examination of research findings pertaining to professional, public, and clinical discourse about medicine and health.

THE RHETORIC OF MEDICINE AND HEALTH

As the name implies, rhetoricians of medicine study persuasion pertaining to medicine and health (see, e.g., Condit, 1999; Derkatch & Segal, 2005; Heifferon & Brown, 2008; Hyde, 1993, 2001; Keränen, 2010b; Lay, 2000; Lyne, 2001; Segal 2000, 2007, 2009; Wells, 2010). Because rhetoricians of medicine recognize that the persuasive components of medicine and health are widespread, dynamic, and individually and collectively experienced, they examine a variety of texts—from semi-private clinical encounters through public, mediated messages, such as films and direct-to-consumer advertisements. The goal, like that of other medical humanities research, is to shed light on the humane dimensions of health care and to highlight its ethical, linguistic, and political dimensions. For researchers in the area known as the rhetoric of medicine the particular texts of interest are those artifacts and symbols that influence the practice and experience of health and illness.

A key concern of rhetoricians who study medicine and health is the use of language to define health and wellness, and disease and illness. Specifically, scholars suggest that health rhetoric is heavily implicated in *medicalization,* the process used to redefine broad human concerns as medical issues that require diagnosis, treatment, therapy, and medicine (Conrad, 2007; Lane, 2007). Shyness and obesity, for example, are two conditions that used to be defined socially but that have, through rhetoric, become subject to medical authority, counseling, and an ever-expanding array of pharmaceutical products. Similarly, patients, medical providers, and everyday citizens use rhetoric to define and redefine both well-known and emerging conditions and to create health and illness identities. As Derkatch and Segal (2005, p. 139) explain:

> The phrase "social anxiety disorder" persuades the very shy person that he or she may be a candidate for drug therapy; the word "breakthrough" persuades the public to imagine medical research as a particularly dramatic sort of enterprise; the phrase "fighting disease" persuades persons that they have failed at something when they cannot stop being ill; the term "survivor" leaves the dead person looking somehow culpable.

As these examples illustrate, the rhetoric we use to talk about health and disease is far from neutral; it subtly asks us to adopt particular health identities (e.g., "the cancer survivor," "the heart patient") and to think of health conditions in certain ways (e.g., "as invaders to be *fought,*" "as problems to be *managed*") in order to take certain courses of action (e.g., to take medication, to forgo surgery).

Beyond defining health and disease and shaping their social and professional meanings, rhetoric also coordinates health care. Patients use language to convince providers to take their medical concerns seriously and to persuade them to prescribe certain treatment regimens or to make referrals to specialists. Health care providers use language to sway patients to accept their diagnoses and follow particular medical treatment plans. Providers similarly use language to move patients through a maze of medical care. Sharf (1990), for example, has argued that doctor-patient exchanges be seen as a kind of "interpersonal rhetoric" where both parties seek to persuade each other using narratives (p. 217), while Berkenkotter (2008) has explored how psychiatry transforms patient narratives into clinically useful formats, such as case histories that fit preferred psychiatric diagnoses. The results of these encounters can be both positive and negative with regard to the experience of health care. Scott (2003) has demonstrated how the flawed argumentation surrounding home HIV testing separates "normal" from "risky" subjects in ways that invite both apathetic and dangerous testing practices. While Sharf's concept of interpersonal rhetoric can potentially promote medical partnerships between patients and practitioners, the rhetoric surrounding HIV testing can have undesirable material and social effects as Scott's findings suggest that certain rhetorical practices surrounding HIV home testing encourage moral attributions, discrimination, and blame. These examples reveal how citizens, patients, and practitioners alike use rhetoric to navigate the complex health care system with both promising and problematic results. In order to get a feel for how rhetoricians make claims about the consequences of the rhetorics of health and medicine, we consider the work of Lisa Keränen (the first author) across professional, public, and clinical contexts. For the remainder of this chapter, Lisa Keränen (in the first person) will detail how a rhetorical perspective helps her move from examination to evaluation, and sometimes, to intervention in the field of medicine.

RHETORIC OF MEDICINE IN A PROFESSIONAL CONTEXT: THE HIPPOCRATIC OATH

One of my earliest studies in the rhetoric of medicine considered the persuasive appeal of the Hippocratic Oath after I repeatedly heard patients invoking the Oath as a reminder to physicians in an intensive care unit about their duty to care for them (Keränen, 2001). Contrary to popular belief, there exists no single, unitary text known as the Hippocratic Oath. Instead, this ancient text, which is believed to have originated in the fourth century BCE, has been molded over the centuries to fit changing medical needs; its rise in the early twentieth century coincided with the professionalization of medicine but included anachronistic and conflicting injunctions. With its mysterious phrases and entreaties to ancient deities like Apollo, Panacea, and Hygieia, what purpose, then, was the seemingly out-of-date Hippocratic Oath serving?

Using theories of *epideictic,* or ceremonial, rhetoric, I analyzed how the contemporary recitation of the Hippocratic Oath functioned for medical professionals, who often recite some reshaped version of it upon graduation from medical school. Epideictic rhetoric is frequently associated with funeral orations and award ceremonies because its explicit function is to praise or blame. However, in the act of praising or blaming, the epideictic often persuades audience members about broader cultural values. Viewed from the lens of epideictic, the Hippocratic Oath can thus be seen as a cultural touchstone that reminds health professionals and non-experts about the far-reaching values of the profession, without providing specific precepts for action. The Hippocratic injunction to "never do harm," for instance, raises a host of questions about treatments that do in fact harm on the road to healing. Such phrasing does not provide practitioners specific guidance, but rather a general ideal. The Oath's specific and outmoded messages about not cutting with stone or not using a pessary matter less, therefore, than its overall celebration of the community of physicians; its rhetorical work is ritualistic and professional. The Oath, in short, reinforces medical authority by invoking and celebrating its widespread professional values.

Close examination of the rhetoric and uses of various versions of the Oath helped me to understand the roles of science and medicine in shaping understandings of illness and physicians' roles as stewards of health within professional contexts. Specifically, the Oath is used to orient practitioners and publics to widely shared beliefs about what medicine ought to be in its idealized form. While the Oath provides an example of how rhetoric is used in professional contexts to instill a sense of medical authority, another study shows how rhetoric is used across public settings to assess medical practice.

RHETORIC ABOUT MEDICINE IN PUBLIC DISCOURSE: COMPETING CHARACTERIZATIONS IN A BREAST CANCER CONTROVERSY

While some of my research addresses professional discourse like the Hippocratic Oath, a large portion of it addresses more traditional terrain for rhetoricians: public discourse about biomedicine broadly construed. The term *biomedicine* refers to the application of biological and life science principles to clinical medicine. It is the dominant way medicine is practiced in the Western world. My book-length study, *Scientific Characters: Rhetoric, Politics, and Trust in Breast Cancer Research,* offers a close rhetorical analysis of news coverage, medical journals, letters to the editors, and cancer pamphlets that chronicle various stages of a science-based controversy to illustrate how public discussion about biomedical science shaped public views of breast cancer research and women's roles as patients and research participants (Keränen, 2010a). The controversy furnishes an example of how publics begin to identify, evaluate, and even influence the course of biomedical science-based discussions that ultimately cultivate our views of illness, our trust in science, and our sense of ourselves as patients.

In 1994, a *Chicago Tribune* headline spread news of a dramatic story: "Fraud in Breast Cancer Research: Doctor Lied on Data for Decade." The controversy surrounding this headline called into question the life's work of Dr. Bernard Fisher, a previously celebrated cancer specialist and women's health advocate. Before the startling 1994 headline, Dr. Fisher's landmark breast cancer research routinely informed decisions regarding women's health, because it had demonstrated that breast-sparing lumpectomy with radiation was as effective as removing the breast for early-state cancers. Tens of thousands of women and their physicians used this finding to guide their cancer decisions. Following the allegations that one of his lead investigators, Dr. Roger Poisson, had falsified data used in this landmark study, public scrutiny of the irreversible, and many argued inexcusable, nature of Dr. Fisher's management of the study, and Dr. Poisson's misconduct, ensued. As more scientists, patients, and advocates spoke up in public about the complex health matter, the controversy undermined trust in the character of Fisher, his research team and findings, and the institution of biomedical science writ large. Fisher was eventually cleared of wrongdoing and his research findings were upheld, but in the meantime, the controversy troubled the public's understanding of the breast cancer experience; foregrounded the relationships among the politics of health, the rhetoric of breast cancer treatment, and the widespread trust in science; and prompted swift public and political response.

In analyzing the progression and meanings of this high-stakes controversy, I made a case for the importance of rhetorically constituted characters in science-based controversies. I argued that in the absence of scientific evidence that they would accept as credible, many of the controversy's stakeholders turned to perceived character as a measure of whose science and medical treatments they should trust. My rhetorical analysis of this controversy tracked how key players employed rhetoric to construct the reputations of people and institutions in order to resolve the controversy. These constructions encouraged particular policy responses and meanings associated with a controversy and therefore bore consequences for our understanding of what it means to be a patient and a potential medical research participant.

After tracking how various publics constructed the characters of Drs. Fisher and Poisson, I analyzed three characterizations that dominated the representation of women across the controversy: *the knowledge consumer* (who relies on accurate knowledge provided by scientists and doctors), *the subject of science* (who acquiesces to medical authority), and *the knowledge partner* (who seeks active partnership in medical decision making). Based on these three representations, I found that women were most frequently cast as consumers or subjects of science and as patients in need of protection from bad medical information; the consequences of these characterizations placed women largely outside of medical decision making as mere recipients of medical information. In this particular case, the portrayal of women as fragile and emotional victims of science worked to maintain the role of science as a dominant source of knowledge and to script women as outsiders to the biomedical research process. The insights offered by this study are relevant to health advocates who understand that policy responses to case-specific controversies more than likely set the tone for how future scientific controversies can and should be handled. Policy implications of rhetorical scholarship, like the ones offered at the end of *Scientific Characters,* can be further demonstrated through my applied work in end-of-life decision making.

RHETORIC OF MEDICINE IN A CLINICAL CONTEXT: DISCOURSES AT THE END OF LIFE

As I was beginning my study of characterization in this major biomedical controversy, I also began shadowing a medical ethicist in an intensive care unit where I witnessed many deathbed interactions between family, unconscious patients, and health care providers. End-of-life discourse is particularly important because twentieth century technological developments ushered in dramatic changes in medical care that could extend lives previously ended. From cardio-pulmonary resuscitation (CPR) to breathing machines, from new conceptions of "brain death" to electrical shocks, such technologies changed the way we think and talk about death and dying. Seventy percent of Americans die in hospitals, nursing homes, or long-term care facilities, even though most want to die at home (CDC, 2005). However, public—and private—discourses about death and dying choices are often lacking (Hyde 1993, 2001).

As a rhetorician, it was clear to me that many end-of-life conversations were leaving most participants frustrated. Haunted by what I was seeing, I set out to examine how the genre of forms that document a patient's end-of-life treatment preferences structure interaction at the bedside of dying patients. A *genre* is a distinct type of discourse that contains recognizable substantive, stylistic, and organizational features; and medical and health care genres include patient charts, electronic medical records, the patient intake interview, and medical forms or the medical case presentation. In this study, I tracked the use of a particular end-of-life decision-making document, a form known as the "'Patient' Preferences Worksheet," at Good Care Hospital, a large, urban, acute care facility in the eastern United States (Keränen, 2007). The "'Patient' Preferences Worksheet" is an example of an ever-evolving genre of forms many hospitals use to determine and document a patient's wishes for interventions, such as CPR, antibiotics, and pain medication at the end of life. In order to understand how the form was influencing end-of-life communication, I combined textual analysis of the form with more than 100 hours of clinical observation and 3 hours of structured group interviews with the primary users of the form. I found that the form framed death and dying in technological—as opposed to ethical, spiritual, and political—terms, and that it subtly encouraged removal of what are commonly referred to as life sustaining technologies. In short, the "'Patient' Preferences Worksheet" and other forms like it seem to signify a significant change in deathbed subjectivity in which patients become subjects who must choose how to die (in this case, most frequently by a decision to remove "life sustaining technologies"). While such forms help routinize the practices surrounding death for providers, they also perform competing functions for patients and families, who often wrestled with the choices presented on the form. The Worksheet, in short, sits at the intersection of a complicated set of discourses about death and dying that converge around the bedside of dying patients; rhetorical analysis can help us untangle these competing vectors.

As I was developing this end-of-life genre study, I began to apply my rhetorical lens on death and dying to a practical project when I partnered with a physician and his team who wanted to improve end-of-life communication skills with the medical residents they were training. Together, we conducted a pilot study of a Palliative Care clinical exercise (Han, Keränen, Lescisin, & Arnold, 2005). This teaching exercise used role-play to model conversations about bad news and end-of-life treatment preferences. At the time, calls for increased training in end-of-life communication skills were frequent, yet we were not aware of any intervention "devised to allow residents to learn and demonstrate communication skills with actual seriously ill patients in real clinical settings, although several experts argue[d] that this would be ideal" (p. 669). The team therefore developed a teaching tool that would allow medical residents to sharpen their skills in actual conversation after discussing and then role-playing (and later debriefing) this communication with a trained mentor, and we introduced this teaching intervention to a class of 60 medical residents. Using survey data and clinical observation, we found that this intervention was feasible and valued by medical residents and their mentors alike. It increased participants' confidence about having such difficult conversations and helped pave the way for further interventions to develop and study end-of-life communication skills. As a humanist who normally practices rhetorical criticism, I was able to partner with social scientists to conduct applied research that made a difference in medical residents' communicative development and training.

Readers of rhetorical analyses of health and medical texts like the ones reviewed in this essay can become more informed patients, critical consumers of medical information, and trained observers of health and illness discourses through the close examination of real-world examples. What the rhetorical perspective offers is sensitivity to the persuasive mechanisms at work in public (and private and clinical) discourse, a vocabulary for assessing potentially problematic and promising trends in medicine, and a platform to begin discussion about the consequences of representing people and institutions in public spaces. The outcome of reading rhetorical studies of health and medicine is that we can weigh in more thoughtfully on public discussions of science and medicine that promise to impact our experiences of illness and our roles as patients, and we can further begin to reconsider our own roles in health and medical contexts.

CONCLUSION

As a perspective, the rhetoric of medicine invites us to consider how health care communication functions as a persuasive exchange and how such communication is ethically and politically-laden. Thus far, we have seen how research in the rhetoric of medicine helps us understand the role of language across professional, public, and clinical settings. Based on what you have read in this chapter, take a moment to assess the medical and health rhetoric that you encounter. What forms of medical and health communication do you participate in on daily, weekly, and annual bases? Which health messages are most persuasive to you, where do they come from, and why? How are distinct genres of medical rhetoric (hospital forms, direct-to-consumer advertisements, medical web sites) and new technologies (electronic medical records, email to providers, health-related smart-phone "apps") changing your communication with health care professionals? How much of your information about health and wellness is gleaned from online sources? In what sorts of communication about the end of life have you and your family engaged? How do public discourses about health and medicine and even science-based controversies affect your understanding of yourself and your health? And, overall, how does your health care communication stack up to the communication discussed in this chapter?

The next time you visit a health care professional, take a moment to take stock of how the language of medicine and the institutional imperatives shape your communication. Who does the talking? How much time is scheduled? Who is trying to persuade whom of what using which means? How do patients and health care providers identify with one another? How do forms, charts, and computer screens enable and constrain your communication? In adopting a rhetorical perspective on health and medicine, you will be examining how your health care communication is shaped by social and symbolic processes with unique but consequential histories, contexts, and functions. In short, you will be examining how rhetoric about medicine and health structures identities, coordinates care, and shapes your understanding of illness and health.

REFERENCES

Berkenkotter, C. (2008). *Patient tales: Case histories and the uses of narrative psychiatry.* Columbia, SC: University of South Carolina Press.

Centers for Disease Control and Prevention [CDC]. (2005). Worktable 309: Deaths by place of death, age, race, and sex. Retrieved from http://www.cdc.gov/nchs/data/dvs/Mortfinal2005_worktable_309.pdf

Condit, C. (1999). *The meanings of the gene: Public debates about human heredity.* Madison: University of Wisconsin Press.

Conrad, J. (2007). *The medicalization of society: On the transformation of human conditions into treatable disorders.* Baltimore, MD: Johns Hopkins University Press.

Derkatch, C., & Segal, J. Z. (2005). Realms of rhetoric in health and medicine. *University of Toronto Medical Journal, 83,* 138–142.

Han, P. K., Keränen, L., Lescisin, D. A., & Arnold, R. M. (2005). The palliative care clinical evaluation exercise (CEX): An experience-based intervention for teaching end-of-life communication skills. *Academic Medicine, 80,* 669–676.

Heifferon, B., and Brown, S. (Eds.). (2008). *The rhetoric of healthcare: Essays toward a new disciplinary inquiry.* Cresswell, NJ: Hampton Press.

Hyde, M. J. (1993). Medicine, rhetoric, and euthanasia: A case study in the workings of postmodern discourse. *Quarterly Journal of Speech, 79,* 201–224.

Hyde, M. J. (2001). *Call of conscience: Heidegger and Levinas, rhetoric and euthanasia.* Columbia: University of South Carolina Press.

Keränen, L. (2001). The Hippocratic Oath as epideictic rhetoric: Reanimating medicine's past for its future. *Journal of Medical Humanities, 21,* 55–68.

Keränen, L. (2007). "'Cause someday we all die": Rhetoric, agency, and the case of the 'patient' preferences worksheet. *Quarterly Journal of Speech, 93,* 179–210.

Keränen, L. (2010a). *Scientific characters: Rhetoric, politics, and trust in breast cancer research.* Tuscaloosa: University of Alabama Press.

Keränen, L. (2010b). Rhetoric of medicine. In S. H. Priest (Ed.), *Encyclopedia of science and technology communication, volume 2* (pp. 639–642). Thousand Oaks, CA: Sage.

Lane, C. (2007). Shyness: How a normal behavior became a sickness. New Haven, CT: Yale University Press.

Lay, M. M. (2000). *The rhetoric of midwifery: Gender, knowledge, and power.* New Brunswick, NJ: Rutgers University Press.

Lyne, J. (2001). Contours of intervention: How rhetoric matters to biomedicine. *Journal of Medical Humanities, 22,* 3–13.

Pew Internet and American Life Project. (2011). Health topics. Retrieved from: http://www.pewinternet.org/Reports/2011/HealthTopics.aspx

Scott, J. B. (2003). *Risky rhetoric: AIDS and the cultural practices of HIV testing.* Carbondale: Southern Illinois University Press.

Segal, J. Z. (2000). Contesting death, speaking of dying. *Journal of Medical Humanities, 21,* 29–44.

Segal, J. Z. (2007). *Health and the rhetoric of medicine.* Carbondale: Southern Illinois University Press.

Segal, J. Z. (2009). Rhetoric of health and medicine. In A. Lundsford et al. (Eds.), *The Sage handbook of rhetorical studies* (pp. 27–246). Thousand Oaks, CA: Sage.

Sharf, B. (1990). Physician-patient as interpersonal rhetoric: A narrative approach. *Health Communication, 2,* 217–231.

Wells, S. (2010). *Our bodies, ourselves and the work of writing.* Palo Alto, CA: Stanford University Press.

World Health Organization [WHO]. (2009). World health statistics. Retrieved from http://www.who.int/whosis/whostat/EN_WHS09_Full.pdf

SECTION 7
INTERCULTURAL COMMUNICATION

The intercultural communication context affords us the opportunity to explore the ways in which culture is a pervasive, yet for the most part, unconscious and taken for granted part of our everyday lives. It is clear that culture, in all its variations, is the manifestation of what it means to belong with a group of people. We express our culture through communication and it is in communication that the differences between our cultural values are exposed. In the following readings you will be asked to explore the ways in which our own culture influences our interactions with others and methods for increasing our intercultural communication competence. The following essays explore intercultural interactions across both the local and everyday cross-cultural types of encounters and the international cross-cultural exchanges. First, Donal Carbaugh (University of Massachusetts Amherst) responds to the question: *How can we best understand intercultural communication when we encounter people from different groups or ethnic backgrounds during our everyday activities, as in our travels, with our extended families, or in work interactions?* Carbaugh explains that in intercultural communication situations we need to attend to communication cues since these can often be misunderstood as they are coded from different points of view. Second, Guo-Ming Chen and Priscilla Young (University of Rhode Island) respond to the question: *What are the ways in which culturally distinctive practices get woven into international and intercultural interactions?* Chen and Young examine the knowledge and skills for being competent in intercultural communication by specifying the dimensions and components of a model of intercultural communication. Third, Tom Nakayama (Northeastern University) responds to the question: *Given the highly racialized society that we live in, how do we communicate more successfully in this context?* Nakayama suggests techniques for adopting a critical approach to intercultural communication that sheds light on the larger structural frameworks that shape intercultural interaction. Throughout these three essays you are provided strategies for increasing your intercultural communication competence.

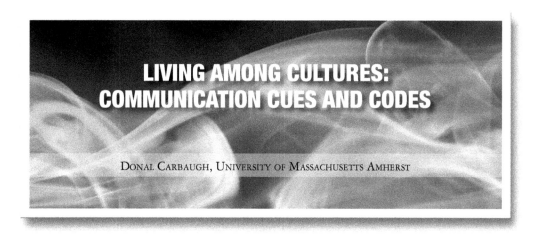

LIVING AMONG CULTURES: COMMUNICATION CUES AND CODES

DONAL CARBAUGH, UNIVERSITY OF MASSACHUSETTS AMHERST

INTRODUCTION

Each of my studies about intercultural communication has begun because something puzzling happened in my social interactions with others. Let me give you a few examples of what I mean by that. At one point, I was teaching classes at the University of Montana, which included several Native American students. In those classes, at times, a Native American student would do something that surprised me, like communicate nonverbally through gesture and demonstration—one "speech" was given primarily this way—rather than verbally. At other times, another Native American student did something I did not expect, such as read from notes rather than speaking in an impromptu way, as part of a specific classroom assignment. That led me to wonder and question not only what these students were doing, but what I was doing, and what I was assuming about "good communication" as a teacher. Those experiences as well as guiding tours in northern Montana, partly on Native American lands and through Glacier National Park, exposed me to Blackfeet people whose ways of living at times contrasted with my own.

Similarly, while working in my university I contacted several people, colleagues and students, from Russia. At times their ways of doing things, such as stating virtues for living a good life rather than talking about the facts of the matter, were puzzling to me. I wondered: Why were they talking about the way things were supposed to be rather than simply reporting the way things actually were? Similarly, while living in Finland, I learned how Finnish ways, especially using silence as a means of communication, were at times unlike what I would do in a similar context, such as talking things out. It seemed to me that no one was talking when I expected a lively verbal exchange. Why was this silent interaction happening? There are many other examples of this sort of intercultural dynamic in our daily lives. Perhaps you can recall several such instances yourself. These examples are sufficient to introduce the research that others and I have done about how each of us communicates in intercultural situations. We find that we do so through means that are distinctive to our own group or upbringing. Much of my research responds to the important question: *How can we best understand intercultural communication when we encounter people from different groups or ethnic backgrounds during our everyday activities, as in our travels, with our extended families or in work interactions?*

We have found two ideas to be particularly helpful in responding to this sort of question. One is the idea of a *communication cue.* As we communicate with each other, we use cues, or signaling devices, mostly in an unthinking way, which are customary in telling others what we mean. When people are in face-to-face interactions, for example, cues come through the language we speak, the way we speak it, the way we hold our faces, the way we gesture, the clothes we wear, our style of hair, the distance we maintain between people, and so on. When we are online, cues are in the language we write, the emoticons we use, the display of visual images, and so on. Cues can include **explicit meanings**, as when we say (or write) the phrase, "we need to talk," and it means exactly what it says. Cues can also include **implicit meanings** as when "we need to talk" means something more, there is a problem and I want you to know about it. In either case, as we communicate, we assume communication cues have shared meanings, and that the people with us understand what we mean when we put things this way. In other words, we assume those with us understand our communication cues, or we would not use them the way we do.

All of our communication involves cues, yet each communication event in which we participate is designed, whether we know it or not, within a distinctive, or special, or to some degree local, or "cultural configuration of cues." This is simply a way of saying we communicate in ways that are customary to us, which we assume others around us understand, based upon our experience with them or upon our membership in human groups. However, we do not communicate through ways that everyone in the world can or will understand! And that is the rub. This point is particularly important when we are involved in intercultural communication. Why? Because others from elsewhere can easily miss a cue about what we mean; just as their cue about what they mean can be easily missed by us. This is of special importance when it comes to cueing and understanding much of the richness in communication exchanges, the more implicit meanings. In a recent book, this particular dynamic, of a cue being unknowingly missed by another, has been discussed as an "invisible misunderstanding" (Carbaugh, 2005). But to understand the rest of the story, we need one more important idea.

When we use a cue, as when we speak about the facts of a matter, we do so typically by assuming such a factual statement will be heard and understood, even appreciated in a particular way. At least for some people in some communities there is the general belief and its attendant value, in some situations, that it is important to state facts truthfully, to speak honestly about things. This belief is of course applied in United States' courts of law. We even take an oath "to tell the truth, the whole truth, and nothing but the truth." We do so because of a particular set of beliefs and values that apply to specific communication practices. We call a particular set of beliefs and values that pertain to a communication practice, a *communication code.*

Many people in the United States have been taught as children that it is valued to speak the truth, it is important to be honest with each other, that even if it is difficult, it is best to be open and to communicate frankly about things. The oft told story about the young boy, George Washington, and his speaking truthfully to his father that he had indeed chopped down the English cherry tree makes the point explicit: speaking truthfully and honestly is valued even if it is difficult to do so (Carbaugh, 1988, pp. 75–77).

As part of one research project, I was watching interactions among Russian people as they interacted with those from the United States. One episode of a television show involved these groups of people. The topic of premarital sex had been raised by the American host, who asked if premarital sex was a problem in Russia. He had asked this problem of American teens before, and they responded by discussing unwanted pregnancies, sexually transmitted diseases, uses of condoms and so on. When asked of Russians, the response was that it is good if a girl is a virgin at the time she is married. Responses from the Russian teens included the importance and value of family life to people and maintaining proper feelings among people. While the Russian responses puzzled the American host, the point follows the idea introduced above: Rather than talk about the facts of the matter, the Russian responses demonstrated a different point, that it is good to talk about what people value, the common ethic of a good life.

Let me describe a similar finding from my research about American and Russian practices. This finding further demonstrates why it is important to study and learn about communication cues and codes. An international group of professors was meeting in order to discuss how best to design a school of business and management. Some participants were from the United States. These professors talked about the difficulties they had with the design of specific programs and courses of study. In particular, at the time of the meeting, there had been economic problems and a high degree of frustration in procuring the proper funds that were needed in order to support their program, its faculty and students. In a nutshell, these professors were speaking honestly about the problems they had encountered in their efforts to design their program. They also felt that speaking this way would encourage others to be honest about their frustrations and difficulties.

Another set of participants at that meeting was from Russia. When they had the chance to speak, they spoke about the importance of their accomplished faculty, the successes of their program, and the degree to which such programs can become a model for others to emulate. In a nutshell, these professors were speaking about the values of a successful program, the virtues of accomplishing what it had been designed to do, and the merit this brought to its faculty and students. They felt that speaking this way would put their program and their university in the best possible light and demonstrate what it offered to the international gathering.

The American professors had spoken truthfully about their difficulties in the hope of addressing them; the Russian professors had spoken about the virtues in such education in the hope of emulating them. The Americans cued their typical style of "speaking honestly" as a sign of open discussion about problems; the Russians had cued "speaking virtuously" as a sign of proper discussion about a university program. In the process, the American professors were talking about problems that the Russians wanted least to hear; the Russians were talking about virtues that the Americans did not expect, for they wanted to address the problems and make the future better! Note that neither communication—cueing the fact of problems or the virtues of a program—is wrong. It is simply that the communication of each is unlike, even unanticipated by the other.

The potential difficulty in dynamics of intercultural communication like these can run deep. If one listens to the Russian cues by using an American code, then things can sound suspect. One might wonder from the view of an American code, why they are talking about virtues when they had been asked a factual question. Why talk about good family life when asked about premarital sex? Or, alternately, why talk about the virtues of a good educational program when asked about the state of one's university program? When heard solely from this American code, it seems something fishy is in the air. They are not talking about the facts. They must be hiding something!

From the Russian code, however, things can be equally as puzzling. What in the world are the Americans doing here? Why are they talking about all these problems and difficulties? We think we are here to discuss at least partly what good there is in human family life, or in university programs. It sounds to us like the Americans do not have any values or virtues at all! Even, at times, these Americans sound like they have no morals—all this talk of premarital sex! This type of dynamic shows how intercultural communication can go when different cues and codes are being used in an intercultural situation.

In another set of studies conducted in Finland and the United States, we found ourselves focusing on how people use and interpret silences in social encounters. In interviews with Finnish foreign exchange students who were living in the United States, I would ask them how they were enjoying school in the U.S. A typical response was that school was fine, but it was hard to concentrate because people were talking all the time. The Finnish students would say it was difficult to find the time to think. I probed further by asking what that meant. Well, they would say, when a teacher asks a question, students usually start talking right away, another student jumps in and says something, then another. The Finnish exchange students would wonder out loud: How am I supposed to think when people are talking all the time?

This study also involved interviewing students from the United States who were exchange students in Finland. I would ask them the same question, how they enjoyed school in Finland—Finnish schools by the way being considered the best in the world by many! American students would often say it was fine but difficult. I asked about the difficulty and part of the response was the report that students do not talk very much. It was difficult to learn, the American students would say, when no one says much of anything.

Parts of these studies were based upon fieldwork in Finland, which involved my teaching in Finnish classrooms. When posing a question in a Finnish classroom, there was often a prolonged period of silence. After experiencing this type of silence for several months, I realized that Finnish students typically believed they should speak in class only when they had something important to say, that was not obvious to anyone else, that was worthy of the teacher's and the other students' time (Carbaugh, 2005). Formulating such a thought into words took some time. And everyone understood that the time it was taking, the prolonged silence, was needed as a space to think deeply and carefully about the matter at hand. In Finnish, there is a kind of educational talk researched by Richard Wilkins called "asia-talk" (Wilkins, 2005, 2009; Wilkins and Isotalus, 2009). It is valued in Finnish classrooms. It involves talking directly and concisely about the subject matter at hand. To do this properly takes time in silence. So, in Finnish communication, the cue of silence is attached through this code to thinking carefully and deeply, as well as to talking directly and concisely. From the view of this Finnish code, then, some American classroom talk can sound rather impulsive and superficial or not well thought out.

By this time you may be wondering why you should care about Native American, Russian, or Finnish cues and codes. After all, you may not have plans to travel to an American Indian reservation, to Russia, or to Finland. But over the next years, or even in your next few days, you will contact people whose ways of living are no doubt different from your customary ways. How will you manage those kinds of situations when they come your way? This can be a real challenge, especially when others, who use other cues and codes, do things you might find at least puzzling if not downright inappropriate or wrong. After all, someone may not speak when you expect them to, or communicate in nonverbal ways when you expect words, or be speaking in a way that feels not quite truthful, or reply to you with a long silence, and so on. Sometimes these matters are simply a matter of an individual's personality; at other times, it is a matter of cultural code. It is an understanding of the latter—the cues and codes—that can help us think through and manage intercultural communication more effectively. Let us conclude with some thoughts about this.

Note that we have been discussing communication practices, or ways of speaking that are customary or shared by people. Through one traditional Native American practice, it is considered most important at times to listen rather than to speak (Carbaugh, 2005, pp. 100–119); in some Russian scenes, it is considered more important to speak about collective virtues than about facts (Carbaugh, 2005, pp. 55–81); in some Finnish scenes, it is considered more important to be silent periodically than to speak (Carbaugh, Berry, and Nurmikari-Berry, 2006). Note that we have not been focusing on individuals or psychological dispositions. One of the important contributions of communication research is its rigorous focus on communication itself, how it is done, its nature, social use, and cultural meanings. The research above helps us do that, to make claims about how people communicate together, thereby shaping their social lives and infusing them with cultural meanings.

It is important to understand this communication focus, what it allows us to understand, and what it does not. If the research is accurate, we can expect to find practices of "listening" in some scenes of Native American; we can expect to find some type of "speaking virtuously" in some Russian scenes; we can expect some Finnish scenes where a kind of silence is appreciated and practiced. BUT, just because these communication patterns are evident and robust in some cultural scenes, does not mean all "Native Americans just listen," "Russians can't speak the truth," or "Finns are silent" any more than it means U.S. Americans are superficial. The findings here are about social patterns and cultural practices of communication, common cues, and codes, not about populations of people. This is an important point. Why, because an inaccurate reading of this research can fall prey to the formulation of negative stereotypes such as "Russians don't speak truthfully" or "Finns are silent." When any one of us reflects for a moment, we do realize that some individuals in Finland indeed talk frequently, just as Russians can speak factually, and so on. So the findings we draw to your attention are about cultural patterns of communication that organize people for a period of time into social events; they are not inherent qualities of a type of person.

The point is important as we live among a diversity of cultures. As we do so, as we enter a work force, or travel, or sometimes even as we marry, we find ourselves among cues we are not sure how to decipher or code. This makes it important for us to watch, listen, and study the communication of others. Good business managers know how to identify the best talents of their workers and to help them work as a team. Part of that talent can involve identifying cues and codes that workers use, and seeing the value they bring to a multicultural team of workers. Good coaches know how to motivate players, increasingly players from different nations or backgrounds, to help them achieve at their highest level. Yet this is not done in one and only one way. That is part of what a good manager or coach today must learn, the variety in cues team members bring and to work productively with them. Similarly, in classrooms, teachers can find a variety of students, from various backgrounds, nations, and ethnicities. Watching what this brings to the classroom, using this to the benefit of education, and designing the social environment with the range in view. This is the challenge and the possibility of studying communication, its diversity of cues and codes!

To summarize then, note that the following can provide a way of studying communication especially in intercultural situations. First, communication includes, whether knowingly or not, cues about shared meaning. These cues can be done in ways that are deliberate and planned, as when one carefully chooses one's language for a public speech. These cues can also be done in a way that is unknowing or unplanned, as the way we hold our faces or our eyebrows. Cues as these can signal meanings that are explicit as when "close the door" means exactly what it says! Cues can also signal meanings that are more implicit as when "close the door" means you are too noisy, my needs are important to you, and I can control what you do by telling you to indeed close that door! Cues, then, are not only planned but unplanned, not only explicit but implicit. By watching and listening for cues, and carefully reflecting upon our own, we can learn about the variety of communication around us.

An important link we have used in our research, and in this brief essay about it, is the linking of cues to codes. Let me finish here with an example about service encounters in convenience stores in Los Angeles, California (Bailey, 2000). Some of these stores are owned and operated by Korean shopkeepers. African-American customers frequent these stores. It is important to both the Korean shopkeepers and the African-American customers to "be respectful" to each other. Yet, how do you show or "cue" respect from one to another? These codes vary! The Korean shopkeeper uses a pattern of verbal reserve, or of saying as little as possible, as a way of giving his customer space and not intruding on the customer's time in the store. The shopkeeper also shows respect in the way merchandise is handed to the customer. The shopkeeper codes these largely nonverbal cues of verbal reserve and nonverbal handing over of the merchandise as "respecting the customer."

The African-American customer at times uses a different set of cues for "respect." He likes some verbal repartee with the shopkeeper. To him, it does not matter so much what is talked about—the weather, sports, merchandise itself, a joke. What does matter is that the shopkeeper becomes verbally engaged with the customer. This cues to the African-American customer that the shopkeeper cares enough to talk with him, to give him some (verbal) time, and to be a part of his trip to the store. Note then, when the Korean shopkeeper cues respect from the vantage of the Korean code—by giving the customer quiet space, he is at the same time cueing a lack of respect from the point of view of African-American code; similarly as the African-American customer cues respect from the vantage of her code—by inviting several verbal exchanges, she is at the same time cueing a lack of respect from the view of the Korean code.

Our summary point about this body of research is this: When we communicate, we use cues that we assume are understood by others. In intercultural communication situations, cues can often be misunderstood as they are coded from different points of view. A way forward is to be able to critically reflect upon the variety of cues others and we use and eventually to better understand how they are coded. At times, intercultural interactions are not easy processes to understand. Yet when we understand communication in this way, it allows us to move onward—not through an unthinking or habitual action and judgment—but by understanding the communication practices better of others and ourselves. This is the way we bring cultural codes into our conversations. And by monitoring this process among family members, workers, and friends, we can improve the ways we are living among cultures!

REFERENCES

Bailey, B. (2000). Communicative behavior and conflict between African American customers and Korean immigrant retailers in Los Angeles. *Discouse & Society, 11,* 86–108.

Boromisza-Habashi, D. (2007). Freedom of expression, hate speech, and models of personhood in Hungarian political discourse. *Communication Law Review, 7,* 54–74.

Braithwaite, C. (1997). Sa'ah naaghai bik'eh hozhoon: An ethnography of Navajo educational communication practices. *Communication Education, 46,* 219–233.

Carbaugh, D. (1988). *Talking American.* Norwood, NJ: Ablex.

Carbaugh, D. (1999). "Just Listen": "Listening" and landscape among the Blackfeet. *Western Journal of Communication, 63,* 250–270.

Carbaugh, D. (2005). *Cultures in conversation.* New York and London: Lawrence Erlbaum Associates.

Carbaugh, D., Berry, M., & Nurmikari-Berry, M. (2006). Coding personhood through cultural terms and practices: Silence and quietude as Finnish "natural way of being." *Journal of Language and Social Psychology, 25,* 1–18.

Covarrubias, P. O. (2008). Masked silence sequences: Hearing discrimination in the college class room. *Communication, Culture & Critique, 1,* 227–252.

Fitch, K. (1998). *Speaking relationally: Culture, communication, and interpersonal connection.* New York, London: The Guildford Press.

Hastings, S. O. (2000). Asian Indian "self-suppression" and self-disclosure: Enactment and adaptation of cultural identity. *Journal of Language and Social Psychology, 19,* 85–109.

Hastings, S. O. (2001). Social drama as a site for the communal construction and management of Asian Indian "stranger" identity. *Research on Language and Social Interaction, 34,* 309–335.

Hymes, D. (1996). *Ethnography, linguistics, narrative inequality: Toward an understanding of voice.* New York: Taylor and Francis.

Katriel, T. (2004). *Dialogic moments: From soul talks to talk radio in Israeli culture.* Detroit, MI: Wayne State University Press.

Leeds-Hurwitz, W. (1990). Culture and communication: A review essay. *Quarterly Journal of Speech, 76,* 85–116.

Milburn, T. (2000). Enacting "Puerto Rican time" in the United States. *International and Intercultural Communication Annual, 23,* 47–76.

Philipsen, G. (1992). *Speaking culturally.* Albany, NY: State University of New York Press.

Philipsen, G. (1997). A theory of speech codes. In G. Philipsen, and T. Albrecht (Eds.), *Developing communication theories* (pp. 119–156). Albany, NY: State University of New York Press.

Philipsen, G. (2002). Cultural communication. In W. Gudykunst and B. Mody (Eds.), *Handbook of international and intercultural communication* (pp. 51–67). Thousand Oaks, CA: Sage.

Philipsen, G., Coutu, L., & Covarrubias, P. (2005). Speech codes theory: Restatement, revisions, and a response to criticisms. In W. Gudykunst, (Ed.), *Theorizing about intercultural communication.* Thousand Oaks, CA: Sage Publications.

Poutiainen, S. (2005). Kulttuurista puhetta deittaamisesta. [Cultural talk about dating.] *Puhe ja kieli, 25:3,* 123–136.

Sajavaara, K., & Lehtonen, J. (1997). The silent Finn revisited. In J. Adam (Ed.), *Silence: Interdisciplinary perspectives* (pp. 262–283). New York: Mouton de Gruyter.

Scollo, M. (2011). Cultural approaches to discourse analysis: A theoretical and methodological conversation with special focus on Donal Carbaugh's cultural discourse theory. *Journal of Multicultural Discourses, 6,* 1–32.

Wieder, L., & Pratt, S. (1990). On being a recognizable Indian among Indians. In D. Carbaugh (Ed.), *Cultural communication and intercultural contact* (pp. 45–64). Hillsdale, NJ: Lawrence Erlbaum Associates, Inc.

Wilkins, R. (2005). The optimal form: Inadequacies and excessiveness within the "asiallinen" [matter-of-fact] nonverbal style in public and civic settings in Finland. *Journal of Communication, 55,* 383–401.

Wilkins, R. (2009). The asiasta puhuminen event. In R. Wilkins, & P. Isotalus (Eds.). *Speech culture in Finland* (pp. 63–84). Lanham, Maryland: University Press of America.

Wilkins, R., & Isotalus, P. (2009). *Speech culture in Finland.* Lanham, Maryland: University Press of America.

Witteborn, S. (2007a). The expression of Palestinian identity in narratives about personal experiences: Implications for the study of narrative, identity, and social interaction. *Research on Language and Social Interaction, 40,* 145–170.

Witteborn, S. (2007b). The situated expression of Arab collective identities in the United States. *Journal of Communication, 57,* 556–575.

Witteborn, S. (2010). The role of transnational NGOs in promoting global citizenship and globalizing communication practices. *Language and Intercultural Communication, 10,* 358–372.

Witteborn, S., & Sprain, L. (2009). Grouping processes in a public meeting from an ethnography of communication and cultural discourse analysis perspective. *International Journal of Public Participation, 3,* 14–35.

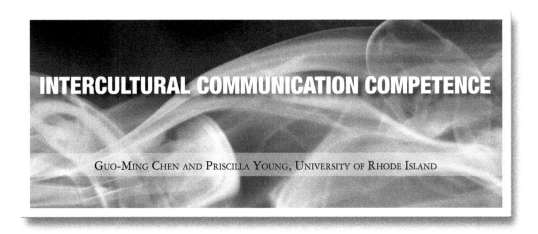

INTERCULTURAL COMMUNICATION COMPETENCE

Guo-Ming Chen and Priscilla Young, University of Rhode Island

INTRODUCTION

Most people probably don't think a lot about how culture affects communication, and vice versa. Generally, we communicate with others the way that our families communicated with us. We listened to and watched the way our parents spoke to and behaved around others, and we followed suit. So, why the interest now in what is called intercultural communication? Isn't everybody basically the same? After all, we're all human beings.

Well, think about these questions: Do you expect to live in the same place where you grew up for the rest of your life? Will the population where you live remain as it is, with no new people moving there? Will the people you work with be of the same background as you, having the same cultural heritage and speaking the same native language? What if you travel to a different country? Will customs be the same? How would you react when speaking to a person who doesn't make eye contact or who politely agrees with all you say? What if you waved at someone whose reaction made you wonder what you did wrong?

These are only a smattering of examples of how culture affects who we are and how we communicate both verbally and nonverbally. The trick, however, is to learn that these behaviors are not necessarily the same for people with backgrounds different from ours. Even more important is to learn that just because we do something in a particular way doesn't mean that others are wrong when they do things in their own way. No one culture is better than another. It just is different. So, in the spirit of questioning, consider the following: How can we best increase our intercultural communication competence when we encounter people from different international cultures during travel, study, or business interactions? This chapter attempts to answer this question by exploring the concept of "intercultural communication competence."

INTERCULTURAL COMMUNICATION COMPETENCE

So what is "intercultural communication competence" (ICC)? ICC can be simply defined as an individual's ability to execute effective and appropriate communication behaviors in order to achieve one's communication goals in an intercultural context. Over the years, intercultural communication scholars have attempted to figure out what the elements of ICC are (e.g., Abe & Wiseman, 1983; Chen, 2009, 2010a; Hammer, Gudykunst, & Wiseman, 1978; Lustig & Koester, 2009; Martin, 1993; Ruben & Kealey, 1979; Spitzberg & Changnon, 2009; Wiseman & Abe, 1986). After a thorough review of the literature of ICC study, Chen (1989) found that the elements specified by scholars can be categorized into four dimensions, and each dimension is comprised of four components (see Figure 1).

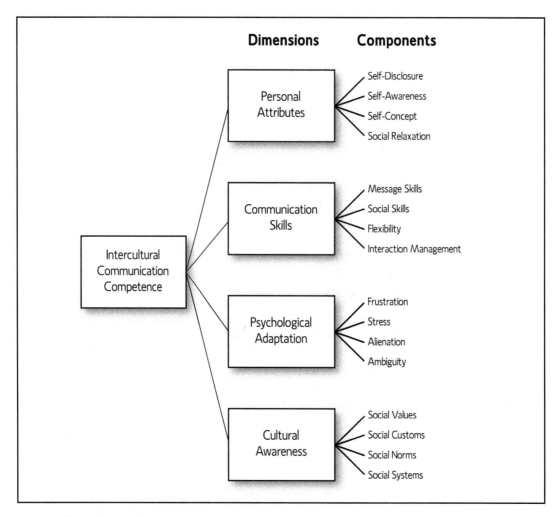

Figure 1. The dimensions and components of intercultural communication competence.

Figure 1 shows that an interculturally competent person possesses four sets of abilities when interacting with people from different cultural backgrounds:

1. **Personal attributes**—referring to having a positive personality, which includes knowing how to disclose oneself appropriately (self-disclosure), knowing oneself (self-awareness), seeing oneself positively (self-concept), and showing little anxiety in interaction (social relaxation).

2. **Communication skills**—referring to knowing how to interact well, which includes being skillful in the verbal and nonverbal language of one's cultural counterpart (message skills), being empathic (social skills), knowing how to behave in different contexts (flexibility), and knowing when to initiate, take turns, and terminate a conversation (interaction management).

3. **Psychological adaptation**—referring to the ability to cope with culture shock, which includes coping with the feelings of frustration, stress, alienation, and uncertainty caused by the ambiguous situation due to cultural differences.

4. **Cultural awareness**—referring to the understanding of the cultural conventions of one's counterpart, including social values, social customs, social norms, and social systems. Figure 1 is a nice illustration of the content of ICC. In order to make the model of ICC even more precise, Chen and Starosta (1996) and Chen (2010b) went one step further to transform Figure 1 into a more aesthetic and theoretical model (see Figure 2), which indicates that ICC can be examined from three perspectives: (1) cognitive—intercultural awareness, (2) affective—intercultural sensitivity, and (3) behavioral—intercultural adroitness. The three perspectives represent the three sides of the equilateral triangle of ICC. Let's use this model to learn more about ICC.

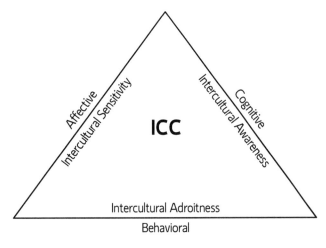

Figure 2. A model of intercultural communication competence.

Intercultural Awareness

The cognitive perspective of ICC, indicating the ability of intercultural awareness, refers to the understanding of distinct cultural features of one's counterpart. It is a process of learning about the beliefs and values or the way of thinking of persons from another culture (Chen & Starosta, 1998–9). To know cultural differences is the first step necessary to reduce ambiguity or uncertainty in intercultural interaction. This will in turn lead to less discomfort, confusion, and anxiety in the process of adapting to a new cultural environment.

According to Kluckhohn (1948), culture is a map. If the cultural map in one's mind is accurate, one will not get lost when interacting with people from that specific culture. It is similar to a geographical map. If the information on the map correctly reflects the streets of the area, one will get to the destination easily. A culture is also like an essay that always has a "theme" running through it (Turner, 1968). In order to know a culture, one needs to know how to properly draw the cultural map or to pull out the cultural theme. The cultural map or cultural theme can be demonstrated by studies on cultural values from scholars like Kluckhohn and Strodbeck (1961), Hall (1976), and Hofstede (1984).

Kluckhohn and Strodbeck (1961) pointed out that cultural values can be understood from five universal problems faced by all human societies: (1) human nature, (2) the relationship between human and nature, (3) time orientation, (4) activity orientation, and (5) relational orientation. Hall (1976) classified human culture into high-context culture and low-context culture. In high-context cultures, such as China and Japan, people tend to be more indirect in expressing themselves and more able to read nonverbal cues; while in low-context cultures, like Switzerland and the United States, people tend to be more verbally expressive and direct in interaction. Hofstede (1984) examined cultural values from the business perspective and found five dimensions, including individualism vs. collectivism, power distance, uncertainty reduction, masculinity vs. femininity, and Confucian dynamism.

Not being aware of the cultural conventions of one's counterpart often leads to misunderstanding in the process of intercultural interaction, which may result in interpersonal conflict, failure in business transactions, or war between nations. The following are a few daily-life examples of cultural differences for you to see how many you are aware of:

1. In Malaysia, people don't use the left hand to eat, hold things, or shake hands, because they think the left hand is not clean.

2. In Korea, gifts shouldn't be wrapped in white paper.

3. In business negotiations, North Americans typically use a factual approach based on logic, Saudi Arabians use an affective approach based on emotions, and Russians use an axiomatic approach based on ideals (Glenn, Witmeyer, & Stevenson, 1977).

4. Mexicans emphasize interpersonal relationships more than being "on time"; thus the way they perceive time tends to be polychromic, which means that they may schedule several events at the same point of time.

There are many ways to assess the degree of one's intercultural awareness (e.g., Kitao, 1981; Kohl, 1984; Moran, Harris, & Moran, 2010; Saville-Troike, 1978). Appendix A is an instrument for testing intercultural awareness developed by Chen (1995). The underlined nation can be replaced by any nation you like, but remember to reverse the scores of different items based on the cultural values of the nation you select for the test.

Intercultural Sensitivity

The affective perspective of ICC is represented by intercultural sensitivity. This refers to the ability to further develop a positive feeling or emotion towards cultural differences in the process of intercultural communication, based on the awareness of cultural characteristics of one's counterpart. This positive emotion includes one's willingness or motivation to understand, acknowledge, respect, and even accept differences of the two cultural beings or groups (Chen & Starosta, 1997). It is important to know that intercultural awareness as the foundation of ICC must be accompanied with intercultural sensitivity in order to reach the authentic state of intercultural understanding. Chen's (1995) study showed that in certain situations (e.g., in a competitive business negotiation), without being interculturally sensitive or using one's heart to understand and empathize with the cultural differences, interactants may take advantage of their counterparts because of understanding their counterparts' culture.

Interculturally sensitive persons usually possess six distinct personal characteristics (Bennett, 1986; Triandis, 1977; Yum, 1989): (1) self-esteem—a strong sense of self-value or self-worth, (2) self-monitoring—the ability to detect the situational constraints in order to behave appropriately, (3) open-mindedness—the willingness to accept differences, (4) empathy—to see the other's point of view from that person's perspective, (5) interaction involvement –responsiveness, perceptiveness, and attentiveness in interaction, and (6) suspending judgment—not jumping to conclusions without having sufficient information. Appendix B is a more recent and valid instrument developed by Chen and Starosta (2000), which readjusts the factors of intercultural sensitivity. You can answer the questions to gauge your level of intercultural sensitivity.

Intercultural Adroitness

The ultimate goal of knowing and being sensitive to cultural differences is to perform effectively in the behavioral level of intercultural interaction. Intercultural adroitness (or intercultural effectiveness) speaks for the behavioral perspective of ICC. It refers to the ability to achieve one's communication goals in intercultural interaction through behavioral performance (Chen, 2007). In other words, intercultural adroitness is demonstrated by one's verbal and nonverbal communication skills that enable the person to be successful and productive in the process of intercultural communication. It is important to remember, however, that the definition of ICC includes appropriateness, so effective communication behaviors must be regulated by this principle because in intercultural interaction one may use unethical means (e.g., violating the cultural rules of one's counterpart) to effectively but inappropriately attain the communication goal.

Studies show that those effective intercultural communication skills include five elements (e.g., Cupach & Imahori, 1993; Martin & Hammer, 1989; Wiseman, 2003): (1) message skills—the ability to employ one's counterpart's verbal and nonverbal behaviors, (2) interaction management—the ability to initiate, take turns, and terminate a conversation, (3) behavioral flexibility—the ability to attend to various information and to use appropriate communication strategies, (4) identity management—the ability to maintain one's counterpart's personal and cultural identities, and (5) relationship cultivation—the ability to establish the interdependent and reciprocal relationship with one's counterpart. Appendix C is a valid instrument developed recently by Portalla and Chen (2010), which you can use to measure your ability of intercultural adroitness.

Finally, you may wonder how can people acquire the ability of ICC? Intercultural training is the answer for this. Scholars and practitioners from different disciplines have developed a variety of intercultural training programs to help people become competent in intercultural interaction. Chen and Starosta (2005) organized those common intercultural training programs into six models: (1) the classroom model—usually applying the curricular offerings of an education system, (2) the simulation model—involving participants in an environment that closely resembles a specific culture, (3) the self-awareness model—training people how psychological forces operate in groups and how their own behaviors influence others, (4) the cultural awareness model—focusing on the understanding of cultural knowledge of one's counterpart, (5) the behavioral model—teaching trainees specific behavioral skills of a specific culture, and (6) the interaction model—directly asking participants to interact with people from a specific culture. Intercultural training is the practical part of intercultural communication study. If you are interested in it, you can use the references at the end of this chapter to gain more information about the topic (e.g., Landis, Bennett, & Bennett, 2003) or take a course dedicated to the topic of Intercultural Communication.

CONCLUSION

The globalization trend continues to dominate the twenty-first century. As a college student, you'll face international students and scholars from different cultures on campus on a daily basis; you may study abroad to fulfill your college course or travel around the world just because the transportation and communication technology makes transnational movement so easy, convenient and less expensive; and you'll compete in the global job market after graduation. All these point to the importance of becoming a global citizen in order to succeed in contemporary human society. Being a successful global citizen means to be able to communicate effectively and appropriately in different cultural contexts. This chapter aims to examine the knowledge and skills for being competent in intercultural communication by specifying the dimensions and components of a model of ICC. Instruments used to measure the ability of each dimension of ICC were also included, so that you can assess you own degree of ICC and further improve it if necessary through participating in different kinds of intercultural training.

From the research perspective it is clear that the approach taken in this chapter to explore the concept of intercultural communication competence is based on the tradition of functionalism or discovery paradigm. In other words, the approach assumes that the elements of ICC can be systematically identified and empirically tested, so that people can acquire ICC through a more scientific method, such as a well-designed intercultural training program. One needs to be aware that in addition to functionalism there are alternative approaches to the study of ICC. For instance, as Young (1996) pointed out, the study of intercultural communication can be addressed from the critical perspective, through which power or ideology embedded in the historical context is involved in understanding the intercultural communication process. In this sense, ICC is conceived as "speaking authentically, accurately, and appropriately with regard to the social relationship, as well as a willingness on the part of those in positions of power to cooperate with those who resist domination" (Kelly 2008, p. 267). To better understand ICC it will be wise to integrate the views from different approaches.

REFERENCES

Abe, H., & Wiseman, R. L. (1983). A cross-cultural confirmation of the dimensions of intercultural effectiveness. *International Journal of Intercultural Relations, 7,* 53 –67.

Bennett, M. J. (1986). A developmental approach to training for intercultural sensitivity. *International Journal of Intercultural Relations, 10,* 179–196.

Chen, G. M. (1989). Relationships of the dimensions of intercultural communication competence. *Communication Quarterly, 37,* 118-133.

Chen, G. M. (1995). *International e-mail debate and intercultural awareness.* Manuscript prepared for a grant project sponsored by the Fund for the Improvement of Postsecondary Education (PIPSE).

Chen, G. M. (2007). A review of the concept of intercultural effectiveness. In M. Hinner (Ed.), *The influence of culture in the world of business* (pp. 95–116). Germany: Peter Lang.

Chen, G. M. (2009). Intercultural communication competence. In S. Littlejohn, & K. Foss (Eds.), *Encyclopedia of communication theory* (pp. 529–532). Thousand Oaks, CA: Sage.

Chen, G. M. (2010a). *A study of intercultural communication competence.* Hong Kong: China Review Academic Publishers.

Chen, G. M. (2010b). *Foundations of intercultural communication competence.* Hong Kong: China Review Academic Publishers.

Chen, G. M., & Starosta, W. J. (1996). Intercultural communication competence: A synthesis. *Communication Yearbook 19,* 353–383.

Chen, G. M., & Starosta, W. J. (1997). A review of the concept of intercultural sensitivity. *Human Communication, 1,* 1–16.

Chen, G. M., & Starosta, W. J. (1998–9). A review of the concept of intercultural awareness. *Human Communication, 2,* 27–54.

Chen, G. M., & Starosta, W. J. (2000). The development and validation of the intercultural sensitivity scale. *Human Communication, 3,* 1–15.

Chen, G. M., & Starosta, W. J. (2005). *Foundations of intercultural communication.* Lanham, MD: University Press of America.

Cupach, W. R., & Imahori, T. T. (1993). Identity management theory: Communication competence in intercultural episodes and relationships. In R. L. Wiseman, & J. Koester (Eds.), *Intercultural communication competence* (pp. 112–131). Newbury Park, CA: Sage.

Glenn, E. S., Witmeyer, D., & Stevenson, K. A. (1977). Cultural styles of persuasion. *International Journal of Intercultural Relations, 1,* 52–66.

Gudykunst, W. B., & Kim, Y. Y. (1992). *Communicating with strangers.* New York: McGraw-Hill.

Hall, E. T. (1976). *Beyond Culture.* Garden City, NY: Anchor.

Hammer, M., Gudykunst, W., & Wiseman, R. (1978). Dimensions of intercultural effectiveness. *International Journal of Intercultural Relations, 2,* 382–393.

Hofstede, G. (1984). *Culture's consequences.* Beverly Hills, CA: Sage.

Kelly, W. (2008). Applying a critical metatheoretical approach to intercultural relations: The case of U.S.-Japanese communication. In M. K. Asante, Y. Miike, & J. Yin (Eds.), *The global intercultural communication reader* (pp. 263–279). New York: Routledge.

Kohls, L. R. (1984). *The values Americans live by: Introduction.* Washington, DC: Meridian House International.

Kitao, K. (1981). The test of American culture. *Technology & Mediated Instruction, 15,* 25–45.

Kluckhohn, F. K., (1948). *Mirror of man.* New York: Harper Collins.

Kluckhohn, F. K., & Strodbeck, F. L. (1961). *Variations in value orientations.* Evanston, Ill: Row, Peterson.

Kohls, L. R. (1988). Models for comparing and contrasting cultures. In J. M. Reid (Ed.), *Building the professional dimension of educational exchange* (pp. 137–153). Yarmouth, ME: Intercultural Press.

Landis, D., Bennett, J. M., & Bennett, M. (Eds.) (2003). *Handbook of intercultural training.* Thousand Oaks, CA: Sage.

Lustig, M. W., & Koester, J. (2009). *Intercultural competence: Interpersonal communication across cultures.* Boston, MA: Allyn and Bacon.

Martin, J. N. (1993). Intercultural communication competence: A review. In R. L. Wiseman & J. Koester (Eds.), *Intercultural communication competence* (pp. 16–29). Newbury Park, CA: Sage.

Martin, J. N., & Hammer, M. R. (1989). Behavioral categories of intercultural communication competence: Everyday communicators' perceptions. *International Journal of Intercultural Relations, 13,* 303–332.

Moran, R. T., Harris, P. R., & Moran, S. V. (2010). *Managing cultural differences: Global leadership strategies for the 21st century.* New York: Elsevier.

Portalla, T., & Chen, G. M. (2010). The development and validation of the intercultural effectiveness scale. *Intercultural Communication Studies, 19*(3), 21–37.

Ruben, B. D., & Kealey, D.J. (1979). Behavioral assessment of communication competency and the prediction of cross-cultural adaptation. *International Journal of Intercultural Relations, 3,* 15–47.

Saville-Troike, M. (1978). *A guide to culture in the classroom.* Rosslyn, VI: InterAmerica Research Associates.

Spitzberg, B. H., & Changnon, G. (2009). Conceptualizing intercultural competence. In D. K. Deardorff (Ed.), *The Sage handbook of intercultural competence* (pp. 2–52). Los Angeles, CA: Sage.

Triandis, H.C. (1977). Subjective culture and interpersonal relations across cultures. In L. Loeb-Adler (Ed.), Issues in cross-cultural research. Annals of the New York Academy of Sciences, 285, 418-434.

Turner, C. V. (1968). The Sinasina "big man" complex: A central cultural theme. *Practical Anthropology, 15,* 16–22.

Wiseman, R. L. (2003). Intercultural communication competence. In W. B. Gudykunst (Ed.), *Cross-cultural and intercultural communication* (pp. 191–208). Thousand Oaks, CA: Sage.

Wiseman, R. L., & Abe H. (1986). Explication and test of a model of communicative competence. *Human Communication Research, 13,* 3–33.

Young, R. E. (1996). *Intercultural communication: Pragmatics, genealogy, deconstruction.* Clevedon, UK: Multilingual Matters.

Yum, J. O. (1989). *Communication sensitivity and empathy in culturally diverse organizations.* Paper presented at the 75th Annual Conference of the Speech Communication Association, San Francisco.

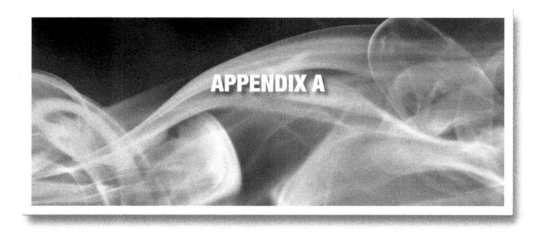

APPENDIX A

INTERCULTURAL AWARENESS INSTRUMENT

DIRECTIONS: Here are several statements about *American* cultural values. Please indicate the extent to which you feel that each statement describes what you think. There are no right or wrong answers. Just answer honestly how you feel by indicating:

    5 = Strongly Agree
    4 = Agree
    3 = Not Decided
    2 = Disagree
    1 = Strongly Disagree

_____ 1. *Americans* are individualists.

_____ 2. *Americans* are doing-oriented.

_____ 3. *Americans* believe that life is basically sad.

_____ 4. *Americans* are high in family mobility.

_____ 5. *Americans* emphasize spiritual life.

_____ 6. *Americans* are open in the family role behavior.

_____ 7. *Americans* are less formal in social interaction.

_____ 8. *Americans* seldom express their opinions openly.

_____ 9. *Americans* emphasize social rank.

_____ 10. *Americans* often refer to each other by first name.

_____ 11. *Americans* are not action-oriented.

_____ 12. *Americans* believe that they are in control over their environment.

_____ 13. *Americans* rely on intermediaries in social interaction.

_____ 14. *Americans* express their opinions directly.

_____ 15. *Americans* are less democratic in the family role behavior.

_____ 16. *Americans* emphasize change more than tradition.

_____ 17. *Americans* do not emphasize status.

_____ 18. *Americans* emphasize the future more than the past.

_____ 19. *Americans* believe that human nature is unchangeable.

_____ 20. *Americans* believe that people are controlled by the supernatural.

Note: The underlined nation's name can be replaced by another nation. Items to be reversed (i.e., 5=1, 4=2, 2=4, 1=5): 3, 5, 8, 9, 11, 13, 15, 17, 19, 20

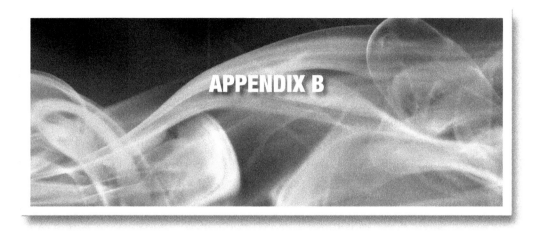

APPENDIX B

INTERCULTURAL SENSITIVITY SCALE

Direction: Below is a series of statements concerning intercultural communication. There are no right or wrong answers. Please work quickly and record your first impression by indicating the degree to which you agree or disagree with the statement. Thank you for your cooperation.

5 = Strongly Agree
4 = Agree
3 = Not Decided
2 = Disagree
1 = Strongly Disagree

_____ 1. I enjoy interacting with people from different cultures.

_____ 2. I think people from other cultures are narrow-minded.

_____ 3. I am pretty sure of myself in interacting with people from different cultures.

_____ 4. I find it very hard to talk in front of people from different cultures.

_____ 5. I always know what to say when interacting with people from different cultures.

_____ 6. I can be as sociable as I want to be when interacting with people from different cultures.

_____ 7. I don't like to be with people from different cultures.

_____ 8. I respect the values of people from different cultures.

_____ 9. I get upset easily when interacting with people from different cultures.

_____ 10. I feel confident when interacting with people from different cultures.

_____ 11. I tend to wait before forming an impression of culturally-distinct counterparts.

_____ 12. I often get discouraged when I am with people from different cultures.

_____ 13. I am open-minded to people from different cultures.

_____ 14. I am very observant when interacting with people from different cultures.

_____ 15. I often feel useless when interacting with people from different cultures.

_____ 16. I respect the ways people from different cultures behave.

_____ 17. I try to obtain as much information as I can when interacting with people from different cultures.

_____ 18. I would not accept the opinions of people from different cultures.

_____ 19. I am sensitive to my culturally-distinct counterpart's subtle meanings during our interaction.

_____ 20. I think my culture is better than other cultures.

_____ 21. I often give positive responses to my culturally different counterpart during our interaction.

_____ 22. I avoid those situations where I will have to deal with culturally-distinct persons.

_____ 23. I often show my culturally-distinct counterpart my understanding through verbal or nonverbal cues.

_____ 24. I have a feeling of enjoyment towards differences between my culturally-distinct counterpart and me.

Note. Items 2, 4, 7, 9, 12, 15, 18, 20, and 22 are reverse-coded before summing the 24 items (i.e., 5=1, 4=2, 2=4, 1=5). Interaction Engagement items are 1, 11, 13, 21, 22, 23, and 24, Respect for Cultural Differences items are 2, 7, 8, 16, 18, and 20, Interaction Confidence items are 3, 4, 5, 6, and 10, Interaction Enjoyment items are 9, 12, and 15, and Interaction Attentiveness items are 14, 17, and 19.

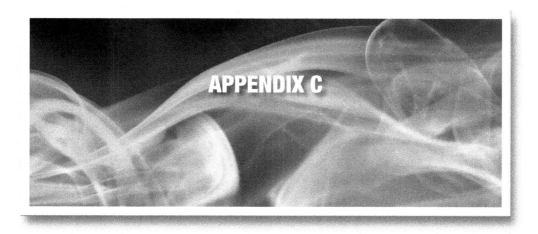

APPENDIX C

INTERCULTURAL ADROITNESS SCALE

Direction: Below is a series of statements concerning intercultural communication. There are no right or wrong answers. Please work quickly and record your first impression by indicating the degree to which you agree or disagree with the statement. Thank you for your cooperation.

5 = Strongly Agree
4 = Agree
3 = Not Decided
2 = Disagree
1 = Strongly Disagree

_____ 1. I find it is easy to talk with people from different cultures.

_____ 2. I am afraid to express myself when interacting with people from different cultures.

_____ 3. I find it is easy to get along with people from different cultures.

_____ 4. I am not always the person I appear to be when interacting with people from different cultures.

_____ 5. I am able to express my ideas clearly when interacting with people from different cultures.

_____ 6. I have problems with grammar when interacting with people from different cultures.

_____ 7. I am able to answer questions effectively when interacting with people from different cultures.

_____ 8. I find it is difficult to feel my culturally different counterparts are similar to me.

_____ 9. I use appropriate eye contact when interacting with people from different cultures.

_____ 10. I have problems distinguishing between informative and persuasive messages when interacting with people from different cultures.

_____ 11. I always know how to initiate a conversation when interacting with people from different cultures.

_____ 12. I often miss parts of what is going on when interacting with people from different cultures.

_____ 13. I feel relaxed when interacting with people from different cultures.

_____ 14. I often act like a very different person when interacting with people from different cultures.

_____ 15. I always show respect for my culturally different counterparts during our interaction.

_____ 16. I always feel a sense of distance with my culturally different counterparts during our interaction.

_____ 17. I find I have a lot in common with my culturally different counterparts during our interaction.

_____ 18. I find the best way to act is to be myself when interacting with people from different cultures.

_____ 19. I find it is easy to identify with my culturally different counterparts during our interaction.

_____ 20. I always show respect for the opinions of my culturally different counterparts during our interaction.

Note. Items 2, 4, 6, 8, 10, 12, 14, 16, and 18 are reverse-coded before summing the 20 items (i.e., 5=1, 4=2, 2=4, 1=5). Behavioral Flexibility items are 2, 4, 14, and 18, Interaction Relaxation items are 1, 3, 11, 13, and 19, Interactant Respect items are 9, 15, and 20, Message Skills items are 6, 10, and 12, Identity Maintenance items are 8, 16, and 19, Interaction Management items are 5 and 7.

GIVEN THAT HIGHLY RACIALIZED SOCIETY THAT WE LIVE IN, HOW DO WE COMMUNICATE MORE SUCCESSFULLY IN THIS CONTEXT?

TOM NAKAYAMA, NORTHEASTERN UNIVERSITY

When many people think about the study of intercultural communication, they are drawn to knowing the most important things that they need to know about communicating successfully in a particular culture. What kinds of nonverbal behaviors should I know about? What do different gestures mean? What kinds of cultural customs should I know about? What are important holidays? I was interested in these topics, but I was far more interested in the larger social structures, such as laws, that brought cultures into contact or kept them apart. Much of this interest was driven by my own history, but I also saw it in the trajectories of other people.

When I went to first grade, I entered a racially segregated elementary school in the Deep South where Jim Crow was still very much alive although it was gasping its last breath as official policy. Race structured everyday life and determined where one lived and went to school, who one married and more. For well over a hundred years, American racial policies have shaped my family's experience. Over the intervening years, many people worked very hard in many different ways to change how we think about race and its place in our society.

Race, racism, and racial differences have been significant influences in U.S. society since its inception. From the first naturalization law that determined only "free, white persons" were eligible to be "Americans," to more recent and enduring racial disparities in health, income, and life expectancy, race continues to shape everyday lives. Race remains a significant issue in our everyday interaction.

How do we communicate more successfully in the context of this highly racialized society we live in? Here I offer some suggestions based upon my work, but these suggestions are certainly not comprehensive. Please add to them as you move forward, based upon your experiences. The world is changing and attitudes about race are changing as well. When I grew up, I could never have imagined a non-white person being elected president. Today, President Barak Obama is president of the U.S., and it is a reflection of changing attitudes in our nation.

And yet older forms of racism re-emerge from time to time to remind all of us how much racial tensions are embedded in our society. For example, in the spring of 2012, the Boston Bruins and the Washington Flyers were in one of the playoff games in the National Hockey League. In this best of seven series, each team had three wins, which sent them to a final seventh game. The winner of the seventh game would move on in the NHL playoffs. The seventh game went into overtime and, in overtime, Joel Ward of the Washington Flyers scored the winning goal. While race seemingly has nothing to do with this hockey game, Twitter lit up with tweets using the N-word to attack Joel Ward. Joel Ward is a black Canadian player who was doing what hockey players try to do: score goals (Karp, 2012). Why do people have to rely upon racial differences to express their disappointment that their team, the Boston Bruins, lost and that their season ended? Yet, this approach continues to reinforce the importance of race in our society and the ways that racial identities are constructed in the public arena.

In this chapter, I want to highlight the importance of taking a critical approach to understanding intercultural communication. A critical approach emphasizes the role of intercultural communication in the context of larger social relations. These social relations can be legal (e.g., immigration laws), ideological (e.g., racism), and economic (e.g., tourists vs. refugees). A critical intercultural communication is concerned with how larger social structures bring some cultures into contact and not others, as well as how they come into contact. Attention to issues of immigration, emigration, refugee status, tourism, study abroad, hate crimes, and many more social issues are important to the scholars of critical intercultural communication as they shape our intercultural experiences.

So what does a critical approach to intercultural communication add to our understanding of intercultural interaction? Well, it means that there are many things you need to think about when you consider who comes into contact with whom and the conditions under which that intercultural contact happens. For example, the Hawaiian Islands have come into the possession of the United States. While the history of this possession is highly contested, people from Hawaii are U.S. citizens and, therefore, can more easily travel or move to the other 49 states of the United States. In contrast, people from Tahiti and the other "Society Islands" are now part of French Polynesia and French citizens. This makes it easier for them to travel to France, to work in France, etc. So, how does a critical intercultural communication orientation help us improve our thinking about intercultural interaction? One the one hand, it may feel daunting to take into account all of the histories, legal relationships, and cultural attitudes that shape our intercultural possibilities, but it is important to do so. Here are some starting points for taking a critical approach to intercultural communication:

1. **Think dialectically.** This means that you should think of the tensions that exist in your cultural identity, as well as in the identity of others. When we developed this model for thinking about how different tensions frame our cultural identities, we were convinced that there are many conflicting tensions that shape our identities. We developed a dialectical approach to intercultural communication (Martin & Nakayama, 1999). For example, I identify as an Asian American when some issues arise, such as more political concerns about racial issues. At other times, I am a Japanese American, but I also know that I am different from, as well as similar to, other Asian Americans and Japanese Americans

in a myriad of ways. On the one hand, I am an individual, but I am also shaped by my racial and ethnic experiences. Sometimes I feel very U.S. American, particularly when I am overseas. Similarly, Michelle Obama may see herself as an African American, but she is both like and unlike other African Americans in many ways. What is your cultural identity and how are you alike and not alike others who share your cultural identity? Sometimes people do not "feel" their cultural identity as strongly as when they are in a context that is the normative or dominant group, such as being a U.S. American overseas.

2. **Be self-reflexive.** In any communication encounter, think about how you are perceived and how that might affect the interpretation of your messages. Various audiences may interpret your communication messages quite differently depending upon whether you are a male or a female, if you are able-bodied or not, if you are old or young, and so on. Think about how your messages might be interpreted depending upon the contexts.

3. **Consider the historical context and the present/future.** We all enter into situations marked by historical events that influence how our communication might be interpreted. What is your cultural identity and how certain are you that your cultural identity might not be categorized differently in the future? How has the past influenced the character of your cultural identity? For example, the United States used to have racial restrictions on immigration. How does this history influence how we understand our cultural identity as U.S. Americans and how we see other U.S. Americans? Would we feel differently if our racial and cultural mix were different, if we had a different history?

   I explored some of these issues in a collection of essays I solicited for the Arizona Humanities Council in a project exploring the history of the interment of Japanese Americans in Arizona and its relevance today. *Transforming Barbed Wire* (Nakayama, 1997) highlights the ways that history has influenced the present and the future.

4. **Be aware of public discourse in the context of private communication.** Our study of California's racial privacy initiative (Flores, Moon, & Nakayama, 2006) focused on the intent of this proposition. In short, it emphasized that your racial identity and racial history are your own private information and the government has no right to ask you about it. However innocent this proposition may seem, it ignited a huge public debate about race, racism, and the ability to take action against racism. If the state has no information on race, how can anyone claim racism? In our study, we found that some people (whites and others) were opposed to the proposition for this same reason. Some whites felt that, as California became a place where whites were a minority, it would be important to have the racial data to prove that whites were discriminated against. Ultimately, we concluded that the debate hinged on the collection of data for healthcare. If healthcare professionals could not collect racial information, the prevalence of particular types of health issues with some racial groups over others might impede the delivery of appropriate healthcare to people in various cultural groups.

   Understanding the debates over what is "public" and what is "private" sheds light on the importance of aspects of our identities and their roles in society. Again, think dialectically about an individual's personal identity and an individual's social identity. We are all members of various collectivities and communities and our identities move through parts that are private, but also parts that are public and configured by social discourses about those identities.

5. **Be aware of the ways that identities can be reconfigured.** We all enter into intercultural conflicts and we need to be aware of the ways that various identities are continually being reconfigured and reconstructed to serve different interests. In our study of the murder of a disabled gay African American man (Moon & Nakayama, 2005), we found that the identities and cultural discourses around the perpetrators of this murder shifted over the period from the murder to the trial. Initially, the perpetrators were seen as part of the community or as "one of us." This image was important to establishing how everyone in the community got along. As more evidence emerged, the identities of the perpetrators began to shift and there was more emphasis on how they enjoyed working on cars and other activities that identified them as from a lower socio-economic class. Once the trial took place, they were clearly defined as poor whites that were not like the rest of the community. In short, this protected the cultural identity of the mainstream community from any connection to attitudes that might result in the murder of a gay, disabled African American man. The reconfiguration of the cultural identities of the perpetrators serves particular purposes. It is not a neutral process, but a process that serves some interests over others.

I observed this same phenomenon in the ways that racial, sexual, and gender identities are negotiated in popular culture. In this study, "Show/down Time" (Nakayama, 1994), I looked at how a popular movie contrasted these identities and the narrative drove a particular story that continually privileged white, heterosexual masculinity. Thus, these dialectical tensions between white and non-white, heterosexuality and homosexuality, and masculinity and femininity need to be understood to see how identities are represented and understood for the narrative to work.

CONCLUSION

As I hope you have seen, it is important to understand the larger social and legal structures that allow or restrain movements of people. A critical approach to intercultural communication sheds light on the larger structural frameworks that shape intercultural interaction. By taking a dialectical approach to the larger social issues that inform intercultural interaction, various issues can be highlighted as influences in intercultural communication. For example, history is always in a dialectical relationship with the present and future. History alone does not determine any outcome, but it shapes and influences the present and future.

There is much more work to be done. In *The Handbook of Critical Intercultural Communication* (Nakayama & Halualani, 2010), we hope to add to the much larger project of building this approach to intercultural communication. The many case studies and theoretical approaches in this collection trace much of the outlines of this much larger project.

REFERENCES

Flores, L. A., Moon, D. G., & Nakayama, T. K. (2006). Dynamic rhetorics of race: California's Racial Privacy Initiative and the shifting grounds of racial politics." *Communication and Critical/Cultural Studies, 3,* 181–201.

Karp, J. (2012, April 26). Boston Bruins racist tweets: Bruins fans target Joel Ward after Game 7. WJLA. Retrieved October 25, 2012 from: http://www.wjla.com/articles/2012/04/boston-bruins-racist-tweets-bruins-fans-target-joel-ward-after-game-7-75320.html

Martin, J. N., & Nakayama, T. K. (1999). Thinking dialectically about culture and communication. *Communication Theory, 9,* 1–25.

Moon, D. G., & Nakayama, T. K. (2005). Strategic social identities and judgments: A murder in Appalachia. *Howard Journal of Communications, 16,* 87–107.

Nakayama, T. K. (1994). Show/down time: "Race," gender, sexuality and popular culture. *Critical Studies in Mass Communication, 11,* 162–179.

Nakayama, T. K. (1997). *Transforming barbed wire: The incarceration of Japanese Americans in Arizona during World War II.* Phoenix: Arizona Humanities Council.

Nakayama, T. K., & Krizek, R. L. (1995). Whiteness: A strategic rhetoric. *Quarterly Journal of Speech, 81,* 291–309.

SECTION 8
INTERPERSONAL COMMUNICATION

The interpersonal communication context focuses on how we convey messages in our dyadic relationships. These relationships (e.g., romantic relationships, friendships), are directly influenced by our communication behavior. Accordingly, interpersonal scholars examine how our communication affects our relationships; for instance, how we develop, maintain, and terminate these voluntary relationships. Some major areas of research in interpersonal communication include personality, language, self-disclosure, perception, emotion, supportive communication, interpersonal skills, and affection. This chapter focuses on three important areas of interpersonal communication research: (1) relational maintenance, (2) first dates, and (3) romantic jealousy. First, Marianne Dainton (La Salle University) reviews how couples maintain their romantic relationships by answering the question: *How can we keep our romantic partners happy by using relational maintenance?* Second, Laura Guerrero (Arizona State University) reviews jealousy research to answer the question: *How do we experience and respond to jealousy in romantic relationships?* Third, Paul Mongeau and Benjamin Wiedmaier (Arizona State University) examine dating research to answer the question: *How can we have better first dates?* Since most of you, if not all of you will find yourselves in a committed romantic relationship at some point in life (if you aren't involved in one already), these research programs will help you understand how to build, maintain, and communicate effectively in romantic relationships. It is after all, communication that can make or break your love life!

RELATIONSHIP MAINTENANCE

Marianne Dainton, La Salle University

Having your heart broken is one of the most miserable things you can go through. Your hopes and dreams for the future are wrenched away from you, and you wonder how you could have been so deluded to think that the other person felt the same way you did, but most of all, you feel completely and utterly rejected. Why *me*? Why don't you love *me*?

Eventually we all survive the heartbreak, but my own experiences with failed relationships made me switch the questions from "why me?" to a more general question of "what makes a relationship work?" The question is an important one; we all have heard the frightening statistic that 50% of marriages in the United States end in divorce. But, rather than focusing on why those marriages fail, I became interested in the other 50%; what makes *those* relationships succeed? For the past 20 years my research has focused on the communication associated with relationship maintenance.

First, I should explain what I mean by relationship maintenance. According to Dindia and Canary (1993), there are actually four different ways to define the concept. The first definition involves efforts to keep the relationship together, regardless of whether the individuals in the relationship are happy or not. We all know people who stay in a relationship for a long time but seem to be miserable in it. This definition implies a simple yes or no answer to the question of maintenance; if you can answer yes, the relationship is still together, and then it has been maintained. If you answer no, the relationship is not still together, then the relationship has not been maintained.

The second definition involves efforts the couple uses to remain satisfied with the relationship. In this scenario, it is not enough to just keep the relationship intact, the partners have to achieve some preferred level of happiness with the relationship. The third definition is a bit broader yet; Dindia and Canary (1993) argued that relationship maintenance might include all efforts to keep a relationship in a desired state. So, this definition includes efforts to maintain a preferred amount of love, liking, commitment, or intimacy, for example. Finally, Dindia and Canary (1993) argued that relationship maintenance might center on keeping a relationship in repair. Unlike the previous definitions, which focus more on "prevention" of problems, this definition centers on "fixing" things when they break. For example, maintenance would involve efforts to resolve an existing conflict, negotiate how to live with an ongoing disappointment, or deal with discovered deception.

My own research uses the third definition. I am interested not only in how couples manage to remain together happily, but also how other important components of the relationship are sustained. What keeps people in love? How do we remain committed to our partners? The rest of this chapter is divided into three distinct areas of focus that are necessary if we want to answer those broader questions,. These include: What types of communication serve as relationship maintenance? What leads some people to engage in these behaviors and others to avoid them? And, what is the effect on the relationship when certain communicative behaviors are used?

MAINTENANCE BEHAVIORS

Believe it or not, researchers did not begin to focus specifically on relationship maintenance until the 1980s. In the fall of 1989, I was in my very first graduate class, Communication in Personal Relationships, taught by Dr. Laura Stafford. Dr. Stafford and Dr. Dan Canary were in the midst of analyzing data for what would turn out to be one of the seminal articles on relationship maintenance, which they published in 1991. However, as I sat in class that semester, Dr. Stafford would give nearly daily updates about what she and Canary had been doing. She challenged the class to critique and extend their work.

Stafford and Canary (1991) asked 77 people to respond to the question "What do you do to maintain your relationship?" Based on their answers, they created a questionnaire and had a different sample of nearly 1,000 people respond to a series of statements about whether they had engaged in those behaviors or not. They used a statistical technique called factor analysis, which collapsed the statements into five different strategies for maintaining relationships. The first was **positivity**, which refers to efforts to be cheerful and optimistic around the partner. **Openness** means having serious discussions about the relationship. **Assurances**, the third strategy they uncovered, occur when people reassure their partners about their love and commitment to the relationship. The fourth strategy Stafford and Canary (1991) uncovered was **social networks**, which means relying on common family and friends. Finally, **sharing tasks** refers to completing responsibilities that the couple face.

Given the challenge given by Dr. Stafford in that class over 20 years ago, my work has focused on extending this original study in two important ways. First, Stafford and Canary focused on *strategies* that people used to maintain relationships, but my own experience suggested to me that people are not always consciously thinking about their relationship and intentionally engaging in behaviors in order to maintain their relationship. Instead, I thought that people often engage in *routine* maintenance behavior, behavior that was not consciously thought about or intentionally acted in order to maintain the relationship. For example, I suspect that giving your partner a kiss goodbye before leaving for work is just part of a daily routine, and not something that a person thinks "oh, I have to kiss him goodbye so that our relationship succeeds." Accordingly, I conducted a study that asked people to report on those sorts of routine maintenance behaviors

(Dainton & Stafford, 1993). We found 12 categories of maintenance. The five behaviors developed by Stafford and Canary (1991) were evident, as well as seven other categories. However, this study simply identified the behaviors, but did not result in a way to measure routine maintenance.

Although Stafford and I uncovered these behaviors in 1991, it would be almost 10 years before we developed a scale to measure them. In 2000, I worked with Stafford and Dr. Stephen Haas to craft a measure of routine maintenance. We surveyed 520 married people and found that the original five behaviors identified by Stafford and Canary (1991) were enacted by partners both routinely and strategically. In addition to those five behaviors, however, we uncovered two additional maintenance behaviors that emerged because we specifically probed about routine behavior: conflict management and advice. **Conflict management** refers to proactive ways to deal with conflict, such as apologizing when you are wrong, and being patient and forgiving with the partner. **Advice** means providing a "reality check" for your partner, and serving as a sounding board for his or her complaints.

Once we uncovered these additional behaviors, I was interested in further exploring the extent to which they were performed routinely or strategically. Dr. Brooks Aylor and I conducted a survey asking people how often they performed each of the seven behaviors strategically (with the explicit goal of maintaining the relationship) and how often they performed the same behavior routinely (without really thinking about why they were performing the behavior). We found that positivity and tasks were performed more routinely than strategically, but that no behaviors were performed more strategically than routinely (Dainton & Aylor, 2002). Interestingly, we also found no relationship between the routine use of a behavior and a strategic use of a behavior. What that means is that the same person who uses assurances strategically is unlikely to also use assurances routinely; it's not that some people just like to use particular behaviors. Instead, clusters of behaviors seem to be used routinely, and clusters of behaviors are likely to be performed routinely. Aylor and I hypothesized that people might use routine maintenance in long-term relationships, but if something happens to break a couple's routine, the relationship partners might switch to strategic maintenance (Dainton & Aylor, 2002). In that case, strategic maintenance might better be understood using the fourth definition of maintenance, which centers on "repair" rather than prevention of problems.

The second way I have critiqued and extended the original Stafford and Canary (1991) study has been through a focus on negative maintenance behaviors. The original five strategies, and the updated seven behaviors, all have a bias towards positive behavior. That is, most of us would agree that these are positive things to do in a relationship. But all of us know that relationships include both positive and negative behavior, good times and bad. In 2005, I was teaching a class in Communication and Personal Relationships, and I expressed my own frustration with this positivity bias. If you have been reading this chapter, you should understand the irony of what is about to be described, because one of my students challenged me on my frustration—if I disagreed with my own work, why didn't I do something about it? Much like my own research was an extension of my professor's classroom challenge, the second major branch of my scholarship has been as a result of my own classroom challenge. My student Jamie Gross and I conducted a study that sought to uncover the negative things that people do to maintain relationships.

Copying the original methods used by Stafford and Canary (1991), we first asked a sample of people about the negative things they do for relationship purposes. We then turned these open-ended data into survey items and conducted a survey asking people to respond to the frequency with which they performed these behaviors. Using factor analysis, we identified six negative maintenance behaviors (Dainton & Gross, 2008). The first negative maintenance behavior is **jealousy induction**, which is an intentional effort to make the partner jealous. Second is **avoidance**, which refers both to avoiding the partner as well as to avoiding topics that might lead to arguments. **Spying** is third. Not surprisingly, this involves checking the partner's mail or phone, or actively talking to the partner's friends to gather information. Next is **infidelity**. Believe it or not, some people report on behaviors ranging from flirting to having sex with other people so that she or he can prevent boredom. **Destructive conflict** is the fifth type of negative maintenance; unlike the more positive conflict management identified earlier, this behavior refers to controlling behavior and seeking arguments. The final behavior is **allowing control**, which references breaking plans with family or friends to be with the partner, avoiding activities that the individual previously enjoyed because the partner doesn't like them, and letting the partner make decisions for him or her. Although this line of research is relatively new for me, others have quickly picked up on the idea, and I will talk about that research in a future section.

WHAT PREDICTS MAINTENANCE BEHAVIOR?

The second major question my research has addressed has been to determine what predicts the use of maintenance behavior. Certainly, an understanding of what people do to maintain relationships, strategically or routinely, positively or negatively, is important. But clearly not everyone engages in maintenance behaviors, otherwise relationships would never end. The second central question I have been focusing on is why some people perform certain maintenance behaviors and why others don't. The answer to this question can be summarized around three distinct variations: sex and gender differences, differences in relationship type, and theoretical predictions.

Sex and Gender Differences

From the very beginning of scholarly research into relationship maintenance, scholars have been interested in whether men and women perform maintenance in a similar fashion. The results from a host of studies indicate that, although men and women typically use the same maintenance behaviors, women tend to use more maintenance overall (see Aylor & Dainton, 2004). However, we should be very careful about the use of the terms *sex* and *gender*. *Sex* refers to biological differences, so if we said women engage in more maintenance than men, we would be suggesting that there are biological reasons for this pattern. *Gender,* on the other hand, focuses on how people are raised to behave. If you were looking at gender differences in communication, then you would be focusing on how feminine people, masculine people, and androgynous people (i.e., people high in both masculinity and femininity) behave. Because previous research found that there are very few biological differences in communication (Canary & Hause, 1993), I conducted two studies looking at how gender might be related to relationship maintenance.

First, I worked with Stafford and Haas to determine whether sex or gender is a better predictor of the use of maintenance (Stafford, Dainton, & Haas,2000). Interestingly, we found a rather small correlation between sex and gender (r = .13). What this means is that, knowing whether someone is a male or female does not help particularly to determine if the person is masculine or feminine. Put in another way, not all men are masculine and not all women are feminine. In this study we found that if you control for someone's gender role, there were only two significant relationships between sex and the use of maintenance: Women were slightly more likely to use openness and shared tasks. Instead, we found that femininity was the single best predictor of all seven pro-social maintenance behaviors. The takeaway piece of advice is that if you want a maintained relationship, you should make sure your partner has either a feminine or an androgynous gender role.

In the second study, Aylor and I looked at sex and gender differences in the routine and strategic use of maintenance behaviors (Aylor & Dainton, 2004). Replicating the study I did with Stafford et al. (2000), we found that gender role was a stronger predictor of maintenance than sex, with sex predicting only one maintenance behavior: the routine use of openness. More interestingly, we found that femininity was a better predictor of routine maintenance, and masculinity was a better predictor of strategic maintenance. This suggests that feminine people tend to think about relationship maintenance as simply part of a daily routine, whereas masculine people tend to operate on a "if it ain't broke, why fix it" model. That is, masculine people tend to approach maintenance as something that is done only when there is a problem that needs to be solved.

Differences in Relationship Type

You may have noticed that I have been using the neutral term of "relationship partner" throughout this chapter. That's because not all relationship types are the same, and a great deal of research has sought to compare married and dating relationships. First, there are clear differences in the maintenance efforts in dating and married relationships. Stafford and Canary (1991) found that married people were more likely than dating people to use assurances, and that dating people were more likely than married people to use openness. Similarly, my work with Stafford (Dainton & Stafford, 1993) indicated that married people were more likely to engage in sharing tasks, whereas dating couples were more likely to use mediated communication to sustain their relationship.

One way to think about these differences might be to think about these groups as ultimately demonstrating different relationship lengths rather than different types of relationships. In my own work, I have found that people engage in less maintenance over time (Dainton, 2000), although the most accurate way to describe this is with a U-shaped curve (Dainton, 2008). That is, after an early high in the amount of maintenance, the use of maintenance steadily drops over time, with it increasing again later in life (usually associated with after the children have left the home). Historically, research has indicated that the birth of children is negatively associated with relationship maintenance, but (good news for prospective parents out there!), it seems that this U-shaped curve is true for both parents and non-parents (Dainton, 2008).

What is particularly interesting is that, although these behaviors are used less frequently over time, people tend to keep their expectations for their partner's use of the behavior fairly high

(Dainton, 2000). This sets them up for potential dissatisfaction, as their expectations are not being met. The best advice I can give for this is that we ought to change our expectations as our relationship changes; "happily ever after" is a pretty difficult standard to achieve.

Theoretical Predictions

It is the rare student who looks forward to a class in communication theory. However, theory often provides us with important insights in how we should behave in everyday life. In my own work, I have used three different theories to help me to understand why some people engage in maintenance and others don't.

The first theoretical approach is social exchange, which takes an economic approach to understanding relationships. Social exchange theory focuses on the rewards and costs associated with being in a relationship. In this approach, the partner's use of pro-social maintenance behaviors would be considered a reward, and one's own use of pro-social maintenance considered a cost. Stafford and Canary's original maintenance study used social exchange theory (Canary & Stafford, 1992, 2001; Stafford & Canary, 1991), with a particular focus on one type of social exchange theory called equity theory. The *Reader's Digest* version of equity theory says that people are happiest when they are receiving the same proportion of rewards to costs as their partner (Sprecher, 1986). If an individual is putting more into the relationship than what s/he is getting out of it, the relationship would be considered under-benefitted; and if the reverse is true—the person is getting more out of it than what they are putting into it—the relationship is considered over-benefitted. Typically about 50% of people in relationships consider themselves to be in equitable relationships, with the remaining 50% divided equally between those who think they are under-benefitted and those that think they are over-benefitted. Stafford and Canary found partial support for this approach, finding that, in general, people who think they have an equitable relationship engage in more pro-social maintenance.

My own research reaches much the same conclusion; equity principles do predict the use of maintenance some of the time. However, this does not hold true for negative maintenance behaviors. That is, one would expect people in equitable relationships would use fewer negative behaviors, and that those in under-benefitted relationships might use more negative maintenance behaviors. However, we found only one relationship between equity and negative maintenance, with over-benefitted people using avoidance less than the other two groups (Dainton & Gross, 2008). Moreover, equity theory did not emerge as the best theoretical predictor in a direct test, which will be described next.

The second theoretical approach is uncertainty reduction theory, which argues that uncertainty is detrimental to relationship stability (Berger, 1987). Two particular forms of uncertainty appear to be most associated with romantic relationships: future uncertainty and mutuality uncertainty. According to Knobloch and Solomon (1999), future uncertainty refers to an individual's feelings of being unsure where the relationship is going, and mutuality uncertainty refers to an individual's insecurity about whether the partner feels the same way that he or she does. In several studies, I have found some evidence that the use of relationship maintenance behaviors is a means for managing uncertainty (e.g., Dainton & Aylor, 2001). In fact, in a direct test certainty (the opposite of uncertainty) was a better predictor of the use of positive maintenance behaviors than was equity, although both certainty and equity together did predict an individual's use of positivity, openness, and conflict management.

The third theoretical approach I have used is attachment theory. Attachment theory suggests that our early relationship with caregivers (usually parents) influences how we see all of our adult relationships (Bartholomew, 1990). Four attachment styles have been identified in research. **Secure** individuals have positive self-esteem and hold positive views of others. **Preoccupied** individuals have negative views of themselves and positive views of others. These people tend to be overly focused on the relationship, and have a tendency to "smother" their partners with care. **Fearful avoidant** types have negative views of both themselves and others. These individuals are terrified of being hurt, and they are most likely to desire being in a relationship but be too afraid to do so. Finally, the **dismissive** attachment style has a positive view of self and a negative view of others. These individuals are most likely to be game-players who do not value, and who do not pay attention to, their relationships with others.

My own work has determined that attachment theory successfully predicts pro-social maintenance use, with secure individuals engaging in all seven pro-social behaviors more than any other group, and dismissive individuals engaging in less of all seven behaviors than any other group (Dainton, 2007). However, the use of maintenance by the other two attachment groups is less clear-cut; I found that preoccupied and fearful avoidant individuals are less likely to use positivity or positive conflict management, but they are more likely to use assurances. It seems that these individuals are quite good at expressing love, but they are not so good at engaging in behaviors that would make them more loveable.

Goodboy and Bolkan (2011) looked at the relationships between attachment and negative maintenance behaviors. As predicted, they found that secure individuals were less likely to use negative maintenance behaviors altogether. More importantly, they found that the other attachments styles were more likely to use negative maintenance behaviors regardless of how satisfied they were. That means that even dismissives, preoccupieds, and fearful avoidants who are happy in their relationships use these anti-social behaviors, with the exception of allowing control.

THE EFFECTS OF MAINTENANCE BEHAVIORS

Throughout this manuscript I have talked at length about a number of different positive and negative maintenance behaviors, but I should caution you that not all behaviors "count" equally. That is, some of these behaviors are much more important than others. Across a number of studies, my own research and that of my colleagues has found that using assurances (both routine and strategic), routine positivity, and positive conflict management is associated with greater relationship satisfaction (e.g., Dainton, 2000; Dainton & Gross, 2008; Stafford & Canary, 1991; Stafford et al., 2000). Conversely, using the negative maintenance behaviors of allowing control, destructive conflict, infidelity, and jealousy induction is negatively associated with satisfaction (Dainton & Gross, 2008; Goodboy, Myers, & Members of Investigating Communication, 2010).

And, surprising to most people, using openness—even though it is considered a pro-social strategy—is negatively related to satisfaction (e.g., Dainton, 2000; Dainton & Aylor, 2002; Stafford et al, 2000). Before you start keeping secrets and lying to your partner, you need to remember that correlation does not equal causation. That is, because of statistical limitations, it might simply be that unhappy people use openness, and not that openness leads to unhappiness. Picture the "big relationship talk." If you are squirming just thinking about it, you might understand why the connection between openness and satisfaction is not as obvious as you might have previously thought.

In the very beginning of this chapter, I indicated that I believe that maintenance has broader implications for relationships than just the link between maintenance and satisfaction. To summarize other findings (e.g., Dainton, Stafford & Canary, 1994; Goodboy et al., 2010; Stafford & Canary, 1991), feelings of love are associated with positivity and tasks. Liking is most associated with positivity, assurances, and relying on social networks, and the use of negative maintenance behaviors is associated with the decreases in liking. Control mutuality (agreeing on who has the right to influence the other in the relationship) is associated with positivity, assurances, and social networks. As for commitment, the most consistent finding is that assurances and sharing tasks are the best pro-social maintenance behaviors, and that all six negative behaviors are associated with lower levels of commitment. Clearly, using assurances and positivity makes the most difference in the maintenance of desired relationship states.

I mentioned an important axiom saying that "correlation doesn't equal causation" just a few paragraphs ago. I should mention that originally maintenance was viewed as both a cause and a consequence of relationship characteristics like satisfaction. That is, we believed that satisfied people used maintenance, which leads to satisfaction, which leads to maintenance, and so on. Since the original study in 1991 we now know this isn't the case. Dainton and Stafford (2000) got their first clue when they conducted a study to see what predicted maintenance. They were surprised to find that satisfaction did not predict the use of any maintenance behaviors, and commitment had only a slight effect on a few behaviors. Directly testing this finding, Canary, Stafford and Semic (2002) surveyed married couples once a month for three months and found that the use of maintenance predicts feelings of satisfaction, commitment, and love, but the reverse is not true. In addition, they found that the effects of maintenance fade rather quickly, so maintenance has to be continuously enacted if you want to sustain your preferred level of satisfaction, love, and the like.

CONCLUSION

Twenty years after beginning a sustained program of research into relationship maintenance, we can conclude that using specific maintenance behaviors, especially being reassuring and being positive, leads to a more satisfying and committed relationship. We know that gender is more strongly associated with using relationship maintenance behaviors than is sex is, so forget about the whole "Men are from Mars, Women are from Venus" thing. We know that relationship maintenance efforts fade over time, which is likely why people tend to become less satisfied over time. However, some types of people are more likely to use more maintenance and remain more satisfied than others.

My research into relationship maintenance leads to the following take-aways:

1. **Be nice.** Have you ever noticed that you can fake being nice to perfect strangers, and then we dump out all of the frustrations of our lives on the person we presumably love the most? Make sure you take time out to be nice, optimistic, and cheerful around your partner. They are supposed to love you in good times and bad, so make sure there are some good times.

2. **Be reassuring.** Never underestimate how frequently you should say, "I love you" or show that you care.

3. **Make it part of your routine.** If you only "remember" to engage in maintenance when things are going badly, you are missing out on the most important form of maintenance. Practice makes perfect.

4. **Find your feminine side.** Remember that gender has very little to do with your biological sex, so women aren't naturally relationship experts. All of us can learn to be more feminine and, in doing so, protect our relationships.

5. **Have realistic expectations.** Relationships change over time, and the amount of time and energy we put into them changes as well. Knowing that we are less likely to engage in maintenance the longer we are together, you should work on making relationship maintenance part of your routine so it feels natural to continue doing it over the long haul. And stop comparing what things are like now compared to what things were like then. Get over the expectations fostered by romance novels and advice columnists.

6. **Work on making things equitable.** If you are under-benefitted, talk about what you need. If you don't get it, you have two choices: Do less yourself, or end the relationship.

7. **Certainty helps, delusion doesn't.** There is always an element of uncertainty in relationships, but if your gut instinct (and your family and friends) suggests that the person doesn't match the intensity of your feelings and that the relationship has no future, you might want to reconsider whether you should maintain the relationship. Yes, you CAN stay together until death do you part, but do you really want to if you don't achieve the satisfaction or commitment you want?

8. **Sometimes it really IS them, not you.** It's the standard break-up line, "it's not you, it's me," but when you are the one being treated badly, it feels like you. Some people really are "bad" at relationships because of the relationship they had with their caregivers. Short of therapy, they aren't likely to change, and they aren't likely to be able to maintain your desired satisfaction or commitment in a romantic relationship. Know that you can change yourself, but you can't change anyone else.

REFERENCES

Aylor, B., & Dainton, M. (2004). Biological sex and psychological gender as predictors of routine and strategic relational maintenance. *Sex Roles, 50,* 689–697.

Bartholomew, K. (1990). Avoidance of intimacy: An attachment perspective. *Journal of Social and Personal Relationships, 7,* 147–178.

Berger, C. R. (1987). Communicating under uncertainty. In M. E. Roloff, & G. R. Miller (Eds.), *Interpersonal processes: New directions in communication research* (pp. 39–62). Newbury Park, CA: Sage.

Canary, D. J., & Hause, K. S. (1993). Is there any reason to study sex differences in communication? *Communication Quarterly, 41,* 129–144.

Canary, D. J., & Stafford, L. (1992). Relational maintenance strategies and equity in marriage. *Communication Monographs, 59,* 243–267.

Canary, D. J., & Stafford, L. (2001). Equity in the preservation of personal relationships. In J. H. Harvey & A. Wenzel (Eds.), *Close romantic relationships: Maintenance and enhancement* (pp. 133–151). Mahwah, NJ: LEA.

Canary, D. J., Stafford, L., & Semic, B. A. (2002). A panel study of the associations between maintenance strategies and relational characteristics. *Journal of Marriage and the Family, 64,* 395–406.

Dainton, M. (2000). Maintenance behaviors, expectations, and satisfaction: Linking the comparison level to relational maintenance. *Journal of Social and Personal Relationships, 17,* 827–842.

Dainton, M. (2003). Equity and uncertainty in relational maintenance. *Western Journal of Communication, 67,* 164–186.

Dainton, M. (2007). Attachment and marital maintenance. *Communication Quarterly, 55,* 283–298.

Dainton, M. (2008). The use of relationship maintenance behaviors as a mechanism to explain the decline in marital satisfaction among parents. *Communication Reports, 21,* 33–45.

Dainton, M., & Aylor, B. A. (2001). A relational uncertainty analysis of jealousy, trust, and the maintenance of long-distance versus geographically-close relationships. *Communication Quarterly, 49,* 172–188.

Dainton, M., & Aylor, B. A. (2002). Routine and strategic maintenance efforts: Behavioral patterns, variations associated with relational length, and the prediction of relational characteristics. *Communication Monographs, 69,* 52–66.

Dainton, M., & Gross, J. (2008). The use of negative strategies for relationship maintenance. *Communication Research Reports, 25,* 179–191.

Dainton, M., & Stafford, L. (1993). Routine maintenance behaviors: A comparison of relationship type, partner similarity, and sex differences. *Journal of Social and Personal Relationships, 10,* 255–272.

Dainton, M., & Stafford, L. (2000). Predicting maintenance enactment from relational schemata, spousal behavior, and relational characteristics. *Communication Research Reports, 17,* 171–180.

Dainton, M., Stafford, L., & Canary, D. J. (1994). Maintenance strategies and physical affection as predictors of love, liking, and satisfaction in marriage. *Communication Reports, 7,* 88–98.

Dindia, K., & Canary, D. J. (1993). Definitions and theoretical perspectives on maintaining relationships. *Journal of Social and Personal Relationships, 10,* 163–173.

Goodboy, A. K., & Bolkan, S. (2011). Attachment and the use of negative relational maintenance behaviors in romantic relationships. *Communication Research Reports, 28,* 327–336.

Goodboy, A. K., Myers, S. A., & Members of Investigating Communication. (2010). Relational quality indicators and love styles as predictors of negative relational maintenance behaviors in romantic relationships. *Communication Reports, 23,* 65–78.

Knobloch, L. K., & Solomon, D. H. (1999). Measuring the sources and content of relational uncertainty. *Communication Studies, 50,* 161–278.

Sprecher, S. (1986). The relation between inequity and emotions in close relationships. *Social Psychology Quarterly, 49,* 309–321.

Stafford, L., & Canary, D. J. (1991). Maintenance strategies and romantic relationship type, gender, and relational characteristics. *Journal of Social and Personal Relationships, 8,* 217–242.

Stafford, L., Dainton, M., & Haas, S. (2000). Measuring routine and strategic relational maintenance: Scale development, sex versus gender roles, and the prediction of relational characteristics. *Communication Monographs, 67,* 306–323.

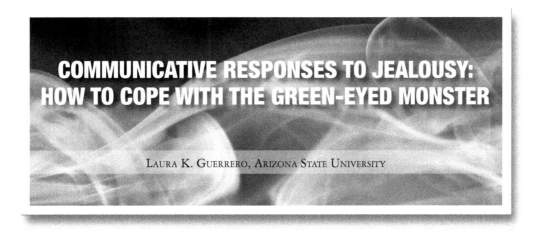

COMMUNICATIVE RESPONSES TO JEALOUSY: HOW TO COPE WITH THE GREEN-EYED MONSTER

Laura K. Guerrero, Arizona State University

For centuries, poets, playwrights, and philosophers have recognized that jealousy is a common yet powerful human emotion. In *Othello,* Shakespeare characterized jealousy as a green-eyed monster. Psychologists and communication scholars have made similar analogies. For example, Brehm (2001) likened jealousy to earthquakes, noting that jealousy runs beneath the smooth surface of many relationships like plates lie waiting to collide under the Earth's crust. At any moment rumblings can surface and the foundation of the relationship might shake! Most people experience these jealous vibrations at least once in their romantic relationships. Sometimes the threat is real and jealousy is well founded. Other times the threat is imagined or exaggerated. In any case, the way people communicate about jealousy is important. In fact, communication helps determine whether jealousy has positive or negative effects on individuals and relationships (Andersen, Eloy, Guerrero, & Spitzberg, 1995; White & Mullen, 1989). Research has therefore attempted to answer two important questions: How do people communicate about jealousy and are some types of jealous communication more helpful or harmful than others?

 Before discussing how people communicate jealousy, it is important to define the concept of jealousy in romantic relationships. *Romantic jealousy* is a cognitive, emotional, and behavioral reaction to the threat that a real or imagined rival is perceived to pose to a person's romantic relationship (Guerrero & Andersen, 1998b; Pfieffer & Wong, 1989; White & Mullen, 1989). Although jealousy is a normal and relatively common emotion, the prospect of losing one's partner to a rival can produce a wide range of jealous thoughts and emotions. Sometimes these thoughts and emotions are pervasive. Carson and Cupach (2000) noted that chronic jealousy is often marked by rumination, which "can be described as obsessive worry about the security of the relationship" (p. 309). Similarly, Bryson (1991) noted that jealous individuals sometimes experience emotional devastation, a syndrome that can include feeling helpless, insecure, confused, fearful, inadequate, depressed, exploited, and taken for granted. Certain types of communication, however, may help individuals cope with jealousy effectively so that they can alleviate these types of negative thoughts and emotions.

Communicative responses to jealousy have been defined as behavioral reactions to jealousy that have "communicative value" and "the potential to fulfill individual and relational goals" (Guerrero, Andersen, Jorgensen, Spitzberg, & Eloy, 1995, p. 272). Messages have communicative value when they are sent with intent and/or interpreted as meaningful by others. In the context of jealousy, messages are sometimes constructed to try to meet such goals as bolstering self esteem, maintaining a relationship, reducing uncertainty, and retaliating against the partner (Guerrero & Afifi, 1998, 1999). Communicative responses to jealousy have been grouped under four broad categories: constructive, destructive, avoidant, and rival-focused (Guerrero, Hannawa, & Babin, 2011).

Constructive Communicative Responses to Jealousy

Although jealousy is often regarded as a negative reaction that has aversive consequences for individuals and relationships, jealousy also has a bright side. Jealousy can reflect love and inject excitement and appreciation into a taken-for-granted relationship, reinforce commitment, and rekindle feelings of attraction and passion (Guerrero & Andersen, 1998b, Pines, 1992). Two communicative responses to jealousy have been identified as generally constructive because they promote positive feelings and relationship satisfaction (Guerrero et al., 1995; Guerrero et al., 2011). The first of these, *integrative communication,* is a style of communication that focuses on problem-solving, constructive criticism, and supportive communication. Integrative communication strategies include calmly questioning the partner about her or his actions and feelings, explaining one's own feelings, and discussing what can be done in the future to prevent jealousy. The second constructive response, *compensatory restoration,* entails trying to maintain the relationship by using such tactics as increasing affection, being a better partner, and spending more time together. Such tactics are often designed to highlight the benefits of the current relationship in comparison to the rival relationship.

Responding to jealousy using these types of constructive communication can be beneficial. People are more likely to use constructive responses when they want to maintain their relationship (Guerrero & Afifi, 1998, 1999) and when they have stronger communal orientations, which means that they are highly responsive to their partner's needs (Cayanus & Booth-Butterfield, 2004). Integrative communication is also related to commitment, and both integrative communication and compensatory restoration are related to being more invested in a romantic relationship (Bevan, 2008). The benefits of using integrative communication appear to extend beyond romantic relationships since siblings also report being happier in their relationships when they use integrative communication to deal with jealousy (Bevan & Stetzenbach, 2007).

One reason constructive responses are beneficial is that partners respond favorably to them. Participants in a study by Yoshimura (2004) read scenarios depicting different ways that their partner might express jealousy to them. Those who read the scenario that represented positive communication (e.g., a combination of integrative communication and compensatory restoration) reported that they would be especially likely to discuss their feelings with their partner, try to be a better partner in the future, and express remorse by appearing hurt or crying. Thus, constructive communicative responses may elicit a more positive response from the partner than other types of communicative responses to jealousy.

Some research, however, suggests that constructive communication alone may not be enough to combat the potentially negative effects of jealousy. Constructive communicative responses are most effective when they are combined with the expression of negative emotions such as hurt (Andersen et al., 1995). In other words, it is not always enough to sit down and have a calm discussion with one's partner. Jealous individuals may also want to show their partner some of their feelings so that their partner understands and empathizes with them. There appears to be a fine line, however, between expressing one's jealous feelings openly and communicating those emotions in a hostile manner.

Indeed, it may be difficult to express jealousy constructively when emotions are strong and jealous thoughts are pervasive. When this is the case, emotions take over and it becomes challenging to cope with jealousy effectively. Research has supported this idea. For example, Guerrero, Trost, and Yoshimura (2005) found that people said they used constructive responses when they were annoyed, but not when they were angry. Anger was related to more negative responses, such as yelling or making accusations. Bryson (1991) also found that people who experience emotional devastation are unlikely to react to jealousy constructively. Another study showed that when people ruminate about their jealous feelings, they are more likely to use all of the communicative responses to jealousy (including compensatory restoration) except for integrative communication (Carson & Cupach, 2000). Taken together, these studies show that when jealousy is accompanied by especially strong negative feelings and pervasive thoughts, it is difficult for people to engage in integrative communication.

Compensatory restoration, on the other hand, is likely to be used when jealous individuals experience high levels of emotional and cognitive jealousy (Bevan, 2008), and when they see their relationship as essential for them to be happy (Carson & Cupach, 2000). Too much compensatory restoration, however, can backfire if it is perceived as desperate or clingy behavior (Guerrero & Afifi, 1998). For example, spending extra time together and saying "I love you" more often can help strengthen the bond between two people, but if one person is doing these things continually, the other person may feel smothered and rebel by wanting more space. The ideal mix of constructive responses to jealousy, then, may consist of high levels of integrative communication with some compensatory restoration and emotional expression mixed in.

DESTRUCTIVE COMMUNICATIVE RESPONSES TO JEALOUSY

In contrast to the constructive responses, Guerrero and her colleagues (2011) identified a set of destructive behaviors that tend to make jealousy worse. These destructive responses, which include negative communication, counter-jealousy inductions, and violent communication, are designed to control the partner or to make the partner feel badly. Many different behaviors fall under the category called negative communication, including giving cold or dirty looks, acting rude, arguing, pulling away, administering the "silent treatment," and showing anger. All of these behaviors are likely to be perceived as punishing by the partner, but they do not cross the line into physical violence.

Violent communication, in contrast, includes behaviors such as hitting or pushing one's partner, throwing dishes or other objects, and threatening physical harm. Research suggests that violent communication is relatively rare following jealousy, although people who do resort to violence often list jealousy as a cause (Guerrero & Andersen, 1998a). This may seem confusing at first, but think of it this way. Among all the responses that people use when they get jealous, violent communication is rare; but among the small population of people who report becoming violent in their relationships, jealousy is often blamed for their actions. Obviously, violent communication should be avoided at all costs. Some people may lose control when jealous or use violence (or threats of violence) as a way to try to control and stop the partner from seeing others. No matter why it is used, however, violent communication almost always leads to relationship destruction in the long run.

Counter-jealousy inductions, which involve trying to make the partner jealous, are a third form of destructive communication about jealousy. When people feel jealous, they sometimes want to make their partner feel jealous in turn. Sometimes counter-jealousy inductions are used as a way to get back at the partner and to even the score. Other times they are used to check for a response. Baxter and Wilmot (1984) referred to this as a type of "secret test" that allows people to reduce uncertainty about their partner's feelings. So if Sarah is jealous because Evan has been spending time with an attractive female friend, she might start spending time with an attractive male friend to see if he notices and cares. If he does, his reaction might reassure her that he still has feelings for her. Counter-jealousy inductions can also be used to try to maintain a relationship (Cayanus & Booth-Butterfield, 2004; Fleischmann, Spitzberg, Andersen, & Roesch, 2005). For example, Sarah might flirt with a good-looking stranger as a way of signaling to Evan that other men find her attractive and he shouldn't take her for granted. Of course, counter-jealousy inductions can backfire. People may not want to put up with someone who plays these kinds of games.

These three destructive responses to jealousy are harmful to relationships in other ways. Not surprisingly, people who use these three responses report being relatively unhappy in their relationships (Andersen et al., 1995; Dainton & Gross, 2008; Guerrero et al., 2011). People may be especially likely to use destructive communication when they are experiencing anxious or possessive types of jealousy (Barelds & Barelds-Dijkstra, 2007). Anxious jealousy is defined as constantly worrying about losing one's partner to someone else. Possessive jealousy is defined as feeling a need to keep tabs on a partner so that rivals cannot get close enough to threaten the relationship. When people have a history of experiencing these types of jealousy, they may find it difficult to control destructive impulses and to remain calm when the next incident of jealousy strikes.

AVOIDANT COMMUNICATIVE RESPONSES TO JEALOUSY

Both constructive and destructive forms of jealous communication involve actively sending a message to one's partner. Avoidant responses are often more passive or reactive. These types of responses focus on avoiding any discussion of jealous feelings. Two different types of avoidant responses are silence and denial (Guerrero et al., 2011). *Silence* involves becoming quiet and not saying very much (if anything) about one's jealous feelings. For example, if Garrett is upset that his girlfriend, Olivia, was flirting with an old friend at a party, he might be less talkative than usual when she returns to his side. If he were purposely giving her the "silent treatment," his behavior would fall under negative communication, but if he were quiet because he just doesn't feel like talking, then Garrett's behavior would be classified as silence. *Denial,* on the other hand, involves inhibiting emotions and pretending not to be jealous. So if Olivia asks Garrett, "What's wrong? You're so quiet" and he responds by saying "nothing" and trying to act as if he isn't upset, then Garrett would be using the denial strategy.

The jury is still out on whether avoidant responses to jealousy are related to being more or less happy in one's relationships. Some studies have found that people are less satisfied in their relationships if they report using avoidant responses (e.g., Andersen et al., 1995). Other studies have found that there is no relationship between avoidant responses and satisfaction (e.g., Guerrero et al., 2011). One study found that silence and denial were related differently to satisfaction (Irvin, 2007). In this study, people reported being the happiest with their relationships when they used silence but not denial to cope with jealousy. This may be because there are times when it is inadvisable to talk about one's jealous feelings too much. Perhaps Garrett has nothing to worry about; Olivia just has a vivacious personality and was excited to see an old friend. Given time, he might learn that Olivia's flirtation with this old friend was harmless and that there was no need to disclose jealous feelings that quickly passed. However, if Olivia asks him about his feelings and he denies them, then this could reflect a deeper communication problem between the two of them.

RIVAL-FOCUSED COMMUNICATIVE RESPONSES TO JEALOUSY

The responses discussed so far focus on communicating with one's partner. However, there are three people involved in a jealousy triangle—the jealous person, the jealous person's partner, and the rival. There are times, then, when the jealous individual communicates with the rival or uses communication to try to find out more information about the rival relationship. Indeed, when people are jealous they often feel uncertain about their partner's feelings and intentions (Afifi & Reichert, 1996; Guerrero & Afifi, 1999). Some forms of rival-focused communication can help alleviate this uncertainty.

Four specific types of rival-focused communication have been identified: surveillance, rival contacts, signs of possession, and rival derogation. *Surveillance* occurs when the jealous person tries to find out about or interfere with the rival relationship by engaging in such behaviors as checking the partner's Facebook page for messages from the rival, calling the partner to see who he or she is with, and spying on the partner. *Rival contacts* involve directly talking to the rival. Jealous individuals sometimes ask rivals questions to assess the seriousness of the threat they pose. They might also confront them and tell them to stay away from their partner. *Signs of possession,* in contrast, involve letting rivals know that one's partner is taken. For example, Garrett might introduce Olivia to a rival as "my girlfriend" and put his arm around her so everyone knows they are together. Finally, *rival derogation* occurs when the jealous individual makes negative comments about the rival. Garrett might tell Olivia that her old friend has "sure let himself go" or mention that he has been unemployed for a while. The key here is that the jealous individual is trying to make the rival look less favorable. In a way, this strategy is similar to compensatory restoration, except that instead of trying to make oneself look better, the jealous person tries to make the rival look worse.

Some rival-focused responses appear to be less helpful than others. Some researchers have argued that it is healthy to use some surveillance behavior because doing so helps one identify and combat potential threats from third parties (Buss, 1988). Similarly, Guerrero and Afifi (1998) found that people who want to maintain their relationships are likely to use surveillance when they get jealous, and Irvin (2007) showed that people who report using signs of possession when they are jealous also say they are happy in their relationships. However, research has also shown that people who see their relationships as satisfying are less likely to report using surveillance and rival contacts when they are jealous (Bevan, 2008; Elphinston & Noller, 2011; Guerrero et al., 2011). People are also more likely to use these types of rival-focused responses when they are experiencing high levels of uncertainty and are ruminating a lot about their feelings (Bevan & Tidgewell, 2009; Carson & Cupach, 2000).

So what do all of these different findings mean? When taken together, they seem to indicate that too much rival-focused communication is unhealthy for individuals and relationships. A small dose of surveillance behavior may help reduce uncertainty and alleviate a jealous person's concerns. However, too much surveillance can be intrusive and even threatening, and it can also signal a lack of trust. Similarly, some signs of possession may ward off potential rivals and let a partner know that she or he is loved, but too many signs of possession may suggest that the jealous person is overly clingy and paranoid. Therefore, if a jealous person feels a need to engage in rival-focused communication, it is advisable to use such behaviors in moderation. It would also be better to reduce uncertainty about jealousy feelings by talking to the partner and using integrative communication rather than surveillance.

CONCLUSION

Jealousy is inevitable in most relationships. But many of its negative consequences can be avoided by using the right communication. When people are feeling jealous, they should understand that sometimes behaviors that seem threatening are not. Perhaps jealousy is unfounded. The best way to find out is to use integrative communication. People should also avoid getting caught in the trap of emotional devastation. Dwelling on jealous feelings makes it more difficult to respond in a constructive manner. It is important for jealous individuals to avoid using destructive communicative responses, especially violent communication and negative communication, if they hope to maintain their relationship. Using certain types of avoidant and rival-focused communication, such as denial, surveillance, and rival derogation, can also be harmful, especially if these behaviors are used in place of more constructive responses like integrative communication and compensatory restoration. Other responses, such as silence and signs of possession, appear to be helpful in some situations but harmful in others. The best strategy of all may be to express one's emotions sincerely and calmly while using a lot of integrative communication and moderate amounts of compensatory restoration. This recipe for constructive communication may help individuals tame the green-eyed monster or at least prevent a major earthquake from disrupting their relationships.

REFERENCES

Afifi, W. A., & Reichert, T. (1996). Understanding the role of uncertainty in jealousy experience and expression. *Communication Reports, 9,* 93–103.

Andersen, P. A., Eloy, S. V., Guerrero, L. K., & Spitzberg, B. H. (1995). Romantic jealousy and relational satisfaction: A look at the impact of jealousy experience and expression. *Communication Reports, 8,* 77–85.

Barelds, D. P. H., & Barelds-Dijkstra, P. (2007). Relations between different types of jealousy and self and partner perceptions of relationship quality. *Clinical Psychology and Psychotherapy, 14,* 176–188.

Baxter, L. A., & Wilmot, W. W. (1984). "Secret tests": Social strategies for acquiring information about the state of the relationship. *Human Communication Research, 2,* 171–201.

Bevan, J. L. (2008). Experiencing and communicating romantic jealousy: Questioning the investment model. *Southern Communication Journal, 73,* 42–67.

Bevan, J. L., & Stetzenbach, K. A. (2007). Jealousy expression and communication satisfaction in adult sibling relationships. *Communication Research Reports, 24,* 71–77.

Bevan, J, L., & Tidgewell, K. D. (2009). Relational uncertainty as a consequence of partner jealousy expressions. *Communication Studies, 60,* 305–323.

Brehm, S. S. (2001). *Intimate relationships* (3rd ed.). New York: McGraw-Hill.

Bryson, J. B. (1991). Modes of responses to jealousy-evoking situations. In P. Salovey (Ed.), *The psychology of envy and jealousy* (pp. 45–62). New York: Guilford.

Buss, D. M. (1988). From vigilance to violence: Tactics of mate retention in American undergraduates. *Ethology and Sociology, 9,* 291–317.

Carson, C. L., & Cupach, W. R. (2000). Fueling the flames of the green-eyed monster: The role of ruminative thought in reaction to romantic jealousy. *Western Journal of Communication, 64,* 308–329.

Cayanus, J. L., & Booth-Butterfield, M. (2004). Relationship orientation, jealousy, and equity: An examination of jealousy evoking and positive communicative responses. *Communication Quarterly, 52,* 237–250.

Dainton, M., & Gross, J. (2008). The use of negative behaviors to maintain relationships. *Communication Research Reports, 25,* 179–191.

Elphinston, R. A., & Noller, P. (2011). Time to face it! Facebook intrusion and the implications for romantic jealousy and relational satisfaction. *Cyberpsychology, Behavior, and Social Networking, 14,* in press.

Fleischmann, A. A., Spitzberg, B. H., Andersen, P. A., & Roesch, S. C. (2005). Tickling the monster: Jealousy induction in relationships. *Journal of Social and Personal Relationships, 22,* 49–73.

Guerrero, L. K., & Afifi, W. A. (1998). Communicative responses to jealousy as a function of self-esteem and relationship maintenance goals: A test of Bryson's dual motivation model. *Communication Reports, 11,* 111–122.

Guerrero, L. K., & Afifi, W. A. (1999). Toward a goal-oriented approach for understanding communicative response to jealousy. *Western Journal of Communication, 63,* 216–248.

Guerrero, L. K., & Andersen, P. A. (1998a). The dark side of jealousy and envy: Desire, delusion, desperation, and destructive communication. In B. H. Spitzberg & W. R. Cupach (Eds.), *The dark side of relationships* (pp. 33–70). Mahwah, NJ: Erlbaum.

Guerrero, L. K., & Andersen, P. A. (1998b). The experience and expression of romantic jealousy. In P. A. Andersen & L. K. Guerrero (Eds.), *The handbook of communication and emotion: Research, theory, applications, and contexts* (pp. 155–188). San Diego, CA: Academic Press.

Guerrero, L. K., Andersen, P. A., Jorgensen, P. F., Spitzberg, B. H., & Eloy, S. V. (1995). Coping with the green-eyed monster: Conceptualizing and measuring communicative responses to romantic jealousy. *Western Journal of Communication, 59,* 270–304.

Guerrero, L. K., Hannawa, A. F., & Babin, E. A. (2011). The communicative responses to jealousy scale: Revision, empirical validation, and associations with relational satisfaction. *Communication Methods and Measures, 5,* 223–249.

Guerrero, L. K., Trost, M. L., & Yoshimura, S. M. (2005). Emotion and communication in the context of romantic jealousy. *Personal Relationships, 12,* 233–252.

Irvin, A. (2007). *Jealousy and relational satisfaction in long-distance versus proximal dating relationships.* Unpublished honor's thesis, Arizona State University, Tempe.

Pfeiffer, S. M., & Wong, P. T. P. (1989). Multidimensional jealousy. *Journal of Social and Personal Relationships, 6,* 181–196.

Pines, A. M. (1992). *Romantic jealousy: Understanding and conquering the shadow of love.* New York: St. Martin's Press.

White, G. L., & Mullen, P. E. (1989). *Jealousy: Theory, research, and clinical applications.* New York: Guilford.

Yoshimura, S. M. (2004). Emotional and behavioral responses to romantic jealousy expressions. *Communication Reports, 17,* 85–101.

HOW TO HAVE BETTER FIRST DATES
(Even if People Don't Have First Dates Anymore)

PAUL A. MONGEAU & BENJAMIN WIEDMAIER, ARIZONA STATE UNIVERSITY

Interpersonal communication theory and research are rarely specific enough that we can say "in order to have a better first date, you need to do these three things" or something of that sort. So many things have to go right for a first date to go well that it's impossible to specify them all (e.g., personality factors, past relational experiences, context, timing, and outside factors), let alone figure out how they have to work together. In the end, *it depends.* We realize that is not a terribly helpful response, but we hope to review what interpersonal and relational communication theory and research have to say about having better first dates in such a way that it is both informative and helpful.

Before we tackle our chapter, we have to discuss two important questions. First, do people still date? We presume that the answer to this question is yes. In a survey we performed in late 2010, nearly 40% of Arizona State students indicated that they were in either a *committed* (30%) or *casual* (9%) dating relationship (Mongeau & Wiedmaier, 2011). The second question is, do people go on first dates? We suspect that the answer to this question is more likely to be no. Paul's research on date initiation (e.g., Mongeau, Serewicz, & Therein, 2004) presumed that one person would call to ask another person out to a future event (e.g., a movie or a concert). From what we hear, students don't do that anymore. So, our topical focus (i.e., first dates) probably doesn't represent the primary way today's college students get together. Therefore, we will focus on the goals associated with first dates and consider how they can be most effectively met in today's campus social culture.

FIRST DATE GOALS

In one of Paul's studies (Mongeau et al., 2004), college students described goals that they wanted to reach while on their most recent first date. Five goals emerged: investigate romantic potential, learn about the partner, establish a friendship, have fun, and have sex. Our chapter will focus primarily on investigating romantic potential and learning about the partner goals because they represent the primary relational first date outcomes. Asking another person on a date was a pretty direct way of communicating romantic, personal, and/or sexual interest. Thus, first dates provided a context for the investigation of romantic interest. Therefore, our chapter will focus on how you can test the relational waters, perhaps without actually going on a first date. In this discussion, we assume that you have an interest in a romantic relationship (i.e., your goals extend beyond hooking up).

INVESTIGATING ROMANTIC POTENTIAL

In the traditional system, romantic interest was expressed through date initiation and interaction during the date, both verbal (what you talk about) and nonverbal (i.e., touch and mild sexual interaction, such as a goodnight kiss). So how can you express and investigate romantic interest when dates aren't initiated and a goodnight kiss seems as outdated as a man tipping his hat to a lady? As we will describe in this chapter, if you want to investigate romantic potential, you need to get the other person alone, do something you both enjoy, and communicate in such a way that you get to know the person better.

Theories of relational development assume that one-to-one interaction is critical to relationship development (Berger & Calabrese, 1975; Stafford, 2008). During that interaction, each person needs to self-disclose, or provide information about the self that the other is unlikely to know. Self-disclosure and relationship development go hand in hand (Derlaga, Metts, Petronio, & Margulis, 1993). So for a first date to go well, both people need to provide new and unique information about the self that the other person will evaluate positively. (For example, disclosing that at the age of eight, you ate an entire outboard motor might be unique, but it is unlikely to be evaluated positively.) In particular, discovering mutual interests and attitudes is important because it is not only important to have a good time on the date, but it is also important to leave the impression that a second and third date might be enjoyable as well (Sunnafrank, 1985). The more things you have in common and the more things you both enjoy doing together, the greater the likelihood that you can get together romantically. So one important task in your first date is to find those common attitudes and interests.

WHO IS YOUR PARTNER?

One of the important factors relevant to a first date is how well you know your partner. When you meet a person for the first time, you tend to go through the standard conversation where you disclose *name, rank, and serial number* (e.g., what's your name, what's your major, where are you from, etc.). When you know the other person well, you are probably far beyond those conversation topics. Both uncertainty reduction theory (Berger & Calabrese, 1975) and predicted outcome value theory (Sunnafrank, 1985) assume that partner knowledge has important implications for what happens on your first date.

First dates (either in the dinosaur sense or the modern one) involve going out and *doing* something. Getting to know your partner (or getting to know the person *better*) is an important first date task. *How* you know your partner is important to getting to know them (better). Is she or he a friend of a friend, part of your friendship group, a classmate in your art history class, or a fellow member of the campus LGBTQ organization? Your connection with the person you are interested in can give important clues as to how and where to get to know him or her better. The hottie in your art history class might be interested in going to the campus art museum. While there, knowing that she is interested in art might help you direct the conversation to issues (both in art and in other areas) where you might have common interests. In the case of the LGBTQ organization member, you could go to a campus lecture on gay rights followed by a trip to a coffee shop. In such cases, your common interest can give you something to talk about away from the madding crowd.

If you don't know the other person very well, you don't have to talk with him/her to reduce uncertainty (Berger & Kellermann, 1983). You can watch how he/she interacts with others (e.g., how he talks with friends at a party, in the dining hall, or in class). Facebook pages tend to be treasure troves of information about the other person's *likes*. For example, if they *like* Skull and Crossbones skateboard helmets and a local tattoo parlor, it might give you a good opening line. ("Would you like to go shred campus sometime?" or "Wanna see my Skull and Crossbones tattoo?") You can also gain information from mutual friends. Friends have always been a good (though potentially biased) source of information and advice about others.

WHAT DO YOU DO ON THE DATE?

At this point, we've talked about the nature of the other person, how you can get to know them (maybe without talking with them), and how that can give you a clue as to what to do on your date. Now we would like to go into greater detail on what you can do on the date.

A first date doesn't have to be dinner at a fancy restaurant and an evening of theatre. It could just as easily be a beer and pub grub and an evening of skateboarding on campus. Whatever your first date activity (even if it isn't a real date), it should be something that you both enjoy doing and, especially, something that you can enjoy doing *together*. Even if you don't know a lot about art, you can go with your classmate to an art museum. Maybe they can teach you a few things. (You might return the favor later by teaching them to skateboard.) It is important that you enjoy yourself on your first date (i.e., it is more rewarding than it is costly), but, again, the estimations of future relational rewards can drive the relationship forward (Sunnafrank, 1985). Finding something (or several things) you can do together can go a long way in making those predictions about the future very positive.

So how can you reach the dual goals of getting to know your partner and investigating romantic potential on the first date? We have several suggestions. First, you should get the other person *alone* so you can get to know him/her (better) in a potentially romantic context. You should get away from your friends and classmates so you can focus primarily on the other person. So going to a party or bar might not make a great first date because it's likely to be noisy, other people will serve as a distraction, and alcohol might interfere with uncertainty reduction. Movies aren't a great choice either because you can't talk during the movie, although it can work if you can talk over a cup of coffee or a glass of wine afterwards.

WHAT DO YOU TALK ABOUT?

OK, you are alone with the attractive person doing something that you both enjoy. An important part of reaching the goals of a first date of getting to know the person and investigating romantic potential involves communication. So choosing what to talk about is really important for having a better first date. What you talk about should follow from your knowledge of the other person and your (mutual) interests. Your self-disclosure is likely even more important when the event isn't an on-record date. You can explicitly communicate and implicitly negotiate your relationship through the what, and how, you self-disclose.

Communicating with the partner to get to know them better represents an important first date goal (e.g., Mongeau, Jacobsen, & Donnerstein, 2007). Communication between close friends is very different from that between relative strangers (Altman & Taylor, 1973; Derlaga et al., 1993), and an important part of that difference has to do with self-disclosure. Morr and Mongeau (2004) found that college students expect considerably more intimate self-disclosure when the date partners are friends rather than strangers. Social penetration theory uses an onion metaphor that helps to explain these findings. All of the information about you is contained somewhere in the onion. The onion's layers represent the *depth* of self-disclosure or how personal the information is. Information at the onion's surface is what can be seen (e.g., age, sex, race, etc.) and information you would disclose to just about anyone (e.g., name, rank, and serial number). As you move through each layer, information becomes increasingly personal (e.g., the number of siblings you have is closer to the surface than your violent family past). At the very core is the information that you communicate only to your closest friends and family members.

In addition, the breadth of self-disclosure represents the number of topic areas that you have opened up to the other person. All possible combinations of breadth and depth are possible. Sometimes friends talk about very few topics (e.g., only skateboarding and tattoos), discuss everything about these topics (surface, intermediate, and core), but rarely discuss other topics. Other friends talk about many topics (e.g., family, friends, hobbies, career goals, sports, entertainment, etc., etc.) but don't talk about anything in much depth. Still others' disclosures are both very wide (covering almost all possible topics) and deep (covering all layers).

Self-disclosures both reflect and build upon the existing relationship (Derlaga et al., 1993; Morr & Mongeau, 2004). Your first-date conversation, then, should be consistent with, *and extend,* what you have communicated before. If you don't know each other very well, you should begin with name, rank, and serial number and work from there. It is in pushing the conversation to places (both in terms of breadth and depth) that it doesn't normally go that can reflect in your romantic intentions when the event isn't a date (Petronio, 2002). At the same time, though, don't push the conversation to the onion's core to signal your romantic interest. Disclosing very personal information too quickly is likely to scare the other person and is likely counterproductive.

When you don't know the other person very well, as the conversation moves from topic to topic, look for things that you (might) have in common and can spend more time talking about. Of course, the 'date' activity should provide you with something to talk about. Don't be afraid to offer other conversation topics, even those you thought about ahead of time. The more things that you have to talk about, the better (Knapp & Vangelisti, 2009).

If you already know your partner pretty well, you've likely opened up several topics of conversation, perhaps at some depth, in the past. If this is the case, you can build off those past conversations and start at that same level of depth (Morr & Mongeau, 2004). If you have enjoyed talking about skateboarding in the past, it would likely make a good conversation starter (particularly if that's the date activity). If what you are trying to do is to roll the relationship forward, you should try increasing breadth by broaching new topics. (Although the same caveat about moving disclosure too deep too quickly applies here as well.) Strategically moving the conversation to new and rarely discussed topics can be a good indicator of romantic interest.

In moving conversations to new levels of breadth and depth, one important element to look for is reciprocity. Put simply, what is your partner doing? Are they matching the increases in breadth and depth? Are they responding nonverbally in a warm and inviting manner (e.g., smiling, forward body lean, and touching)? This would suggest that they approve of the move to new areas and are comfortable discussing these areas. If, on the other hand, your partner is quiet and providing surface-level responses, it's possible that they aren't comfortable with the escalation. (Though it's also possible that they are just nervous or apprehensive, which is where looking at their behavior in other contexts might come in handy).

Computer-Mediated Communication. As you are surely aware, social media and other computer-mediated communication (CMC), such as text and instant messaging, email, and Internet sites such as Facebook, have fundamentally changed the way that people communicate when dating. Potential dating partners employ CMC to (among other things) self-disclose, seek information, and initiate dates (Scissors, 2011). When we don't know another person very well, as is often the case when we begin hanging out, CMC is the preferred mode of seeking information about others, because not only are we unable to see the person's immediate reactions to our requests (whether a flirty one-liner or a corny date initiation), we can also spend more time constructing our messages than we are able to in face-to-face contexts (Westerman, 2008).

There is a potential problem, however, with the *exclusive* use of CMC early on in relationships. Modality switching (i.e., moving communication from online to face-to-face; i.e., FtF) research suggests a letdown effect, such that the longer partners communicate exclusively through CMC, the less attraction and perceived intimacy there tends to be once partners do eventually communicate FtF (Ramirez & Zhang, 2007). While the participants in this study met and communicated exclusively via CMC *before* face-to-face, it is not a stretch to hypothesize that if you meet someone at a party, then begin to chat it up with the person via CMC for a while, a similar letdown effect may occur once the second face-to-face meeting occurs.

Don't get us wrong. There's nothing wrong with CMC so long as you mix in FtF conversation (if you can). Thus, CMC is an excellent tool for early information seeking, but if you met via CMC and you think this is a person you would want to date, move the interaction offline sooner rather than later (Ramirez, Walther, Burgoon, & Sunnafrank, 2002).

CONCLUDING THOUGHTS

As we close, we want to reinforce two important points: moderation and communication. We will consider each topic in turn.

The importance of moderation. Aristotle, the ancient Greek rhetorician, frequently advocated the importance of moderation, and we think that this holds true in first dates. Moderation in first dates is important in terms of expectations, communication, drinking, and sexual activity.

First, don't expect too much (and too quickly) from your first date. First dates are more a place to *investigate* whether a romantic transition is *possible* rather than where it is likely to happen (Mongeau et al., 2004). So just because things didn't magically turn romantic on your first date doesn't mean that you've failed. Sometimes people are nervous or uncertain on first dates and don't come across as positively as they could. The first date is likely a success if it motivates you to go on a second date (and a third one, etc.). Sometimes that's all you can ask for.

We've already noted the importance of not disclosing too much too quickly. Remember the onion metaphor. First dates are not a race to get to the onion's core. Relational development is gradual as partners expose (metaphorically) themselves slowly over time. On the first date, sometimes all you can do is see what you have in common and decide whether you want to see the other person again. Communicating everything about yourself on a first date is likely a good way of making sure that a second date doesn't happen.

Third, you have probably noticed that when we suggested date activities, we were more likely to suggest going to a coffee shop than to a bar or a party. We aren't teetotalers (we both like the occasional pint or three), but on a first date, where the primary goal is likely to get to know the other person and/or to investigate romantic potential, drinking a lot can be problematic. Assuming that you want to gauge your partner's romantic interest, as well as to present yourself in a positive relational light, getting drunk is probably problematic. Having one or two drinks is unlikely to be an issue. If you are nervous or need a push into the next layer of the onion, it might even be helpful. Binge drinking, from the perspective of having a better first date, probably won't be.

Another reason that excessive drinking is counterproductive to having better first dates is that it is frequently paired with hookups (Bogle, 2008). While it is certainly true that sexual interaction is an important part of what it means to be in a romantic relationship, it can be rather confusing on a first date (especially if it's not an on-record date). For example, consider Chris and Tom, who are classmates who go to a party together. At the party, they flirt while binge drinking and end up engaging in sexual intercourse. Was this a first date or a hookup? Does this represent investigating romantic potential or is it a drunken grope? If your goal is to initiate a romantic relationship, this sort of relational uncertainty may be counterproductive because it might suggest that all you are interested in is the person's body. (It's OK to be interested in your partner's body, but you should be interested in other parts as well.)

As with communication and alcohol consumption, moderation in sexual interaction is likely most effective when your goal is to initiate a romantic relationship with a first date. Some moderate amount of sex might communicate that you are interested in your partner (both body and mind). At the same time, not going *all the way* (as they used to say in Paul's college days) can communicate that the sexual interaction at the end of the date is *not* a hookup and that you *are* interested in seeing, and communicating with, the person again. We understand that this runs counter to the hyperspeed nature of sexual interaction on many college campuses these days (Bogle, 2008); however, allowing your sexual interaction to get too far ahead of the breadth and depth of your self-disclosure and feelings of warmth and closeness is probably uncomfortable and inhibits relational development (Metts, 2004).

Importance of communication. Our other takeaway message focuses on the importance of interpersonal communication in making first dates better. Sometimes the best first dates just happen and don't involve anything other than talking. Communication, for the most part, is how to achieve reduced uncertainty and to investigate romantic potential first date goals. Relational development generally takes longer than one date, so effective communication is important both for the event itself and for what comes after it.

Interpersonal communication plays a critical role in making better first dates. The nature of self-disclosure and the nature of relationships are "mutually transformative" (Derlaga et al., 1993, p. 8). Steve Duck (1994) says that we talk our relationships into existence. How a romantic relationship differs from a close friendship or from friends with benefits is primarily in the way that partners communicate with each other. First dates are sometimes difficult because they represent that point where couples start to communicatively construct a romantic relationship. So many things aren't clear and so many things can go wrong that the communicative tasks seem daunting. Sometimes, first dates do not generate romantic relationships, but they do play important roles in relational communication in budding relationships.

REFERENCES

Altman, I., & Taylor, D. A. (1973). *Social penetration: The development of interpersonal relationships.* Oxford, England: Holt, Rinehart & Winston.

Berger, C. R., & Calabrese, R. J. (1975). Some explorations in initial interaction and beyond: Toward a developmental theory of interpersonal communication. *Human Communication Research, 1,* 99–112.

Berger, C. R., & Kellerman, K. (1983). To ask or not to ask? Is that a question? In R. N. Bostrom (Ed.), *Communication Yearbook 7* (pp. 342–368). Newbury Park, CA: Sage.

Bogle, K. A. (2008). *Hooking up: Sex, dating, and relationships on campus.* New York: NYU Press.

Derlaga, V. J., Metts, S., Petronio, S., & Margulis, S. T. (1993). *Self-disclosure.* Newbury Park, CA: Sage.

Duck, S. W. (1994). *Meaningful relationships: Talking, sense, and relating.* Newbury Park, CA: Sage.

Knapp, M. L., & Vangelisti, A. L. (2009). *Interpersonal communication and human relationships* (6th ed.). Boston: Allyn & Bacon.

Metts, S. (2004). First sexual involvement in romantic relationships: An empirical investigation of communicative framing, romantic beliefs, and attachment orientation in the passion turning point. In J. H. Harvey, A. Wenzel, & S. Sprecher (Eds.), *The handbook of sexuality in close relationships* (pp. 135–158). Mahwah, NJ: Erlbaum.

Mongeau, P. A., Jacobsen, J., & Donnerstein, C. (2007). Defining dates and first date goals: Generalizing from undergraduates to single adults. *Communication Research, 34,* 526–547.

Mongeau, P. A., Serewicz, M. C., & Therrien, L. (2004). Goals for cross-sex first dates: Identification, measurement, and contextual factors. *Communication Monographs, 71,* 121–147.

Mongeau, P., & Wiedmaier, B. (2011). *Is dating really dead? Investigating the college hookup culture.* Paper presented to the National Communication Association, New Orleans, LA.

Morr, M. C., & Mongeau, P. A. (2004). First-date expectations: The impact of sex of initiator, alcohol consumption, and relationship type, *Communication Research, 31,* 3–35.

Petronio, S. (2002). *Boundaries of privacy: Dialectics of disclosure.* Albany, NY: State University of New York Press.

Ramirez, A. Jr., & Zhang, S. (2007). When online meets offline: The effect of modality switching on relational communication. *Communication Monographs, 74,* 287–310.

Ramirez, A. Jr., Walther, J. B., Burgoon, J. K., & Sunnafrank, M. (2002). Information-seeking strategies, uncertainty, and computer-mediated communication: Toward a conceptual model. *Human Communication Research, 28,* 213–228.

Scissors, L.E. (2011, May). *We like each other, now what? Examining initial email messages from speed-date matches.* Paper presented at the annual meeting of the International Communication Association, Boston, MA.

Stafford, L. (2008). Social exchange theories. In L. Baxter & D. Braithwaite (Eds.), *Engaging theories in interpersonal communication: Multiple perspectives* (pp. 377–390). Thousand Oaks, CA: Sage.

Sunnafrank, M. (1985). Predicted outcome value during initial interactions: A reformulation of uncertainty reduction theory. *Human Communication Research, 13,* 3–33.

Westerman, D. (2008). How do people really seek information about others? Information seeking across Internet and traditional communication channels. *Journal of Computer-Mediated Communication, 13,* 751–767.

SECTION 9
INSTRUCTIONAL COMMUNICATION

The instructional communication context focuses on how instructors and students communicate and how student learning is affected. Instructional communication scholars examine how an instructor's behavior in the classroom influences students' learning and communication, how students' orientations and traits affect their communication, and how the instructor-student relationship is developed. Some major areas of research in instructional communication include the instructor's use of power, instructor misbehaviors, the instructor's use of effective teaching behavior (e.g., humor, clarity), student communication apprehension, student compliance, and student learning. This chapter focuses on three important areas of instructional communication research: (1) student email writing, (2) student public speaking anxiety, and (3) effective student communication. First, Keri Stephens (University of Texas at Austin), Marian Houser (Texas State University-San Marcos), and Renee Cowan (University of Texas San Antonio) discuss how students can write better emails by answering the question: *How can students craft more competent emails to instructors?* Second, Chris Sawyer and Amber Finn (Texas Christian University) review communication apprehension research to answer the question: *How can students better cope with public speaking anxiety in the college classroom?* Third, Alan Goodboy and Matthew Martin (West Virginia University) examine student communication research to answer the question: *How can students communicate effectively with their instructors?* Since you are likely a student in college at this very moment, these research findings have a direct relevance to your life. Moreover, since you will have to write many emails, give several speeches, and talk with your instructors quite often, these findings can help your classroom communication encounters progress more smoothly. In the end, we hope you get more out of your college experience by enacting some minor changes in thinking and communication behavior.

DID I REALLY SEND THAT? CRAFTING EFFECTIVE EMAILS TO PROFESSORS

Keri K. Stephens, University of Texas at Austin, Marian L. Houser, Texas State University-San Marcos & Renee L. Cowan, University of Texas San Antonio

Warning: You are about to read actual email messages sent from students to professors.

Grammar and punctuation have not been altered in any way:

> **Message 1 (sent unsigned):** My parents are mad that I signed up for your 350 lab class. They think it's too late. They still want me to come home every weekend. So is there any way I can be placed into one of your lab classed that are earlier or another day?

> **Message 2:** Howdy Mr. Smith. I'm in your Thursday night class. I want to let you know/ask you if it's cool if I can attend your Tuesday night class on Oct. 20th. I know we have a test but on the 15th I have floor seats for the miley cyrus concert and I don't want to mis it =]...Gracias.

> **Message 3:** hey teach, so sorry i was absent yesterday. These legal matters are killing me. but im not making excuses. i was just wondering if it would be too much trouble to let me know where i stand on absences in both my classes i am fortunate enough to have you as an instructor for. im trying to get my lawyer to help me work my court appearances around my class schedule. Thanks.

> **Message 4:** Dr.Smith, I spoke with you abut this already, and the fact that I couldn't even make it to the bathroom without going on myself. Its not that I didn't want to come to class, it wa s matter of I could not physically make it to class one, and two why would you want me to spread that to the rest of the class and then put them and or you out for a week or so? This is ridicules, how are we expected to be in class when its not physically possible. Next time I'll just come to class an dpuke on the floor or shit mypants, if that will make you happy and keep mepassing the class. See you in class.

It is highly likely these students, if given the opportunity to review their email message, would wonder "Wow! Did I really send that?" While these are extreme examples, almost every professor who has taught for more than a year has a similar extreme email case to share. It is difficult to speculate what causes students to decide to hit the send key after composing these messages. Is it the stress that students feel about making that 'A,' or is the message written so quickly that the student does not think twice about how a professor might react toward their less than ideal message? Regardless of the reason, it is highly likely that students do not have their requests granted when their emails are misunderstood, confusing, and do not meet the expectations of the professors.

This chapter focuses on using research to better understand how students can best use email to communicate with professors. As there is considerable evidence to suggest that the student-instructor relationship is extremely valuable and creates many positive outcomes for the student, it is important to understand the impact of proper vs. improper messages (Frymier & Houser, 2000; Pogue & Ahyun, 2006; Witt, Wheeless, & Allen, 2004). The following example will be used throughout this chapter and is a more common type of email many students send to professors today—one resembling a text message. This message is very casual in tone and is considered quite informal, nonetheless, students sending these emails are evaluated quite harshly (Wilson, 2005).

Subject: mting?

Hey, I read chapter 9 and attended class but still don't get it. r u going 2 b in your office this afternoon can I come by if you are. tb

This chapter begins by discussing the concept of audience analysis and uses this to elaborate on the professor-student communication relationship. In addition, specific features of email messages are examined, followed by a discussion of email use beyond college and in the workplace. When you complete this chapter you should be more aware of the benefits of thinking about your email before you hit the send key.

USING EMAIL WITH PROFESSORS

Email is a dominant form of professor-student communication and interaction (Hassini, 2006; Hinkle, 2002; Jones, 2002). Research on email use in this context can really help students understand why they need to carefully consider their specific email actions that bother professors. This form of written communication is personal and often one-on-one, so it provides an ideal opportunity to build a relationship or to ruin a potential relationship.

Professors: An Important Audience

Communication students are typically taught to analyze their audience before they attempt to communicate. Audience analysis is often stressed in the public speaking context where students learn to craft openings that capture the attention of the audience and include details in the speech body that appeal to them (Beebe, Beebe, & Ivy, 2010). This analysis is also very important in interpersonal interactions because these communication events typically occur more frequently than speeches, and audience analysis increases the effectiveness of communication. This is especially the case when the audience is a professor and the message from the student is a request of some type.

Research suggests that requests are the most frequent type of email message sent from a student to a professor (Duran, Kelly, & Keaton, 2005). Virtually every student will need to make a request of a professor at some time during their college career. Some requests are very simple, such as setting up a meeting during or outside of office hours. Other requests require a bit more persuasion, such as a request to miss class or to have an assignment re-graded. How you craft your email message has a direct impact on (a) whether the professor complies with your request, (b) his/her perception of your credibility, and (c) whether he/she likes you (Stephens, Houser, & Cowan, 2009). Well-written, grammatically correct, and organized messages are received more positively (Bunz & Campbell, 2004; Jessmer & Anderson, 2001; Waldvogal, 2007). This helps to overcome the issue of imposing additional costs or burdens—e.g., time to read and comprehend the message—on the message receiver. Well-crafted emails demonstrate goodwill on the part of the students because they have taken their time writing the messages (Jessmer & Anderson, 2001), and thus the professor views them as more credible (Stephens, Cowan, & Houser, 2011).

Many students nod their heads at this point, because this makes sense when they stop and think about their audience. This is, after all, a professor who has some amount of authority over them. But often students simply do not stop to think before typing the message, or they say, "If they know me, then it does not matter if I send a sloppy email." Students also defend their decisions for sending quick overly-casual emails to professors by claiming, "My professor is young, like me, so I am sure they find quick messages acceptable." These may seem like logical conclusions, but the research does not support these rationalizations.

Millennial professors and email. Few people will argue that the members of Generation Y (or Millennials) use technology differently than people in prior generations (Lancaster & Stillman, 2002). Students born between 1982 and 2000 are considered part of the Millennial generation because of their advanced technology use, and most traditional college-aged students are considered part of this generation. Research suggests Millennials are confident in how they use technology (Howe & Strauss, 2000), and they tend to violate email quality and structure expectations more often than people over 30 years of age (Extejt, 1998). Stephens, et al. (2009) specifically examined whether there were differences in how younger professors viewed email violations when compared to professors from older generations. In their study of the perceptions of students' overly casual emails, they found very few age effects on email perceptions. Thus, regardless of age, professors had very similar negative reactions to overly casual emails. Some younger professors did not view these email professionalism violations more permissively, which suggests that students should proceed cautiously.

Their study did find that younger professors are engaging in more text messaging (Stephens & Rains, 2011), and throughout the higher education community there are increasing informal reports that some professors are requesting students text them in addition to using email. However, this does not suggest students have free reign to send casual and sloppy messages. Research also suggests that email is used more by an older generation, while younger people rely on mobile phones, text messaging, and instant messaging (Kim, Kim, Park, & Rice, 2007).

Familiarity and email. It makes sense that once people become more familiar, email formality can decrease, but the research on professor-student email conversations does not suggest this. In their experimental study examining the effect of familiarity on a professor's willingness to comply with a simple request for a meeting with a student, Stephens, et al. (2009) discovered the results differed depending on whether professors' or students' opinions were asked. In their study, familiarity (how well a professor knows a student) does not affect how a professor evaluates a student's credibility, the professor's attitude toward a message, feeling of liking, or willingness to grant a meeting. Students *believed* that when professors did not know they were sending the message, professors were more willing to grant a meeting request if the message was more formally constructed (Stephens et al., 2011). This suggests that students might pay closer attention when they don't know a professor, but then become less worried about message quality when they become more familiar with them. Keep in mind that this is only one study and that these findings might differ depending on the context. But remember that, regardless of familiarity with a student, a professor's view on the email does not change. So students need to continue to remain professional in their email communication even as they get to know their professors.

A day in the life of a professor. To better understand why professionalism in communication matters in a college environment, let's examine what it is like to be in a professor's shoes. When a student's email appears in the inbox of a professor, it is highly likely to be mixed within 25 to 50 other messages. Some of these messages come from other students, and not necessarily from students in the same classes. In addition to students' emails, professors receive emails about departmental committees, university news, research grant information, letters of recommendation requests from former students, textbook adoption materials, volunteer requests from student organizations, and emails from co-authors and journal editors, just to mention a few. Combine the broad diversity of the messages with the reality that professors have busy days and many of the research findings regarding how professors examine and evaluate email messages make a lot of sense.

Pulling these findings together, it becomes clear there is a type of organizational and institutional norm that guides professors' interpretations of emails. Professors are in an organizational role where their job includes teaching and evaluating student work. Receiving a carelessly constructed email from any student might make that role more prominent and create a situation where students are harshly evaluated for sloppy emails (Stephens et al., 2011). Professors worry when they receive emails with grammatical errors and shortcuts because they dread having to read and grade papers (which are often much longer) from a student who opts not to take the time to write a proper email.

Writing Effective Emails for Professors

So far, this chapter has focused primarily on the perception of students who write overly-casual email messages, but research also provides guidance on the specific components of email messages that likely matter the most. For example, do you like long emails that drone on for pages? Probably not, and the research says that most of us prefer concise emails that are well-crafted and to the point (Crowther & Goldhaber, 2001).

There are some differences in opinions concerning what is problematic, especially when comparing professors and students. Two specific email items were found especially frustrating for professors:

those with the absence of the author's name in the message and those using shortcuts like those found in text messages (Stephens et al., 2009). Both of these issues bothered students significantly less than professors. Again, try and put yourself in a professor's shoes; this might help to clarify the following research findings. For example, imagine reading a message that is unsigned, in an inbox full of unread messages. The professor looks everywhere in the message to figure out who sent it, but only finds the email address of kl523478@txstate.edu. The professor thinks, "Do I have a student with the initials KL in any of my four classes?" Then the professor wonders if the letters are even the student's initials. In a frustrated state, the professor does not know how to respond. Now imagine being a professor and receiving an email from a student that includes the acronym "LOL." The professor wonders, "Does that student want me to laugh out loud, or are they sending me an uncomfortable amount of love?" Of course, this assumes the professor is familiar with text messaging acronyms, which is related to another research finding regarding professors' dislike of shortcuts.

So what about openings, closings, signature blocks, and the all-important subject line? Research provides some guidance on these issues as well. "Hey" or "Howdy" is a bit abrupt for a professional email and simply avoiding a greeting altogether is not prudent. Several research studies suggest that people need to include greetings such as Dear, or Hello and include a person's name (Bunz & Campbell, 2005; Waldvogal, 2007). In addition, unless advised otherwise, never refer to your professor as Mr. or Mrs. when Dr. is their formal title (Yagoda, 2003). If you do not know your professors' titles, you should simply ask them or look them up on the Internet to see if they have completed their Ph.D. When you are ending your message you should include a closing, as it sends an appropriate politeness cue (Bunz & Campbell, 2005), and be sure to sign your name as the author of the message (Pirie, 2000; Stephens et al., 2009). It is also extremely important to use the subject line and to include specificity that will encourage others to open the message (Crowther & Goldhaber, 2001; Focazio, 1997). People are increasingly overloaded and email is to blame in many situations (Farhoomand & Drury, 2002).

Avoiding email pitfalls and crafting thoughtful messages will not go unnoticed, which is especially important if you are making a request. A final consideration is to understand that your email address sends a message about who you are as a person. Imagine being a professor and receiving an email from *biglovemama@utexas.edu*. Many students never consider that their actual email address sends an additional message above and beyond the content of the message. Not only does this send the wrong message to a professor, but it is also unprofessional as you consider graduating and entering the workplace (and perhaps even asking for that all important letter of recommendation).

USING EMAIL BEYOND COLLEGE

While there will be varied organizational norms for how to use email in the places you work, much of what we have discussed here provides a conservative approach for you to manage your impression as you begin your career. Wilson (2005) warns college graduates to pay close attention because sending improper emails can send a negative impression to important and powerful audiences, such as managers, colleagues, and customers. One of the advantages of taking a communication course is that you learn how to observe others and to adapt your communication to fit their needs and create a win-win situation for both of you. Not all organizations will want extremely formal emails, so it is important for you to learn how this tool is appropriated in a given environment (Ducheneaut & Watts, 2005). Also consider that mobile devices like iPhones® and BlackBerries® are frequently used in workplace environments, and sending and receiving messages from these smaller devices presents challenges to crafting well-written messages with limited character subject lines (Stephens et al., 2009). A good workplace email reference guide is *Send,* by Shipley and Schwalbe (2008), op-ed editor of the *New York Times* and Hyperion Books' editor-in-chief. This popular press book provides humorous, yet real examples of how people have ruined careers by not being cognizant of email etiquette. They also provide many tips for how to successfully communicate through email.

Using Email with Other Communication Technologies

Email is still a dominant form of communication between many students and professors (Jones, 2002), and it is often considered a professional way to communicate (Stephens & Heller, 2010). Yet it is important to remember that email is not used in isolation because students and working professionals often use a mix of communication technologies, including text messaging, social media, instructional tools like Blackboard, phone, and even face-to-face (FtF) communication (Stephens, Sørnes, Rice, Browning, & Sætre, 2008). Recent research suggests that using a combination of communication technologies—e.g., email followed by FtF communication—is more persuasive than simply using email or FtF repetitively (Stephens & Rains, 2011). In their study of using multiple messages to persuade college students to visit career services, Stephens and Rains (2011) found that overload—defined as having more messages than people want—plays a pivotal role in why using a mix of communication technologies matters. These findings point to another tip when interacting with professors: Vary the medium you use to communicate. Instead of sending repeated emails it is often prudent to handle some conversations in person rather than through repeated emails.

CONCLUSION

If you have not felt a bit uncomfortable yet about past email messages you have sent, you are probably in the minority. Most of us are guilty of firing off a last minute email or of using shortcuts to compose an email on a mobile device. These mistakes can be costly. This chapter should have reminded you that the messages you send to professors are worth the time to get them correct and understood. Hopefully you understand more about how your audience (professors) views your message in the context of the other 25 to 50 waiting in their inbox at the same time. It doesn't matter how well you know your professor, or if your professor is young, professionalism is expected in this environment. Even though it is tempting to use shortcuts, especially when you are using mobile phones, don't include them in emails. Remember to sign your emails with your name, use descriptive subject lines, and focus on appropriate greetings. It is important that you learn how these mistakes impact your life as a college student because if you remember the importance of professionalism now, it will serve you well into your professional career. btw...gtg!

REFERENCES

Beebe, S.A., Beebe, S. J., & Ivy. D. K. (2010). *Communication: Principles for a Lifetime* (4th ed.). Boston: Allyn and Bacon.

Bunz, U., & Campbell, S. W. (2004). Politeness accommodation in electronic mail. *Communication Research Reports, 21,* 11–25.

Crowther, G., & Goldhaber, G. (2001). Effective e-mail revisited. *Harvard Management Communication Letter, 4,* 12.

Ducheneaut, N., & Watts, L. A. (2005). In search of coherence: A review of e-mail research. *Human-Computer Interaction, 20,* 11–48.

Duran, R. L., Kelly, L., & Keaton, J. A. (2005). College faculty use and perceptions of electronic mail to communication with students. *Communication Quarterly, 53*(2), 159–176.

Extejt, M. M. (1998). Teaching students to correspond effectively electronically. *Business Communication Quarterly, 61,* 57–67.

Farhoomand, A. F., & Drury, D. H. (2002). Managerial information overload. *Communications of the ACM, 45,* 127–131.

Focazio, M. (1997). How effective is your email? *Getting Results for the Hands on Manager, 42,* 7.

Frymier, A. B., & Houser, M. L. (2000). The teacher-student relationship as an interpersonal relationship. *Communication Education, 49,* 207–219.

Hassini, E. (2006). Student-instructor communication: The role of email. *Computers & Education, 47,* 29–40.

Hinkle, S. E. (2002). The impact of e-mail use on student-faculty interaction. *Journal of the Indiana University Student Personnel Association,* 27–34.

Howe, N., & Strauss, W. (2000). *Millennials rising: The next great generation.* New York: Vintage.

Jessmer, S., & Anderson, D. (2001). The effect of politeness and grammar on user perceptions of electronic mail. *North American Journal of Psychology, 3,* 331–346.

Jones, S. (2002). The Internet goes to college: How students are living in the future with today's technology. Retrieved from http://www.pewinternet.org/Reports/2002/The-Internet-Goes-to-College.aspx

Kim, H., Kim, G. J., Park, H. W., & Rice, R. E. (2007). Configurations of relationships in different media: FtF, email, instant messenger, mobile phone, and SMS. *Journal of Computer-Mediated Communication, 12*(4). Online at http://jcmc.indiana.edu/vol12/issue4/kim.html.

Lancaster, L. C., & Stillman, D. (2002). *When generations collide: Who they are, why they clash, how to solve the generational puzzle at work.* New York: HarperCollins.

Pirie, R. (2000). Ask an expert: Email etiquette= e-mail effectiveness. *CA Magazine, 133,* 11.

Pogue, L., & Ahyun, K. (2006). The effect of teacher nonverbal immediacy and credibility on student motivation and affective learning. *Communication Education, 55,* 331–344.

Shipley, D., & Schwalbe, W. (2008). *Send: The essential guide to email for office and home.* New York: Random House, Inc.

Stephens, K. K. (2007). The successive use of information and communication technologies at work. *Communication Theory, 17*(4), 486–509.

Stephens, K. K. (2008). Optimizing costs in workplace instant messaging use. *IEEE Transactions on Professional Communication, 51,* 369–380.

Stephens, K. K., Cowan, R. L., & Houser, M. L. (2011). Organizational norm congruency and interpersonal familiarity in email: Examining messages from two different status perspectives. *Journal of Computer Mediated Communication, 16,* 228–249.

Stephens, K. K., & Heller, A. (2010). 2010 US Census Coverage Measurement Residence Hall Report. Washington DC: US Census Bureau

Stephens, K. K., Houser, M. L., & Cowan, R. L. (2009). R U able to meat me: The impact of students' overly casual email messages to instructors. *Communication Education, 58,* 303–326.

Stephens, K. K., & Rains, S. A. (2011). Information and communication technology sequences and message repetition in interpersonal interaction. *Communication Research, 38,* 101–122. doi:10.1177/0093650210362679.

Stephens, K. K., Sørnes, J. O, Rice, R. E., Browning, L. D., & Sætre, A. S. (2008). Discrete, sequential, and follow-up use of information and communication technology by managerial knowledge workers. *Management Communication Quarterly, 22,* 197–231.

Waldvogal, J. (2007). Greetings and closings in workplace email. *Journal of Computer-Mediated Communication, 12,* 456–477.

Wilson, E. V. (2005). Persuasive effects of system features in computer-mediated communication. *Journal of Organizational Computing and Electronic Commerce, 15*(2), 161–184.

Witt, P. L., Wheeless, L. R., & Allen, M. (2004). A meta-analytical review of the relationship between teacher immediacy and student learning. *Communication Monographs, 71,* 184–207.

Yagoda, B. (2003, June 13). What should we call the professor? *The Chronicle of Higher Education, 49* (40), B20. Retrieved from http://chronicle.com

Yates, B. L., Adams, J. W., & Brunner, B. R. (2009). Mass communication and journalism faculty's perceptions of effectiveness of email communication with college students: A nationwide survey. *Learning, Media, and Technology, 24,* 307–321.

LEARNING TO COPE WITH SPEECH ANXIETY THE NATURAL WAY

CHRIS R. SAWYER & AMBER N. FINN, TEXAS CHRISTIAN UNIVERSITY

We begin this chapter with a short vignette about a student named Miriam, a college sophomore taking her first course in communication. Confident in every other aspect of her academic life, she avoids any class that requires speaking in public. However, her basic speech course is required at the university, and today Miriam is giving her dreaded first speech. Detailed, hardworking, and always prepared, Miriam has devoted most of her preparation time to researching and writing multiple drafts of her presentation. Not much effort was made in rehearsing delivery because her main goal is to muddle through this assignment by reading from her extensive notes. Suddenly she realizes that she's the next to make a presentation. Her heart begins to pound and her breathing becomes shallow. Worrisome thoughts race through her mind. The instructor calls her name and soon afterwards the "moment of truth" finally arrives. Standing behind a lectern, she faces her fellow students for the first time. How will Miriam react to this new situation? Will her anxiety symptoms continue to escalate and make this the single most stressful event of her life? Perhaps she will discover that presenting speeches isn't so bad after all, or she might even enjoy the experience. What about the reactions of the audience and her teacher, how will they perceive her performance? Will they see through her attempts to cover up her insecurities or simply not notice them at all?

Modern communication scholars have posed these questions, and many others like them, when trying to account for speaker anxiety levels before, during, and after giving public speeches. Those who are new to this issue are often amazed to discover its complexity and the richness of theories offered to explain it. Despite the tireless efforts of many prominent scholars, a complete account of speech anxiety has yet to appear in scholarly writings.

The purpose of this chapter is to present a brief summary of how one simple approach to this problem called narrow-banding (Behnke & Sawyer, 1998) has helped to advance our knowledge of how students can better manage the negative effects of speech anxiety in classroom speeches.

EARLY SPEECH ANXIETY RESEARCH

For more than 70 years, communication scholars have attempted to examine the relationships among the various forms of public speaking state anxiety. In his summary of early "stage fright" research, Clevenger (1959) was uncertain whether the methods used to measure anxiety at that time were valid. Moreover, it was unclear to him whether those methods represented differing aspects of the same construct or if definitional problems were at fault. Shortly after Clevenger's paper was published, however, it became evident that the progress of early speech anxiety researchers was impeded by conceptual weaknesses.

Spielberger (1966) differentiated *state* and *trait* anxiety using factor analytic techniques pioneered by Cattell and Scheier (1958). A state is a *transitory* condition, which means that it varies over time. Traits, on the other hand, are stable and may reflect basic individual differences such as personality dimensions. Essentially, what distinguishes traits from states comes down to "how do you generally feel" (trait) versus "how do you feel at a given moment in time," usually "right now" (state). Prior to Spielberger, the ways anxiety was measured in studies of communication were often ambiguous or excessively broad. These limitations were overcome by the State-Trait Anxiety Inventory (STAI A-State) (Spielberger, Gorsuch, and Lushene, 1970), which became the most widely used measure of public speaking state anxiety in empirical studies.

Spielberger's state-trait distinction was a valuable breakthrough for communication scholars. A good example of a trait anxiety measure used in our field is McCroskey's (1982) Personal Report of Communication Apprehension (PRCA-24). Trait measures of anxiety, like the PRCA-24 among others, are useful because the way speakers describe their general level of speech anxiety today tends to be very similar to how they will report it in the future. As a result, instruments such as the PRCA-24 can help identify students who might suffer discomfort on future speech assignments. Public speaking *state* anxiety, on the other hand, refers to how speakers feel during a particular speech, as opposed to all others they've ever presented (Behnke & Sawyer, 1998). Because each speaking situation is unique, speakers cannot be expected to respond in exactly the same way every time they make a presentation. Moreover, unlike traits, states fluctuate with time, which makes them useful for answering a variety of questions where the trait approach would be impractical. The work covered in this chapter focuses on state rather than trait communication apprehension.

MEASUREMENT AND CONCEPTUAL ISSUES

Before discussing the contributions of this research, a number of concepts should be laid out along with a basic vocabulary. First, by far the most common method of conducting speech anxiety research is simply to ask speakers to share their experiences using interviews and surveys. Self-reported data of this type are easy to obtain and usually provide good accounts of feelings, worry, and other psychological variables. In other speech anxiety research, trained observers watch video recordings of speeches looking for telltale signs of nervousness. However, not all can be seen by the naked eye. The third and last strategy involves direct measurement of physical changes in a speaker's body, such as increases in heart rate brought on by the stress of giving a speech. Together these approaches to speech anxiety research are called the three **modes of experience**. Each way of knowing and observing makes a unique contribution to our understanding of the problem. Although we've found that speaker self-reported anxiety is most useful to our work, we have also used physiological (Finn, Sawyer, & Behnke, 2009; Roberts, Sawyer, & Behnke, 2004) and behavioral (Finn, Sawyer, & Behnke, 2003) indices of speech anxiety.

Another idea is called **unrolling the ball of string**. Imagine that you are holding a ball of cotton string in the palm of your hand. Unwinding it, you realize that the ball is actually made up of different colored stands of twine and yarn connected end to end. As an analogy, "unrolling the ball of string" means measuring state anxiety at particular moments throughout the speech, rather than for the speech as a whole. This approach reveals insights into the reactions of speakers left undetected when they are asked to describe their overall feeling during a presentation. Some of these have surprising results, especially for students enrolled in introductory courses.

This leads us to the concept of state anxiety milestones. **Milestones** are specific moments before, during, and immediately following a public speech through which specific psychological events occur (Behnke & Sawyer, 1999). In much of our research, we ask speakers to tell us how they felt at various times, such as one minute before speaking, during the first and last minutes of their presentations, and for the minute immediately following their speeches. These are known respectively as the anticipation, confrontation, adaptation, and release milestones. The use of milestones to gauge the state anxiety levels of speakers is also called *narrow-band measurement* (Behnke & Sawyer, 1998).

Speech State Anxiety Pattern Types

Plotting speaker state anxiety before, during, and after public speaking reveals at least two competing emotional processes, namely, **habituation** and **sensitization** (Behnke & Sawyer, 2001a; Finn, Sawyer, & Behnke, 2003). When examined across the four milestones, most speakers report their highest level of psychological state anxiety during the anticipation milestone, approximately one minute before presenting the speech. Anxiety levels begin to decline during the first minute of speaking, also known as the "moment of truth" or confrontation milestone. State anxiety levels then continue to decrease through the last minute of the speech and the minute after the speech or the adaptation and release milestones. The resulting *monotonic decreasing function* is consistent with the phenomenon of habituation, in which humans become progressively more comfortable in the presence of fear arousing stimuli. Approximately two-thirds to three-quarters of all speakers studied in patterns studies display this overall shape and are called *habituators*.

Generally, a secondary pattern accounts for the remaining speakers and reflects a contrary process called sensitization. For these speakers, psychological anxiety is elevated during the anticipation milestone but rises dramatically and peaks during confrontation. Anxiety then declines gradually during the remainder of the speech and through the release milestone. Speakers who display this inverted V-shaped pattern are called *sensitizers*. Several facts have been established concerning speakers with this pattern type. Sensitizers adapt more slowly to public speaking than habituators (Sawyer & Behnke, 2002) and experience more body sensations of distress (Horvath, Huner, Weisel, Sawyer, & Behnke, 2004). Compared to habituators, sensitizers report higher levels of anxiety sensitivity (Behnke & Sawyer, 2001b), affect intensity, and sensitivity to punishment (Clay, Fisher, Xie, Sawyer, & Behnke, 2005). Sensitization during public speaking appears to be the function of high trait anxiety combined with reactivity to stressful stimuli (Harris, Sawyer, & Behnke, 2006; Roberts, Finn, Harris, Sawyer, & Behnke, 2005).

Making Sense of the Findings

Each of the findings discussed above is consistent with recent advances in our understanding of how emotions are processed. Specifically, anxiety is an adaptive process that promotes survival in hostile or dangerous environments (LeDoux, 1996). It consists of a constellation of symptoms or reactions, including increased physiological arousal (increased heart rate), heightened vigilance, stress reactions, and rumination or worry, which are connected to our evolutionary development as a species (Gray & McNaughton, 2000). Our vignette at the start of the chapter contained many of these characteristics. Miriam's speaking behavior, which we did not describe, would likely reflect a condition known as behavior inhibition, including monotone vocal cues, deadpan facial expressions, and rigid or non-existent gestures (Mulac & Sherman, 1974; Finn, Sawyer, & Behnke, 2003). According to this perspective, once behavior inhibition sets in it will continue to influence speaker behaviors until the level of perceived threat diminishes.

Interestingly, state anxiety naturally declines with exposure to a feared stimulus, so long as speakers experience little or no real harm (McNally, 2007). Suppose that Miriam avoids speaking in public because she worries that audiences will behave unfavorably towards her. In this case, a supportive audience will promote the habituation response because what the speaker fears most never materializes. One anxiety management strategy that makes use of this principle is exposure therapy (Foa, Huppert, & Cahill, 2006). Under this strategy, a mild to moderate anxiety reaction is first induced by presenting a fear arousing stimulus. Then, continued exposure to the stimulus is maintained while negative consequences are controlled.

In the communication classroom, a convenient method for implementing exposure therapy is the TRIPLESPEAK assignment (Dubner & Mills, 1984). In TRIPLESPEAK, the speech class is divided into four groups. Students assigned to one of the groups are speakers while each of the other groups serves as audiences. Every speaker makes a brief presentation to each of the audiences in turn. These brief multiple exposures have the effect of reducing the threat of giving a speech. As the perceived level of threat diminishes, speakers become less inhibited and more comfortable, and they experience less distress. Moreover, habituation during these initial presentations continues to help speakers on subsequent assignments (Finn, Sawyer, & Schrodt, 2009).

Summarizing the concepts and information covered in this chapter, several principles emerge. First, anxiety affects the physiological, behavioral, and psychological reactions of speakers. Consequently, it is among one of the greatest barriers to student success in introductory communication courses, especially those requiring public speaking assignments. Next, instruments like the PRCA-24 were designed to measure traits, which by definition do not change over time. Therefore, it is more appropriate to focus on *states* when assessing the progress of students. Otherwise, substantial gains in speaker confidence will go undetected when using trait measures alone. Besides, only about half of the variance in speech state anxiety is a function of trait anxiety. The remaining 50% stems from speaker adaptation while speaking along with some situational variance (Harris, Sawyer, & Behnke, 2006). Third, "unrolling the ball of string" called public speaking state anxiety requires looking at specific moments in which critical events occur called milestones. Habituators differ mainly from sensitizers at the "moment of truth" or confrontation. Therefore, preparing students for the first minute of the presentation may be critical to the extent to which they benefit from class speaking assignments. Last, instructors can embed exposure within a variety of classroom assignments such as TRIPLESPEAK. As a result, students can get the benefits of greater confidence during confrontation without the embarrassment of feeling singled out for special treatment.

Most stage fright researchers are motivated by the compassionate impulse to help others and to relieve discomfort. Here are three suggestions based on the information presented in this chapter that could potentially enhance your life as a public speaker.

Don't forget to breathe. Many of the anxious speakers we've studied report physical sensations, such as chest pressure, palpitations, and shortness of breath. Symptoms such as these are part of the fight-flight reflex and can be neutralized to some degree through proper breathing. A few minutes before you are scheduled to speak, consciously begin to take deep breaths, inhaling through your nose, and filling up your abdomen. Hold each breath for just a few seconds and then exhale quietly through your nose. You should start feeling more relaxed within a few cycles of deep breathing. Also, breathing from your stomach when giving speeches can help you to project your voice so that you can be heard clearly by everyone in the audience.

Remember, the worst part is over very early. The physical symptoms of state anxiety are uncomfortable for a reason. They act like an alarm system warning you of some potential threat. Over the years, we've learned that those speakers who can get through the "moment of truth" at the outset of a presentation become progressively less anxious as they continue to speak. Consequently, it's important for you to be able to speak continuously for at least the first minute of the presentation. We recommend rehearsing the initial minute or two of your speech and taking notes or other memory aids with you to the lectern. After speaking for about a minute or so, you should begin to notice fewer stress sensations and greater comfort.

Start small and work your way up. Once you've learned the fundamentals of preparing and giving speeches during your introductory communication course, make a point to give short speeches occasionally in front of small but friendly audiences outside of class. Volunteering to make an announcement to a small social gathering of friends is a good place to start. Look for opportunities to speak and gradually increase the length of your speeches, presenting them to slightly larger groups each time. Most of our students who have used this strategy report greater confidence when making formal public speeches to large gatherings.

Many of the great orators throughout history began their careers with fear and trepidation. Despite this, they became confident and well composed speakers with diligent practice and the support of others. The same can be true for you.

REFERENCES

Behnke, R. R., & Sawyer, C. R. (1998). Conceptualizing speech anxiety as a dynamic trait. *Southern Communication Journal, 63,* 160–169.

Behnke, R. R., & Sawyer, C. R. (1999). Milestones of anticipatory public speaking anxiety. *Communication Education, 48,* 165–172.

Behnke, R. R., & Sawyer, C. R. (2001a). Public speaking arousal as a function of anticipatory activation and autonomic reactivity. *Communication Reports, 14,* 73–85.

Behnke, R. R., & Sawyer, C. R. (2001b). Patterns of psychological state anxiety in public speaking as a function of anxiety sensitivity. *Communication Research Reports, 19,* 156–166.

Bode, G. (2010). A racing heart, rattling knees, and ruminative thoughts: Defining, explaining, and treating public speaking anxiety. *Communication Education, 59,* 70–105.

Cattell, R. B., & Scheier, I. H. (1958). The nature of anxiety: A review of thirteen multivariate analyses comprising 814 variables. *Psychological Reports, 4,* 351–388.

Clay, E., Fisher, R. L., Xie, S., Sawyer, C. R., & Behnke, R. R. (2005). Affect intensity and sensitivity to punishment as predictors of sensitization (arousal) during public speaking. *Communication Reports, 18,* 111–120.

Clevenger, T. (1959). A synthesis of experimental research in stage fright. *Quarterly Journal of Speech, 45,* 134-145.

Dubner, F. S., & Mills, F. O. (1984). TRIPLESPEAK: A teaching technique to multiply successful speech performance. *Communication Education, 33,* 168–172.

Finn, A. N., Sawyer, C. R., & Behnke, R. R. (2003). Audience-perceived anxiety patterns of public speaking. *Communication Quarterly, 51,* 470–481.

Finn, A. N., Sawyer, C. R., & Behnke, R. R. (2009). A model of anxious arousal for public speaking. *Communication Education, 58,* 417–432.

Finn, A. N., Sawyer, C. R., & Schrodt, P. (2009). Examining the effect of exposure therapy on public speaking anxiety. *Communication Education, 58,* 92–109.

Foa, E. B., Huppert, J., & Cahill, S. P. (2006). Emotional processing theory. In B. O. Rothbaum (Ed.), *Pathological anxiety: Emotional processing in etiology and treatment* (pp. 3–24). New York: Guilford Press.

Gray, J. A., & McNaughton, N. (2000). *The neuropsychology of anxiety: An enquiry into the functions of the septo-hippocampal system.* Oxford, UK: Oxford University Press.

Harris, K. B., Sawyer, C. R., & Behnke, R. R. (2006). Predicting speech state anxiety from trait anxiety, reactivity, and situational influences. *Communication Quarterly, 54,* 213–226.

Horvath, N. R., Huner, M. C., Weisel, J. J., Sawyer, C. R., & Behnke, R. R. (2004). Body sensations during speech performance as a function of public speaking anxiety type. *Texas Speech Communication Journal, 29,* 65–72.

LeDoux, J. E. (1996). *The emotional brain.* New York: Simon and Schuster.

McCroskey, J. C. (1982). Oral communication apprehension: A reconceputalization. In M. Burgoon (Ed.), (6th ed., pp. 136–170). Beverly Hills, CA: Sage.

McNally, R. J. (2007). Mechanisms of exposure therapy: How neuroscience can improve treatments for anxiety disorders. *Clinical Psychology Review, 27,* 750–759.

Mulac, A., & Sherman, R. A. (1974). Behavioral assessment of speech anxiety. *Quarterly Journal of Speech, 60,* 134–143.

McNally, R. J. (2007). Mechanisms of exposure therapy: How neuroscience can improve treatments for anxiety disorders. *Clinical Psychology Review, 27,* 750–759.

Roberts, J. B., Finn, A. N., Harris, K. B., Sawyer, C. R., & Behnke, R. R. (2005). Public speaking state anxiety as a function of trait anxiety and reactivity mechanisms. *Southern Communication Journal, 70,* 161–167.

Sawyer, C. R., & Behnke, R. R. (1999). State anxiety patterns for public speaking and the behavior inhibition system. *Communication Reports, 12,* 33–41.

Sawyer, C. R., & Behnke, R. R. (2002). Reduction in public speaking state anxiety during performance as a function of sensitization processes. *Communication Quarterly, 50,* 110–121.

Spielberger, C. D. (1966). *Anxiety and behavior.* New York: Academic Press.

Spielberger, C. D., Gorsuch, R. L., & Lushene, R. E. (1970). Manual for state-trait anxiety inventory. Palo Alto, CA: Consulting Psychological Corporation.

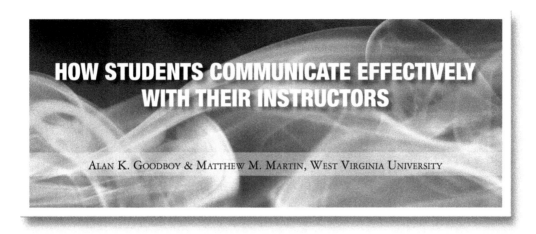

HOW STUDENTS COMMUNICATE EFFECTIVELY WITH THEIR INSTRUCTORS

ALAN K. GOODBOY & MATTHEW M. MARTIN, WEST VIRGINIA UNIVERSITY

In your communication classes you learn that the nonverbal and verbal messages you send often have a great impact on how others perceive and interact with you. How you communicate plays a role in your ability to influence others, to get others to like you, and to initiate and maintain good relationships. This is also true in the student-instructor relationship; how you communicate with your instructors will help determine how well you achieve your educational and relational needs in the classroom (Mottet, Frymier, & Beebe, 2006). Based on research in instructional communication, we will discuss in this chapter how you can adapt your communication strategies in order to communicate more competently (i.e., appropriately and effectively) with your instructors.

Sometimes students send messages (whether intentional or not) that instructors decode as students not being interested, not being prepared, not taking the course seriously, or being overall disrespectful. Although we are now both professors, obviously we were also once students. And we acknowledge that we were not always model students (or as some of our students might point out, not always model instructors). At times, we might have told our instructors that we did not have to study that much for their classes because they were easy. Or maybe we sat there in class with a baseball hat covering our sunglass covered eyes. Possibly we grunted when our instructor asked us an open-ended question. Maybe instead of giving serious answers, we made jokes or told off-topic stories. Or spent our time flirting with girls (almost always unsuccessfully). We gave little thought to what our instructors thought about us, or at times, we might have been under the wrong assumption that our instructors found us entertaining and engaging. In reality, most of the time we did want our instructors to like us and we wanted to participate constructively in the class. How we communicated, however, sent a different message.

Did you ever want an instructor to think that you were smart, funny, or likeable? This desire is not unnatural; rather, it is common occurrence because research suggests that many students identify with their instructors (Chory & Goodboy, 2010), see their instructors as similar to themselves (Goodboy & Myers, 2007), and even view their instructors as someone they would consider as potential friends and want to spend time with (Weiss & Houser, 2007). When there are good relationships between students and their instructors, there is plenty of evidence that shows that students learn more and have greater affect for the course content. In other words, if you are able to communicate appropriately and effectively with your instructors, you will have greater success in the classroom and you will find the overall experience more enjoyable. In the next few pages, we will explore what research has shown to be effective student communication behaviors. We'll start by explaining why students communicate with their instructors in the first place.

STUDENT MOTIVES FOR COMMUNICATING

In each of your classes, you are going to have a relationship with your instructor. How you communicate with your instructor is going to have a great impact on the relationship and how your instructor communicates with you. Students communicate with their instructors for a variety of reasons (Martin, Myers, Mottet, 1999, 2002). First, students communicate for the **functional motive** to gain information about the course material or content (e.g., ask for clarification about what is being taught). When students communicate for the **relational motive**, they attempt to develop a personal relationship with their instructor (e.g., become friends with their instructor). Students who communicate for the **participatory motive** show that they understand the material (e.g., offering an example in class). Students who communicate for the **excuse-making motive** attempt to explain why work is late or inadequate (e.g., making up an excuse for missing a test). Finally, students who communicate for the **sycophancy motive** suck up to the instructor to create a favorable impression (e.g., telling the instructor how great the class is).

At times, how instructors communicate in the classroom influences their students' communication. For instance, student motives are influenced when instructors engage in positive classroom behavior such as self-disclosure (Cayanus, Martin, & Goodboy, 2009), assertiveness (Myers, Martin, & Mottet, 2002), and confirmation with students (Goodboy & Myers, 2008). On the contrary, student motives are also influenced by instructors who engage in negative behavior, such as verbal aggression (Myers, Edwards, Wahl, & Martin, 2007), misbehavior (Goodboy, Myers, & Bolkan, 2010), and abuse of power (Goodboy & Bolkan, 2011).

You might find these three studies particularly relevant in your life as a student. First, a study by Myers (2006) found that students who have high quality relationships with their instructors (i.e., in-group instead of out-group status) communicate more for relational, functional, and participatory, and sycophancy motives, but they avoid using excuse-making. Another study (Goodboy, Martin, & Bolkan, 2009) found that students who had satisfying conversations with their instructors communicated for the same reasons. A third study (Knapp, 2010) found that when students talk to their instructors for the relational and participatory motives, instructors are more satisfied with their job and are more likely to talk with students outside of class, and when students communicate for the relational motive, instructors reported being more motivated at work.

Considering these findings together collectively, students can form high quality and satisfying relationships with their instructors by avoiding excuse-making and communicating for relational, functional, and participatory reasons. Students can also help instructors enjoy their job more and encourage communication outside of class by communicating for the relational and participatory motives. Now that we know why students talk with their instructors, and how their motives can help foster positive outcomes with their instructors, we will now focus on how students can secure favorable classroom outcomes through their nonverbal behaviors.

STUDENT RESPONSIVENESS AND NONVERBAL IMMEDIACY

Competent students focus on communicating nonverbal responsiveness with their instructors (Frymier, 2005). **Responsiveness** refers to a student's "capacity to be sensitive to the communication of others, to be a good listener, to make others comfortable in communicating, and to recognize the needs and desires of others" (Richmond & McCroskey, 1998, p. 93). Student nonverbal responsiveness, which is also known as nonverbal immediacy (Barringer & McCroskey, 2000), is communicated to an instructor by engaging in immediacy behaviors, such as **smiling, nodding your head, making eye contact, forward learning, answering questions, displaying pleasant facial expressions, using vocal variety, and taking notes** (Mottet, 2000). By communicating these simple behaviors to an instructor, a plethora of useful outcomes can be obtained in a college course.

First, when students display nonverbal responsiveness, instructors grant students more relational power in the classroom and give higher scores/grades on essay evaluations (Mottet, Beebe, Raffeld, & Paulsel, 2005). Second, student nonverbal responsiveness empowers instructors, as it causes them to believe they have the ability to influence student performance in the classroom (i.e., instructor self-efficacy) and increases their satisfaction with teaching (Mottet, Beebe, Raffeld, & Medlock, 2004). Third, student nonverbal responsiveness makes instructors like students more (Mottet & Beebe, 2006) and increases their likelihood of complying with student requests and giving preferential treatment, such as raising final grades, tutoring students, extending due dates, permitting absences, offering extra credit, and letting out class early (Mottet, Beebe, Raffeld, & Paulsel, 2004). Fourth, student nonverbal responsiveness is related to instructor perceptions of student credibility, interpersonal attraction, and projections of student success in the classroom (Barringer & McCroskey, 2000). Fifth, responsive students tend to enjoy their classes more, learn more, and earn higher grades (Frymier, 2005; Harper & Hughey, 1986; Mottet & Beebe, 2006). It is obvious, then, that student nonverbal responsiveness pays off for students in many important ways. Students who wish to succeed in their coursework would be well-advised to communicate responsiveness to their instructors, as their instructors tend to reciprocate to students in meaningful ways.

STUDENT AFFINITY-SEEKING STRATEGIES

A final program of research that is useful for students to understand focuses on **student affinity-seeking strategies**. Affinity-seeking refers to how people communicate to get others to like them and to feel positively toward them (Bell & Daly, 1984). Students use a variety of affinity-seeking strategies (27 of them to be exact!) to get their instructors to like them. These strategies along with examples of each are listed in the following table:

Student Affinity-Seeking Strategies	Examples
Altruism—Helping or assisting your instructor	Handing out course evaluations
Achievement—Showing hard work ethic	Earning straight A's on assignments
Assume Control—presenting yourself as a leader	Giving input that helps the entire class
Assume Equality—Presenting yourself as an equal	Acting like a peer or friend
Comfortable Self—Acting comfortable with your instructor	Being yourself
Concede Control—Letting the instructor take charge	Asking for help with a paper
Conversational Rule Keeping—Following rules of talking	Raising your hand
Dynamism—Presenting yourself as enthusiastic	Showing excitement in class
Elicit Disclosures—Encouraging the instructor to talk	Asking questions about your instructor's life
Facilitate Enjoyment—Making class enjoyable	Telling a funny story
Flirting—Using flirtatious behavior	Smiling and laughing a lot
Gifts—Giving the instructor a gift	Giving a birthday card
Inclusion of Other—Including your instructor in events	Inviting your instructor to lunch
Influence Perceptions of Closeness—Increasing closeness	Telling your instructor he/she is a friend
Listening—Paying close attention to what your instructor says	Listening attentively during class
Nonverbal Immediacy—Using nonverbal cues	Making eye contact and nodding
Openness—Being open in communicating	Disclosing personal interests
Personal Autonomy—Seeming independent and free thinking	Challenging ideas in class
Physical Attractiveness—Looking good	Dressing nice for class
Presenting Interesting Self—Sounding interesting	Telling a unique story about yourself
Requirements—Meeting all course requirements	Coming to class always prepared
Self-Concept Confirmation—Complimenting your instructor	Telling your instructor he/she is smart
Self-Inclusion—Seeing the instructor often	Saying hello during office hours
Sensitivity—Showing caring and concern	E-mailing an ill/absent instructor
Similarity—Acting similar to your instructor	Talking about mutual interests
Supportiveness—Showing support for your instructor	Telling a noisy class to be quiet
Trustworthiness—Acting like a trustworthy student	Reporting a test cheating incident

Strategies From Wanzer (1998). * = increases instructor liking of student (Wanzer, 1995).

Of course, students do not necessarily use all of these strategies in their courses, depending on their communication preferences and style, nor do they use many of these strategies in a simultaneous manner. But instructors do tend to like students more if they use these strategies (Wanzer, 1995). Although students who enjoy talking to their instructors tend to use these strategies in general (Goodboy, Bolkan, Myers, & Zhao, 2011), research suggests that students typically prefer to use conversational rule keeping, nonverbal immediacy (which is what we discussed previously as responsiveness), self-inclusion, elicit disclosure, requirements, listening, and achievement (Goodboy, Bolkan, Beebe, & Shultz, 2010; Wanzer, 1998). However, the strategies of **conversational rule keeping, comfortable self, dynamism, and facilitate enjoyment** produce the most liking with instructors (Wanzer, 1995). Even though many students believe some of the other student-affinity seeking strategies "work" to make an instructor like them more, some strategies have little to no effect on instructors. Specifically, students should avoid using flirting, gifts, assume control, assume equality, and physical attractiveness, for instance, as their "go to" strategies because they have no effect on an instructor's liking. Don't be alarmed if you have used some of these strategies in the past, however, because *none* of the 27 student-affinity seeking strategies will actually decrease an instructor's liking of you! It's just that some strategies work better than others, and now you know which ones work the best. Please refer to the table for the entire list of strategies that work (indicated by *) to increase liking.

CONCLUSION

In this chapter we only touch on some of the communication variables that come into play in the student-instructor relationship. And we focus on what students can do to be more competent— obviously quite a bit of the student-instructor relationship is based on instructor characteristics and the context. If students would perceive an instructor as incompetent, unfair, and egocentric, it would definitely complicate matters for those students that want to have a positive learning experience and a good student-instructor relationship with that instructor (Goodboy, 2011; Goodboy & Bolkan, 2009). But focusing on **you**—what can you do to communicate more appropriately and effectively with your instructors:

- If you have questions about the course material or instructions that are unclear to you (or you want clarification about a grade), ask your instructor questions. Students that report talking to their instructors for functional reasons report learning more and having greater affect for their instructors.

- Participate in class if the instructor is encouraging participation. Your instructor will view it positively and you will become more engaged in the class, i.e., you will learn more and the class will be more enjoyable.

- It is OK to explain special circumstances to an instructor (e.g., you missed a class because you were in the emergency room getting stitches), but avoid habitually making excuses with your instructor. If the only communication you have with your instructor involves you making excuses, it will be difficult to have a positive student-instructor relationship.

- Talk to your instructors before and after class, as well as when you see them outside of the classroom. Many instructors want to know their students beyond the formal classroom structure (and in the lecture class, it is difficult to establish any type of student-instructor relationship without additional communication).

- Listen in class; there are many positive learning outcomes related to listening in class, but beyond listening, appear to be listening. Look at the instructor and provide nonverbal responsiveness to the instructor. Instructors like to see students paying attention.

- Relatedly, try to look happy to be in class. This does not mean you have to be overly cheerful or phony in your behaviors, but some individuals tend to have a look on their faces that they are bored to death and would rather be anywhere else but in the classroom. While this might be true at times, some students are unaware of the messages they are sending their instructors. Instructors are more comfortable and satisfied when it appears that their students are interested and are having a pleasant time.

- Communicate respect to your instructors and to your fellow students. This sounds easy and like common sense, but making offensive comments or personal attacks against the instructor or fellow classmates is hugely detrimental to your relationships in class, including your relationship with your instructor.

- Remember that your instructor is not your adversary. You might not find the instructor socially attractive (i.e., you might not want to have any type of friendship with the instructor), but at least for a given course, you will have a student-instructor relationship. Do what you can to make this relationship as positive and constructive as possible.

The information here does not guarantee that the instructor will like you and/or that you will receive an A in a particular course. We will guarantee you, though, that if you regularly use the behaviors promoted in this chapter, you will learn more, have better classroom experiences, and have more positive student-instructor relationships.

REFERENCES

Barringer, D. K., & McCroskey, J. C. (2000). Immediacy in the classroom: Student immediacy. *Communication Education, 49,* 178–186.

Bell, R. A., & Daly, J. A. (1984). The affinity-seeking function of communication. *Communication Monographs, 51,* 91–115.

Cayanus, J. L., Martin, M. M., & Goodboy, A. K. (2009). The relation between teacher self-disclosure and student motives to communicate. *Communication Research Reports, 26,* 105–113.

Chory, R. M., & Goodboy, A. K. (2010). Power, compliance, and resistance in the classroom. In D. L. Fasset, and J. T. Warren (Eds.), *SAGE handbook of communication and instruction* (pp. 181–199). Los Angeles: Sage.

Chory-Assad, R. M. (2002). Classroom justice: Perceptions of fairness as a predictor of student motivation, learning, and aggression. *Communication Quarterly, 50,* 58–77.

Frymier, A. B. (2005). Students' classroom communication effectiveness. *Communication Quarterly, 53,* 197–212.

Goodboy, A. K. (2011). Instructional dissent in the college classroom. *Communication Education, 60,* 296–313.

Goodboy, A. K., & Bolkan, S. (2009). College teacher misbehaviors: Direct and indirect effects on student communication behavior and traditional learning outcomes. *Western Journal of Communication, 73,* 204–219.

Goodboy, A. K., & Bolkan, S. (2011). Student motives for communicating with instructors as a function of perceived instructor power use. *Communication Research Reports, 28,* 109–114.

Goodboy, A. K., Bolkan, S., Beebe, S. A., & Shultz, K. (2010). Cultural differences between United States and Chinese students' use of behavioral alteration techniques and affinity-seeking strategies with instructors. *Journal of Intercultural Communication Research, 39,* 1–12.

Goodboy, A. K., Bolkan, S., Myers, S. A., & Zhao, X. (2011). Student use of relational and influence messages in response to perceived instructor power use in American and Chinese college classrooms. *Communication Education, 60,* 191–209.

Goodboy, A. K., Martin, M. M., & Bolkan, S. (2009). The development and validation of the student communication satisfaction scale. *Communication Education, 58,* 372–396.

Goodboy, A. K., & Myers, S. A. (2007). Student communication satisfaction, similarity, and liking as a function of attributional confidence. *Ohio Communication Journal, 45,* 1–12.

Goodboy, A. K., & Myers, S. A. (2008). The effect of teacher confirmation on student communication and learning outcomes. *Communication Education, 57,* 153–179.

Goodboy, A. K., Myers, S. A., & Bolkan, S. (2010). Student motives for communicating with instructors as a function of perceived instructor misbehaviors. *Communication Research Reports, 27,* 11–19.

Harper, B. H., & Hughey, J. D. (1986). Effects of communication responsiveness upon instructor judgment grading and student cognitive learning. *Communication Education, 35,* 147–156.

Knapp, J. L. (2010). The influence of students on instructor out-of-class communication, job satisfaction, and motivation. *Human Communication, 13,* 171–196.

Martin, M. M., Myers, S. A., & Mottet, T. P. (1999). Students' motives for communicating with their instructors. *Communication Education, 48,* 155–164.

Martin, M. M., Myers, S. A., & Mottet, T. P. (2002). Student motives for communicating in the college classroom. In J. L. Chesebro, & J. C. McCroskey (Eds.), *Communication for teachers* (pp. 35–46). Boston: Allyn & Bacon.

Mottet, T. P. (2000). Interactive television instructors' perceptions of students' nonverbal responsiveness and their influence on distance teaching. *Communication Education, 49,* 146–164.

Mottet, T. P., & Beebe, S. A. (2006). The relationships between student responsive behaviors, student socio-communicative style, and instructors' subjective and objective assessments of student work. *Communication Education, 55,* 295–312.

Mottet, T. P., Beebe, S. A., Raffeld, P. C., & Medlock, A. L. (2004). The effects of student verbal and nonverbal responsiveness on teacher self-efficacy and job satisfaction. *Communication Education, 53,* 150–163.

Mottet, T. P., Beebe, S. A., Raffeld, P. C., & Paulsel, M. L. (2004). The effects of student verbal and nonverbal responsiveness on teachers' liking of students and willingness to comply with student requests. *Communication Quarterly, 52,* 27–38.

Mottet, T. P., Beebe, S. A., Raffeld, P. C., & Paulsel, M. L. (2005). The effects of responsiveness on teachers granting power to students and essay evaluation. *Communication Quarterly, 53,* 421–436.

Mottet, T. P., Frymier, A. B., & Beebe, S. A. (2006). Theorizing about instructional communication. In T. P. Mottet, V. P. Richmond, & J. C. McCroskey (Eds.), *Handbook of instructional communication: Rhetorical and relational perspectives* (pp. 255–282). Boston: Allyn & Bacon.

Myers, S. A. (2006). Using Leader-Member Exchange Theory to explain students' motives to communicate. *Communication Quarterly, 54,* 293–304.

Myers, S. A., Edwards, C., Wahl, S. T., & Martin, M. M. (2007). The relationship between perceived instructor aggressive communication and college student involvement. *Communication Education, 56,* 495–508.

Myers, S. A., Martin, M. M., & Mottet, T. P. (2002). Students' motives for communicating with their instructors: Considering instructor socio-communicative style, student socio-communicative orientations, and student gender. *Communication Education, 51,* 121–133.

Richmond, V. P., & McCroskey, J. C. (1998). *Communication: Apprehension, avoidance, and effectiveness* (5th ed.). Boston: Allyn & Bacon.

Wanzer, M. B. (1995). *Student affinity-seeking messages and teacher liking: Subordinate initiated relationship building in superior-subordinate dyads.* Unpublished doctoral dissertation, West Virginia University, Morgantown, WV.

Wanzer, M. B. (1998). An exploratory investigation of student and teacher perceptions of student-generated affinity-seeking behaviors. *Communication Education, 47,* 373–382.

Weiss, S. D., & Houser, M. L. (2007). Student communication motives and interpersonal attraction toward instructor. *Communication Research Reports, 24,* 215–224.

SECTION 10
MEDIA COMMUNICATION

Beginning with the invention of writing and paper, humans have sought to amplify and extend their communication across time and space. The context of media communication both examines the use of particular communications media and critiques the forms and practices of the media in contemporary society. Mediated communication has served as a large influence in shaping our sense of who we are, how we are positioned in the world, and what is important to pay attention to (and subsequently what we can ignore and thereby dismiss as unimportant). The following essays explore the proliferation, influence, and place of contemporary forms of mediated communication in our everyday lives. First, Mark Andrejevic (The University of Queensland) responds to the question: *In what ways is the proliferation of interactive media (scanning your grocery card, casting a vote on* American Idol, *and purchasing the latest phone app) and reality television programming damaging our ability to enact citizenship in our democracy?* In responding, Andrejevic questions the assumption that the Internet will increase our ability to participate more actively in democracy and afford us more power as consumers. In reality, Andrejevic argues, we may be more caught up in voting for our favorite *American Idol* candidate than for the next President of the U.S., and we may increasingly be giving up more and more information about our buying habits and behaviors so as to be more the dupes of successful marketing programs. Second, Kenneth Lachlan and Ashleigh Shelton (University of Massachusetts Boston) consider the question: *How does violent video game play affect individuals' thoughts, feelings, and behavior?"* Lachlan and Shelton explore the nuanced research findings, which suggest that the more realistic the violence (the possibility of which is enhanced as the graphics technology advances), the greater the effects on aggression in the players. Third, Kent Ono (University of Utah) and Myra Washington (University of New Mexico) take a critical cultural studies approach to addressing the question: *How do representations of cultural others in popular media shape our understanding of ourselves and our place in society?* Their work asks us to question the stereotypes we have developed as a result of our own exposure to the enduring historical (mis)representations of cultural others in media that are mostly negative or inaccurate and rarely nuanced or complex. One could argue that the media genie is out of the bottle and that the best we can now do is to engage with these media in a more critical and thoughtful fashion.

252

SURVEILLANCE AND DEMOCRACY IN THE DIGITAL ERA

Mark Andrejevic, The University of Queensland

A NEW ERA OF DEMOCRACY?

It has become one of the truisms of the digital era that the rise of so-called interactive media—technologies that allow viewers to respond, to provide information about themselves, and to create their own media content—is a form of democratization. We are told that the Internet will empower consumers and citizens, that more participation means greater control over the media, and that even seemingly trivial forms of "interactive" popular culture like reality TV represent a new era of cultural democratization, in part because "anyone" can become a celebrity. Such accounts tend to equate interactivity with participation and participation with democracy. The result is a rather indiscriminate use of the term "democratization" —one that tends to de-politicize it and to equate it with greater market choice, new forms of commercial customization, and enhanced forms of public participation in consumer culture. A society in which viewers can vote for their favorite contestants on a singing contest may be a more participatory one, but it is not necessarily a more democratic one—at least if the term is to retain any vestige of political meaning.

Such accounts need to be tempered by the recognition that the Pop Idol franchise and its various spinoffs can thrive in authoritarian as well as in democratic societies. Often the forms of so-called participation on offer in the digital era are simply techniques for collecting information about consumers and viewers. These techniques serve as strategies for offloading the work of market research onto consumers by finding ways to induce them to provide more detailed information about themselves, their friends, their behavior and their consumer preferences. This chapter considers the ways in which the equation of new forms of interactivity with participation serves as an alibi for surveillance without necessarily enhancing forms of democratic self-rule.

SURVEILLANCE AND PARTICIPATION IN THE DIGITAL ECONOMY

If we are to understand democracy as a system in which members of the public participate meaningfully in setting the political goals of their society as well as the means for achieving them, it becomes clear that participation in marketing to ourselves is something altogether different. Increasingly, the interactive economy allows viewers, consumers, and citizens to participate by expressing their preferences and providing feedback, but this is something quite different from democracy, because users do not shape the goals that this information serves: usually increased sales and profits for private entities. Successful reality TV franchises like *Britain's Got Talent* and *Pop Star,* for example, dispense with the need for focus group testing of new artists, since the audience serves as a nationwide, or in some cases, even a region-wide focus group. Interactive web sites that provide "free" services do so in exchange for the ability to collect and use information about consumers. Google provides us with mail and document storage, driving maps, and a search engine in exchange for the ability to capture increasingly detailed information about our behavior and preferences. Facebook gives us a way to stay in touch with our friends and to share pictures with them in exchange for access to detailed information about our social lives and behavior. In both cases, this information is used in ways that are often not transparent to us in order to market to us more effectively. In the digital era, those who have access to the technology are entering a more interactive world, and a more monitored world, but not necessarily a more democratic one.

This observation is not meant to dismiss the potential of interactive media to enhance democracy but rather to emphasize that such media will not necessarily do so of their own accord. If we want a more democratic society, we will have to bend the technology to fit our purposes rather than relying on a misguided faith in the technology to empower the citizenry on its own. Perhaps most importantly, we will have to address the very real asymmetries in power and knowledge that are coming to characterize the so-called information society. For example, businesses and governments will be able to collect and store more information about the behavior of consumers and citizens than ever before, but it will be harder for people to find out exactly what information is collected about them and who has access to it. The easier and more comprehensive data collection becomes as an oft overlooked byproduct of interactivity, the harder it is to keep track of which institutions are gathering what information for which purposes. Is it even possible to specify the entire range of information that smart phone applications or companies like Google and Facebook collect about us when we use their services? At this point, perhaps the most reasonable response is to assume that *everything* we do using interactive devices and services is recorded and stored—at least temporarily. We encounter this fact regularly when we go online and find ads that are related to web sites we may have visited in the past, places or commodities we have mentioned in our emails, or search terms we may have entered online. If you visit a web site devoted to weight loss, for example, expect to find ads for diet products or services inserted in the content of future web sites that you visit, or even alongside your email messages when you check them online.

As more of our personal, professional, and social lives come to rely upon interactive digital platforms from social networking sites to smart phones, we should assume that most of the details of our movements, our interactions, and our purchases are recorded. We should further understand that much of this information can become available to the state and its various monitoring and surveillance apparatuses, which have become increasingly comprehensive and less transparent in the post-9/11 era (Andrejevic, 2007, pp. 161–163)

Viewed from this perspective, the era of enhanced interactivity is not so much one of citizen and consumer empowerment but one characterized by glaring asymmetries in monitoring and surveillance practices. Admittedly, this is just one lens through which to look at the recent development of the information society—there are also new possibilities for commerce, new forms of political and cultural journalism, new forms of sociability and information sharing, and so on. All of these have the potential to contribute to the process of political deliberation, research, and participation. The lens of surveillance is an important one, however, because of the potential impact it has on power relations in contemporary society and also because it tends to be overlooked by more celebratory accounts of new media. We are much more likely to hear about the conveniences of digital media than about their use for monitoring and surveillance. And we are much more likely to hear about the "democratizing" character of the information era than the new and asymmetrical forms of surveillance it enables.

While it is important to acknowledge the very real conveniences and advances associated with the development of digital media technologies, it is also important to address the implications they have for questions of surveillance and power. In return for the many conveniences and advances provided by digital media, we have unthinkingly committed ourselves to the unprecedented privatization of the infrastructure for our social and communicative lives. We tend to treat the companies that populate this infrastructure like Google and Facebook almost as public utilities, entrusting them with the content of our lives and paying for their free services with our personal information.

It is tempting to imagine, at least in media savvy circles, that this exchange is a matter of informed consent—that we understand precisely what we are surrendering in return for access to interactive services—but the fact is, even those few who carefully peruse terms of service agreements and privacy policies have only the vaguest idea of what information is captured about them and how it is used. The policies themselves are general, vague, and subject to ongoing change without notice. Those who own the infrastructure of the digital world we are coming to inhabit set the terms of the exchange and the rest of us are obliged to accept them or go without.

We might describe the migration of our communicative lives onto commercially monitored platforms as a process of digital "enclosure"—one whereby a growing range of activities, transactions, and interactions become encompassed by the monitoring embrace of an interactive (virtual) space (for more on the notion of digital enclosure see Boyle, 2003). Accompanying this movement is a not-so-subtle shift in social relations: not so much the end of privacy, but the privatization and commodification of personal information at an unprecedented level. The process of digital enclosure clearly has a spatial component, insofar as it relies on the expansion of an interactive communication infrastructure that includes broadband and cellular, as well as digital TV and radio. As these networks encompass new spaces, they enter into a monitored, interactive, "virtual" enclosure. These can intersect with and overlap one another. We might, for example, log onto the Internet over morning coffee via smart phone or laptop—thereby generating information about our location, browsing habits, email use, and so on. During the course of the day, we might use GPS systems, cellular networks, and various kinds of "smart" cards to pay tolls, ride mass transit, or shop. All of these interactive systems lend themselves to the generation of cybernetic information: feedback about the transactions and interactions they enable. This feedback becomes the property of private companies that can store, aggregate, sort, and, in many cases, sell the information to others.

The promise of interactivity comes into its own in the realm of politics—the realm from which the popular reception of new media as democratic is drawn. The rhetoric is a familiar one: Now anyone (who has access) can talk back, can have their voice heard, and can create their own media content. Everyone (who has access) has become a publisher, a creator, a participant in our public culture. For example, the claims of new media theorist and game designer Celia Pearce (1997) neatly complement those of ubiquitous political consultant and cyber-celebrant Joe Trippi (2004). Both invoke the promise of technologically facilitated democratic revolution as a natural outcome of digital media. As Pearce puts it, "The digital age introduces a new form of international socialism, a new kind of democracy that Marx never even imagined" (1997, 180). The story of the political deployment of the Internet is, according to Trippi, a story of the revitalization of democracy: "Most of all it's the story of people standing up and making themselves heard. It's the story of how to engage those Americans in a real dialogue, how to reach them where they live, how to stop *selling* to them and start *listening* to them" (2004, XX). This opposition is a misleading one. The emerging model of data-driven relationship marketing undermines the opposition described by Trippi: The sellers are able to sell more effectively precisely because they are able to listen more efficiently.

The real question that needs to be addressed is how new media technologies are being turned to political ends not in theory, but in *practice*. And increasingly this means the use of monitoring and marketing strategies by politicians. It is one thing to say with Joe Trippi that the Internet could be the "most democratizing innovation we've ever seen," (2004, p. 235) and quite another to consider the ways in which it is being used as one of the most powerful technologies for centralized information gathering, sorting, and management that we've ever seen. Political consultants—never far behind the marketers—have realized for some time that market research algorithms can yield information that is useful not just for selling products, but for recruiting voters. The problem was finding cheap and efficient ways to gather and sort the information. One political consultant, for example, recalled how research revealed several decades ago, "that Mercury owners were far more likely to vote Republican than owners of any other kind of automobile—data that was so constant across the country . . . that it couldn't possibly have been the product of chance. 'We never had the money or the technology to make anything of it . . . But of course, they do now'" (Gertner, 2004, B1).

Just as background details like education level, place of residence, and reading habits help predict what types of products a consumer is likely to buy, they can serve as reliable indicators of which hot-button political issues voters care about. At least that's what political consultants are telling parties and candidates. As the former head of the Republican National Committee put it, "We can tailor our message to people who care about taxes, who care about health care, who care about jobs, who care about regulation—we can target that way" (Gertner, 2004, p. B1). The result is a change in the mode of address adopted by political campaigners. Instead of tailoring a general message designed to maximize common appeal and minimize offense, the goal is to target individuals and groups based on key motivating issues. Whereas the prevailing political wisdom had been to avoid districts heavily populated by opposition party voters, target marketing allowed for tactical poaching: "The advantage of data-based targeting is that political field operatives can home in on precisely the voters they wish to reach—the antiabortion parishioners of a traditionally Democratic African American church congregation, for instance" (Edsall, 2006, p. A1).

This "niche-marketing" approach requires the same asymmetry of information in the political as in the commercial realm: the accumulation of detailed information about consumers combined, ideally, with a corresponding *lack* of information about alternatives (or undesirable aspects of the product being pushed) on the part of consumers. As one political consultant put it: "The nightmare scenario is that the databases create puppet masters" (Gertner, 2004, p. B1). In this nightmare vision—the one whose monitoring apparatus is currently being assembled by political consultants and database experts in anticipation of upcoming elections, "every voter will get a tailored message based on detailed information about the voter. The candidate would know what schools the voter went to, any public records that showed they supported some cause, any court case they've been involved in. There might even be several different messages sent by a candidate to the same home—one for the wife, one for the husband and one for the 23-year-old kid" (Gertner, 2004, p. B1). Far from public empowerment and democratic rebellion, such a scenario envisions what one commentator describes as "a nearly perfect perversion of the political process": "The candidate knows everything about the voter, but the media and the public know nothing about what the candidate really believes" (Gertner, 2004, p. B1).

Like marketers, political data-miners can harness emerging interactive technologies to the ends of political research. Consider, for example, the case of Knowledge Networks, an instant polling company founded by two Stanford political scientists who realized, like market researchers before them, the information-gathering capability of interactive communication technology. Knowledge Networks turned the TiVo model of interactive content delivery into an instant political polling mechanism by spending millions of dollars to equip more than 40,000 homes of selected viewers with Web TVs. The viewers received the interactive TV device—their portal into the digital enclosure—free of cost in exchange for agreeing to spend 10 minutes a week answering pollsters' questions over the Internet (Lewis, 2000, pp. 65 ff.). In addition to the weekly polls, the Web TVs gather detailed information about viewing habits and Web surfing behavior that can be used to create profiles of the respondents. The device that is used to gather instant responses to, for example, the performance of candidates during a political debate, also collects a constant stream of information about viewers even when they aren't directly engaged in the polling process.

One of the reasons for the increasing value of information captured within the embrace of the digital enclosure is that it does double- and triple-duty: for marketing, policing, and campaigning, By embracing sites of domesticity, leisure, and labor, and permitting always-on connectivity, the interactive digital enclosure provides information not just in discrete packets—a survey here, a focus-group there—but a continuous flow of data.

In a world in which digital media are used to create better informed citizens and to provide them with the means for engaging in public deliberation, for expressing themselves, and for holding their elected officials accountable, the Internet may well enhance democracy. However, in a world in which interactive media are used to monitor citizens and consumers more thoroughly in order to market to them more effectively, there is no guarantee that the ability to interact strengthens modern democracies. The world imagined by marketers and political consultants is all too often one in which interactive technology can be used to perfect strategies for target marketing and the centralized management of public opinion by political elites.

Possible Futures

At stake in these alternative versions of the future—one of empowerment, the other of centralized control—is the very meaning of the term "democratic participation." By participation, do we simply mean the ability to provide increasingly detailed information about ourselves? If so, then the offer of participation can double as an alibi for the perfection of marketing strategies— both political and commercial. If, however, by participation, we mean a conscious, considered, informed, and meaningful contribution to the governing process, it is important to distinguish this at every turn from a version of participation that equates submission to detailed monitoring with participation. Democratic politics promises public participation all the way up, as it were, to the goal-setting process itself. A second element of democracy—one emphasized by constitutional scholar Cass Sunstein (2002)—is the creation of optimal conditions for public deliberation *about* shared goals. As Sunstein suggests, the adoption of marketing and advertising techniques by political campaigns ignores an important difference between consumer decisions and political decisions. The former relate to individual preferences and only indirectly influence society as a whole, whereas the latter are explicitly about collective decisions that (directly) influence society as a whole. My decision to buy a particular laundry detergent does not have broader social consequences in quite the same way as does my vote for a new school tax proposal or a Congressional candidate. Moreover, as Sunstein argues, political participation envisions a decision-making process that "does not take individual tastes as fixed or given. It prizes democratic self-government, understood as a requirement of 'government by discussion,' accompanied by reason-giving in the public domain" (Sunstein, 2002, p. 37).

The database-informed customized campaign model of political marketing transposes the perfection of what Sunstein might describe as a consumerist model onto the political process. Far from contributing to democratic participation and deliberation, the version of interactivity envisioned by the database consultants and target marketers offers to perfect a cybernetic form of public relations: the customization of marketing appeals based on detailed profiles of individual voters. The consequences of this model of interactivity are threefold: the further disaggregation of the citizenry, the facilitation of sorting and exclusion when it comes to information access, and the further normalization of surveillance as a legitimate political tool.

Database politics transforms government publicity into target marketing and citizen publicity into increasingly precise market research. It equates submission to detailed forms of monitoring with democratic participation—and feedback with shared control. In so doing, it reduces what

Sunstein calls citizen sovereignty—the collective expression of shared political concerns arrived at through public deliberation—to what he calls consumer sovereignty—the "individualized" preferences of the shopper. In so doing, it further enables the importation of marketing and public relations strategies into the political process. The goal of these strategies is not to become increasingly responsible to the public will, but to find ways of managing it more effectively before it expresses itself in action. As media theorist Jodi Dean observes, "Perhaps paradoxically, the very means of democratic publicity end up leading to its opposite: private control by the market" (Dean, 2002, p. 150). Avoiding this outcome depends on our will to distinguish between meaningful participation and the process of providing marketers with more information about ourselves. It will depend on developing media technologies that serve the interests of citizens in addition to those of consumers.

REFERENCES

Andrejevic, M. (2007). *iSpy: surveillance and power in the interactive era.* Lawrence, KS: University of Kansas Press.

Boyle, J. (2003). The second enclosure movement and the construction of the public domain. *Law and Contemporary Problems, 66,* 147–178.

Dean, J. (2002). *Publicity's secret: How technoculture capitalizes on democracy.* Ithaca: Cornell University Press.

Edsall, T. (2006). Democrats' data mining stirs an intraparty battle. *The Washington Post,* March 8, A1.

Gertner, J. (2004). The very, very personal is political. *The New York Times Magazine,* 15 February, B1.

Lewis, M. (2000). The two-bucks-a-minute democracy. *The New York Times Magazine,* 5 November, 65–72.

Pearce, C. (1997). *The interactive book.* New York: Penguin.

Sunstein, C. (2002). *Republic.com.* Princeton, NJ: Princeton University Press.

Trippi, J. (2004). *The revolution will not be televised.* NY: ReganBooks.

VIDEO GAME VIOLENCE

KENNETH A LACHLAN & ASHLEIGH SHELTON, UNIVERSITY OF MASSACHUSETTS BOSTON

Not unlike the Internet and cell phones, video games are such a significant part of our popular culture that it is hard to imagine a time before they existed. With their initial reputation as a novelty or a toy in the early 1970s, video games quickly expanded into a multi-billion-dollar industry by the mid-1980s (Wolf, 2001), and the popularity of video game entertainment has continued to rise over the past few years. In 2010, the game industry reaped colossal profits of more than $20 billion in the U.S. Goldberg (2011) reports that 77% of households play video games, and people are now spending more money on video games than on music, movies, and DVDs, lending support to the suggestion that video game play is displacing other media use (Slocombe, 2005).

While popular commentary about video game violence rages, we have yet to answer the question: Do violent video games cause aggression, do those who already have violent tendencies choose to play games with aggressive themes, or are video games simply a reflection of our culture's fascination with and glorification of violence? Recent research suggests that there may be a connection between game play and aggressive tendencies. At the same time, specific types of content may have a stronger impact on game players in terms of aggression, as may the extent to which game players adapt to their environment.

VIOLENT VIDEO GAMES AND USER RESPONSES

The gradual increase in video game use across the U.S. has led policymakers and researchers to consider its effects on attitudes, behaviors, and beliefs. In a study of game players' usage habits, Sherry, Lucas, Greenberg, and Lachlan (2006) found that children, adolescents, and adults of both sexes spend a substantial amount of time playing video games. On average, males in their early teens spend about 11 hours playing console games every week. Most American households have at least one game console, with about a third of these game consoles located in bedrooms or other places where game play goes unmonitored (Kaiser Family Foundation, 1999).

Both casual observation and scientific research (see below) indicate that video games contain lots of violence and aggression. As video games have become more sophisticated over the years (think about how different *Frogger* and *Halo* are in terms of realism), these portrayals of violence have become faster paced, more graphic, and more realistic. A number of early studies tried to tie together game play and aggressive attitudes or worldviews (Dominick, 1984). Wiegman and Van Shie (1998) found that children who played video games more often were identified by their classmates as more aggressive. Similar correlations between video game play and aggressive tendencies have been reported in studies looking at both children (Dominick, 1984; Lin & Lepper, 1987) and adults (Anderson & Dill, 2000).

While these studies are informative and offer some evidence of a link between game play and aggression, they are based on self-reports and evaluation by others, as well as other loosely linked factors. In other words, while we can say that there is a link here, these studies don't give us any reason to believe that game play *causes* aggression. Fortunately, a number of experimental studies have explored the causal link between video game play and aggression, at least in terms of short term responses. Anderson and Ford (1986), Ballard and Lineberger (1999), Anderson and Dill (2000), and others have looked at actual behaviors following game play. They have found that when provoked, adults who have just played a violent video game are more likely to do rather unpleasant things to others when given the opportunity. These include administering long, loud blasts of obnoxious noise, or forcibly immersing someone's hand in ice-cold water. While it is scientifically unethical to conduct studies such as these with children, there are a few less severe studies that indicate a causal relationship between video game play and aggression among kids. For example, Shutte, Malouf, Post-Gordon, and Rodasta (1987) exposed seven-year olds to either a violent or a non-violent video game. When given a chance for "free play" with a Bobo doll, the children who played the violent game were more likely to abuse the Bobo doll or to *attack each other* than were those playing the non-violent game.

TELEPRESENCE, THE FEELING OF "BEING THERE"

The notion that there is some kind of connection—be it a correlation or a causal link—between video game play and aggression is clearly not a new one. There have, however, been some new developments in our thinking over the last 10 years or so. Sherry (2001) published what researchers call a meta-analysis, or a mathematical evaluation of all of the major studies that have been published linking video games and aggression. This study revealed that, among other things, the strength of the relationship between game playing and aggression is increasing over time. In other words, the newer the study, the stronger the link between the two. This has led researchers to start thinking about how video games may have changed over the decades, and the ways in which these changes may impact subsequent responses by game players. Put another way: *Why is this relationship stronger than it used to be?*

Obviously, video games have changed in terms of their realism, intensity, and graphicness. Simple graphic representations of tanks and missiles as crude squares on a green background have been replaced by life-like, three dimensional avatars, advanced artificial intelligence, realistic interactions, and competitive game play environments against other gamers. These realistic game environments may lead to a psychological experience known as *telepresence,* in which game players feel as though they have left their physical world and have become immersed in a mediated one. At this point, a sense of separation from the "real world" breaks down, and people may be more likely to respond to mediated characters as though they were real, and they may also be more likely to acquire attitudes, beliefs, and action tendencies from their reactions to these characters.

Lombard and Ditton (1997) define presence as "a psychological state or subjective perception in which even though part or all of an individual's current experience is generated by and/or filtered through human-made technology, part or all of the individual's perception fails to accurately acknowledge the role of the technology in the experience" (Lombard, 2000, cited in Bracken, 2006, p. 725). Steuer (1992) and others argue that situational factors related to the game user, such as the level of experience with the medium and general aptitude at adapting to mediated environments, may also play a role in the level of presence one experiences, and the degree to which one may acquire attitudes and action tendencies. It is not difficult to see that video games are far more complex and realistic than they used to be, and that individuals are spending more time with video games than they have in the past. If this is the case, then people may be becoming more adept at these complex interactions, and more susceptible to learning aggressive thoughts and scripts from them.

A study by Tamborini, Eastin, Skalski, Lachlan, Fediuk, & Brady (2004) has offered at least initial evidence of this type of process. In this particular study, participants were assigned to play or to observe violent and non-violent video games. The results revealed that participants experienced higher levels of presence when playing, as opposed to watching video game play. They also discovered that those observing a non-violent game were found to express less hostility when provoked than those playing or watching a violent game. While the connections here are somewhat loose, they do suggest that presence may play a role in whether or not video game play leads to subsequent aggression.

THINKING ABOUT VIDEO GAME CONTENT

In addition to concerns regarding the experience of presence and realism, scholars have also turned their attention to the specific types of violence we can expect in video games, how often they occur, who is involved, and what this violence looks like. In one of the earliest studies of this kind, Braun and Giroux (1989) evaluated 21 arcade games in an attempt to figure out how often violence takes place. They observed that roughly three quarters of the games they looked at featured death or destruction of some kind; not surprisingly, games with themes related to war or crime were more likely to feature this kind of content. A number of years later, Haninger and Thompson (2004) examined "T" rated games, in order to get an idea of the violence in kids' games and what kind of violence might happen deeper into the games. They found that about 90% of the games required the use of violence, while 69% required the killing of other game characters.

While these studies provide useful data, they fail to acknowledge the specific contexts in which video game violence may occur. This is problematic, given decades of research in other media suggesting that certain types of violence may be more or less likely to engender aggressive responses in viewers. Of note, much of the research in film violence suggests that violence that is rewarded, justified, committed with weapons, repetitive in nature, graphic, committed by liked characters, or committed by attractive characters may be especially powerful as behavioral models that people will want to imitate. Given this knowledge, Smith, Lachlan, and Tamborini (2003) looked at the ways in which these context elements changed across games rated for different age groups, as well as the relative frequency of violent interactions in these contexts. Looking at the top 60 games from the 1999 calendar year, they identified individual acts of violence and their context, using the coding scheme from the National Television Violence Study. They found that games rated for mature audiences featured an average of 4.59 acts of violence per minute, over four times the rate found on television. Further, the context of violence in games rated for these audiences was cause for concern, as violence in these games was more likely to repeat violence, gun violence, and bloodshed and gore.

The authors published a number of follow-up studies, looking at the same data in different ways. One study revealed that gun violence is rampant in video games (Smith, Lachlan, Pieper, Boyson, Wilson, Tamborini, & Weber, 2004). Of equal concern, this gun violence is typically presented alongside other problematic contextual features. These include a lack of realism, justification for the violent act, and repetitive gun violence that may systematically desensitize.

A second follow-up study looked at the physical attributes of violent game characters, since past research evidence has shown that people are more likely to model behavior after individuals they find attractive or perceive as similar to themselves (Lachlan, Smith, & Tamborini, 2005). This study revealed that violent game perpetrators are often presented as white males, and it adds that video games are especially popular with white male adolescents. When looking at the results across these three studies, a concerning picture begins to emerge. The world of video games, according to these data, is full of repetitive violence, violence that frequently involves guns, and violence committed by characters that look like the people who are most commonly playing the games.

While the studies by Braun and Giroux, Haninger and Thompson, and Lachlan and colleagues are valuable, they overlook some of the nuances of video game play. As stated earlier, the experience of presence is likely to have an impact on game play experiences, as is the psychological makeup of the individual game player. Experience playing a particular game or video games in general may mitigate the decisions one makes in a virtual environment, as may one's general level of comfort ability with interactivity. These content studies are based on analytic techniques that were developed for linear media, such as television and film, and may not lend themselves all that well to interactive media such as video games (Schmierbach, 2010). Fortunately, there is one study in the literature that has attempted to address some of these concerns.

Lachlan and Maloney (2008) attempted to take a first look at the relationship between game player attributes and aggressive content. In a sense, they decided to look at how video game violence would manifest itself in decisions made by game players within the interactive environment. The authors randomly assigned a large number of game players (160) to a small number of games (4), to see how content would change from player to player depending on these attributes and experiences. They found that the frequency of violence and the context in which it might be found varied greatly from player to player. They also found that certain player attributes predicted violent behavior in the game, and that these causes were not the same from game to game.

In some games, physical aggressiveness and argumentativeness predicted certain types of violent acts, while in others psychoticism or vigilateism positively predicted the number of certain violent acts. Across all games, experienced presence *negatively predicted gun violence.* In fact, across the board, presence was negatively associated with violent acts of all kinds. At first glance, this seems to contradict our earlier reasoning about the relationship between immersive experiences and aggression. Lachlan and Maloney (2008), however, offer an alternate viewpoint on these processes, and one that begs us to look deeper into the interactive nature of video game violence.

While not formally measured in their study, Lachlan and Maloney, along with their research assistants, noted that just because someone committed a lot of violence did not mean that the person was doing it well. In examining tape recordings of the game play, they noticed that there were a number of players who didn't grasp the game very well and proverbially "shot at everything that moved." Game players that struggled to navigate the game environment often sprayed off dozens of rounds of ammunition in no particular direction. By contrast, those that seemed to adapt well to the interactive environment actually committed fewer acts of violence. This is because they knew how to use aggressive acts to accomplish goals, such as killing enemies, destroying buildings, and moving on to more advanced levels of the game.

This observation forces us to question our real concerns about the nature of violent video game content and its effects on attitudes, behaviors, and beliefs. While media scientists have traditionally thought of violence in very simple "more = bad" terms, this picture may be incomplete. Should we be concerned about the game player who staggers around not knowing what he is doing, or the game player who very methodically knows how to kill in order to accomplish goals? The instrumental nature of violence has gone relatively unexamined in the video game literature, and its consideration is essential if we are to further disentangle the relationship between violent game play and subsequent aggressive attitudes and behaviors.

CONCLUSION

Bearing in mind the standing that video games occupy culturally, it cannot be ignored that social effects are present. Research indicates there is a small, but significant, overall effect of video game play on aggression, and this effect is positively related to the *type* of game violence (Sherry, 2001). That is, realistic, sanitized, justified, humorous, and rewarded violent acts committed by an attractive or similar looking character are linked to greater effects on aggression than violence that is unwarranted and fantastical and that results in negative consequences or punishments. Additionally, certain video game genres tend to be more violent and can have greater effects on aggression. First-person shooter, fighting, action, and adventure games are often more violent and have a tendency to reward players with points, bonus rounds, new weapons, and extra lives for carrying out the most brutal acts imaginable.

The development of technological innovations, such as high-definition game graphics, surround sound, accelerometers, increased processing speed, rumble features, on-controller speakers, touch screens, improved hard-drive memory, and more naturally mapped controllers are increasingly immersing media users in interactive worlds of violence. With these advancements in intensity and graphicness of video games, children will have trouble distinguishing between reality and fantasy and could easily be influenced by the images, characters, and scenarios on the screen (Villani, Olson & Jellinek, 2005).

The fact that many of the most popular video games contain violent themes has people debating whether the effects on attitudes, behaviors, and beliefs can be attributed to intrinsic or extrinsic factors. Does exposure to a perpetual diet of video game violence and hostility make people more aggressive, or are naturally aggressive people more drawn to violent content? This chicken-or-egg conundrum deserves further exploration, and additional research on the interactive nature of video game violence is essential to our understanding of the impacts and consequences of this ever-evolving technology. Furthermore, continued research in this area can help shed light on real world problems and concerns. As parents, teachers, and policymakers become increasingly concerned with the impact of video games on physcial and psychological health, this research can help us determine the types of content that are problematic, the extent to which they are problematic, and the role that the skills and personalities of individual game players play in this whole process. Armed with this body of knowledge, parernts may be able to make better decisions about buying games for their kids, policymakers may be better able to suggest rating and content management guidelines, and game players may become more aware of the effects that their own gaming may have on them.

REFERENCES

Anderson, C. A., & Dill, K. E. (2000). Video games and aggressive thoughts, feelings, and behavior in the laboratory and in life. *Journal of Personality and Social Psychology, 78,* 772–790.

Anderson, C. A., & Ford, C. M. (1986). Affect of the game player: Short-term effects of highly and mildly aggressive video games. *Personality and Social Psychology Bulletin, 12,* 390–402.

Ballard, M. E., & Lineberger, R. (1999). Video game violence and confederate gender: Effects on reward and punishment given by college males. *Sex Roles, 41,* 541–558.

Bracken, C. C. (2006). Perceived source credibility of local television news: The impact of television form and presence. *Journal of Broadcasting and Electronic Media, 50,* 723–741.

Braun, C. M. J., & Giroux, J. (1989). Arcade video games: Proxemic, cognitive, and content analyses. *Journal of Leisure Research, 21,* 92–105.

Dietz, T. (1998). An examination of violence and gender role portrayals in video games: Implications for gender socialization and aggressive behavior. *Sex Roles, 38,* 425–442.

Dominick, J. R. (1984). Videogames, television violence, and aggression in teenagers. *Journal of Communication, 34,* 136–147.

Goldberg, H. (2011). *All your base are belong to us: How fifty years of videogames conquered pop culture.* New York: Three Rivers Press.

Haninger, K., & Thompson, K.M. (2004). Content and ratings of teen-rated video games. *Journal of the American Medical Association, 291* (7), 856–865.

Kaiser Family Foundation (1999). *Kids & media @ the new millennium: A comprehensive national analysis of children's media use.* Menlo Park, CA: Kaiser Family Foundation.

Lachlan, K.A., & Maloney, E.K. (2008). Game player characteristics and interactive content: Exploring the role of personality and telepresence in video game violence. *Communication Quarterly, 56* (3), 284–302.

Lachlan, K.A., Smith, S.L., & Tamborini, R. (2005). Models for aggressive behavior: The attributes of violent characters in popular video games. *Communication Studies, 56* (4), 313–329.

Lin, S., & Lepper, M. R. (1987). Correlates of children's usage of videogames and computers. *Journal of Applied Social Psychology, 17,* 72–93.

Lombard, M. (2000). *The concept of presence: Explication statement.* Available online at http://www.temple.edu/ispr/index.htm. Retrieved July 16, 2011.

Lombard, M. & Ditton, T. (1997). At the heart of it all: The concept of presence. *Journal of Computer Mediated Communication, 3*(2). Retrieved July 27, 2011, from http://www.ascusc.org/jcmc/vol3/issue2/lombard.html.

Schmierbach, M. (2010). Content analysis of video games: Challenges and potential solutions. *Communication Methods and Measures, 3,* 147–171.

Sherry, J. (2001). The effects of violent video games on aggression: A meta-analysis. *Human Communication Research, 27,* 409–431.

Sherry, J., Lucas, K., Greenberg, B.S., & Lachlan, K.A. (2006). Video game uses and gratifications as predictors of use and game preference. In P. Vorderer and J. Bryant (Eds.), *Playing computer games: Motives, responses, and consequences.* Cresskill, NJ: LEA.

Shutte, N. S., Malouf, J. M., Post-Gordon, J. C., & Rodasta, A. L. (1987). Effects of playing videogames on children's aggressive and other behaviors. *Journal of Applied Social Psychology, 18,* 454–460.

Slocombe, M. (2005). Men spend more money on video games than music: Nielsen report. *Digital-Lifestyles.* Available online at: http://digitallifestyles.info/display_page.asp?section=cm&id=2091. Retrieved July 30, 2011.

Smith, S. L., Lachlan, K. A., & Tamborini, R. (2003). Popular video games: Quantifying the presentation of violence and its context. *Journal of Broadcasting and Electronic Media, 47,* 58–76.

Smith, S. L., Lachlan, K. A., Pieper, K. M., Boyson, A. R. Wilson, B. J., Tamborini, R., & Weber, R. (2004). Brandishing guns in American Media: Two studies examining how often and in what context firearms appear on television and in popular video games. *Journal of Broadcasting and Electronic Media, 48* (4), 584–606.

Steuer, J. (1992). Defining virtual reality: Dimensions determining telepresence. *Journal of Communication, 42,* 73–93.

Tamborini, R., Eastin, M., Skalski, P. D., Lachlan, K. A., Fediuk, T., & Brady, R. (2004). Violent virtual video games and hostile thoughts. *Journal of Broadcasting and Electronic Media, 48,* 335–357.

Villani, V.S., Olson, C.K. & Jellinek, M.S. (2005). Media literacy for clinicians and parents. *Child and Adolescent Psychiatric Clinics of North America, 14,* 523-553.

Wiegman, O., & Van Shie, E. G. M. (1998). Video game playing and its relations with aggressive and prosocial behavior. *British Journal of Social Psychology, 37,* 367–378.

Wolf, M. J. P. (2001). Space in the video game. In M. J. P. Wolf (Ed.), *The medium of the videogame* (pp. 51–75). Austin, TX: University of Texas Press.

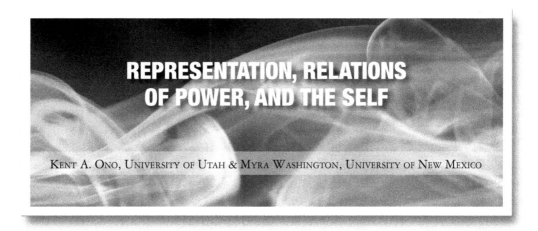

REPRESENTATION, RELATIONS OF POWER, AND THE SELF

Kent A. Ono, University of Utah & Myra Washington, University of New Mexico

Season 5 of the UK reality television show *Celebrity Big Brother* was both its highest rated season and its most controversial. The scandal of the season involved the racist verbal abuse of housemate and famed Bollywood star Shilpa Shetty by housemates Danielle Lloyd (model), reality TV star Jade Goody, her boyfriend Jack Tweed, Goody's mother Jackiey Budden, and singer Jo O'Meara. Instances of abuse included: Budden referring to Shetty as "the Indian" rather than using her name, Tweed making monkey noises while calling her a "f******g c***," Lloyd commanding Shetty to "f*** off home . . . [because] she can't even speak English properly," and Goody attacking Shetty's authenticity and class status by telling her to go live in a "slum," while also referring to her as "Shilpa poppadum" (Singh, 2007; Revoir, 2007; Blake, 2007; Bashir, 2007).

London's mayor, Ken Livingston, criticized broadcaster Channel 4 for pandering to racism by selecting and airing such racist clips, simply in order to gain a larger audience and more advertisers (Blake, 2007). Viewers responded to Shetty's treatment on the show by filing nearly 50,000 complaints during the month-long season with Britain's television regulator, the Office of Communication (Ofcom). Ultimately, Ofcom found Channel 4 breached the broadcasting code by making "serious editorial misjudgements (sic)." As a result, Channel 4 was required to apologize on air and broadcast unedited transcripts of the even more racist unaired moments (Conlan, 2007). Advertisers responded by pulling their ads and sponsorships.

The already infamous season 5 also touched off an international media melee when Indians burned an effigy of the producers of the show during then Minister of Finance Gordon Brown's visit to India. Prime Minister Tony Blair made a statement in an attempt to salvage Britain's reputation after Shetty's treatment on the show became international news. The *Celebrity Big Brother* scandal was revealing, because it showcased not just the racism of the contestants on the show, but correspondingly (through the evolving information about the editing and broadcasting of select clips) the producers and editors as well, who chose to air many of the filmed segments, implying their tacit approval of Shetty's verbal harassment by bullies.

This essay takes a critical cultural studies approach to addressing the question: *How do representations of cultural others in popular media shape our understanding of ourselves and our place in society?* In an attempt to answer this question, we do not conduct audience, spectatorship, or reader response analysis to determine precisely how, intellectually, physiologically, or psychologically, representations of cultural others in popular media affect our bodies and our psyches. Nor do we distribute and analyze survey questionnaires or conduct laboratory observations of how images of cultural others shape self-understandings of people and their social positions in the world. Rather, we draw on critical cultural research to theorize the relationship between such representations of cultural others in order to address the notion of selves and of positionality. By *critical cultural,* we mean an approach that addresses relations of power, power situated in multiple ways and that ranges from class to race to mobility, for instance, and that forges new theoretical and methodological vistas in the process by borrowing and re-conceiving disciplinary modalities (see Ono, 2009a; Ono, 2011). We also have *praxis* in mind, how knowledge of this can shape our actions and the world around us. Stuart Hall has addressed this very question in his work on representation, both in a lecture captured in video form, *Stuart Hall: Representation and the Media* (Jhally, 1997), as well as in his book, *The Work of Representation* (1997). Hence, we are indebted to him for many of our insights about this subject, even as we work to build upon his work in order to answer the question posed above.

Hall begins by explaining that each of us has our own "conceptual map," or "maps of meaning," or "frameworks of intelligibility," which Hall uses as synonyms. By these terms, he is suggesting that people see the world through memories of the experiences they have had. That is, people only remember certain things, and they largely remember things they have experienced; hence, one's own unique combination of overlapping experiences leads an individual to having the particular conceptual map she does. As he says in the video,

> **Now it could be the case that the conceptual map which I carry around my head is totally different from yours, in which case you and I would interpret or make sense of the world in totally different ways. We would be incapable of sharing our thoughts or expressing ideas about the world to each other. In fact, each of us probably does understand and interpret the world in a unique and individual way. (p. 19)**

What Hall suggests is that what we remember remains internal to us unless we voice it, tell others, and make it public, what he calls "externalization." Thus, we have memories of what happened to us—our experiences—but only those memories that we vocalize or share in some other way become publicly accessible and available for public consumption, discussion, and comparison to others' conceptual maps.

Historically, representations of people of color were controlled by dominant media industries that were overseen and operated almost exclusively by members of the dominant white racial elite, at least until the civil rights era of the 1950s, the 1960s, and the 1970s (the vast majority still are, by the way) (Noam, 2009). Because those white men did not necessarily know a lot of people of color intimately, hang around people of color, or live in their neighborhoods, for instance, the externalizations put out there by the media did not directly correspond in any real or useful way to the actual lived experiences of people of color. Those externalizations, which emerged out of the experiences of those who made those images, were, therefore, stereotypes, representations that were produced and circulated that came, not from people of color on the ground, but from those with little real knowledge, access, or lived relationship with people of color. Furthermore, those images that some people have called "false" ones were quoted or cited by other media; hence, a well of such images existed as a kind of archive of imagery of people of color that had little to do with their lived realities and experiences (hooks, 1992; Ono, 2009b, 2010; Hall, 2003; Collins, 2000). Those images were odd, indeed, as those representations were neither created by those being represented, nor by people who knew people of color well, which explains how such sometimes bizarre images became the reigning stereotypes of our media culture.

One might argue that, at least during the time period when the vast majority of media images of people of color were not their own externalizations, if one were to see, and hence consume, images of people of color, one was forced to consume images that were not self-made ones, but ones made by others, whose ideas of people of color were neither well informed nor often complimentary.

Many have written that when one does not see images of people like oneself, when one does not see images of people like oneself that are heroes and leads, and when one does not see images of people like oneself that are kind, sensitive, complimentary, and complex, it is possible to have a distorted sense of one's own social position within society and one's social position and worth, as well as one's meaningfulness within society (Dixon & Linz, 2000; Gross, 2001; Ting-Toomey, 2005; Tang, 2007; Morgan, Shanahan & Signorielli, 2009; Martins & Harrison, 2011). Not seeing one's image represented on screen, or seeing one's image in a way that is alienating—hence is quite detached from one's own experience of self-identity—can be psychologically traumatizing. But, seeing problematic representations of people of color also affects those who are not members of the group being represented, including members of the racially dominant society.

So, for members of the dominant culture, images that reinforce problematic images of minority groups means living in a vacuum and operating in a world that is not real. It is fantasy, and it can lead to assumptions, beliefs, decisions, and whole ways of being based on those images that not only are not self-serving, but that may ultimately be socially troubling, as well as ultimately self-defeating. Kent Ono and Vincent Pham (2009) have suggested this in their discussion of yellowface, a practice not unlike blackface, where non Asian Americans played Asian Americans in the theatre, in films, and on television:

> **Yellowface also serves a psychosocial function, mediating both the psychological perception of Asians and Asian Americans and the social interaction with them. It allows audiences to think the masquerading actor is both like and not like an Asian or Asian American. Like blackface, yellowface is a form of racial masquerade, a masquerade in which the audience knows the actor is masquerading, that they are not actually Asian. (p. 47)**

They go on to say:

> **Yellowface has a social dimension as well, for it was originally created for the pleasure of white audiences. Hence, it has more to do with the way white people relate to each other than it does with a genuine, humane relationship with Asians and Asian Americans. As Tchen suggests, 'The visual language of yellowface came to signify a universe of meanings having far more to do with the host culture than with who and what were originally being represented' (1999, p. 129.) . . .**

Tchen says, 'Viewers who believed these representations became imprisoned in a world of racial caricatures and power relations" (Ibid).

Essentially, then, images from the past that continue into the present that were part of historical subjugation and of social separation and stratified racial and classed subservience, and that may continue to do so, facilitate the ability for divisions to exist between the superordinate and subordinate group and group members, thereby having the effect of producing and reproducing, structurally, social positions and locations. It is the case that media are rarely discussed in relationship with structural racism, but part of what we argue here in this essay is in fact that media representations of minority group members are in fact absolutely basic to any theory of institutional and structural racism.

To clarify some of what we have argued, we briefly take up the specific case of mixed race people here. Currently, discourses of a "new" multiracial identity are being circulated in hopes of more easily negotiating those divisions between superordinate and subordinate groups as mixed race people act as a bridge between races. In this way, multiracial people function as a barometer of sorts for the state of race relations, whereas, historically, mixed race people have been represented as the "ultimate race problem." Now, they are proffered both as the solution to the race problem and as the impetus for the (illusory) declining significance of race (Squires, 2007, p. 2). The changes in racial categorization schema in the 2000 Census has given multiracial people political legitimation; now, they are using mass media for cultural legitimation. Squires (2007) makes note of this fact as she reconciles multiracial visibility with the current media landscape:

Multiracial-identified people have built up an impressive set of texts, theories, organizations, and political projects aimed at reconceptualizing mixed race identity, interracial family life, interracial adoption, and state-sanctioned racial terminology to combat and debunk racist myths and practices that oppress multiracial people. Mass media have been important arenas for this project of redefinition. Through publications targeted at multiracial families and individuals, Web sites, best-selling autobiographies, talk show interviews, press conferences, public testimony at government hearings, and 'outing' of multiracial celebrities, multiracial people have used media to disseminate new images and descriptions of their identities and experiences (Squires, 2007 p. 10).

Multiracial exceptionalism, or the hope that multiracial people will transcend race and heal racial divisions, is not the answer to how popular media can better represent cultural others. Having progressed from enduring tropes that rendered mixed race people either invisible, tragic, hybrid degenerates, or the quintessential basis of the "race problem," the current representations of multiracial people do, minimally, demonstrate the power of visibility. Their popularity currently also demonstrates the unequal operation of power, especially when comparing how rapidly mixed race people as a group have increased their visibility within media, and how other groups are still dealing with negative representations and continued marginalization by both media and society.

Representations of cultural others in media are an important source of information through which both dominant and subordinate groups construct their identities, attitudes, and beliefs. However, as a source of information, a number of factors, including media ownership, and enduring historical (mis)representations of others, have resulted in selective depictions that, when existing, are mostly negative or inaccurate and are rarely nuanced or complex. Included in these misrepresentations are instances when people of color offer their own representations, positive and negative, because those representations are still part of a media system in which they have little control. A steady stream of these images (or lack thereof), have been detrimental to the psychosocial development of members of those groups, distorting one's sense of worth and sense of belonging, and reinforcing the idea that the political and cultural exclusion of many marginalized groups is warranted. The higher visibility of mixed race people, rather than being heralded as the solution to the race problem, should be taken as one group's quest to challenge the legacy of the under/mis-representation of cultural others in media and culture. Their emergence has challenged their previously static depictions, and they have been able to shift the meanings attached to historically derogatory images. Recognizing mixed race success cautiously in this realm means also recognizing the privilege mixed race people have been afforded, especially considering that other groups similarly have been attempting to shift representations and meanings attached to their images. However, as groups continue to challenge their characterizations in media and work toward dismantling racial hierarchies by creating connections in contrast to media produced divisions between groups, new social realities may be created for media to model. And, new, more productive identities may be forged.

REFERENCES

Bashir, M., (Anchor) & Wright, D. (Reporter). (2007). Bigot brother? Reality racism. [Television], *Nightline:* ABC.

Blake, J. (Reporter). (2007). Bigot Brother? [Television], *CNN News*.

Browne, A., O'Connor, A., Webster, P., & Sherwin, A. (2007, January 18). Reality TV creates a very surreal diplomatic crisis, *The Times (London)*.

Collins, P. H. (2000). Mammies, matriarchs, and other controlling images. *Black feminist thought: Knowledge, consciousness, and the politics of empowerment* (2nd ed., pp. 69–96). New York: Routledge.

Conlan, T. (2007, May 24). Channel 4 forced to air Big Brother apologies, *The Guardian*. Retrieved from http://www.guardian.co.uk/media/2007/may/24/bigbrother.channel4.

Dixon, T. L., & Linz, D. (2000). Overrepresentation and underrepresentation of African Americans and Latinos as lawbreakers on television news. *Journal of Communication, 50*(2), 131–154.

Gross, L. (2001). *Up from invisibility: Lesbians, gay men, and the media in America.* New York: Columbia University Press.

Hall, S. (1997). The work of representation. In S. Hall (Ed.), *Representation: Cultural representations and signifying practices* (pp. 13–64). London: Sage.

Hall, S. (2003). The whites of their eyes: Racist ideologies and the media. In G. Dines, & J. M. Humez (Eds.), *Gender, race, and class in media: A text-reader* (pp. 89–93). Thousand Oaks, CA: Sage.

Hooks, B. (1992). *Black looks: Race and representation.* Boston, MA: South End Press.

Jhally, S. (Director), & Hall, S. (Lecturer). (1997). Stuart Hall: Representation and the media [video]: Media Education Foundation.

Martins, N., & Harrison, K. (2011). Racial and gender differences in the relationship between children's television use and self-esteem: A longitudinal panel study. *Communication Research*. March 16, 2011.

Morgan, M., Shanahan, J., & Signorielli, N. (2009). Growing up with television: Cultivation processes. In J. Bryant, & M. B. Oliver (Eds.), *Media effects: Advances in theory and research* (3rd ed., pp. 34–49). New York: Routledge.

Noam, E. M. (2009). *Media ownership and concentration in America.* Oxford: Oxford University Press.

Ono, K. A. (2011). Critical: A finer edge. *Communication and Critical Cultural Studies, 8*(1), 93–96.

Ono, K. A. (2010). Postracism: A theory of the 'post'-as political strategy. *Journal of Communication Inquiry, 34*(3), 227–233.

Ono, K. A. (2009a). Critical/Cultural approaches to communication. In W. F. Eadie (Ed.), *21st century communication: A reference handbook* (pp. 74–81). Thousand Oaks, CA: Sage.

Ono, K. A. (2009b). Power Rangers: An ideological critique of neocolonialism. In *Contemporary media culture and the remnants of a colonial past* (pp. 71–87). New York: Peter Lang.

Ono, K. A., & Pham, V. (2009). *Asian Americans and the media*. Cambridge, UK: Polity Press.

Revoir, P. (2007, January 17). 10,000 complain over the 'racists' of Big Brother, *Daily Mail*.

Singh, A. (2007, January 15). Big bro viewers complain of racism towards Shilpa, *The Evening Standard*.

Squires, C. (2007). *Dispatches from the color line: The press and multiracial America*. Albany, NY: SUNY Press.

Tang, M. (2007). Psychological effects on being perceived as a 'model minority' for Asian Americans. *New waves: Educational research and development, 11*(3), 11–16.

Ting-Toomey, S. (2005). Identity negotiation theory: Crossing cultural boundaries. In W. B. Gudykunst (Ed.), *Theorizing about intercultural communication* (pp. 211–233). Thousand Oaks, CA.: Sage.

SECTION 11
NONVERBAL COMMUNICATION

The nonverbal communication context focuses on the messages we send as behaviors without verbal communication or words/language. Nonverbal communication scholars typically examine different nonverbal codes of communication, including physical appearance, haptics (touch), oculesics (eye behavior), proxemices (use of space), chronemics (use of time), facial behavior, kinesics (gesture and movement), vocalics (sound of voice), and environmental cues. Nonverbal scholars consider how the many unspoken behaviors we communicate send important messages simultaneously (for example, our nonverbal communication in an interview). Some major areas of research in nonverbal communication include physical attraction, nonverbal deception, nonverbal differences across cultures, nonverbal greetings, emotional displays in facial behavior, social messages of smiling, the use of color and clothing choices, and scents and smells in environments. This chapter focuses on three important areas of nonverbal communication research: (1) deception/lying, (2) flirting/seduction, and (3) nonverbal skills in communication competence. First, Timothy Levine (Michigan State University) reviews deception research to answer the question: *How can we tell if someone is lying to us?* Second, Betty La France (Northern Illinois University) reviews flirting research to answer the question: *What nonverbal cues are effective when flirting?* Third, Brian Spitzberg (San Diego State University) examines how we can display communication competence by answering the question: *Which nonverbal skills are important for communicating competence?* Many of us are unaware of the nonverbal messages we send and how important these messages can be. Whether it is during an job interview, a date, an important presentation, or even when trying to get out of a speeding ticket, our nonverbal cues serve to help or hurt us. The research reviewed in this chapter can help you sort out the bad advice you may have been given about detecting when someone is lying, flirting with someone, or communicating competence in general. Sometimes, the words you say are much less important than the nonverbal actions you use. This research explains the importance of these actions in commonly occurring situations.

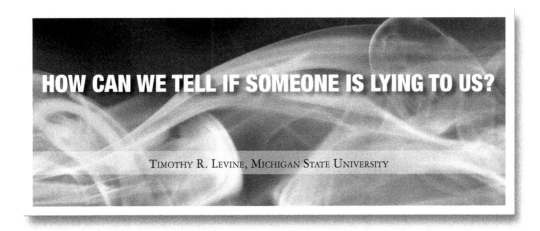

HOW CAN WE TELL IF SOMEONE IS LYING TO US?

TIMOTHY R. LEVINE, MICHIGAN STATE UNIVERSITY

Hi. My name is Tim Levine and I am a Professor of Communication at Michigan State University. Before MSU, I was on the faculty at the University of Hawaii. I have been asked to write a little bit about myself and especially about my research. You might find what I do interesting. I study deception.

This has been a big year for me. I am finishing up a series of deception experiments funded by the National Science Foundation. Those findings have led to a new theory I call Truth Default Theory. I believe my new findings may forever change how we understand deception and deception detection. Besides my recent findings and new theory, I won a distinguished faculty award from my university. And, just a couple of days ago, my 100th and 101st journal articles were accepted for publication. I figure publishing 100 articles before age 50 is not too bad. But, you might ask, what motivates all this research? What gets Dr. Levine up in the morning besides a good cup of coffee (or two)?

Deception is an exciting area to research for many reasons. For one, it brings me into contact with many interesting people. I have met spies and spy catchers, special forces guys, and professional interrogators. I have done training for police and secretive federal agencies. But, I don't have a security clearance and I don't want one. I work for a public university, and I make all my ideas and research findings public though publication. I may study deception, but I strive for transparency and openness, especially in science. I also value trust and honesty in communication and in my relationships with others.

A question I am often asked is how I came to study deception. I know deception researchers who started researching deception in order to try and understand their own gullibility. They got burned by a big lie from someone they trusted. My path into deception research, however, was more mundane. I did not get involved in the topic because I was naturally interested in the topic in the first place but instead because one of the professors (Dr. Steve McCornack) was interested in deception. At first, I was just the research assistant and was along for the ride. I went to graduate school to study persuasion, not deception. But, one question led to another, and, well, here I am. I got sucked in. Now I'm an internationally recognized expert in deception.

There are two big reasons I stuck with research on deception as my career evolved. One has to do with something called counter-intuitive findings. One of the big criticisms of much social science research is that so much social science just documents the obvious. It is common sense. A counter-intuitive finding is a result of research that goes against common sense. If all we needed were common sense, there is little need for research. But, when research brings you knowledge that you cannot come by otherwise, that makes research fun, interesting, and important. In deception, common sense does not always hold and this makes deception an interesting thing to research. To show you what I mean, try answering these two questions:

1. What is the best way to tell if someone is lying to you?

2. True or False: It is easier to detect a lie from someone you know well than from a stranger.

For the answers to these and other questions, read on.

The second reason I got sucked into deception research was there was opportunity. I became convinced early on that most deception theory was wrong-headed. It was mythology, not science. It pointed attention in the wrong direction. Research, it seemed to me, disproved the theory. Because I believed that existing theory was flawed, I saw opportunity. Deception and deception detection provided a puzzle to solve. If old theory was wrong, what was the truth about deception? It has taken me almost 25 years of research to come up with answers I am happy with, but the puzzle pieces are really starting to fit together now and each new finding is more and more impressive. In short, the reason to do research is to learn something new. Deception provided me with a topic about which there was little existing valid knowledge, many misconceptions to correct, and so much to learn. Some people like researching topics upon which there is good prior research to build on and where knowledge needs only a little fine tuning. Not me. I was looking for a challenge, and deception provided that for me.

Deception is defined as knowingly misleading another person (Levine & Kim, 2010). A **lie** is a subtype of deception that involves deceiving someone by saying something that is known to be false. For greater discussion of these definitions, see Levine and Kim, (2010). For ease, I use lying and deception interchangeably here. The intricacies of definitions are boring and not important for the current discussion. Let's just simulate the definition and move on to common misconceptions, key findings, and answering the question asked in the title of this chapter.

First, consider question #1 above. How can you tell if someone is lying to you? Did you answer that a liar won't look you in the eye? Or maybe you guessed that liars fidget or act nervous? This is what research says most people think. A psychologist named Charley Bond (Bond & The Global Deception Research Team, 2006) surveyed people in 75 different countries asking just this question. By far, the #1 answer worldwide was a lack of eye contact. People everywhere think liars won't look you in the eye while lying. Other common answers had to do with acting nervous or anxious.

Most people think that liars have nonverbal tells that give them away. Yet, in research looking at the behaviors of both truth-tellers and liars, there is no scientifically supported evidence that a lack of eye contact signals deceit (DePaulo et al., 2003). Eye contact has no validity as a deception tell. Zero. Fidgeting is not very informative either. In fact, most specific nonverbal behaviors are near worthless as signals of lying. Some research supports some nonverbal deception cues, but other findings do not, and in the end it tends to be a wash. Forty years of research on nonverbal deception cues has led to a dead end in lie detection. Not everyone agrees on this, but I find the evidence convincing. Research disproves common sense and conventional wisdom.

It was findings such as these that clued me into the belief that most deception theory is probably misguided. You see, most deception theory is all about nonverbal communication as the path to detecting lies. Since the 1970s, most thinking about deception and deception detection was guided by variations on psychologist Paul Ekman's idea of **leakage**. If you have seen the TV show, *Lie to Me,* you will know something about this idea. Basically, the idea is that it is easy to control what you say, but the truth leaks out though facial expressions and body language. According to leakage and related theories, if you know how to read nonverbal behaviors, you can detect lies.

The idea that paying attention to nonverbal behaviors is actually misleading guided one of my most recent series of experiments (Levine et al., 2011). People who present themselves as confident, composed, and friendly tend to be believed. We say such people have an honest demeanor. Other people who come off as standoffish, anxious, or uncertain tend to be disbelieved and have a dishonest demeanor. We found this to be true regardless of who was witnessing and judging the communication. We replicated our findings with college students, college professors, and federal agents, and with people from a different country who didn't even understand what was being said. Some people are just seen as more sincere than others. The thing is though, the things that make people believable are not the same things that are valid predictors of actual honesty or deception. People believed sincere acting people, not sincere people. It matters how smooth, confident, and friendly a communicator was, not how honest the person was. So, when people base judgments of others' honesty based on how those people are acting (i.e., their demeanor; do they look honest, have good eye contact, appear confident and composed, etc.), they are wrong much of the time. This makes accuracy at detecting deception near chance (Levine et al., 2011). And this is just what most deception detection experiments find. People are only slightly better at chance at distinguishing truths from lies in deception experiments (Bond & DePaulo, 2006).

In a somewhat related recent experiment, my students randomly assigned research participants to either watch the show *Lie to Me* or a different crime drama named *Numb3rs,* or they were in a control group that did not watch a show. *Lie to Me* depicts an expert who can detect lies by reading nonverbal communication, and the show claims to be based on real science. In our experiment (Levine, Serota & Shulman, 2010), the participants who watched *Lie to Me* were the least adept at deception detection compared to the other groups, but they were also the most cynical. That is, the *Lie to Me* viewers thought more people were lying than others but were the least accurate at telling truths from lies. In particular, they tended to disbelieve honest people.

But, I am ahead of myself. My thinking about deception was initially influenced by a well-documented finding called **truth-bias**. Truth-bias is the tendency to believe others regardless of whether or not the person is actually honest (Levine, Park & McCornack, 1999). The term was originally coined by McCornack and Parks (1986). Every study I have ever done, and I have done many, has supported truth-bias. People tend to believe others more often than not.

The truth-bias finding led my wife (Dr. Hee Sun Park, also a communication professor, and also a deception researcher) to the idea of **the veracity effect** (Levine, Park, & McCornack, 1999). Veracity has to do with if something is true or false, honest or dishonest. The idea is that a sender's honesty (or veracity) affects accuracy at detecting truths and lies. As I said previously, overall, research shows that people are near chance at distinguishing truths from lies (Bond & DePaulo, 2006). Research, as you now know, also finds that people are truth-biased. Because people tend to believe others more often than not, if the person they are talking to is honest, then they are correct in believing them. If the person is actually lying, however, they tend to be wrong and are fooled. Although people are a little better than chance at distinguishing truths and lies, they get honest statements right much more often than lies. Accuracy for truths is above 50%, but accuracy for lies is below 50%. The veracity of the message affects accuracy, hence the "veracity effect."

By the way, people tend to believe the people they know even more often than strangers. That is, the closer your relationship with someone, the more you will tend to be truth-biased. Because truth-bias blinds us to another's lies, we tend to be slightly worse at detecting deception in people we know best. This is the answer to question two above. The answer is false. It is easier to detect lies in strangers (McCornack & Parks, 1986). It was cool findings like these that made me want to work with Professor McCornack and kept me into deception research.

Truth-bias led to another of my recent interesting findings. As I mentioned, people are truth-biased in my studies. I began to wonder why. Generally, when students participate in research, they know things are not always what they seem. Especially if you know you are in a deception experiment, wouldn't that make you suspicious? My thinking was, if people are truth-biased even when they know they are in a deception experiment, this truth-bias must really be powerful and deeply ingrained in people.

Back in the late 1980s and 1990s I thought of truth-bias as flawed thinking. It is called a bias after all. It must be irrational. Or, is it? What if most people were honest most of the time? Then believing others makes good sense. Truth-bias might actually be functional. This led me to research how often people lie.

My colleagues and I (Serota, Levine, & Boster, 2010) did a nationally representative survey asking 1,000 adults in the USA how often they had lied in the past 24 hours. How many lies have you told today? What do you think the results were?

The results were that the average was between one and two lies per day. But, most people said they did not lie at all. A few people, in contrast, lied a whole lot. Almost half of the reported lies were told by just 5% of the sample. I call this finding **a few prolific liars**. Most people are honest most of the time, but there are a few people who lie a whole lot. As a consequence, the average number of lies (1.6 lies per day) does not reflect the average person (who reports zero lies).

We have now replicated the few prolific liar findings several times. We have surveyed college students and high school students and got access to prior research as well as a new large survey from England. The pattern holds up. Most people are usually honest, but there are a few chronic liars out there. So, maybe truth-bias is not so much of a bias after all. Maybe people believe others more often than not because people are in fact honest more often than not. Communication would not work well if you had to second guess everything you were told or read.

There is one interesting variable we have found so far that predicts how often people lie. Age. Older people lie less. High school students report lying twice as often as college students. College students lie more than older adults. Our findings suggest honesty increases with age for most people. Most (but not all) people grow out of lying, so to speak, and only lie occasionally as needed.

So far, we have learned that people tend to be truth-biased and that truth-bias may not be a bias at all because people tend to be honest about most things most of the time. But, people are not always honest and people don't always believe others. This led me to research when people actually lie (Levine, Kim & Hamel, 2010) and when people think others lie (Levine, Kim & Blair, 2010).

Generally, people lie for a reason. That is, they lie when they have a motive to do so. However, the motives that prompt deception are not any different than those that guide honest communication. People want to gain desirable outcomes and avoid undesirable outcomes. People want to create a positive impression and maintain autonomy. When the truth works in a person's favor, or at least does not interfere with their goals and desires, almost everyone is honest (Levine, Kim & Hamel, 2010). It is only when the truth is a problem that the question of deception arises. So, for example, if a significant other gives you a gift that you like, you would almost certainly be honest in expressing your opinion of the gift. It is only when the gift is disliked and you have to worry about hurting the gift-giver's feelings or appearing ungrateful that the temptation to lie occurs.

Perhaps because people lie for a reason and are typically honest absent a motive to lie, people consider motive when judging the honesty of others. I call this idea the **Projected Motive Model** (Levine, Kim & Blair, 2010). Charlie Bond independently had the same idea, although his paper has not been published yet as of this writing. The idea of projecting motive is that we tend to believe others when they lack an obvious motivation to lie, but truth-bias is diminished greatly when we think someone might have a reason to lie. An obvious example is when someone is trying to sell us something. In my experiments, I showed people videos of people who denied cheating or confessed to cheating. The confessions were almost always believed. Why would people say they cheated when they didn't? They have no apparent motive. But, denials were believed less often.

So, people are honest more often than not. When they do lie, it is because the truth poses some problem that provides a motive to lie. Having a motive to lie does not mean that a person will lie because some people are honest anyway. But, people who do not have a motive to lie are almost always honest. Thus, it makes sense that people tend to believe others, unless they think the other person has some motive to lie. When people infer that others have a reason to lie, that is, they project a motive, they become suspicious.

How then can we test our suspicions to see if someone is actually lying or not? I have already told you about Charlie Bond's study asking people how do we know when someone is lying. The number one answer was that they won't look you in the eye. Most other common answers, you will remember, centered on other aspects of nonverbal communication, like acting nervous.

You will also remember, I hope, that such beliefs have little validity. Eye contact is not a valid deception cue.

My wife had a clever idea. We did a study asking the question a slightly different way. Instead of asking people their beliefs about how to detect deception, we asked people to think of a recent but memorable situation where the actually discovered a lie. Try this yourself. Can you think of a time you discovered, uncovered, or recognized a lie? How did you do that? How did you know you were lied to?

In our study (Park, Levine, McCornack, Morrison, & Ferrar, 2002) titled , **How People Really Detect Lies**, we asked 200 participants to describe, in detail, a lie that they had detected. The results were very different than Charley Bond's eye contact findings. The detected lies in our data were uncovered though the use of various sorts of evidence rather than through the observation of nonverbal behaviors. There was information from third parties. Other people provided information that contradicted the lie. People used physical evidence. For example, a roommate denied using a computer owned by another roommate, but her login name was in a login spot. People confessed. The person being lied to already knew the truth, so the lie failed. In all, 98% of the reported instances of discovered deception involved discovery methods other than eye contact and other nonverbal clues. Further, most lies were detected after the fact at some later point in time. Leakage had little to do with it.

The idea that people use evidence to detect deception led us to the idea of **Content in Context** (Blair, Levine, and Shaw, 2010). By content, we mean paying attention to what someone says rather than how they say it. We distinguish between communication content (the words and what the words mean) and **demeanor** (how someone presents themselves; do they seem honest). While deception research has traditionally focused on demeanor and nonverbal cues, we think content is more valuable so long as the communication context is understood. Context has to do with the situation surrounding the communication. We believe that listening to what is said and comparing that to what is known given the context can be useful in detecting lies. In our series of experiments, providing people with valid context information greatly improved their ability to detect lies (Blair, Levine, & Shaw, 2010).

In conclusion, deception is an intriguing area of research. Over the past 25 or so years, I have become increasingly obsessed with the questions about when and how can people detect lies. One finding has led to another and I think my persistence in research has finally paid off. When I started doing research on deception, most research was based on the idea that lies could be detected by careful and knowledgeable observation of nonverbal behaviors. My earlier understanding of the research findings was that people couldn't really detect lies at rates much better than chance, and that truth-bias was a nearly inescapable cloud obscuring people's judgment. After years of research, I now think that truth-bias is healthy and adaptive. It makes good sense to believe most people most of the time because most people are for the most part honest. To catch lies, focus not on nonverbal behaviors but instead consider if the person has a motive to lie, listen to what the person is saying, and assess if what is said makes sense given what you know about the context. That is how you can detect a lie.

REFERENCES

Blair, J. P., Levine, T. R., & Shaw, A. J. (2010). Content in context improves deception detection accuracy. *Human Communication Research, 36,* 423–442.

Bond, C. F., & DePaulo, B. M. (2006). Accuracy of deception judgments. *Personality and Social Psychology Review, 10,* 214–234.

Bond, C. F., & The Global Deception Research Team (2006). A world of lies. *Journal of Cross-Cultural Psychology, 37,* 60–74.

DePaulo, B. M., Lindsay, J. J., Malone, B. E., Muhlenbruck, L., Charlton, K., & Cooper, H. (2003). Cues to deception. *Psychological Bulletin, 129,* 74–118.

Levine, T. R., & Kim, R. K. (2010). Some considerations for a new theory of deceptive communication. In M. Knapp & M. McGlone (Eds.), *The Interplay of Truth and Deception* (pp. 16–34). New York: Routledge.

Levine, T. R., Kim, R. K., & Blair, J. P. (2010). (In)accuracy at detecting true and false confessions and denials: An initial test of a projected motive model of veracity judgments. *Human Communication Research, 36,* 81–101.

Levine, T. R., Kim, R. K., & Hamel, L. M. (2010). People lie for a reason: Three experiments documenting the principle of veracity. *Communication Research Reports, 27,* 271–285.

Levine, T. R., Park, H. S., & McCornack, S. A. (1999). Accuracy in detecting truths and lies: Documenting the veracity effect. *Communication Monographs, 66,* 125–144.

Levine, T. R., Serota, K. B., & Shulman, H. (2010). The impact of Lie to Me viewers actual ability to detect deception. *Communication Research, 37,* 846–856.

Levine, T. R., Serota, K. B., Shulman, H., Clare, D. D., Park, H. S., Shaw, A. S., Shim, J. C., & Lee, J. H. (2011). Sender demeanor: Individual differences in sender believability have a powerful impact on deception detection judgments. *Human Communication Research, 37,* 377–403.

Levine, T. R., Shaw, A., & Shulman, H. (2010). Increasing deception detection accuracy with strategic questioning. *Human Communication Research, 36,* 216–231.

McCornack, S. A., & Levine, T. R. (1990). When lovers become leery: The relationship between suspicion and accuracy in detecting deception. *Communication Monographs, 57,* 219–230.

McCornack, S. A., & Parks, M. R. (1986). Deception detection and relationship development: The other side of trust. In M. L. McLaughlin (Ed.), *Communication yearbook 9* (pp. 377–389). Beverly Hills, CA: Sage.

Park, H. S., Levine, T. R., McCornack, S. A., Morrison, K., & Ferrara, M. (2002). How people really detect lies. *Communication Monographs, 69,* 144–157.

Serota, K. B., Levine, T. R., & Boster, F. J. (2010). The prevalence of lying in America: Three studies of reported deception. *Human Communication Research, 36,* 1–24.

FLIRTING: WHAT NONVERBAL CUES ARE EFFECTIVE?

BETTY H. LA FRANCE, NORTHERN ILLINOIS UNIVERSITY

A look across a bar. A loud laugh at someone's joke. A coy smile. Brushing against someone's arm. Leaning forward. These nonverbal behaviors are examples of flirtatious cues in that they convey relational interest. Flirting is crucial for relationships—especially in the early stages. The next several paragraphs will present a short summary of the research that has examined nonverbal behaviors that are considered flirtatious. This review addresses key issues that have been raised as a result of these investigations. Furthermore, the flirtatious nonverbal behaviors perceived most effective are also discussed.

For a variety of reasons, answering the simple question regarding the effectiveness of flirtatious nonverbal cues is not easy. There are two main reasons for the difficulty in addressing this question. First, effectiveness can only be determined after considering the goal or objective of a particular action. In this case, assessing the effectiveness of a particular nonverbal cue can only be accomplished after addressing which flirting goal is being considered. As will be discussed, Henningsen (2004) found that there are several reasons why people flirt. So, the reason why someone is flirting will drive the assessment regarding the effectiveness of her or his behavior. A second reason why it is difficult to answer the question posed in the title of this review is that there have only been a few investigations that specifically examine how a single nonverbal cue leads to some predicted outcome. There are different ways of addressing each reason, and the following review offers many answers to the effectiveness question.

Henningsen (2004) defines flirting as the use of those verbal and nonverbal communicative behaviors or cues that are used to cultivate a relationship, which includes sexual contact. This definition clearly indicates that flirting is often associated with the start of a romantic relationship. As Henningsen (2004) also notes, however, men and women use flirtatious behaviors in other types of relationships and for other reasons. Consequently, it is often the case that the same communication cues considered flirtatious in one setting (e.g., eye contact between a man and a woman at a bar) are interpreted as friendly in another setting (e.g., eye contact between a man and a woman in a hallway at work) (Abbey, 1987). Research has shown that the same verbal and nonverbal communicative behaviors typically associated with flirting appear in cross-sex romantic and platonic (i.e., nonsexual) relationships (Egland, Spitzberg, & Zormeier, 1996), and they have also been seen in therapeutic settings (Scheflen, 1965). Oftentimes confusion about how to perceive nonverbal behavior has led to a wide variety of awkward interactions. Imagine hanging out with someone you like at a bar; you are attracted to this person. You think things are going well, and you would like to pursue a sexual relationship. You think this person is really into you. At the end of the night, the person turns to you and remarks what a good friend you are. This example reflects a common experience, and it has—in part—prompted the scientific study of flirting.

Research on flirting has quite a long and exciting history, and a large number of nonverbal communication behaviors thought to indicate flirting have been identified (Abbey, Cozzarelli, McLaughlin, & Harnish, 1987; Clark, Shaver, & Abrahams, 1999; Edgar & Fitzpatrick, 1993; Egland, Spitzberg, & Zormeier, 1996; Grammer, 1990; Greer & Buss, 1994; Koeppel, Montagne-Miller, O'Hair, & Cody, 1993; Kowalski, 1993; La France, 2010; Moore, 1985, 2002; Rose & Frieze, 1993; Simpson, Gangestad, & Biek, 1993). These behaviors can be categorized into the traditional nonverbal cue categories: kinesics, haptics, proxemics, oculesics, vocalics, physical appearance, and facial expressions (see Table 1 for a list of identified nonverbal communication cues).

Flirting is a crucial courtship behavior (Clark, Shaver, & Abrahams, 1999; Grammer, 1990; Henningsen, 2004; Hall, Carter, Cody, & Albright, 2010; Moore, 2002; Singh, 2004), and courtship is comprised of verbal and nonverbal cues that express romantic relational interest in another as well as advertise oneself as a quality partner (Grammer, 1990; Moore, 1985). Moore (2002) aptly notes that flirting behaviors are comprised of "courtship signals," which include "nonverbal behaviors [that] serve to attract and maintain the attention of a potential partner" (p. 97). Women and men readily flirt and use nonverbal communication strategically to initiate relationships (Clark et al., 1999). Thus, research focusing on flirtatious nonverbal behavior has examined cross-sex interactions that presume heterosexual participants have the potentiality to be sexually interested in each other. These early interactions between people contain courtship signals, which happen during the beginning stages of a relationship. People—scholars included—overwhelmingly associate flirtatious behaviors with the beginning of a heterosexual, sexual (short-term or long-term) relationship.

There is increasing and compelling evidence that flirting to accomplish sexually-driven goals is guided by adaptive evolutionary processes (Buss, 1998; Schmitt, 2005). Sexual Strategies Theory (Buss & Schmitt, 1993) proposes that men and women engage in strategic behaviors that reflect "selection pressures," which developed over years of evolution (p. 205). The different evolutionary pressures men and women faced have led them to use different short-term and long-term strategies to find a mate (Buss, 1998; Buss & Schmitt, 1993, Simpson et al., 1993; Schmitt, 2005). Some of these strategies include using specific nonverbal behaviors that reflect the adaptations people have made. As such, these nonverbal cues have developed as part of their repertoire of flirtatious behavior. Examining flirtatious behaviors from the evolutionary perspective is useful because it suggests that nonverbal cues are used, they are used strategically, and that nonverbal behaviors represent—in part—preferences that are adaptations to evolutionary mating pressures. For

TABLE 1 List of Nonverbal Flirting Behaviors

Adaptor	Nod head
Arch back	Occasionally glance downward
Arm flex	Open body posture
Body orientation	Open legs with gap between thighs
Breast touch	Parade
Brush	Play footsies with them
Buttock pat	Pout
Coy smile	Primp
Engage in extended eye contact	Protrude chest
Expose skin	Put your arm around someone
Eyebrow flash	Rub neck
Fondling	Rub shoulder
Gaze into eyes	Shoulder flex
Giggle	Sit next to each other
Go out of way to be close	Skirt hike
Grab and kiss someone	Smile
Grab hand and pull towards you	Touch cheek, neck, shoulder
Groom and dress	Touch hand
Hair flip	Touch them occasionally
Head tilt	Touch yourself
Head toss	Trunk flex
Hold hand	Use animated/expressive voice
Intimate tone of voice	Use hand gestures
Laugh	Vocal fluency
Lean close to/toward them	Wave
Lip lick	Wear attractive clothes
Lipstick application	Wear revealing clothing
Maintaining eye contact	Whisper
Move close	Worry about appearance
Neck presentation	

example, men's ability to use nonverbal cues to convey social status, access to resources, and interest in commitment would be beneficial (from an evolutionary perspective) because women's mate selection preferences include looking for clues to a man's suitability for parenthood (Buss & Schmitt, 1993).

Perhaps the starkest example of a nonverbal cue that developed in response to evolutionary mate pressures is physical attractiveness. Specifically, Buss and Schmitt (1993) argue that, for men, a woman's level of physical attractiveness (e.g., clear skin, symmetry) is a cue representing her reproductive capability. Empirical evidence demonstrates that physical attractiveness—regardless of culture—is a powerful nonverbal code for mate selection, especially for men (Buss, 1989, 1998; Singh, 2004). Although certain physical characteristics are considered attractive because of cultural expectations (e.g., blond hair), other attributes have been found to be attractive across cultures. For example, female images at a normal weight with a 7.0 waist-to-hip ratio have been rated as most attractive compared to lower or higher ratios (Buss, 1998; Singh, 2004). Clearly, physical attractiveness is an effective nonverbal flirtatious cue, and individuals perform a host of behaviors that enhance their level of attractiveness (e.g., using lipstick to highlight lips, wearing short skirts to accentuate toned leg muscles). In fact, merely commenting on another person's physical attractiveness is one of the top ten effective ways to encourage a sexual encounter (Greer & Buss, 1994). To date, empirical investigations assessing the importance that women place on finding a physically attractive mate have found that women do not place as much value on that particular nonverbal cue as do men (Schmitt, 2005). There are, however, other cues—such as social status—to which women attend and that also influence the impact of physical attractiveness on sexual attitude (van Straaten, Engels, Finkenauer, & Holland, 2008).

Studies where specific nonverbal cues during cross-sex interactions were the focus have presented somewhat contradictory findings regarding the effectiveness of particular behaviors. For example, Grammer (1990) found certain nonverbal behaviors were consistently rated as indicating interest (see Table 2). The nonverbal cue that was the most consistent indicator of interest was body openness. Generally speaking, women signal interest by opening their posture through opening their arms and/or legs. By contrast, a lack of interest was communicated through closed arms or legs. Men, on the other hand, do not consistently open their bodies (legs or arms) to signal interest (see Table 2). Similar to the differences seen for disinterested males, Simpson, Gangestad, and Biek (1993) also found that, for men, an open body position means a lack of interest.

Other nonverbal behaviors for signaling relational interest have also been found. For example, establishing eye contact and smiling demonstrate attention and interest in a dyadic partner; conversely, looking downward or away communicates disinterest (Koeppel et al., 1993; Moore, 2002; Simpson et al., 1993). In addition to eye contact and smiling, women also communicate their interest in men by tilting their heads and flashing their eyebrows (Grammer, 1990; Simpson et al., 1993). Furthermore, Grammer, Honda, Juette, and Schmitt (1999) demonstrated that women who are interested in men move more slowly during their interactions than do women who are not interested. Men, however, show no change in movement related to their interest in women.

In addition to studying the effectiveness of specific flirtatious nonverbal behaviors, differences in how men and women judge nonverbal cues have been measured. For example, Moore (2002) found some similarities and differences in the ways that men and women judged women's nonverbal flirtatious behaviors. Both men and women rated women's laughter, smiling, touching, and coy smiling positively. Men rated other nonverbal behaviors (e.g., shirt hike, lip lick, hair flip) more positively than did women. That is, men perceive a greater range of nonverbal behavior as conveying flirtatiousness than do women.

Although other studies have found that certain flirtatious nonverbal behaviors are effective, Grammer et al. (1999) found no consistently performed nonverbal behavior related to how interested men and women reported to be in their opposite sex interactions. Men and women used not one nonverbal cue across cultures that communicated relational interest consistently.

TABLE 2 Women and Men's Highest Rated Nonverbal Behaviors that Signal Interest (Grammer, 1990)

Dyad Type	Women's Nonverbal Behavior	Men's Nonverbal Behavior
Female interested—Male interested	Head turned away Head tilted away Open arms Hands touch body Lean back and turns away	Lean forward and turns toward Head akimbo* Legs crossed and open
Female uninterested—Male interested	Hands touch face Head turned toward Head tilted toward Lean back and turns toward	Hands touch head Lean back and turned toward Head akimbo
Female interested—Male uninterested	Head turned toward Head tilted toward Legs crossed and open Lean back and turned away	Arms crossed Head turned away Head tilted toward Legs crossed and closed
Female uninterested—Male uninterested	Lean back Legs crossed and closed Hands touch arms	Open arms Open legs Lean forward

*Head akimbo = "angle between body and arm [is] greater than 45 degrees and the hands [are] folded in the neck region . . ." (Grammer, 1990, p. 214)

If a sexual encounter is a desired goal or outcome of flirtatious behavior, it is important to understand that particular nonverbal behaviors are seen as more effective than others for having sex. Greer and Buss (1994) demonstrated that there are several acts or tactics men and women employ to increase the probability of having sex with someone. Some of these cues are nonverbal flirtatious behaviors. For example, for women, increasing sexual touch and non-sexual touch are in the top ten of most effective strategies women use to have sex with men. Interestingly, men's most effective tactics include behaviors that are accomplished using nonverbal communication. If men are able to use specific nonverbal flirtatious cues to demonstrate that they are committed and attentive, they are more likely to engage in sex.

Similar to Greer and Buss's (1994) findings, La France (2010) found that there are particular nonverbal communication cues that increase the likelihood that sex occurs. She asked research participants to evaluate the nonverbal and verbal communication cues that occur during the traditional sexual script (i.e., a script that details a casual sexual encounter that begins at a bar and ends with the participants having sex at the woman's apartment). La France (2010) found that when the man described in the script kisses the woman at the bar, all other communication after that nonverbal cue led participants to believe that sex would likely happen. Furthermore, once the couple in the hypothetical scenario arrived at the woman's house, research participants were confident that sex would happen. The only other nonverbal behavior that was instrumental in increasing perceptions that sex *would* happen during this casual sexual encounter was when the man kissed the woman after she stated that she thought things were "moving too fast" (La

France, 2010, p. 318). Taken together, these results demonstrate that seemingly small flirtatious nonverbal cues make a large impact in accomplishing a desired end: sex.

Certain flirtatious nonverbal cues have been consistently associated with increased romantic and sexual interest (e.g., smiling), and men and women are able to identify positive and negative nonverbal flirting behaviors accurately (Moore, 2002). To interpret extant research findings as portraying that there are clear unambiguous markers or nonverbal cues that will always lead to a specific desire, such as sex, is a mistake. Contrary to popular thought, flirting is a complex communication activity, and a large part of the complication arises in the haziness inherent in the use of nonverbal communication. For many situations, including flirtatious situations, nonverbal cues are vague and can be used strategically for communicating desires in a way that does not injure one's self-esteem (or image) should those desires be unreciprocated (Grammer, 1990). Expressing interest nonverbally allows one to determine if another person is receptive to advances without the high risk of embarrassment that a verbal statement may make. The ambiguity of nonverbal communication also allows for the possibility of using several additional nonverbal behaviors in response to a target's behavior (Grammer, 1990). The haziness that is a positive attribute of flirtatious interactions also allows people to pursue multiple goals using flirtatious behaviors as a tactic. For example, Henningsen (2004) found that people pursue multiple goals or objectives when they flirt. In fact, the top two most common single reasons people identified for engaging in flirtatious behavior was to increase the intimacy of a relationship (labeled relational motivation) and for fun (i.e., to have a good time). So, imagine if one person uses touch to have a good time and another person uses touch to promote a sexual encounter. At the end of the interaction, both people will most likely be unhappy, confused, and angry.

Another reason why flirting is more complicated than the mere identification of one or two effective nonverbal behaviors is because of the larger context in which flirting takes place. If the same flirtatious nonverbal behavior can produce different meanings in the same context, then it is not absurd to conclude that the same nonverbal cues will mean something different depending on the situation in which they are communicated (Henningsen, Henningsen, & Valde, 2006; Moore, 1985). Consistent with this idea, Grammer, Kruck, and Magnusson (1998) argue that, ". . . communication in courtship is a slow process in which the sender slowly reveals his/her intentions, and the receiver seems to sum up different combinations of courtship signals over time" (p. 7). This view of relationship initiation suggests that flirtatious nonverbal cues cannot be usefully interpreted (or employed) singularly. Rather, people use and perceive sets of nonverbal cues over time and in different contexts, the meanings for which change depending on all the characteristics of a given situation.

As an alternative to relying on specific flirtatious nonverbal cues, Hall, Carter, Cody, and Albright (2010) have persuasively argued that people should think about the entire context of flirting when making judgments about what certain verbal statements and nonverbal cues mean. They identified five styles (traditional, physical, sincere, playful, and polite) of flirting that reflect individuals' personalities and their dispositions toward conveying romantic interest in another person. These general flirting styles provide an indication of what specific nonverbal behaviors may be used to show interest in another person. For example, Hall et al. (2010) found that individuals who were extraverted (i.e., outgoing, sociable) were more likely to have physical, sincere, and playful flirting styles. La France, Heisel, and Beatty (2004) found that extroverts exhibited more nonverbal behavior, such as smiling, inflected speech, gesturing, body contact, and facial expressions, than did introverts. Taken together, these studies demonstrate that people who engage in physical, sincere, and playing flirting should, on average, smile, use inflected speech, actively gesture, engage in body contact, and use facial expressions more than people who have different flirting styles when in situations where romantic behavior is normative.

Given the previous discussion and list of nonverbal communication cues listed in Table 1, it should be apparent that some nonverbal behaviors clearly indicate romantic interest while others could be interpreted otherwise. It takes significant cognitive effort to process nonverbal behaviors and that effort increases substantially as the number of nonverbal cues used during an interaction increases (La France, Heisel, & Beatty, 2007). As such, people can (and do) make mistakes in determining whether another person is flirting with them. In fact, Haselton and Buss (2000) provide evidence demonstrating that people make consistent mistakes—or errors in judgment— in perceiving nonverbal behaviors during cross-sex interactions. The errors that people make, they argue, are systematically biased in one's evolutionary favor (i.e., the error is the least costly from an evolutionary perspective). During cross-sex interactions, men overestimate women's sexuality, including flirtatiousness, and women underestimate men's level of commitment (Haselton & Buss, 2000; Henningsen & Henningsen, 2010; La France, Henningsen, Oates, & Shaw, 2009). Consequently, when interacting with women, it is in a man's best interest to misperceive that women are interested in him (despite that, in reality, they are not), and it is in a woman's best interest to misperceive that men are not committed to her (when, in reality, they are). Men and women use nonverbal cues when making assessments regarding another's interest and commitment levels, and people make systematic errors when interpreting these cues.

SUMMARY

The research reviewed in the preceding paragraphs (and indeed that investigate flirting) rely on heterosexual participants who are engaged in cross-sex interactions. This review provides evidence demonstrating that although there are certain nonverbal behaviors—such as eye contact, a smile, a kiss—that are perceived to be effective flirtatious behaviors, it is more useful to take into consideration the larger context (e.g., the setting) to determine whether nonverbal behaviors are effective. Furthermore, there are several different reasons why people flirt, so it is crucial to recognize *why* someone is (or why *you* are) flirting to avoid awkward situations and hurt feelings. Finally, although people make systematic and evolutionarily advantageous mistakes when interpreting flirtatious nonverbal behavior, those errors are uncomfortable for people who experience them. Thus, it is worthwhile to understand that the interpretation of flirtatious nonverbal cues, and their effectiveness, is not as straightforward as previously assumed.

REFERENCES

References marked with an asterisk indicate studies from which the list of nonverbal flirting behaviors was drawn.

Abbey, A. (1987). Misperceptions of friendly behavior as sexual interest: A survey of naturally occurring incidents. *Psychology of Women Quarterly, 11,* 173–194.

*Abbey, A., Cozzarelli, C., McLaughlin, K., & Harnish, R. J. (1987). The effects of clothing and dyad sex composition on perceptions of sexual intent: Do women and men evaluate these cues differently? *Journal of Applied Social Psychology, 17,* 108–126.

Buss, D. M. (1989). Sex differences in human mate preferences: Evolutionary hypotheses tested in 37 cultures. *Behavioral and Brain Sciences, 12,* 1–49.

Buss, D. M. (1998). Sexual strategies theory: Historical origins and current status. *The Journal of Sex Research, 35,* 19–31.

Buss, D. M., & Schmitt, D. P. (1993). Sexual strategies theory: An evolutionary perspective on human mating. *Psychological Review, 100,* 204–232.

*Clark, C. L., Shaver, P. R., & Abrahams, M. F. (1999). Strategic behaviors in romantic relationship initiation. *Personality and Social Psychology Bulletin, 25,* 709–722.

*Edgar, T., & Fitzpatrick, M. A. (1993). Expectations for sexual interaction: A cognitive test of the sequencing of sexual communication behaviors. *Health Communication, 5,* 239–261.

*Egland, K. L., Spitzberg, B. H., & Zormeier, M. M. (1996). Flirtation and conversational competence in cross-sex platonic and romantic relationships. *Communication Reports, 9,* 105–117.

*Grammer, K. (1990). Strangers meet: Laughter and nonverbal signs of interest in opposite-sex encounters. *Journal of Nonverbal Behavior, 14,* 209–236.

Grammer, K., Honda, M., Juette, A., & Schmitt, A. (1999). Fuzziness of nonverbal courtship communication unblurred by motion energy detection. *Journal of Personality and Social Psychology, 77,* 487–508.

Grammer, K., Kruck, K. B., & Magnusson, M. S. (1998). The courtship dance: Patterns of nonverbal synchronization in opposite-sex encounters. *Journal of Nonverbal Behavior, 22,* 3–29.

*Greer, A. E., & Buss, D. M. (1994). Tactics for promoting sexual encounters. *The Journal of Sex Research, 31,* 185–201.

Hall, J. A., Carter, S., Cody, M. J., & Albright, J. M. (2010). Individual differences in the communication of romantic interest: Development of the Flirting Styles Inventory. *Communication Quarterly, 58,* 365–393.

Haselton, M. G., & Buss, D. M. (2000). Error management theory: A new perspective on biases in cross-sex mind reading. *Journal of Personality and Social Psychology, 78,* 81–91.

Henningsen, D. D. (2004). Flirting with meaning: An examination of miscommunication in flirting interactions. *Sex Roles, 50,* 481–489.

Henningsen, D. D., & Henningsen, M. L. M. (2010). Testing error management theory: Exploring the commitment skepticism bias and the sexual overperception bias. *Human Communication Research, 36,* 618–634.

Henningsen, D. D., Henningsen, M. L. M., & Valde, K. S. (2006). Gender differences in perceptions of women's sexual interest during cross-sex interactions: An application and extension of cognitive valence theory. *Sex Roles, 54,* 821–829.

*Koeppel, L. B., Montagne-Miller, Y., O'Hair, D., & Cody, M. J. (1993). Friendly? Flirting? Wrong? In P. J. Kalbfleisch (Ed.), *Interpersonal communication: Evolving interpersonal relationships* (pp. 13–32). Hillsdale, NJ: Lawrence Erlbaum Associates.

*Kowalski, R. M. (1993). Inferring sexual interest from behavioral cues: Effects of gender and sexually relevant attitudes. *Sex Roles, 29,* 13–36.

*La France, B. H. (2010). What verbal and nonverbal communication cues lead to sex?: An analysis of the traditional sexual script. *Communication Quarterly, 58,* 297–318.

La France, B. H., Heisel, A. D., & Beatty, M. J. (2004). Is there empirical evidence for a nonverbal profile of extraversion?: A meta-analysis and critique of the literature. *Communication Monographs, 71,* 28–48.

La France, B. H., Heisel, A. D., & Beatty, M. J. (2007). A test of the cognitive load hypothesis: Investigating the impact of number of nonverbal cues coded and length of coding session on observer accuracy. *Communication Reports, 20,* 11–23.

La France, B. H., Henningsen, D. D., Oates, A., & Shaw, C. M. (2009). Social-sexual interactions?: Meta-analyses of sex differences in perceptions of flirtatiousness, seductiveness, and promiscuousness. *Communication Monographs, 76,* 263–285.

*Moore, M. M. (1985). Nonverbal courtship patterns in women: Context and consequences. *Ethology and Sociobiology, 6,* 237–247.

*Moore, M. M. (2002). Courtship communication and perception. *Perceptual and Motor Skills, 94,* 97–105.

*Rose, S., & Frieze, I. (1993). Young singles' contemporary dating scripts. *Sex Roles, 28,* 499–509.

*Scheflen, A. E. (1965). Quasi-courtship behavior in psychotherapy. *Psychiatry, 28,* 245–257.

Schmitt, D. P. (2005). Fundamentals of human mating strategies. In D. M. Buss (Ed.), *The handbook of evolutionary psychology* (pp. 258–291). Hoboken, NJ: John Wiley & Sons, Inc.

*Simpson, J. A., Gangestad, S. W., & Biek, M. (1993). Personality and nonverbal social behavior: An ethological perspective of relationship initiation. *Journal of Experimental Social Psychology, 29,* 434–461.

Singh, D. (2004). Mating strategies of young women: Role of physical attractiveness. *The Journal of Sex Research, 41,* 43–54.

van Straaten, I., Engels, R. C., Finkenauer, C., & Holland, R. W. (2008). Sex differences in short-term mate preferences and behavioral mimicry: A semi-naturalistic experiment. *Archives of Sexual Behavior, 37,* 902–911.

NONVERBAL SKILLS FOR COMMUNICATING COMPETENTLY

BRIAN H. SPITZBERG, SAN DIEGO STATE UNIVERSITY

A commonplace assumption is that nonverbal behavior matters more in the communication of meaning than does verbal communication. This is not a very accurate claim, because it depends significantly on the context and what meanings are being interpreted (e.g., detecting deception versus getting directions from someone), and because nonverbal behavior can rarely be realistically separated from verbal behavior in everyday interactions (Barrick, Shaffer, & DeGrassi, 2009; Motley, 1993). Furthermore, translating such an aphorism into practical advice is not easy. Consider the following train of thought:

- You never get a second chance to make a first impression.

- To make a good first impression, *make eye contact.*

- To make a good first impression, make an *appropriate* amount of eye contact.

- To make a good first impression, make an appropriate amount of eye contact for the particular type of *relationship* you have with the others in the situation.

- To make a good first impression, make an appropriate amount of eye contact for the particular type of relationship you have with the others *in the situation for that particular culture.*

We all know that making a good impression on others is vital to our success in life, and that making a good impression depends on our nonverbal behavior. Skill in nonverbal communication can significantly affect who we develop intimate relationships with (Place, Todd, Penke, & Asendorpf, 2009), our academic success (Witt, Wheeless, & Allen, 2004), our occupational success (Barrick, Shaffer, & DeGrassi, 2009; Peterson, 1997), and our mental and physical health (Floyd et al., 2005). But how can we translate such findings into learnable skills? It is easy to recommend things like "a firm handshake," "good eye contact," and "a smile." What is far, far more difficult to know in advance is how *much of and in what manner* such behaviors are needed in any given communication encounter (how firm a handshake, how much eye contact, how big a smile, etc.).

This chapter seeks to provide some guidance for these questions. In particular, it seeks to address *which nonverbal skills are important for communicating competence.*

KEY CONCEPTS

Nonverbal behavior consists of the entire domain of a person's observable actions, conscious and unconscious. This includes, for example, averting eye contact and the blush a person reveals at feeling embarrassed, as well as the firm handshake and the smile at greeting someone. *Nonverbal communication* consists of all nonverbal behaviors that result in you or others attributing meaning to actions that do not involve words (Buck & VanLear, 2002). Some nonverbal communication is highly symbolic, such as *iconic* gestures in particular cultural contexts (e.g., the peace sign, the hitchhiking thumb, the "crazy" sign of circling a finger at one's head, etc.).

Nonverbal communication has many potential relationships with verbal communication. In relationship to verbal communication, nonverbal communication can *complement* interaction (e.g., pointing in a given direction while describing how to get to the bookstore), *contradict* (e.g., your eyes dilate while trying to keep a deadpan face when dealt a good hand in a game of poker), *substitute* (e.g., nodding "yes" or "no" instead of saying "yes" or "no"), or *regulate* (e.g., raising your hand to indicate you want a turn to talk in class).

Although nonverbal communication generally lacks many features of language (e.g., it has less formal syntax and semantic rules), it is also very similar to language in many ways. American sign language, for example, is a set of nonverbal skills for representing language. Lip-reading and reading Braille are ways of understanding language through the nonverbal behaviors of sight and touch. Wearing a uniform or a badge is a way of communicating a lot of information nonverbally that can also be communicated verbally. If a picture can say a thousand words, it illustrates the complex interrelation between these modes of communicating.

A nonverbal communication *skill* is a repeatable sequence of behaviors capable of achieving some specified goals. You might be able to toss a basketball into a hoop by accident, but this does not qualify you as a professional basketball player. To be considered skilled, you must be able to consciously identify a goal and to be able to call forth a set of actions that provide a reasonable likelihood of achieving these goals at least some of the time (e.g., Spitzberg, 2003). As a skill, it is always capable of improvement, so that the level and quality of goal achievement can increase as you refine your skills through experience, practice, feedback, and analysis. So professional poker players and actors generally get better at their crafts the more they systematically study their crafts, seek qualified feedback, and train toward improvement.

The reality is, people rarely care about a skill by itself—what they care about is whether or not a given skill produces desirable outcomes. We don't care per se whether or not someone can ask a question or make eye contact. We care whether they perform these skills in ways that lead to personally, relationally, or socially desirable outcomes. In evaluating skills, we are generally concerned less with whether or not the skill is performed, and more about whether or not the skill is performed *competently* (Spitzberg, 2009a, 2009b). The judgment of a skill's competence is, in turn, generally based on two judgments—appropriateness and effectiveness. *Appropriateness* is the judgment that a skill is legitimate or fitting in a given context. Smiling during a funeral tends to be evaluated differently than smiling at a party (unless the funeral is a wake or a similar cultural episode). *Effectiveness* is the judgment that a skill has successfully accomplished a preferred outcome. This is not to say that the skill achieved a satisfying outcome, because there are no-win situations in which the most effective thing to do is to do what produces the least costly or harmful outcomes. From this perspective, there are two key components to nonverbal skills: the things we are able to *do* nonverbally (i.e., skills), and the judgments we make about the quality of those skills (i.e., competence, which is a function of appropriateness and effectiveness).

GUIDING PRINCIPLES

Before identifying valuable nonverbal skills, a few important principles require consideration. First, having nonverbal skills is not the same thing as using them. You may be *able* to smile and make eye contact, but you may not be motivated to in a given situation, and you may not know how in a particular context (e.g., how much to smile when someone compliments you—too much and you might look egotistical, too little and you might look unappreciative). Thus, *competence is a function of motivation, knowledge, and skills.*

Second, *the competence of nonverbal skills depends on the context* (Spitzberg & Brunner, 1991). In general, we view people who match our own nonverbal behavior, and who engage in affectionate behavior, to be more competent (Floyd & Erbert, 2003; Floyd et al., 2005). However, in any given context, these kinds of behavior can be threatening or harassing (Erbert & Floyd, 2004; Spitzberg, 1993, 1994). Traditionally, there are at least five levels of understanding the nature of a context: cultural, chronological, situational, relational, and functional.

At the *cultural* level, the context is the patterns of intergenerational beliefs, values, attitudes, and behavioral rituals of a group of people (Spitzberg & Chagnon, 2009). Different cultures have somewhat different expectations for what constitutes competent nonverbal behavior in any of the other levels of a communication context. At the *chronological* level, the context involves all those aspects of timing that affect communication, such as what constitutes "showing up on time," speaking pace or rate, the timing with which certain actions are considered appropriate or inappropriate (e.g., when should a "first kiss" occur in a dating relationship), and so forth. At the *situational* level, communication occurs in different physical environments. Temperature, expansiveness of physical space, background noise, the comfort or discomfort of seating or standing arrangements, the color of the environment, and so forth, all can significantly affect what nonverbal communication skills are most appropriate. At the *relational* level, different skills are likely to be considered competent in different types of relationships, and at different stages of relationships. You probably have a very different level of informality with a best friend or a romantic partner than you do with your coworkers, or with your teacher, or your boss, or your classmates who are mere acquaintances. Finally, at the *functional* level, which nonverbal skills are most competent depend significantly on what the purpose or objectives of the communication encounter are. You are likely to need somewhat different nonverbal skills to manage a conflict encounter than you do a courtship or a flirtation encounter.

Related to this contextual principle is a corollary: *Too much of any skill is likely to be incompetent.* Textbooks often say things like "make eye contact when meeting someone" and "dress up for a job interview," but it should be obvious to any casual observer that one can make too much eye contact and dress up too elaborately or formally for a job interview. Research clearly indicates that most nonverbal skills are curvilinear to competence—that is, a moderate amount of the skill is viewed as more competent than too little, or too much (Spitzberg, 2003, 2009a; Spitzberg & Cupach, in press). Related to this principle is the fact that having more skills does not mean they will be used in the most competent ways. For example, research shows that the more socially skilled adolescents are, the better they are at lying successfully (Feldman, Tomasian, & Coats, 1999).

Third, *nonverbal skills in practice are always intertwined with verbal skills.* Just as someone can look very physically attractive, until they open their mouth, so can any nonverbal skill be undone by the verbal skills that accompany it (or don't accompany it). For example, the ability to detect deception depends significantly on verbal interrogation skills; relying on nonverbal behaviors alone achieves accuracy rates no better than chance (Bond & DePaulo, 2006, 2008).

Fourth, *nonverbal skills can be understood at macro and micro levels.* Some nonverbal skills are best considered for the sake of learning at relatively specific levels of analysis. For example, it is relatively easy to think about smiling, eye contact, dress, and gestures as relatively specific and isolated types of skills that can be learned and enacted. Other skills, however, are far more macro or composite in nature. For example, research has investigated the ability to *accurately perceive,* or to "read," nonverbal behavior, including the skills of interpreting emotions (Elfenbein & Ambady, 2002; Elfenbein et al., 2010), romantic interest (Place, Todd, Penke, & Asendorpf, 2009), and detecting deception (Bond & DePaulo, 2006, 2008; Hartwig & Bond, 2011; Park, Levine, McCornack, Morrison, & Ferrara, 2002). Research has also examined the ability to *accurately express* emotions in ways that can be easily or accurately interpreted by others (Elfenbein et al., 2010), to communicate power (Carney, Hall, & LeBeau, 2005), to deceive (Sporer & Schwandt, 2006, 2007), communicate affection (or immediacy: Witt, Wheeless, & Allen, 2004) or warmth (Floyd & Morman, 1998). Others have studied the ability to *match* (i.e., reciprocate similar skills and actions, such as smiling when another person smiles) or to *compensate* (i.e., to reflect the opposite type of skill or action, such as leaning back when someone leans toward you) another's nonverbal actions (Andersen, Guerrero, Buller, & Jorgensen, 1998; Floyd & Erbert, 2003).

NONVERBAL SKILLS

The study of nonverbal communication has historically divided nonverbal skills into domains of study that reflect a particular channel or mode of behavior: *haptics* (the study of touch); *oculesics* (the study of eye contact, gaze, dilation, etc.); *kinesics* (the study of body movement, including facial expressions, body lean, nodding, gestures, etc.); *proxemics* (the study of use of space, such as personal space); *chronemics* (the study of the use of time as communication); and *paralinguistics* (the study of the nonverbal aspects of speech, such as rate, pitch, prosody, volume, etc.). These domains work well enough for examining the more *micro* nonverbal skills, but they tend to blur when considering *macro* level nonverbal skills, which tend to be comprised of multiple forms of behavior that cross over these domains of activity.

There are two broad ways of considering macro-level nonverbal skills. One is the *dimensional* approach, which attempts to identify the underlying dimensions of nonverbal communication skills. You can think of an underlying dimension as an essential evaluative theme that ranges along two ends of a continuum, often from low to high, or across opposites. For example, Gallagher et al. (2005) identified six dimensions of doctor-patient interactions: *immediacy/affection* (e.g., communicated coldness vs. warmth), *similarity/depth* (e.g., showed liking vs. disinterest), *receptivity/trust* (e.g., communicated sincerity and openness vs. closedness), *composure* (e.g., calm and posed vs. tense), *formality* (e.g., casual vs. formal), and *dominance* (e.g., communicated higher status vs. equal status). These and other basic dimensions have been identified across a variety of nonverbal interactions (e.g., Burgoon & Hale, 1987).

Another approach to dimensions attempts to bridge the macro- and micro-levels of nonverbal communication skills. Research indicates that most nonverbal behaviors can be grouped into four skill clusters, or dimensions (Spitzberg, 2008; Spitzberg, Brookshire, & Brunner, 1990). These skills include *attentiveness skills* (i.e., attention to, interest in, and concern for the conversational partner), *composure skills* (i.e., confidence, assertiveness, and relaxation), *expressiveness skills* (i.e., animation and variation in verbal and nonverbal forms of expression, including face, voice, body, and opinion), and *coordination skills* (i.e., the non-disruptive negotiation of speaking turns, conversational initiation, and conversational closings). These skills appear to represent the vital functions of asserting oneself (i.e., composure, expressiveness) as well as of orienting to the other person(s) in the encounter (i.e., attentiveness and coordination). In any communication encounter, competent nonverbal skills will function at their most macro level to enable the appropriate and effective promotion of one's own interests, as well as the interests of the other persons involved in the encounter.

A second approach to macro-level nonverbal skills is to identify specific skills that are important to particular contexts or interaction functions. Research has, for example, examined the nonverbal skills involved in competent flirtation (e.g., Egland, Spitzberg & Zormeier, 1996), courtship (e.g., Moore, 2010), negotiation (e.g., Curhan & Pentland, 2007), teaching (Andersen, Andersen, & Jensen, 1979), health interactions (e.g., Crane & Crane, 2010), and successful sales (e.g., Taute, Heiser, & McArthur, 2011), just to name a few. The likelihood is that scholars in the pursuit of identifying important nonverbal skills will have investigated any given area of professional or career pursuit, hobby, sport, or interest. If you have the motivation, then you can obtain the knowledge and the skills through further education, both through your own efforts and the efforts of your instructors.

Given the principles discussed earlier, it is possible to consider research across these academic traditions and to speculate on the most general competent nonverbal skills. Research at the micro-level of nonverbal skills has tended to show, all other things being equal (i.e., across a wide variety of contexts, and not accounting for any particular feature of a given context), that the communication skills listed in Table 1 tend to be strongly associated with competent communication (Spitzberg, 2007; Spitzberg et al., 1990; Spitzberg & Dillard, 2002).

TABLE 1

Generally competent micro-level nonverbal skills

Appropriate lean toward partner (neither too forward nor too far back)

Appropriate posture (neither too closed/formal nor too open/informal)

Avoiding nonverbal adaptors (i.e., nervous "ticks" like twirling hair or tapping a foot or pen)

Avoiding response latencies (i.e., minimizing awkward silences between speaking turns)

Expressive or regulative head movements, such as head nods in response to partner statements

Facial expressiveness (neither blank nor exaggerated)

Moderate eye gaze (i.e., steady direction of eyes toward other interactants)

Moderated speaking volume

Moderately disproportionate talk time (i.e., talking 60–70% of the proportionate time based on the interaction time allowed and the number of participants)

Occasional eye contact

Occasional moderated smiles and/or laughter

Occasional, well-timed gestures to emphasize or regulate what is being said

Speaking fluency (pauses, silences, "uh," etc.)

Speaking rate (neither too slow nor too fast)

Vocal confidence (neither too tense/nervous nor overly confident sounding)

Vocal variety (neither overly monotone nor dramatic voice)

For any more macro-level contextual type of skill, research has indicated various skills that are associated with the function of interest. For example, in communicating affection in romantic relationships, skills such as holding hands, kissing on lips and cheeks, putting an arm around the shoulder, sitting close, hugging, and looking into each other's eyes are generally appropriate (Floyd & Morman, 1998). In contrast, communicating warmth and affection (also referred to as immediacy) in an educational context involves making eye contact, relaxed body posture, gestures, casual touching (e.g., on the shoulder), smiles, less formal dress, open body position and posture, vocal expressiveness, and proximal movement through the classroom (Andersen et al., 1979). In contrast, if you want to communicate power rather than immediacy or affection, nonverbal skills portray inattention to others, initiation of handshake, invasive proximity behavior, touch initiation, gaze, eye contact while speaking, assertive or aggressive facial expression, gestures, fewer self-touching behaviors, upturned head orientation, and erect posture (Carney et al., 2005).

CONCLUSION

Nonverbal communication research has generated a rich set of findings about how to communicate competently. In general, communication competence will be facilitated by nonverbal behaviors that reveal an interest in and attentiveness toward others, that display an ability to smoothly manage the ebb and flow of conversation, that reveal emotions and intended meanings through expressive behavior, and that demonstrate a calm and collected demeanor suggesting that one is in control of his or her own behavior. Beyond this, these actions should be adapted to the particular function of the situation, the place, the type of relationship, and the cultural expectations.

As the rapid evolution of media continues to converge across face-to-face and distance contexts, and as the media themselves become richer in allowing all people to communicate their entire verbal and nonverbal "presence" in encounters, the more important that nonverbal communication is likely to become. Even though nonverbal communication tends to be more unconsciously controlled than verbal communication, it is still subject to learning, practice, and feedback. Assuming you are motivated to enhance your nonverbal skills in any given context, it is likely that scholars have already conducted important research in the area, pointing to specific activities or behaviors that you could identify and begin to incorporate into your everyday communication. As but one example that may apply to many of you reading this chapter, research has shown that a casual touch of a patron can significantly increase the tips that waiters earn and increase the sales a sales associate makes (Guéguen, Jacob, & Boulbry, 2007). It seems that research sometimes can pay off.

REFERENCES

Andersen, J. F., Andersen, P. A., & Jensen, A. D. (1979). The measurement of nonverbal immediacy. *Journal of Applied Communications Research, 7,* 153–180.

Andersen, P. A., Guerrero, L. K., Buller, D. B., & Jorgensen, P. (1998). An empirical comparison of three theories of nonverbal immediacy exchange. *Human Communication Research, 24,* 501–536.

Barrick, M. R., Shaffer, J. A., & DeGrassi, S. W. (2009). What you see may not be what you get: Relationships among self-presentation tactics and ratings of interview and job performance. *Journal of Applied Psychology, 94,* 1394–1411.

Bond, C. F., Jr., & DePaulo, B. M. (2006). Accuracy of deception judgments. *Personality and Social Psychology Review, 10,* 214–234.

Bond, C. F., Jr., & DePaulo, B. M. (2008). Individual differences in judging deception: Accuracy and bias. *Psychological Bulletin, 134,* 477–492.

Buck, R., & VanLear, C. A. (2002). Verbal and nonverbal communication: Distinguishing symbolic, spontaneous, and pseudo-spontaneous nonverbal behavior. *Journal of Communication, 52,* 522–541.

Burgoon, J. K., & Hale, J. L. (1987). Validation and measurement of the fundamental themes of relational communication. *Communication Monographs, 54,* 18–41.

Carney, D. R., Hall, J. A., & LeBeau, L. S. (2005). Beliefs about the nonverbal expression of social power. *Journal of Nonverbal Behavior, 29,* 105–123.

Crane, J., & Crane, F. G. (2010). Optimal nonverbal communications strategies physicians should engage in to promote positive clinical outcomes. *Health Marketing Quarterly, 27,* 262–274.

Curhan, J. R., & Pentland, A. (2007). Thin slices of negotiation: Predicting outcomes from conversational dynamics within the first 5 minutes. *Journal of Applied Psychology, 92,* 802–811.

Egland, K. L., Spitzberg, B. H., & Zormeier, M. M. (1996). Flirtation and conversational competence in cross-sex platonic and romantic relationships. *Communication Reports, 9,* 105–118.

Egland, K. L., Stelzner, M. A., Andersen, P. A., & Spitzberg, B. H. (1995). Perceived understanding, nonverbal communication, and relational satisfaction. In J. E. Aitken, & L. J. Shedletsky (Eds.), *Intrapersonal communication processes* (pp. 386–396). Plymouth, MI: Midnight Oil/Annandale, VA: Speech Communication Association.

Elfenbein, H. A., & Ambady, N. (2002). On the universality and cultural specificity of emotion recognition: A meta-analysis. *Psychological Bulletin, 128,* 203–235.

Elfenbein, H. A., Foo, M. D., Mandal, M., Biswal, R., Eisenkraft, N., Lim, A., & Sharma, S. (2010). Individual difference in the accuracy of expressing and perceiving nonverbal cues: New data on an old question. *Journal of Research in Personality, 44,* 199–206.

Erbert, L. A., & Floyd, K. (2004). Affectionate expressions as face-threatening acts: Receiver assessments. *Communication Studies, 55,* 254–270.

Feldman, R. S., Tomasian, J. C., & Coats, E. J. (1999). Nonverbal deception abilities and adolescents' social competence: Adolescents with higher social skills are better liars. *Journal of Nonverbal Behavior, 23,* 237-249.

Floyd, K., & Erbert, L. (2003). Relational message interpretations of nonverbal matching behavior: An application of the social meaning model. *Journal of Social Psychology, 143,* 581–597.

Floyd, K., & Morman, M. T. (1998). The measurement of affectionate communication. *Communication Quarterly, 46,* 144–162.

Floyd, K., Hess, J. A., Miczo, L. A., Halone, K. K., Mikkelson, A. C., & Tusing, K. J. (2005). Human affection exchange: VIII. Further evidence of the benefits of expressed affection. *Communication Quarterly, 53,* 285–303.

Gallagher, T. J., Hartung, P. J., Gerzina, H., Gregory, S. W., Jr., & Merolla, D. (2005). Further analysis of a doctor-patient nonverbal communication instrument. *Patient Education and Counseling, 57,* 262–271.

Guéguen, N., Jacob, C., & Boulbry, G. (2007). The effect of touch on compliance with a restaurant's employee suggestion. *International Journal of Hospitality Management, 26,* 1019–1023.

Hall, J. A., Blanch, D. C., Horgan, T. G., Murphy, N. A., Rosip, J. C., & Mast, M. S. (2009). Motivation and interpersonal sensitivity: Does it matter how hard you try? *Motivation and Emotion, 33,* 291–302.

Hartwig, M., & Bond, C. F., Jr. (2011). Why do lie-catchers fail? A lens model meta-analysis of human lie judgments. *Psychological Bulletin, 137,* 643–659.

Levine, T. R., Shaw, A., & Shulman, H. C. (2010). Increasing deception detection accuracy with strategic questioning. *Human Communication Research, 36,* 216–231.

Motley, M. T. (1993). Facial affect and verbal context in conversation: Facial expression as interjection. *Human Communication Research, 20,* 3–40.

Moore, M. M. (2010). Human nonverbal courtship behavior—A brief historical review. *Journal of Sex Research, 47,* 171–180.

Park, H. S., Levine, T. R., McCornack, S. A., Morrison, K., & Ferrara, M. (2002). How people really detect lies. *Communication Monographs, 69,* 144–157.

Peterson, M. S. (1997). Personnel interviewers' perceptions of the importance and adequacy of applicants' communication skills. *Communication Education, 46,* 287–291.

Place, S. S., Todd, P. M., Penke, L., & Asendorpf, J. B. (2009). The ability to judge the romantic interest of others. *Psychological Science, 20,* 22–27.

Spitzberg, B. H. (1993). The dialectics of (in)competence. *Journal of Social and Personal Relationships, 10,* 137–158.

Spitzberg, B. H. (1994). The dark side of (in)competence. In W. R. Cupach, & B. H. Spitzberg (Eds.), *The dark side of interpersonal communication* (pp. 25–49). Hillsdale, NJ: Erlbaum.

Spitzberg, B. H. (2003). Methods of skill assessment. In J. O. Greene & B. R. Burleson (Eds.), *Handbook of communication and social interaction skills* (pp. 93–134). Mahwah, NJ: Erlbaum.

Spitzberg, B. H. (2007). *CSRS: The conversational skills rating scale—An instructional assessment of interpersonal competence* (NCA Diagnostic Series, 2nd Edition). Annandale, VA: National Communication Association.

Spitzberg, B. H. (2008). Perspectives on nonverbal communication skills. In L. K. Guerrero, & M. L. Hecht (Eds.), *The nonverbal communication reader: Classic and contemporary readings* (pp. 21–26). Long Grove, IL: Waveland.

Spitzberg, B. H. (2009a). Axioms for a theory of intercultural communication competence [invited article, Japanese Association of Communication and English Teachers]. *Annual Review of English Learning and Teaching, No.14,* 69–81.

Spitzberg, B. H. (2009b). Interpersonal communication competence and social skills. In W. Donsbach (Ed.), *International encyclopedia of communication* (pp. 2486–2492). Oxford: Blackwell Publishing.

Spitzberg, B. H., Brookshire, R. G., & Brunner, C. C. (1990). The factorial domain of interpersonal skills. *Social Behavior and Personality, 18,* 137–150.

Spitzberg, B. H., & Brunner, C. C. (1991). Toward a theoretical integration of context and competence inference research. *Western Journal of Speech Communication, 56,* 28–46.

Spitzberg, B. H., & Chagnon, G. (2009). Conceptualizing intercultural communication competence. In D. K. Deardorff (Ed.), *The SAGE handbook of intercultural competence* (pp. 2–52). Thousand Oaks, CA: Sage.

Spitzberg, B. H., & Cupach, W. R. (1989). *Handbook of interpersonal competence research.* New York: Springer-Verlag.

Spitzberg, B. H., & Cupach, W. R. (in press). Interpersonal skills. In M. L. Knapp, & J. A. Daly (Eds.), *Handbook of interpersonal communication* (4th ed). Newbury Park, CA: Sage.

Spitzberg, B. H., & Cupach, W. R. (2012). Epilogue: The power of the dark side. In T. J. Socha, & M. Pitts (Eds.), *The positive side of interpersonal communication* (pp. 313–321). New York: Peter Lang.

Spitzberg, B. H., & Dillard, J. P. (2002). Meta-analysis, social skills, and interpersonal competence. In M. Allen, R. Preiss, K. Dindia, B. Gayle, & N. Burrell (Eds.), *Interpersonal communication: Advances through meta-analysis* (pp. 89–107). Mahwah, NJ: Erlbaum.

Sporer, S. L., & Schwandt, B. (2006). Paraverbal indicators of deception: A meta-analytic synthesis. *Applied Cognitive Psychology, 20,* 421–446.

Sporer, S. L., & Schwandt, B. (2007). Moderators of nonverbal indicators of deception: A meta-analytic synthesis. *Psychology, Public Policy, and Law, 13,* 1–34.

Taute, H. A., Heiser, R. S., & McArthur, D. N. (2011). The effect of nonverbal signals on student role-play evaluations. *Journal of Marketing Education, 33,* 28–40.

Witt, P. L., Wheeless, L. R., & Allen, M. (2004). A meta-analytical review of the relationship between teacher immediacy and student learning. *Communication Monographs, 71,* 184–207.

SECTION 12
ORGANIZATIONAL COMMUNICATION

The organizational communication context focuses on how members of organizations communicate in work environments. Organizational communication scholars examine how workplace relationships are influenced at the macro (e.g., entire organization) and micro levels (e.g., individual coworker relationships). Some major areas of research in organizational communication include organizational identification, organizational culture, organizational power, organizational assimilation, and organizational structures. This chapter focuses on three important areas of organizational communication research: (1) organizational dissent, (2) the meaning of work, and (3) work/life balance. First, Jeffrey Kassing (Arizona State University) reviews research on organizational dissent by answering the question: *What issues cause employee dissent in the workplace and how do employees dissent?* Second, George Cheney (Kent State University; The University of Waikato) and Theodore Zorn (The University of Waikato) review research on meaningful work to answer the question: *What is the meaning of work and how do we make work meaningful?* Third, Patrice Buzzanell (Purdue University) examines work/life balance research to answer the question: *How can we sustain commitments to the work and personal aspects of our lives?* As college students, you're not just here to have fun (we hope!). We know that you have another goal too: to obtain a fulfilling career after college. The organizational communication research reviewed in this chapter will better prepare you for when employees complain and express contradictory views, as well as help you understand how to have a meaningful career while maintaining a social life. All of this research collectively may help you prepare for communication tied to all organizations.

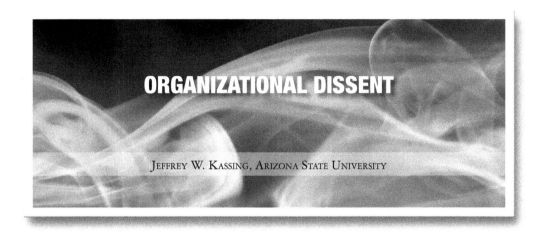

ORGANIZATIONAL DISSENT

Jeffrey W. Kassing, Arizona State University

At a fundamental level expressing disagreement is part and parcel of American culture. Our cultural values ensure this. Yet, there is one place, perhaps the place where we spend most of our adult lives, which restricts freedom of speech. That place is the workplace. It is here that we hold our tongues, carefully choose what we say, and temper our opinions. We do so because the risks of speaking out at work are considerable (Waldron & Kassing, 2011). We may put our jobs, careers, and livelihood on the line when we speak out. So we confront an unusual paradox when we go to work. We value and uphold the principles of free speech culturally, yet we check those very principles at the proverbial office door each morning. The prevalence and acceptance of this paradox raises interesting questions about how and why employees express dissent within organizations, and it frames organizational dissent as a pertinent line of communication inquiry. This chapter highlights that line of inquiry by considering the question: What issues cause employee dissent in the workplace and how do employees dissent?

Before discussing why and how employees dissent, some definitions should be put in place. Organizational dissent refers to the expression of disagreement or contradictory opinions about workplace policies and practices (Kassing, 1998). Expressing dissent, then, entails separating or distancing oneself from the majority and taking a stance that is in opposition to the prevailing position. Organizational dissent naturally requires contradiction and disagreement (Kassing, 1997, 2011a). This does not, however, mean that it will be destructive to the organization. Rather, this is one of several commonly held misconceptions about organizational dissent. To the contrary, organizational dissent can offer important corrective feedback that helps organizations identify problematic practices and policies that could prove damaging and debilitating if left unaddressed (Hegstrom, 1995; Kassing, 1997).

What other assumptions do we make about dissent that should be reconsidered? Well, people often associate dissent with conflict. Dissent can certainly bring about conflict, but it does not always do so (Kassing, 1997; Redding, 1985). Additionally, people tend to believe that dissent occurs clearly and often exclusively in response to unethical actions. While this is one key reason why people express dissent, it is only one of many (Kassing & Armstrong, 2002). Another common misconception is the idea that dissent stems from dissatisfaction. This may be the case, but dissatisfied employees are not the only ones who express dissent. In fact, research suggests that employees dissent out of a desire to fix problems in the workplace and to protect their companies from risk (Sprague & Ruud, 1988). Furthermore, we tend to liken dissent to open protest, something shared loudly and widely. But realistically it can be comparatively quiet, shared with colleagues around the office and with friends and family outside of work (Kassing, 1998). Similarly, we expect dissent to be adversarial. But it can be constructive in nature too as it may be delivered with suggestions for improving the situation (Kassing, 2002). Dissent therefore can be offered in the spirit of helpfulness (Redding, 1985). Thus, dissent expression is related to but independent from conflict, happens in response to all manner of events and issues, and is shared by both satisfied and dissatisfied employees. And it can be expressed openly or selectively as well as constructively or destructively (Kassing, 2007, 2011a).

With these conceptual parameters in mind, we can now consider what causes employees to express dissent in the first place. Kassing (1997) suggested that there are three crucial pieces to the dissent equation: the dissent triggering event, the spheres of influence that affect dissent expression, and the dissent audience. Accordingly, a dissent trigger starts the process in motion (Kassing, 1997; Kassing & Armstrong, 2002). This is an event that is deemed serious enough to warrant attention—a situation that is grave enough to move an employee to express dissent despite the attendant risks. Many factors can serve as dissent triggers, including employee treatment, organizational change, decision making, inefficiency, roles and responsibilities, performance evaluation, ethics, and preventing harm to customers and coworkers (Kassing & Armstrong, 2002). In addition, dissent routinely triggers as a result of some shortcoming in supervision (Kassing, 2007).

Once a dissent trigger escalates to the point where an employee feels strongly that it must be addressed, the employee considers individual, relational, and organizational spheres of influence, in conjunction with personal goals (Garner, 2009), before deciding with whom to share dissent. Sorting through these spheres of influence allows employees to address two basic questions. First, will I be perceived as adversarial or constructive? Second, what is the likelihood of experiencing some measure of retaliation for expressing dissent? While some modern organizations have made considerable strides in being more dissent tolerant, affording employees greater latitude in expressing and sharing their opinions (Cheney, 1995; Hegstrom, 1990), the majority of workplaces continue to restrict employee voice even as they intend to honor and promote it (Stohl & Cheney, 2001; Van Dyne, Ang, & Botero, 2003). Thus, many employees operate under the assumption that they may experience retaliation for speaking out about issues. Accordingly, they rely upon individual, relational, and organizational influences to inform their decisions about how and with whom to express dissent (Kassing, 1997).

These spheres of influence help employees choose an audience for their dissent. Dissent audiences include: management, coworkers, and family and friends outside of work (Kassing, 1997, 1998; Kassing & Armstrong, 2002). Expressing dissent to management is known as articulated or upward dissent. This is dissent that is shared directly and openly with supervisors, management, or others higher in the chain of command. It happens when employees determine that they will be viewed as constructive and are unlikely to experience retaliation. For example, managers tend to express more upward dissent than their non-management counterparts (Kassing & Armstrong, 2001; Kassing & Avtgis, 1999). So too do employees who feel comfortable and confident with their organizational standing (Kassing, 2000a; Payne, 2007).

Sharing dissent with coworkers of the same or a similar rank has been called latent or lateral dissent. The term latent refers to the fact that dissent readily exists in organizations but goes unheard by management. Lateral denotes that this form of dissent expression moves laterally within organizations—being shared vertically across levels of the organization rather than being directed upward to management. Latent/lateral dissent occurs when employees feel that it is too risky to express their disagreement with management directly, but still feel that dissent should be heard by others in the organization. In these instances they turn to coworkers as a sounding board. Latent/lateral dissent appears to be favored by non-management workers, by employees who are not as invested in their organizations, and by organizational members who exercise less influence in their workplaces (Kassing, 1998; Kassing & Armstrong, 2001; Kassing & Avtgis, 1999).

Displaced dissent gets directed to family members and non-work friends. It is a type of dissent expression that winds up being displaced outside organizations as employees intentionally seek out and express dissent to people who are not affiliated with their respective workplaces. This type of dissent occurs when people recognize that they most certainly will be perceived as adversarial and risk retaliation. Thus, they turn to the safer and insulated channels of expression that organizational outsiders provide. Outsiders offer counsel, advice, and support with little risk to the dissenter. So while displaced dissent fails to help the organization, it serves an important function for organizational members. Research findings indicate that people rely on displaced dissent when they are new and inexperienced and when they are considering terminating their employment (Kassing & Dicioccio, 2004; Kassing, Piemonte, Goman, & Mitchell, 2012). That is, at times when seeking the guidance of others can prove particularly pertinent.

While these types of dissent expression have traditionally been conceptualized as distinct from one another, the advent of social media has shown how they can in fact overlap (Gosset & Kilker, 2006). Researchers, for example, studied what are known as gripe sites or sucks sites. These are Web pages that current or former employees, as well as customers, use to vent their frustration and to express their disagreement with a given organization's practices. Such sites have proliferated in the past decade and many organizations have devoted considerable time and energy to shutting these sites down. Gosset and Kilker's (2006) work revealed that what by definition would be considered displaced dissent, as it was not shared within the traditional confines of the organization, wound up functioning more like upward dissent. Accordingly, former and current employees expressed dissent in their postings knowing full well that management would be reading their comments. Thus, displaced and upward dissent combined in a novel way as a result of social media's capability to provide anonymity while targeting a particular readership (i.e., management).

Employees come to share dissent with one of these audiences based on their assessment of how individual, relational, and organizational influences converge. Individual influences include the personality and communication traits that people bring into their respective organizations. For example, people who like to argue seem to be more inclined to express dissent to management (Kassing & Avtgis, 1999). Similarly, those who are confident that they control what happens to them more so than external factors (i.e., possess an internal locus of control) favor expressing dissent to management (Kassing & Avtgis, 2001). In contrast, people who are more verbally aggressive by nature and those who believe that external factors exercise greater control in their lives appear to share dissent with their coworkers more readily (Kassing & Avtgis, 1999, 2001).

In addition, individual influences also take into account how people feel about their respective organizations. Are they more or less satisfied, committed, loyal, and engaged? Research illustrates that people who are more satisfied with work express upward dissent to management compared to those who are less satisfied (Kassing, 1998). Similarly, those who have a stronger connection with their workplace—those who identify more clearly and strongly with the organization as well as those who have higher levels of organization-based self esteem—favor upward dissent expression (Kassing, 2000a; Payne, 2007). Apparently work engagement associates strongly with upward dissent as well (Kassing et al., 2012). And those who choose to express dissent to management also appear to avoid emotion based coping strategies for dealing with stress (Kassing, 2011b).

In contrast, employees who are less committed to their organizations express more lateral and displaced dissent, as do those employees who believe that they exercise little personal influence in their respective organizations (Kassing, 1998). Dissent expression also varies in response to employee burnout. Apparently employees suffering from burnout reduce their expression of lateral dissent to coworkers (Avtgis, Thomas-Maddox, Taylor, & Richardson, 2007). Moreover, employees who express lateral and displaced dissent reportedly rely on emotional venting when dealing with stress and give greater consideration to leaving their respective organizations (Kassing, 2011b; Kassing et al, 2012).

Relational influences include the types of relationships we maintain with our supervisors, managers, coworkers, and colleagues (Kassing, 1997). In contrast to the aforementioned study on social media, early research showed that employees preferred to express dissent most readily in face-to-face interactions with their supervisors (Sprague & Ruud, 1988). Not surprisingly, when employees believe that they have strong relationships with their superiors they express more upward dissent to management and direct less lateral dissent to coworkers (Kassing, 1998, 2000b). Coworker relationships also factor into dissent expression. In fact, concern for coworkers has surfaced as a consistent reason people report feeling the need to express dissent (Kassing & Armstrong, 2002; Sprague & Ruud, 1988). In some cases, concern for coworkers is a stronger reason for expressing dissent than unethical issues (Kassing & Armstrong, 2002).

The final set of influences—organizational—considers the impact that organizational structure, culture, and climate have on dissent expression (Kassing, 1997, 2000a). Organizational structure concerns the systematic arrangements that dictate reporting, tasks, and relationships within organizations. These are the formal and tangible aspects of organizations that influence how work gets accomplished. Apparently, dissenters feel more confident and influential sharing their concerns in smaller versus larger organizations (Miceli & Near, 1992). Other organizational facets, like the degree to which an organization operates bureaucratically with centralized or decentralized reporting can affect dissent expression as well (King, 1999). Organizational climate and culture are the facets of organizational life that take shape through the daily interactions of members sharing stories, recounting events, and enacting rituals. Organizational climate and culture inform employees about how tolerant their organizations will be with regard to hearing employee dissent. This often manifests in how organizations make decisions and the degree to which employees feel these decision making processes are fair. How fair employees perceive their organizations to be when it comes to making decisions has a clear impact on how they express dissent (Goodboy, Chory, & Dunleavy, 2009; Kassing & McDowell, 2008). Some organizations are clearly more tolerant of dissent than others and employees come to learn these tolerance levels as they develop an understanding of an organization's culture (Hegstrom, 1990; Pacanowsky, 1988). Not surprisingly, when employees recognize that their organizations are more tolerant of dissent they share more upward dissent with management (Kassing, 1998, 2000a).

Although dissenters can share their concerns with various audiences, upward dissent presents the greatest challenge to employees (Kassing, 2007, 2009a, 2009b, 2011a). As a result, employees express upward dissent strategically, choosing from a variety of different approaches (Kassing, 2002). These range from providing solutions and evidence to going around your boss and threatening to quit and vary with regard to perceived effectiveness and utility (Kassing, 2005).

Direct-factual appeal is a proactive and competent strategy (Kassing, 2005), which involves "supporting one's dissent claim with factual information derived from some combination of physical evidence, knowledge of organizational policies and practices, and personal work experience" (Kassing, 2002, p. 195). When using this strategy, employees actively collect evidence and summon their experience. In doing so, they buoy their concerns with facts, evidence, and workplace experience. As a result, they avoid unfounded opinions, unnecessarily aggressive attacks, and misdirected complaints. Furthermore, accompanying one's dissent claim with evidence shifts attention away from the individual dissenter and toward the issue at hand.

Solution presentation involves presenting a solution to the perceived problem that has triggered dissent. This strategy demonstrates a willingness to be proactive in addressing the concern on behalf of the dissenter and therefore is seen as widely effective and appropriate (Kassing, 2002, 2005). Employees have offered solutions that address a range of issues and vary in their viability. This highlights the fact that the feasibility of a solution is less pertinent than the act of offering one in the first place (Kassing, 2011a). Solutions presentation can be used in conjunction with direct factual appeals so that solutions accompany the direct evidence generated for a given issue (Kassing, 2002).

Circumvention is the act of going around one's immediate boss or supervisor in order to air a concern with someone higher in the chain of command (Kassing, 2002, 2007, 2009a). It is not used as frequently as direct-factual appeal and solution presentation strategies, but it is used somewhat routinely. People justified circumventing their bosses for three predominant reasons: supervisor inaction, supervisor poor performance, and supervisor indiscretion (Kassing, 2009a). Supervisor inaction led to circumvention when employees felt that their supervisors' continual dismissal of or disregard for their concerns warranted the attention of other audiences. In these instances, employees attempted multiple times to share their concerns with an inattentive or dismissive supervisor or they assumed that the supervisor would be inattentive and dismissive.

Inaction or suspected inaction resulted in circumvention in both cases. Circumvention also occurred when employees believed that their bosses were failing to perform their respective duties well or when they were taking advantage of their supervisory status, using it as the basis for capricious and unjustifiable decisions. Finally, employees circumvented supervisors when there were clear breeches of company policy. These instances included cases of deceit, theft, poor judgment, and harassment (Kassing, 2009a). Circumventing one's supervisor is no small undertaking as it resulted in superior-subordinate relational decline the majority of the time (Kassing, 2007). However, there were many cases in which it produced some form of relational stability or even improvement. This happened, for example, when supervisors recognized that circumvention was necessary to get movement from upper management on issues they were unable to address at their supervisory level.

Threatening resignation, as the name suggests, involves using the threat of quitting one's job as a means to draw attention to the severity of the situation. This strategy confronts the organization and supervisor with an ultimatum, fix the situation or lose the employee. For this reason it is not a strategy to be used regularly and in fact serves as an option of last resort in many instances (Kassing, 2009a). Although it does not occur too often, it does surface in particular types of situations (Kassing, 2002, 2011a). Employees have threatened resignation when their safety has been put in jeopardy by a job requirement or an organizational failure to address a dangerous circumstance. Threatening resignation also surfaces when employees confront a direct and serious affront to their integrity and image and when they reach an impasse with their supervisors (Kassing, 2011a). In the former case, employees respond to a direct attack on their work, personality, or standing in the company with the threat of resignation, whereas in the latter case they do so because they finally come to the point where they recognize that an intolerable and untenable situation with their direct supervisor will not change without the threat of resignation. When threatening resignation, employees reveal how far they are willing to be pushed before they decide to push back. This can occur instantaneously as in cases of safety, harm, and personal affronts, or it can be reached over time when employees finally determine that a longstanding and ongoing situation will not change unless they take dramatic action. Employees do not threaten such dramatic action though without recognizing that it could mean they would in fact have to quit their jobs (Kassing, 2002, 2011a).

The final upward dissent strategy is repetition. This strategy involves revisiting an issue on several occasions across a given period of time with the intention of drawing some resolution from management (Kassing, 2002, 2009b). When enacting repetition, employees rely upon and use the other upward dissent strategies discussed here, with the intention of keeping a topic alive without overstating it. This can be challenging as supervisors can grow weary of hearing the same concerns repeatedly, but also effective as it demonstrates employees' undeterred desire to see the issue addressed satisfactorily. Employees, then, must be cautious about the impressions they create when practicing repetition. Thus, they tend to use proactive and competent strategies initially and more often (e.g., solution presentation, direct factual appeal) and only move to less competent ones later (i.e., circumvention and threatening resignation). Employees also must give consideration to how often and how frequently they should raise the same concern (Kassing, 2009b). Should it be brought up weekly or monthly, every other day, or once every few weeks? Additionally, repetition seems to be affected by supervisors' responses. When supervisors delay addressing dissent claims, employees stretch repetition out and let it transpire for longer. In contrast, when supervisors became irritated and annoyed with hearing dissent about the same issue repeatedly, employees shortened the length of time they were willing to practice repetition.

In conclusion, employees face any number of triggering events at work that will lead them to feel they need to express dissent. They must then work through a host of influences that will help them determine with whom they should share their dissent. They can share it with management, with coworkers, or with family members and friends outside of work. If they choose to share dissent with management, employees can enact several different strategies for expressing upward dissent. Doing so will require consideration of which tactics to use, how often to use them, and how supervisors react to those tactics.

Dissent expression in organizations is an interesting line of inquiry, one that has garnered considerable attention (Kassing, 2011a). It is relevant to anyone who confronts the need to share disagreement and contradictory opinions at work. Understanding what causes dissent and how people go about expressing it is an important communication skill that will serve employees well. Once familiar with the possibilities, dissenters can know and understand why they feel the need to speak out, can determine who to talk to about their concerns, and can decide how best to express those concerns. When this happens both individuals and organizations stand to benefit.

REFERENCES

Avtgis, T. A., Thomas-Maddox, C., Taylor, E., & Richardson, B. R. (2007). The influence of employee burnout syndrome on the expression of organizational dissent. *Communication Research Reports, 24,* 97–102.

Cheney, G. (1995). Democracy in the workplace: Theory and practice from the perspective of communication. *Journal of Applied Communication Research, 23,* 167–200.

Garner, J. T. (2009). Strategic dissent: Expressions of organizational dissent motivated by influence goals. *International Journal of Strategic Management, 3,* 34–51.

Goodboy, A. K., Chory, R. M., & Dunleavy, K. N. (2009). Organizational dissent as a function of organizational justice. *Communication Research Reports, 25,* 255–265.

Gossett, L. M., & Kilker, J. (2006). My job sucks: Examining counterinstitutional web sites as locations for organizational member voice, dissent, and resistance. *Management Communication Quarterly, 20,* 63–90.

Hegstrom, T. G. (1990). Mimetic and dissent conditions in organizational rhetoric. *Journal of Applied Communication Research, 18,* 141–152.

Hegstrom, T. G. (1995). Focus on organizational dissent: A functionalist response to criticism. In J. Lehtonen (Ed.), *Critical perspectives on communication research and pedagogy* (pp. 83–94). St. Ingbert, Germany: Rohrig University Press.

Kassing, J. W. (1997). Articulating, antagonizing, and displacing: A model of employee dissent. *Communication Studies, 48,* 311–332.

Kassing, J. W. (1998). Development and validation of the Organizational Dissent Scale. *Management Communication Quarterly, 12,* 183–229.

Kassing, J. W. (2000a). Exploring the relationship between workplace freedom of speech, organizational identification, and employee dissent. *Communication Research Reports, 17,* 387–396.

Kassing, J. W. (2000b). Investigating the relationship between superior-subordinate relationship quality and employee dissent. *Communication Research Reports, 17,* 58–70.

Kassing, J. W. (2002). Speaking up: Identifying employees' upward dissent strategies. *Management Communication Quarterly, 16,* 187–209.

Kassing, J. W. (2005). Speaking up competently: A comparison of perceived competence in upward dissent strategies. *Communication Research Reports, 22,* 227–234.

Kassing, J. W. (2007). Going around the boss: Exploring the consequences of circumvention. *Management Communication Quarterly, 21,* 55–74.

Kassing, J. W. (2009a). Breaking the chain of command: Making sense of employee circumvention. *Journal of Business Communication, 46,* 311–334.

Kassing, J. W. (2009b). In case you didn't hear me the first time: An examination of repetitious upward dissent. *Management Communication Quarterly, 22,* 416–436.

Kassing, J. W. (2011a). Dissent in organizations. Cambridge: Polity.

Kassing, J. W. (2011b). Stressing out about dissent: Examining the relationship between coping strategies and dissent expression. *Communication Research Reports, 28,* 225–234.

Kassing, J. W., & Armstrong, T. A. (2001). Examining the association of job tenure, employment history, and organizational status with employee dissent. *Communication Research Reports, 18,* 264–273.

Kassing, J. W., & Armstrong, T. A. (2002). Someone's going to hear about this: Examining the association between dissent-triggering events and employees' dissent expression. *Management Communication Quarterly, 16,* 39–65.

Kassing, J. W., & Avtgis, T. A., (1999). Examining the relationship between organizational dissent and aggressive communication. *Management Communication Quarterly, 13*(1), 76–91.

Kassing, J. W., & Avtgis, T. A. (2001). Dissension in the organization as a function of control expectancies. *Communication Research Reports, 18,* 118–127.

Kassing, J. W., & DiCioccio, R. L. (2004). Testing a workplace experience explanation of displaced dissent. *Communication Reports, 17,* 111–120.

Kassing, J. W., & McDowell, Z. (2008). Talk about fairness: Exploring the relationship between procedural justice and employee dissent. *Communication Research Reports, 25,* 1–10.

Kassing, J. W., Piemonte, N. M., Goman, C. C., & Mitchell, C. A. (2012). Dissent expression as an indicator of work engagement and intention to leave. *Journal of Business Communication.*

King, G. (1999). The implications of an organization's structure on whistleblowing. *Journal of Business Ethics, 20,* 315–326.

Miceli, M. P., & Near, J. P. (1992). *Blowing the whistle: The organizational and legal implications for companies and employees.* New York: Lexington Books.

Pacanowsky, M. E. (1988). Communication in the empowering organization. In J. Anderson (Ed.), *Communication yearbook, 11* (pp. 356–379). Beverley Hills: Sage.

Payne, H. J. (2007). The role of organization-based self-esteem in employee dissent expression. *Communication Research Reports, 24,* 235–240.

Redding, W. C. (1985). Rocking boats, blowing whistles, and teaching speech communication. *Communication Education, 34,* 245–258.

Sprague, J. A., & Ruud, G. L. (1988). Boat-rocking in the high technology culture. *American Behavioral Scientist, 32,* 169–193.

Stohl, C., & Cheney, G. (2001). Participatory processes/paradoxical practices: Communication and the dilemmas of organizational democracy. *Management Communication Quarterly, 14,* 349–407.

Van Dyne, L., Ang, S., & Botero, I. C. (2003). Conceptualizing employee silence and employee voice as multidimensional constructs. *Journal of Management Studies, 40,* 1359–1392.

Waldron, V. R., & Kassing. J. W. (2011). *Managing risk in communication encounters: Strategies for the workplace.* Thousand Oaks, CA: Sage.

WHAT DO WE KNOW AND WHAT WE CAN LEARN ABOUT MEANINGFUL WORK (From the Standpoint of Communication)?

GEORGE CHENEY, KENT STATE UNIVERSITY AND THE UNIVERSITY OF WAIKATO
& THEODORE E. ZORN, JR., THE UNIVERSITY OF WAIKATO

WHAT IS THE MEANING OF MEANINGFUL WORK TODAY?

The quest for meaning in work has taken many different forms over the centuries and across cultures. Joanne Ciulla's (2000) book *The Working Life* is one of the best accounts of the meanings and roles of work in people's lives that we have read. Her historical and contemporary analyses open up our thinking about the nature of work, reminding us that what counts as work for one person may not count for someone else. For example, the elites in ancient Athens denigrated physical labor as "mere work" and sought to relegate it to others, including slaves. Yet, those same elites were engaged in the public work of the community, the city-state—activity that they valued, but they did not consider "work" as such. In many cultures of the world, just as political, cultural, and spiritual domains are not set apart from the fabric of life, so work is interwoven into community practices and traditions.

Sociologists of work and organizations, along with industrial-organizational psychologists, have probably had the most to say about what constitutes meaning*ful* work—that is, work that is both satisfying and that confers meaning to the person or group (e.g., Bowie, 1998; Gardner, Csikszentmihalyi, & Damon, 2001). However, in the past decade or so, organizational communication scholars have also begun to ponder this question, both probing what had been taken for granted about the settings and activities of work and seeking to advance our understanding of how work can be more meaningful for people during these turbulent economic times (e.g., Cheney, Zorn, Planalp, & Lair, 2008; Dempsey & Sanders, 2010; Kisselbaugh, Berkelaar, & Buzzanell, 2009).

Certainly one of the most important points to take from a broad-based examination of work over human history and across cultures is that however it gets defined and performed, people have certain goals associated with it. Even when, for example, someone defines her work or position as "just a job" and in a way containing that domain and saying it's not so important, she has clear preferences for what she seeks in the work experience (Cheney, Lair, Ritz, & Kendall, 2010). While a particular job may not point to career advancement, be lucrative, or have associations with lofty goals, it can still be imbued with desires and meanings in terms of goal attainment, health, and camaraderie.

Questions about meaningful work are suggestive of communication-based analyses because of the centrality of meaning to communication studies. For example, we are led in the beginning of such investigations to ask questions of individuals like: "What does your work mean to you?" "In what ways is your work meaningful?" And, "What are the most important ways your work could be made more meaningful for you?" These are important practical questions that allow us to investigate the topic further while perhaps provoking people to think about their own assumptions. For example, in her research on careers, Patrice Buzzanell (e.g., Buzzanell & Lucas, 2006; Kisselbaugh et al., 2009) regularly asks university students to reflect on these and related questions, to help them get at their most basic concerns and hopes. Meanings are also reflected in and shaped by our discussions with others. For example, in his research on "encore careers"—the notion of moving into new forms of work as one reaches or approaches traditional retirement age—Zorn and his colleagues asked "How do you talk about your move with others?" and "How do you feel about these conversations?" (Simpson, Richardson, & Zorn, in press).

In important ways, "macro" or broad studies of the economy, work, and organizations are being connected with "micro" studies of individual and group work experience. This is occurring through two avenues: the happiness research, which is taking serious human goals at every level (e.g., Diener, Ng, Harter, & Arora, 2010); and practical examinations of community resilience and sustainability (e.g., Magis, 2010). These are fairly new developments. Traditionally scholars tended not to bridge different levels of analysis, such as individual, group, organization, community, and society. The forging of micro and macro perspectives has occurred for three reasons.

First, there has been a growing recognition that certain areas of economics had become divorced from people's experiences. That is, within both academic and popular circles, the economy and the market came to be something "abstracted" from human experience rather than closely tied to it. The ways we talk about the economy and the market in the news, for example, illustrate this clearly: We place the "market" in a position of control over everything, hovering above us like Adam Smith's (1776) "invisible hand" even though he used that metaphor only once in his book, *Wealth of Nations* (Werhane, 1989).

A second reason is the extreme turbulence in the global economy since the recession began in 2007. Within this context, many people are questioning their work and roles, sometimes out of necessity because of layoffs or furloughs and sometimes because of choice in terms of making a career change or reducing the role of work in their lives altogether (Schor, 1992, 2010).

The third reason that scholars are thinking more in terms of micro-macro links is that the happiness literature has greatly expanded and influenced disciplines ranging from psychology (e.g., Diener & Seligman, 2004) to economics (e.g., Layard, 2005), history (e.g., Hecht, 2007) and political science (e.g., Lane, 2000). That is, questions are now being asked about the market's relationship to happiness as well as to more specific considerations of the happiness of an individual. In this regard, there has been a revival of interest in Aristotle's notion of *eudaimonia,* traditionally translated as happiness in English but now more commonly associated with "flourishing" (Fredrickson &

Losada, 2005). And, flourishing brings together the individual's goals and desires with finding a place in society and helping to serve societal needs.

As for organizations, which serve mediating functions between the individual and the larger society, how do they figure into this? Because we serve organizations in a variety of capacities, as employees, consumers, citizens, spokespersons, negotiators, regulators, etc., it's natural to consider how an organization, industry, or sector is providing for meaningful work and human flourishing (Cheney et al., 2008). This leads to a very practical and ethical reconsideration of organizational culture, for example, zeroing in on the aspects of work culture that truly support human needs and advancement (Grawitch, Gottschalk, & Munz, 2006; Pratt & Ashforth, 2003). In a certain sense, this orientation is not new, having first appeared at the dawn of the Human Relations Movement in the 1930s, when concern for "job satisfaction" first took off. Today the approach is more holistic thanks to ideas from systems theory (of the 1950s onward) as well as from the organizational culture movement (from the 1980s onward). We all understand deeply how organizations both enable us and constrain us, but posing questions about individual and group flourishing casts a somewhat brighter light on even the most self-acclaimed progressive workplaces and employing organizations (Grant, Christianson, & Price, 2007; van Marrewijk, 2004).

One of the most popular banners in the world of organizations today is *entrepreneurship,* and this refers to both independent individual activity and to transformative initiatives within and by organizations (du Gay, 1996). This term and its connotations are very important, even inspiring, around the world. But like any other slogan, "entrepreneurship" can become a gloss over important issues and can actually serve to divert attention from some of the ways that individuals, organizations, and the market are interdependent (Gill, 2010). This we see especially in a time of great economic upheaval and uncertainty, where a call for individual initiative cannot fully make up for lack of security more generally (Cremin, 2011). Ultimately, we must ask what organizations can do in the face of dire market conditions and individual insecurity. It may well be that what we used to think of as the *exceptions* to job, work, and career experience—what we would generally call nonstandard work (Firkin, de Bruin, & Spoonley, 2002) or contingent employment (Smith, 2010)—is now the norm. Still, accepting the idea that individuals and groups ought to be more entrepreneurial begs important questions about market functioning and the roles and policies of private business, government, and the non-profit sector.

WHAT CAN COMMUNICATION SAY ABOUT MEANINGFUL WORK AND ITS KEY DIMENSIONS?

As we have already seen a bit, communication-centered analyses focus attention on key terms, on meanings, and on the process by which new developments turn into trends. In addition, communication offers us tools to examine claims and debates about meaningful work. Finally, communication helps us to analyze the interrelationships of those elements as well as to keep in mind how they are cast in the discourses of organizations, business, popular culture, and governmental policy (Cheney et al., 2008).

Through a survey of the multidisciplinary literature on meaningful work and through contributions of organizational communication scholars themselves, we suggest the following list of key dimensions. In some ways, this list reflects eight decades of research on what makes work meaningful for people, beginning with the studies of job satisfaction, which strove to show that the happy worker was the productive worker; see e.g., Argyris, 1964. It continued through W. Charles Redding's (1972) proposed Ideal Managerial Climate, or IMC (with its key elements of trust, openness, supportiveness, participative decision making, and its emphasis on high-performance goals), and findings from recent studies of happiness and the nature of work. In other ways, though, the list includes reflection on the terms themselves, as we are conscious of the various connotations or associations.

Valued Purpose: One of the most consistent themes in the research on meaningful work is the notion that we value work that has a clear sense of purpose, especially when the purpose itself is valued. For example, Levy (2005) argues that achieving goals that transcend our individual interests—goals that are "bigger than us"—makes work meaningful. Similarly, Gardner and colleagues (2001) stress the importance of knowing that one's work makes a contribution to society.

Self-realization: Nearly every study of meaningful work emphasizes the importance of using and developing our skills and abilities. Our sense of worth is enhanced when we discover our talents, use those talents, and enhance our sense of competence by improving them. For example, Bowie (1998) and Levy (2005) both argue that a sense of meaningfulness is derived by developing our capacity for rational thought, as we do when solving problems. Terez's (2002) interview-based research found that people especially valued work that fit with their abilities.

Autonomy, agency, and self-determination are highly desired by nearly all employees, as revealed in the U.S. national surveys in *What Workers Want* (Freeman & Rogers, 1999) and *What Workers Say* (Freeman, Boxall, & Haynes, 2007). Bowie (1998) also argues for the centrality of work that is "freely entered into . . . . [and] allows the worker to exercise her autonomy and independence" (p. 1083).

Variety and Interest: From the beginning of job design and enrichment programs in the 1930s (http://en.wikipedia.org/wiki/Job_enrichment), there has been a recognition of the tension between routinization and variety. Either too much constancy or too much change presents a problem for the individual worker. Mitroff and Denton's (1999) survey research found that work that was interesting was among the top characteristics that contributed to a sense of meaning.

Participation and Voice is a consistently emphasized aspect of work and empowerment, from the contexts of work teams to social movements and new media (e.g., Seibold & Shea, 2001; Stohl & Cheney, 2001). Extensive survey research on U.S. employees led Yankelovich (1978) to the conclusion that work is meaningful to the extent that it involves enabling participation in decision making.

Network embeddedness and support: Here it is important to think of yourself as a part of a network that extends beyond work and beyond your immediate circles of close family, friends, and colleagues. In a sense, this dimension combines notions of social support with elements of wider connection and solidarity. Cheney's research in the Mondragón cooperatives of the Basque Country, Spain (e.g., 1999, 2009), reveals how nuanced and multi-facted the idea and practices of solidarity can be.

Trust and ethical confidence: One of the single most discussed concepts today in the management literature as well as in self-help books is trust. Why is this? And, what kinds of trust do we seek? Trust has reemerged dramatically in the study of organizations in part because of scandals in all sectors and in part because of a perceived breakdown in functions of the market, but also because of a deeper realization of the importance of trust at all levels of society—from main street to Wall Street (Kramer, 2006). We mention trust here because of how it helps to provide a foundation of security and confidence for job performance, and that's precisely why it was featured in Redding's (1972) IMC.

SO, WHAT CAN THIS RESEARCH MEAN FOR YOU, IN WORK AND LIFE?

We would like to close this brief discussion by highlighting a few things to think about as you make your own choices for jobs, professions, career, and work life.

Consider *the individual life cycle and career path*—including new angles on professional development in terms of narratives and reinterpretations of career. The notion of encore career, which we mentioned earlier, suggests that we may change our thinking about what's important in our work at different points in our lives (Simpson et al., in press). Some people who worked to make ends meet for most of their lives find that they want something different when they have the opportunity to reflect on the next stage of their lives. Consider these questions: What kind of story or stories do you want to be able to tell in five years, ten years, or towards the end of your career? Do you think of career as something that belongs to you, or something that links you to work, organizations, profession, people, and places?

Challenge assumptions about *self-fulfillment,* especially considering turbulent economic conditions. All of us have been trained through many messages to think of traditional success indicators: a high salary, prestige, lots of possessions, public acclaim, and so on (Schor, 1992), but many people find that these are ultimately unfulfilling. Some questions for reflection: What versions or aspects of success are most important to you? And, how much time do you want to devote to obtaining that kind of success?

Emphasize *connection and community* in your life, sorting out the ways in which you would like work to contribute to these goals versus maintaining autonomy and independence. The research on belonging (see Baumeister & Leary, 1995) has firmly established the basic nature of the need for connection to others. A question for reflection: How do you think about connection and community in terms of your range of mediated and non-mediated or partially mediated relationships?

Explore *humane and ethical work cultures* and the organizational structures and supports required to establish and maintain them (see May, 2011). This relates to how we approach organizations (for example, in an interview), as well as how we operate within them. Some questions for reflection: In what ways can organizations be more inspiring for you? And, how can you contribute to this as an employee?

Come to terms with *limits of the productivity and growth paradigms.* Today there are new perspectives on resources, growth, and productivity (Hamilton, 2003). This is a good thing because we no longer assume that unlimited economic growth is possible. On the other hand, there is tremendous uncertainty about the future. For all of us, this means heightened attention to sustainability with respect to the various environments in which we operate but also with regard to our own activities.

Work is an important part of all our lives. We spend a significant amount of our time at and around work. And, if you're reading this chapter, there's a good chance that you're spending a significant amount of time and money *preparing* for work. It is worth considering, then, what will make your work meaningful. Our research, and that of other scholars, hints at some of the important issues that are valuable to consider in reflecting on the work that you do now and will do in the future.

REFERENCES

Argyris, C. (1964). *Integrating the individual and the organization.* New York: Wiley.

Baumeister, R. F., & Leary, M. R. (1995). The need to belong: Desire for interpersonal attachments as a fundamental human motivation. *Psychological Bulletin, 117*(3), 497–529.

Bowie, N. E. (1998). A Kantian theory of meaningful work. *Journal of Business Ethics, 17* (9/10), 1083–1092.

Boxall, P., Freeman, R. B., & Haynes, P. (Eds.). (2007). *What workers say: Employee voice in the Anglo-American workplace.* Ithaca, NY: Cornell University Press.

Buzzanell, P. M., & Lucas, K. (2006). Gendered stories of career: Unfolding discourses of time, space, and identity. In B. Dow & J. Wood (Eds.), *The Sage handbook on gender and communication* (pp. 161–178). Thousand Oaks: Sage

Cheney, G. (1999). *Values at work: Employee participation meets market pressure at Mondragon,* Cornell University Press, Ithaca, NY.

Cheney, G. (2009). Arizmendi topaketak. Mondragōn, Basque Country, Spain: Gizadibea.

Cheney, G., Lair, D. J., Ritz, D., & Kendall, B. E. (2010). *Just a job? Communication, ethics, and professional life.* New York: Oxford University Press.

Cheney, G., Zorn, T. E., Planalp, S., & Lair, D. (2008). Meaningful work and personal/social well-being: Organizational communication engages the meanings of work. *Communication Yearbook, 32,* 138–185.

Ciulla, J. (2000). *The working life.* Pittsburgh, PA: Three Rivers Press.

Cremin, C. (2011). *Capitalism's new clothes: Enterprise, ethics and enjoyment in times of crisis.* London: Pluto Books.

Dempsey, S. E., & Sanders, M. L. (2010). Meaningful work? Nonprofit marketization and work/ life imbalance in popular autobiographies of social entrepreneurship. *Organization, 17*(4), 437–459.

Diener, E., Ng, W., Harter, J., & Arora, R. (2010). Wealth and happiness across the world: Material prosperity predicts life evaluation, whereas psychosocial prosperity predicts positive feeling. *Journal of Personality and Social Psychology, 99*(1), 52–61.

Diener, E., & Seligman, M. E. P. (2004). Beyond money: Toward an economy of well-being. *Psychological Science in the Public Interest, 5*(1), 1–31.

du Gay, P. (1996). *Consumption and identity at work.* London: Sage.

Firkin, P., de Bruin, A., & Spoonley, P. (2002). Managing non-standard work arrangements: Choices and constraints. *Journal of Sociology, 38*(4), 425–441.

Fredrickson, B. L., & Losada, M. F. (2005). Positive affect and the complex dynamics of human flourishing. *American Psychologist, 60*(7), 678–686.

Freeman, R., Boxall, P., & Haynes, P. (2007). *What workers say: Employee voice in the Anglo-American workplace.* Ithaca, NY: ILR Press.

Freeman, R. B., & Rogers, J. (1999). *What workers want.* Ithaca, NY: Cornell University Press.

Gardner, H., Csikszentmihalyi, M., & Damon, W. (2001). *Good work: When excellence and ethics meet.* New York: Basic Books.

Gill, R. (2011). A superhero on Utah's silicon slopes? The construction and practice of entrepreneurial identities at the nexus of religion, gender, and place. Doctoral Dissertation. University of Utah, Salt Lake City, UT.

Grant, A. M., Christianson, M. K., & Price, R. H. (2007). Happiness, health, or relationships? Managerial practices and employee well-being tradeoffs. *Academy of Management Perspectives, 21*(3), 51–63.

Grawitch, M. J., Gottschalk, M., & Munz, D. C. (2006). The path to a healthy workplace: A critical review linking healthy workplace practices, employee well-being, and organizational improvements. *Consulting Psychology Journal, 58*(3), 129–147.

Hamilton, C. (2003). *Growth fetish.* Sydney: Allen & Unwin.

Hecht, J. M. (2007). *The happiness myth: The historical antidote to what isn't working today.* New York: HarperOne.

Job enrichment. http://en.wikipedia.org/wiki/Job_enrichment

Kisselbaugh, L., Berkelaar, B. L., & Buzzanell, P. M. (2009). Discourse, gender, and the meaning of work. *Communication Yearbook, 33* (259–299).

Kramer, R. M. (Ed.). (2006). *Organizational trust: A reader.* New York: Oxford.

Lane, R. (2000). *The loss of happiness in market democracies.* New Haven, CT: Yale University Press.

Layard, R. (2005). *Happiness: Lessons from a new science.* New York: Penguin.

Levy, N. (2005). Downshifting and meaning in life. *Ratio, 18*(2), 125–247.

Magis, K. (2010). Community resilience: An indicator of social sustainability. *Society Natural Resources, 23*(5), 401–416.

May, S. K. (2011). Ethical engagement. In G. Cheney, L. T. Christensen, T. E. Zorn, Jr., & S. Ganesh (Eds.), *Organizational communication in an age of globalization: Issues, reflections, practices* (2nd ed., p. 438). Prospect Heights, IL: Waveland.

Mitroff, I. I., & Denton, E. A. (1999). *A spiritual audit of corporate America.* San Francisco: Jossey-Bass.

Pratt, M. G., & Ashforth, B. E. (2003). Fostering meaningfulness in working and at work. In K. S. Cameron, J. E. Dutton, & R. E. Quinn (Eds.), *Positive organizational scholarship: Foundations of a new discipline* (pp. 309–327). San Francisco: Berrett-Koehler, pp. 664–703.

Redding, W. C. (1972). *Communication within the organization: An interpretive review of theory and research.* New York: Industrial Communication Council, Inc.

Schor, J. B. (1992). *The overworked American.* New York: Basic Books.

Schor, J. (2010). *Plentitude: The economics of true wealth.* New York: Penguin.

Seibold, D. R., & Shea, B. C. (2001). Participation and decision making. In F. M. Jablin, & L. L. Putnam (Eds.), *The new handbook of organizational communication.* Thousand Oaks, CA: Sage.

Simpson, M., Richardson, M., & Zorn, T. E. (in press). "Out the door," "back for more," or "new horizons": Multiple meanings for encore careers. *Work, Employment & Society.*

Smith, A. (1776). *An inquiry into the nature and causes of the wealth of nations.* London: W. Strahan and T. Cadell.

Smith, V. (2010). Review article: Enhancing employability: Human, cultural, and social capital in an era of turbulent unpredictability. *Human Relations, 63*(2), 279–300.

Stohl, C., & Cheney, G. (2001). Participatory processes/paradoxical practices: Communication and the dilemmas of organizational democracy. *Management Communication Quarterly, 14,* 349–407.

Terez, T. (2002). *22 keys to creating a meaningful workplace.* Avon, MA: Adams Media Corporation.

van Marrewijk, M. (2004). The social dimension of organizations: Recent experiences with Great Place to Work assessment practices. *Journal of Business Ethics, 55,* 135–146.

Werhane, P. H. (1989). The role of self-interest in Adam Smith's Wealth of Nations. *Journal of Philosophy, 86*(11), 669–680.

Yankelovich, D. (1978). The meaning of work. In J. M. Roson (Ed.), *The worker and the job: Coping with change.* Englewood Cliffs, NJ: Prentice-Hall.

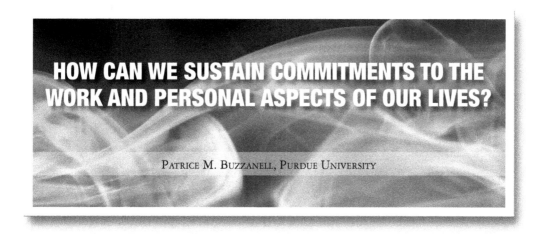

HOW CAN WE SUSTAIN COMMITMENTS TO THE WORK AND PERSONAL ASPECTS OF OUR LIVES?

Patrice M. Buzzanell, Purdue University

The question, how can we sustain commitments to the work and personal aspects of our lives, embeds several ideas that are worth defining. At the heart of this question is the notion of "sustainability." When most people think of sustainability, they typically associate the term with ecological concerns, environmental problems, and technical, scientific, and engineering efforts to design solutions for the global grand challenges of our times (e.g., http://www.grandchallenges. org/Pages/Default.aspx and http://www.engineeringchallenges.org). These grand challenges typically address the depletion and desirable endurance of resources and societal infrastructures for the betterment of humankind. There are many definitions and much effort, including funded large-scale projects from such organizations as the U.S. National Science Foundation (www.nsf. gov/funding/pgm_summ.jsp?pims_id=501027) and Coca-Cola (www.thecoca-colacompany. com/.../foundation_guidelines.html), geared toward conceptualizing and solving sustainability issues. Indeed, the word "sustainability" produces 97,800,000 hits in an early September 2011 Google™ search.

Regardless of its context in environmental, community, or other concerns, the underlying premise and importance of sustainability has to do with the processes underlying, and the long-term effects of, our lifestyles. Here we might question whether and how our energy consumption or recycling efforts contribute to better air, water, and landscape qualities. We might also think about our overall resource use patterns and our abilities to generate alternative resources or to utilize resources differently. Our goals might center on our potential contributions to our own and to our community's efforts to engage in sustainable living.

My research takes a somewhat different look at sustainability. To me, a central question is how we, as individuals and as members of different collectivities, can work toward engaging in both our careers and in our personal lives in fulfilling ways. I ask the question in this way because "work-family balance" sets us up for failure if we believe that these two, and only two, aspects must be equally present at all times. Instead, I look for sustainable communication processes that enlarge what we mean by work and family as well as other personal life involvements. I also use "career" rather than work because it is not the doing of work itself that is the issue but the overwhelming conflation of one's career status (i.e., positive views of advancement, prestige, status, salary, and benefits) with one's identity that is problematic. Instead, I define career as the themes underlying our work over the course of our lifetimes, as well as the job, occupational, and institutional structures that coincide with these themes (see Berkelaar & Buzzanell, 2011; Buzzanell & Lucas, 2006). I take for granted that sustainability efforts would be ongoing, changeable, and socially constructed with full consideration of the diverse materialities in our lives.

I take a social constructionist viewpoint, meaning that knowledge is co-constructed based on personal experiences and conditions of our lives (see Buzzanell, 1995). This stance means that realities endure because of the historically, politically, culturally, and socially embedded nature of taken-for-granted views, but also that these same realities can be revised or reinvented from scratch. Sustainability, then, is not simply application of appropriate technologies to increase the structural endurance of material and human systems, but it is the ongoing design of problem definition, application, construction, testing, and transformation of the discourses and materialities to create sustainable and fulfilling lifestyles. The use of "discourses" means that we engage in everyday talk that implicates and is implicated by cultural formations, or understandings such as economy, time, career, gender, race, family, workplace priorities, profit, justice and fairness, and so on, to make such everyday talk sensible. These cultural formations are the products of powerful societal forces to maintain the status quo. As we reflect on the conduct of our career and personal lives, we can ask whose interests are served by the ways we prioritize career as advancement. Often we find that the prevailing interests being served and sustained are corporate and consistent with the values of the dominant group (e.g., owners and managers aligned with traditional ways of thinking about and doing things; see Buzzanell, 1994, 2000; Buzzanell & Goldzwig, 1991).

To explain my argument more fully, I want to discuss (a) why focusing on career-personal life sustainability is so important, (b) how my research has approached career-personal life sustainability, and (c) what communicative processes might enhance our ability to create and sustain viable and fulfilling lifestyles.

WHY CAREER AND PERSONAL LIFE SUSTAINABILITY?

Let me begin by providing some examples of why I believe that our language surrounding and efforts to achieve work-family balance are inadequate.

On April 1, 2010, a "Rhymes with Orange" comic entitled "the work/life balance" depicted a male manager saying to a woman seated opposite him at his desk: "Yes, I hired you to work half days. A half day is twelve hours. What's the problem?"

In a second case, the *Harvard Business Review* published an article on "Extreme jobs: The dangerous allure of the 70-hour workweek" (Hewlett & Luce, 2006) that described the exhilarations and costs when men and women from around the globe who work in high risk, time intensive, and high salary careers commit well over 70 hours per week to their jobs. They love their work and the excitement of doing things well that no one has done before. But they cannot keep up the pace for more than a couple of years or they burn out and their families pay high costs in terms of marital dissolutions and children's problems at school and with illegal substances. These workers in the highest income bracket worldwide are not the only ones who succumb to "no limits" career ideologies and behaviors (for Chinese ideologies, see Lucas, Liu, & Buzzanell, 2006; for lack of time for family and friends voiced by workers at Indian call centers, see Pal & Buzzanell, 2008). Many people are urged to find their passion or "calling" so that they will enjoy working the expected hours over their lifetimes (Berkelaar & Buzzanell, 2011). Even when structures are in place to curtail excessive work styles, such as policies in place in Sweden, individuals find ways to surreptitiously usurp constraints both to meet work demands and to achieve higher performance evaluations and awards (Wieland, 2011).

Finally, Sarah Dempsey and Matthew Sanders (2011) analyzed social entrepreneurs' popularized accounts of their goals and lifestyles. In their autobiographies, John Wood, founder of Room to Read, Greg Mortenson, founder of the Central Asia Institute, and Wendy Kopp, founder of Teach for America, describe their commitment to helping others without much reflection on, and clear acceptance of the self-sacrifice required through underpaid and unpaid labor, and total commitment to their organizations regardless of losses to family, health, and other life aspects.

In each of these instances, the assumption is that work—especially careers oriented toward the welfare of others—should always be prioritized over other life aspects. As we can see from these examples, women and men succumb to the allure of an identity associated with exciting and meaningful work. But they may simply need to work long hours to meet bosses' expectations and employability security. It is not simply these research participants who express concerns about their lifestyles, their abilities to keep up, their lack of time for friends and family, their chagrin at missing children's school and extracurricular events, and so on. Men and women who engage in full-time employment and caregiving express family first, but their actions and their concerns about their behavioral inconsistencies with their family and work ideologies tell a very different story (Buzzanell & D'Enbeau, 2009; Buzzanell, D'Enbeau, & Duckworth, 2010; D'Enbeau, Buzzanell, & Duckworth, 2009, 2010; Duckworth & Buzzanell, 2009). Moreover, single adults without dependent children or partners are expected to work long hours, weekends, and holidays because they do not have "family" (Lucas & Buzzanell, 2006; Young, 1996). Families where members have chronic illnesses or disabilities have tremendous strains on their abilities to have their capabilities and needs understood by others and to have any release from career and personal life pressures and uncertainties (e.g., Buzzanell, 2003, 2006, 2008).

HOW HAS MY RESEARCH CONTRIBUTED TO CAREER-PERSONAL LIFE SUSTAINABILITY?

My research evolved from asking why our identities are so tied to our work and careers (Buzzanell & Goldzwig, 1991) to how members of particular groups are thwarted in their attempts to attain recognition of competence and career potential because of who they are rather than what they do or are capable of doing (Buzzanell, 1995; Buzzanell & Lucas, 2006); and to why we steadfastly believe that the talented and hardworking will rise to the top regardless of gender, race/ethnicity, class, and other differences, and despite formidable evidence to the contrary (Buzzanell, 2000). I've used surveys, analyses of popular culture and media, interviews, U.S. Department of Labor data, and participant observation to study these questions. I admit that my questions often assume that women and men want advancement. However, I recognize that some place greater value on time with their newborns and other members of their extended family networks (Buzzanell, Waymer, Tagle, & Liu, 2007) and simply being able to pay bills and to provide for their loved ones (D'Enbeau, Buzzanell, & Duckworth, 2009, 2010; Duckworth & Buzzanell, 2009; Lucas & Buzzanell, 2004). In the course of examining why and how policies, organizational practices, and members' everyday talk curtail individuals' means of achieving what they want in their careers and personal lives, I studied communication surrounding family leave.

Family leave is not always enacted in practice as it is designed in the operating procedures of Human Resources (HR) and governmental policies. It is supposed to create a safe space in which families can birth or adopt children and care for sick and dying family members without losing their jobs or career opportunities (for descriptions of U.S. laws and policies, see Buzzanell & Liu, 2005; see also Liu & Buzzanell, 2004, 2006). For instance, in examining maternity leaves, Meina Liu and I (Buzzanell & Liu, 2005) found that women struggled to enact productive employee identities while they were pregnant to show that they were the same good workers albeit different in appearance and familial responsibilities. Meina Liu and I (2004) found that most (75%) of the women who reported being discouraged at their work and career prospects at the times of their leaves did not return to or left their employers soon after their maternity leaves ended. They left mainly because their bosses relied on (a) stereotypes about women (e.g., women with infants are not reliable), (b) traditional justice ethics (e.g., equal treatment standards prompted their supervisors to treat women with difficult pregnancies the same way they would treat other women and men); (c) guilt (e.g., many women felt guilty because coworkers had to handle their workloads; see also D'Enbeau & Buzzanell, 2010); and (d) surveillance (e.g., their bosses monitored their activities, including bathroom breaks, and did not adjust procedures even when the women had doctors' notes requesting accommodations). Our findings suggested that training and dialogue about differential superior-subordinate expectations, rights, responsibilities, and ethical stances might assist people in creating a mutually beneficial situation (and avoid potential litigation).

Furthermore, my colleagues and I (Buzzanell, Meisenbach, Remke, Bowers, Liu, & Conn, 2005) argued that managerial women who did not need to work for financial reasons and who enjoyed their careers often made sense of their work and family choices by constructing a "good *working* mother image." They conformed to and molded this image discursively and materially. They did so by reporting their (a) arrangement of good quality childcare, (b) pride in handling arrangements (without partners' assistance), and (c) pleasure in being both workers and mothers simultaneously. These findings indicate that the popularized divide between stay-at-home and employed mothers is deep. Indeed, women may attempt to justify their career and personal life choices in ways that preclude inclusion of women who do not subscribe to the same logics. My research as well as that of others indicates that alliances among women and men who voice different interests in, and rationales for, their lifestyles can prove very difficult. Without collaboration among these women and men, viable policies, laws, and practices cannot be created and used to transform our everyday career and personal life communication for sustainable fulfillment.

HOW CAN WE CREATE AND SUSTAIN VIABLE AND FULFILLING LIFESTYLES?

Individuals and their families—rather than societal structures and work-family ideologies—are blamed when they cannot manage everything (Buzzanell, Dohrman, & D'Enbeau, 2010). Many researchers have discussed the kinds of discursive and structural interventions necessary for long-term change. As a start, to truly accommodate women's and men's interests, governmental and organizational conceptualizations of "family" would need to be expanded to account for neighbors, friends, "fictive kin," and extended family, as well as biological and legal family members (Lucas & Buzzanell, 2006). In addition, structural changes should include: government- and corporate-supported quality child and elder care, paid family leaves, after-school/evening/weekend programs for dependents so that caregivers can work shifts, and adequate respite care for those handling the family members' chronic or end-of-life needs. From a practical standpoint, investments into families and children are less costly than lack of investment. If caregivers cannot earn funds through paid labor, then they need to acquire unemployment. If children do not receive good quality care and education, and elders (or dependents with chronic illnesses or disabilities) do not have adequate day facilities and home-based medical assistance, then businesses lose productivity as their employees' attention is diverted away from their work and taxpayers foot a higher bill for remedial training, hospital care, and, in worst case scenarios, for rehabilitation centers and prisons. Society loses their children's potential contributions. Many researchers have calculated these cost-benefit ratios, with the bottom line being that structural changes and investments in human resources pay for themselves.

With these arguments, one would think that it would be fairly easy to set policies, laws, and practices in motion to create better quality of life for citizens. But it is not "simply" a matter of revising structures and policies. Nor is it simply a matter of showing people how to manage time or resources better (e.g., Medved, 2004; Sotirin, Buzzanell, & Turner, 2007). Rather, long-term solutions require further research on ways to break the hold of managerialist and traditional career communication. For instance, Meisenbach, Remke, Buzzanell, and Liu (2008) described how discourse favors organizational motives rather than women's own interests in maternity leaves and returns to paid work. Additional research could examine how policies themselves act as agents to sustain or modify the status quo.

But beyond more research, what can we do to make our careers and personal lives more fulfilling and sustainable? My own and others' communication research indicates that key processes involve disassembling and critiquing everyday discourses and cultural formations about work-family balance to determine how we can transform our talk and the discourses and structures that prohibit sustainable and fulfilling lifestyles. The next step involves collaboration with others to effect structural change.

REFERENCES

Berkelaar, B., & Buzzanell, P. M. (2011, November). *Imagined possibilities: Examining the paradoxes and tensions of calling in the contemporary marketplace.* Paper presented to the National Communication Association, conference held in New Orleans, LA.

Buzzanell, P. M. (1994). Gaining a voice: Feminist organizational communication theorizing. *Management Communication Quarterly, 7,* 339–383.

Buzzanell, P. M. (1995). Reframing the glass ceiling as a socially constructed process: Implications for understanding and change. *Communication Monographs, 62,* 327–354.

Buzzanell, P. M. (2000). The promise and practice of the new career and social contract. In P. M. Buzzanell (Ed.), *Rethinking organizational and managerial communication from feminist perspectives* (pp. 209–235). Thousand Oaks, CA: Sage.

Buzzanell, P. M. (2003). A feminist standpoint analysis of maternity and maternity leave for women with disabilities. *Women & Language, 26* (2), 53–65.

Buzzanell, P. M. (2006). Pondering diverse work-life issues and developments over the lifespan. *Electronic Journal of Communication, 16.* Available at http://www.cios.org/www/ejc/v16n34.htm

Buzzanell, P. M. (2008). Necessary fictions: Stories of identity, hope, and love. *Communication, Culture, & Critique, 1,* 31–39.

Buzzanell, P. M. (2010). Resilience: Talking, resisting, and imagining new normalcies into being. *Journal of Communication, 60,* 1–14.

Buzzanell, P. M. (2010, November). *Seduction and sustainability: The politics of feminist communication and career scholarship.* Carroll C. Arnold Distinguished Lecture presented to the National Communication Association, conference held in Chicago, IL. Webcast: http://hosted.verticalresponse.com/394897/b55625f227/1714500491/886b4deb98/

Buzzanell, P. M., & D'Enbeau, S. (2009). Stories of caregiving: Intersections of academic research and women's everyday experiences. *Qualitative Inquiry, 15,* 1199–1224.

Buzzanell, P. M., D'Enbeau, S., & Duckworth, J. (2010). What men say about women: Fathers contemplate work-family choices and motherhood. In S. Hayden, & L. O'Brien Hallstein (Eds.), *Contemplating maternity in the era of choice: Explorations into discourses of reproduction* (pp. 291–311). Lanham, MD: Lexington Press.

Buzzanell, P. M., Dohrman, R., & D'Enbeau, S. (2010). Problematizing political economy differences and their respective work-life policy constructions. In D. K. Mumby (Ed.), *Reframing difference in organizational communication studies: Research, pedagogy, practice* (pp. 245–266). Thousand Oaks, CA: Sage.

Buzzanell, P. M., & Goldzwig, S. (1991). Linear and nonlinear career models: Metaphors, paradigms, and ideologies. *Management Communication Quarterly, 4,* 466–505.

Buzzanell, P. M., & Liu, M. (2005). Struggling with maternity leave policies and practices: A poststructuralist feminist analysis of gendered organizing. *Journal of Applied Communication Research, 33,* 1–25.

Buzzanell, P. M., & Lucas, K. (2006). Gendered stories of career: Unfolding discourses of time, space, and identity. In B. J. Dow, & J. T. Wood (Eds.), *The Sage handbook of gender and communication* (pp. 161–178). Thousand Oaks, CA: Sage.

Buzzanell, P. M., Meisenbach, R., Remke, R., Bowers, V., Liu, M., & Conn, C. (2005). The good working mother: Managerial women's sensemaking and feelings about work-family issues. *Communication Studies, 56,* 261–285.

Buzzanell, P. M., Waymer, D., Tagle, M. P., & Liu, M. (2007). Different transitions into working motherhood: Discourses of Asian, Hispanic, and African American women. *Journal of Family Communication, 7,* 195–220.

Dempsey, S., & Sanders, M. (2011). Meaningful work? Nonprofit marketization and work/life imbalance in popular autobiographies of social entrepreneurship. *Organization, 17,* 437–459.

D'Enbeau, S., & Buzzanell, P. M. (2010). Managing work, life, and family: Informal parenting support systems. In D. Braithwaite, & J. T. Wood (Eds.), *Casing interpersonal communication: Case studies in personal and social relationships* (pp. 109–114). Dubuque, IA: Kendall Hunt.

D'Enbeau, S., Buzzanell, P. M., & Duckworth, J. (2009). Money or family/Money for family: Fatherhood dilemmas for men of differing socioeconomic classes. In E. Kirby, & M. C. McBride (Eds.), *Case studies in gender communication* (pp. 92–98). Dubuque, IA: Kendall Hunt.

D'Enbeau, S., Buzzanell, P. M., & Duckworth, J. (2010). Problematizing classed identities in fatherhood: Development of integrative case studies for analysis and praxis. *Qualitative Inquiry, 16,* 709–720.

Duckworth, J., & Buzzanell, P. M. (2009). Constructing work-life balance and fatherhood: Men's framing of the meanings of both work and family. *Communication Studies, 60,* 558–573.

Hewlett, S. A., & Luce, C. B. (2006). Extreme jobs: The dangerous allure of the 70-hour workweek. *Harvard Business Review, 84* (12), 49–58.

Kirby, E., & Krone, K. J. (2002). "The policy exists but you can't really use It": Communication and the structuration of work-family policies. *Journal of Applied Communication Research, 30,* 50–77.

Liu, M., & Buzzanell, P. M. (2004). Negotiating maternity leave expectations: Perceived tensions between ethics of justice and care. *Journal of Business Communication, 41,* 323–349.

Liu, M., & Buzzanell, P. M. (2006). When workplace pregnancy highlights difference: Openings for detrimental gender and supervisory relations. In J. H. Fritz, & B. L. Omdahl (Eds.), *Problematic relationships in the workplace* (pp. 47–68). New York: Peter Lang.

Lucas, K., & Buzzanell, P. M. (2004). Blue-collar work, career, and success: Occupational narratives of sisu. *Journal of Applied Communication Research, 32,* 273–292.

Lucas, K., & Buzzanell, P. M. (2006). Employees "without" families: Discourses of family as an external constraint to work-life balance. In L. H. Turner, & R. West (Eds.), *The family communication sourcebook* (pp. 335–352). Thousand Oaks, CA: Sage.

Lucas, K., Liu, M., & Buzzanell, P. M. (2006). No limits careers: A critical examination of career discourse in the U.S. and China. In M. Orbe, B. J. Allen, & L. A. Flores (Eds.), The same and different: Acknowledging diversity within and between cultural groups. *International and intercultural communication annual 28* (pp. 217–242). Thousand Oaks, CA: Sage.

Medved, C. E. (2004). The everyday accomplishment of work and family: Exploring practical actions in daily routines. *Communication Studies, 55,* 128–45.

Meisenbach, R., Remke, R., Buzzanell, P. M., & Liu, M. (2008). "They allowed": Pentadic mapping of women's maternity leave discourse as organizational rhetoric. *Communication Monographs, 75,* 1–24.

Pal, M., & Buzzanell, P. M. (2008). The Indian call center experience: A case study in changing discourses of identity, identification, and career in a global context. *Journal of Business Communication, 45,* 31–60.

Sotirin, P., Buzzanell, P. M., & Turner, L. (2007). Colonizing family: A feminist critique of family management texts. *Journal of Family Communication, 7,* 245–263.

Young, M. (1996). Career issues for single adults without dependent children. In D. T. Hall & Associates (Eds.), *The career is dead—Long live the career: A relational approach to careers* (pp. 196–219). San Francisco: Jossey-Bass.

Wieland, S. (2011). Struggling to manage work as a part of everyday life: Complicating control, rethinking resistance, and contextualizing work/life studies. *Communication Monographs, 78,* 162–184.

SECTION 13
PERSUASION COMMUNICATION

Persuasion is a pervasive phenomenon affecting our everyday lives on both an interpersonal and a social scale. Persuasion has been the subject of considerable and focused scholarship since antiquity; however, advances in media technology have added a layer of complexity to the study. Altering the beliefs, attitudes, values and behaviors of others is a challenging task. In the three essays in this section, the authors explore strategies for increasing our effectiveness in influencing others. First, Robin Nabi (University of California, Santa Barbara) responds to the question: *How do evoked emotions (e.g., anger, fear) affect our attempts to be persuasive?* She examines the research to answer the question as to when and how inducing fear, guilt, or humor in an audience enhances the likelihood of their being persuaded to agree with us. Second, Daniel O'Keefe (Northwestern University) considers the question: *How can we increase the success rate of compliance requests?* O'Keefe and others who have researched this topic have discovered that one way to enhance the chances that people will agree to your request is by first getting them to *refuse* a different request (*Door in the Face*). Third, Larry Hosman (University of Southern Mississippi) answers the question: *How can we use powerful (and avoid powerless) language to persuade others?* Hosman explains that linguistic markers of powerlessness such as tag question hedges have a very real impact on the way others perceive you, the quality of your argument, and the persuasiveness of your message in inducing attitude change. Understanding the research on which strategies are effective and which are ineffective in inducing others to change their beliefs, values, attitudes, and behaviors can help you to be more effective in winning friends and influencing others.

THE PERSUASIVE INFLUENCE OF EMOTION

Robin L. Nabi, University of California, Santa Barbara

In everyday life, we are bombarded with persuasive messages in the media. One cannot watch television or surf the Internet without exposure to attempts at persuasion. Yet, decades of persuasion research have documented just how challenging it can be to alter the beliefs, attitudes, and especially the behaviors of others. Indeed, one of the key challenges in persuasion is simply securing the attention of the audience in the first place. Given message exposure is a necessary condition for that message to have any chance at achieving its desired effect, this is a critical issue in all persuasion endeavors. As such, numerous strategies have been employed to capture audience attention, and primary among these is the use of emotional appeals. The assumption is that by using scary, angering, or even amusing messages, the audience will not only be more likely to pay attention to the message but also, given their emotional state, be more motivated to yield to its claims. But is this truly the case? Are audiences more likely to yield to a persuasive message that evokes an emotional response?

As we look to the research literature on emotional appeals, it is clear that the answer to this question is not a simple one. Sometimes emotions facilitate attitude and behavior change; other times they actually interfere. Further, different emotions may affect the persuasive process differently, so generalizations across emotions are unlikely to hold. Understanding how each emotion influences how people think and choose to act, then, is critical not only to the choice of whether to use an emotional appeal or not but also how to design one that has the greatest chance of achieving its goals.

The overwhelming majority of the research on emotion and persuasion has centered around fear arousal and its effects on both message processing and the outcomes of attitudes, behavioral intentions, and behaviors, though increasing attention is being paid to the persuasive influence of other emotional states, like guilt and amusement. This chapter overviews what is currently known about the persuasive effect of different emotions and the implications of this knowledge for successful message design. In essence, the research question this chapter addresses is: *How do evoked emotions (e.g., fear, anger) affect our attempts to be persuasive?*

FEAR APPEAL RESEARCH

The fear appeal literature has cycled through several theoretical perspectives over the past 50 years (see Nabi, 2007, for a more detailed discussion). First, fear was thought to be akin to drive states, like hunger, motivating people to adopt message recommendations expected to alleviate their unpleasant feelings (Hovland, Janis, & Kelley, 1953). But when research showed fear appeals sometimes led to successful persuasion and other times backfired, scholars began thinking about fear not simply as a motivational state but as a cognitive one as well (Leventhal, 1970). That is, scholars asserted that sometimes fear may promote rational thought, allowing people to focus on how to best protect themselves from a threat, which increases the chances they will adopt the message's recommendations. However, fear as a motivational state may lead people to engage in counterproductive responses, like denial or reactance (message resistance stemming from perceiving an unjust restriction to one's freedom to choose; Brehm, 1966), and thus to reject the message's recommendations. As conceptualization of fear's cognitive components progressed, scholars determined that four cognitions, or thoughts, are necessary to the success of a persuasive appeal. First, a person must see a threat as something that is severe, or potentially very dangerous. Second, a person must see themselves as susceptible to that threat. Combined, these two perceptions lead to the emotion of fear. Whether that fear leads to effective action is in part dependent on two other judgments: response efficacy, or whether there is an action that can help one to avoid that threat, and self-efficacy, or whether the person believes she can actually perform that action (Rogers, 1975, 1983; Witte, 1992).

So imagine we have the goal of changing the behavior of texting while driving. How might we try to persuade drivers to stop this dangerous behavior? Using the model of fear appeals outlined above, we must first point out how severe the consequences are for performing the behavior. We could use statistics (e.g., texting while driving is more than twice as dangerous as drinking and driving), or we might depict a fatal accident caused by a driver distracted while texting. We would also note that the audience is susceptible to those negative outcomes to the extent they text while driving, even if only on occasion. We then offer an effective response to help the audience see that they can avoid the scary possibility of a fatal car accident by, for example, suggesting the driver put the cell phone in the back seat, out of reach to avoid temptation. Finally, we would indicate that this is a behavior that is easily accomplished. According to theories like the protection motivation model (PMM; Rogers, 1975, 1983) and the extended parallel process model (EPPM; Witte, 1992), this message structure should increase the chances that this message will change the audience's behavior and thus reduce the incidence of texting while driving.

However, though this message design may increase the chances of persuasion over messages that do not evoke fear, it in no way guarantees persuasive success. Some audience members will not perceive the danger, and thus won't experience fear. Some won't believe the outcome will happen to them and thus have no motivation to change their behavior. And still other audience members will think the response won't work or that they can't actually do it. Indeed, some might even avoid listening to the message to avoid feeling fear at all. Thus, though our fear appeal may work for some, the audience's perception of the message information is highly variable, which makes persuasive success hard to secure.

Still, evidence does support a small to moderately sized positive relationship between fear arousal and attitude, behavioral intention, and behavior change; and meta-analyses, or statistical reviews, of the fear research suggest that the cognitions identified in the PMT, and later in the EPPM, are important to fear appeal effectiveness. Still, there are significant holes in our knowledge. First, no model of fear appeals has been endorsed as fully capturing the process of fear's effects on decision making and action (see Mongeau, 1998; Witte & Allen, 2000). To the extent message features evoke perceptions of susceptibility and severity, as well as response and self-efficacy, fear may generate persuasion, but how these constructs relate to one another is still unclear. Additionally, questions about whether severity and susceptibility information should always be explicitly included in a message, or whether "implicit" fear appeals might be more effective, have also been raised (Nabi, Roskos-Ewoldsen, & Dillman Carpentier, 2007). That is, evidence suggests that when audiences are very knowledgeable about a subject, including information about the severity and susceptibility of a threat in a fear appeal may actually be more irritating than fear inducing and, thus, less effective. Indeed, the research on fear appeals is rather complicated by the fact that fear appeals often evoke emotions other than just fear, like anger, sadness, or disgust, (Dillard, Plotnick, Godbold, Freimuth, & Edgar, 1996), which makes it difficult to assess the effects of fear versus these other emotions. Thus, in sum, though fear appeals generally give a persuasive advantage over non-fear-based messages, there is still much work to be done in linking the theory of fear appeals to appropriate message design.

THE PERSUASIVE EFFECT OF GUILT

Unlike fear appeals, there has been minimal theorizing regarding the effects of guilt on attitude change. Still, there is some discussion in the research literature about how one might evoke guilt and the conditions under which it may be effective in persuasive contexts (O'Keefe, 2002). Guilt is typically evoked when people feel they have violated an internalized norm (Lazarus, 1991), like "one shouldn't lie" or "one shouldn't cause harm to another." Thus, creating the perception that one has transgressed against, or harmed, another person is likely to evoke guilt in one's audience. Further, people are likely to feel more guilt over transgressions when there is some preexisting interpersonal relationship. That is, a person will likely feel guiltier after lying to a friend than to a stranger. Once guilt is aroused, a person is motivated to alleviate that uncomfortable state by making amends to the wronged party. For example, if you've lied to your parents, you might voluntarily do some extra chores around the house. This action may not undo the lie, but it does offer a benefit to the harmed party while also helping to reestablish your view of yourself as a good person, all of which helps to alleviate guilt. Given guilt is such an uncomfortable state, people are motivated to reduce it quickly. Making amends is one way to reduce guilt, but people also eliminate guilt through various forms of rationalization, for example, by denying they did something wrong or by convincing themselves the harmed party deserved what they got.

Of course the question here is: Does guilt help or harm persuasion? The answer is, unsurprisingly, it depends. Early studies of guilt in interpersonal contexts assumed that guilt would increase compliance with requests from strangers, and research seemed to support that hypothesis (e.g., Carlsmith & Gross, 1969; Freedman, Wallington, & Bless, 1967). Indeed, meta-analysis results support a positive linear relationship between interpersonal transgression and compliance (O'Keefe, 2000). Further, guilt has also been shown to be effective in interpersonal contexts with stronger relational ties (Baumeister, Stillwell, & Heatherton, 1994).

However, interestingly, evidence from media-based studies suggests a *negative* linear relationship in that the stronger the guilt appeal in a media message (e.g., a telethon to raise money for victims of famine or flood), the less persuasive the message may be (O'Keefe, 2000). This effect tends to be attributed to the fact that high levels of guilt are associated with high levels of anger (Pinto & Priest, 1991), which short-circuits attitude change if the anger is directed at the source of the message (Nabi, 2002b). The striking contrast between guilt in interpersonal versus media contexts is likely a function of the lack of interpersonal connection between the media message source and the audience. This does not mean, however, that guilt cannot be a successful media strategy. Rather, care must be taken in message design to minimize the likelihood of resistance.

Based on the theoretical conceptualization of guilt, as well as the small body of empirical literature, it is clear that media messages should be subtle in pointing out possible transgressions (e.g., not eating healthy or exercising frequently enough) or anticipated transgressions (e.g., not donating to a worthy cause or sponsoring a child in a developing country) to keep guilt arousal moderate and to minimize the chances of reactance. Next, to the extent a familiar and likeable source (e.g., a celebrity) can be used in the message, the perception of an interpersonal relationship may increase, and thus increase the audience's tolerance for the guilt experience. Third, guilt messages should provide very clear and easy to perform behaviors that can be performed quickly to alleviate the guilt. If there is too much time passage between message exposure and opportunity to act, the likelihood that the guilt will dissipate by some other means (e.g., denial) greatly increases, thus reducing the chances the audience will comply with the recommended action. Finally, media messages may wish to tap into anticipated guilt. That is, rather than leave the audience feeling guilty over past mistakes, messages can help audiences see how they can avoid feeling guilty by altering their behavior to avoid creating future harm (e.g., don't text and drive so that you won't feel guilty about causing an accident at some point in the future) (Lindsey, 2005). These are just a few suggestions for how to design more effective guilt appeals, though more theorizing and research is needed to substantiate these claims.

HUMOR AND PERSUASION

A third area of emotion and persuasion that has received notable attention is the role of humor in advertising. Although there is a general sense that funny advertisements are effective, in fact, reviews of the humor literature have concluded that they are generally no more persuasive than their non-humorous equivalents (see Weinberger & Gulas, 1992). That is, as long as the commercials contain the same content, serious and humorous presentations are equally effective. Importantly, however, such reviews have noted that humor may enhance message attention and source liking. Given, as noted earlier, that message attention is a necessary, though not sufficient, condition for persuasive success, the fact that funny messages garner greater attention means that they may, in fact, have an inherent persuasive advantage in a competitive media environment. However, though humor may offer an advantage in terms of capturing attention, if not implemented properly, it may undermine that advantage if the humor distracts from, rather than is integrated with, the main point of the message. For example, the GEICO cavemen commercials are arguably effective because the cavemen are so directly tied to the product name and slogan. However, the concepts of "cavemen" and "car insurance" are not naturally linked, so it is possible that though people may remember and like the commercials, they may have difficulty remembering with what product they are associated, thus undermining their effectiveness in terms of purchase behavior.

With the increasing popularity of political satire programs, such as the *Daily Show* and the *Colbert Report,* there has been an upswing in interest in examining the process through which humor may have persuasive influence. For example, Nabi, Moyer-Gusé, and Byrne (2007) argue that humor may not have immediate persuasive effect because though audiences attend closely to the message, they discount it as a joke that is not intended to persuade, thus minimizing the message content's effects on their attitudes. However, they also posit that this type of processing may lead to a "sleeper effect" such that the persuasive effect of humor may emerge after some time has passed (see also Appel & Richter, 2007, and Young, 2008). Clearly, future research would benefit from closer examination of the contexts, processes, and timing of humor's effect in media-based persuasive efforts.

GENERAL THEORETICAL FRAMEWORKS FOR EMOTIONAL APPEALS

Despite the focus on a very limited number of emotions thus far, there is growing interest in understanding the effects of a range of emotions in the processing of persuasive messages (see Nabi, 2007, for a more extensive discussion) and emerging models attempt to examine those processes. For example, the cognitive functional model (CFM; Nabi, 1999) attempts to explain how message-relevant negative emotions (e.g., fear, anger, sadness, guilt, disgust) affect the direction and stability of persuasive outcome based on three constructs—emotion-driven motivated attention to the issue at hand, motivated processing of the message, and expectation that the message will provide reassurance from the negative situation presented. An initial test of the model (Nabi, 2002a) offered support for some, though not all, of the model's propositions, but as it awaits future tests, the CFM offers insight into the process through which a range of discrete emotions, not just fear, influences message processing and outcomes.

In a similar vein, Nabi (2003, 2007) posits an emotions-as-frames model to explain the effects of more general media exposure on attitudinal and behavioral outcomes. In this model, emotions are conceptualized as frames, or perspectives, through which incoming stimuli are interpreted. The model first notes that certain message features are likely to evoke various discrete emotions. These emotional experiences, moderated by individual differences (e.g., prior knowledge, coping style), are predicted to influence both accessibility of information in the mind as well as information seeking in the environment, which ultimately generate emotion-consistent decisions and action. Nabi argues that through this perspective we may ultimately have a better understanding of the potentially central role emotions may play in determining how a range of media messages, including those designed to persuade, might impact attitudes and behaviors.

Despite these advances, there is much that is still unknown about the effects of emotions on persuasive outcomes. We know little about the conditions under which various negative emotions, like anger or sadness, contribute to persuasive outcomes. Additionally, there has been very little attention to positive emotions, like hope and pride, in motivating attitude and behavior change. Beyond the types of emotions investigated, we also need to know more about the conditions under which emotions draw attention to messages versus generate message avoidance. Of course, once attention is gained, it is critical that the rest of the message be structured appropriately for the audience. Understanding the delicate balance between gaining attention and harnessing it to intended effect has been an elusive challenge in the area of emotional appeals and persuasion, and future research would be well served by tackling this difficult message design issue.

Further, there has been surprisingly little attention to the types of themes that are likely to evoke particular emotions in specific target audiences. For example, the assumption in fear appeal research is that people are scared by threats to their physical body, most especially by thoughts of death. Yet fears of disability (e.g., paralysis, blindness) or disfigurement may prove equally, and sometimes more, frightening than death. Further, not all fears are rooted in physical well-being. Younger audiences are more likely to view themselves as invulnerable to serious physical calamity. However, given that teenagers and young adults are still forming their identities, threats to social acceptance may be far more salient, and thus more frightening, to such audiences than threats to physical well-being. Thus, social harm-based fear appeals may be more effective for such audiences than physical harm-based fear appeals. Future research would be well-served by considering not simply a greater range of emotional responses, but also by matching message content and features to the desired emotional arousal for particular target audiences.

CONCLUSION

At their most functional, emotional states can facilitate attention to persuasive messages and motivate productive action. However, they can also deter desire to attend to a message and lead to rationalization processes that interfere with persuasive success. To this point, fear is the only emotion that has been the focus of substantial theorizing in the domain of emotion and persuasion. Other emotions, like guilt and humor, are in their nascent stages of development, and still other emotions, like anger, sadness, and hope, have been subject to only very limited empirical attention. Indeed, there are still many open questions about the conditions under which fear appeals, as well as other emotional appeals, facilitate attitude and behavior change.

Ultimately, the successful use of emotion to persuade requires, first, a solid understanding of the various emotional states so that one can choose the emotion that is most consistent with one's goals. For example, fear may be useful to alert people to behaviors they don't see as dangerous (e.g., texting while driving), whereas hope may be more useful to motivate people to continue to attempt to change hard-to-change behaviors (e.g., quitting smoking). Second, care must be taken not to arouse emotions that may be counterproductive, like anger, which may generate reactance against the message's goals, or disgust, which may lead audiences to tune out a message. Finally, it is important that emotional appeals convey a sense of response and self-efficacy, so audiences know what they are to do and that they are able to do it. As we await greater theoretical development across the array of emotional appeals that may be used, these guidelines may help us achieve the benefits, while avoiding the pitfalls, of the use of emotion in persuasive contexts.

REFERENCES

Appel, M., & Richter, T. (2007). Persuasive effects of fictional narratives increase over time. *Media Psychology, 10,* 113–134.

Baumeister, R. F., Stillwell, A. M., & Heatherton, T. F. (1994). Guilt: An interpersonal approach. *Psychological Bulletin, 115*(2), 243–267.

Brehm, J. (1966). *A theory of psychological reactance.* New York, Academic Press.

Carlsmith, J. M., & Gross, A. E. (1969). Some effects of guilt on compliance. *Journal of Personality and Social Psychology, 11*(3), 232–239.

Dillard, J. P., Plotnick, C. A., Godbold, L. C., Freimuth, V. S., & Edgar, T. (1996). The multiple affective outcomes of AIDS PSAs: Fear appeals do more than scare people. *Communication Research, 23,* 44–72.

Freedman, J. L., Wallington, S. A., & Bless, E. (1967). Compliance without pressure: The effect of guilt. *Journal of Personality and Social Psychology, 7*(2), 117–124.

Hovland, C. I., Janis, I. L., & Kelley, H. H. (1953). *Communication and persuasion.* New Haven, CT: Yale University Press.

Lazarus, R. S. (1991). *Emotion and adaptation.* New York: Oxford University Press.

Leventhal, H. (1970). Findings and theory in the study of fear communications. In L. Berkowitz (Ed.), *Advances in experimental social psychology* (Vol. 5, pp. 119–186). New York: Academic Press.

Lindsey, L. L. M. (2005). Anticipated guilt as behavioral motivation: An examination of appeals to help unknown others through bone marrow donation. *Human Communication Research, 31,* 453–481.

Mongeau, P. (1998). Another look at fear-arousing persuasive appeals. In M. Allen, & R. W. Preiss (Eds.), *Persuasion: Advances through meta-analysis* (pp. 53–68). Cresskill, NJ: Hampton.

Nabi, R. L. (1999). A cognitive-functional model for the effects of discrete negative emotions on information processing, attitude change, and recall. *Communication Theory, 9,* 292–320.

Nabi, R. L. (2002a). Anger, fear, uncertainty, and attitudes: A test of the cognitive-functional model. *Communication Monographs, 69,* 204–216.

Nabi, R. L. (2002b). Discrete emotions and persuasion. In J. Dillard, & M. Pfau (Eds.), *Handbook of Persuasion* (289–308). Thousand Oaks, CA: Sage.

Nabi, R. L. (2003). The framing effects of emotion: Can discrete emotions influence information recall and policy preference? *Communication Research, 30,* 224–247.

Nabi, R. L. (2007). Emotion and persuasion: A social cognitive perspective. In D. R. Roskos-Ewoldsen, & J. Monahan (Eds.), *Social cognition and communication: Theories and methods* (pp. 377–398). Mahwah, NJ: Erlbaum.

Nabi, R., Moyer-Gusé, E. & Byrne, S. (2007). All joking aside: A serious investigation into the persuasive effect of funny social messages. *Communication Monographs, 74,* 29–54.

Nabi, R. L., Roskos-Ewoldsen, D., & Dillman-Carpentier, F. (2007). Subjective knowledge and fear appeal effectiveness: Implications for message design. Health Communication.

O'Keefe, D. J. (2000). Guilt and social influence. In M. E. Roloff (Ed.), *Communication yearbook 23* (pp. 67–101). Thousand Oaks, CA: Sage.

O'Keefe, D. J. (2002). Guilt as a mechanism of persuasion. In J. P. Dillard, & M. Pfau (Eds.), *The persuasion handbook: Developments in theory and practice* (pp. 329–344). Thousand Oaks, CA: Sage.

Pinto, M. B., & Priest, S. (1991). Guilt appeals in advertising: An exploratory study. *Psychological Reports, 69,* 375–385.

Rogers, R. W. (1975). A protection motivation theory of fear appeals and attitude change. *Journal of Psychology, 91,* 93–114.

Rogers, R. W. (1983). Cognitive and physiological processes in fear appeals and attitude change: A revised theory of protection motivation. In J. T. Cacioppo, & R. E. Petty (Eds.), *Social psychophysiology* (pp. 153–176). New York: Guilford.

Weinberger, M. G., & Gulas, C. S. (1992). The impact of humor in advertising: A review. *Journal of Advertising, 21,* 35–59.

Witte, K. (1992). Putting the fear back into fear appeals: The extended parallel process model. *Communication Monographs, 59,* 329–349.

Witte, K. (1994). Fear control and danger control: A test of the extended parallel process model (EPPM). *Communication Monographs, 61,* 113–134.

Witte, K., & Allen, M. (2000). A meta-analysis of fear appeals: Implications for effective public health campaigns. *Health Education & Behavior, 27,* 591–615.

Young, D. (2008). The privileged role of the late-night joke: Exploring humor's role in disrupting argument scrutiny. *Media Psychology, 11,* 119–142.

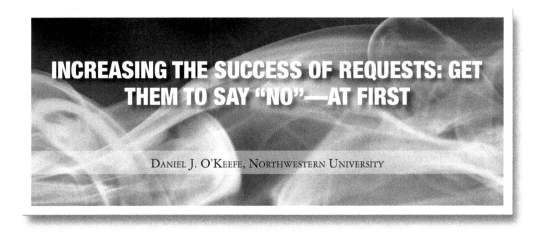

INCREASING THE SUCCESS OF REQUESTS: GET THEM TO SAY "NO"—AT FIRST

DANIEL J. O'KEEFE, NORTHWESTERN UNIVERSITY

Making a request of someone is a common communication task. We ask favors of people, we seek charitable donations from others, we ask people to volunteer for worthy causes, and so on. So how might the success of such requests be increased? Research has found that—somewhat surprisingly—one way to enhance the chances that people will agree to your request is by first getting them to *refuse* a different request.

THE DOOR-IN-THE-FACE STRATEGY

This strategy for increasing the success of requests is known as the "door-in-the-face" (DITF) strategy. The strategy consists of initially making a large request—one that is so large that the person turns it down. Then you make the second, smaller request—the one you're really interested in. The idea is that the person's initially having (metaphorically) closed the door in your face will make the person more likely to agree to your second request than if you had just presented that request all by itself.

Here's a classic example of the strategy (Cialdini et al., 1975, Experiment 1). In this experiment, people on campus sidewalks were approached by a student who indicated that he or she represented the county youth counseling program. People were randomly assigned to a control condition or an experimental condition. In the control condition, the requester made only one request (the "target" request, the one the requester wanted people to agree to). People in this condition were asked whether they would volunteer to chaperone a group of juveniles from the detention center on a two-hour trip to the local zoo; only 17% agreed to this request.

In the DITF (experimental) condition, before that target request was made, people were first asked whether they would volunteer to spend two hours a week for a minimum of two years as an unpaid counselor at a local juvenile detention center. As you might imagine, no one agreed to this huge request. Then the requester made the smaller target request (about chaperoning a trip to the zoo).

Even though this second request was exactly the same as the request in the control condition, in the DITF condition 50% of the people agreed. That is, the compliance rate nearly *tripled*.

Obviously, the DITF strategy can dramatically increase the likelihood that people will agree to your requests. If you make an initial large request that people decline, this can make them much more willing to agree to a second, smaller request.

MODERATING FACTORS

As this study illustrates, the DITF strategy *can* produce dramatic increases in request compliance. But the strategy is not always so successful. Sometimes it's a good strategy to use (it boosts the compliance rate a lot), but sometimes it's not helpful at all. Quite a bit of research has been conducted concerning the DITF strategy, and researchers have learned a great deal about the conditions under which the strategy is more or less successful. These conditions are conveniently described as a set of "moderating factors," that is, factors that moderate (influence) the success of the DITF strategy.

Four specific moderators are worth mentioning here (for a fuller account and additional discussion, see Dillard, Hunter, & Burgoon, 1984; Fern, Monroe, & Avila, 1986; O'Keefe & Hale, 1998, 2001). Each of these factors influences the success of the DITF technique, that is, influences the degree to which using the strategy leads to an increase in request success (compliance rate) above what is found in a control condition in which only the target request is made.

First, the DITF strategy is more successful—there's a bigger increase in request compliance— when the same person makes the two requests than when different people make the two requests. If a different person makes the second request, the strategy isn't as effective.

Second, the strategy is more successful when the two requests have the same beneficiary as opposed to benefiting different recipients. If the first request benefits an environmental-protection group and the second request benefits a traffic-safety group, the strategy won't be as effective as it would have been if both requests had had the same beneficiary.

Third, the strategy is more successful with prosocial requests—ones that benefit society at large or people in need (requests of the sort made by charitable groups, civic-benefit organizations, and the like)—than with non-prosocial requests, such as from businesses or other profit-seeking organizations. That is, charities get a bigger boost (in compliance rates) from using this strategy than businesses do. Just to be clear: The point here is not that requests from charities are more successful than requests from businesses. The point is that charities get a bigger *increase* in compliance rates by using the DITF strategy than businesses do (a bigger increase over the success rate seen in control conditions); using this strategy helps charities more than it does businesses.

Fourth, the strategy is more successful if there is little or no delay between the two requests. For example, if the second request comes a week or more after the first request, the DITF strategy isn't nearly as helpful as when the second request comes right after the first request is refused.

Notice that in the classic study described earlier, the conditions were perfect for finding a large effect of using the DITF strategy: The same person made the two requests, the two requests benefited the same people (the juveniles at the detention center), the requests were prosocial (helping those juveniles through the county youth counseling program), and there was no delay between the two requests. This is exactly the recipe for DITF success—exactly the set of circumstances under which using the DITF strategy is most advantageous.

Knowing about these moderating factors is important for two reasons. First, these factors make clear the conditions under which deploying this strategy is likely to be most useful—or, expressed the other way round, the conditions under which using the strategy may not be very helpful. For example, imagine that a marketing research firm wants to get people to volunteer to answer a 20-question survey about a local business. Should they use the DITF strategy and start by asking people to complete a 100-question survey? Probably not. Because the requests would come from a marketing firm, not a prosocial organization, the DITF strategy is unlikely to be very helpful in boosting compliance rates.

Of course, it's possible to know that a social influence strategy can work, and to know some of the moderating factors, without necessarily knowing *why* the strategy works. But knowing how and why an influence strategy works—that is, having a good explanation of the strategy's effects—is helpful. If nothing else, knowing why a strategy works makes it easier to see when that strategy might be most useful.

And this brings us to the second way in which identifying moderating variables is valuable: The moderating factors constrain the potential *explanations* for why this strategy works. A satisfactory explanation has to show why the various moderator variables work as they do. For example, a good explanation of DITF effects has to explain why it makes a difference whether the same person makes both requests. We know that that's a moderating factor—one that influences how successful the strategy is—so presumably the underlying mechanism (the mechanism that drives the strategy) must somehow be affected by whether the same person makes both requests. In short, any good explanation of why the DITF strategy works has to explain why those moderating variables have the effects they do.

EXPLAINING THE STRATEGY'S EFFECTS

So what explains the success of the DITF strategy? Why does it work the way it does? The explanation is actually a little complicated, because it involves a combination of two different processes: reciprocity and guilt.

Reciprocity is a widely-recognized, fundamental principle governing human relationships (Cialdini, 2009, pp. 18–50). The core idea is that we should try to repay others for things they do for us—"repay" not necessarily with money, but with a matching action. If a casual acquaintance invites you to a party, you'll feel some pressure to invite that person to your next party; if you pick up the check when we go out for lunch one day, I'm expected to reciprocate the next time we go out; and so on. One can see reciprocity at work in a variety of ways and a variety of settings. For example, in negotiating or bargaining situations, it commonly takes the form of reciprocating concessions. In such situations, the general expectation is that if one side makes a concession, the other side is supposed to reciprocate by making a concession of its own. For instance, in labor-management negotiations, if management agrees to increased pay for workers, perhaps the labor union then agrees to reduced benefits.

Applied to the DITF strategy, the idea is that the sequence of requests makes the situation look like one of these bargaining situations. The requester initially starts off with a large request, which gets refused—so then the requester makes a concession, by making a smaller (second) request. This naturally puts some pressure on the other person to reciprocate that concession—and the easy way to reciprocate is to agree to that second request.

Reciprocity provides a good basis for understanding one particular moderating factor, namely whether the two requests come from the same person. When the two requests do come from the same person, it's apparent that that person is making a concession—making a smaller request than the person originally asked for. But if a different person makes the second request, then no one has made a concession; the second request is smaller than the first, but the second requester has not made a concession (because that person did not make the first request).

However, reciprocity, by itself, does not illuminate some other aspects of DITF effects. Consider, for example, that it matters (to the success of the strategy) whether the requests are prosocial. There is no apparent reason why this should be true if reciprocity is the only driving force behind the DITF strategy (cf. Cialdini & Goldstein, 2004, p. 601). That is, a reciprocity-based account, by itself, leaves some moderator variables unexplained.

And that's where the second process comes in: guilt. The idea is that when the DITF strategy works, it works because refusal of the first request makes the person feel guilty—and in order to alleviate those guilt feelings, the person agrees to the second request (O'Keefe & Figgé, 1997, 1999). Rejecting worthy requests is just the sort of thing that might make people feel guilty. And guilt is an emotion with built-in motivating force; when people feel guilty, they characteristically report having reactions such as feeling like undoing what they did, wanting to make up for what they did wrong, and wanting to make amends (Roseman, Wiest, & Swartz, 1994, p. 215; Tangney, Miller, Flicker, & Barlow, 1996).

Guilt provides a good basis for understanding the effects of three specific moderating factors. Why does the DITF strategy work better when the two requests have the same beneficiary? Because a person gets more guilt reduction by agreeing to a request that benefits the same individual (or group) that was injured by the rejection of the first request. In that classic DITF experiment, it's easy to imagine that a person would feel guilty about not helping those juveniles at the detention center (feel guilty about turning down the first request)—and so would jump at the chance to help those same kids by saying "yes" to the second request (but cf. O'Keefe, 2002, pp. 336–337).

Why is the strategy more helpful when the requests are prosocial (charitable requests, rather than from businesses)? Because people probably feel guiltier about rejecting a charity than they do about rejecting a business—and since they feel more guilt, they're more eager to find a way to reduce that guilt. That is, feeling more guilt makes them more eager to agree to the second request.

And why is it important that the second request comes right after the first one? Because over time, people's feelings of guilt will surely fade away—and so if the requester comes back a week later with the second request, people might not be feeling guilty any more.

So neither reciprocity nor guilt seems, on their own, sufficient to explain why the DITF strategy works—but the combination of those two processes makes for a very satisfying picture. Turning down the first request makes people feel guilty. The presentation of the second, smaller request represents a concession by the requester, which naturally invites a reciprocal concession. And accepting the second request provides both a means of reciprocating the concession and a means of reducing guilt.

Because guilt and reciprocity are the driving forces behind the success of the DITF strategy, when considering whether to employ the DITF strategy, it will to useful to ask: "If the person turns down my first request, are they likely to feel guilty about that? And when I make the smaller second request, are they likely to feel any pressure to reciprocate my concession?"

For example, some people are more likely in general to experience feelings of guilt than other people are (e.g., Tangney, 1990). Since arousal of guilt feelings is central to how the DITF strategy works, presumably the strategy should be especially effective for people who are naturally guilt-prone. The strategy might not be quite so helpful when directed at people who aren't especially susceptible to guilt feelings.

CONCLUSION

You can increase the chances that people will agree to a request if, before making it, you first make a large request that people refuse. To maximize the effectiveness of this strategy, four specific conditions should be met: One person should make both requests, the two requests should benefit the same person or group, the requests should be prosocial (socially beneficial), and the second request should be made right after the first one is refused.

REFERENCES

Cialdini, R. B. (2009). *Influence: Science and practice* (5th ed.). Boston, MA: Pearson.

Cialdini, R. B., & Goldstein, N. J. (2004). Social influence: Compliance and conformity. *Annual Review of Psychology, 55,* 591–621.

Cialdini, R. B., Vincent, J. E., Lewis, S. K., Catalan, J., Wheeler, D., & Darby, B. L. (1975). Reciprocal concessions procedure for inducing compliance: The door-in-the-face technique. *Journal of Personality and Social Psychology, 31,* 206–215.

Dillard, J. P., Hunter, J. E., & Burgoon, M. (1984). Sequential-request persuasive strategies: Meta-analysis of foot-in-the-door and door-in-the-face. *Human Communication Research, 10,* 461–488.

Fern, E. F., Monroe, K. B., & Avila, R. A. (1986). Effectiveness of multiple request strategies: A synthesis of research results. *Journal of Marketing Research, 23,* 144–152.

O'Keefe, D. J. (2002). Guilt as a mechanism of persuasion. In J. P. Dillard & M. Pfau (Eds.), *The persuasion handbook: Developments in theory and practice* (pp. 329–344). Thousand Oaks, CA: Sage.

O'Keefe, D. J., & Figgé, M. (1997). A guilt-based explanation of the door-in-the-face influence strategy. *Human Communication Research, 24,* 64–81.

O'Keefe, D. J., & Figgé, M. (1999). Guilt and expected guilt in the door-in-the-face technique. *Communication Monographs, 66,* 312–324.

O'Keefe, D. J., & Hale, S. L. (1998). The door-in-the-face influence strategy: A random-effects meta-analytic review. *Communication Yearbook, 21,* 1–33.

O'Keefe, D. J., & Hale, S. L. (2001). An odds-ratio-based meta-analysis of research on the door-in-the-face influence strategy. *Communication Reports, 14,* 31–38.

Roseman, I. J., Wiest, C., & Swartz, T. S. (1994). Phenomenology, behaviors, and goals differentiate discrete emotions. *Journal of Personality and Social Psychology, 67,* 206–221.

Tangney, J. P. (1990). Assessing individual differences in proneness to shame and guilt: Development of the Self-Conscious Affect and Attribution Inventory. *Journal of Personality and Social Psychology, 59,* 102–111.

Tangney, J. P., Miller, R. S., Flicker, L., & Barlow, D. H. (1996). Are shame, guilt, and embarrassment distinct emotions? *Journal of Personality and Social Psychology, 70,* 1256–1269.

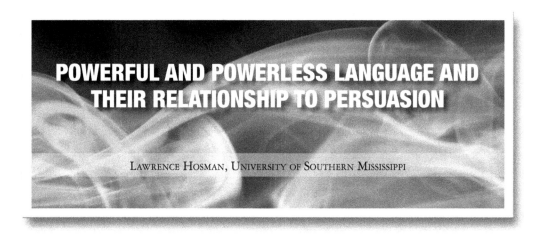

POWERFUL AND POWERLESS LANGUAGE AND THEIR RELATIONSHIP TO PERSUASION

LAWRENCE HOSMAN, UNIVERSITY OF SOUTHERN MISSISSIPPI

Imagine being a juror and hearing a witness testify like the following:

"Um . . . I'm pretty sure I saw the defendant come around the corner and rob the woman. He sort of grabbed her purse. Uh . . she was kind of scared, you know?"

What impression did you form of this person? Are they confident? Are they uncertain? Are they powerful? Would you believe their account of the robbery?

Image the same situation and having a witness testify like the following:

"I saw the defendant come around the corner and rob the woman. He grabbed her purse. She was scared."

What impression did you form of this person? Were they confident? Uncertain? Powerful? Would you believe their account of the robbery? Which of the two descriptions do you find more persuasive?

These are the sorts of questions I try to answer. I look at the language people use and how it affects the impression formed of them and their persuasiveness. More specifically, I look at language that may cause people to see speakers as powerful or powerless, and then I look at whether it helps or hurts speakers' abilities to persuade others. So, the question I'm going to answer for you in this chapter is: *How can we use powerful (and avoid powerless) language to persuade people?*

The study that was most important to my research on powerful and powerless language was conducted by professors at Duke University, led by William O'Barr (Erickson, Lind, Johnson, & O'Barr, 1978). These researchers observed 150 hours of courtroom communication and found that those low in power in the courtroom (witnesses, for example) spoke in a distinctive way. When speaking, they tended to be overly polite ("sir"), hedged ("sort of," ""kind of"), filled their hesitations ("um," "er"), used tag questions (a statement with a question "tagged" onto the end, such as "that's what happened, isn't it?"), and unnecessary or "empty" intensifiers ("really," "awesome"). They labeled this powerless language. Those high in power (judges, attorneys) tended to speak not using that language, and this was called powerful language. As social scientists, they wanted to further support their observations and conducted a research study where they wrote courtroom testimony that mirrored these differences. Since the impressions formed of speakers are important to their persuasive success, these researchers asked people for their impressions of the speaker using powerful or powerless language. Their findings can be summarized simply—receivers find speakers using powerless language to be less credible, less powerful, less likeable, and more culpable for a crime than speakers using powerful language.

This single study began research that has continued over thirty years. Much of my early research (Hosman, 1989; Hosman & Wright, 1987; Wright & Hosman, 1983) looked at the impressions created by communicators using powerful and powerless language. This research generally supported the original O'Barr study—if speakers want to be perceived favorably, they should use powerful language and avoid powerless language.

One concern raised was that much of the early research focused on the legal communication context. Was it possible that powerful language was better than powerless language only in a legal context? Several researchers and I tried answering this question by conducting research in other contexts—employment interviews (Parton, Siltanen, Hosman, & Langenderfer, 2002), crisis-intervention contexts (Bradac & Mulac, 1984a), classroom contexts (Haleta, 1996), and computer-mediated contexts (Adkins & Brashers, 1995). In each of these contexts, essentially the same results were found—powerless language created a more negative impression of the speaker than did powerful language.

In the early 1990s, this research took a new direction—one that is still my primary research interest. This direction looked at whether power and powerless language affected persuasion. To study these effects most of this research has used either a persuasion theory called the Elaboration Likelihood Model (ELM) or the Heuristic Systematic Model (HSM). These are called dual-process models because they view persuasion as occurring via one of two routes. One route is labeled a "central" or "systematic" route where receivers carefully scrutinize a message's argument and evidence and are persuaded based on this scrutiny. The other route is labeled a "peripheral" or "heuristic" route in which receivers quickly analyze something in the message and are persuaded based on this quick judgment. The question driving this research was whether powerful or powerless language would cause receivers to use the central or peripheral route when listening to a persuasive message. Would, for example, powerful language cause receivers to carefully scrutinize the persuasive message? Might powerless language cause receivers to use the peripheral route, form a quick impression of the speaker, and be persuaded based on this quick analysis?

The earliest study was done by Jim Bradac and his colleagues (Gibbons, Busch, & Bradac, 1991). They looked at whether powerful and powerless language differed in its persuasive impact and impression formation. In their study, people read a speech advocating that students should take comprehensive exams in order to receive an undergraduate degree. This comprehensive exam would test students over everything covered in their undergraduate career. In one version of the speech, the language was powerful, while in the other the language was powerless. Otherwise the speeches were identical. They found the pattern observed before—a speaker using powerful language was perceived more positively than a speaker using powerless language. However, what they did not find was that powerful language was more persuasive than powerless language. This was a puzzle—a speaker who uses powerful language is perceived more positively than a speaker who hedges, hesitates, and uses tag questions, but is not any more persuasive.

A number of researchers, including me, were puzzled. Some found that the original study seemed an unusual finding—they found that powerful language was, indeed, more persuasive than powerless language (Sparks, Areni, & Cox, 1998; Sparks & Areni, 2008). Other studies supported the original finding by Jim Bradac—that powerful language was more persuasive than powerless language (Hosman, Huebner, & Siltanen, 2002).

How do you resolve these contradictory findings? One answer is that there's more to persuasion than the way one speaks. For instance, isn't the quality of the argument used by the speaker important? What if a speaker uses a high quality argument (sound reasoning, excellent, credible information), but delivers it with hedges, hesitations, and the like? Or what if a speaker uses powerful language but also has a weak argument (biased information, fallacious reasoning)?

Other researchers and I have been trying to answer these types of questions. Thomas Holtgraves and his research partners (1999) looked at whether the quality of a speaker's arguments is important and found that it is. Using powerful language leads receivers to perceive the message as having high quality arguments and this leads to persuasion. Conversely, using powerless language leads receivers to perceive the message's arguments to be of low quality and thus hurt persuasion. Other researchers have observed similar effects (Areni & Sparks, 2005). So, the language you use to express your ideas will affect how people perceive the quality of your ideas. Powerless language will lead people to see your arguments as weak.

I have found (Hosman, Huebner, & Siltanen, 2002) that if one used powerful language, it did not affect how the receivers thought about one's supporting material. However, if one spoke using a weak argument, powerful language could overcome that weakness and cause receivers to think positively about the content of what was said.

Another way of thinking about powerful and powerless language emerged after the Erickson study in 1978. Powerful and powerless language are comprised of a number of elements (hedges, hesitations, and the like), but do they all contribute equally or similarly to the impressions formed or to the persuasion that occurs? In fact, some of the components may work in contradictory ways. For example, powerless language includes hedges ("sort of," "kind of"), which weaken the force of a statement or express speaker uncertainty about the topic, but it also contains intensifiers ("awesome," "definitely") that would seem to strengthen the force of a statement or express speaker certainty. So how is it that these elements work together, or is it possible that some have little effect on impressions and others have a substantial effect on impressions? Or, if each element is bad by itself, does more than one element "double" the bad effect? So other researchers and I began to look at how the individual parts work when by themselves and when combined with other elements. One important study (Bradac & Mulac, 1984b) looked at a number of elements individually to see how powerful they were perceived in an employment interview. What this study found was that hesitations and tag questions were perceived as most powerless. Other elements like hedges and intensifiers were perceived as neither powerful nor powerless. So, at least in an employment interview, an interviewee shouldn't use filled pauses or tag questions ("I have good computer skills, don't you think?"), but being polite is an asset.

In other studies (Hosman, 1989; Hosman & Wright, 1987; Wright & Hosman, 1983), I looked at how combinations of these elements worked. These studies found two general patterns. First, not using any powerless language element is best. Second, the presence of any one element (tag question, hesitation, hedge, and so forth) damaged the impression formed of the speaker. Using more than one did not do additional damage to one's impression.

As with the research on powerless and powerful language, the research on the elements turned to their persuasive impact. Do hedges, tag questions, or the like have negative impact on persuasion? Several studies (Blankenship & Holtgraves, 2005; Holtgraves & Lasky, 1999) first looked at how several elements affect persuasion or attitude change. These studies found that some components hurt persuasion, while others have minimal impact. In particular, hedges and hesitations hurt persuasion—when speakers hedge or hesitate, their persuasive efforts will be hurt.

Hedges represent an unusual case, however. Although the original research saw hedges as powerless because they qualified a speaker's statement and indicated that the speaker was uncertain, others point out that hedging one's statements is very appropriate. Few things are absolutely black or white, and thus hedging is a way for a speaker to be accurate. Scientists, for example, are trained to qualify or hedge their findings, because they are only probably true, not absolutely true. Durik, Britt, Reynolds, and Story (2008) observed that a speaker could hedge one of two types of statements—statements involving data or statements involving interpretation. So, a speaker could say "global warming might be causing more droughts" or say "*Descendants* is probably the best movie this year." What these researchers found is that hedging a data statement has a negative effect on persuasion, while hedging a statement of interpretation does not have a negative effect. Apparently, if you hedge a data statement it indicates that you are unsure of the facts, which hurts your credibility. Hedging one's interpretation may merely indicate that a speaker is uncertain of their opinion or recognizes that others may disagree with them, but it is not as bad to do so.

Why do these effects occur? Why is powerless language evaluated more negatively than powerful language? Why are certain powerless elements like hesitations or hedges evaluated negatively? Researchers have come up with three explanations. They are an uncertainty explanation, a control-of-others explanation, and a control-of-self explanation.

The uncertainty explanation is pretty simple. It says that when a speaker uses a powerless style they are perceived to be uncertain or tentative about what they are saying and we don't like uncertain people—they aren't credible, attractive, or persuasive. Imagine a witness at a trial who, when asked if they committed a crime, says "Uh, I'm kind of sure I didn't, don't you think?" Compare this to the witness who says "No, I didn't." This also applies to particular elements, such as hesitations. Hesitations communicate that a speaker is uncertain about what he or she said, and this hurts his or her credibility and persuasiveness. Several studies (e.g., Hosman & Siltanen, 1994) are supportive of the uncertainty explanation.

The control-of-others explanation is different. It says that we like people who are powerful, particularly if they are influential and effective. Powerless language indicates someone who is not influential or effective, or who does not control others. This language is therefore evaluated negatively. Conversely, powerful language indicates a person in power, who influences others or is effective, and this causes receivers to evaluate the person positively.

A third explanation is a control-over-self explanation. Powerless language is hesitant, hedging, polite, and questioning, which creates a picture of a person who "doesn't have it together." Powerful language, on the other hand, is straightforward and direct. It reflects a person who is in control of him- or herself—and is self-assured.

Some studies (Hosman & Siltanen, 1994) have tried to see which of the two control explanations is best. They found that powerless language is evaluated as having less control-over-others as well as less control-of-self than powerful language. However, when looking at which explanation was better, they found that the control-over-others explanation was stronger and thus better explained how powerful and powerless language work. Therefore, if you want to be perceived as influential and effective, do not use powerless language.

There is one last question that this research has looked at—what role does the speaker's biological sex play in the persuasion process? Does it make a difference whether the speaker using a powerful or powerless language is a man or a woman? Do men and women evaluate powerful and powerless language differently? When the research began in the late 1970s, Robin Lakoff (1975) had presented an intriguing, but controversial idea—that women speak with a particular style—a powerless style. Women, she argued, hedged a great deal, used empty intensifiers, were very polite in their speech, and exhibited other features. She claimed that powerless language was a woman's style of speech. The O'Barr and Atkins 1980 study undermined this idea, showing that it was status and power, not biological sex, which were important. But, gender and power are linked together. Despite great strides in a number of areas, women tend to be less powerful and have less status than men, and it's difficult to separate gender and power. Thus, the biological sex of the speaker may be important as to how powerful and powerless language is reacted to.

Early on, several studies looked at whether biological sex affected how receivers perceived powerless or powerful language. These studies were very inconsistent in what they found. Some studies (Bradac & Mulac, 1984b; Erickson et al., 1978) found that a receiver's biological sex affected how powerful and powerless language were perceived. Other studies (Hosman & Wright, 1987; Wright & Hosman, 1983) found that a receiver's biological sex made no difference in how powerful or powerless language was perceived.

At this point the best that can be said about the relationship between a receiver's biological sex and the perceptions of powerful and powerless language is that it is puzzling and much more complex than originally thought. In fact, since the early 2000s few researchers have looked at biological sex in their studies of power of language and persuasion. One study that did (Areni & Sparks, 2005) found that a speaker's biological sex did not make a difference. Most importantly, overly simplistic stereotypes, such as women can speak too assertively, are not warranted.

CONCLUSION

Since powerful and powerless language have been studied for years, some conclusions are clear. Speakers using powerless language such as hesitations or filled pauses, tag questions, and hedges can hurt perceptions of their credibility, likeability, and argument quality, and will also hurt their ability to persuade others. Speakers who do not use powerless language are perceived positively—they are perceived as credible, likeable, and using high quality arguments, and they will be persuasive.

As a communicator, you should remember that how you say something can be as important as what you say. Whether in a legal setting, employment context, or public speaking context, using powerless language can negatively affect how you are perceived by others and whether you will be able to persuade them.

REFERENCES

Adkins, M., & Brashers, D. E. (1995). The power of language in computer-mediated groups. *Management Communication Quarterly, 8,* 289–322.

Areni, C. S., & Sparks, J. R. (2005). Language, power and persuasion. *Psychology and Marketing, 22,* 507–525.

Blankenship, K. L., & Holtgraves, T. (2005). The role of different markers of linguistic powerlessness in persuasion. *Journal of Language and Social Psychology, 24,* 3–24.

Bradac, J. J., & Mulac, A. (1984a). Attributional consequences of powerful and powerless speech styles in a crisis-intervention context. *Journal of Language and Social Psychology, 3,* 1–19.

Bradac, J. J., & Mulac, A. (1984b). A molecular view of powerful and powerless speech styles: Attributional consequences of specific language features and communicator intentions. *Communication Monographs, 51,* 307–319.

Durik, A. M., Britt, M. A., Reynolds, R., & Storey, J. (2008). The effects of hedges in persuasive arguments: A nuanced analysis of language. *Journal of Language and Social Psychology, 27,* 217–234.

Erickson, B., Lind, E. A., Johnson, B. C., & O'Barr, W. M. (1978). Speech style and impression-formation in a court setting: The effects of "powerful" and "powerless" speech. *Journal of Experimental Social Psychology, 14,* 266–279.

Gibbons, P., Busch, J., & Bradac, J. J. (1991). Powerful versus powerless language: Consequences for persuasion, impression formation, and cognitive response. *Journal of Language and Social Psychology, 10,* 115–133.

Haleta, L. L. (1996). Student perceptions of teachers' use of language: The effects of powerful and powerless language on impression formation and uncertainty. *Communication Education, 45,* 16–28.

Holtgraves, T. M., & Lasky, B. (1999). Linguistic power and persuasion. *Journal of Language and Social Psychology, 18,* 196–205.

Hosman, L. A. (1989). The evaluative consequences of hedges, hesitations, and intensifiers: Powerful and powerless speech styles. *Human Communication Research, 15,* 383–406.

Hosman, L. A., Huebner, T. M., & Siltanen, S. A. (2002). The impact of power-of-speech style, argument strength, and need for cognition on impression formation, cognitive responses, and persuasion. *Journal of Language and Social Psychology, 21,* 361–379.

Hosman, L. A., & Siltanen, S. A. (1994). The attributional and evaluative consequences of powerful and powerless speech styles: An examination of the "control over others" and "control of self" explanations. *Language & Communication, 14,* 287–298.

Hosman, L. A., & Wright, J. W., II. (1987). The effects of hedges and hesitations on impression formation in a simulated courtroom context. *Western Journal of Speech Communication, 51,* 173–188.

Lakoff, R. (1975). *Language and woman's place.* New York: Harper Colophon Books.

O'Barr, W. M., & Atkins, B. K. (1980). "'Women's language' or 'powerless language.'" In S. McConnell-Ginet, R. Borker, & N. Furman (Eds.), *Women and Language in Literature and Society* (pp. 93-110). New York: Praeger.

Parton, S. R., Siltanen, S. A., Hosman, L. A., & Langenderfer, J. (2002). Employment interview outcomes and speech style effects. *Journal of Language and Social Psychology, 21,* 144–161.

Sparks, J. R., & Areni, C. S. (2008). Style versus substance: Multiple roles of language power in persuasion. *Journal of Applied Social Psychology, 38,* 37–60.

Sparks, J. R., Areni, C. S., & Cox, K. C. (1998). An investigation of the effects of language style and communication modality on persuasion. *Communication Monographs, 65,* 108–125.

Wright, J. W., II, & Hosman, L. A. (1983). Language style and sex bias in the courtroom: The effects of male and female use of hedges and intensifiers on impression formation. *Southern Speech Communication Journal, 48,* 137–152.

SECTION 14
POLITICAL COMMUNICATION

It is not uncommon to hear an undergraduate student proclaim being uninterested in "political stuff." So one might reasonably ask the question of who exactly is or should be interested in political communication. The context of political communication addresses how people come together in attempting to influence their world. Political communication can occur at the local, regional, national, or even international (or global) level. The research widely demonstrates that college students are increasingly disengaged from political life. The three authors in this section explore our engagement in contemporary political life. First, Robert Ivie (Indiana University, Bloomington, USA) addresses the question: *How can we, as citizens of democracy, engage productively with others despite our political differences?* Ivie suggests we adopt the stereoscopic gaze as a strategy of perspective taking that can facilitate our communication across a divided citizenry. Second, Mitchell McKinney (University of Missouri) considers directly the motivations that might decrease the apathy of college students such as yourself as he answers the question: *How can we encourage college students to participate in a more political life (e.g., voting)?* Third, Trevor Parry-Giles (National Communication Association) and Sean Luechtefeld (University of Maryland, College Park) consider the question: *How does campaign communication influence who we vote for?* They examine research about the role of campaign speeches, campaign advertisements, and campaign debates in determining who we are likely to vote for. Throughout these three essays you are challenged with the potential for increasing your own engagement in politics and civic life.

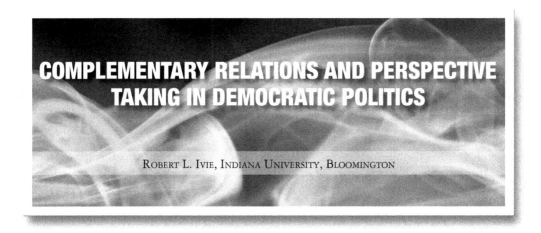

COMPLEMENTARY RELATIONS AND PERSPECTIVE TAKING IN DEMOCRATIC POLITICS

ROBERT L. IVIE, INDIANA UNIVERSITY, BLOOMINGTON

As citizens of a democracy, we are challenged to engage our political differences with one another productively, which is not an easy challenge to meet. We are more likely to throw our hands up in despair, or to just withdraw from politics entirely, than to deliberate our differences constructively. Our tendency is to speak of our political adversaries as if they are our enemies (Mouffe, 2005, pp. 19–21). We readily demonize them by calling them "Liars! Cheaters! Evildoers!" (De Luca and Buell, 2005). Such accusations mark the demise of civil debate and the decline of democracy, at least in those moments of acrimony.

Indeed, democracy is more difficult to practice than to profess. It is not simply a matter of voting periodically for one's favorite candidate for political office. It is a politics of deliberation among adversaries. Especially in a complex society of competing interests and diverse identities, our differences become barriers to agreement. Opposing a common enemy is about our only incentive to unite with one another, especially when we perceive some individual or party as hostile to our wellbeing or antagonistic to our fundamental beliefs and values. Democracy is achieved, even if temporarily, only when we overcome this powerful temptation to create enemies out of political adversaries (Ivie, 2008b, p. 454). How is that democratic moment realized?

CIVILITY AND EQUALITY

William Norwood Brigance (1952) was a discerning speech teacher who understood that the biggest challenge facing a democratic people is to learn how to live together by persuading rather than coercing one another. Rhetoric, he taught, can serve the democratic purpose of constructing healthy human relations. It isn't easy to meet this rhetorical standard of talking out our differences instead of engaging in a war of words, but it is perhaps the ultimate test of collective self-governance. Brigance believed in teaching citizens to resist discourses of hatred and fear (Ivie, 2008a, pp. 267, 271).

Yet, our differences can be substantial enough to put us politically at odds with one another in a competitive society, where typically one person's gain is considered another person's loss. Additionally, perspectives vary significantly from person to person and group to group. Different sets of people see the world from divergent vantage points. Their differing points of view are reflected in the ways they speak to and about one another, the attitudes they adopt toward politics, the stereotypes they indulge, the culture wars they engage, and the political positions they endorse or dispute (Lakoff, 1996).

In short, political life is necessarily agonistic in some degree, but democracy breaks down when, as political philosopher Chantal Mouffe (2000, pp. 13, 102–103) observes, antagonism goes too far and adversaries become enemies for lack of a shared symbolic space. We need to establish a point of identification to compensate for our substantial differences.

Seeking a full consensus on divisive political issues is an elusive goal at best, even under ideal circumstances. Fortunately, unanimity of opinion is unnecessary for democracy to work within a pluralistic society. Engaging in a productive contestation of political opinions does presume, though, a degree of common ground and a minimum of civility toward one's opponents. We cannot deliberate with those we take to be sheer enemies. Accordingly, it is important to consider how shared symbolic space, as a necessary condition of democratic civility, can be realized.

To address this matter, we need to consider the tension that exists between the democratic value of equality and the political condition of hierarchical antagonism—a condition in which a single order of truth and virtue enables one class of citizens to benefit at the expense of others. If we assume that civility in a democracy is premised in some way on egalitarian relationships of some kind, but also that politics operates on a principle of hierarchy that is conducive to antagonism, must we further assume that equality requires the leveling of our differences and the elimination of hierarchy so that we all might be treated as equivalent to one another in every important respect? This leveling assumption seems culturally improbable at best.

While equality and community are two of democracy's highest ideals of political solidarity, along with a commitment to consensual decision-making (Hanson, 1985, p. 51), a tension exists in the tradition of liberal democracy between the values of equality and competition, community and freedom, solidarity and individualism. This tension reflects the broader problem of hierarchy in democratic politics and raises the question of which order of ideas, values, and interests should prevail. For example, should protecting the individual's wealth, freedom, and rights from government encroachment be valued over providing for the welfare of the society at large? Should the state regulate private enterprise, restrict gun ownership, fund abortions, legalize gay marriage, or not?

The tension embedded in these kinds of issues cannot be resolved by abolishing hierarchy from politics. Hierarchy is intrinsic to symbolic action in general and to political communication in particular. We are forever ranking and ordering various aspects of our political world, including whether it is more important to balance the national budget, to increase military spending, or to provide better health care. We struggle over which groups most and least deserve government funding or tax breaks. Debate can become intense, hostile, and unproductive. Ranking and ordering among competing values, interests, and people is a political constant and a recurring source of alienation. We are faced, therefore, with adapting rather than abandoning the principle of hierarchy, with deepening and broadening political hierarchies, in order to enhance the democratic process of consensual decision-making in an ongoing context of agonistic politics.

COMPLEMENTARY RELATIONS

Rather than thinking of political alienation as a lack of democratic equality, where equality is taken to mean an improbable condition of equivalency or sameness among a diverse citizenry, the problem of hierarchical antagonism can be understood as a function of the absence of complementary relations. From this vantage point, the possibility comes into view of articulating a relationship of equality in which differences between political adversaries complement one another enough to constitute a shared symbolic space. The democratic answer to hierarchical antagonism may be to establish mutually advantageous webs of interdependency.

For this purpose, we must consider political equality in a way that is compatible with self-interest and simultaneously responsive to the needs of the larger community. As Kenneth Burke (1950/1969, p. 141) has noted in *A Rhetoric of Motives,* the principle of hierarchy is always at work even in a "scheme of equality." Just as there can be unidirectional schemes of inequality (for example, where owners are valued above workers, men above women, whites above people of color, or Christians above Muslims), there also can be bidirectional schemes of equality (for example, if the welfare of employers and employees alike is understood to intersect at the point where sustainable profits for owners and the continuing productivity of workers require fair labor practices).

Bidirectional schemes or hierarchies of equality are grounded in a discourse of interdependence (Fry, 2007, pp. 220–221) to compensate for the otherwise divergent and divisive interests of citizens deliberating in a pluralistic political culture (Ivie, 2010, p. 242). The diverse members of the political community, with their complex identities, are understood to complement one another in different ways to their mutual advantage. They even rely in some measure on the fulfillment of another's goals for the attainment of their own goals. Within this construction of equality, they are not automatically reduced to and disadvantaged by the color of their skin, their ethnicity, their religious affiliation, their age, gender, sexual orientation, or socioeconomic status. Their composite identity as democratic citizens implicitly traverses and interconnects discrete features of their social identity. An often-untapped potential to identify across conventional lines of division exists within this tacit matrix of political identity.

The category of consumer or the role of parent, for example, cuts across divisions of class, race, and gender in ways that can be imagined as relevant to political issues such as product safety or public education. Beyond the discovery of a common interest in these issues, citizens may realize that they depend on one another to generate a critical mass of public support for specific proposals, that they contribute unique perspectives and resources to the public deliberation of those proposals, or even that ignoring the needs of some can cause trouble and lead to negative consequences for privileged others.

This notion of complementary relations is not a leveling construction of equality in which everyone is considered identical and treated in the same way, but instead is a multifaceted image of crosscutting ties (Fry, 2007, p. 216). Conceptions of self-interest are extended and transformed into a conjointly empowering web of interdependencies (Ivie, 2011, p. 379). Equality, understood as a kind of positive symbiosis, operates in the political context of what Gerard Hauser (1999, pp. 64–67, 72) identifies as the reticulate public sphere—a complex web, or latticework, of overlapping discursive spaces with permeable boundaries.

Where the complexity of interconnected political identities and discursive processes is acknowledged and hierarchy is distributed asymmetrically, no one party necessarily dominates another party despite its superiority in a specific domain of value, at least not without diminishing itself. All parties are superior to one another in discoverable and distinctive ways. Moreover, two or more parties in a complementary relationship do not necessarily perceive the nature of their interdependency from the same vantage point. No single perspective determines political reality. All parties perceive from their own point of view how they are enhanced by the strengths of others, and they must see enough benefit to themselves to sustain a given hierarchy of equality (Ivie, 2012, p. 102).

This conception of complementary relations compensates for political divisions. It does not eliminate or transcend all differences, nor supplant the contestation of democratic politics by achieving a unanimity of opinion or harmonious perspective, but instead transforms the relationship of differences (Ivie, 2010, p. 242). It resists the tendency of political adversaries to treat each other as sheer enemies and promotes more constructive deliberation by articulating a shared symbolic space. It serves as a model of political communication to promote and facilitate productive democratic deliberation rather than as an ideal that will be fully realized or that will resolve all political differences.

PERSPECTIVE TAKING

Envisioning complementary relations is an act of perspective taking, which can be enhanced by assuming the attitude of the stereoscopic gaze (Ivie, 2007b, pp. 46–47, 51–52). As a mode of reflective perspective taking, the stereoscopic gaze is a useful metaphor, a rhetorical trope that draws on the language of vision and position to elevate our estimation of an adversary's humanity and increase our capacity for self-critique. By shifting our angle of view, it allows us to adjust the way we look at others. It provides a humanizing corrective to the demonizing tendencies of people engaged in political conflict.

The stereoscopic gaze is a rhetorical device for putting us in a productive frame of mind and establishing a constructive orientation toward our political opponents. As such, it involves a double articulation of perspective taking in which, first, we speculate on the motives of our adversaries from what we take to be their point of view toward the matters in dispute and, second, we speak critically of ourselves from what we imagine to be the perspective of others, including adversaries, allies, and bystanders.

This rhetorical turn positions us better to articulate the strategic points of interdependency that constitute complementary relations. It also enables us to engage in self-critique by indirection. Rather than condemn ourselves, which would be an uncomfortable and unlikely step for a politically engaged citizen to take, we can reflect back upon our position obliquely from the assumed perspective of what others might say about us. This shift of perspective enables us to complicate the narrow and simplistic framework of right versus wrong, good versus evil.

In a dramatic historical example of this process of perspective taking, President John F. Kennedy adopted a stereoscopic gaze toward Chairman Nikita Khrushchev in an attempt to diffuse the Cuban missile crisis of 1962 (Ivie, 2007b, pp. 38–46). By raising the question of motive, Kennedy attempted to understand Khrushchev's viewpoint and to avoid succumbing to simplistic Cold War demonology. He asked his advisers why the Soviets would want to place missiles in Cuba. This opened a discursive space for speculating on the enemy's point of view, which enabled Kennedy to observe that the U.S. presence in Berlin could look bizarre from the perspective of the Soviet Union and even to acknowledge that America's Western European allies might see the U.S. as slightly demented for risking a nuclear war over a few missiles in Cuba that did not, in any event, alter the overall balance of power.

Perceiving an adversary with motive and purpose suggested to Kennedy that Khrushchev was not completely irrational and that he should be given an opportunity to negotiate a de-escalation of the crisis. It also helped Kennedy to see that his Cold War rival shared a common interest in avoiding a nuclear holocaust and that they needed one another's cooperation to realize that goal. They became strategically yoked to one another, each complementing and depending upon the other's contribution to difficult negotiations. Kennedy eventually grasped that he had to treat Khrushchev as an equal, just as Khrushchev came to realize he could not intimidate Kennedy, proposing instead that they normalize U.S.-U.S.S.R. relations on a principle of peaceful competition so that together they might avoid the lunacy of nuclear suicide. Neither could achieve a stable peace without the contributions of the other.

The stereoscopic gaze exercises what John Paul Lederach (2005, p. ix) calls our "moral imagination" for peace-building, which he defines as the *"capacity to imagine something rooted in the challenges of the real world yet capable of giving birth to that which does not yet exist"* (his italics). Through this creative act we "speak to the hard realities of human affairs" with "the capacity to envision a canvas of human relationships" (Lederach, 2005, p. x). People begin to "imagine themselves in a web of relationships even with their enemies" (Lederach, 2005, p. 34). They suspend judgment long enough to watch for metaphors, such as avoiding the lunacy of nuclear suicide, that locate points of intersection and that enable them to perceive a relational interdependency from their separate points of view.

A sense of human connectivity can emerge through an apt metaphor that re-synthesizes experience and confounds the projection of evil onto a political adversary (Ivie, 2005b, p. 68; Ivie, 2011, p 380). By invoking the names of his grandchildren, Israeli Prime Minister Menachem Begin, with the assistance of mediator Jimmy Carter, was able to bridge his differences with Egyptian President Anwar Sadat enough to negotiate a historic peace accord at Camp David in 1978 (Carter 1995; Carter 1998). Seeing like a grandfather enabled him to grasp the human dimensions of the conflict at a critical moment when the negotiations apparently were doomed to failure. Carter has continued to coach seemingly intractable Israeli and Palestinian political leaders since then in the ways of perspective taking.

The relationship of hierarchies of equality based on complementary relations to the stereoscopic gaze and its double articulation of perspective taking is requisite to constructive deliberations in a pluralistic society. It is also suggestive of related modes of productive political communication. Speaking in the humanizing language of political friendship, for instance, helps to bridge distrust and disdain between adversaries who operate from different perspectives and pursue competing interests. The language of political friendship, as Danielle Allen (2004, pp. 140–159) explains in an adaptation of Aristotle's *Rhetoric,* is an egalitarian alternative to the politics of civic warfare—an alterative based on an attitude of respect and cultivated, for example, by a rhetorical articulation of trust, overlapping aspirations, shared histories, common adversities, convergent values, and similar character traits (see also Ivie, 2007a, pp. 168–171). Dissent is another mode of productive political communication when adversaries are careful to balance their sharp criticisms with reassuring expressions of shared values, thereby utilizing what might be called the double gesture of nonconforming solidarity (Ivie, 2005a). The rhetoric of reconciliation, as analyzed by Erik Doxtader (2003), is yet another approach to reflexive perspective taking that aims to reduce political alienation in order to promote a more constructive contestation of opinions (see also Ramsbotham, Woodhouse, and Miall, 2011, pp. 246–261).

Each of these discourses of reconciliation, nonconforming solidarity, and political friendship resonates with the kind of perspective taking required to achieve the democratic moment of civility in an otherwise acrimonious and violent era of polarization and alienation. Sojourner Jim Wallis, speaking as a Christian evangelical leader and faith-based peace activist, breaks with the rhetoric of demonization that characterizes post-9/11 America when he calls to account the martial spirit of the politically mobilized religious right. Toward this end, he invokes a stereoscopic gaze (Ivie, 2007b, pp. 47–51). He poses a question of motivation, asking why so many people are angry with the U.S., as a way of motivating an act of perspective taking. The humanizing aesthetic of his discourse crafts crosscutting ties and transcends the belligerent attitude of narrow nationalism by, for example, adopting the transnational viewpoint of a worldwide Christian church, so that Christian Americans might become more humble, more empathetic, more self-critical, more open to the international critics of U.S. imperialism, more aware of the "dark places within us and within our nation" (quoted in Ivie, 2007b, p. 48), more thoughtful about the conditions of poverty and hopeless desperation that fuel the evil of terrorism, and less tempted by easy certainties of a national theology of war.

From a larger vantage point of the church worldwide, Wallis prompts Christian America to reflect on the widespread global resentment of U.S. militarism rather than automatically rejecting critics as terrorist sympathizers. Minimally, he suggests, American Christians ought to consider what other Christians around the world think of what the U.S. does. Peacemaking rather than self-righteous warfare, he argues, is the principal vocation of Christians working together across national boundaries to enhance the security and justice of a troubled world.

Peering into the darkness of the nation's collective soul is the complement of gazing into the plight of the desperate victims of grinding poverty and political displacement. This is the double optic Wallis uses to reveal the interdependency between draining the swamps of injustice and reducing the threat of terrorism. "God's politics," he insists, "reminds us of the people our politics always neglects—the poor, the vulnerable, the left behind. God's politics challenges narrow national, ethnic, economic, or cultural self-interest, reminding us of the much wider world and the creative human diversity of all those made in the image of the creator" (Wallis, 2005, p. xv).

CONCLUSION

Democracy, as a politics of contested opinions and divergent perspectives, isn't easy to practice productively in a pluralistic society, especially where adversaries are inclined to demonize one another on religious, ideological, or other grounds. The primary concern of democratic citizens, therefore, is to communicate across lines of division in a manner that does not reduce political opponents to the status of enemies. Civility presumes a common regard for the democratic value of equality, even under conditions of hierarchical antagonism. Given that hierarchy is endemic to political communication in a liberal democracy, articulating hierarchies of equality based on complementary relations is more culturally plausible than treating everyone as identical. Adopting the stereoscopic gaze as a strategy of perspective taking facilitates the recognition of crosscutting ties and the expression of complementary relationships of interdependency among an otherwise divided citizenry. Citizens are more capable of acknowledging the humanity of their adversaries and critiquing their own limitations when they practice a perspective-taking discourse such as the stereoscopic gaze.

How we choose to address our political adversaries will either increase or decrease the chance of debating our political differences productively. The easy and most common choice is to demonize those with whom we strongly disagree. The more difficult but constructive choice is to articulate a common symbolic space that makes deliberation possible. Developing the habit of perspective taking to foster the crosscutting ties of complementary relations will help us to make the constructive choice more readily and thus to meet the challenge of democratic citizenship better, instead of withdrawing from politics in despair.

REFERENCES

Allen, D. S. (2004). *Talking to strangers: Anxieties of citizenship since Brown v. Board of Education.* Chicago: University of Chicago Press.

Brigance, W. N. (1952). *Speech: Its techniques and disciplines in a free society.* New York: Appleton-Century-Crofts.

Burke, Kenneth. (1950/1969). *A Rhetoric of motives.* Berkeley: University of California Press.

Carter, J. (1995). *Keeping faith: Memoirs of a president.* Fayetteville: University of Arkansas Press.

Carter, J. (1998, 25 October). "Remarks by President Jimmy Carter." Sadat Lecture for Peace, University of Maryland, online at http://sadat.umd.edu/lecture/lecture/carter.htm Accessed August 17, 2011.

De Luca, T., & Buell, J. (2005). *Liars! cheaters! evildoers! Demonization and the end of civil debate in American politics.* New York: New York University Press.

Doxtader, E. (2003). Reconciliation—A rhetorical concept/ion. *Quarterly Journal of Speech, 89,* 267-292.

Fry, D. P. (2007). *Beyond war: The human potential for peace.* New York: Oxford University Press.

Hanson, R. L. (1985). *The Democratic imagination in America.* Princeton, New Jersey: Princeton University Press.

Hauser, G. (1999). *Vernacular voices: The rhetoric of publics and public spheres.* Columbia, South Carolina: University of South Carolina Press.

Ivie, R. L. (2005a). Democratic dissent and the trick of rhetorical critique. *Cultural Studies <-> Critical Methodologies, 5,* 276–293.

Ivie, R. L. (2005b). Web-watching for peace-building in the new communication order. *Javnost—The Public, 12,* 61–78.

Ivie, R. L. (2007a). *Dissent from war.* Bloomfield, Connecticut: Kamarian Press.

Ivie, R. L. (2007b). Finessing the demonology of war: Toward a practical aesthetic of humanizing dissent. *Javnost—The Public, 14,* 37–54.

Ivie, R. L. (2008a). Speaking democratically in the backwash of war: Lessons from Brigance on rhetoric and human relations. In T. F. McDorman, & D. Timmerman (Eds.), *Rhetoric and democracy* (pp. 265–280). East Lansing, MI: Michigan State University Press

Ivie, R. L. (2008b). Toward a humanizing style of democratic dissent. *Rhetoric & Public Affairs, 11,* 454–458.

Ivie, R. L. (2010). Depolarizing the discourse of American security: Constitutive properties of positive peace in Barack Obama's rhetoric of change. In E. Demenchonok (Ed.), *Philosophy after Hiroshima* (pp. 233–261). Newcastle, UK: Cambridge Scholars Publishing.

Ivie, R. L. (2011). Hierarchies of equality: Positive peace in a democratic idiom. In G. Cheney, S. May, & D. Munshi (Eds.), *The handbook of communication ethics* (pp. 374–386). New York: Routledge.

Ivie, R. L. (2012). Democracy and militarism. In Kostas Gouliamos, and Christos Kassimeris (Eds.), *The marketing of war in the age of new-militarism* (pp. 89–106). New York: Routledge.

Lakoff, G. (1996). *Moral politics.* Chicago: University of Chicago Press.

Lederach, J. P. (2005). *The moral imagination: The art and soul of building peace.* New York: Oxford University Press.

Mouffe, C. (2000). *The democratic paradox.* London: Verso.

Mouffe, C. (2005). *On the political.* London: Routledge.

Ramsbotham, O., Woodhouse, T., & Miall, H. (2011). *Contemporary conflict resolution.* 3rd ed. Cambridge, UK: Polity Press.

Wallis, J. (2005). *God's politics: A new vision for faith and politics in America.* New York: Harper San Francisco.

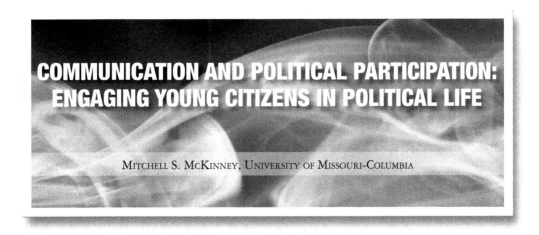

COMMUNICATION AND POLITICAL PARTICIPATION: ENGAGING YOUNG CITIZENS IN POLITICAL LIFE

MITCHELL S. MCKINNEY, UNIVERSITY OF MISSOURI-COLUMBIA

The political engagement of young citizens, and particularly their participation in voting activity, represents a longstanding concern of communication scholars and those interested in U.S. citizens' engagement in democratic life. The fact that older citizens vote in larger numbers than young voters by itself is not a new phenomenon nor is it necessarily surprising. This has always been so, largely because of the less settled and still developing (economically, educationally, politically, socially, etc.) nature of younger citizens. Still, if we view voting in national elections as a gage of young citizens' involvement in political and civic (public) matters, recent evidence suggests actual improvement in young voters' electoral performance that provides some reason to believe our youngest citizens are now more engaged than ever before. This chapter will first describe historical trends in young citizens' electoral engagement. Second, the chapter will discuss how young citizens are engaged politically through campaign communication, and particularly with new media and communication technologies; and, finally, this chapter will conclude with a brief discussion of the continuum of political and civic activities that constitute the engaged citizen.

YOUNG CITIZENS' POLITICAL ENGAGEMENT THROUGH VOTING

First, it is important to note that our understanding of political engagement should not be reduced to the singular—yet crucial—act of voting. As will be discussed later in this chapter, a citizen's involvement in political and civic affairs can take many forms. Yet, the casting of one's ballot in an election can be viewed as something of a "threshold" expression of citizen engagement. In fact, we might examine the act of voting as a form of political communication, an important civic message. The voting message is much more than a statement of support by a citizen in the practical selection of one's local, state, or national leaders, but a communicative activity that constructs the individual as an engaged member of the larger political community, thus investing the citizen with responsibilities for the common good. There is ample evidence to suggest that regular voters do make better citizens. Robert Putnam (2000, p. 35), in his comparative analysis of voters and nonvoters, explains:

> **Like the canary in the mining pit, voting is an instructive proxy measure of broader social change. Compared to demographically matched nonvoters, voters are more likely to be interested in politics, to give to charity, to volunteer, to serve on juries, to attend community school board meetings, to participate in public demonstrations, and to cooperate with their fellow citizens on community affairs. It is sometimes hard to tell whether voting *causes* community engagement or vice versa, although some recent evidence suggests that the act of voting itself *encourages* volunteering and other forms of good citizenship.**

In tracing the voting behaviors of young citizens, we find that of all voters it has been our youngest citizens who have traditionally been among the least represented at the ballot box. Until most recently, only about one-third of 18 to 29-year-olds regularly vote in presidential elections, compared to approximately two-thirds of those 30 and older (Levine & Lopez, 2002). When the voting age was lowered (from 21 years of age) to include 18-year-olds in 1972, young voters achieved their "high-water mark" of electoral participation at 55.4%. For the next 20 years, the participation of young citizens in presidential elections charted a steady decline. Then, in 1992, driven largely by young citizens turning out in greater numbers to vote for Bill Clinton, youth voting increased to 52%, young citizens' highest rate of participation since 1972. With his saxophone and shades on late night TV, to his MTV appearance with college students (where he responded "Usually briefs" to the burning question from a young female voter "Is it boxers or briefs?"), candidate Clinton appealed directly to young citizens using their language and media. This achievement in youth voting, however, was short lived as 18 to 29-year-olds followed their 1992 increased participation by recording their lowest level of voter turnout in 1996 (at 34%), once again returning young citizens to their more traditional one-third rate of participation in presidential balloting (Levine & Lopez, 2002).

Following the 1996 presidential election, there was much lamenting from scholars, pundits, and political campaign practitioners regarding young citizens' disengagement in political and civic affairs (see, for example, Kaid, McKinney, & Tedesco, 2000; McKinney & Banwart, 2005; McKinney, Kaid, & Bystrom, 2005). Curtis Gans (2005, p. 79), Director of the Committee for the Study of the American Electorate, wrote of the "decline of American civic participation." He described the "apparent dangers for our democratic system" caused by an intergenerational pattern of civic disengagement in which nonvoting young citizens were now growing into disengaged older citizens. In short, Gans' assessment of voting data in presidential elections since the 1960s found that the ranks of our more active senior voters were not being replenished with replacement voters who had taken up their civic responsibility in their formative years as young citizens.

Beginning with the 2000 presidential election, and much in response to young citizens' historic low voter participation in 1996, it seemed that a national movement was afoot to get young citizens involved in the political process. From MTV's "Rock the Vote" and "Choose or Lose" to P. Diddy and Lil' Kim's "Vote or Die" advertising blitzes, voting was marketed to young citizens as the "hip" thing to do. Candidates and their campaigns, too, joined this civic chorus with their targeted appeals to young voters. Since 2000, we've now witnessed three successive presidential elections in which the electoral participation of young citizens has actually increased; and, during this same period, the gap between more older vs. fewer younger citizens voting has diminished with each election since 2000 (New Census Data, 2009). Voter turnout for 18 to 29-year-olds increased from 34% in 1996 to 40.3% in 2000, compared to 64.6% for citizens 30 and older (a 24.3% gap). In 2004, younger voters' rate of voting increased again to 49%, compared to older voters at 67.7% (an 18.7% gap); and, finally, in 2008, younger voters recorded a 51.1% rate of participation, compared to older voters' 67% participation (a gap of 15.9%).

Indeed, the 2008 electoral performance of young citizens was historic on several fronts. With a 51% turnout in 2008, young citizens achieved their second highest turnout in a presidential election since 1972 (New Census Data, 2009). Perhaps even more noteworthy was the fact that while young voters increased their turnout in 2008, the rate of older citizens voting (those 30 and over) actually declined from their 2004 level of participation—the very first time since 1972, when 18-year-olds first voted in a presidential election, that young voter participation rose while older citizens' participation decreased. Also, in 2008, African-American voters ages 18-29 achieved the highest turnout ever recorded (58%) by any racial or ethnic group of young citizens; and 2008 was the very first time the percentage of registered young African-American voters outnumbered young white voters (New Census Data, 2009).

For more than a decade now, young citizens have begun to reverse their steady decline in electoral participation, yet to what factor or factors might we attribute their improved electoral performance? While there are many considerations that influence voter mobilization and participation in elections, there does seem to be convincing evidence that the influence of political communication—and particularly campaign messages targeted specifically to young citizens using the language, modes, and channels of communication most common to these voters—has resulted in young citizens' greater engagement in electoral politics. The next section provides a brief case study describing the campaign communication that attracted historic numbers of youth voters in the 2008 presidential election.

The Political Engagement of Digital Natives

Young citizens' overwhelming support of Barack Obama in the 2008 presidential contest provides a compelling case study in how a candidate's campaign communication can succeed in targeting younger voters. As Figure 1 illustrates, Obama received his widest margin of support from 18 to 29-year-olds, with these voters choosing Obama by more than two to one (68% to 32%) over John McCain. So why would our youngest citizens be so drawn to candidate Obama? During the 2008 election the Obama campaign devoted considerable time and campaign resources to organizing and mobilizing our nation's first generation of "digital natives"—those young voters for whom digital technologies have always been part of their lives.

Team Obama was quite successful in crafting campaign appeals with which young voters easily identified, and it was always careful to adopt the very language and communicative practices of young citizens (Palfrey & Gasser, 2008). *The New York Times* described Obama's loyal following as "Generation O," and it noted that Obama's relationship with these voters was based largely on a

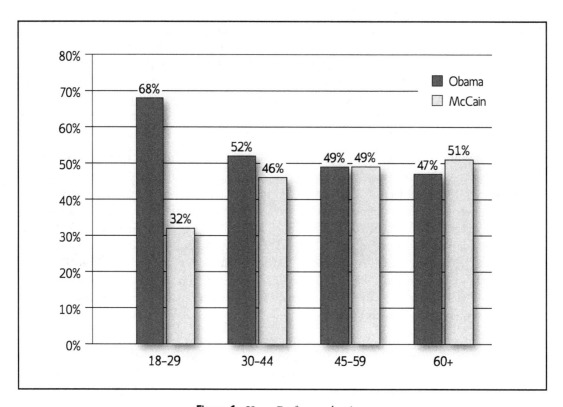

Figure 1. Voter Preference by Age

Source: Young Voters in the 2008 Presidential Election (www.civicyouth.org)

constant stream of digital communication that forged a rather intense and personal relationship between the candidate and his supporters. Barack Obama's personalization of his communication with his digital following is perhaps best illustrated in a message he sent on the evening of his election, just seconds after the national news networks declared him the winner. His very first message as president-elect, even before he addressed the nation and the world to herald his historic victory, was a text sent to his throng of digital followers that was signed simply "Barack" and informing them "I'm about to head to Grant Park to talk to everyone, but I wanted to write to you first. All of this happened because of you . . . we just made history" (Cave, 2008).

From YouTube to Twitter, to blogs, texting, and social networking, a variety of new forms and channels of communication emerged as a key feature of campaign 2008. Historian Max Friedman (2009, p. 343) concluded, "this was the election in which new media played a more important role than ever before in American history." The Pew Internet and American Life Project (2008) found that more than half of all Americans (54%) reported using the Internet to get news about the 2008 campaign. Clearly, in the emerging era of digital politics, this election demonstrated that candidates' campaign communication must now meet the expectations and communicative practices of a growing number of "netizens" whose political engagement is increasingly performed through various forms of digital messaging. Friedman (2009, p. 344) suggested we might best understand the 2008 presidential selection by considering the leading candidates' "technologized" images:

> ... consider the hip sensibility of Obama's campaign versus the old-school consultants around the [Hillary] Clinton machine, and it becomes clear why the leading Democratic campaigns were sometimes compared to the clash between Apple and Microsoft. Obama was the Mac, of course: youthful, creative, nimble, forward-looking, and sleekly stylish; Clinton was the PC—massive, corporate, sitting atop a huge pile of capital and a legacy of brand recognition and market share that favored a conventional, risk-averse strategy struggling to patch over the basic flaws in its original design. John McCain, though ... who had never sent an e-mail ... was an IBM Selectric. (p. 344)

This case study of Barack Obama's campaign messaging and appeals to young citizens is not to suggest that he became president of the United States solely because he was more skillful than his opponents in adopting the Internet and digital technologies as a campaign communication tool. Presidential campaigns are won and lost based on a myriad of reasons, including, among other factors, candidates' abilities to successfully frame their message (the crafting of a vision and development of image), while also attempting to frame their opponent in desired ways, as well as the ability to strategically craft and target appropriate messages for particular audiences, the ability to mobilize one's base supporters, and, of course, the ability to raise the hundreds of millions of dollars now needed to wage a successful presidential campaign. Overall, it is useful to consider a presidential campaign as an enterprise fully grounded in communication principles and processes, an activity that includes a communicator (candidate) crafting persuasive appeals (message/image) for desired audiences (targeted voters), with strategically developed messages delivered via appropriate communication channels or media. In the end, winning and losing an election has much to do with a candidate's ability to communicate effectively—or not.

As one traces the history of American campaigning and elections, viewing a parallel history of the development of communication media and technologies is useful (see, for example, Schudson's *The Good Citizen*). From handbills and broadsides, to party parades and the rise of the partisan press, to U.S. Senate candidates Lincoln and Douglas debating throughout Illinois, FDR's fireside radio chats, Eisenhower's first televised presidential campaign spots,[1] Kennedy and Nixon's nationally televised debates, Lyndon Johnson's "Daisy Girl" ad,[2] to Bill Clinton's shades and saxophone[3] and boxers or briefs, political leaders and candidates have long sought innovative ways, often adopting the latest in communication media and technologies, to reach the public and targeted audiences with their appeals. This abbreviated chronicling of just a few of the high—and perhaps some low—points in political communication history demonstrates the evolutionary nature of political campaign communication. It is also important to realize that the arrival of the so-called "digital revolution" in political communicating did not instantaneously emerge in campaign 2008. For well over a decade, the Internet and the so-called "new" digital technologies were evolving as an increasingly important part of our political communication landscape.

After very limited use of the just emerging Internet during his 1992 campaign, Bill Clinton launched the first White House web site in 1994 (Whillock, 1997); and within the next few years, and certainly by 2000, web sites and e-mail lists were common communication tools and practices for political office holders and candidates at all levels. Perhaps as a prelude to campaign 2008, Howard Dean's 2004 Democratic presidential primary bid demonstrated the Internet's social networking utility for political campaigning as thousands of supporters were organized through "meet ups" and mobilized as Dean campaign volunteers. The Dean campaign also established the Internet's effectiveness as a tool for raising campaign cash (Trippi, 2004). Finally, before "Obama Girl" went viral in 2008,[4] or even before Hillary Clinton's primary campaign was spoofed in 2007 with the "Hillary 1984" Apple parody ad (titled Vote Different),[5] the power of citizen-generated video in political campaigns was discovered by U.S. Senate candidate George Allen in 2006 when he was filmed at a rural Virginia campaign rally by a staffer working for his opponent who uploaded Allen's "macaca" moment to a video-sharing web site that had been in existence for just over a year, YouTube.[6]

Thus, by 2008, the "digital revolution" in presidential campaign communication was ripe, and BarackObama.com was there to lead the revolution. Friedman (2009, p. 345) provides this description of Obama's digital campaign operation: ninety paid staffers on the Obama Internet team, who built a 13 million address e-mail list, sending out more than 1 billion e-mail messages by election day, maintaining an Obama presence on 15 different social networking sites—such as Facebook, MySpace, and BlackPlanet—with over 2 million supporters' profiles created on MyBarackObama.com, with these volunteers organizing approximately 200,000 "meet up" events; and, on election day alone, Obama's Facebook friends sent over 5 million messages reporting they had just cast their ballot for Barack Obama and urging their friends to do the same.

President Obama's 2012 re-election effort shows little sign of ceding the social media race to any of his potential Republican challengers, as the online digital media and technology magazine *Mashable* asks the question "Who's winning the Twitter and Facebook 2012 presidential election?" It reports that "President Barack Obama's Facebook and Twitter following leaves Republican presidential candidates in the dust . . . and Obama still is the social-media-savvy candidate who reaches out to voters on the online platforms where they communicate" (Skelton, 2012). As of February, 2012, more than 25.2 million people "like" Barack Obama on Facebook, compared to Mitt Romney's Facebook following of 1.5 million people, the largest of any Republican candidate. Also, Barack Obama has just over 12.5 million Twitter followers, with President Obama personally tweeting an average of four times a day, while Newt Gingrich is the 2012 Republican candidate with the largest Twitter following at just over 1.4 million followers.

CONCLUSION

This chapter's focus on Barack Obama's success in attracting young voters through the use of digital technologies in his 2008 presidential bid, and his continuing use of social media in his re-election effort, serves as illustration to support two central arguments regarding young voters' political and electoral engagement. First, when candidates strategically target and craft appeals designed particularly for young citizens, these voters respond. As previously noted, the two elections in which young voters came near matching their cohort's record high rate of participation in 1972—Bill Clinton's campaign of 1992 and Barack Obama's 2008 campaign—happen to be elections in which the candidates, both regarded as "new" or younger generation candidates, devoted considerable time and campaign resources to communicate with young citizens, and these campaigns communicated by adopting the language and channels used most by young citizens. In both instances, young voters responded in record numbers.

A second central theme of this chapter is that young citizens have now recorded more than a decade—three successive presidential elections—of improved electoral engagement. This period of greater young citizen engagement also marks the decade in which political campaigns have increasingly adopted new communication technologies and digital media as important tools of campaign communication. It is likely no coincidence that young citizens, representing the largest numbers and quickest "early adopters" of these communication technologies, have become increasingly engaged in the political process during this same period.

While voter participation in presidential elections is often used as the most common bit of data to illustrate citizens' political engagement, as argued earlier in this chapter voting behavior is only one component of civic activity. Indeed, there are countless ways in which citizens might fulfill their civic responsibilities. In their classic book *Modes of Democratic Participation,* Verba, Nie, and Kim (1971) point out that political participation constitutes a wide range of specific actions carried out by citizens who seek to influence the selection of their elected representatives and the policy-related decisions made by public officials. When considering the many ways of enacting one's role as the engaged citizen, we might envision a broad continuum of participatory civic activities, ranging from least passive to more active involvement.

On the passive pole of this continuum, citizens can at the very least, if they wish to remain informed, attune to the most readily available political and campaign media messages. As consumers of political information, even here there are ranges of passivity and activity. For example, it would take less effort to listen to a quick network or cable news update, or to refrain from changing the television channel when a candidate's political ad appears, than the effort required to read a news article, view a televised candidate debate, or seek out political information on the Internet. Progressing along the continuum of civic engagement, other forms of participation in civic life that might require greater effort or motivation would be to sign a petition, to display a campaign yard sign or bumper sticker, to donate money to one's preferred cause or candidate, or to engage in a discussion of social or political issues with others. Still other more demanding activities might be to e-mail an elected official or to post a political comment or letter online, to attend a political rally or meeting, to volunteer in a campaign, or perhaps even to run for office. Somewhere on this continuum, one might argue much closer toward the "passivity" pole, would be perhaps our most expected form of civic participation, casting one's ballot every two or four years on Election Day.

The various activities of civic and political engagement described here position the simple, yet powerful, act of voting as but one value or practice upon which our democracy rests. Beyond voting, however, democracy is also found in individual citizens' many acts of joining, volunteering, serving, attending, meeting, participating, giving, and, perhaps most importantly, communicating and cooperating with other citizens. These are the very communicative behaviors and forms of citizen expression that result in the achievement of a participatory democracy. The notion of a vibrant democracy requires the participation and representation of all segments of society. Certainly, the voices of our youngest citizens constitute a vital part of our democracy. The evidence presented in this chapter suggests that when political candidates acknowledge and incorporate the concerns of young citizens as an important part of their campaign message, and communicate with these citizens using the language and modes of communication most readily adopted by young voters, these good citizens respond with enthusiasm.

REFERENCES

Cave, D. (2008, November 9). Generation O gets its hopes up. *The New York Times,* p. ST1. Retrieved from http://www.nytimes.com/2008/11/09/fashion/09boomers.html

Friedman, M. P. (2009). Simulacrobama: The mediated election of 2008. *Journal of American Studies, 43*(2), 341–356.

Gans, C. (2005). Low voter turnout and the decline of American civic participation. In M. S. McKinney, L. L. Kaid, D. G. Bystrom, & D. B. Carlin (Eds.), *Communicating politics: Engaging the public in democratic life* (pp. 79–85). New York: Peter Lang.

Kaid, L. L., McKinney, M. S., & Tedesco, J. C. (2000). *Civic dialogue in the 1996 presidential campaign: Candidate, media, and public voices.* Creskill, NJ: Hampton Press.

Levine, P., & Lopez, M. H. (2002). *Youth voter turnout has declined, by any measure.* Retrieved December 1, 2002, from www.civicyouth.org/research/areas/pol_partic.htm.

McKinney, M. S., & Banwart, M. C. (2011). The election of a lifetime. In M. S. McKinney, & M. C. Banwart (Eds.), *Communication in the 2008 election: Digital natives elect a president* (pp. 1–9). New York: Peter Lang.

McKinney, M. S., & Banwart, M. C. (2005). Rocking the youth vote through debate: Examining the effects of a targeted debate message on the intended audience. *Journalism Studies, 6,* 153–163.

McKinney, M. S., Kaid, L. L., & Bystrom, D. G. (2005). The role of communication in civic engagement. In M. S. McKinney, L. L. Kaid, D. G. Bystrom, & D. B. Carlin (Eds.), *Communicating politics: Engaging the public in democratic life* (pp. 3–26). New York: Peter Lang.

New Census Data Confirm Increase in Youth Voter Turnout. (2009, April 28). *The Center for Information & Research on Civic Learning & Engagement.* Retrieved June 15, 2009 from www.civicyouth.org.

Palfrey, J., & Gasser, U. (2008). *Born digital: Understanding the first generation of digital natives.* New York: Basic Books.

Pew Internet and American Life Project. (2008, June 15). *The Internet and the 2008 election.* Retrieved July 15, 2009 from www.pewinternet.org

Putnam, R. D. (2000). *Bowling alone: The collapse and revival of American community.* New York: Simon & Schuster.

Schudson, M. (1998). *The good citizen.* Cambridge, MA: Harvard University Press.

Skelton, A. (2012, February 18). Who's winning the twitter and facebook presidential election? *Mashable.com,* p. 9. Retrieved from http://mashable.com/2012/02/18/presidential-election-infographic/

Trippi, J. (2004). *The revolution will not be televised: Democracy, the Internet, and the overthrow of everything.* New York: HarperCollins.

Verba, S., Nie, N. H., & Kim, J. (1971). *Modes of democratic participation: A cross-national comparison.* Beverly Hills, CA: Sage.

Whillock, R. K. (1997). Cyber-politics: The online strategies of '96. *American Behavioral Scientist, 40,* 1208–1225.

ENDNOTES

1. Presidential candidate Dwight Eisenhower's 1952 ads, the first use of televised advertising in a presidential campaign, can be viewed at: http://www.livingroomcandidate.org/

2. Lyndon Johnson's "Daisy Girl" ad can be viewed at The Living Room Candidate site (above), or also at: http://www.youtube.com/watch?v=ExjDzDsgbww

3. Presidential candidate Bill Clinton's appearance on the Arsenio Hall Show can be viewed at: http://www.youtube.com/watch?v=VTkUeb6zQFA&feature=related

4. The original Obama Girl video (titled "Crush on Obama") can be viewed at: http://www.youtube.com/watch?v=wKsoXHYICqU

5. The Hillary Clinton 1984 Apple parody ad (titled "Vote Different") can be viewed at: http://www.youtube.com/watch?v=6h3G-lMZxjo

6. George Allen's Macacca moment campaign video clip (titled "George Allen introduces Macacca") can be viewed at: http://www.youtube.com/watch?v=r90z0PMnKwI

POLITICAL CAMPAIGN COMMUNICATION
AND CAMPAIGN OUTCOMES

TREVOR PARRY-GILES, NATIONAL COMMUNICATION ASSOCIATION
& SEAN LUECHTEFELD, UNIVERSITY OF MARYLAND

INTRODUCTION

The great Athenian sophist Isocrates once said that humans are different from animals "because there has been implanted in us the power to persuade each other and to make clear to each other whatever we desire." With this power, this capacity to persuade, he said we have "escaped the life of wild beasts, . . . and we have come together and founded cities and made laws and invented arts." Isocrates lived almost 3,000 years ago in a society that was the first human experiment in democracy and self-government. We've come a long way since ancient Greece. But we still believe that speech and persuasion are important—we still believe that such speech sets us apart from the "wild beasts." What's more, we are still engaged in a democratic experiment and we still use communication, in a variety of forms, to perform and to persuade, to win votes and change minds.

Isocrates and the other ancient rhetoric teachers really didn't worry about the effect of rhetoric on people—they assumed that rhetoric was important and had impact. But in the centuries since, teachers and scholars of communication have worked hard to try to reach some conclusions about the effect of communication on audiences and listeners. In a political campaign, in particular, scholars, teachers, and practitioners all ask: *How does campaign communication influence who we vote for?*

Answering that question is harder than it might seem. For one thing, there is an awful lot of "campaign communication" over the course of a given political election contest. From the ads to the speeches, from the debates to the coverage by the news media, there's just a whole lot of communication that happens in a political campaign. Trying to decide which example of campaign communication, which speech or ad or debate, had the most influence on voters is almost impossible. The other major problem is that people's voting behavior is complicated—it's hard to say why people vote the way they do, and it's especially hard to say, with certain linear causality, that campaign communication or a specific example of campaign communication causes people to vote the way they do.

Our research examines political discourse from a rhetorical perspective. As rhetorical critics of political discourse we study how texts possess and manifest particular meanings for public audiences and we make arguments about those meanings and their ideological and political consequences. So when we write about ads (Parry-Giles, 2010) or television shows (Parry-Giles & Parry-Giles, 2006) or Gilded Age political and social campaigns (Luechtefeld, 2010), we mostly write about how these texts mean what they do. We might discuss how they circulate through the political culture or with various audiences, but we generally don't reach specific conclusions about the effects of those texts, much less their particular effect on audiences' voting behaviors. Some people do reach such conclusions, and we will review the research that does exist that tries to answer the question of how does campaign communication influence who we vote for? In particular, we'll look at research about campaign speeches, campaign advertisements, and campaign debates.

POLITICAL SPEECHES

Over the course of a political campaign, candidates will deliver literally hundreds of speeches. What's more, those speeches will be taped and videoed and may recirculate on YouTube, campaign websites, or as email attachments to supporters and journalists. Candidates will give stump speeches and policy speeches, fundraising speeches and thank you speeches, after-dinner speeches and inspirational speeches. They will talk to thousands if not millions of people. But does any of this oratory matter?

Part of the problem with assessing the impact of political campaign speeches on an election's outcome is the fact that candidates give speeches for a lot of different reasons to a lot of different audiences and there's not usually anyone there trying to measure whether or not the speech makes any kind of difference. There's some sense that giving all these speeches is important, or else candidates wouldn't do it. Part of the ritual of political campaigning in America is that candidates hold rallies, give speeches, and shake hands. And in every election, the news media will present images and narratives from average voters where someone will usually say something like "I wasn't sure who to vote for until I saw Candidate X speak today—now I'm sure." At the anecdotal level, then, we know that these speeches sometimes make a difference.

In 1949, one scholar did try to measure the effect of a political campaign speech on a specific group of listeners. Wayne Thompson, from the University of Illinois, taped a speech by Thomas E. Dewey, the 1948 Republican candidate for president. The speech was presented in Chicago just a few days before the election, on October 26, 1948. One hundred thirty-eight students from the University of Illinois were presented with a survey that asked about their opinions and impressions of Governor Dewey. Then they listened to the speech and were asked to fill out another survey. Thompson (1949) discovered that there was not real impact from the speech on the students' attitudes about the soundness of Dewey's ideas, but that there was an impact on the esteem in which the students held Dewey's speaking skills. Moreover, there were little to no impact listening to the speech on attitudes about Dewey's candidacy though there was some impact on the intensity of people's attitudes toward Dewey. In short, the speech didn't really make much of a difference.

Since Thompson's (1949) study, a few others tried to measure the effect of other aspects of the speech-giving process in political campaigns. Based on his coding of hand gestures at the 2004

Democratic National Convention, Streeck (2008) calls for more "systematic" research into how audiences respond to gesturing in campaign speaking and "everyday communication" (p. 181). Another study, this one from Germany, assessed the reactions of audience members at a campaign rally for former German Chancellor Helmut Kohl and compared them to reactions from viewers who saw the event on television. This study discovered that there wasn't much of a difference in how people viewed Kohl or his speech based in how they encountered the oratory. In other words, TV viewers and actual audience members had similar reactions to the politician's oratory (Donsbach, Brosius, & Mattenklott, 1993).

In the end, it's really hard to say that a political speech has a direct and immediate impact on campaign outcomes or on actual voting behaviors. A speech may contribute to a set of reasons or cognitions or emotions that a voter may give for the decision she makes at the polls, but no one can really prove that a specific political campaign speech is the only (or even the primary) reason why voters vote the way they do, and thus, why campaigns come out the way they do. We subscribe, instead, to a mosaic theory of political effects—that each of the speeches or ads or debates or events or direct mail appeals that voters encounter over the span of a campaign contributes a small piece to a larger picture of voter impressions, attitudes, and emotions. Some parts of the mosaic are bigger and some are smaller, but none are so significant that they actually determine campaign outcomes. The trick, it seems, is figuring out what the larger picture means and how it is shaped and comes to influence voter decision-making.

POLITICAL ADVERTISING

As is the case with political speeches, measuring the effects of political advertising is a complicated and often impossible endeavor. First, researchers find it difficult to isolate the effects of political advertising on candidate choice from the effects of other campaign communication on candidate choice. For example, because voters are often exposed to political speeches in conjunction with advertisements, understanding the extent to which each medium plays a role in persuading voters can be futile. Second, researchers find it difficult to isolate the effects of political campaign communication from other candidate-related messages. While those running for office would like their messages to have no competition, public conversations about campaigns are inundated with messages from news media outlets, bloggers, social media websites, and a variety of other sources. Finally, measuring the effects of political advertising is complicated by the nature of exposure to advertising as a variable. Far more than mere exposure matters in determining whether a political ad will have an effect on its audience, including frequency of exposure, attention to the message, and audience members' likelihood to recall the message. Researchers' inability to control for these factors makes measuring the effects of political advertising difficult.

Despite these challenges, a number of studies have sought to measure the effects of political advertising. For example, Huber & Arceneaux (2007) studied exposure to spot ads featuring Al Gore and George W. Bush during the 2000 presidential election and found that whether or not voters were persuaded depended, at least in part, on exposure to ads. Of course, whether a voter is persuaded is itself insufficient in determining candidate choice—factors like turnout and campaign fatigue influence the likelihood a voter will cast his ballot a certain way, even despite his propensity to be persuaded. A more recent study conducted by Kaid, Fernandes, & Painter (2011) also sought to determine the effect of exposure to spot ads on candidate choice. Their experiment with 1,165 young voters in the 2008 presidential election found that while exposure to spot ads could influence voters' perception of the candidates, it could not predict whether voters would mobilize for that candidate.

Perhaps, then, these studies allow us to conclude that determining the effects of political advertising is a fruitless process. Other scholars have reached such a conclusion, finding that measuring the extent to which voters are moved to behave is at best tedious. As far back as the early 1980s, Meadow & Sigelman (1982) used a fictitious ad about a real congressional candidate to test the effect of the ad and ultimately found that measuring such effects using manufactured research stimuli—often the only choice available for those conducting political experiments—frequently leads to results that are at best hard to make sense of and at worst outright inaccurate. Likewise, Goldstein & Ridout (2004) have eloquently illustrated in their research how measuring effects can be difficult, suggesting that political scientists (and communication scholars, presumably) have a long way to go in developing a mechanism for measuring the impact of spot ads.

To be sure, all of this is not to suggest that there is little to be gained from studying political advertising. In their analysis, Goldstein & Ridout (2004) make a useful distinction between direct and indirect campaign communication effects and argue that despite scholars' general inability to measure *direct* effects (i.e., whether exposure to a political ad leads to voting for the sponsoring candidate), we have done a better job of measuring *indirect* effects (e.g., whether exposure to a political ad increases voter knowledge, apathy, or fatigue). This distinction confirms the work of researchers like Pinkleton, Um, & Austin (2002), who, in their study of negative campaign advertising, find that although exposure to attack ads increases viewers' disgust with the sponsoring campaign, there is little evidence to suggest that voters with higher levels of disgust are unlikely to vote for the candidate with whose campaign they are disgusted. Indeed, this and similar research (Kaid, 1997; Kaid & Chanslor, 2004) suggest that while we are far from devising a means of measuring the effect of political advertising on candidate choice, we are much better equipped to understand other ways in which political advertising influences voters.

In short, despite our best efforts, we still have a long way to go in terms of understanding how political ads influence elections. Because of the difficult nature of isolating political advertising from other campaign communication, isolating campaign communication from other candidate-related messages, and integrating the complexities of exposure as a variable for measurement, communication scholars and political scientists can look forward to a future dedicated to harnessing what we do know about political advertising and how it might better inform our research.

POLITICAL DEBATES

The first debate between candidates vying for the presidency was probably the 1948 radio debate in the Oregon Republican primary between Thomas Dewey and Harold Stassen. Of course, most people think the first debates were the famous 1960 debates between John F. Kennedy and Richard Nixon, and those were, in fact, the first *general* election presidential debates. Despite a gap in presidential debates during the 1960s and 1970s, ever since 1976, general election presidential debates have become a ritualized part of the campaign process. What's more, candidate debates happen up and down the ballot, with debates happening between candidates for a lot of public offices, from judge to assessor to member of Congress. But do these debates really matter—do they deserve all the attention they get?

As with political speeches and political ads, it's really difficult to measure the effects of political debates. A group of scholars (The Racine Group, 2002) convened in 2001 and 2002 to assess what political communication research reveals about the effects and factors emerging from political debates, and they reached a number of conclusions that still hold true today.

First, the format of political debates makes a difference in how people view and perceive those debates. If there are many debates versus just a few, if the debates are face-to-face clashes between two candidates or multi-candidate question-and-answer sessions, if the questions come from journalists or voters, if candidates are allowed follow-up rebuttals—all of these format aspects and many others will influence how political debates contribute to campaign outcomes and impressions.

Second, the participants in a political debate will make a difference. Things like candidate gender, the race of a candidate, and how the person looks on stage and appears in comparison to opponents in a debate, can all leave an impression on voters. Just think back to the 2008 presidential election debates—it made a big difference in those debates (in the primary and the general election) that one of the debaters was an African-American man while another of the debaters (in the Democratic primaries) was a woman.

Third, context matters in political debates. Political debates in a primary campaign are different and mean different things to voters than do general election political debates. At the presidential level, especially, general election debates are a big deal, attracting millions of viewers and becoming almost national events of some importance, like the Super Bowl or the Academy Awards. That's not the case with the scores of down ballot debates that may only get airtime on the local public access channels or the PBS affiliate. The context of the campaign and the timing of the debate may make a big difference in how people perceive the debate or even if they know it happens at all.

Fourth, what candidates say in debates can make a big difference in campaign outcomes. While it's difficult to prove for sure, when a candidate gets off a good one-liner or makes a serious mistake in a debate, it can often have a significant impact on their subsequent coverage by the news media and their future debate performances. What's more, these campaign debate moments become the stuff of political legend. President Gerald Ford and Ronald Reagan are often remembered, critically or fondly, for what they said in presidential debates. In a related sense, alongside the words that matter in political debates is the manner of their presentation. Research indicates that voters respond not only to the messages that candidates offer but how they say them—their modes of presentation and things like body language and style of speech.

Finally, political debates also have an impact because of how they are covered by the news media. Television commentators and newspaper writers will often pronounce a particular candidate the "winner" of the debate and insta-analysis will dissect and parse out even the most minute phrase or facial tick for loads of possible meaning. Voters don't simply watch debates and react to them in an unfiltered way. And, sometimes, if they don't see the debates at all, they will still see bits and pieces of them in news stories or recaps. How the news media filter, frame, evaluate, and repackage political debates can have a real impact on voter impressions.

CONCLUSION

We return, in the end, to our mosaic theory of campaign effects. Speeches, ads, debates—regardless of the type of political communication that comes from candidates and campaigns, it is virtually impossible to say with any certainty that a single communication message, event, or moment is the only factor influencing campaign outcomes. Instead, they are bits and pieces of the larger campaign picture. Trying to figure out which piece matters most or has the biggest impact may ultimately be a fool's errand, especially as we keep adding more and more pieces to the mosaic. Now, alongside speeches, ads, debates, and other forms of direct candidate communication, we have to add Web ads, and email solicitations, and tweets from candidates, and Facebook updates, and YouTube videos. At bottom, we might just end up studying how and why candidates communicate politically in a variety of ways to a large array of public audiences rather than trying, and failing, to accurately and singularly know the effects of political communication on campaign outcomes.

The mosaic approach to political communication also liberates us as consumers, listeners, audience members, and citizens of such communication. We are free to consume and consider a whole range of political messages, secure in the confidence that no single message, no precise ad or debate or speech, has the power to definitively decide anything or to control and determine our votes. Knowing this, our sense of politics, our ability to function as citizens and critics of political communication, is enhanced and intensified. It's a little scary, though, to know that it's our job, rather than that of the candidates and their campaigns or the news media, to make sense of all of the many campaign messages that bombard us every election cycle. Citizenship in a democracy is hard work, but it's also immensely important and inherently satisfying. That's the challenge we face, those are the obstacles to overcome, if democracy is to work and we are to help it work.

REFERENCES

Donsbach, W., Brosius, H-B., & Mattenklott, A. (1993). How unique is the perspective of television? A field experiment on the perception of a campaign event by participants and television viewers. *Political Communication, 10,* 37–53.

Goldstein, K., & Ridout, T. N. (2004). Measuring the effects of televised political advertising in the United States. *Annual Review of Political Science 7,* 205–226.

Huber, G. A., & Arceneaux, K. (2007). Identifying the persuasive effects of presidential advertising. *American Journal of Political Science, 51,* 961–981.

Kaid. L. L. (1997). Effects of the television spots on image of Dole and Clinton. *American Behavioral Scientist, 40,* 1085–1094.

Kaid, L. L., & Chanslor, M. (2004). The effects of political advertising on candidate images. In K. L. Hacker (Ed.), *Presidential candidate images* (pp. 133–150). New York: Rowman & Littlefield.

Kaid, L. L., Fernandes, J., & Painter, D. (2011). Effects of political advertising in the 2008 presidential campaign. *American Behavioral Scientist, 55,* 437–456.

Luechtefeld, S. (2010). A petition in boots: Jacob Coxey's constitution of citizenship in 1894. Unpublished paper presented at the National Communication Association Convention, San Francisco, CA.

Meadow, R. G. & Sigelman, L. (1982). Some effects and noneffects of campaign commercials: An experimental study. *Political Behavior, 4,* 163–175.

Parry-Giles, T. (2010). Resisting a 'treacherous piety': Issues, images, and public policy deliberation in presidential campaigns. *Rhetoric & Public Affairs, 13,* 37–64.

Parry-Giles, T., & Parry-Giles, S. J. (2006). *The prime-time presidency:* The West Wing *and U.S. nationalism.* Urbana: University of Illinois Press.

Pinkleton, B. E., Um, N., & Austin, E. W. (2002). An exploration of the effects of negative political advertising on political decision making. *The Journal of Advertising, 31,* 13–25.

Streeck, J. (2008). Gesture in political communication: A case study of the Democratic presidential candidates during the 2004 primary campaign. *Research on Language & Social Interaction, 41,* 154–186.

The Racine Group. (2002). White paper on televised political campaign debates. *Argumentation & Advocacy, 38,* 199–218.

Thompson, W. N. (1949). A study of the attitude of college students toward Thomas E. Dewey before and after hearing him speak. *Speech Monographs, 16,* 125–134.

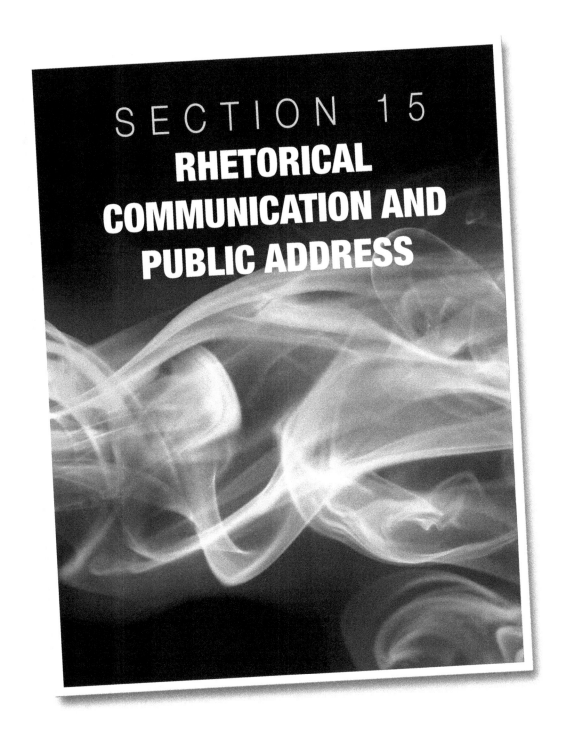

SECTION 15

RHETORICAL COMMUNICATION AND PUBLIC ADDRESS

Several of the essays you have read in the text explore the various contexts from a rhetorical or critical perspective. The importance of the study of rhetoric to the discipline of communication studies cannot be ignored, and rhetoric itself is a significant context of communication studies. Rhetoric is most simply understood as the study of social influence, in particular how people use symbols as a means for achieving social cooperation and fulfilling human potential. We live our lives in a world shaped via rhetoric. What we know, how we think, how we act are the result of the way we, and those around us, use language and other forms of symbolic expression. Rhetoric has enjoyed a dynamic and complex history. Rhetorical studies have been a significant part of humanity's education since before the time of Plato and Aristotle. Today, rhetoric—the attempt by one person or group to influence another through strategically selected and stylized symbolical action—is enjoying renewed popularity in Western culture. The three essays in this section study how human beings use symbols to influence thought and action in public life, i.e., rhetoric. First, Carole Blair (University of North Carolina at Chapel Hill) explores the question: *How and why might one assume the role of a tourist-critic when visiting places of public memory?* She suggests that when visiting memorials we should engage in citizenship by adopting the role of the tourist-critic, so that we can judge for ourselves what commitments we wish to make to these memorials. Second, Celeste Condit (University of Georgia) considers the question: *What are far-reaching practical consequences for the genetic revolution in terms of prenatal testing, new drugs, and new agricultural products?* Condit advocates that we cannot simply turn decisions over to experts if we want democratically made decisions that are likely to be good for most of us, and that this is not necessary, even in a highly technical society. Third, Raymie McKerrow (Ohio University, Athens) explores the question at the heart of rhetorical studies: *Why should we all engage in critical civic discourse?* He encourages us to be more active, more critical, and more civil in our public interactions. Each of these authors explores how rhetorical research can be utilized in encouraging us to become more active and effective change agents in an increasingly complex symbolical world.

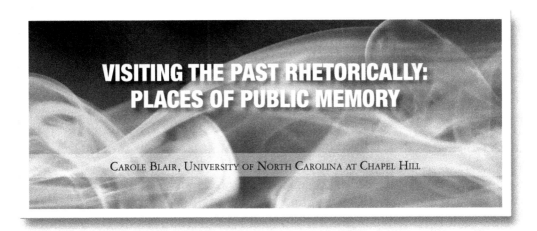

VISITING THE PAST RHETORICALLY: PLACES OF PUBLIC MEMORY

CAROLE BLAIR, UNIVERSITY OF NORTH CAROLINA AT CHAPEL HILL

Memory tourism is an important cultural phenomenon (and industry) worldwide. You have probably been on a trip that was at least partly devoted to visiting memory places, like history and heritage museums, preservation sites, battlefields, cemeteries, or commemorative monuments or memorials. If you are like most American visitors, you may have approached these sites as educational experiences; you visited them to learn about particular moments of the past that have been deemed sufficiently important to be marked physically on the landscape. Places of public memory typically are thought of as sites where we can absorb important lessons from the past. They aren't usually thought of as attempts to persuade us to a particular belief, to convince us that a specific value should be uppermost among the principles that guide our lives, or to influence our action toward a specific goal. Put another way, we may have our critical radar turned to low when we visit such places. Perhaps it is because we typically understand places of public memory to represent opportunities of learning about the past *rather than* of persuasion or influence about the present that we are likely to find them so credible and to accept their versions of the past rather unquestioningly (Rosenzweig & Thelen, 1998, pp. 91, 113).

Typical views of them notwithstanding, places of public memory are rhetorical through and through. Yes, they are installations or artworks that teach. But teaching, especially teaching about public culture, is a mode of political socialization—it offers what Biesecker (2004) has called a pedagogy of citizenship (p. 229). Moreover, any memory site itself has a past; someone or some group constructed it at a particular time and place with a clear purpose and to foster particular kinds of responses. That is one reason that places of public memory are so frequently contested. You may be familiar with recent conflicts over the size, placement, and designs of the World War II Memorial in Washington or of the September 11 memorial at the World Trade Center site. Very often conflicts about representing the past are ways of arguing about our shared present and future, about the character of our collective, and about our values and identities within it.

Places of public memory advocate particular attitudes about the events or individuals they commemorate, promote different images of the nation-state or other collective, and endorse specific modes of citizenship. When studying places of public memory, thus, rhetorical critics tend to ask questions about *what* these places propose as a shared past, present, and future. And they ask *whether* and *how* such public sites influence their visitors about the past and/or about national identity or responsibilities of citizenship. In short, critics inquire as to the very different imaginings of the world, the nation, ideal citizens, and modes of belonging that public memory places nominate for their visitors' political investments. In this chapter, I hope to answer the question of why and how we should adopt a more critical attitude when we visit public memory places, which can help us understand ways in which these sites influence us in perhaps unexpected ways. Since the international landscape is decorated by thousands of places of public memory, I will focus most here on examples of what rhetoricians and other communication scholars have helped us to understand about U.S. memory sites.

THINKING SPATIALLY AND EXPERIENCING ASKEW

Critics of public memory sites typically work from a premise that their targets are not simply visual artifacts; they are material (Ott & Dickinson, 2009). Hence the importance of the notion of "experience" (Clark, 2004), rather than simply sightseeing. We certainly do look at places of public memory, but we also walk through them, hear their sounds, and touch the surfaces we are allowed to touch. Some new museums have deliberately created "themed smells," of wilderness areas or of trench warfare for example, to create a sense of "authenticity" for visitors. Even our sense of taste may be enticed and sweeten the experience of a memory place, if, for example, the site's concession or a nearby street vendor has sold us an ice cream cone. Although nothing would preclude such considerations of sensate experience in the study of other rhetorical phenomena (Blair, 2001, p. 276), the place-ness of these memory sites *forces* the issue of our inherent contextualization within spatial domains. Dickinson, Ott, and Aoki (2006) ask us to think about ourselves as occupying an "experiential landscape" that takes account of both physical and cognitive features of place. That idea prompts us to consider the "precinct" of a spatial experience (where, for example, are the experiential boundaries of the Jefferson Memorial?) and to contemplate how visitors are urged into a particular position vis-à-vis the memory place and its setting (what does the Jefferson Memorial suggest to visitors about the proper mode of being a citizen?).

Of course, these are not the ways that visitors are expected to experience a place of public memory; hence the notion of "experiencing askew."[1] When most visitors make a pilgrimage to the Franklin Delano Roosevelt Memorial, their completely reasonable presumption is that they will learn about FDR. But *what* about FDR will they learn? And how? Why does this Washington, DC memorial include sculpted figures of people in a bread line during the Great Depression or, for the first time ever in a presidential memorial, a statuary figure of a First Lady? Why does this memorial

---

[1] With apologies to Žižek and his title, *Looking Awry*. Although his is perhaps a more attractive locution, I have modified it to imply a fuller array of sensate experience than simply looking. And I've modified it because most of the work addressed here is not influenced directly or deeply, perhaps to its detriment, by Žižek or Lacan.

contain two different sculptural representations of President Roosevelt, and why—and with what effect—are they placed where they are? Does it matter that the selective openness of the design of this memorial allows us to glimpse other, major memorials in Washington, DC, but not others? Do these features tell us about FDR or about the concerns and values of the people sponsoring, planning, and designing the memorial? Perhaps both, but surely more about the latter. Note the difference here: These questions are about the FDR *Memorial,* not about FDR, except in a very indirect way. They are about the memorial's rhetoric—about how it invites us to occupy a particular identity, and to think of its subject matter in particular ways relevant to our present experience of the site. Such questions lead to experiencing the memorial askew—from a different vantage point and at a different angle than what we're accustomed to as visitors. One of the many contributions of this already large and growing literature is that it has taught us to experience these places with our critical radar turned back on and with some new questions to pose of the places. If rhetorical criticism is, among other things, about offering readers different ways of understanding or responding to a critical target, of enhancing readers' critical repertoire, the ongoing rhetorical criticism of public memory sites surely has had that kind of impact.

THE POLITICS OF PUBLIC MEMORY PLACES

Although those who visit places of public memory often invest a fair amount of trust in the messages they offer, some places simply get history wrong (Loewen, 1999). Those cases, though, are relatively rare. Usually the past isn't actually misrepresented; it is represented in a partial, sometimes highly partisan way (Blair, Dickinson, & Ott, 2010, pp. 9–10). For example, Greg Dickinson, Brian L. Ott, and Eric Aoki (2005) have argued that the Buffalo Bill Museum, one of five museums in Cody, Wyoming's Buffalo Bill Historic Center (BBHC), trivializes historical encounters between Native peoples and European settlers. It does so by telling Western history through artifacts and narratives about Buffalo Bill's Wild West Show, itself a fictional spectacle that carnivalized the violence of those historic encounters. Steps away is the Plains Indian Museum, which they argue (Dickinson, Ott, & Aoki, 2006) positions visitors in a stance of distanced reverence with respect to Native American culture and absolves European-American visitors of the social guilt attending cultural conquest (pp. 28–29). These deeply politicized narratives are reinforced in another of the BBHC's museums, the Cody Firearms Museum, where, these authors argue, the guns are silent and presented as artworks, not as lethal weapons (Ott, Aoki, & Dickinson, 2011). In their essay on the Draper Museum of Natural History (also a part of the BBHC), they conclude powerfully and importantly that the site "affords its visitors the possibility of practicing and performing [a role the Museum advocates] even as they learn about it" (Aoki, Dickinson, & Ott, 2010, p. 261). They point out that that this is an example of "one of the powerful rhetorical consequences of memory places" in that it is a "site of enactment and performance of the memories and the values memory encodes" (261). Their argument is that we may be encouraged by a memory place to perform the very political actions it advocates, not just somewhere else, but inside the memory place, essentially practicing for such enactments later, beyond its borders.

Those who would construct public memory sites usually face profound difficulties: Most pasts are not *wholly* celebratory, and sometimes those pasts cast gloomy shadows on our present (e.g., Zelizer,

1995). It cannot seriously be considered an accident that the interest among U.S. rhetorical critics in studying public memory sites was kicked up in the 1980s and early 1990s by a most unusual new memorial—the Vietnam Veterans Memorial (VVM) in Washington, DC, which seemed to capture not only various cultural broodings about the conflict, but also to contest the often self-congratulatory features of traditional commemoration. At least seven essays in communication journals appeared during those years that focused on the VVM (Haines, 1986; Foss, 1986; Carlson & Hocking, 1988; Ehrenhaus, 1988a; Ehrenhaus, 1998b; Ehrenhaus, 1989; Blair, Jeppeson, & Pucci, 1991). It is almost certainly because of the politics of the VVM and the jarring public conflict about its design in the early 1980s that rhetorical critics' attention was drawn to it.

The conflict over the design of the VVM was, in part, about "proper" modes of commemorating; some objected to its black granite composition, others to its lack of physical height, and still others to its seemingly endless listing of names of the dead. Those objections, though, were also about how we should remember the Vietnam conflict. The VVM's original design was a chronicle of death; opponents believed it should have a more redemptive message about the war. The project was allowed to go forward only after a compromise added to the memorial site a sculptural representation of three soldiers—all very much alive and alert—and a U.S. flag. Far from resolving anything, that compromise rendered the memorial a site of perpetual symbolic struggle over how to remember the war (Blair, Jeppeson, & Pucci, 1991). And it provoked further conflict; the addition of the sculpture prompted some women's groups to question why there was no prominent representation of the many women who had served in Vietnam. That secondary conflict led to another sculptural augmentation in 1993, the Vietnam Women's Memorial. Of course, the VVM was not in any sense unique in being contested; even the Lincoln and Jefferson Memorials and the Washington Monument generated major public conflict before and during their construction, as difficult to believe as it may be now to imagine Washington, DC without one or more of those memorials. As Prosise (2003) has noted, attending to the conflicts that have arisen in the invention of a public memory site helps us to consider different, often useful, perspectives on the site (pp. 363–364). It also helps us to understand what is at stake politically in their having been constructed.

Most critical analyses of public memory sites deal explicitly with the political character of these important places, often raising flags about how muted or even stifled—but still powerful—the political representations or enactments may be. Many rhetorical critics focus on explicitly difficult pasts—of racial and ethnic violence, genocide, colonialism, and/or senseless death—and their representations at places of public memory (e.g., Hasian & Wood, 2010). Among these critics, Atwater and Herndon (2003) emphasize that it is vital "for the past, however painful, to be remembered," (25) for it has profound effects upon our present, our identity, and our political culture. Some rhetorical critics too have begun to remark on the changing face of civil religion as it is marked in U.S. public memory sites (e.g., Halloran & Clark, 2006; Blair, 2007), a promisingly rich way of considering the politics of these sites and to account for some of their rhetorical power—their sometimes astonishing capacities to create their own auras of "authenticity," to make claims for their own significance that overshadow the events or persons they purportedly represent, or even to bid for a status for themselves as sacred (Blair, Dickinson, & Ott, 2010, pp. 25–32).

RE-HISTORICIZING AND RE-CONTEXTUALIZING

For many different reasons, the past of a public memory place can be lost to those in charge of its interpretation and thus also to most visitors. Among the reasons are institutional neglect or a desire to reinscribe the place because of the difficulty of its own history (e.g., Prosise, 1998). For example, much of the history of U.S. First World War monuments and cemeteries constructed in Europe in the 1920s and 1930s, is unknown to the very agency tasked with their onsite interpretation to visitors. These places bear enormous significance—individually as historical artworks, together as the largest commemorative building enterprise undertaken by the federal government to that point, and as one of the first U.S. experiments in blurring the lines between commemoration and diplomacy (Blair, Balthrop, & Michel, 2007). But the American Battle Monuments Commission's top brass considered itself for many of the intervening years simply a caretaking agency, with concerns of horticulture and masonry more important than memory or interpretation. One of the consequences is that people in the organization now know little about the sites they care for. Their good fortune is that there is a wealth of material in various U.S. collections, particularly the National Archives. Still, scholars—among them rhetorical critics— are only now making a serious attempt to restore some of those sites' histories.[2]

The histories of other sites are "lost," or at least not volunteered to visitors, apparently because of a desire to put aside a difficult history (Prosise, 1998). Mount Rushmore seems just such a case. This national memorial, which often is touted as a monument to U.S. presidents or as a monument to the growth of the nation, was actually dreamed up by locals as a way to bring tourism to South Dakota. Its sculptor, Gutzon Borglum, had clearly in mind a monument to U.S. national imperialism, evident even in the earliest contract forged between him and the founding memorial association, which called for a "memorial to the continental expansion of the Republic of the United States of America" (qtd. in Blair & Michel, 2004, 169). It is little wonder that the National Park Service would like to distance itself politically from the original purposes behind Rushmore and especially from the history of Native American ownership of the Black Hills. But such evasions have consequences, among them an erosion of faith in the organizations entrusted with the heritage of such sites. Perhaps the most serious consequence, though, is that U.S. citizens are positioned as untrustworthy audiences of their own country's imperfect past. That is a view of our fellow citizens that most rhetorical critics reject, and so part of the critical task is to restore to such problematic sites their difficult histories. At least we think that those three million visitors to Mount Rushmore every year ought to be able to access more precisely what the planners of this extraordinary place believed they should honor. Sometimes the work of critics to "recover" these histories can even have the effect of inducing officials to change the interpretation they present to visitors to a site (e.g., Aden, 2010).[3]

---

[2] In recent years, these sites have begun to garner a bit more attention, including from communication scholars. See, e.g., Seitz (2009); Iles (2006); Blair, Balthrop, & Michel (2007).

[3] Even in my limited experience, administrators and interpreters at various sites have taken up some of our work in presenting those sites to visitors. I know of that happening at the Civil Rights Memorial in Montgomery, AL and the St. Mihiel American Cemetery near Thiaucourt, France. Reportedly, the Astronauts Memorial Foundation actually altered the physical context of the Astronauts Memorial at Cape Canaveral, Florida, as a result of Neil Michel's and my critique. It would be very surprising if these were unique cases.

Rhetorical critics have also lent insight to the memory places they study by their choices of how to contextualize these places, whether politically, historically, geographically, economically, etc. This contextualization and re-contextualization is one of the values of Dickinson, Ott, & Aoki's (2005 & 2006) notion of the "experiential landscape," noted earlier. And indeed those authors do place the BBHC and their analyses of it within their experience of driving through "the West" to arrive at the museum. Similarly, Neil Michel and I expanded the geographical context within which we attempted to understand the Astronauts Memorial, in order to attempt to make sense of visitors' reactions to it in light of its proximity to Disney World (Blair & Michel, 1999). Other scholars have considered the relationships, contrasts, and sometimes-mutual effects of local and national memorials that are purportedly about the same or similar subject matter (e.g., Edwards, 2010; Bodnar, 2010). Still others have considered a theoretical concept developed about discourse to assess its applicability to a memorial site (e.g., Veil, Sellnow, & Heald, 2011).

Teresa Bergman has considered the orientation films at various public memory locations to inquire about what site officials have wished to emphasize in advance for visitors. Particularly interesting is her analysis of places where there have been multiple orientation films that replaced each other over time, enabling us to understand changing interpretive patterns at the sites over time (Bergman, 2003; Bergman, 2008). Balthrop, Blair, & Michel (2010) tried another kind of contextualization—considering the World War II Memorial in terms of various aspects of its dedication ceremony—in order to account for what most public commentators and critics had considered a virtually illegible public memory site. Another approach my coauthors and I believe fruitful is to consider together various commemorative sites of the same era, so that their similarities and differences emerge clearly; sometimes we have compared those from the U.S., and, at other times, contextualized with similar memorials internationally (Blair, 1999; Blair & Michel, 2007; Blair, Balthrop, & Michel, 2011). Still another approach is for multiple scholars to take up critical analyses of the same public memory site, as happened spontaneously with the VVM in the 1980s and 1990s, and as has happened purposefully and productively in Morris's (2011) collection of critiques of the AIDS Memorial Quilt. In each grouping are wonderfully nuanced ways of understanding and responding to each of these important memorials, reinforcing the value of multiple critical standpoints brought to bear and the many valuable insights these different angles of scholarly approach have to offer.

FOSTERING COLLECTIVE (AND RESTRICTED) IDENTITIES

We observed earlier that places of public memory offer to visitors a kind of pedagogy of citizenship (Biesecker, 2004, p. 229). Barbour elaborates the significance of this observation by noting that, "Memorial sites are used as classrooms of American history, teaching visitors what it means to be American. These civics lessons define what people and events should be remembered . . . for tourists engaged in pilgrimages of civic identity" (101). If these sites teach us what it means to be American, they also, at least by implication, tell us who or what is not so American, thereby valuing and devaluing particular peoples, events, and even whole cultural histories. One of the most robust inquiries in the rhetorical study of public memory sites has been precisely about such important issues of approved and disapproved identities, inquiring about how U.S. citizens of color are represented and valued, and about how rights movements, particular the Civil Rights Movement, have been remembered in public memory sites.

Although many rhetorical analyses of public memory sites take note of missing voices, missing cultural identities, and missing perspectives on what it "means to be an American," a number of scholars train their attention very specifically on public memory and race. We are fortunate to have a relatively large number of rhetorical critiques of U.S. memory sites that address race most explicitly.[4] For example, Richard Marback's 1998 and 2008 essays on Detroit's *Monument to Joe Louis*, otherwise known as "The Fist," offer two interestingly divergent, but still systemically consistent, accounts of the importance of this unusual commemorative artwork and of how significant such works can be in our lives. "The Fist" is a bronze sculpture of a black forearm and fist, suspended by cables from an open pyramidal frame, meant to honor Lewis, a famous African-American boxer. It was dedicated in 1986, a period of urban revitalization with substantial corporate investment. It has been a source of endless discussion and controversy because of its ironic and contested representation of African American masculinity. Marback's second essay was motivated by "The Fist" having been vandalized; he focuses attention on the vandals' expressed desire to "unclench the fist," of course an impossible aspiration for a cast bronze hand. Victoria Gallagher and Margaret LaWare take up "The Fist," noting too the vandalism of the sculpture, but also offering a rich interpretive position nourished by a consideration of the origins of the installation, its commissioning by Time, Inc., and its various instantiations as a "counter-monument," despite its corporate origins.

Since the late 1980s, a large number of major museums and memorials have sprung up that remember events and figures from the Civil Rights Movement. They have been of serious interest to a number of rhetorical critics of memory sites. Gallagher's work offers the most systematic study of them (1995, 1999, 2004, 2006). She has concluded that some of these memory places tell a tale of Civil Rights achievements, without much attention to the often violent resistance to the Movement. Such a skewed narrative seems to imply, contrary to the historical record, that there has been little opposition to efforts for racial justice in the U.S. Even some of these sites that acknowledge the opposition of the past address the present as if it were free of racial anxiety or conflict, thanks to the success of the Movement. However, Gallagher (2004) and others have called our attention to Civil Rights sites that tell the story in far more nuanced ways. For example, Montgomery, Alabama's Civil Rights Memorial and Civil Rights Memorial Center are not plagued with that problematic progress narrative,[5] and they address directly troubling racial tensions of the present, asking their visitors to actively oppose racial and other injustices in the present.[6]

---

[4] In addition to the examples described, see Armada (1998); Armada (2010); and Reyes (2010). Only some of the essays in the Reyes collection address memory places.

[5] Nor, DeLaure (2011) argues, is the International Civil Rights Center and Museum, in Greensboro, North Carolina, one of the most recently opened sites in the Civil Rights memory landscape.

[6] Also see Blair and Michel (2000) and Blair (2007), on the character of the Civil Rights Memorial and Memorial Center. Though not related to the Civil Rights Movement, a parallel case emerges in Schowalter's trenchant analysis (2009) of the Smithsonian's National Museum of the American Indian; he suggests that it too has the capacity of critical art, "*dis*preserving" visitors' standard narratives about what "Indianness" is, allowing visitors to rearticulate new understandings (273).

Of these more hopeful assessments of how contemporary public commemoration has treated race, the question must be asked, and Mark McPhail asks it (2010), of whether such exemplars of critical public art really make any difference in people's actions, once they leave a commemorative site. McPhail is dubious, and he has a right to be. Given the near impossibility of tracking museum and memorial visitors after they've left a site, it is unlikely that this question could be answered with a reasonable degree of certainty. Still, there have been some new developments that train our critical attention upon visitor reception.

RECEPTION AND PLACEMAKING

Studies of visitors' reception, their reactions to places of public memory, have been so far quite limited. We may never be able to answer the poignant question of effects McPhail raises, for the simple reason that researchers rarely have access to memory place visitors once those individuals leave the vicinity of the site. Still, there is virtue in inquiring even about immediate reactions of visitors, and that work has begun. Even then, there are serious impediments to such inquiries, For example, when Neil Michel and I were studying the Astronauts Memorial (1999), we were curious about why other people didn't seem to pay any attention to it, despite its looming four-story presence and its (we thought) fascinating message. It was something of a conundrum. We could have asked people why they weren't attending to the memorial, but then we would have called their attention precisely to what they were ignoring. So, we had to seek other, less direct ways to try to account for the attention deficit.

Some critics have begun to use guest registers and interviews as ways of getting at visitors' reactions, at what they bring to a site, and the uses to which visitors may put it. For example, Noy (2008) made a study of visitor books at the Ammunition Hill National Memorial Site in Israel. Noy's approach was not to simply record and categorize responses, but to consider the writing in these guest registers as performances of place, as active projections of meaning onto their surroundings (p. 179). As he points out, the visitor books are themselves public communicative media (p. 175); they should provoke critical examination, just as surely as do the memory sites. Noy's position seems quite close to the notion of placemaking (and perhaps re-making) that a number of geographers have forwarded in recent years (e.g., Massey, 2005). Essentially, the position is that the uses to which people put a place make it what it is, at least temporarily.[7] It is not far afield from the position that Michael Bowman (2010) forwards by means of field studies and interviews with visitors to the Mary Queen of Scots House and Visitor Centre, in Jedburgh, Scotland. His delightful interviews (which read a lot like conversations) with other visitors suggest not only that memory site tourists aren't dupes, but that they actively construct the site as they go through it, affectively, performatively, and cognitively, and that they are perfectly capable of responding critically. For example, Bowman reports this response from a visitor: "'Oh, I loved the lock of hair, of course . . . . Well, I liked the *story* about the hair just as much—who found it, etcetera—who

---

[1] So-called spontaneous shrines or memorials, which seem to just "spring up" on a site relevant to a violent or disruptive event, are also good examples of placemaking. They have been studied critically by Jorgensen-Earp and Lanzilotti (1998); and by Kennerly (2002).

knows if it's really hers [Mary's] or not?" (p. 210). Finally, Dickinson's study of Old Pasadena (1996) suggests that in various kinds of traversals of a memory landscape (e.g., walking or driving), visitors reflect upon not only the place but their own identities.

CONCLUSION

It is my hope that this chapter has offered a sense of how fresh, fruitful, and exciting this burgeoning area of scholarship is. No doubt you will find other insights from even a brief look at the rhetorical literature on places of public memory. Certainly, neither theoretical nor practical implications of these studies have been exhausted, and there always are new commemorative sites to study or older ones to reconsider. As more rhetoricians begin to consider sites outside U.S. borders (e.g., Katriel, 1994), there almost certainly will be many new considerations, assumptions, and historical reconceptualizations to be made.

If you like your spaces less overtly littered with symbols of the past or of death, many of the insights developed in research about public memory sites have had useful carry-over in studies of other kinds of landscapes. Indeed, you might recognize some of the figures involved in that kind of work. Some study everyday places, like shopping malls (Stewart & Dickinson, 2008), health food stores (Dickinson & Maugh, 2004), or coffee shops (Dickinson, 2002). Others have studied theme park attractions (Balthrop & Blair, 2003), fantasy places concocted by Hollywood in unlikely locations like northern Iowa (Aden, Rahoi, & Beck, 1995), or outdoor art installations (Zagacki & Gallagher, 2009). A large and growing group of scholars has taken up the exciting study of urban communication (e.g., Burd, Drucker, & Gumpert, 2007; Fleming, 2008), an area that is now so dynamic that it would require a whole separate review of work dealing with communication, space, and place. This interesting scholarship shares with studies of places of public memory the recognitions that we are never outside of space, that where we are located matters, and that it matters rhetorically. The other thing it shares with the studies I've focused on here is how interesting it can be to be a tourist-critic.

If you assume the role of the tourist-critic, you will be enacting citizenship by: (1) attending to the politics of commemorative places; (2) noticing how these memory places are designed to invoke certain reactions and commitments from you and other visitors; (3) reflecting upon the historical, political, and geographical contexts in which these places are situated, and how re-contextualizing them rhetorically allows you to see them in a new light; (4) understanding how our senses of identity are shaped by memory places; and (5) equipping yourself to judge whether the rhetoric of a particular place of memory is one with which you would like to identify.

REFERENCES

Aden, R. C. (2010). Redefining the 'Cradle of Liberty': The President's House controversy in Independence National Historical Park. *Rhetoric and Public Affairs, 13,* 77–105.

Aden, R. C., Rahoi, R. L., & Beck, C. S. (1995). 'Dreams are born on places like this': The process of interpretive community formation at the Field of Dreams site. *Communication Quarterly, 43,* 368–380.

Aoki, E., Dickinson, G., & Ott, B. L. (2010). The master naturalist imagined: Directed movement and simulations at the Draper Museum of Natural History. In G. Dickinson, C. Blair, & B. L. Ott, (Eds.), *Places of public memory: The rhetoric of museums and memorials* (pp. 238–265). Tuscaloosa: University of Alabama Press.

Armada, B. J. (1998). Memorial agon: An interpretive tour of the National Civil Rights Museum. *Southern Communication Journal, 63,* 235–243.

Armada, B. J. (2010). Memory's execution: (Dis)placing the dissident body. In G. Dickinson, C. Blair, & B. L. Ott (Eds.), *Places of public memory: The rhetoric of museums and memorials* (pp. 216–237). Tuscaloosa: University of Alabama Press.

Atwater, D. F., & Herndon, S. L. (2003). Cultural space and race: The National Civil Rights Museum and MuseumAfrica. *Howard Journal of Communications, 14,* 15–28.

Balthrop, V. W., & Blair, C. (2003). Discursive collisions: A reading of 'Ellen's Energy Adventure.' In F. H. van Eemeren, J. A. Blair, and C. A. Willard (Eds.), *Proceedings of the Fifth Conference of the International Society for the Study of Argument* (pp. 119–123). Amsterdam, The Netherlands: Sic Sat.

Balthrop, V. W., Blair, C., and Michel, N. (2010). The presence of the present: Hijacking 'the Good War'? *Western Journal of Communication, 74,* 170–207.

Barbour, J. L. B. (2010). Review essay: Stirring up and smoothing out the landscapes of commemoration: authenticity, building, and consumption in public memorials. *Quarterly Journal of Speech, 96,* 89–102.

Bergman, T. (2003). A critical analysis of the California State Railroad Museum's orientation films. *Western Journal of Communication, 67,* 427–448.

Bergman, T. (2008). Can patriotism be carved in stone? A critical analysis of Mt. Rushmore's orientation films. *Rhetoric and Public Affairs, 11,* 89–112.

Biesecker, B. (2004). Renovating the national imaginary: A prolegomenon on contemporary paregoric rhetoric. In K. R. Phillips (Ed.), *Framing public memory* (pp. 212–247). Tuscaloosa: University of Alabama Press.

Blair, C. (1999). Contemporary U.S. memorial sites as exemplars of rhetoric's materiality. In J. Selzer, & S. Crowley (Eds.), *Rhetorical bodies* (pp. 16–57). Madison: University of Wisconsin Press.

Blair, C. (2001). Reflections on criticism and bodies: Parables from public places. *Western Journal of Communication, 65,* 271–294.

Blair, C. (2007). Civil rights/civil sites: ' . . . Until Justice Rolls Down Like Waters . . . '. *National Communication Association Carroll C. Arnold Distinguished Lecture, 2006.* Boston: Allyn and Bacon.

Blair, C., Balthrop, V. W., & Michel, N. (2007). "Arlington-sur-Seine: War commemoration and the perpetual argument from sacrifice." In F. H. van Eemeren, J. A. Blair, C. A. Willard, & B. Garssen (Eds.), *Proceedings of the Sixth Conference of the International Society for the Study of Argument* (pp. 145–151). Amsterdam, The Netherlands: Sic Sat, 2007.

Blair, C., Balthrop, V. W., & Michel, N. (2011). The arguments of the tombs of the unknown: Relationality and national legitimation. *Argumentation: An International Journal, 25,* forthcoming.

Blair, C., Dickinson, G., & Ott, B. L. (2010). Rhetoric/Memory/Place. In G. Dickinson, C. Blair, & B. L. Ott (Eds.), *Places of public memory: The rhetoric of museums and memorials* (pp. 1–54). Tuscaloosa: University of Alabama Press.

Blair, C., Jeppeson, M. S., & Pucci, E., Jr. (1991). Public memorializing in postmodernity: The Vietnam Veterans Memorial as prototype. *Quarterly Journal of Speech, 77,* 263–288.

Blair, C., & Michel, N. (1999). Commemorating in the theme park zone: Reading the Astronauts Memorial. In T. Rosteck (Ed.), *At the Intersection: Cultural studies and rhetorical studies* (pp. 29–83). New York: Guilford.

Blair, C., & Michel, N. (2000). Reproducing civil rights tactics: The rhetorical performances of the Civil Rights Memorial. *Rhetoric Society Quarterly, 30,* 31–55.

Blair, C., & Michel, N. (2004). The Rushmore effect: Ethos and national collective identity. In M. J. Hyde (Ed.), *The ethos of rhetoric* (pp. 156–196). Columbia: University of South Carolina Press.

Blair, C., and Michel, N. (2007). The AIDS Memorial Quilt and the contemporary culture of public commemoration. *Rhetoric and Public Affairs, 10,* 595–626.

Bodnar, J. (2010). Bad dreams about the Good War: Bataan. In G. Dickinson, C. Blair, & B. L. Ott (Eds.), *Places of public memory: The rhetoric of museums and memorials* (pp. 139–159). Tuscaloosa: University of Alabama Press.

Bowman, M.S. (2010). Tracing Mary Queen of Scots. In G. Dickinson, C. Blair, & B. L. Ott (Eds.), *Places of public memory: The rhetoric of museums and memorials* (pp. 191–215). Tuscaloosa: University of Alabama Press.

Burd, G., Drucker, S. J., and Gumpert, G. (Eds.) (2007). *The urban communication reader.* Creskill, NJ: Hampton.

Carlson, A. C., & Hocking, J. E. (1988). Strategies of redemption at the Vietnam Veterans' Memorial. *Western Journal of Speech Communication, 52,* 203–215.

Clark, G. (2004). *Rhetorical landscapes in America: Variations on a theme from Kenneth Burke.* Columbia: University of South Carolina Press.

DeLaure, M. B. (2011). Remembering the sit-ins: Performing public memory at Greensboro's International Civil Rights Center and Museum. *Liminalities: A Journal of Performance Studies, 7,* http://liminalities.net/7-2/ICRCM.pdf.

Dickinson, G. (1997). Memories for sale: Nostalgia and the construction of identity in Old Pasadena. *Quarterly Journal of Speech, 83,* 1–87.

Dickinson, G. (2002). Joe's rhetoric: Starbucks and the spatial rhetoric of authenticity. *Rhetoric Society Quarterly, 32,* 5–28,

Dickinson, G., & Maugh, C. M. (2004). Placing visual rhetoric: Finding material comfort in Wild Oats Market. In C. A. Hill, & M. Helmers (Eds.), *Defining visual rhetorics* (pp. 259–276). New York: Lawrence Erlbaum.

Dickinson, G., Ott, B. L., & Aoki, E. (2005). Memory and myth at the Buffalo Bill Museum. *Western Journal of Communication, 69,* 85–108.

Dickinson, G., Ott, B. L., & Aoki, E. (2006). Spaces of remembering and forgetting: The reverent eye/I at the Plains Indian Museum. *Communication and Critical/Cultural Studies, 3,* 27–47.

Edwards, J. L. (2010). Ethnic contradiction and reconciliation in Japanese internment memorials. In G. M. Reyes (Ed.), *Public memory, race, and ethnicity* (pp. 73–95). Newcastle upon Tyne, UK: Cambridge Scholars Publishing.

Ehrenhaus, P. (1988a). Silence and symbolic expression. *Communication Monographs, 55,* 41–57.

Ehrenhaus, P. (1988b). The Vietnam Veterans Memorial: An invitation to argument. *Argumentation and Advocacy, 25,* 54–64.

Ehrenhaus, P. (1989). The wall. *Critical Studies in Mass Communication, 6,* 94–98.

Fleming, D. (2008). *City of rhetoric: Revitalizing the public sphere in metropolitan America.* Albany: SUNY Press.

Foss, S.K. (1986). Ambiguity as persuasion: The Vietnam Veterans Memorial. *Communication Quarterly, 34,* 326–340.

Gallagher, V. J. (1995). Remembering together? Rhetorical integration and the case of the Martin Luther King, Jr. Memorial. *Southern Communication Journal, 60,* 109–119.

Gallagher, V. J. (1999). Memory and reconciliation in the Birmingham Civil Rights Institute. *Rhetoric and Public Affairs, 2,* 303–320.

Gallagher, V. J. (2004). Memory as social action: Projection and generic from in civil rights memorials. In P. A. Sullivan & S. R. Goldzwig (Eds.), *New approaches to rhetoric* (149–171). Thousand Oaks, CA: Sage.

Gallagher, V. J. (2006). Displaying race: Cultural projection and commemoration. In L. J. Prelli (Ed.), *Rhetorics of display* (pp. 177–196). Columbia: University of South Carolina Press.

Gallagher, V. J., & LaWare, M. R. (2010). Sparring with public memory: The rhetorical embodiment of race, power, and conflict in the *Monument to Joe Louis.* In G. Dickinson, C. Blair, & B. L. Ott, (Eds.), *Places of Public Memory: The Rhetoric of Museums and Memorials* (pp. 87–112). Tuscaloosa: University of Alabama Press.

Haines, H. H. (1986). 'What kind of war?' An analysis of the Vietnam Veterans Memorial. *Critical Studies in Mass Communication, 3,* 1–20.

Halloran, S. M., and Clark, G. (2006). National park landscapes and the rhetorical display of civic religion. In L. J. Prelli (Ed.), *Rhetorics of display* (pp. 141–156). Columbia: University of South Carolina Press.

Hasian, M., and Wood, R. (2010). Critical museology, (post)colonial communication, and the gradual mastering of traumatic pasts at the Royal Museum for Central Africa (RMCA). *Western Journal of Communication, 74,* 128–149.

Iles, J. (2006). Recalling the ghosts of war: Performing tourism on the battlefields of the Western Front. *Text and Performance Quarterly, 26,* 162–180.

Jorgensen-Earp, C. R., & Lanzilotti, L. A. (1998). Public memory and private grief: The construction of shrines at the sites of public tragedy. *Quarterly Journal of Speech, 84,* 150–170.

Katriel, T. (1994). Sites of memory: Discourses of the past in Israeli pioneering settlement museums. *Quarterly Journal of Speech, 80,* 1–20.

Kennerly, R. M. (2002) Getting messy: In the field and at the crossroads with roadside shrines. *Text and Performance Quarterly, 22,* 229–260.

Loewen, J. W. (1999). *Lies across America: What our historic sites get wrong.* New York: New Press.

Marback, R. (1998). Detroit and the closed fist: Toward a theory of material rhetoric. *Rhetoric Review, 17,* 74–91.

Marback, R. (2008). Unclenching the fist: Embodying rhetoric and giving objects their due. *Rhetoric Society Quarterly 38,* 46–65.

Massey, D. (2005). *For space.* London: Sage.

McPhail, M. L. (2010). Stones the builders rejected: Freedom Summer, Kent State, and the politics of public amnesia (pp. 96–119). In G. M. Reyes (Ed.), *Public memory, race, and ethnicity* (pp. 73–95). Newcastle upon Tyne, UK: Cambridge Scholars Publishing.

Morris, C.E., III. (Ed.) (2011). *Remembering the AIDS Quilt.* East Lansing: Michigan State University Press.

Noy, C. (2008). "Mediation materialized: The semiotics of a visitor book at an Israeli commemoration site. *Critical Studies in Media Communication, 25,* 175–195.

Ott, B. L., Aoki, E., & Dickinson, G. (2011). Ways of (not) seeing guns: Presence and absence at the Cody Firearms Museum. *Communication and Critical/Cultural Studies, 8,* 215–239.

Ott, B. L., and Dickinson, G. (2009). Visual Rhetoric and/as Critical Pedagogy. In A. A. Lundsford, K. H. Wilson, & R. A. Eberly (Eds.), *The Sage handbook of rhetorical studies* (pp. 391–405). Thousand Oaks, CA: Sage.

Prosise, T. O. (1998). The collective memory of the atomic bombings misrecognized as objective history: The case of the opposition to the National Air and Space Museum's atom bomb exhibit. *Western Journal of Communication, 62,* 316–347.

Prosise, T. O. (2003). Prejudiced, historical witness, and responsible, collective memory and liminality in the Beit Hashoah Museum of Tolerance. *Communication Quarterly, 51,* 351-366.

Reyes, G. M. (Ed.). (2010). *Public memory, race, and ethnicity.* Newcastle upon Tyne, UK: Cambridge Scholars Publishing.

Rosenzweig, R., & Thelen, D. (1998). *The presence of the past: Popular uses of history in American life.* New York: Columbia University Press.

Schowalter, D.F. (2009). Disarticulating American Indianness in the National Museum of the American Indian. In Biesecker, B.A., and Lucaites, J.L. (Eds.), *Rhetoric, materiality, and politics* (pp. 253–276). New York: Peter Lang.

Seitz, D. W. (2009). 'Let him remain until the judgment in France': Family letters and overseas burying of U.S. World War I soldiers. In U. D. Hebel (Ed.), *Transnational American memories* (pp. 215–242). Berlin: Walter deGruyter.

Stewart, J., & Dickinson, G. (2008). Enunciating locality in the postmodern suburb: FlatIron Crossing and the Colorado lifestyle. *Western Journal of Communication 72,* 280–307.

Veil, S. R., Sellnow, T. L., & Heald, M. (2011). Memorializing crisis: The Oklahoma City National Memorial as renewal discourse. *Journal of Applied Communication Research, 39,* 164–183.

Zagacki, K. S., and Gallagher, V. J. (2009). Rhetoric and materiality in the Museum Park at the North Carolina Museum of Art. *Quarterly Journal of Speech, 95,* 171–191.

Zelizer, B. (1995). Reading the past against the grain: The shape of memory studies. *Critical Studies in Mass Communication, 12,* 214–223.

Žižek, S. (1992). *Looking awry: An introduction to Jacques Lacan through popular culture.* Cambridge, MA: MIT Press.

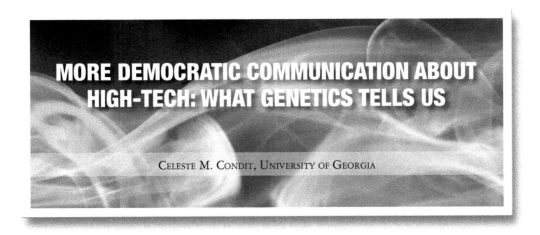

MORE DEMOCRATIC COMMUNICATION ABOUT HIGH-TECH: WHAT GENETICS TELLS US

CELESTE M. CONDIT, UNIVERSITY OF GEORGIA

The U.S. Constitution set an exceedingly ambitious agenda for a nation. Its preamble announced the government's goals as "to form a more perfect Union, establish Justice, insure domestic Tranquility, provide for the common defense, promote the general Welfare, and secure the Blessings of Liberty to ourselves and our Posterity." The tradition of democratic governance that this novel constitution sought to enact included the broadest possible realm of self-determination for individuals in their private lives *and* the shaping of collective actions necessary to secure these blessings through a process the Declaration of Independence had described as based in the "consent of the governed."

This was already a tall order in 1787, but the expansion of complex technological products into every aspect of contemporary life has created even greater challenges to the enactment of democratic ideals. The fundamental ideal of democracy assumes that all citizens are capable of understanding the benefits and costs of various decisions, both for their own lives and for "the people" as a whole. In contrast, a technologically oriented society presumes and requires extensive specialization. Different individuals are responsible for knowing the thousands of different techniques and facts necessary for creating and operating technologies such as water treatment plants, food safety standards, air traffic control, drug safety and enforcement, toxic chemical control, Internet creation and access, weapons technology, bureaucratic management, economic regulation, etc. No one individual can know all the information necessary for comparing and choosing among all the possibilities in an advanced technological society. How, then, is it possible to have truly democratic decision-making in a society pervaded by complex technologies?

This is a question that scholars in rhetoric have been deeply concerned about (Farrell & Goodnight, 1981; Ceccarelli, 2011). Since Aristotle's time, scholars in rhetoric have been concerned about how public decisions can be well made. Public decisions are those related to collective governance, such as decisions by nations, states, cities, or other large, non-homogeneous organizations. Because debate and discussion are typically the most visible ways in which different individuals and groups contribute to public decision processes in democratic organizations, rhetoricians have often focused on public speeches, debates, and discussions. In recent years, however, they have branched out to study deliberation processes in a wider range of venues, largely because they believe that public or social decisions are influenced by communication that goes on in these venues. Thus, scholars studying "rhetoric of science" have been interested in scientific communication, in part because such communication influences the many public decisions that involve technological products (such as weapons, Internet privacy, or patents for genes).

My research has sought to understand how the tensions between technological expertise and the need for everyone to make decisions about technology in a democracy actually are getting accomplished in the U.S. today, both in individual lives and in shared governance. I am trying to use this understanding to identify ways to lessen the impact of the tensions between democratic governance and technological expertise. I have focused my work on such genetic technologies as prenatal testing, personal health genomics, and genetic modifications in agriculture because they provide an interesting and important area of contemporary technologies. In this essay, I will share with you not only some of the far-reaching and practical consequences for the genetic revolution, but also two guidelines developed from this communication research about how to enhance our capacities to make better decisions about these technologies.

GENETIC TECHNOLOGIES AND US

The arrival of knowledge and technologies about genetics in the twentieth century is arguably one of the most profound developments in human history. At its most radical, genetic knowledge might have the consequence of changing the boundaries of what it means to be human. Thinking about genetics has led some people to consider removing particular characteristics from the human lineage (including cystic fibrosis, "gay genes", short height, and deafness) and led other people to consider adding new characteristics to the human lineage (including protection from radiation and shorter stature for space travel, chlorophyll, e-mortality, gills, fluorescent hair, and anti-balding). In the shorter term, people are already eating genetically modified food and, based on genetic tests, making decisions about whether to have children, which embryos to implant or abort, whether to remove both their breasts and their ovaries, what kinds of foods to eat, what racial group they identify with, and what kinds of medical tests to undergo.

All of these decisions are not just a matter of technical computation. When deciding to eat a cereal with genetically modified corn or soybean oil in it, one doesn't just ask questions such as "which crop uses less water" or "which costs more"? The decision engages a broad set of values: "How much do I value a cheaper product? How much do I value environmental sustainability? How much uncertainty about the safety of the product for my health am I willing to tolerate?"

These decisions are also rarely just individual decisions. Deciding to get a genetic test has implications for one's whole family, because one shares one's genes with them. If a test reveals one has a gene that increases the risk of a serious disease, then one is probably not going to be able to get life insurance. This not only means one's family is not financially protected, it also means that one's children's ability to get life insurance is also threatened (because their chance of having that risk-conferring version of the gene is now known to be much higher than average).

The complexity of these relational and value-based considerations is magnified when we move to the level of governmental decision-making. At this level, the questions might include: "What is a sufficient level of health testing for genetically modified organisms?" "What is a sufficient level of environmental testing?" "Does it matter if this product drives out small farmers or shifts profits from farmers to chemical companies?"

Because of the role of values and contexts, people who are "experts" about genetics have only a minor contribution to make to the decision processes for both individuals and the society. Unfortunately, our society has tended to assume that expert knowledge about the details of technology should carry most, if not all, of the weight when it comes to such decision processes. Instead of seeing experts as having small contributions to make to shared decisions, we have a proclivity to turn over whole domains of decision-making to experts based solely on their detailed knowledge of the technical aspects in an area. This is undemocratic and not necessary even in a technologically advanced society. It also tends to bias decisions in inequitable ways, because—as I will illustrate shortly—technical specialists such as medical researchers, nuclear energy engineers, or nanotech scientists tend to be biased, even in their technical estimates. They tend to overestimate the effectiveness of the technologies they can generate, downplay the risks of those technologies, and overemphasize the harms of doing without the technologies. In contrast, lay people use sophisticated, multi-input approaches that guide them to consider a broader range of factors in their judgments. This difference can be identified by a rhetorical approach that compares the metaphors, statistics, and cost-benefit analyses used by specialists to those used by the general public.

METAPHORS ABOUT GENES

My research team has identified the errant expectations for easy and powerful applications from genetic knowledge encouraged by the metaphors used by geneticists (Condit, 1999). We've looked at metaphors because such forms of speech tend to express complex relationships in vivid ways. Metaphors therefore accomplish a lot of work for speakers and writers in a short amount of space or time. Scientists also frequently use metaphors as translation devices to communicate complex ideas to the public (Nerlich & James, 2009). For both of these reasons, metaphors provide a good place for rhetorical critics to focus in order to understand what scientists are suggesting to the public.

The metaphors used by experts about genetics have tended to compare genes to scientific objects that had previously produced relatively quick and powerful technological benefits. Some of the earliest comparisons were to atoms. Genes were said to be like the atoms of biology. Humanity's scientific understanding of atoms had enabled the production not only of the impressive power of nuclear applications, but also of most modern chemical products. If genes were like atoms, then putting money into research on genes should produce similar rapid and wide-ranging technological power.

An even more common and persistent metaphor compared genes to various kinds of "codes" (Condit, 2011; Knudsen, 2005). Genes and DNA were often described as the "code of life." Unlike the "atom" metaphors, these coding metaphors actually capture a great deal about the characteristics of DNA. There is a descriptive resonance and utility in describing DNA as made up of chemical "letters," which can be "read" by the body. As you can see, however, these metaphors draw on the vocabularies of computer technologies. At the time, computer technologies were rapidly and impressively expanding their contributions to human life. So this metaphor was attractive to scientists and science promoters in part because it implied that, if genes were like biological computers, understanding genetics better should enable us to have a massive expansion in biological technology. This expectation was further increased because thinking about DNA as a "code" or a set of "letters" implied that these letters could be easily rearranged. Scientists talked about "snipping out" genetic "instructions" that were unwanted and replacing them with new instructions (Schmeck, 1985). This way of thinking about genes produced a widespread promotion of "gene therapy," which suggested that the next wave of medicine would entail using genes like they were drugs.

Scientists were quick to articulate the promise of gene therapy. In 1990, *The New York Times* quoted Wally Steinberg saying, "After the year 2000, one of every two or three ethical drugs will turn genes on or off" (Rifkin, 1990). That deadline was obviously not met, but when it was up, the most visible pioneer scientist in the area, W. French Anderson, predicted that gene therapy would produce major medical "products" before the end of the *next* decade (Anderson, 1999). This prediction also proved wrong. You can't just snip out a gene like you can delete a letter on your computer, because genes are embedded in complex biological systems.

Not only did thinking about genes as though they were easily re-writeable "code" encourage scientists to overestimate how easy it would be to produce "gene therapies," it also encouraged scientists to discount the risks. After all, how fatal can it be to rewrite a piece of code? Thus, for example, early in the research on gene therapy, people raised the question of whether inserting foreign genes into people might cause cancer. This risk was instantly dismissed; as the *New York Times* reported, "Most experts think the risk would be extremely small . . ." (Schmeck, 1985, p. 130). This judgment turned out to be wrong—even efforts at gene therapy that have had some success in combating diseases have turned out to cause leukemia, as well as other fatal responses to the therapies ("FDA Halts," 2003; Pollack, 2007; Stolberg, 1999).

Scientists thus tended to use metaphors about genes that compared them to other successful technologies, and this encouraged excessively rosy expectations. In contrast, my team's research has shown that lay people have not widely adopted the "coding" or "atom" metaphors for genetics—even though the mass media routinely have pushed the coding metaphors at them. Instead, the general public seems to utilize metaphors that incorporate the sense that genes are both difficult to control and contain a sense of risk (Condit, 2009; Gronnvoll & Landau, 2010). They describe genes as "viruses," or they combine discussions of genes with considerations of behavior or the environment by talking about behaviors as "triggers" that activate unwanted genetic effects, or as something that adds "fuel to the fire" that is the gene; or they describe a gene as being a "strike" against you that can then be added to (more strikes) by behavior. Such metaphors incorporate more elements than did the genetic scientists' metaphors (including both environmental impacts and genetic ones), as well as being more cautious about risks. In these ways, the general public's metaphors are more inclusive and appropriate for decision-making than those utilized by the "experts."

I am not arguing that we shouldn't have spent money on genetic research. I am, however, arguing that the narrowness and somewhat misleading character of the metaphors that geneticists have used and promoted illustrate why we should not trust experts in genetics alone to decide how much money to spend, where it should be spent, and what kind of ethical controls should be included in research. Like everyone else, experts in genetics have biased perspectives, and those biases show up in their selection of metaphors. Our national discussion about such decisions therefore needs to include and take seriously the perspectives of non-specialists, including experts in other dimensions of the issue—social scientists, rhetorical critics, or ethical leaders—but also each of us with our own individual perspectives, interests, affiliations, and concerns. Similar biases show up in the medical genetics community's use of statistics, and these biases have implications for our decisions about personal health as well as for decisions about governance.

SCARE STATISTICS VS. LIFE EXPERIENCE

In general, medical geneticists tend to play up the sense that bad genes produce very high risks, whereas the general public often has a more moderate reaction to the risk. For example, one study showed that genetic counselors counted a risk of 6% for having a child with a genetically based health challenge as "moderate," but the majority of their patients felt that level of risk was "low" or "very low" (Wertz, Sorenson, & Heeren, 1986). The genetic counselors thought a risk of 25% was "high," but the patients felt that 25% was only a "moderate" level of risk, because the expected outcome was "probably normal." Why might the counselors have had these biases toward treating a given risk level as more severe? The most cynical explanation is that geneticists make their work important by exaggerating the risks, but there are other possible explanations.[8] Whatever the cause of the difference, geneticists endorse a higher sense of risk, and for some kinds of decisions at least, the less exaggerated risk perceptions of the general public might well be more appropriate. This pattern is also evident in the case of breast cancer genetics.

One of the most famous "breakthroughs" in genetics research was the discovery that about 5 to 10% of cases of breast cancer in women had a genetic basis, which could be traced largely to variations in two genes called BRCA1 and BRCA2. Having an alteration in one of these genes increases the risk

---

[8] One explanation is simply that they became genetic counselors precisely because they evaluated genetic risks as more serious than other people do. Another explanation is that these counselors had seen the effects of severe genetic conditions frequently, and patients had not. (That, of course, is a biased perception, caused by their working conditions, rather than by the data itself.) A third explanation is that the counselors were thinking at the "population" level, whereas the lay people were thinking at the individual level. If one is thinking about the whole population, having 25% of cases with positive tests produce children with severe health problems is a large number. Thus, one might say that this is a "high" level of risk, because it will produce a "high" number of children with diseases. In contrast, for an individual woman, a 25% risk means that, indeed, her child will probably be normal. So this might well appear to be a moderate level of risk.

one will get breast cancer, ovarian cancer, or prostate cancer (among other cancers), but it ⟨ ⟩s not mean that one will definitely get any of these diseases. Just how much the genetic variati   will increase the risk depends on precisely where in the gene the disruption is, other genes one ⟨ ⟩ries, and environmental and behavioral factors. The measured range for breast cancer, for exampl   is as low as 28% to as high as 85% (Narod & Foulkes, 2004). So what are women typically told   out the risks for breast cancer? My analysis of representations by organizations on the Internet at   by physicians' comments on the Internet indicate that women mostly are told that the risk is "8   %" or "up to 80%," and sometimes they are told that it is "85%." While it may be accurate to   se the "up to" formula, this way of presenting the risks clearly slants decisions toward testing   d medical intervention, because it gives women no idea of what the low end of the range might   , and making the high end concrete and specific but the low end vague means women are likely   focus on the high end of the range. Hearing that the risk is "between 28% and 80%" would like produce a different set of calculations for women, because other research shows that people ten to assess risks as moderate if they fall in the range from 20% to 70% and to perceive them as higl only when they are in the 80% to 100% range (Cameron, Sherman, Marteau, & Brown, 2009).

Why might non-geneticists rate these cancer risks lower and medical geneticists rate them higher? Geneticists are only focusing on one thing—the potential for a specific disease and its prevention. In contrast, the rest of us have to worry about far more than the chance of getting one disease. Not only are we worried about heart disease, diabetes, and car accidents, but we also have to worry about our ability to get insurance, to take care of our friends and family, to get our work done, and to wedge in some sleep and fun. When geneticists see people failing to adopt the often radical "prevention" approaches—for example, removing both their breasts and their ovaries or taking strong drugs with side effects—they think people are behaving irrationally, and so they may be tempted to scare them into the behaviors that the geneticists think are correct. But maybe the geneticists are the ones who are wrong here? The research of Marli Huijer (2009) on prenatal testing for breast cancer has shown how people actually can and do incorporate a wider range of information into decisions that concern the use of technologies.

Huijer analyzed the public stories told by women whose families carry the risk-associated versions of the BRCA genes. Some of these women chose to have genetic tests; others chose not to have these tests. She found that these women's decisions were responsive to their family's experiences with this hereditary breast cancer, as well as to the family values, and to the resources available to the family. In some families, the experience with BRCA had been devastating to family members. They had lost many mothers, children, or aunts to the cancer at young ages, with devastating consequences, sometimes exacerbated by the nature of family values and relationships, sometimes exacerbated by the family's lack of resources. Other families had not lost many family members, and those who had died had been older, or losses had been better absorbed due to family structure or other factors. Still other families manifested different combinations of disease severity, age of onset, resources, and relationships. One can see these families as making decisions that reflect the accumulated experience of their families within the specific conditions for which they have to make their decisions. It is impossible for an outsider such as a genetic counselor or a physician to match this complex experience and knowledge. Indeed, the very idea of "expert" knowledge has been that knowledge is context-free; thus, the experts' knowledge by definition would not match the specific contexts and conditions that most individuals faced. Crediting the experiential knowledge of family members as at least equal in importance to the technical information from the medical geneticists seems essential to getting to good health decisions for individuals and their families.

COST-BENEFIT ESTIMATES

These examples show that expert knowledge tends to be biased in the direction of heightened estimates of risk for a problem and excessively rosy expectations for technological benefit. Experts also tend to downplay the risks that arise from a technology. You have probably heard dozens of cases of experts reassuring you that every possible technology—from nuclear power plants to cell phones to chemical preservatives to oil drilling rigs—is low in its risks. And you've seen that these "low" risks actually often have high consequences—from contaminating whole swaths of land through radiation fallout (Chernobyl in 1986 and the Japanese nuclear power plants in 2011) to terrible pollution of the seas and oceans (Exxon-Valdez 1989, & the BP Oil Deepwater Drilling Explosion in 2010). This pattern is explained by looking at the genetic experts' treatment of the risks associated with genetically modified organisms in agriculture.

The first thing to say about these risks is that no one really knows what the full range of risks is. Very little research has been done to assess *long-term* health risks or *long-term* environmental risks; most risk assessment is short term (e.g. allergic reactions, small-scale controlled experiments on contained plots of land), whereas long-term research is essentially conducted by monitoring what happens post-release or post-market (Winter, 2008). But, more fundamentally, it is impossible to know with certainty in advance the impacts of all of the possible applications of any new technology. Sound risk estimates require good empirical measures across many conditions, and such measures can't exist with new technologies, especially when many of the applications have not yet even been imagined.[9]

In spite of the limited evidence, and the historical record associated with high-impact technologies, the chorus from the experts has been close to unanimous in downplaying risks: "there is no evidence that the modified foods approved for human consumption are harmful" (Pollack, 2000). In contrast, the publics of various nations have tended to view the risks as of substantially greater concern (Ferretti & Lener, 2008). Experts and the general public evaluate these imperfectly predictable risks differently because they have different things at stake. For experts, their jobs and therefore their world-views are bound up with producing new products using these genetically based technologies. They stand to gain a lot if the new technologies move forward, and the chance that they will experience personal risk consequences is relatively low. For the specialists, the risk-benefit trade-offs are very good. In contrast, for a member of the general public, a slightly cheaper tomato, or even one that holds up to long-distance transportation better,

---

[9] Based on experience with other high-impact technologies, a good prediction would be that we will experience relatively isolated negative effects from rapid and widely applied genetic modification of living beings, but that a few of these may be of high impact.

is not a very big benefit to weigh against the relatively unknown, probably low, but potentially serious consequences of GMO. Because the public disagrees with the specialists, the specialists keep insisting that the risks are low and that the public is stupid or uninformed (Ferretti & Lener, 2008; de Boer, McCarthy, Brennan, Kelly, & Ritson, 2005). But the disagreement really arises from the disparate benefits anticipated in the face of uncertain risks.

TRUTH AND CONSEQUENCES

When we make public decisions about technology, whether to restrict it, to regulate it, to fund research into it, or to buy it for public purposes, we cannot simply "ask the experts." The research I have shared with you has indicated that specialists—whether physicians or oil engineers—will not give us unbiased decisions, and they probably won't provide as good a set of decisions as if a wide variety of perspectives, experiences, and expertise is included and heard in the discussions that produce the decisions. Unfortunately, exclusive reliance on narrow technical specialties often occurs today. In the case of the GMO controversy, for example, surveys show that the majority of the public wants labeling of products with regard to whether they contain genetically modified content or not (Costa-Font, Gil, & Traill, 2008). Nevertheless, when such legislation or regulatory rulings have come up for consideration in the U.S., genetic, economic, and industry "experts" have prevented them from coming into practice, arguing that it would inappropriately "scare" the public (Reiss, 2002). These experts believe that since they "know" that GMO is safe, then there is no reason for nations to add on the cost of separating GMO products from others in the food chain and labeling them (Reiss, 2002). In a democracy, however, we should not let the narrow specialists make these decisions for us (Lappe, 2002). The economists can tell us the approximate costs of labeling, and the geneticists can tell us the mathematical range of known risks, and then we, the people, should make the decisions, considering all of the different factors we know about and all of the values we can bring to bear on the decision process. Our judgment shouldn't be short-circuited by claims that the experts don't want to scare us.

WHAT TO DO?

But how can we do that? It is difficult to resist the vociferous insistence of specialists that they know what they are talking about, and we don't. After all, how many of us know what the real risk of breast cancer is? It is only by poring through many complicated research papers that I have been able to figure out that the risk figures given to the public by medical genetics specialists tend to be slanted toward the high end.

A two-pronged strategy is available. In cases where you personally have a serious interest or investment (for example, you have a lot of breast cancer in your family, or you are concerned about a particular area of legislation) you should do extra research to get behind the public story presented by the experts. This isn't easy, but thousands of lay people have proven that it is possible, especially when people band together and share with each other. In families where there is a genetic disease, the family members often become more expert than the doctors with whom they consult (because a doctor deals with lots of diseases but the family focuses on one). In the legislative arena, the Web now enables us to share our collective, non-expert knowledge and to help each other "get up to speed."

The second prong is to adjust the risk estimates we hear from experts based on our understanding that the interests of the general public are different from the interests of experts in most cases. This means that from the perspective of the general public, experts will typically be exaggerating the risks of a condition, exaggerating their ability to easily solve it, or down-playing the risks involved in their solutions. This pattern does not require dismissing completely what the experts have to say, but rather tempering their estimates.

By coming to understand how typical patterns of communication shape scientific products, we have learned that we cannot simply turn decisions over to experts if we want democratically made decisions that are likely to be good for most of us, and that this is not necessary, even in a highly technical society. Instead, as individuals and as members of the public, we need to do the hard work to combine the narrow knowledge of specialists with our broader contextual knowledge and experience. Democratic decision-making is possible in a technological society, but it requires pooling different kinds of knowledge, a task that requires an emphasis on communication.

REFERENCES

Anderson, W. F. (1999, December 12). The long horizon of gene therapy, interview with Dr. W. French Anderson. *The New York Times,* p. BU4.

Cameron, L. D., Sherman, K. A., Marteau, T. M., & Brown, P. M. (2009). Impact of genetic risk information and type of disease on perceived risk, anticipated affect, and expected consequences of genetic tests. *Health Psychology, 28,* 307–316.

Ceccarelli, L. (2011). Manufactured scientific controversy: Science, rhetoric, and public debate. *Rhetoric and Public Affairs, 14,* 195–228.

Condit, C. (1999). *The meanings of the gene: Public debates about heredity.* Madison, WI: University of Wisconsin Press.

Condit, C. M. (2009) Dynamic feelings about metaphors for genes: Implications for research and genetic policy. *Genomics, Society and Policy 5,* 44–58.

Condit, C. M. (2011, in press). How we feel with metaphors for genes: Implications for understanding humans and forming genetic policies. In N. M. P. King, and M. J. Hyde (Eds.), *Bioethics, public moral argument, and social responsibility,* (123–140). New York: Routledge.

Costa-Font, M., Gil, J. M., Traill, W. B. (2008). Consumer acceptance, valuation of and attitudes towards genetically modified food: Review and implications for food policy. *Food Policy, 33,* 99–111.

De Boer, M., McCarthy M., Brennan M., Kelly A. L., & Ritson, C. (2005). Public understanding of food risk issues and food risk messages on the island of Ireland: The views of food safety experts. *Journal of Food Safety, 25,* 241–265.

Farrell, T. B. & Goodnight, G. T. (1981). Accidental rhetoric: the root metaphors of Three Mile Island. *Communication Monographs, 48,* 271–300.

Ferretti, M. P. & Lener M. (2000). Lay public or stakeholder participation in authorization for GMO products in the European Union. *Review of Policy Research, 25,* 507–525.

FDA halts dozens of gene-therapy trials. (2003, January 15). *USA Today,* p. 08d.

Gronnvoll, M., & Landau, J. (2010). From viruses to Russian roulette to dance: A rhetorical critique and creation of genetic metaphors. *Rhetoric Society Quarterly, 40,* 46–70.

Huijer, M. (2009). Storytelling to enrich the democratic debate: The Dutch discussion on embryo selection for hereditary breast cancer. *Biosocieties, 4,* 223–238.

Knudsen, S. (2005). Communicating novel and conventional scientific metaphors: A study of the development of the metaphor of genetic code. *Public Understanding of Science, 14,* 373–392.

Lappé, M. (2002). Labeling should be mandatory. *Nature Biotechnology, 20,* 1081–1082.

McCluskey, J. J. (2000). Read the warning . . . THIS PRODUCT MAY CONTAIN GMOs. *Choices: The Magazine of Food, Farm & Resource Issues, 15* (2), 08865558.

Narod, S. A., Foulkes, W. D. (2004). BRCA1 and BRCA2: 1994 and beyond. *Nature Reviews on Cancer, 4,* 665–676.

Nerlich B., and James, R. (2009). "The post-antibiotic apocalypse" and the "war on superbugs": Catastrophe discourse in microbiology, its rhetorical form and political function. *Public Understanding of Science, 18,* 574–590.

Pollack, A. (2000, September 26). Labeling genetically altered food is thorny issue. *The New York Times,* p. A1.

Pollack, A. (2007, September 18). Death in gene therapy treatment is still unexplained. *The New York Times,* p. A22.

Reilly, P. R. (2000). Public concern about genetics. *Annual Review of Genomics and Human Genetics, 01,* 485–506.

Reiss, M. (2002). Labeling GMO foods—the ethical way forward. *Nature Biotechnology, 20,* 868.

Rifkin, G. (1990, August 5). Lining up for potential gene therapy profits: The new treatments could radically change the drug industry. *The New York Times,* p. F9.

Schmeck, H. M. Jr. (1985, November 10). The promises of gene therapy. *The New York Times,* pp. 116–130.

Stolberg, S. G. (1999, December 9). FDA officials fault Penn team in gene therapy death. *The New York Times,* p. A22.

Wertz, D., Sorenson, J. R., & Heeren, T. C., (1986). Clients' interpretation of risks provided in genetic counseling. *American Journal of Human Genetics, 39,* 253–264.

Winter, G. (2008). Nature protection and the introduction into the environment of genetically modified organisms: Risk analysis in EC multilevel governance. *Reciel: Review of European Community & International Environmental Law, 17,* 205–220.

ENGAGING A CRITICAL VOICE AS A RHETORICAL CITIZEN

RAYMIE E. MCKERROW, OHIO UNIVERSITY

My approach in this brief essay is to raise awareness about how one can act within an everyday world to make a difference. I take my cue from a third-wave feminist writer who observed "The revolution starts in your house" (McCarry, 2001, p. 247). While she was writing about how each individual can act in small ways, from the home outward, to change the status of women in society, the phrase applies more broadly to civic engagement regardless of one's own position in society.

The first question the title of this essay might raise is "what's a critical voice?" And, just as important, what does 'engage' mean? Before answering that, ask yourself: Is my life perfect as is? Am I the "perfect being" I want myself to be? If you answer in the negative in response to one or both, then you begin to realize what is at stake in "engaging a critical voice." You critique your dress and appearance, rehearse and then review the shortcomings of your attempts to convince friends of something as simple as skipping studying to attend a party, bemoan your ill-conceived attempt at humor at the party, and otherwise satisfy the aphorism "you are your own best critic." Years ago, Michael Calvin McGee coined the phrase "the rhetorical impulse." [1978] He used this phrase in response to the seemingly never-ending desire to improve one's own world—whether it implies doing better on an exam, getting friends to listen to your ideas, or even repairing damaged interpersonal relationships. Language—the use of rhetoric to assist in making your environment better at a specific moment in time—is a central resource in engaging your voice. Of course, it is more than that; the sounds you make—how you speak to others and the facial expressions you use, the animated way in which your body moves in relation to your words and sounds—all impact how that "impulse to change the world for the better" will work (Goodale, 2011). In any case, engaging the rhetorical impulse reflects a desire to do right by your own view of how you might live your life in the moment. As another quick gloss on the same issue, consider the oft-used phrase "language matters." Don Imus's ill-conceived attempt at humor in referring to the women's basketball players at Rutgers mattered—his words belied the mythic pronouncement that "sticks and stones may break my bones, but words will never harm me" (Lee & Morin, 2009). In the present, referring to the Federal Reserve Board Chair as committing a treasonous act were he to print money is another instance where language labels you as well as the other you are 'naming.' Engaging a critical voice is not without responsibility.

The second question this title may raise is "what is a rhetorical citizen and why does that matter?" A while ago, I wrote the following in an attempt to answer this question:

> **A focus on the citizen as a rhetorical agent, as one who expresses or enacts citizenship via symbolic means, cuts across race, sex, gender, and class lines. It is inclusive with respect to one's activity within the public sphere as well—whether one is a social activist or passive participant in the life of the community. It allows a conception of citizenship to be formulated that responds to the place where one enacts citizenship, whether as part of the public or as part of a specific 'counterpublic.' The sense of rhetoric implied here as "symbolic" suggests what the rhetorical critic Kenneth Burke would endorse: any act, whether via words or gestures, signs or even dress, that invites an interpretation regarding how that act is to be understood or taken by others, is a rhetorical expression. In this sense, Picasso's famous painting, "Guernica"–painted as a response to war–functions rhetorically as an expression of an artist's enactment as a "citizen of the world." (McKerrow, 2010, pp.78–79).**

What this brief introduction brings us to is the central question animating this essay: *"Why should we all engage in critical civic discourse?"* As you quickly realize, asking this question raises the stakes from everyday interpersonal interactions to acts that may take place on the public stage, with consequences that are more far-reaching. If you understand that the principles that apply to engaging a critical voice are the same, regardless of the significance of the consequences to you or to others around you, you are well on your way to grasping the significance of this larger question.

As we engage this question, there are three preliminary issues to address: (1) what is the relationship between *citizen* and *citizenship?*; (2) what is the distinction between *what people do* and *how they perform* citizenship?; and (3) is there a space for the enactment of citizenship? With respect to the first issue, a relevant response would be "engaging in citizenship is the right of citizens." While that seems a straightforward and non-problematic response, it isn't quite that simple.

As Robert Asen (2004) has noted in an important essay, and one I shall draw on in building a case for engagement, "when viewed as a mode of public engagement, citizenship appears as a performance, not a possession" (p. 205). What this means is that the focus is not on the rights you possess by virtue of being named a citizen, as that excludes any actions by, for example, illegal immigrants. As Jesse David Cisneros (2011) has argued, protests by those considered "illegals" can be understood as "a rhetorical enactment of US citizenship" (p. 28).

Acting like a citizen, then, may encompass those who have yet to be thought of in those terms. The actions of Antonio Diaz Chacon, "who chased down a suspected child abductor" are those we might call an expression of citizenship, yet Chacon does not yet have legal residential status in the US (N. M. Hero, 2011, August 2011, p. A9).

While this example privileges a focus on "what people do," that is not the only approach to consider with respect to engaging social others in matters of public importance. Asen (2004) offers the strategic counter:

Rather than asking what counts as citizenship, we should ask: how do people enact citizenship? Reorienting our framework from a question of *what* to a question of *how* usefully redirects our attention from acts to action. Inquiring into the *how* of citizenship recognizes citizenship as a process (p. 191).

As the second issue suggests, the 'how' is an important component, and one that lends itself to a focus on what people say in enacting citizenship—it reorients our focus from such acts as voting to what Asen describes as a discourse theory of citizenship. This perspective permits a focus on performance as a *"mode of public engagement."* In Asen's (2004) words: "In drawing attention to citizenship as a process, a discourse theory recognizes the fluid, multimodal, and quotidian enactments of citizenship in a multiple public sphere" (p. 191). "Mode" is simply a shorthand term for how people engage others—and that covers such a broad range of possible means as to defy clear description. Nonetheless, an example or two would be useful! Consider the phrase used in describing the principles and practices of speaking in public: *The only rule is that there are no rules.* What this means, in practice, is something you already know: What worked in one situation will not necessarily work in what appears to be a similar new situation. You can be as confident as possible that your rhetorical approach to an "imperfection" in your life will work wonderfully well, only to be shown the door (metaphorically if not literally) in engaging the social other. In a more public setting, the rules for what is permissible keep changing. Regardless of your politics, you have heard political candidates for the presidency utter the most unimaginable things—sometimes at the cost of their own candidacy. Current Texas Governor Rick Perry's allusion to the Chair of the Federal Reserve Board engaging in a "treasonous act" were he to print new money is just one example. You can pick several phrases from Sarah Palin's candidacy as Vice President as another example. Public acts have consequences that are beyond the control of social mores, political establishments, or civic associations to control completely.

The third issue is a tricky one: who has access to the public sphere (however that phrase is understood). That is, who can speak to whom with what expected impact? You know from your own experience that you might be able to speak in a social setting, only to have your views summarily ignored (while another person says pretty much the same thing and is praised for his contribution). That you cannot speak at all may not have come to your attention. Yet, to what extent do the homeless have a voice in society, or are they constantly being spoken of, and for, by others? To what extent do the poor have a voice? Asen (2004) recounts the contemporary views of those who are pessimistic about "ordinary citizens" having much of an impact, while other commentators are much more positive. Space does not allow here a lengthy discussion of the pros and cons related to whether there is even a "public sphere" we can enter and have the expectation our voice will be heard. I prefer to take the positive, more optimistic (yet realistic) approach; to do less is to give in to defeatism and to award the victory to the pessimists, and that also means letting bureaucrats, technical advisors, political pundits, and others hold sway over the "untutored masses"—the *hoi polloi.* As a realist, it also means that you may need to become socially and politically more active in making room for yourself at the public "table." It may mean protesting exclusion, running like-minded people for political office, etc. to ensure that where absence is the given status, your presence becomes the counter move. I don't want to sugarcoat the possibilities—but rather want to suggest that when entry is denied for reasons of race, class, religion, sexuality or other bogus rationale, it becomes imperative to challenge the exclusion.

This brings us to the central question raised earlier regarding "Why?" As I have noted in another essay:

> **Why should you act (or not)? What are the motives for enacting citizenship that mean something to you? When you refuse to have a political sign on your yard, is it because you disagree with the candidate's views (or party affiliation), or is it simply that such signs are aesthetically offensive? Is the latter a non-essential reason—one that devalues your role as a citizen? (McKerrow, 2010, p. 79)**

The question that is raised goes to the heart of the matter: Inaction, or denial of a proposed action, may constitute your means of expressing citizenship. Either is an action that expresses a particular meaning for others to interpret. If your motive in not voting is to send a message to civic society, how do you control the interpretation that is put on your "non-action that is an action?" You run the risk of being perceived as shirking your responsibilities as a citizen if you do not permit the sign because you see it as damaging your viewscape. All you can do in this setting is to express the motive underlying the action and let the consequences fall as they will. The prospects for being misunderstood, or understood and damned are daunting, and sufficient to consider not engaging in civic discourse for any reason.

While this is a potential reality, I want to switch the focus from the pessimism implicit in the preceding discussion to a more positive view of the prospects for engagement. Critical, civic discourse may be engaged in without necessarily engaging politics at the local, regional, or national level—at least not in the context of political campaigns. Exhorting a neighbor to assist in a March of Dimes campaign, or talking volunteers into an effort to clean up a city park are modes of public engagement. Talking the company you work for into supporting a fundraising bike ride is a mode of engagement. Obviously, appearing at a city council meeting to lambaste the elected representatives over some perceived mishandling of a city issue engages politics more directly—but it also means you are exercising voice in a critical, and hopefully, civil manner.

This latter raises an issue that I've been advancing for the past decade: Is there ever a space for incivility in the performative enactment of one's citizenship? As we perform our sense of what it means to be a citizen within a community, I have argued that we need to retain the potentiality for incivility, however hard that may be to accomplish. The nature of "incivility" is the critical concern, as I want to distinguish it from what goes under the rubric "hate speech." There are four characteristics of the rhetoric of hate that can be applied in an analysis of its expression.[1] First, hate, and the crimes that result from its expression and resultant action, creates an adversarial relation in order to justify behavior. In the Matthew Shepard case, one of the individuals involved initially constructed a false story, wherein Matthew "came on to them" in a straight bar and they refused his overture, only later to decide to "teach him a lesson."[2] That story is symptomatic of

---

[1] I owe Kathryn Olson's 2002 analysis a large debt in this review of hate speech.

[2] Matthew Shepard was a victim of a hate crime, perpetrated because he was a homosexual. He was attacked, beaten, tied to a fence and left to die in early October, 1998 outside Laramie, Wyoming. A movie, *The Laramie Project* (2002), chronicled his story.

the "win-lose" mindset that is inherent within adversarial conflict. To be sure, not all adversarial encounters will result in hate speech or hate crimes, but it does appear that all expressions of hate, and actions connected to those expressions, are rhetorically constructed in adversarial terms. Losing once in this "war" does not deter future actions, any more than losing one game means the players give up and the season is lost. Hate groups are in it for the long haul—beating them once, whether on the street or in a courtroom, is not the end of the relationship.

Second, hate is not so much "personalized" as in the expression "I hate YOU" but rather "I hate you BECAUSE . . ." And you can fill in the "class" term—poor, white, Black, Hispanic, gay, and on through the seemingly never-ending possibilities. In this sense, hate rhetoric is highly impersonal. The "YOU" as victim is interchangeable—it could be any "you" that happens to be in my vicinity, my sphere of influence, as I engage in an act of hateful expression or, worse, visit violence on your physical being. In effect, claiming that "I am gay, white, Black or . . . . fill in the phrase . . . . But that is not all that I am" falls on deaf ears—for all that you are is **singularity** in the mind of the other.

Third, a corollary to the impersonal nature of the class relationship is the rhetorical distance that one constructs in an attitude of hate. During the Vietnam War, police were referred to as "Pigs" —it is much easier to kick a pig when it is down than a real live human being. We did the same to the Germans and Japanese in World War II. In fact, one might claim that the rhetorical necessity in wartime is to depersonalize the enemy—to distance oneself from the human behind the name. One rhetorical response to distancing has been rhetorical re-appropriation. In the earlier example, the police, realizing that pigs are among the cleanest of the barnyard animals, embraced "pig power" as a symbol—one which inured them to the radicals' chants. Similarly, in our time, 'queer' is being re-appropriated as a term, not of derision, but one depicting solidarity.

Fourth, the expression of dominance and superiority underlies hate toward another. This brings us full circle to the outcome of the adversarial relation—from the perspective of the hater —it is not enough to merely hate, but to show the object of that hatred that we exist, and that we will not be deterred in our fight to maintain our position. Its expression serves, internal to the hate group, to establish commonality and, in some instances, superiority among one's peers. There is sufficient evidence to suggest that, for the perpetrator of hate, it "feels good" to give voice to virulent rhetoric or to act violently toward the other—and to be able to stand tall among one's peers in the aftermath of the event can be a powerful incentive to initiate action. An outcome is that the rhetoric of hate is often expressed as part of a group act. It may be the single voice of a drunk college student (or his father during "Dad's day"—it does happen, unfortunately) toward a person presumed to be gay or lesbian or—again, you can fill in the "marker"—but it is spoken within the frame of a circle of friends whose ensuing laughter is all the more incentive to continue "flogging" the other with one's creative expressions—ever more virulent and mocking as "naming the other" continues.

These four "traits" of hateful rhetoric are not intended to be exhaustive, but they do serve to frame the kind of symbolic reality that is created through their expression. These traits do not however, function as an answer to a complex question: When is speech hateful? On the one hand, you know it when you hear it. Some instances are clearly self-evident. That is not the case in all such instances. If I were to claim that "gays should not be in the classroom as instructors," am I expressing a hateful utterance, or am I expressing a value judgment that presumes one's gayness can influence others to become likewise? Can we maintain the two interpretations as mutually exclusive? As silly as I *personally* think that latter position is, from a professional vantage point, I must acknowledge its presence within the presumably educated community.

Discourse that contains elements of these four attributes of hateful rhetoric are not what I have in mind in suggesting that there are times that "getting along" with the social other for the sake of peace and harmony is not the right answer. The principle that I wish to advance here is that:

> **[N]either tolerance nor civility function as a guarantor of mutual respect. I need not acknowledge the other as a social being in reality, while at the same time giving the very public sense that I am in fact doing just that. It is in this sense that civility, to the extent that it is a privileged outcome, may only foster a climate that is destructive of the possibility of dissent, to say nothing of the elimination of any prospect for meaningful dialogue. (McKerrow, 2012)**

What I hope to suggest with the foregoing is that, while one avoids discourse that borders on hateful speech, one can still be critical in ways that some will see as acts of incivility. The consequences of those actions need to be considered in taking this approach, as it may mean that you lose more ground than you gain. One need look only at the "debt default" rhetoric of late 2011 to see how uncivil labeling of the social other, while eschewing "hatefulness," nonetheless put parties at such odds as to virtually foreclose on the possibility of communicating with each other. At the same time, being open to the possibility that a more forceful approach may build solidarity within your own group, while putting the other on notice that your patience is running thin, may well prove to be, in the long run, a more useful rhetoric.

So, why engage at all? I could offer all sorts of good reasons, from "it is your civic duty" to "you will gain confidence" to "you will be able to enact social change." You know all of these already. If they haven't had much impact on you to date, exhorting you to engage social others on matters of social, economic, political importance will fail. I will, however, attempt to provide a response to this central question that you may not have thought of. The answer, for me, is simple (and this term is not to be confused with "simplistic," for it most assuredly is not): "Enacting a civil, or at times uncivil discourse . . . is not simply an option to consider, but a fundamental necessity of being actively human (McKerrow, 2001, p. 281).

REFERENCES

Asen, R. (2004). A discourse theory of citizenship. *Quarterly Journal of Speech, 90,* 189–211.

Cisneros, J. D. (2011). (Re)Bordering the civic imaginary: Rhetoric, hybridity, and citizenship in La Gran Marcha. *Quarterly Journal of Speech, 97,* 26–49.

Goodale, G. (2011). *Sonic persuasion: Reading sound in the recorded age.* Urbana, IL: University of Illinois Press.

Lee, R., & Morin, A. (2009). Using the 2008 presidential election to think about "playing the race card." *Communication Studies, 60,* 376–391.

McCarry, S. (2001). Selling out. In B. Findlen (Ed.), *Listen up: Voices from the next generation* (pp. 247–52). Berkeley, CA: Seal Press.

McGee, M. C. (1978). The rhetorical impulse. Unpublished manuscript, Department of Communication Studies, University of Iowa, Iowa City, IA.

McKerrow, R. E. (2001). Coloring outside the lines: The limits of civility. *Vital Speeches of the Day, (February 15, 2001), 67,* 278–81.

McKerrow, R. E. (2012). Principles of Rhetorical Democracy, *Retor,* 2 (1), 94–113.

McKerrow, R. E. (2010) Citizenship. In R. Jackson (Ed.), *Encyclopedia of identity* (Vols. 1–2; Vol. 1: 78–80). Thousand Oaks, CA: Sage.

N. M. hero who saved girl says he's illegal immigrant. (2011, August 21) *The Athens Messenger,* p. A9

Olson, K. M. (2002). Detecting a common interpretive framework for impersonal violence: The homology in participants' rhetoric on sport hunting, 'hate crimes,' and stranger rape." *Southern Communication Journal, 67,* 215–244.

CPSIA information can be obtained
at www.ICGtesting.com
Printed in the USA
LVHW020255150623
749726LV00002B/2